# Target Germany

# Target Germany

## No. 186 Squadron 1944-1945

Steve C Smith

BOMBER COMMAND BOOKS
An imprint of
MENTION THE WAR PUBLICATIONS

www.bombercommandbooks.com

First published in the United Kingdom in 2022 by Mention the War Ltd. Merthyr Tydfil, CF47 0BH, Wales.



Cover design: Topics – The Creative Partnership www.topicdesign.co.uk

Cover image: Keith Aspinall, used with the kind permission of Pat Aspinall.

A CIP catalogue reference for this book is available from the British Library.

ISBN 9781915335104

# Table of Contents

# Acknowledgements

This book would not have been possible without the generous help of a number of individuals. I want to thank the following long-term friends for their usual support and help, especially Simon Hepworth, Greg Harrison, Liz Evans, Graham Howard and Chris Ward. A very special thanks to Jock Whitehouse, a respected author, historian and artist who has done so much to preserve the aviation history of East Anglia.

A very special thanks to Fay McPherson, Susan Griffin, Duncan Knight and Dennis Godfrey and his family in Australia for allowing me to use their photographs and documents throughout this book. Also, Chris Cussen, Janet Hunt and Graham Smith, both of whom have helped tremendously. Also, a thank you to the late James Sharpe. James was very keen from the outset for a book being written on No.186 Squadron. James would keep me on my toes and motivate me to keep plugging away. I was in contact with James a week before he sadly died. I am so glad I had the opportunity to know such a wonderful man. I would also like to show my sincere appreciation to Kelvin Youngs, who, over the years, has provided me with a wealth of material for my book projects. His excellent website, Aircrew Remembered, is worth visiting.

A very special thanks to Di Abblewhite, who, on numerous occasions, supplied me with a wealth of material on individual airman. Thanks Di. As usual a big thank you to Peter Wheeler of the RNZAF Bomber Command Association. Also, the following for their assistance and support, Errol Martyn in New Zealand, Joop Hendrix, Dr Theo Boiten and Bob Collis. A special thank you to Louisa Bush of the Lincolnshire Aviation Centre. I also like to acknowledge the help of two excellent websites/forums that have provided, on numerous occasions, the answers to many difficult questions, RAF Commands and 12 O'Clock High. A special thanks to Pat Aspinall, wife of the late Keith Aspinall, artist and friend. Pat very kindly allowed me to use Keith's wonderful painting, 'Predator' for the cover. Lastly, Tony Hibberd who very kindly supplied the memorial photographs, and Nigel Perry for his help.

Unfortunately, I could not obtain any help from the RAAF in Australia, which was disappointing as the RAAF influence on the squadron was vast. This also applies to the No.90 Squadron Association. They did not reply to my many letters or emails requesting help. Who did was Les Turner of the No.90 Squadron Research Group. Thanks Les! To the dozens of people who supplied snippets of information, or a photo, my sincere thanks.

Regrettably, unlike in my previous books, I did not have the opportunity of meeting and talking with the veterans. Sadly, this meant that the squadron history is lacking somewhat in personal anecdotes, the human side of the bomber war, which is, to me, essential. I must express regret for the quality of some of the photographs. Unfortunately, it has been somewhat challenging to obtain photographs depicting No.186 Squadron due to its relatively brief operational existence. For that reason, I have chosen to include some that are inferior. However, from a historical point of view, they are unique.

Finally, let me apologise in advance for the inevitable errors. I have tried to give the facts using primary source material, which some of you may know is notoriously unreliable. I have attempted to ensure that this book gives an honest appraisal of the squadron's activities between October 1944 and July 1945. Mistakes were made by the squadron, the Group and Bomber Command. We should not shy away from discussing this and writing about it. A sanitized history is no history and does not do justice to the overall success and achievements of the young men and women of Bomber Command.

*This book is humbly dedicated to all those who served on No.186 Squadron.*

*In memory of*

*James Sharpe*

*who sadly passed away just a few weeks before completion of this book.*

*A very special thanks to my wife Jill, who despite fighting her own battles continues to give me her love, support and encouragement to carry on with my research . Thanks Hun.*

# Preface

Towards the final months of the bomber offensive of WW2, No.3 Group RAF Bomber Command formed a number of new bomber squadrons equipped with the excellent Avro Lancaster. One of these new squadrons was number 186.

Partially formed from 'C' Flight of No.90 Squadron in October 1944, this new squadron would start operating almost immediately from its base at RAF Tuddenham. Almost from conception, the squadron was staffed by battle-hardened veterans brimming with operational experiences. The man given command of the new squadron was Wing Commander Giles DFC. It was an inspirational choice.

Wing Commander Giles DFC style of command and his willingness to operate regularly against some of the most heavily defended targets in Germany inspired every member of the squadron, from the humble Erk to his senior Flight Commanders. The squadron's success was in no small measure also influenced by the selection of his hand-picked Flight Commanders, Squadron Leader Percy Reynolds of 'A' Flight and Squadron Leader Mervyn Leyshon AFC of 'B' Flight. These men embodied the squadron's exceptional spirit and courage, and determination. Like any squadron, success in the air would not have been possible without the hard work of those on the ground. Number 186 Squadron was fortunate, it had amongst its ranks outstanding Groundcrews, WAAF's and support staff. They did their bit too, and this should never be forgotten. Nor should the significant contribution of the RAAF, RNZAF and RCAF personnel who operated throughout the squadron's brief operational existence. The Australian influence especially was a crucial factor in the squadron's many achievements.

With the war in Europe over in May 1945, the squadron's fate was sealed. In July 1945, the squadron was disbanded without any fanfare. The young crews were posted or on their way home. The once vibrant Offices and Sergeants Mess or Flight Commanders Officers were now eerily silent.

Post-war, the achievements of No.186 Squadron, RAF Bomber Command hardly gets a mention in books on the bomber offensive. Like the Group it operated with, the squadron tucked away in rural East Anglia is considered by many authors and eminent historians to have played a secondary role compared to the Lincolnshire base groups during the lengthy and costly Bomber Offensive. They could not be more wrong.

This is the history of a single squadron that played a pivotal role in destroying Germany's oil and transport facilities. Each member of the squadron can be justly proud, as can their relatives. Their story is one of heroics and perseverance in getting the job done.

Steve C Smith

June 2022

# Foreword

I have taken the unusual step of asking three people to write the forward to this book. A wife, a son and finally a daughter. Three very different perspectives.

.- .-.. .-- .- -.-- ... / .-. . -- . -- -... . .-. . -..

**"They were some of the best years of my life!"**

This was the answer my husband Gerald McPherson gave when asked how he faced the dangers of flying over enemy territory in a Lancaster Bomber.

Gerald was the rear gunner in Flight Lieutenant Alexander Jeffery Clarson's crew, known as "Clarson's Mob "and they completed their tour of 39 operations in 186 Squadron, Bomber Command on 9th April 1945. Unlike many of his comrades, Gerald was always willing to share his experiences and he emphasised how fortunate he was to survive and live to tell the tale, when so many of his friends never returned home to their loved ones.

He gave all the credit for their crew's survival to the superb flying skills of their Captain and Pilot, Jeff Clarson. As Gerald so often said "*He was an outstanding pilot and a good friend. We were a close-knit crew, we were like brothers".*

If only Gerald was here today to read Steve's book about his beloved Squadron, he would have been so pleased and proud to be a part of it. Sadly, my dearest Gerald passed away on 27th July 2021 at the age of 96. Thank you, Steve, for your dedication in recording the experiences of the brave airmen of 186 Squadron. Because of you their stories will live on, and they will never be forgotten.

*In the words of Henry Longfellow:*

*"Lives of great men all remind us*
*We can make our lives sublime*
*And departing leave behind us*
*Footprints on the sands of time".*

**Fay McPherson**
April 2022

.- / --. . -. . .-. .- - .. --- -. / --- ..-. / .... . .-. --- . ...

***'This was heroism'***

Bomber Command was formed with Whitley's Wellingtons, Blenheims and Hampdens. Which at the beginning of the War was no match for the German Air Force. Then things changed with the introduction of Stirling's, Halifax's and Lancaster's. These Bomber Command then divided into groups.

This book is about one of the less known squadrons, No.186 of No.3 Group, formed at RAF Tuddenham in 1944. The crews came together from No.90 Squadrons C Flight which had recently converted from the Short Stirling to the Avro Lancaster in June 1944.

My father's pilot was Flying Officer Ted Ritson DFC. My father, Flight Lieutenant J Sharpe, was Ted's Flight Engineer throughout their tour. Ted sadly passed away in February 1997 in his 90s. My father died on December 14th 1954, after a motorcycle accident. I was privileged to meet Ted's daughter and her husband, two very nice people with whom I have contact most weeks.

Unfortunately, my father and Ted hardly ever commented on the War. However, seeing some of Ted's operational flights during the War, one stood out. A bombing operation to the Ruhr. Ted's Lanc lost an engine over the English Channel. With my father's help, Ted continued the operation to the target and bombed it, returning safely back to base. This was heroism. Sadly some paid with their lives.

This book on No.186 Squadron consists of photos and family comments from those who served on the squadron. Seeing and handling Ted's DFC made me think of all the hours day and night of which the crews never returned.

For those interested, I have had a stone memorial placed in the beautiful garden of remembrance at RAF Tangmere in Chichester. This is to remember my Father, Ted Ritson and all of those who lost their lives.

**James Sharpe**
April 2022

... - .-. .. -.- . / .... .- .-. -.. / ... - .-. .. -.- . / ... ..- .-. .

***"Clarson's Mob".***

On a visit home to Cairns, North Queensland in 1986 to see my Step-Mother Ray, a passing comment about Dad started my search to find out about him and his crew.

"You know your Father was awarded a Medal for flying during the War, he was a brave man and a brilliant pilot. He flew Lancasters which were a very big aircraft"

I knew nothing at all about my Father's exploits during WW11 as he would not speak about that time and we were all teenagers not interested in our Dad's war stories. He has passed away at the tender age of 59 on the 18th of November 1982 the chance was gone. A few snippets were overheard by we children, listening at the door as the adults all drank and conversed with friends on one of the many "Parties" at our home. I forgot all about this conversation until much later after Ray's passing in 1997. Amongst her "Precious Items" kept in a blue suitcase was the DFC Medal in its original box as well as numerous personal photos that my siblings and I don't recall seeing when we were growing up.

The Distinguished Flying Cross and all other medals, including the Bomber Command Clasp awarded in 2014 were placed in a Montague in Memory of Alexander Jeffery Clarson F/Lt 426251 and his Crew and gifted to the Cairns RSL Club displayed in The Kokoda Hall Museum.

Fast forward to 2006 the start of my Ancestry Tree "The Clarson Sisters". My search starts with the help of my Sister Jane Dean. Computer skills being somewhat limited at this time, we fond very little information on the 186 Bomber Squadron we tried to piece together the names of his crew from a photo taken on the wing of "M" their favourite Lancaster just days before their last Operation. Dad has written all of the names on the end of this photo and of all of them I found his Rear Gunner Gerald McPherson who lived in Melbourne with his wife Fay. This relationship was the start of a "Treasure Chest of Information" and a wonderful friendship for the years to follow continuing today with Fay after Gerald's passing in 2021. Fay and Gerald both provided so many insightful stories and photos to round out memories of a very missed Father.

Kelvin Youngs from Air Crew Remembered was enormously helpful putting together a memorial page for our Father Alexander Jeffery "Jeff" Clarson and his brother Kenneth David who died in an aircraft accident in Iceland on the 7th of November 1944. From here more stories emerged and contacts made who filled in gaps and increased our knowledge. I might point out that until a few years ago I had no idea how many crew were really involved in and flew with the 186. This came to light while I was working recently with the Virtual War Museum Australia providing extra details about Dad and his Crew "Clarson's Mob". The researchers have compiled a marvellous story about how the Squadron was formed, operated and disbanded. Here we are in 2022 with Steve Smith's book "Target Germany" researched with such dedication building further clarity on the 186 Lancaster Bomber Squadron. Honouring all of the brave men who climbed into their aircraft knowing full well there was a real chance of not returning to base.

Thank you Steve for allowing all who are left and in thirst of knowledge of this particular Squadron the 186 Squadron, to know more simply by reading your story.

**Susan Clarson-Griffin, Proud Daughter of Jeff Clarson**
**Western Australia**

Postscript : Sadly, just a few days after I received the above, James passed away.

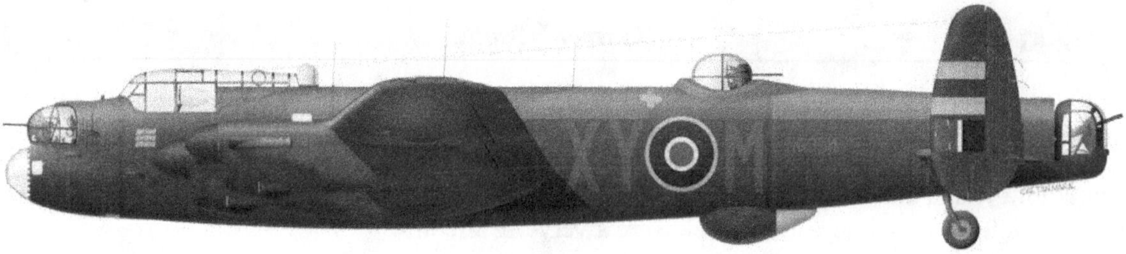


# October 1944

## *'Into the Fray'*

On October 5th, 1944, the ranks of No.3 Group RAF Bomber Command were increased by the formation of a new squadron to be numbered 186 Squadron. This new two-flight squadron created and authorised by Bomber Command Letter BC/521717/13/org would consist of 20 Avro Lancaster bombers. The formation of this new squadron came with a cost, especially to No.90 Squadron.

It would be the RAF Tuddenham based No.90 Squadron that would form the nucleus of No.186, it would lose its entire 'C' Flight, including its flight and deputy flight commander, in all 14 crews and 10 aircraft would effectively be gone in one swoop. Both squadrons would form part of No.32 Base.

At this stage, no commanding officer had yet arrived, the squadron was effectively being commanded by No.90 Squadron's commanding officer, W/Cdr A.J Ogilvie AFC, DFC. Things were moving in the right direction with the arrival in the afternoon of A/F/Lt J.S Walker, who would skilfully fill the role of Adjutant. On the day of the squadron's formation, RAF Tuddenham was very much on a war footing and taking the fight to Nazis Germany. Twenty-five crews had been detailed and briefed for an attack on Saarbrucken that night, seven of which included future 186 Squadron crews, Flying Officers L Smith and S Smith, R.E Roach and F.C Hoskin RCAF, Pilot Officer P.D Kelsey and finally Flight Sergeant H.S Young. All returned safely to RAF Tuddenham. On October 6$^{th}$, the first batch of pilots reported to the squadron on completion of No.56 Course at No.3 Lancaster Finishing School based at RAF Feltwell.

| Name | Rank | Air Force | Posted From | Date |
|---|---|---|---|---|
| I Graham | F/O | RNZAF | No.3 LFS | 06/10/1944 |
| J Liddel | F/O | RAFVR | No.3 LFS | 06/10/1944 |
| B.R Tait | P/O | RAFVR | No.3 LFS | 06/10/1944 |
| R Hanson | P/O | RAFVR | No.3 LFS | 06/10/1944 |

The arrival of these four crews put yet more strain on the already stretched facilities of RAF Tuddenham, and it was soon realised that the best option was to process the new arrivals and instantly send them on leave! Other than the laborious work of trying to organise the squadron October 7$^{th}$ was comparatively quiet until the transfer of the first batch of Lancasters moved over to 186 from 90 Squadron. It was then that the Adjutant and his senior NCO Sgt Tarrant's work really began. All were brand new aircraft delivered almost direct from either Armstrong Whitworth or Austin Motors manufacture during the last week of September. The squadron's remaining Lancasters were languishing at No.32 Base awaiting collection.

| Serial | Mark | Maker | Date | Via |
|---|---|---|---|---|
| NG137 | Mk.B.I | Armstrong Whitworth | 07/10/1944 | No.90 Squadron |
| NG140 | Mk.B.I | Armstrong Whitworth | 07/10/1944 | No.90 Squadron |
| NG146 | Mk.B.I | Armstrong Whitworth | 07/10/1944 | No.90 Squadron |
| NG147 | Mk.B.I | Armstrong Whitworth | 07/10/1944 | No.90 Squadron |
| NG148 | Mk.B.I | Armstrong Whitworth | 07/10/1944 | No.90 Squadron |
| NG149 | Mk.B.I | Armstrong Whitworth | 07/10/1944 | No.90 Squadron |
| NG174 | Mk.B.I | Armstrong Whitworth | 07/10/1944 | No.90 Squadron |
| NG175 | Mk.B.I | Armstrong Whitworth | 07/10/1944 | No.90 Squadron |
| NG176 | Mk.B.I | Armstrong Whitworth | 07/10/1944 | No.90 Squadron |
| NN720 | Mk.B.I | Auston Motors | 07/10/1944 | No.90 Squadron |

To date, no ground equipment had been received. However with the reduction from 3 to 2 flights, No.90 Squadron provided a motley collection of 17 vehicles, and so the squadron was beginning to take shape. October 9th 1944, was an important day for the squadron. Who at No.3 Group HQ was behind the selection of the squadron's first commanding officer will never be known, but their choice was inspiring. The man chosen was 34-year-old Canadian Wing Commander John Hassell Giles DFC. Born in Shanghai, China, in 1910, W/Cdr Giles had already seen considerable active service over Burma and India flying Curtis Mohawk fighters with 5 Squadron, whom he briefly commanded from Dum Dum airfield. More recently, with No.90 Squadron flying Short Stirlings. He had arrived with his crew in December 1942 and immediately took over 'A' Flight, where he served continuously until December 1943. With the departure of W/Cdr J.C Claydon DFC in June 1943, S/Ldr Giles was promoted to Wing Commander rank and given command. With No.90 Squadron, he was awarded a DFC in August 1943. Finally, in December 1943, after a full year of operations that had seen the squadron and Bomber Command suffer crippling losses, he was posted to the RAF Staff College for a rest. Affectionally known as 'Farmer' Giles, he somehow survived a year of continuous operations. On the same day as the new commanding officer's arrival, 14 complete crews from 90 Squadron's 'C' Flight were officially posted to No.186 Squadron.

| No. | Name | Rank | Air Force | Posted From | Date |
|---|---|---|---|---|---|
| 1 | R.P Madden | A/F/O | RCAF | 90 Squadron | 09/10/1944 |
| 2 | F.C Hoskin | F/O | RCAF | 90 Squadron | 09/10/1944 |
| 3 | W.T Jennings | A/F/Lt | RCAF | 90 Squadron | 09/10/1944 |
| 4 | S.Smith | A/F/Lt | RAFVR | 90 Squadron | 09/10/1944 |
| 5 | T.Phillips | A/F/O | RAFVR | 90 Squadron | 09/10/1944 |
| 6 | P. Kelsey | A/F/O | RAFVR | 90 Squadron | 09/10/1944 |
| 7 | L. Smith DFC | A/F/O | RAFVR | 90 Squadron | 09/10/1944 |
| 8 | R.E Roach | A/F/O | RAFVR | 90 Squadron | 09/10/1944 |
| 9 | E.E Ritson | F/O | RAFVR | 90 Squadron | 09/10/1944 |
| 10 | C.J Wait | F/O | RAFVR | 90 Squadron | 09/10/1944 |
| 11 | A.C Powell | A/F/Lt | RAFVR | 90 Squadron | 09/10/1944 |
| 12 | J.H Gibson | A/F/O | RAFVR | 90 Squadron | 09/10/1944 |
| 13 | H.S Young | Sgt | RAFVR | 90 Squadron | 09/10/1944 |
| 14 | F.J Cook | Sgt | RAAF | 90 Squadron | 09/10/1944 |

The first of the section leaders arrived on the 10th. From No.1651 Conversion Unit came A/F/Lt W Earle, the new squadron Navigation Leader, followed by A/F/Lt E Buckland, Gunnery Leader fresh from No.3 Group Air Gunners School. Finally, F/Lt B Holman, Bombing Leader, arrived from No.1657 Conversion Unit. Bernard 'Bill' Holman was a pre-war Police Officer. Born in 1914, in Kent, he had joined the Police Force in 1935 on his 21st birthday! After his training, he would be attached to the

Avro Lancaster Mk.B.I NG149 XY-G. This aircraft was one of the batch of ten Lancasters supplied by No.90 Squadron's 'C' Flight. After a long and illustrious association with No.186 Squadron, this Armstrong Whitworth built Lancaster was transferred to No.300 Squadron in September 1945.

Police Force in Margate. He married his fiancée Margarete in October 1939, a month to the day of declaration of war. Being in a reserved occupation, it was not until July 1941 that Bernard got his wish and joined the RAF. In February 1942, he set sail for South Africa to undertake his initial training. In September 1942, he was back in Britain, having docked in Liverpool. January 1943 found Bernard posted for conversion at No.1651 HCU at RAF Waterbeach. On completion, he and his crew were posted to No.15 Squadron, where he served until May 1943. In June, he was posted to No.90 Squadron. There followed yet another posting in September, this time to No.623 Squadron at RAF Downham Market. Having completed his first tour, Bernard was posted as an instructor to No.1651 CU in October 1943. Four months later in January 1944, he completed a Bombing Leaders Course at RAF Manby. Now, fully refreshed, Bernard would join a squadron brimming with experience.

The following day the final two section leaders arrived at RAF Tuddenham, F/O A.G Portway, Engineering Leader fresh from a stint at No.3 Lancaster Finishing School and New Zealand Signals Leader. Flying Officer G Baxter RNZAF arrived from No.1657 CU having previously flown with both No.214 and No.75(NZ) Squadron. Two more crews arrived via 3 LFS during the afternoon. One was captained by A/S/Ldr P Reynolds, who would fill the post of 'A' Flight Commander. He was accompanied by twenty-two-year old former insurance clerk from Montreal, Pilot Officer G Templeton RCAF. Southend born Percy Reynold's operational career stretched back to 1941. In that year, he was severely injured when taking off for a raid on Cherbourg in Vickers Wellington Mk.Ic Z8860. Three minutes after take-off, the Wellington crashed at 21.15 hours two miles N.E of Oakington (Rampton) and burst into flames. One of the crew was killed, three seriously injured, and one slightly. Percy sustained serious burns and an injured leg resulting in him being admitted to Addenbrookes Hospital. It was his first operation as captain. It was not his first crash. On August 3rd, he was a second pilot aboard Wellington R1088, which forced landed and burnt out at Rodgerous Field, Park Farm, East Bravorne. On this occasion, Percy received a few cuts and bruises.

A further two more crews joined the now growing ranks on No.186 Squadron on the 12th, both arriving from 3 LFS. New Zealander F/O K.J Orman and Australian P/O E.R Barton RAAF gave the squadron a distinct Antipodean feel. With the squadron reaching its effective establishment in crews, the need for accommodation and office space was becoming a priority. On the 12th, W/Cdr Giles DFC, and the squadron Adjutant, along with all available Orderly Room Staff, moved to its new if but temporary Squadron Headquarter situated opposite the stations, R&I Hanger. The post of 'B' Flight commander was finally filled with the arrival of Welshman A/S/Ldr M. Leyshon AFC on the 13th, another 214 Squadron veteran. Wing Commander Giles DFC now had all his senior staff in place. Each brought a wealth of operational experience.

On the 14th, W/Cdr Giles DFC and nine of his crews participated in the daylight raid against Duisburg alongside No.90 Squadron. All but one crew would be flying aircraft still officially on strength of No.90 Squadron.

Form B.660 – October 14th, 1944 (D): Target : Duisburg 'Cod'

| Rank | Surname | Initial | Airforce | Serial | Code | Role | Results |
|---|---|---|---|---|---|---|---|
| W/Cdr | Giles DFC | J | | NF987 | R | Main Force | Duty Carried Out. |
| F/Lt | Powell | A.C | | LM160 | W | Main Force | Duty Carried Out. |
| F/O | Ritson | E.E | | LM617 | X | Main Force | Duty Carried Out. |
| F/O | Hoskin | S | | LM618 | U | Main Force | Duty Carried Out. |
| F/O | Madden | R.P | RCAF | HK613 | Y | Main Force | Duty Carried Out. |
| F/O | Phillips | T | | LM165 | T | Main Force | Duty Carried Out. |
| F/O | Roach | R.E | | PD336 | P | Main Force | Duty Carried Out. |
| F/O | Gibson | J.H | | NG148 | B | Main Force | Duty Carried Out. |
| F/Sgt | Cook | F | RAAF | LM188 | S | Main Force | Duty Carried Out. |
| Sgt | Young | H | | HK622 | Z | Main Force | Duty Carried Out. |

This raid was part of a special operation which has received scant recognition in the history of Bomber Command. On October 13th, 1944, Sir Arthur Harris received the directive for Operation Hurricane, its aim was simple; *'In order to demonstrate to the enemy in Germany generally the overwhelming superiority of the Allied Air Forces in this theatre ... the intention is to apply within the shortest practical period the maximum effort of the Royal Air Force Bomber Command and the VIIIth United States Bomber Command against objectives in the densely populated Ruhr.'* No doubt Bomber Command HQ was aware that this directive was coming, giving it time to prepare. The first part of the directive began on the early morning of the 14th. Bomber Command had not operated for 48 hours giving the command ample time to assemble 1,013 aircraft.

All of the No.186 Squadron's contingent returned safely to RAF Tuddenham, it was an excellent start.[1] Serious damage was inflicted on Duisburg. However, worse was to come that night. Having returned to their bomber bases spread across the east of England, the ever resilient and hard-working groundcrews quickly repaired, refuelled, and bombed up their charges. It was a magnificent effort by everyone.

[1] *The 186 ORB does not record either operation against Duisburg. This maybe the result of all Administrational functions being undertaken by 90 Squadron up until October 16th.*

In a show of unimaginable force, over 1000 bomber crews were again briefed for a return visit to Duisburg, ten being provided by the Squadron. Remarkably all apart from F/O T Phillips and crew would be operating again, Phillips being replaced by F/O L Smith DFC. Sadly, however the Squadron's luck would run out on this night.

Form B.661 – October 14th, 1944 (N): Target : Duisburg

| | | | | | | | |
|---|---|---|---|---|---|---|---|
| W/Cdr | Giles DFC | J | | NF987 | R | Main Force | Duty Carried Out. |
| F/Lt | Powell | A.C | | LM160 | W | Main Force | Duty Carried Out. |
| F/O | Ritson | E.E | | LM617 | X | Main Force | Duty Carried Out. |
| F/O | Hoskin | S | | LM618 | U | Main Force | Duty Carried Out. |
| F/O | Madden | R.P | RCAF | HK613 | Y | Main Force | Duty Carried Out. |
| F/O | Roach | R.E | | PD336 | P | Main Force | Duty Carried Out. |
| F/O | Gibson | J.H | | NG148 | B | Main Force | Duty Carried Out. |
| F/Sgt | Cook | F | RAAF | LM165 | T | FTR | **MISSING** |
| Sgt | Young | H | | HK622 | Z | Main Force | Duty Carried Out. |
| F/O | Smith DFC | L | | NG186 | S | Main Force | Duty Carried Out. |

The crews began to depart RAF Tuddenham just before 23.00 hours heading firstly to Reading then crossing the English Coast at Beachy Head. The raid was planned in two waves, separated by 2 hours. The first phase was to commence at 01.29hrs by 675 bombers, followed at 03.20 hours by a further 330 bombers. In near perfect weather the force entered German airspace. The crews of No.186 Squadron were briefed for the first phase of the attack. The fires from the earlier day raid were visible when still over 100 miles from Duisburg. Opposition was minimal, the German controllers had been completely taken unawares as the first Red and Green Target Indicators started to fall over the port area. Flak over the city was classified as moderate and searchlights were rather ineffective during the early stages. Despite the lack of opposition Duisburg's flak would claim the squadron's first crew. Flight Sergeant F.J Cook RAAF and crew were reported missing when their Lancaster LM165 WP-T crashed near the railway station of Meidrich, Germany at 01.34 hours killing on all board. Four bodies were recovered and initially buried in the North Cemetery at Duisburg-Hamborn.

| | | |
|---|---|---|
| Type | Avro Lancaster Mk.I **LM165 WP-T** | Armstrong Whitworth |
| Taken on Charge | 12/06/1944 (90 Squadron) | |
| Cat E Missing | 15/10/1944 | |
| Struck Of Charge | 15/10/1944 | |
| Total Flying Hours | 220.05 hours | |
| Take-Off Time | 22.52 hours | |
| Bomb Load | 11 x 500lb + 4 x 500lb GP | |
| | | |
| | **CREW** | |
| Pilot | F/Sgt Francis John Cook. Aus/429526 RAAF | Runnymede Panel 260 |
| Navigator | Sgt Kenneth Morrell.1397720 RAFVR | Runnymede Panel 234 |
| Bomb Aimer | Sgt Kenneth Brian Howell.1581325 RAFVR | Runnymede Panel 231 |
| Wireless Operator | Sgt George Irving Read. 22215997 RAFVR | Runnymede Panel 236 |
| Mid Upper Gunner | Sgt William Purnell-Edwards. 605673 RAFVR | Runnymede Panel 236 |
| Rear Gunner | Sgt John Robert Sunley.1623987 RAFVR | Runnymede Panel 238 |
| Flight Engineer | Sgt Frederick William James.1896671 RAFVR | Runnymede Panel 232 |
| | | |
| Posted History | 3 LFS – 90 Squadron – 186 Squadron 09/10/44 | |
| Operations Flown | 1 | |
| Buried | N/A | |

The Air Forces Memorial at Runnymede commemorates by name over 20,000 men and women of the air forces, who were lost in the Second World War during operations from bases in the United Kingdom and North and Western Europe, and who have no known graves. They served in Bomber, Fighter, Coastal, Transport, Flying Training and Maintenance Commands, and came from all parts of the Commonwealth. Some were from countries in continental Europe which had been overrun but whose airmen continued to fight in the ranks of the Royal Air Force.

Despite the bodies of Sergeants Sunley, Purnell-Edwards, Morrell and Read being reportedly buried in the Duisburg-Hamborn Cemetery, post war the Royal Air Force Missing Research and Enquiry Service (MRES) were unable to locate the graves and the crew were classified as 'Missing, presumed killed'. William Purnell-Edward was from Co. Dublin, the Irish Republic.

In total 4,040 tons of high explosive and 500 tons of incendiaries were dropped during the night. Five Lancasters and 2 Halifaxes were lost. Nearly 9,000 tons of bombs had thus fallen on Duisburg in less than 48 hours. Local reports are difficult to obtain. The Duisburg Stadtarchiv does not have the important Endbericht — the final report. Small comments are available however: *'Heavy casualties must be expected.' 'Very serious property damage. A large number of people buried.' 'Thyssen Mines III and IV: About 8 days loss of production.'* It had been a staggering show of force by RAF Bomber Command. The euphoria on the squadron however was muted by the loss of a crew.

Form B.663 –October 15th, 1944 (N): Target : Wilhelmshaven 'Kipper'

| | | | | | | | |
|---|---|---|---|---|---|---|---|
| F/Lt | Powell | A.C | | LM160 | W | Main Force | Duty Carried Out. |
| F/O | Ritson | E.E | | LM617 | X | Main Force | Duty Carried Out. |
| F/Sgt | Young | H | RAAF | HK622 | Z | Main Force | Duty Carried Out. |
| F/O | Madden | R.P | RCAF | LM618 | U | Main Force | Duty Carried Out. |

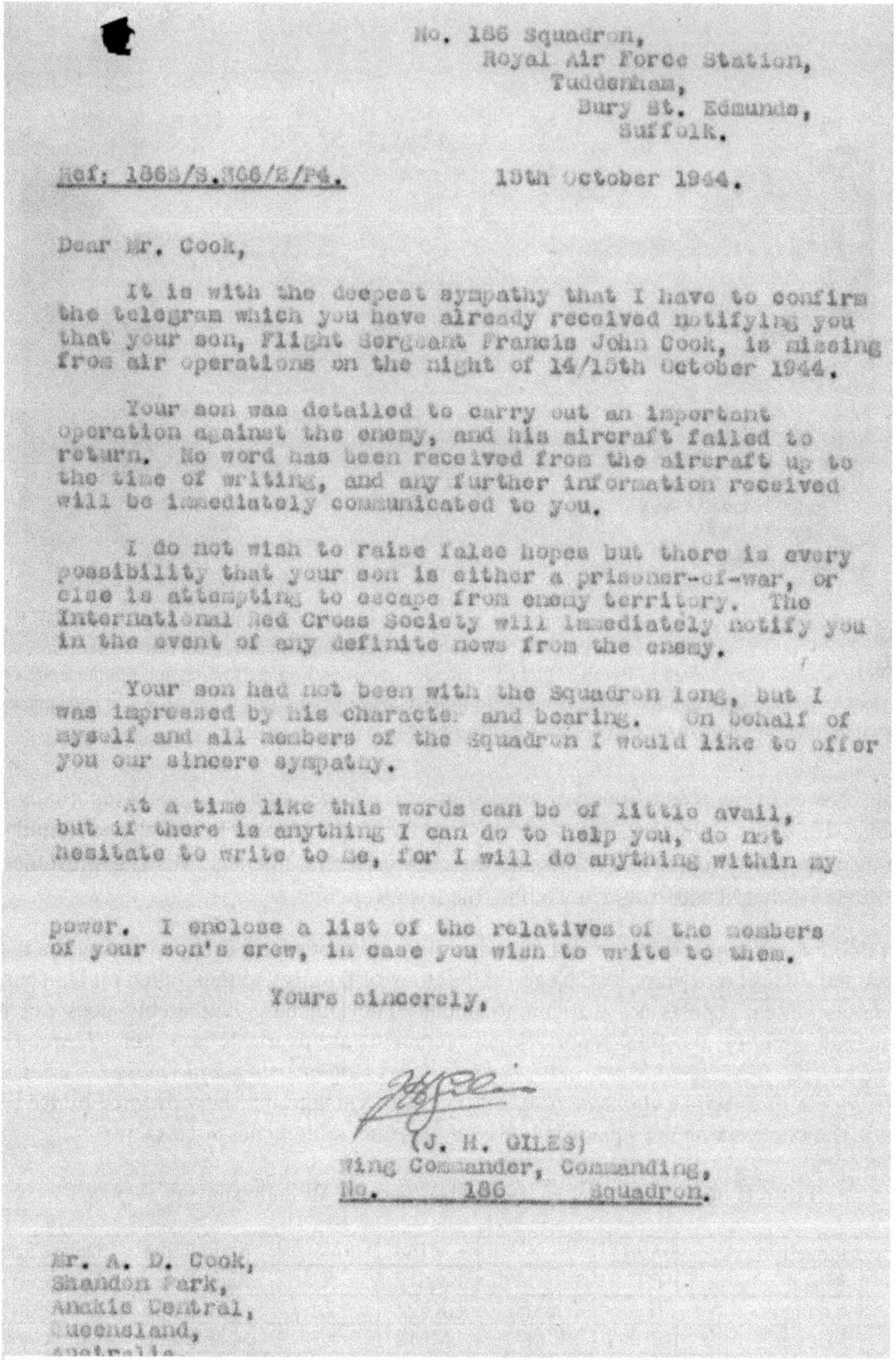

No. 186 Squadron,
Royal Air Force Station,
Tuddenham,
Bury St. Edmunds,
Suffolk.

Ref: 186S/S.306/2/P4. 15th October 1944.

Dear Mr. Cook,

It is with the deepest sympathy that I have to confirm the telegram which you have already received notifying you that your son, Flight Sergeant Francis John Cook, is missing from air operations on the night of 14/15th October 1944.

Your son was detailed to carry out an important operation against the enemy, and his aircraft failed to return. No word has been received from the aircraft up to the time of writing, and any further information received will be immediately communicated to you.

I do not wish to raise false hopes but there is every possibility that your son is either a prisoner-of-war, or else is attempting to escape from enemy territory. The International Red Cross Society will immediately notify you in the event of any definite news from the enemy.

Your son had not been with the Squadron long, but I was impressed by his character and bearing. On behalf of myself and all members of the Squadron I would like to offer you our sincere sympathy.

At a time like this words can be of little avail, but if there is anything I can do to help you, do not hesitate to write to me, for I will do anything within my power. I enclose a list of the relatives of the members of your son's crew, in case you wish to write to them.

Yours sincerely,

(J. H. GILES)
Wing Commander, Commanding,
No. 186 Squadron.

Mr. A. D. Cook,
Shandon Park,
Anakie Central,
Queensland,
Australia.

The reality of war. The squadron had not been formed ten days before Wing Commander Giles DFC would sign the first of what would become a regular letter to the family of crews who Failed to Return. Wing Commander Giles DFC has expressed his and his squadron's sorrow of losing the crew of Flight Sergeant Cook RAAF. The reality is the crew probably only met the Commanding Officer once on arrival and at a briefing. Such was the intensity of operations.

The important shipyards and dock area of Wilhelmshaven were the intended targets on the early evening of October 15th. Four squadron crews would participate, F/Lt A 'Sandy' Powell, F/O's R Madden R RCAF and E Ritson and F/Sgt H Young. Remarkably, each had flown on the two Duisburg operations. The squadron very nearly notched up another loss when F/Sgt Herbert Young was fortunate to survive the attention of Wilhelmshaven's ferocious flak. While over the target at 19,000 feet, a burst of flak exploded so close to Lancaster HK622 XY-Z that it wrenched the control column out of the hands of the pilot, forcing it into a 4000 feet dive. He finally regained control at 15,000 feet. On the crew's return, they reported, *'parachute and equipment flung out of aircraft'* How or why this happened is unclear. Both gunners aboard F/Lt A.C Powell's Lancaster passed out due to oxygen starvation on the return trip when the supply to both turrets froze. Sergeant R.J Dack, Mid-Upper Gunner, and Sgt L.Grice, Rear Gunner, were found unconscious. They, and the rest of the crew had been lucky that a prowling fighter had not intercepted them.

October 16th, 1944, was an important day in the history of No.186 Squadron. The squadron took sole responsibility for all administrational and operational activities from this date. Since its formation, No.186 had been conjoined with No.90 Squadron and as such much of the day-to-day activities were under the supervision of its parent squadron. On October 17th, the squadron was informed that it would be required for a daylight operation to Bonn the following day. It would coincide with a milestone in the No.3 Group history. This would be the first major operation by the Group in the new independent role which its commander, Air Vice-Marshal R. Harrison, had been granted. Although only approximately 40 of the group's Lancasters had been fitted with the G-H blind-bombing device, No.3 Group were to operate predominately on days where cloud covered the target. The device was no stranger to the group which used it with some limited success in 1943 before it was withdrawn on the orders of the C-in-C Bomber Command. It was No.218 (Gold Coast) Squadron who were tasked over the winter of 1943 and Spring of 1944 to experiment and develop G-H under operational conditions. Their pioneering work was the catalyst for the Group's success over the last 8 months of the war. Air Vice-Marshal Harrison requested that Bonn, a relatively intact and important town, should be the target for this first operation. Possibly so that post raid reconnaissance photographs could show the results of the first G-H raid without the effects of other bombing, confusing the interpretation of the photographs. Twelve crews were detailed and briefed for the operation.

Fourteen crews from 90 Squadron would join them. The assembled crew would have been given strict instructions to format on specific G-H equipped aircraft at the briefing. These aircraft would be identified by two horizontal yellow bars on the rudders. Marking on this occasion would be provided by RAF Methwold's No.218 Squadron, at that time No.3 Group's premiere G-H specialist and No.149 Squadron. No squadrons of No.32 Base had yet to be fitted with G-H and would rely heavily on Methwold and No.33 Base over the coming weeks and months. Strict adherence to the speeds and altitude was essential. A speed of 165 R.A.S on the run into target and 160 R.A.S with bomb doors open over the target was given, and a stepped bombing altitude between 16,500 feet and 17,500 feet. It was stressed that timing was vital. Crews were warned that they must bomb at their allotted time. For many of the old hands, these strict instructions could not have been any further from the rather generous times over target experienced in the campaigns of 1943 or early 1944. This was a new type of bombing, and flying discipline was critical for both survival and success.

At 07.58 hours, on an overcast morning, 'A' Flight's S/Ldr P Reynolds lifted Lancaster NG174 XY-A off the tarmac, two minutes later 'B' Flight's S/Ldr M Leyshon AFC was airborne in Lancaster LM188 XY-S. Once airborne, the squadron headed towards its departure point of Bradwell Bay on the Essex Coastline. None of the 12 Lancasters had yet to be equipped with GH, and it would not be until the new year that sets would become available.

## Form B.665 – October 18th, 1944 (D): Target : Bonn 'Shark'

| | | | | | | | |
|---|---|---|---|---|---|---|---|
| S/Ldr | Reynolds | P | | NG174 | XY-A | Follower | Duty Carried Out. |
| F/O | Graham | I.D | RNZAF | NG148 | XY-B | Follower | Duty Carried Out. |
| F/O | Wait | C.J | | NG147 | XY-C | Follower | Duty Carried Out. |
| P/O | Tait | B.R | | NG137 | XY-D | Follower | Duty Carried Out. |
| P/O | Templeton | G.M | RCAF | NG146 | XY-E | Follower | Duty Carried Out. |
| F/O | Smith | L | | NG140 | XY-F | Follower | Duty Carried Out. |
| S/Ldr | Leyshon AFC | M | | LM188 | XY-S | Follower | Duty Carried Out. |
| F/O | Smith | S | | LM618 | XY-U | Follower | Duty Carried Out. |
| F/Lt | Powell | A.C | | LM160 | XY-W | Follower | Duty Carried Out. |
| F/O | Ritson | E.E | | LM617 | XY-X | Follower | Duty Carried Out. |
| F/O | Madden | R.P | RCAF | HK613 | XY-Y | Follower | Duty Carried Out. |
| F/O | Liddell | J.B | | HK622 | XY-Z | Follower | Duty Carried Out. |

Conditions over Bonn were ideal, giving both the attackers and the defenders an opportunity to engage. At 11.00 hours the first marker flares arched their way down towards Bonn. Crews were generally pleased with the accuracy, New Zealander F/O I.D Graham RNZAF dropped his mixed HE and incendiary load from 17,000 feet remarking upon his return, *'Identified target visually, built-up area. Results Successful attack, many fires'.* Squadron Leader M Leyshon AFC watched with some satisfaction as numerous 4000 pounders exploded on both sides of the river Rhine, with many landing on the west bank. Not all the crews were pleased, however, F/O E.E Ritson reported at de-briefing *'Incendiary attack rather haphazard'* while F/O S Smith at the controls of Lancaster MK.III LM618 XY-U stated, *'Formation rather unsatisfactory, bombing seemed fairly scattered on both sides of the river'.*

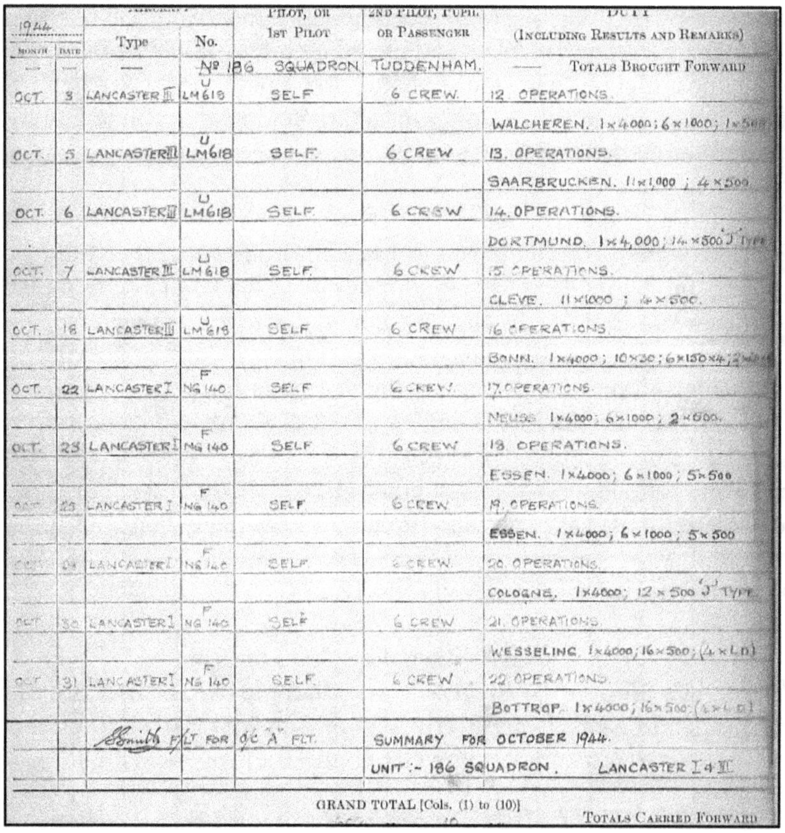

| 1944 Month | Date | Type | No. | Pilot, or 1st Pilot | 2nd Pilot, Pupil or Passenger | Duty (Including Results and Remarks) |
|---|---|---|---|---|---|---|
| — | — | — | Nº 186 | SQUADRON | TUDDENHAM. | — Totals Brought Forward |
| OCT. | 3 | LANCASTER III | U LM618 | SELF | 6 CREW. | 12 OPERATIONS. |
| | | | | | | WALCHEREN. 1×4000; 6×1000; 1×5[illegible] |
| OCT. | 5 | LANCASTER III | U LM618 | SELF | 6 CREW | 13. OPERATIONS. |
| | | | | | | SAARBRUCKEN. 11×1,000 ; 4×500 |
| OCT. | 6 | LANCASTER III | U LM618 | SELF | 6 CREW | 14. OPERATIONS. |
| | | | | | | DORTMUND. 1×4,000; 14×500 'J' TYPE |
| OCT. | 7 | LANCASTER III | U LM618 | SELF | 6 CREW | 15. OPERATIONS. |
| | | | | | | CLEVE. 11×1000 ; 4×500. |
| OCT. | 18 | LANCASTER III | U LM618 | SELF | 6 CREW | 16 OPERATIONS. |
| | | | | | | BONN. 1×4000; 10×30; 6×150×4; [illegible] |
| OCT. | 22 | LANCASTER I | F NG140 | SELF | 6 CREW. | 17. OPERATIONS. |
| | | | | | | NEUSS 1×4000; 6×1000; 2×500. |
| OCT. | 23 | LANCASTER I | F NG140 | SELF | 6 CREW | 18 OPERATIONS. |
| | | | | | | ESSEN. 1×4000; 6×1000; 5×500 |
| OCT. | 25 | LANCASTER I | F NG140 | SELF | 6 CREW | 19. OPERATIONS. |
| | | | | | | ESSEN. 1×4000; 6×1000; 5×500 |
| OCT. | 28 | LANCASTER I | F NG140 | SELF | 6 CREW. | 20. OPERATIONS. |
| | | | | | | COLOGNE. 1×4000; 12×500 'J' TYPE |
| OCT. | 30 | LANCASTER I | F NG140 | SELF | 6 CREW | 21. OPERATIONS. |
| | | | | | | WESSELING. 1×4000; 16×500; (4×L.B.) |
| OCT. | 31 | LANCASTER I | F NG140 | SELF | 6 CREW | 22 OPERATIONS. |
| | | | | | | BOTTROP. 1×4000; 16×500; (4×L.B.) |
| | | S Smith F/LT FOR | O.C. "A" FLT. | | SUMMARY FOR | OCTOBER 1944. |
| | | | | | UNIT :- 186 SQUADRON. | LANCASTER I & III |

GRAND TOTAL [Cols. (1) to (10)] Totals Carried Forward

Left: A page from Log Book of 'A' Flights Sidney Smith. This page records Sidney's sorties from No.12 to No.22 and lists the operation to Bonn on October 16th, 1944, Sidney's 16th operation. It is interesting to note that in the space of just one month, Sidney flew a total of 11 operations. This graphically shows the intensity of operations and how quickly a tour could be completed compared to 1943.

An excellent photograph of Sidney Smith. Twenty-four-year old Sidney was born in Blyth, on the windswept Northumberland coast in 1919. He followed the usual route for a No.3 Group crew at the time, No.1657 HCU, No.3 Lancaster Finishing School, before joining 'C' Flight of No.90 Squadron. Sidney undertook his first operation on September 5th 1944, against Le Havre. By the time he was transferred to No.186 Squadron, he had completed 11 operations.

CYMRU AM BYTH ( Wales Forever) adorns the Lancaster of Squadron Leader M Leyshon AFC. He was personally handpicked to join the squadron and given command of 'B' Flight. Mervyn Leyshon had completed his first tour flying the Vickers Wellington with No.214 Squadron in 1942. A gifted pilot and excellent Flight Commander, his time on 186 Squadron was sadly cut short.

The last squadron crew to land back at RAF Tuddenham was F/Lt A.C Powell at the controls of Lancaster LM160 XY-W at 13.17 hours. All the Tuddenham crews returned, some showing visible signs of damage. Three Lancasters had been hit over Bonn, HK613 XY-Y, the most seriously, severe damage being inflicted to the starboard wing. Canadian P/O B.R Tait had the fuselage of Lancaster NG137 XY-D punctured. Also hit was F/O J.B Liddel, who had his starboard engine nacelle peppered by flak fragments. Both crews had just returned from their first operation.

No.186 Squadron Reported Flak Damage 18/10/1944

| Serial | Code | Damage Reported | Repairs / Notes |
|---|---|---|---|
| HK622 | **XY-Z** | Starboard engine nacelle. | Repaired on Squadron. |
| HK613 | **XY-Y** | Starboard Wing. | Repaired on Squadron. |
| NG137 | **XY-D** | Fuselage. | Repaired on Squadron. |

There was no time to celebrate the squadron's first 'official' operation. The following night, the squadron was required to provide 15 crews against two separate targets at Stuttgart, which would be attacked with a four-hour interval. It would prove to be a frustrating night and costly night. One crew was withdrawn prior to take-off. The first of twelve crews to depart was W/Cdr Giles DFC at 17.29 hours, he was immediately followed by NG174 XY-A flown by S/Ldr Percy Reynolds. The crews made landfall over the French coast at Cayeux-Sur-Mer. It was here that the crew of F/O L Smith DFC was forced to abort with a defective rear turret aboard Lancaster LM188 XY-S. The first phase of the attack was divided into three waves, with the Path Finder's opening the attack at 20:30 hours.

Form B.666 – October 19th, 1944 (N): Target : Stuttgart 'Barbel 'D'

| | | | | | | | |
|---|---|---|---|---|---|---|---|
| W/Cdr | Giles DFC | J.H | | LM160 | XY-W | Main Force | Duty Carried Out. |
| S/Ldr | Reynolds | P | | NG174 | XY-A | Main Force | Duty Carried Out. |
| F/O | Wait | C.J | | NG147 | XY-C | Main Force | Duty Carried Out. |
| F/O | Graham | I.D | RNZAF | NG176 | XH-H | MISSING | FTR |
| P/O | Templeton | G.M | RCAF | NG146 | XY-E | Main Force | Duty Carried Out. |
| P/O | Gibson | J.H | | NN720 | XY-K | Main Force | Duty Carried Out. |
| P/O | Tait | R.R | | NG175 | XY-J | Main Force | Duty Carried Out. |
| F/O | Madden | R.P | RCAF | HK661 | XY-R | Main Force | Duty Carried Out. |
| F/O | Roach | R.E | | HK650 | XY-T | Main Force | Duty Carried Out. |
| F/O | Smith DFC | L | | LM188 | XY-S | Main Force | Duty Not Carried Out. |
| F/O | Ritson | E.E | | LM617 | XY-X | Main Force | Duty Carried Out. |
| F/O | Liddell | J.B | | HK606 | XY-V | Main Force | Duty Carried Out. |
| P/O | Hanson | R.A | | HK613 | XY-Y | Main Force | Duty Carried Out. |
| | | | 2nd Phase | | | | |
| F/O | Kelsey | P.D | | LM618 | XY-U | --- | Withdrawn. |
| F/O | Roach | R.E | | HK650 | XY-T | Main Force | Duty Carried Out. |
| F/Lt | Jennings DFC | W.T | RCAF | NG148 | XY-B | Main Force | Duty Carried Out. |

Number 186 Squadron crews were evenly divided over all three waves. The early marking was severely hampered by thick cloud, the red target indicators being quickly swallowed up. Squadron Leader P Reynolds was at the controls of Lancaster NG174 XY-A. Flying at 17,000 feet, he deposited his single 4000 pounder and 1500 four-pound incendiaries at 20.33 hours. Apart from the flak which punctured the bomb aimers position of F/O E.E Ritson's Lancaster LM617 XY-X and shattered the windscreen of Lancaster NN720 XY-K flown by P/O J.H.Gibson the presence of German fighter flares was a more ominous sign of trouble. Wing Commander Giles DFC was unable to drop his 4000lb Cookie on what appeared to be a concentration of Red and Yellow Target Indictors. Despite his and his bomb aimer's best efforts, the cookie stubbornly refused to drop. It was subsequently jettisoned. Having deposited their bombs, the crews started the long journey home. At 20.46 hours, P/O R.A. Hanson was flying over Wachendorf at 8000 feet when the rear gunner reported a fighter flare on the port beam. Almost immediately, an FW190 fighter was observed 300 yards to port, the rear gunner Sgt R.C Thomas gave the order to corkscrew at the same time opening fire, Sgt S.C Rogers joined him in the mid-upper turret. Both gunners claimed that the FW190 was hit as it dived to starboard. No damage was reported to Lancaster HK613 XY-Y or injuries to the crew. On return, the following was submitted by the crew. Interestingly no single engine fighters are reported to have been airborne on this night.

| A surprise attack from behind a fighter flare. Immediate evasive action taken, and enemy fighter broke off the attack and dived to starboard. Not seen again. |
|---|

Not so lucky was the crew of New Zealander F/O I.D Graham RNZAF. They were intercepted and shot down at around 20.50 hours by a prowling night fighter. Avro Lancaster XY-H NG176 is reported to have crashed between the villages of Mattexey and Clezentaine, 20 miles South of Luneville, France, killing all on board. There is a possible, but unconfirmed claimant for the destruction of NG176, Lt Clemens Ostrowizki of 1./NJG6, who 'claimed' four bombers that night. Thirty-year-old Ian Graham was older than most on the squadron, born in Auckland in January 1914, he sailed to the United Kingdom in December 1941. Ian spent the first two years in England as a Flying Instructor flying Oxfords. His arrival at Tuddenham on October 6th had previously seen him and his crew training at 29 Operational Training Unit, No.1657 Con Unit, and finally No.3 Lancaster Finishing School. The bodies of the crew were initially buried at Luneville, then moved to the American Cemetery at Andilly. Finally, post-war, the crew were reinterred in the Choloy War Cemetery, France. The Army Graves Service initially created the cemetery for the re-burials of casualties recovered from isolated sites, communal cemeteries, and small churchyards in north-eastern France.

| Type | Avro Lancaster Mk.I **NG176 XY-H** | Armstrong Whitworth |
|---|---|---|
| Taken on Charge | 07/10/1944 via 90 Squadron. | |
| Cat E Missing | 20/10/1944 | |
| Struck Of Charge | 01/11/1944 | |
| Total Flying Hours | N/K | |
| Take-Off Time | 17.35hrs | |
| Bomb Load | 1 x 4000lb + 1500 x 4lb IB | |
| | **CREW** | **GRAVE** |
| Pilot | F/O Ian Dundee Graham NZ413407 RNZAF | 2.B.3 |
| Navigator | Sgt William Raine 1565370 RAFVR | 2.B.2 |
| Bomb Aimer | F/O John Robert Frees Aus/429404 RAAF | 2.B.4 |
| Wireless Operator | F/O John Duncan McFarlane NZ421981 RNZAF | 2.B.5 |
| Mid Upper Gunner | Sgt Henry Alan Sumner 1335456 RAFVR | 2.B.7 |
| Rear Gunner | Sgt Frank Evans 1146235 RAFVR | 2.B.1 |
| Flight Engineer | Sgt Edward Brunskill 1514782 RAFVR | 2.B.6 |
| | | |
| Posted History | 1657 CU / No.3 LFS / 186 Squadron 6/10/1944 | |
| Operations Flown | 2 | |
| Buried | **CHOLOY WAR CEMETERY** | |

At 21.15 hours, the mid-upper gunner of F/O J.B Liddell spotted the unmistakable outline of a single-engine fighter on the starboard quarter against the white clouds. At 700 yards, Sgt P.L.W Scott, the rear gunner, identified the fighter as a Bf109. The crew, now fully alert, braced themselves for the inevitable attack. Sergeant N.H Clydesdale sitting in his mid-upper turret, gave a running commentary on its position to his pilot while the rear gunner scanned below and behind for another fighter. Finally, at 600 yards, the Bf109 turned into attack from the starboard quarter, opening fire immediately. Both gunners instantly returned fire as the Lancaster was thrown into a steep corkscrew to starboard. The

The crew of New Zealander Flying Officer Ian Graham RNZAF. L-R Sergeant Edward Brunskill (Flight Engineer) Pilot. Flying Officer John MacFarlane RNZAF (Wireless Operator), Sergeant William Raine (Navigator), Sergeant Henry Sumner (Mid Upper Gunner), Sergeant Frank Evans (Rear Gunner), and Flying Officer John Frees RAAF (Bomb Aimer). The photo was taken at the wedding of William Raine. Via Kelvin Young.

fighter's aim was slightly off as tracer fire passed harmlessly above the Lancaster. Thankfully, the gunner's aim was better. Strikes were observed hitting the fuselage as the Bf109 dived to port. This was confirmed by the wireless operator who was standing at the Astro Dome. The fighter was not seen again. Wing Commander Giles DFC finally managed to drop his 4000 pounder in the North Sea on route home. While most of the squadron were making their way home looking forward to their beds, three crews were getting ready to participate in the second phase of the attack. The first crew airborne was F/Lt W.T Jennings RCAF, a former 90 Squadron crew in Lancaster NG148 XY-B at 22.10 hours. Twenty-seven-year-old Welland Jennings, was born in Fort Garry, Manitoba and had previously served 12 months in the Canadian Army before joining the RCAF. One crew failed to take off when the brake pressure aboard Lancaster LM618 XY-U dropped below the minimum PSI required. Despite patiently waiting to build up the air pressure F/O P.D Kelsey was given the red. He was too late for take-off. The attack commenced at 01.00 hours as planned and was carried out through 9/10th cloud. The glow of the fires from the earlier raid could be seen despite the cloud cover. The Path Finder dropped Wanganui flares were rather dispersed, resulting in what appeared to be a scattered raid. Contrary to F/O R.E Roach's somewhat cautious remarks on return, '*Bombing widespread, inconclusive raid*' severe damage had been inflicted to Stuttgart's central and eastern districts. The squadron was not required on the 20th and instead welcomed two crews from No.3 LFS, Australian P/O Rex Cogler RAAF and P/O Edgar Field. The squadron did not participate in an all No.3 Group daylight raid against the coastal battery at Walcheren on the 21st but was required to prepare 14 crews for a raid directed against Neuss instead. This was later cancelled and put back 24 hours. On the 22nd, No.186 Squadron prepared nine crews for No.3 Group's second all G-H operation. The target was the city of Neuss. The first crew away from RAF Tuddenham was F/O S Smith at the controls of Lancaster NG140 XY-F at 12.52 hours. Once he and the squadron were safely airborne they headed for the Group assembly point. What followed next

F/O Ian Dundee Graham NZ413407 RNZAF

Sgt William Raine 1565370 RAFVR

F/O John Robert Frees Aus/429404 RAAF

F/O John Duncan McFarlane NZ421981 RNZAF

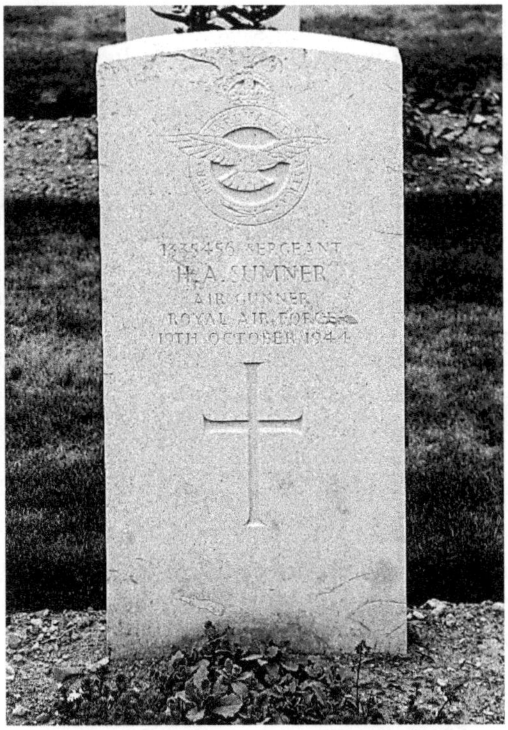


Sgt Henry Alan Sumner 1335456 RAFVR

Sgt Frank Evans 1146235 RAFVR

Sgt Edward Brunskill 1514782 RAFVR

was a shambles. The No.3 Group Records Book reported *'Faulty Forming-up'*. In amongst the monstrous clouds, Lancasters were jockeying all over East Anglia trying desperately to locate their allotted G-H leaders.

Form B.672 – October 22nd, 1944 (D): Target : Neuss 'Ray'

| | | | | | | | |
|---|---|---|---|---|---|---|---|
| F/O | Smith | S | | NG140 | XY-F | Follower | Duty Carried Out. |
| F/O | Templeton | G.M | RCAF | NG146 | XY-E | Follower | Duty Carried Out. |
| F/Lt | Powell | A.C | | LM160 | XY-W | Follower | Duty Carried Out. |
| F/O | Kelsey | P.D | | LM618 | XY-U | Follower | Duty Carried Out. |
| F/O | Smith | L | | LM188 | XY-S | Follower | Duty Carried Out. |
| F/O | Ritson | E.E | | LM617 | XY-X | Follower | Duty Carried Out. |
| F/O | Liddell | J.B | | HK622 | XY-Z | Follower | Duty Carried Out. |
| F/O | Hanson | R.A | | HK613 | XY-Y | Follower | Duty Carried Out. |
| S/Ldr | Reynolds | P | | NG174 | XY-A | Follower | Duty Carried Out. |

Flying Officer S Smith reporting, *'Arrived at group rendezvous point ten minutes early, no G-H aircraft seen, joined up with four other G-H aircraft'*. Finally, and surprisingly without any collisions, the 100 Lancasters first gathered and then departed in some resemblance of a formation. The Lancasters headed towards the departure point of Orford Ness on the Suffolk Coast. The squadrons of No.32 Base were again reliant on the G-H equipped aircraft of RAF Methwold, which provided 15 G-H crews plus 15 reserves due to technical issues with the mobile G-H station at Antwerp. The first marker flares were to drop at exactly 16.00 hours - H-Hour. However, despite the briefing for strict adherence to timings, flares began arching towards Neuss at 15.55 hours. The squadron's crews quickly bombed these early markers. Flying Officer E.E Ritson, who was on his 11th operation, reported, *'Bombing very scattered, but when this aircraft dropped bombs, seven others dropped simultaneously'*. Squadron Leader P Reynolds saw two Methwold G-H Leaders fire white Verey flares just before the run into the target. This was the signal that their G-H set was unserviceable. He was lucky to format on one of the reserve G-H aircraft in time to drop his 1 x 4000lb + 2 x 500lb MC + 6 x 1000lb AN-M59 from 15,000 feet. Flak was moderate to heavy and accurate, with the only casualty being F/O J.B Liddell, who reported flak damage to the front turret and bomb aimer's position aboard Lancaster HK622 XY-Z. Once again, the returning crew's pessimism regarding accuracy proved unfounded. Over 90 houses and three industrial buildings were utterly destroyed, and over 500 houses and 18 industrial premises seriously damaged. No aircraft were lost from the raid.

No.186 Squadron Reported Flak Damage 22/10/1944

| Serial | Code | Damage Reported | Repairs / Notes |
|---|---|---|---|
| HK622 | **XY-Z** | Front Turret, forward section. | Repaired on Squadron. |

Bomber Command directed its Hurricane-force against Essen on the early evening of October 23rd. 1,055 aircraft — 561 Lancasters, 463 Halifaxes, and 31 Mosquitoes would be deployed. This was the largest raid on Essen so far in the war, and the number of aircraft despatched excluded the Lancasters of 5 Group. Number 3 Group provided a respectable 172 Lancasters with RAF Tuddenham squadrons supplying 16 Lancasters each. The first crew away was that of S/Ldr P Reynolds at 16.14 hours at the controls of Lancaster NG174 XY-A. The No.3 Group contingent departed over Beachy Head, its squadrons evenly distributed over the six waves. It was on this operation the squadron notched up two early returns. The crew of F/Sgt L.A Green was the first when they lost the A.S.I and Gee aboard Lancaster HK606 XY-V soon after crossing the coast. They were followed by F/O L Smith DFC at the controls of LM188 XY-S. Lionel Smith had experienced problems with his starboard inner engine over the North Sea but continued on. However, it was soon realised that they would never reach the target, so he turned for home. Only the previous month while operational with No.90 Squadron, Smith and his crew had been hit by flak while attacking Calais. The mid-upper gunner had been seriously injured, and the Lancaster severely damaged. Despite this, the crew pressed on with the attack and bombed the target. Back over Suffolk, the crew were obliged to make a wheel-up landing at Friston, Suffolk. For his action, on this day, he was awarded the DFC in November.

A nice view of both mid-upper and rear turrets aboard Avro Lancaster Mk.B.I NG146 XY-E. This aircraft was part of the batch of ten transferred to No.186 from No.90 Squadron in October 1944. A favourite aircraft of Flying Officer G.M Templeton RCAF, who skippered XY-F on twenty-three raids.

Form B.673 – October 23rd, 1944 (N): Target : Essen 'Bullhead'

| | | | | | | | |
|---|---|---|---|---|---|---|---|
| S/Ldr | Reynolds | P | | NG174 | XY-A | Main Force | Duty Carried Out. |
| F/O | Barton | E.R | RAAF | NG148 | XY-C | Main Force | Duty Carried Out. |
| F/O | Wait | C.J | | NG147 | XY-C | Main Force | Duty Carried Out. |
| F/O | Tait | R.R | | NG137 | XY-D | Main Force | Duty Carried Out. |
| F/O | Smith | S | | NG140 | XY-F | Main Force | Duty Carried Out. |
| F/O | Templeton | G.M | RCAF | NG146 | XY-E | Main Force | Duty Carried Out. |
| F/Lt | Powell | A.C | | LM160 | XY-W | Main Force | Duty Carried Out. |
| F/O | Kelsey | P.D | | LM618 | XY-U | Main Force | Duty Carried Out. |
| F/O | Smith DFC | L | | LM188 | XY-S | Main Force | Duty Not Carried Out. |
| F/O | Madden | R.P | RCAF | HK661 | XY-R | Main Force | Duty Carried Out. |
| F/O | Oman | K.G | RNZAF | HK659 | XY-Q | Main Force | Duty Carried Out. |
| F/O | Roach | R.E | | HK650 | XT-T | Main Force | Duty Carried Out. |
| F/Sgt | Green | L.A | | HK606 | XY-V | Main Force | Duty Not Carried Out. |
| P/O | Gibson | J.H | | NN720 | XY-K | Main Force | Duty Carried Out. |
| F/O | Hanson | R.A | | HK613 | XY-Y | Main Force | Duty Carried Out. |
| F/O | Ritson | E.E | | LM617 | XY-X | Main Force | Duty Carried Out. |

The weather on the route to Essen was appalling. Thunderous clouds up to 17,000 feet made navigation difficult. Conditions did not improve over the target area with 7/10th to 10/10th cloud conditions. The planned ground marking using Oboe was quickly altered to emergency 'Wanganui', resulting in the Path Finder markers being initially scattered and late. Flying Officer S Smith was part of the fourth wave scheduled to bomb between 19.42 hours to 19.46 hours, *'PFF opened the attack late, impossible to identify their flares because they were dropped singly. Eventually, they dropped a combination of three on which bombing was carried out.* The later arrivals had the benefit of a number of fires which could be seen through the murk. These fires appeared reasonably large as the last bombers passed over the aiming point. The raid was the heaviest yet inflicted on the unfortunate city. Severe damage was caused, with an estimated 607 buildings destroyed and 812 seriously damaged. Unlike previous attacks, the bombers were now fielding more high explosive bombs as opposed to incendiaries. It was considered at Bomber Command HQ that anything worth burning had already been destroyed.

It was a busy day on the squadron on the 24th, with the arrival of three crews from the Mildenhall based No.15 Squadron. The three Australian captains were Acting Flying Officer Alan Fleming RAAF and F/O Robert Powers RAAF and George Williamson RAAF. On the same day, the squadron's commanding officer W/Cdr J.H Giles attended an investiture at Buckingham Palace to receive his award from His Majesty The King. It was a special day for the squadron. RAF Station Tuddenham welcomed two Halifaxes on return from Essen, a Canadian crew from No.425 RCAF Squadron and from RAF Lissett, a No.158 Squadron aircraft.

The crew of Flying Officer Kenneth Orman RNZAF are photographed sitting on Lancaster HK659 XY-Q 'Queenie'. This was Ken's favourite aircraft completing an impressive twenty-six operations during his 38 raid tour.

Essen was on the receiving end once again on the 25th. Seventeen aircraft were detailed and briefed for the late afternoon attack. On what was becoming the norm, the first away was the irrepressible S/Ldr P Reynolds at the controls of his regular aircraft, Lancaster NG174 XY-A, at 13.03 hours. The crews once again crossed the English Coast over Orford Ness on the Suffolk coast, then headed out over the North

Sea towards Ostend, where the formation picked up its sizeable fighter escort. A total of seven RAF Mustang squadrons and fourteen Spitfire squadrons would give penetration, target, and withdrawal cover to the lumbering bombers. The squadrons of 3 Group would be evenly distributed over the raid. Two aiming points were to be attacked with three waves per target. The weather, as forecast by the Met Officer at briefing, was for once spot on. Solid cloud covered the route. Over the target, the cloud had broken up slightly, affording the crews brief glimpses of the devastation below. Unlike the previous operation, all sixteen crews reached the target. The first to bomb at 15.39 hours was F/O C.J Wait aboard Lancaster NG147 XY-C. They quickly identified many red target skymarkers, which they bombed from 20,000 feet. Five crews experienced hang-ups due to icing. The worst affected was F/O J.B Liddell aboard Lancaster HK606 XY-V, who had to jettison almost his entire bomb load. Once the most feared of targets, Essen offered relatively little opposition. Only one Lancaster flown by P/O E/L Field sustained damage, a flak fragment in the port outer engine.

Essen was once again severely hit despite the initial reports of scattered bombing. The once-mighty war producing hub of Nazi Germany was now a shattered wasteland. Much of the vital smaller factories had been dispersed throughout Germany. The mighty Krupps works were almost a shell of its former glory. Some targets, however, could not be moved. The coal mines and steelworks remained and would continue to be attacked, bringing more destruction to the people of Essen.

Form B.675 –October 25th 1944 (D): Target : Essen 'Bullhead'

| | | | | | | | |
|---|---|---|---|---|---|---|---|
| S/Ldr | Reynolds | P | | NG174 | XY-A | Follower | Duty Carried Out. |
| F/O | Barton | E.R | RAAF | NG148 | XY-B | Follower | Duty Carried Out. |
| F/O | Wait | C.J | | NG147 | XY-C | Follower | Duty Carried Out. |
| F/O | Templeton | G.M | RCAF | NG146 | XY-E | Follower | Duty Carried Out. |
| F/O | Smith | S | | NG140 | XY-F | Follower | Duty Carried Out. |
| F/O | Tait | R.R | | NG137 | XY-D | Follower | Duty Carried Out. |
| F/O | Gibson | J.H | | NN720 | XY-K | Follower | Duty Carried Out. |
| F/Sgt | Green | L.A | | LM618 | XY-U | Follower | Duty Carried Out. |
| F/O | Orman | K.G | RNZAF | HK659 | XY-Q | Follower | Duty Carried Out. |
| F/O | Madden | R.P | RCAF | HK661 | XY-R | Follower | Duty Carried Out. |
| F/O | Williamson | G.E | RAAF | LM188 | XY-S | Follower | Duty Carried Out. |
| F/O | Roach | R.E | | HK650 | XY-T | Follower | Duty Carried Out. |
| F/O | Hanson | R.A | | LM617 | XY-X | Follower | Duty Carried Out. |
| F/O | Liddle | J.B | | HK606 | XY-Y | Follower | Duty Not Carried Out. |
| F/O | Field | E.L | | NG149 | XY-G | Follower | Duty Carried Out. |
| W/O | O'Brien | J.D | RAAF | HK613 | XY-Y | Follower | Duty Carried Out. |
| F/O | Hoskin | F.C | RCAF | NG175 | XY-J | Follower | Duty Carried Out. |

The only crew reporting damage was 'A' Flight's F/O E.L Field. The once feared flak defences of Essen and the 'Happy Valley' appeared to have lost its reputation on this occasion.

No.186 Squadron Reported Flak Damage 25/10/1944

| Serial | Code | Damage Reported | Repairs / Notes |
|---|---|---|---|
| NG149 | **XY-G** | Port Outer engine nacelle. | Repaired on Squadron. |

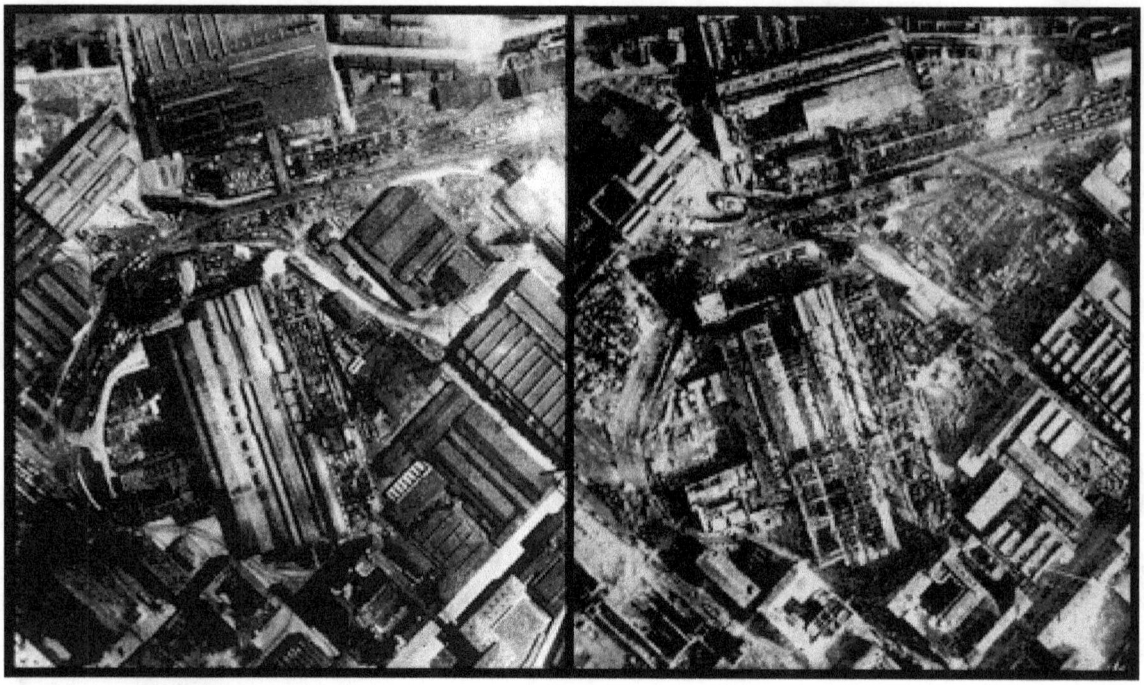

Krupps Work at Essen. On the left the works before No.3 Groups raid on October 23rd/24th 1944. On the right, the works showing the considerable damage inflicted.

The chemical works at Leverkusen were the target for an all 3 Group daylight raid on the 26th. The squadron would provide ten crews, led on this occasion by 'B' Flight commander, Squadron Leader Mervyn Leyshon AFC and his eight-man crew aboard HK661 XR-R. This was the first recorded operation of an 8-man crew on the squadron. The additional crew member occupied the mid-under gun position. Vickers Armstrong, Birmingham, built HK661, arrived on the squadron on October 12th. It was one of the Lancasters explicitly built to accommodate the 8000lb and 12,000lb super cookies gradually becoming more dominant within the group. To accommodate these new bombs, the standard H2S radome was removed. A singular or twin machine gun of various calibre ranging from .303, .30 to .5in were fitted in its place. Twenty-five-year-old Leyshon started his operational tour in 1941, completing his first tour on Wellingtons with 214 Squadron in August 1942.

Form B.676 –October 26th 1944 (D): Target : Leverkusen : GS116

| | | | | | | | |
|---|---|---|---|---|---|---|---|
| F/O | Powers | R.C | RAAF | NG174 | XY-A | Follower | Duty Carried Out. |
| F/Lt | Fleming | A.J | RAAF | NG140 | XY-F | Follower | Duty Carried Out. |
| F/O | Wait | C.J | | NG147 | XY-C | Follower | Duty Carried Out. |
| F/O | Barton | E.R | RAAF | NG137 | XY-D | Follower | Duty Carried Out. |
| P/O | Gibson | J.H | | NN720 | XY-K | Follower | Duty Carried Out. |
| S/Ldr | Leyshon AFC | M | | HK661 | XY-R | Follower | Duty Carried Out. |
| F/O | Madden | R.P | RCAF | LM188 | XY-S | Follower | Duty Carried Out. |
| F/Sgt | Green | L.A | | LM618 | XY-U | Follower | Duty Carried Out. |
| F/O | Liddell | J.B | | HK606 | XY-V | Follower | Duty Carried Out. |
| W/O | O'Brien | J.D | RAAF | HK650 | XY-T | Follower | Duty Carried Out. |

Once airborne, the entire force converged 10,000 feet over the historic cathedral town of Bury St Edmunds. Here the non G-H aircraft would form up on their selected G-H Leaders. The squadrons of RAF Tuddenham would once more be reliant on the G-H equipped squadrons of Methwold. After some careful flying, the squadron's ten crews positioned themselves in the standard Vic formation behind their 'Leader' and flew first to Orford Ness and then to Ostend. The force was once again provided with fighter escort in the form of four RAF Mustang squadrons as they entered German air space skirting Munchen Gladbach. The G-H ground stations appeared to have been working exceptionally well as 31 of the 35 G-H Lancasters provided on the raid marked on their sets. 186 Squadron was part of the first wave over Leverkusen. Tucked close behind their leaders, the bomb aimers in the nose watched intently as the bombs began to drop from their Leader's 33-foot-long bomb bays. Instantly, salvo after salvo of bombs started dropping. Some of the more experienced crews checked their position using H2S. One such crew was F/O CJ Wait, who dropped 1 x 4000lb + 1950 x 4lb incendiaries from 16,800 feet at 15.28 hours, *'Identified G-H Leader, aircraft bombs falling. Results checked on H2S and bombing appeared O.K'.* Leverkusen was utterly cloud covered as the first bomb loads exploded 3 miles below, flak opposition over the target was described as accurate and predicted, but this soon became ineffective. No enemy fighters were seen. As the last wave left the target, smoke was seen rising through the clouds. The crews were confident that the chemical works had been hit. A No.3 Group report recorded the following about the raid. *'It seems that a good time was had by all, with all crews much more enthusiastic about the possibilities of G-H than has been the case in the past.*

On return to RAF Tuddenham, some crews were not happy with their G-H Leaders, F/O J.B.M Liddell, *'Bombed on a Green flare from unidentified G-H aircraft as our own G-H aircraft had swung to port just previous to target, owing to a burst of flak around him and then fired a Red'.* Also unhappy was Australian F/O E.R Barton RAAF, he noted on his return, *'G-H Leader changed speed too often and weaved too much'.* There was a growing feeling within the squadron and No.32 Base that they could do better!

On the morning of the 27th, the squadron was informed it would be required to attack Hannover that afternoon, and 18 crews would be required. Frustratingly soon after the Lancasters were bombed up and fuelled the operation was cancelled due to adverse weather over the continent. The squadron recorded the award of the DFC to Canadian, F/O Welland Jennings RCAF on this date. The award may have been won while he was on No.90 Squadron, but No.186 saw this as an excellent opportunity to have a party in the traditional manner! The Citation reads.

*One night in September 1944 this officer was pilot of an aircraft detailed for a mine-laying operation. When more than 200 miles from the target the aircraft came under anti-aircraft fire and was hit. The starboard mainplane, aileron and flap were damaged, making the aircraft difficult to control. Some airspeed was lost. Nevertheless, Flying Officer Jennings flew on to the target to complete his task and afterwards returned to base where he made a safe landing under difficult conditions. His determination was typical of that which he has shown throughout his tour.*

There is another recommendation for the award, which was put forward by commanding officer of 90 Squadron, W/Cdr A.J Ogilvie, and this gives a far better insight into the exploits of this brave young Canadian.

*On the night of 11/12 September 1944, this officer was pilot of a Lancaster aircraft detailed to lay mines in the vicinity of Stettin. While still approximately 250 miles from the mining area, his aircraft received three direct hits from heavy flak, causing severe damage to the starboard mainplane, aileron and flap. In spite of the fact that the aircraft became extremely difficult to control, and the airspeed decreased by 15 miles per hour, he carried on to complete his mission successfully, and made a safe landing on return to base. This instance of fine determination to press home the attack on the enemy is typical of the spirit with which this officer has performed all his operational tasks. On a previous occasion his aircraft was attacked by a night fighter while approaching the target at Russelheim. As a result, the rear gunner was fatally wounded, but on this mission, too, the attack was pressed home to a successful conclusion and landing carried out away from base. His recent outstanding performance, combined with his previous excellent and steady operational record, is worthy of recognition and | strongly recommend the immediate award of the Distinguished Flying Cross.*

The heavy gun emplacements at Flushing W6 (J/106) on the Island of Walcheren would be the target for No.32 Base's three squadrons on the 28th. Number 186 Squadron would provide just four crews for the early morning attack on what would promise to be a busy day. Three large 150mm calibre guns of 9./MAA202 Naval Battery were strategically positioned to oppose any naval movement in the Scheldt Estuary. It was No.32 Base's job to knock them out. With a new Allied offensive to take place on November 1st, these guns had to be destroyed. The first crew away from Tuddenham was that of W/Cdr J.H Giles DFC at the controls of Lancaster HK662 XY-P at 08.12 hours. Flying with him in the 2nd pilot role was Australian F/Sgt Jeff Clarson RAAF.[2] who had arrived via No.3 LFS three days prior.

Gun Battery W15, located at Westkapelle, destroyed on October 28th, 1944. These and other similar calibre guns would have wreaked havoc on any seaborne landing.

Form B.678 –October 28th 1944 (D): Target : Flushing : Gun Emplacements

| | | | | | | | |
|---|---|---|---|---|---|---|---|
| W/Cdr | Giles DFC | J.H | | HK662 | XY-P | Main Force | Duty Carried Out. |
| F/Lt | Powell | A.C | | LM160 | XY-W | Main Force | Duty Carried Out. |
| F/O | Liddle | J.B | | LM167 | XY-X | Main Force | Duty Carried Out. |
| F/O | Hanson | R.A | | HK613 | XY-Y | Main Force | Duty Carried Out. |

*[2] The 186 Squadron ORB does not record pilot's operations in the 2nd pilot role. This entry is an exception.*

A fresh-faced Flight Sergeant Jeff Clarson RAAF looks slightly apprehensive before starting his operational tour with No.186 Squadron. Over the coming weeks and months, he would prove to be an excellent captain and courageous and gifted bomber pilot.

The attack by just fifty aircraft from No.3 Group would be controlled by Wing Commander William Watkins DSO DFC DFM, officer commanding No.15 Squadron at RAF Mildenhall. Time over the target was scheduled for 10.00 hours, and for once the squadron would have a chance to carry out visual bombing if conditions allowed. There would be no Path Finder markers to aim at. It was down to the bomb aimers to find and then accurately bomb the reinforced casements. Thankfully, the weather conditions were ideal, giving the participating crews unhindered visibility as they arrived over the target between 7,000 - 8,000 feet. Opposition on the run into target consisted of moderate light flak. However, it quickly changed to accurate heavy flak over the aiming point. All four crews dropped their mixed 4000lb, 1000 and 500 pounders at 10.01 hours. A terrific red explosion quickly followed. Flying Officer J.B Liddell commented, *'Identified visually, sea wall picked out. Target well plastered, bombs landed straight across A.P'.* Equally impressed was F/O R.A Hanson, at de-briefing Ron Hanson simply reported, *'concentrated bombing'*. One Lancaster was seen to be hit, and crash, the rear gunner aboard HK613 XY-Y was F/Sgt R.C Thomas, he recalls, *'The weather at the time was good, visibility clear, so we had a good view of the raid. Going into the attack on the battery, I saw a Lancaster crash from my position in the rear turret'*. The Lancaster was a No.90 Squadron aircraft flown by F/O R Higgins. There were no survivors. With the four crews safely back from Flushing, it was the turn of 15 Squadron crews to inflict more misery on Cologne. The Lancasters of No.1 Group would be the first over Cologne, followed by the squadrons of No.3 Group who were timed to start bombing at 15.43 hours.

Ted Ritson and crew photographed in front of Lancaster NG353 XY-X. On completing their Lancaster Conversion at No.3 LFS, they began their tour with No.90 Squadron's 'C' Flight in September 1944. The crew had completed five operations before transfer to 'B' Flight of No.186 Squadron.

Form B.679 –October 28th 1944 (D): Target : Cologne : 'Trout G'

| | | | | | | | |
|---|---|---|---|---|---|---|---|
| S/Ldr | Reynolds | P | | NG174 | XY-P | Main Force | Duty Carried Out. |
| F/O | Barton | E.R | RAAF | NG148 | XY-B | Main Force | Duty Carried Out. |
| F/Sgt | Young | H.S | | NG147 | XY-C | Main Force | Duty Carried Out. |
| F/O | Tait | R.R | | NG137 | XY-D | Main Force | Duty Carried Out. |
| F/Lt | Smith | S | | NG140 | XY-F | Main Force | Duty Carried Out. |
| P/O | Field | E.L | | NG149 | XY-G | Main Force | Duty Carried Out. |
| F/O | Hoskin | F.C | RCAF | NG175 | XY-J | Main Force | Duty Carried Out. |
| F/O | Powers | R.C | RAAF | NN720 | XY-K | Main Force | Duty Carried Out. |
| F/O | Templeton | G.M | RCAF | NG146 | XY-E | Main Force | Duty Carried Out. |
| F/O | Madden | R.P | RCAF | HK661 | XY-R | Main Force | Duty Carried Out. |
| F/O | Williamson | G.E | RAAF | LM188 | XY-S | Main Force | Duty Carried Out. |
| F/Lt | Roach | R.E | | HK650 | XY-T | Main Force | Duty Carried Out. |
| F/Sgt | Green | L.A | | HK606 | XY-V | Main Force | Duty Carried Out. |
| W/O | O'Brien | J.D | RAAF | HK622 | XY-Z | Main Force | Duty Carried Out. |
| F/O | Orman | K.G | RNZAF | HK659 | XY-Q | Main Force | Duty Carried Out. |

Weather conditions over Cologne were ideal, as seen in the Target Photograph taken by the crew of Flying Officer Barton from 20,000 feet. Note the destroyed Cologne - Mulheim Bridge.

The fifteen Lancaster's of 186 Squadron were scheduled to bomb between Zero hour and 15.49 hours from between 17,000ft and 22,000 feet. The route to target went as planned meeting little if any opposition, but as the squadron neared the target, the flak quickly intensified. Heavy predicted flak was particularly uncomfortable, given the lack of cloud. Cologne would have two aiming points, AP 'G' and AP 'H', No.3 Group had been selected to bomb AP 'G'. The Path Finders had, in the face of accurate flak, dropped several precise red TI's, which were clearly seen against the smoke rising from the first wave's attack. Three crews were hit by flak on their bomb runs, S/Ldr P Reynolds sustained slight damage to the starboard inner engine aboard NG174 XY-A. Canadian F/O G.M Templeton RCAF had the mid-upper turret perspex punctured, and a chunk of propeller blade shot away at 14.46 hours. Also hit was Lancaster HK622 XY-Z flown by Australian J.D O'Brien RAAF and crew. They had the starboard fin lacerated by flak. Weather conditions over the target meant that visual observation was possible, S/Ldr P Reynolds, *'40 seconds after bombing, a terrific explosion took place. Smoke was seen rising to 9000 feet, Bombing well concentrated around A.P.'* Flying Officer F.C.C Hoskins was at 20,000 feet aboard Lancaster NG175 XY-J. He confirmed the accuracy back at Tuddenham, *'Identified on picking out Marshalling Yards. Bombing heavily concentrated. Good trip'.* Flight Sergeant L.A Green had just closed his bomb door, having dropped his single 4000 pounder and 12 x No.14 Clusters when a burst of flak exploded too close for comfort. A large hole appeared in the starboard wing's trailing edge, a reminder that the German gunners below still had plenty of fight in them. The crews began landing back at RAF Tuddenham just before 18.00 hours. The attack by over 700 aircraft was devastating. Mulheim and Zollstock, situated both north and south of the centre of the attack, were in chaos. Over two thousand blocks of flats, fifteen industrial premises, two police stations, and many other buildings were in ruins. The railways and harbour were also hard hit, as was the cities power station, all for the loss of seven crews from the attacking force.

No.186 Squadron Reported Flak Damage 28/10/1944

| Serial | Code | Damage Reported | Repairs / Notes |
|---|---|---|---|
| NG174 | **XY-P** | Starboard inner engine. | Repaired on squadron. |
| NG146 | **XY-E** | Prop blade damaged. Mid Upper turret holed. | Repaired on squadron |
| HK622 | **XY-Z** | Starboard fin damaged. | Repaired on squadron |
| HK606 | **XY-V** | Starboard wing. | Repaired on squadron |

That night the squadron was ordered to prepare five crews for a raid, which was subsequently cancelled. Squadron Leader M Leyshon AFC presided over an attack against Westkapelle 'B' on the morning of October 29th. The target was two heavy casement pillboxes on the edge of a dyke. Visibility over the target was good. Oboe equipped Mosquitoes of No.109 Squadron dropped a number of Red Flares from 22,000 feet which fell slightly southwest and northwest of the aiming point.

Form B.680 –October 29th 1944 (D): Target : Westkappelle :

| | | | | | | | |
|---|---|---|---|---|---|---|---|
| S/Ldr | Leyshon AFC | M | | HK662 | XY-P | Main Force | Duty Carried Out. |
| F/Sgt | Clarson | J | RAAF | HK682 | XY-L | Main Force | Duty Carried Out. |
| F/O | Wait | C.J | | LM160 | XY-W | Main Force | Duty Carried Out. |
| P/O | Gibson | J.K | | HK613 | XY-Y | Main Force | Duty Carried Out. |
| F/O | Ritson | E.E | | LM617 | XY-X | Main Force | Duty Carried Out. |

The error was quickly identified, and the Master Bomber Squadron Leader Harry Davies DFC of No.7 Path Finder Squadron ordered his Deputy to re-mark with Greens. This he did with some accuracy. The five crews of No.186 Squadron were over the target at 11.00 hours. Three crews, F/O E.E Ritson, P/O J.H Gibson and F/Sgt A.J Clarson RAAF on his first operation as captain, experienced no trouble and were confident that their bombs hit the target. Squadron Leader Leyshon AFC was unhappy with his first run over the aiming point, so he decided to make a second run from 8,000 feet. This time he was happy, remarking on his return, *'Concentrated bombing apart from 1 stick in sea 1 ½ miles short'.* Flying Officer C.J Wait experienced electrical failure aboard LM160 XY-W, which resulted in his bomb load falling chiefly to port of the casements exploding near a breach in the sea wall. On return all the crews agreed that it was an excellent effort. The only criticism was that the Master Bomber seemed to give his instructions rather too fast. The crewing up and training process for most of F/Sgt Jeff Clarson RAAF crew had not been without tragedy. Jeff Clarson had joined the crew late after they had suffered

A marvellous photograph of the Fraser-Nash mid-upper turret of Lancaster XY-Q HK659. The smiling gunner is Sergeant Geordie Bennett, he was part of Ken Orman's RNZAF crew.

a run of bad luck. The crew had lost their original Wireless Operator in March 1944 when he was asked to join a crew on a gunnery exercise over the North Sea. Unfortunately, the aircraft he was flying in was forced to ditch. Sadly, 22-year-old Sgt Charlie Smallwood drowned. A replacement was quickly found in the shape of Australian Wireless Operator Sgt Wilbert Perry. On completing No.41 Course at No.3 LFS at RAF Feltwell, the crew were posted on July 17th 1944, to No.15 Squadron, based at RAF Mildenhall. They had only just settled into squadron life when their skipper, F/Sgt Eric Haughton RNZAF, joined the crew of F/Lt T.G Reynolds for operational experience. The crew, along with Eric, took off from RAF Mildenhall on July 24th 1944, for a raid on Stuttgart. They never returned, the victim of a prowling night fighter. All aboard Lancaster LM 142 LS-A were killed. Tragically, the crew of F/Lt Reynold were on their 29th operation when lost. The loss of their skipper was a tremendous blow to the crew. Now pilotless, the survivors found themselves in an unenviable position. Over the previous months, they had become a tight-knit group. Confident in each individual's ability, they requested to stay together. Thankfully, No.15 Squadron's Commanding Officer, W/Cdr W.D Watkins DFC DFM, respected their wishes, and they were posted back to No.1651 HCU to find a new skipper. It was at No.1651 HCU that fate played a part. The crew were joined by another Australian, F/Sgt Jeff Clarson RAAF. It was a fortunate union for all concerned. It was an early briefing for 12 crews on the morning of October 30th. The target was the synthetic oil storage tanks at Wesseling. It would be an all No.3 Group attack. Wesseling was an important target. It had long been associated with hydrogenating large quantities of imported oil. Situated on the Rhine bordering Cologne, it had received scant attention from Bomber Command. This was to change dramatically. In what was becoming a bit of a ritual, the first crew away was 'A' Flight's S/Ldr P Reynolds at the controls of NG174 XY-Y at 08.50 hours. Once airborne the now familiar routine saw the squadrons of No.32 Base form up with the G-H equipped squadrons of RAF Methwold 10,000 feet above Bury St Edmunds.

Form B.681 –October 30th 1944 (D): Target : Wesseling : GQ1510

| | | | | | | | |
|---|---|---|---|---|---|---|---|
| S/Ldr | Reynolds | P | | NG174 | XY-A | Follower | Duty Carried Out. |
| F/Lt | Fleming | A.J | RAAF | NG148 | XY-B | Follower | Duty Carried Out. |
| F/O | Wait | C.J | | NG147 | XY-C | Follower | Duty Carried Out. |
| F/O | Tait | R.R | | NG137 | XY-D | Follower | Duty Carried Out. |
| F/O | Templeton | G.M | RCAF | NG146 | XY-E | Follower | Duty Carried Out. |
| F/Lt | Smith | S | | NG140 | XY-F | Follower | Duty Carried Out. |
| F/O | Barton | E.R | RAAF | NG149 | XY-G | Follower | Duty Carried Out. |
| F/O | Hoskin | F.C | RCAF | NG175 | XY-J | Follower | Duty Carried Out. |
| F/O | Gibson | J.H | | NN720 | XY-K | Follower | Duty Carried Out. |
| F/O | Madden | R.M | RCAF | HK622 | XY-P | Follower | Duty Carried Out. |
| F/Lt | Roach | R.E | | HK650 | XY-T | Follower | Duty Carried Out. |
| F/Lt | Powell | A.C | RCAF | LM160 | XY-W | Follower | Duty Carried Out. |

Once in their allotted Vics, the formation headed to the market town of Diss, slowly gaining altitude until they departed England over Orford Ness. The Lancasters picked up their fighter escort of 18 squadrons of Spitfires over Ghent, Belgium. A further seven squadrons of RAF Mustangs would provide target support. The squadron would be part of the first wave over the target briefed to bomb between 11.57 and 12.00 hours. The aiming point was the synthetic fuel-producing Union Rheinische Braunkohlen Kraftstoff A.G works. On leaving the English coast, the formation encountered a layer of thick cloud that seemed to cover the entire region of the Low Countries and the Ruhr. A misinterpretation of the G-H release pulse some 6 miles short of the aiming point caused confusion, and some crews started to release their bomb loads. The error was quickly realised, but the damage had been done. Wesseling would be spared the attention of 40 Lancaster bomb loads from No.33 Base. Flak on the run into and over the target was intense. One of the first hit was the crew of F/Lt A.C Powell. Tucked closely behind his allotted G-H Leader, both were severely damaged by flak a minute before bombing. Lancaster LM160 XY-W shuddered under the impact of three flak bursts that bracketed both aircraft. It was immediately apparent that they were in trouble. The rear gunner, Sgt L.Grice, informed his pilot that he had been injured. Flak splinters had entered the rear turret and embedded themselves in his right thigh and lower leg at the same time rendering his turret unserviceable. The damage was not confined to the rear. The cockpit windscreen was holed in several places, an oil pipe was punctured, and the port inner engine was rendered useless. For his actions on this raid, the rear gunner, Sgt Leonard Grice, would be recommended for a DFM. Also hit was the pilot, who also received a flak wound to his right thigh. Another crew in trouble was F/O E.R Barton RAAF. They were hit by predicted flak at 11.58 hours, the mid-upper turret was smashed, the starboard inner engine hit, the main plane holed, and starboard tyre believed punctured aboard Lancaster NG149 XY-G. Despite the spirited defences, the crews dropped their bombs on a number of what appeared to be accurate sky markers. All the crews dropped on their allotted G-H Leaders, S/Ldr P.Reynolds summed up the raid back at debriefing, *'A fairly concentrated attack'*. There were a couple barbed comments by some of the participating crews aimed at their G-H Leaders on return, F/O J.H Gibson reported, *'G-H aircraft did not keep on track and led us over Cologne !'*. Canadian F/O R.M Madden RCAF sarcastically reported, *'Straightforward trip, apart from the G-H Leader not turning up !!'*. Flying Officer E.R Barton RAAF and crew landed Lancaster NG149 XY-G at RAF Newmarket as instructed due to suspected tyre damage. Flight Lieutenant A.C Powell flew home on three engines, and he was the last to land back at RAF Tuddenham. On return to RAF Tuddenham, F/Lt A.C Powell was admitted to the SSQ while his rear gunner was transported to the RAF Hospital at Ely.

No.186 Squadron Reported Flak Damage 30/10/1944

| Serial | Code | Damage Reported | Repairs / Notes |
|---|---|---|---|
| NG149 | **XY-G** | Extensive damage. | Repaired on squadron. |
| LM160 | **XY-W** | Rear and forward fuselage. | Repaired on squadron |

One of the squadron's most respected crews during its early days was Flight Lieutenant Sandy Powell. They are seen here in front of Lancaster LM160 XY-W 'William the Konkerer'. When transferred to No.186 they had completed 15 operations. By the end of their operational tour they would be one of the squadron's most highly decorated crews with two DFCs and two DFMs. The crew are L-R Sergeant Norman Wilman DFM (Wireless Operator), Sergeant Joe Firth (Flight Engineer), Flying Officer William 'Bill' Picton (Bomb Aimer), Flight Lieutenant Sandy Powell DFC (Pilot), Sergeant Bob Dack (Mid Upper Gunner), Flying Officer Bob Hunter DFC RCAF (Navigator) and Sergeant Len Grice DFM (Rear Gunner).

That evening eight crews were again briefed for a return visit to Cologne. They would join a force of over 900 bombers on an Oboe-marked attack. Wing Commander J.H Giles DFC was airborne at 18:02 hours. He had commandeered the crew of his 'B' Flight Commander, S/Ldr M Leyshon AFC, for this raid. There was one early return, a gunner aboard F/Sgt H.S Young's crew was taken ill, forcing the crew's early return while over the North Sea. Cologne would be on the receiving end of the squadron's first use of the 8000-pound super-cookie on this raid. Two crews would be chosen to carry these monsters, the unfortunate F/Sgt Young at the controls of HK682 XY-L and F/O E.L Field aboard NG176 XY-H.

Form B.683 – October 30th 1944 (N) : Target : Cologne : 'Trout D'

| | | | | | | | |
|---|---|---|---|---|---|---|---|
| F/O | Field | E.L | | NG176 | XY-H | Main Force | Duty Carried Out. |
| F/Sgt | Young | H.S | | HK682 | XY-L | Main Force | Duty Not Carried Out. |
| F/O | Orman | K.G | RNZAF | HK659 | XY-Q | Main Force | Duty Carried Out. |
| W/Cdr | Giles DFC | J.H | | HK661 | XY-R | Main Force | Duty Carried Out. |
| F/O | Williamson | G.R | RAAF | LM188 | XY-S | Main Force | Duty Carried Out. |
| F/Sgt | James | W.C | RAAF | LM167 | XY-X | Main Force | Duty Carried Out. |
| F/O | Hanson | R.A | | HK613 | XY-Y | Main Force | Duty Carried Out. |
| F/O | Liddell | J.B | | HK622 | XY-Z | Main Force | Duty Carried Out. |

The entire force of over 900 bombers took a southerly approach across France to confuse the German night fighters. The weather turned out to be a little more uncomfortable than forecast by the Met Officer back at RAF Tuddenham. Cloud tops extended between 14,000 and 20,000 feet causing icing to some

Not the best of photographs but an important one nevertheless. Flight Lieutenant William Bernard Holman. An experienced second tour Bomb Aimer. William would fill the Bombing Leader role from October 1944 until July 1945. After the war, he returned to the Police Force. He died aged just 58 in 1972.

aircraft. One of the crews affected was F/O G.H Williamson RAAF, *'Severe icing in the clouds making handling extremely difficult'*. In between the clouds and the icing, a full moon illuminated the Lancasters making the air gunners slightly uneasy. On the run into the target, F/O E.L Field was unfortunate to be bracketed by flak. Severe damage was inflicted to NG176 XY-H. The larger modified bomb doors were severely damaged, as was the tailplane and port inner engine. Despite the damage, the plucky crew continued onto the target. The cloud over Cologne was thankfully below the briefed bombing height and did not interfere with the Path Finders, who dropped a number of Green Sky markers. The squadron crews began their bomb runs at 21.00 hours. Bombing appeared concentrated, the glow of a number of large fires could be seen below the clouds as the squadron left the target area. The last over the target and almost five minutes behind the rest of No.3 Group was the crew of F/O Field. The damage to the port inner engine had meant a reduction in speed. At 21.13 hours, the 8000lb + 3 x 1000 + 4 x 500lb HE was dropped on a bunch of Green Sky markers. Immediately after bombs away, the engine, which was now producing oily grey smoke, was feathered. Once again, Cologne was on the receiving end of a devastating raid. Damage to civilian property was particularly hard hit, especially in the suburbs of Braunsfeld and Klettenberg situated to the west of Cologne.

No.186 Squadron Reported Flak Damage 30/10/1944

| Serial | Code | Damage Reported | Repairs / Notes |
|---|---|---|---|
| NG176 | **XY-H** | Port Inner Engine, tailplane, and bomb doors. | Repaired on squadron. |

The last daylight raid of October was an all No.3 Group affair. The target was the Welheim synthetic oil plant at Bottrop. The squadrons of Methwold would once again have the responsibility of leading elements of No.32 Base on this operation. RAF Tuddenham provided 24 crews evenly divided between both squadrons. As usual, Squadron Leader P Reynolds was the first away at 11.46 hours. The remainder of the squadron followed in one-minute intervals.

Form B.684 – October 31st 1944 (D) : Target : Bottrop : Welheim Synthetic Oil Plant : 'GQ1536'

| | | | | | | | |
|---|---|---|---|---|---|---|---|
| S/Ldr | Reynolds | P | | NG174 | XY-A | Follower | Duty Carried Out. |
| F/Lt | Field | A.J | RAAF | NG148 | XY-B | Follower | Duty Carried Out. |
| F/O | Wait | C.J | | NG147 | XY-C | Follower | Duty Carried Out. |
| F/O | Tait | RR | | NG137 | XY-D | Follower | Duty Carried Out. |
| F/O | Templeton | G.M | RCAF | NG146 | XY-E | Follower | Duty Carried Out. |
| F/Lt | Smith | S | | NG140 | XY-F | Follower | Duty Carried Out. |
| F/O | Hoskin | F.C | RCAF | NG175 | XY-J | Follower | Duty Carried Out. |
| F/O | Gibson | J.H | | NN720 | XY-K | Follower | Duty Carried Out. |
| F/O | Madden | R.M | RCAF | HK662 | XY-P | Follower | Duty Carried Out. |
| F/Sgt | Green | L.A | | HJ650 | XY-T | Follower | Duty Carried Out. |
| W/O | O'Brien | J.D | RAAF | HK684 | XY-O | Follower | Duty Carried Out. |
| F/O | Ritson | E.E | | HK606 | XY-V | Follower | Duty Carried Out. |

Forming up over Bury St Edmunds was accomplished quickly and efficiently. Crews were slowly becoming familiar with the procedure. The formation of over 101 Avro Lancaster's would pick up their fighter escort of RAF Mustangs over the continent. Some barbed criticism was aimed at Bomber Command HQ over recent days concerning the apparent inability of the bomber crews to adhere to planned times and altitudes as briefed on daylight raids. It was HQ Fighter Command's opinion that there seemed to be a relatively relaxed attitude by some groups about flying discipline. On two recent operations over Germany, the formation was reported to be nearly 25 miles in length and a staggering 3 miles wide on the approach to the target. The fighter escort had been stretched to its limit. Thankfully, on each occasion there were no fighter encounters. Exning House, No.3 Group HQ were obviously made aware of the concerns of the Fighter-boys and instructed the Group's squadron commanders to rigorously enforce flying discipline. On approaching the German border, the RAF fighter escort estimated the No.3 Group formation at 10-15 miles in length, but much narrower than previous raids. It was an improvement of sorts. The first markers started to appear at 14:56 hours, No.186 Squadron would follow the G-H equipped squadrons of No.149 and No.218 over the target between 15:00 hours and 15:03 hours. Predicted flak was plentiful and accurate over the target area, F/O G.M Templeton RCAF was hit almost immediately as he started on his bomb run. The port side of Lancaster NG146 XY-E took the full force of a flak burst. Practically the entire fuselage between the rear turret and mid-upper was like a colander. Miraculously both Canadian gunners were uninjured. Also lucky was the crew's navigator Australian F/Sgt F.J McKey RAAF. He was sitting at his navigation table when a piece of flak ripped through his navigational panel, missing him by just a few inches. Despite the vicious flak all the squadron managed to bomb, Flight Lieutenant A.J Fleming RAAF, *'Results difficult to see own G-H aircraft at target owing to the sun. Bombing appeared concentrated, possibly to east of town.'* The flak claimed one Lancaster, which was seen to explode over the target area. It was later established that it was a crew from No.90 Squadron, F/Lt J Ward RNZAF. They were on their 34th operation. There were no survivors. The squadron started landing just before dusk, all were convinced that it had been an accurate raid.

No.186 Squadron Reported Flak Damage 31/10/1944

| Serial | Code | Damage Reported | Repairs / Notes |
|---|---|---|---|
| NG146 | **XY-E** | Fuselage. | Repaired on squadron. |

Cologne rounded off the month operationally. Five crews, skippered by two Australians, one New Zealander, a Welshman, and an Englishman, were set to departed RAF Tuddenham just after 18:30 hours. The crew of S/Ldr Leyshon AFC was withdrawn at the last minute due to illness of the pilot, which was the start of a series of ongoing health issues that would befall the experienced Welshman.

Form B.685 – October 31st 1944 (N) : Target : Cologne : 'Trout'

| | | | | | | | |
|---|---|---|---|---|---|---|---|
| S/Ldr | Leyshon AFC | M | | HK662 | XY-P | Main Force | WITHDRAWN |
| Sgt | Cowley | N.C | | HK682 | XY-L | Main Force | Duty Carried Out. |
| F/O | Barton | E.R | RAAF | NG137 | XY-D | Main Force | Duty Carried Out. |
| F/Sgt | James | W.C | RAAF | HK622 | XY-Z | Main Force | Duty Carried Out. |
| F/O | Orman | K.G | RNZAF | HK659 | XY-Q | Main Force | Duty Carried Out. |

They would join over 400 bombers from No.1,3,4, and 8 Groups on an Oboe marked attack. Once airborne, the No.3 Group contingent headed towards Reading on the western edge of London. Along with the Group's offering of seventy-three aircraft, the armada turned southeast to depart over Beachy Head. The four crews would be part of the fourth and final wave timed over the target between 21:10 and 21:14 hours. Once again, solid cloud blanketed western Europe from the French coast onwards, a solid mass of cloud varying in height from 9,000 feet to 15,000 feet prevented any visual ground observation. Over the doomed city, the crews quickly identified many Red, White and Green Wanganui flares that were quickly bombed. Opposition over Cologne was slight, giving the crews a trouble-free bomb run. Flight Sergeant W.C James RAAF and crew were at 20,000 feet aboard Lancaster HK622 XY-Z, *'Identified on Red and white flare. Glow reflected in the cloud, markers flares concentrated'.* What followed was a concentrated attack. All crews reported seeing an extensive red glow below the clouds. A number of what was believed to be fighter contrails were seen. Some crews considered jet-propelled fighters caused them. However, No.3 Group HQ dismissed this as high flying Mosquitoes. The last crew to land and finish off a hectic 48 hours was Sgt C Cowley at the controls of

HK682 XY-L at 22:45 hours. The crew bade farewell to recently awarded F/O Welland Jennings DFC on the 31st , he was posted to RCAF 'R' Depot for repatriation, he would serve in the RCAF until 1946.

CREWS POSTED IN OCTOBER 1944

| No | Date | Captain | Posted From |
|---|---|---|---|
| 1 | 06/10/1944 | F/O I Graham RNZAF and crew | 3 L.F.S Feltwell |
| 2 | 06/10/1944 | F/O J Liddell and crew | 3 L.F.S Feltwell |
| 3 | 06/10/1944 | P/O R Hanson and crew | 3 L.F.S Feltwell |
| 4 | 06/10/1944 | P/O B.R Tait and crew | 3 L.F.S Feltwell |
| 5 | 09/10/1944 | W/Cdr J.H Giles DFC | 3 Group HQ |
| 6 | 09/10/1944 | P/O R.P Madden RCAF and crew | 90 Squadron |
| 7 | 09/10/1944 | F/O F.C Hoskin RCAF and crew | 90 Squadron |
| 8 | 09/10/1944 | F/O W.T Jennings DFC RCAF and crew | 90 Squadron |
| 9 | 09/10/1944 | P/O S Smith and crew | 90 Squadron |
| 10 | 09/10/1944 | P/O T Phillips and crew | 90 Squadron |
| 11 | 09/10/1944 | P/O P Kelsey and crew | 90 Squadron |
| 12 | 09/10/1944 | P/O L Smith and crew | 90 Squadron |
| 13 | 09/10/1944 | F/O R.E Roach and crew | 90 Squadron |
| 14 | 09/10/1944 | F/O E.E Ritson and crew | 90 Squadron |
| 15 | 09/10/1944 | F/O C.J Wait and crew | 90 Squadron |
| 16 | 09/10/1944 | P/O A.C Powell and crew | 90 Squadron |
| 17 | 09/10/1944 | P/O J.H Gibson and crew | 90 Squadron |
| 18 | 09/10/1944 | P/O G.M Templeton RCAF and crew | 90 Squadron |
| 19 | 09/10/1944 | Sgt H.S Youngs and crew | 90 Squadron |
| 20 | 09/10/1944 | Sgt F.J Cook RAAF and crew | 90 Squadron |
| 21 | 11/10/1944 | P/O G.M Templeton RCAF and crew | 3 L.F.S Feltwell |
| 22 | 12/10/1944 | F/O K.J Orman RNZAF and crew | 3 L.F.S Feltwell |
| 23 | 12/10/1944 | P/O E.R Barton and crew | 3 L.F.S Feltwell |
| 24 | 12/10/1944 | S/Ldr M Leyshon AFC and crew | 3 L.F.S Feltwell |
| 25 | 12/10/1944 | S/Ldr P Reynolds and crew | 3 L.F.S Feltwell |
| 26 | 12/10/1944 | F/Sgt L.A Green and crew | 3 L.F.S Feltwell |
| 27 | 12/10/1944 | Sgt N.C Cowley and crew | 3 L.F.S Feltwell |
| 28 | 18/10/1944 | W/O J.D O'Brien RAAF and crew | 3 L.F.S Feltwell |
| 29 | 20/10/1944 | P/O R.J Gogler and crew | 3 L.F.S Feltwell |
| 30 | 20/10/1944 | P/O E.L Field and crew | 3 L.F.S Feltwell |
| 31 | 22/10/1944 | P/O G.E Williamson RAAF and crew | 15 Squadron |
| 32 | 22/10/1944 | F/O R.C Powers RAAF and crew | 15 Squadron |
| 33 | 22/10/1944 | P/O A.J Fleming RAAF and crew | 15 Squadron |
| 34 | 25/10/1944 | F/Sgt A.J Clarson RAAF and crew | 3 L.F.S Feltwell |
| 35 | 25/10/1944 | F/Sgt W.C James RAAF and crew | 3 L.F.S Feltwell |

Thus ended October 1944. It had been a good start by the squadron despite the loss of two crews. Everyone had performed remarkably well, considering the limited time the squadron had been together. The hard-pressed Maintenance Staff and the squadron armourers had shown that they could take on any challenge given the operational demands being placed upon them. Particular praise was directed at the back-room staff under the capable guidance of the Squadron Adjutant F/Lt J.S Walker. The squadron had dropped a total of 688.8 tons of bombs over 13 raids, amounting to 644 flying hours. Over the month, Wing Commander Giles DFC welcomed many battle-hardened veterans posted onto the squadron during October. Both his Flight Commanders had been selected on their ability. It was a tremendous privilege as described by Squadron Leader M. Leyshon AFC, *'The posting to 186 Squadron was excellent news to me. Apparently, a number of squadron leaders were considered, and it was wonderful to be selected.'* Other than the need to rely on other squadrons for G-H bombing the squadron found itself in a buoyant mood. The squadron would have to wait for the delivery and installation of the G-H apparatus, although the sets were becoming increasingly available No.186 would just have to be patient and wait its turn.

October 1944 (Part 2) : Avro Lancaster Delivery.

| ToC Date | Serial | Code | Maker | Mark | From |
|---|---|---|---|---|---|
| 12/10/1944 | HK650 | XY-T | Vickers Armstrong | Mk.B.I | Works |
| 12/10/1944 | HK661 | XY-R | Vickers Armstrong | Mk.B.I | Works |
| 14/10/1944 | HK659 | XY-Q | Vickers Armstrong | Mk.B.I | Works |
| 15/10/1944 | HK606 | XY-V | Vickers Armstrong | Mk.B.I | No.90 Squadron |
| 15/10/1944 | HK613 | XY-Y | Vickers Armstrong | Mk.B.I | No.90 Squadron |
| 15/10/1944 | HK622 | XY-Z | Vickers Armstrong | Mk.B.I | No.90 Squadron |
| 15/10/1944 | LM160 | XY-W | Armstrong Whitworth | Mk.B.I | No.90 Squadron |
| 15/10/1944 | LM188 | XY-S | Armstrong Whitworth | Mk.B.I | No.90 Squadron |
| 15/10/1944 | LM617 | | A.V Roe | Mk.B.I | No.90 Squadron |
| 15/10/1944 | LM618 | XY-U | A.V Roe | Mk.B.I | No.90 Squadron |
| 16/10/1944 | PD374 | | Metropolitan Vickers | Mk.B.I | Works |
| 18/10/1944 | NF994 | | Armstrong Whitworth | Mk.B.I | 5 M.U |
| 19/10/1944 | HK662 | XY-P | Vickers Armstrong | Mk.B.I | Works |
| 22/10/1944 | HK680 | XY-H | Vickers Armstrong | Mk.B.I | Works |
| 24/10/1944 | HK682 | XY-L | Vickers Armstrong | Mk.B.I | Works |
| 24/10/1944 | HK684 | XY-O | Vickers Armstrong | Mk.B.I | Works |
| 24/10/1944 | HK685 | | Vickers Armstrong | Mk.B.I | Works |
| 26/10/1944 | HK664 | | Vickers Armstrong | Mk.B.I | Works |
| 31/10/1944 | HK688 | XY-M | Vickers Armstrong | Mk.B.I | Works |

Any squadron was only as good as its ground staff. At RAF Stradishall, No.186 Squadron come up trumps. The dedication and pride in their work was only equalled by that of the Air Crew. A smiling bunch of Airmen and WAAFs are photographed outside the Technical Repairable Stores building in 1944. The identity of the Squadron Leader and his team are sadly unknown. Note the solitary aircrew member, rear, fifth from right.

# November 1944

## *'The Battle for Oil'*

The squadron welcomed another batch of recently trained crews from No.3 Lancaster Finishing School on the 1st, F/Sgt F Fernley, P/O J.E Tonks and Australian D.F.J Godfrey RAAF all three having successfully completed No.60 Course.

A relaxed-looking Flight Sergeant Dennis Frederick John Godfrey RAAF. Born in Tooting, England, he would like his fellow Aussies pilots carve out a reputation as a courageous and excellent captain.

Brummie Pilot Officer John Edward Tonks RAFVR. His operational career paralleled that of Dennis Godfrey and Frederick Fernley, his fellow No.60 Course pilots. Each would complete a hectic operational tour.

The squadron was not required for the attack on Oberhausen on the night of November 1st. It was a welcome reprieve, if only for 24 hours. On the 2nd, the squadron made ready 18 crews for a daylight attack on the Fischer Tropsch synthetic oil plant at Homberg/Meerbeck, located northwest of Duisburg. The group put up a respectable 180 Lancasters who departed over the small seaside town of Orford Ness.

Form B.686 – November 2nd, 1944 (D) : Target : Homberg : Fischer Tropsch synthetic oil plant: 'GQ1511'

| | | | | | | | |
|---|---|---|---|---|---|---|---|
| F/O | Barton | E.R | RAAF | NG174 | XY-A | Follower | Duty Carried Out. |
| F/Lt | Fleming | A.J | RAAF | NG148 | XY-B | Follower | Duty Carried Out. |
| F/O | Wait | C.J | | NG147 | XY-C | Follower | Duty Carried Out. |
| F/O | Tait | R.R | | NG137 | XY-D | Follower | Duty Carried Out. |
| F/O | Gibson | J.H | | NN720 | XY-K | Follower | Duty Carried Out. |
| F/O | Hoskin | F.C | RCAF | NG175 | XY-J | Follower | Duty Carried Out. |
| F/O | Field | E.L | | NG140 | XY-F | Follower | Duty Carried Out. |
| F/Sgt | Young | H.S | | HK682 | XY-L | Follower | Duty Carried Out. |
| W/O | O'Brien | J.D | RAAF | HK684 | XY-O | Follower | Duty Carried Out. |

| | | | | | | | |
|---|---|---|---|---|---|---|---|
| Sgt | Cowley | N.C | | HK662 | XY-P | Follower | Duty Carried Out. |
| F/O | Orman | K.G | | HK659 | XY-Q | Follower | Duty Carried Out. |
| W/Cdr | Giles DFC | J.H | | HK661 | XY-R | Follower | Duty Carried Out. |
| F/Lt | Roach | R.B | | HK650 | XY-T | Follower | Duty Carried Out. |
| F/O | Williamson | G.E | RAAF | LM618 | XY-U | Follower | Duty Carried Out. |
| F/Sgt | Green | L.A | | HK606 | XY-V | Follower | Duty Carried Out. |
| P/O | Gogler | R.J | RAAF | LM617 | XY-X | Follower | Duty Carried Out. |
| F/O | Liddell | J.B | | HK622 | XY-Z | Follower | Duty Carried Out. |
| F/O | Hanson | R.A | | HK613 | XY-Y | Follower | Duty Carried Out. |

Wing Commander J.H Giles DFC climbed away from RAF Tuddenham at 11:24 hours at the helm of 'B' Flight Lancaster, HK661 XY-R. He was joined once again by the crew of S/Ldr Leyshon AFC. Fighter escort would be provided by nine squadrons of European based Spitfires and over the target four squadrons of Mustang Mk.III's from England. The weather was for once as forecast by the Met Officer back at base. The crews had an opportunity to appreciate nature at its most beautiful, a mass of white cottonwool like clouds below and an icy inky blue sky above. The only sign of war was the sight of over one hundred sleek Spitfires darting around looking for trouble.

It was not until the force was five miles from the target that the flak gunners below made their presence known. The accuracy was uncannily good from the outset. Predicted flak had the height almost immediately. The attack would be carried out over three waves timed to be over the target at 14:00 hours. The G-H equipped squadrons of RAF Methwold would be responsible for leading the second and third waves. Twenty-six G-H crews would attack at 14:02 hours, leading 52 followers drawn from No.33 Base. This wave included No.186 Squadron's contribution. The third wave timed at 14:06 hours would be guided onto the target by six G-H aircraft and just ten followers from No.32 Base, plus two non G-H aircraft of Methwold. A further fifty-seven Lancasters of No.32 Base would be required if, due to the weather, an experimental G-H Wanganui marking attack was ordered. If not, they would be part of the third and final wave. HQ No.3 Group had quickly realised that to obtain the best results out of G-H, an accurate method of marking was essential. They did not have to look far for guidance. The Path Finder Force, who historically had been rather unhelpful, reluctantly shared their knowledge. They had developed various methods to mark targets by day and night using Oboe. It was now up to No.3 Group to refine these existing methods and adapt them to suit their particular requirements.

The first wave of bombers found the oil refinery almost clear of cloud. Almost to the second, the first bombs started to arch towards the target below. In amongst the High Explosives and incendiaries were a new type of Green sky-marker used for the first time. Over the target area, the flak had reached an intensity that many crews had never experienced. Flying 90 seconds behind the first wave, the squadron crews had an excellent opportunity to observe the bombing accuracy of the lead group and the intensity of the flak. A massive explosion was observed over the target area due to either a collision or the premature explosion of a cookie. It was an ominous sight. Red and Green flares were tightly grouped as the squadron started on their bomb runs at 14.00 hours, and three Lancasters were immediately hit. Flying Officer G.E Williamson RAAF was at the controls of Lancaster LM618 XY-U when flak disabled the two port engines. Lancaster HK650 XY-T flown by F/Lt R.B Roach was hit in the bomb gear. Tragically a piece of flak entered the navigator's position and struck the navigator F/O W.S Cowan RCAF in the head, killing him instantly. Unable to drop their bomb load, the crew continued over the target. To add to the crew's problems, they were hit by a 4lb incendiary dropped from above. Thankfully it passed through the wing without igniting the fuel tanks or damaging the engines. Also hit was the Lancaster flown by F/Sgt L A Green. The bomb aimer Perspex dome was shattered, making for a cold and draughty return flight. Lancaster LM617 XY-Y, flown by Australian P/O R.J Gogler RAAF, had its bomb bay and bomb doors badly holed, resulting in his 4000-pounder falling into the target. If the flak were not enough to contend with, some crews experienced frustrating hang-ups. Both F/O C.J Wait and F/Sgt L.A Green had a single incendiary cluster hang up, while F/O J.H Gibson had five, four of which were later jettisoned. The most seriously affected were F/O E.L Field, who had seven of his 14 troublesome clusters refusing to drop, while P/O R.J Gogler RAAF brought back eleven No.14 Clusters despite every effort to jettison them. Flying Officer F.C.G Hoskin RCAF had three clusters fail to release even after the jettison bars were pulled. In his effort to drop the stubborn incendiaries, his violent jinking damaged the bomb bay doors and resulted in his flight engineer sustaining a knock to his head.

The only squadron fatality on the November 2nd operation to Homberg was navigator Flying Officer Walter Sidney Cowan RCAF.

Severe icing was the culprit for the failure to drop. There was extraordinarily little the crews could do to prevent this, given the freezing conditions. Finally, after three murderous minutes over the aiming point, the battered formation finally cleared the murderous flak after accurately dropping most of its bombs on the burning oil complex below. It now found itself facing the long flight home. Heading towards Eindhoven, dozens of Lancasters were observed with one or even two feathered engines. Many aircraft showed apparent signs of trouble. A number of Lancasters were spotted in trouble including numerous with smoking engines. One such crew was that with F/O George Williamson RAAF at the controls of Lancaster LM618 XY-U. Both port engines had been feathered as a result of flak while on the bomb run. Now, unable to maintain height, the crew desperately jettisoned everything they could to reach the comparative safety of the Allied front line. The 28-year-old from Rockhampton, Queensland, showed remarkable piloting skill managing to fly the severely damaged Lancaster as far as Zeeland, Holland. It was here the solid cloud had finally dispersed enough to give the crew a visual of the terrain below. Circling over the small town of Lewedorp, the crew desperately looked for a place to crash land. Below them were positioned the 186th Field Regiment of the Royal Artillery. Sensing the aircraft was

The sorry looking wreckage of Lancaster LM618 XY-U photographed a few days after its forced landing in Nieuwe Kraaijertpolder at Lewedorp, Zeeland, November 2nd 1944.

in trouble, they signalled and indicated they were friendly. At 15:10 hours, F/O Williamson carried out a crash landing in a waterlogged minefield close to the Notenhoeve farm at Nieuwe-Kraaijertpolder. The predominately RAAF crew immerged, shaken but alive.

The squadron started landing back at RAF Tuddenham just after 15.15 hours. The weary crews trudged to de-briefing, where they received cocoa or hot chocolate liberally laced with rum. The crews were confident that the oil refinery had been severely damaged if not destroyed. New Zealand K.G Orman RNZAF remarked, *'Our bombs hit the plant'*. Wing Commander J.H Giles DFC commented, *'Bombing very concentrated, large columns of smoke visible'*. Flying Officer R.A Hanson was equally confident of success, *'4000lb or 8000lb burst on the factory buildings'*. The success came at a cost. Six Lancaster crews failed to return, RAF Mildenhall lost three crews, two from XV Squadron and one from No.622 Squadron. The RAF Witchford based No.195 Squadron lost two crews. A further 67 Lancasters reported flak damage on return. The body of the 26-year-old F/O Walter Cowan RCAF was taken to the station morgue. He would be buried on November 8th at Brookwood Cemetery. The crew's bomb aimer, F/O P.J Bray, was admitted overnight to SSQ for bruising and 'hysteria'. The horror of witnessing the death of a crewmate was too much for the young airman. The station doctor, obviously sympathetic to his condition, ordered that he be grounded for 48 hours.

No.186 Squadron Reported Flak Damage 02/11/1944

| Serial | Code | Damage Reported | Repairs / Notes |
|---|---|---|---|
| HK606 | **XY-V** | Front perspex. | Repaired on squadron. |
| LM617 | **XY-X** | Bomb Bay. | Repaired on squadron |
| HK650 | **XY-Y** | Bomb Bay. | Repaired on squadron |
| LM618 | **XY-U** | Both port engines. Forced Landed. | SoC |
| NG175 | **XY-J** | Bomb doors buckled due to jinking aircraft. | Repaired on squadron |

## Lancaster Mk.III LM618 XY-U 'Uncle'

| | | |
|---|---|---|
| Avro Lancaster Mk.III | A.V Roe, Yeadon | |
| T.o.C | 10/10/1944 via No.90 Squadron | |
| Cat Ac/FB Missing | 02/11/1944 | |
| S.o.C | 16/11/1944 | |
| Total Flying Hours | 267.30 | |
| Take-Off Time | 11.29 hours | |
| Bomb Load | 1 x 4000lb + 12 x No.14 Clusters | |
| | **CREW** | |
| Pilot | Flying Officer G.E Williamson A426933 RAAF | Safe |
| Navigator | Flight Sergeant K.H Turner 1458457 RAFVR | Safe |
| Bomb Aimer | Flying Officer E Winton 153353 RAFVR | Safe |
| Wireless Operator | Warrant Officer A.E Stiles A423349 RAAF | Safe |
| Mid Upper Gunner | Flight Sergeant W.P Burton A432748 RAAF | Safe |
| Rear Gunner | Flight Sergeant H.K Coombe A433197 RAAF | Safe |
| Flight Engineer | Sergeant A.E Piggin 976406 RAFVR | Safe |
| Posted Via | No.15 Squadron, RAF Mildenhall. | |
| Operations Flown (186) | 3 | |
| Buried | N/A | |

The forward section of Lancaster LM618 XY-U. It was an excellent piece of airmanship by the pilot Flying Officer G.E Williamson to crash land the badly damaged Lancaster without serious injury to his crew.

The squadron was not required on the 3rd but received instructions it would be needed the following day for an attack on a steel works at Solingen.

On November 3rd, 1944, 3 Group HQ sent a secret telegram to HQ Bomber Command setting out its planned installation programme of all its available G-H sets to the squadrons within the group. The initial problems with production of ***George-Henry*** were now finally being resolved, if but slower than expected. Number 3 Group felt that to get the greatest benefit from G-H it was necessary to introduce all the available sets into all the squadrons within the group as quickly as possible. Only two squadrons had been fully equipped, RAF Methwolds No.149 and No.218 Squadron while 514 Squadron had a single flight operational. The plan was for each two-flight squadron to be provided with six G-H aircraft, twelve crews with between 10 and 20 sortie experience were to be trained in the use of G-H. In a similar fashion each three-flight squadron was to be provided with nine aircraft and eighteen trained crews. The squadrons to be equipped were as follows.

No.32 Base

| | |
|---|---|
| 90 Squadron – RAF Tuddenham | 6 G-H Sets |
| 186 Squadron – RAF Tuddenham | 6 G-H Sets |
| 622 Squadron – RAF Mildenhall | 6 G-H Sets |

No.33 Base

| | |
|---|---|
| 75 (NZ) Squadron - RAF Mepal | 9 G-H Sets |
| 115 Squadron – RAF Witchford | 6 G-H Sets |
| 514 Squadron – RAF Waterbeach | 6 G-H Sets |

The production of the G-H sets was now becoming more regular, which meant installation was carried out as soon as the sets were delivered. There was, however, one problem, training. The single Type 77 Trainer available to No.3 Group was at full capacity training crews almost around the clock. It took approximately five hours per crew to be sufficiently trained to operate and manipulate the G-H set. Number 3 Group had requested an additional set in the summer. However, its long-awaited arrival never materialised despite repeated requests. There was one possible solution, but it required the cooperation of the Path Finders, something that was not always forthcoming. They had four fully operational Type 55 Trainers, which they used for Oboe training. The boffins at No.3 Group believed that the Type 55 could be modified and converted to a Type 77 Trainer with some adjustment. It was decided that this would be the best option in the short term but would need the intervention of HQ Bomber Command to apply pressure on the Path Finder Force to comply. The steelworks at Solingen was the target for the squadrons of No.3 Group on the afternoon of November 4th. Situated in North Rhine-Westphalia, some 20 miles east of Düsseldorf, Solingen was one of eight targets listed on No.3 Group's *'Priority List No.1'*. The squadron detailed and briefed 18 crews. However, this was reduced just before take-off when fluid was observed trickling from the starboard outer engine radiator of Lancaster HK682 XY-L. Flying Officer Phillips had no option but to abort the operation and return to his dispersal for repair. The squadron was led away by S/Ldr M Leyshon AFC and crew aboard Lancaster HK661 XY-R. Three recent arrivals, F/Sgt Fernley and P/O's Tonks and Godfrey RAAF would be undertaking their first operation. It was very nearly the first and last for the young Australian, Godfrey.

Form B.688 – November 4th, 1944 (D) : Target : Solingen 'A'

| | | | | | | | |
|---|---|---|---|---|---|---|---|
| F/O | Barton | E.E | RAAF | NG174 | XY-A | Follower | Duty Carried Out. |
| F/Sgt | Fernley | F | | NG148 | XY-B | Follower | Duty Carried Out. |
| F/O | Wait | G.J | | NG147 | XY-C | Follower | Duty Carried Out. |
| F/Lt | Smith | S | | NG140 | XY-F | Follower | Duty Carried Out. |
| F/O | Field DFC | E.L | | NG149 | XY-G | Follower | Duty Carried Out. |
| F/O | Hoskin | F.C | RCAF | NG175 | XY-J | Follower | Duty Carried Out. |
| P/O | Tonks | J.S | | NN720 | XY-K | Follower | Duty Carried Out. |
| F/O | Phillips | T | | HK682 | XY-L | - | WITHDRAWN |
| Sgt | Cowley | N.C | | HK688 | XY-R | Follower | Duty Carried Out. |
| W/O | O'Brien | J.D | RAAF | HK684 | XY-O | Follower | Duty Carried Out. |
| F/O | Kelsey | P.D | | HK662 | XY-P | Follower | Duty Carried Out. |
| F/O | Orman | K.G | RNZAF | HK659 | XY-Q | Follower | Duty Carried Out. |

| | | | | | | | |
|---|---|---|---|---|---|---|---|
| S/Ldr | Leyshon AFC | M | | HK661 | XY-R | Follower | Duty Carried Out. |
| F/O | Smith DFC | L | | LM188 | XY-S | Follower | Duty Carried Out. |
| P/O | Godfrey | D.F | RAAF | HK606 | XY-V | Follower | Duty Carried Out. |
| F/Lt | Powell | A.C | | LM160 | XY-W | Follower | Duty Carried Out. |
| F/O | Gogler | R.J | | HK613 | XY-Y | Follower | Duty Carried Out. |
| F/O | Liddell | J.B | | HK622 | XY-Z | Follower | Duty Carried Out. |

A total of 177 Lancasters lifted off from No.3 Group's bases spread throughout East Anglia. In the vanguard of the formation was No.186 Squadron. The Group crossed the Belgium coast where the fighter escort consisting of three squadrons of Spitfires and six squadrons of RAF Mustangs made contact near St Trond. The bomber stream headed towards the target crossing the Rhine between Bonn and Koblenz. The now fully recovered Flight Lieutenant A.C Powell was obliged to jettison two 1000 pounders over Germany when he could not climb Lancaster LM160 XY-W to the briefed bombing height of 19,000 feet. Once again, both No.218 and No.149 Squadrons would act as G-H Leaders for the opening waves timed to attack at 14:00 hours. Each G-H aircraft was equipped with 3 Red Marker flares to which their followers would drop on their release. Flak over the target was unusually light. Other than the 7/10th cloud over the target, making accessing accuracy tricky, all, however, appeared well. The first two squadron crews to bomb were S/Ldr M Leyshon AFC and F/O L.Smith DFC at 14:00 hours. Squadron Leader Leyshon reported *'Identified on Red TI flares and visually. Good trip, no results observed'.* Pilot Officer D Godfrey RAAF had just settled into his bomb run at 19,000 feet when there was a yell from the rear gunner. Sitting directly above them was another Lancaster with its 33ft bomb bay wide open oblivious to the Lancaster below. To the rear gunner's horror, the first bombs started to fall. By a miracle, all the bombs dropped missed except one, which gave the rudder a glancing blow. The crew had been fortunate. A few seconds or a few yards either way would have meant disaster.

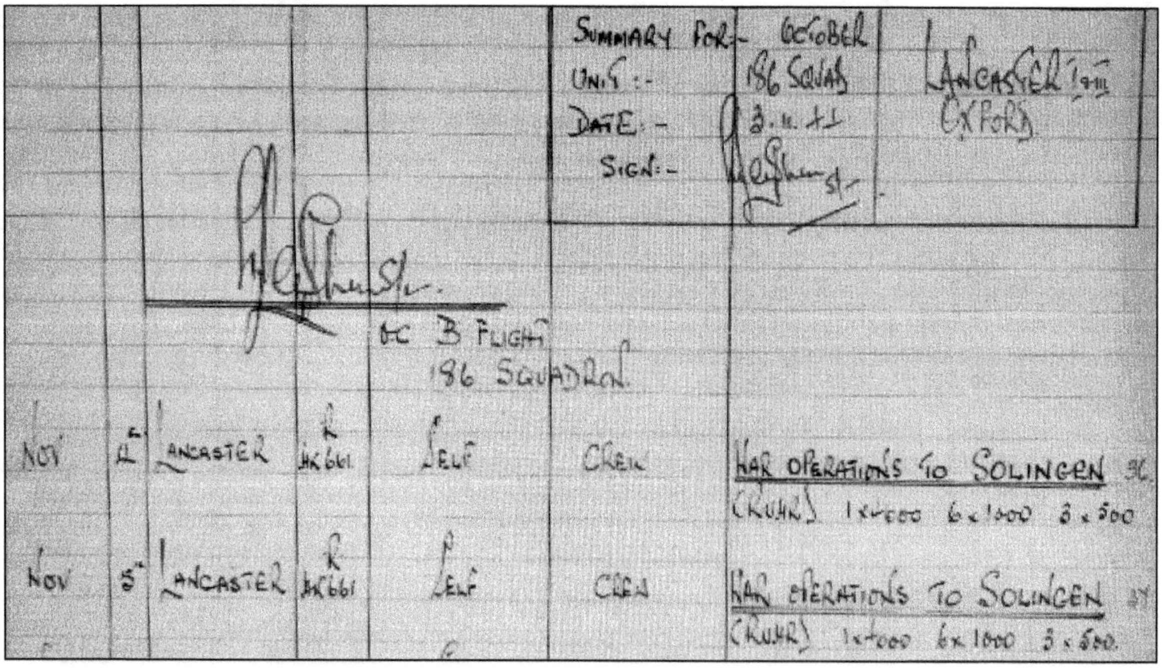


A page from the Log Book of 'B' Flight Commander, Squadron Leader Leyshon AFC. This page records his 36th and 37th operation, both to Solingen.

Rear Gunner Sergeant Norman 'Cisco' Haikney. His first operation was nearly his last when the crew of Pilot Officer Godfrey RAAF were bombed from above over Solingen. Sadly despite the best endeavours of No.3 Group HQ, this frightening experience, often with tragic results, continued until VE Day.

It was a relatively subdued de-briefing back at RAF Tuddenham. The squadron crews reported the marker flares strung out on the approach to target, and only a handful of crews managed to observe bombs exploding in the general area of the town. While the squadron was over Germany the crew of F/O G.E Williamson RAAF had arrived back on the squadron having firstly being deposited at RAF Northolt. The crew were immediately sent on leave.

It was no surprise, given the partial success that instructions were received from No.3 Group HQ informing the squadron of another attack on Solingen the next day, the squadron would be required to provide an impressive 19 crews. It was an early morning briefing for the crews at RAF Tuddenham, W/Cdr J.H Giles DFC briefed the 133 airmen who would return to Solingen and its defences. All 19 crews safely departed RAF Tuddenham just after 10 am and made for Orford Ness along with 156 No.3 Group Lancasters. One crew skippered by F/Sgt F Fernley very nearly did not take off. Various technical problems aboard HK650 XY-T required the frantic intervention of the ground crew. Finally, ten minutes late, 'B' Flight F/Sgt Fernley managed to take off. It was an excellent effort on the part of the crew on only their second operation. While the squadron was battling its way towards Germany, another crew arrived from No.3 LFS. Pilot Officer Frederick Mason and crew had successfully completed Course No.61 at RAF Feltwell. They would join the ranks of 'B' Flight on arrival at RAF Tuddenham.

<u>Form B.689 – November 5th, 1944 (D) : Target : Solingen 'A'</u>

| | | | | | | | |
|---|---|---|---|---|---|---|---|
| F/O | Barton | E.E | RAAF | NG174 | XY-A | Follower | Duty Carried Out. |
| W/Cdr | Giles DFC | J.H | | NG148 | XY-B | Follower | Duty Carried Out. |
| Sgt | Cowley | N.C | | NG147 | XY-C | Follower | Duty Carried Out. |
| F/O | Tait | R.R | | NG137 | XY-D | Follower | Duty Carried Out. |
| P/O | Tonks | J.E | | NG146 | XY-E | Follower | Duty Carried Out. |

| | | | | | | | |
|---|---|---|---|---|---|---|---|
| F/Sgt | Young | H.S | | NG140 | XY-F | Follower | Duty Carried Out. |
| F/O | Field DFC | E.L | | NG149 | XY-G | Follower | Duty Carried Out. |
| F/O | Hoskin | F.C | RCAF | NG175 | XY-J | Follower | Duty Carried Out. |
| F/O | Gibson | J.H | | NN720 | XY-K | Follower | Duty Carried Out. |
| F/O | Phillips | TT | | HK682 | XY-L | Follower | Duty Carried Out. |
| W/O | O'Brien | J.D | RAAF | HK684 | XY-O | Follower | Duty Carried Out. |
| F/O | Kelsey | P.D | | HK662 | XY-P | Follower | Duty Carried Out. |
| F/O | Orman | K.G | RNZAF | HK659 | XY-Q | Follower | Duty Carried Out. |
| S/Ldr | Leyshon AFC | M | | HK661 | XY-R | Follower | Duty Carried Out. |
| F/O | Smith DFC | L | | LM188 | XY-S | Follower | Duty Carried Out. |
| F/Sgt | Fernley | F | | HK650 | XY-V | Follower | Duty Carried Out. |
| P/O | Godfrey | D.F | RAAF | LM160 | XY-W | Follower | Duty Carried Out. |
| F/O | Gogler | R.J | RAAF | HK613 | XY-Y | Follower | Duty Carried Out. |
| F/O | Liddell | J.B | | HK622 | XY-Z | Follower | Duty Carried Out. |

Wing Commander Giles DFC was airborne in Lancaster NG148 XY-B. He had chosen to take the crew of the relatively inexperienced F/Sgt L.A Green with the exception of the crew's navigator, who was replaced by the Squadron Navigation Leader F/Lt W Earle. If No.3 Group HQ at Harraton House had hoped for clear conditions, they would have been disappointed. Thick cloud blanketed the whole of the route from the English coast to the target. As per the preceding day's effort, the squadrons of Methwold would supply the bulk of the G-H crews. Of the forty G-H crews despatched, twenty-seven would be supplied by Methwold. These would be spread over the 1st, 3rd, and 4th waves timed to bomb between 13:00 hours and 13:10 hours. The techniques used on the 4th were once again deployed. On this occasion, both the red markers and bombing appeared concentrated. Twelve of the squadron crews opened the attack at 13.00 hours. The remainder were divided over the proceeding waves. Flak that emanated from what appeared to be just one flak battery gave the crews an almost untroubled approach to the target. Wing Commander J.H Giles DFC dropped 1 x 4000lb + 6 x 1000lb + 6 x 500lb from 18,000 feet at 13:03 hours, he reported on return , *'Identified on Navigation Aids, Exceptionally good Leader'.*[3] Once again, opinions differed on the accuracy of the attack. Squadron Leader M Leyshon AFC commented, *'Flares rather scattered'* while New Zealander F/O K.G Orman RNZAF stated, *'Bombing seemed concentrated'*. One thing was certain the G-H leaders appeared to have impressed not only the Squadron Commander but also F/O L Smith DFC, who told the Intelligence Officer at de-briefing, *'Leading aircraft was very reliable'*. Over thirteen hundred houses and eighteen industrial premises were destroyed, plus numerous properties were damaged. The lessons learnt over the previous raids were now slowly being put to good effect as the confidence in the accuracy of G-H rapidly increased throughout the group. On crossing the channel on the return route, the crews encountered low clouds and pouring rain, which resulted in four crews landing at alternative airfields. Two landed at RAF Woodbridge, and one apiece at the fighter station at RAF Rockford, Essex and RAF Mendlesham, the home of the B17 Flying Fortress equipped 34th Bombardment Group. On the 6th, S/Ldr Leyshon AFC flew the squadron's Oxford to Southend, accompanied by fellow pilots, F/O's Orman RNZAF and Smith DFC as well as his usual wireless operator, F/O A.J Oyler and bomb aimer, F/O H.W Richards. It is presumed it was to pick up the crew of F/Sgt F Fernley who diverted on return from Solingen the previous day.

[3] There is some confusion with the 186 Squadron ORB concerning GH or 'Navigational Aid'. For some unexplained reason, the Intelligence Officer, or Adjutant, refers to crews bombing on 'Navigational aids. This term is frustratingly used when aircraft are known to have bombed on a GH Leader. Because there is no distinction between the two, i.e., bombing/marking on GH, or simply bombing on a GH aircraft, the author has copied what is written in the Squadron Form 541 and tried to cross-referenced this information with the No.3 Groups Operational Records Book (Air25). However, even this cross-checking, has resulted in numerous contradictions.

Another Rear Gunner starting his operational career at this time was Flight Sergeant Gerald McPherson RAAF. He flew with fellow Aussie, Flight Sergeant Alexander Clarson RAAF. Born November 14th 1924, in Dimboola, Victoria, Gerald worked pre-enlistment as a Bank Clerk.

Peter Kelsey is seen here with the rank of Flight Sergeant. His stay on No.186 Squadron was brief for all the right reasons. Peter flew a wide range of operations from low-level Short Stirling supply drops to the French Resistance to daylight precision raids on German industry. He is reported to have said when asked about operational stress. "Oh stiff upper lip, chaps. All of us had the sense to know that that was the only way of looking at it. There was no alternative way. It's no good going to the corner and crying." He died in 2020.

The raid on Solingen concluded the first tour of F/O Peter Kelsey. He had flown just four operations with the squadron since his arrival. His tour started with No.90 Squadron flying Short Stirlings in May 1944.

In other publications, there is a suggestion that this operation may have been the first G-H operation flown by No.186 Squadron. This has caused much chaos over the years. The problem is caused by the Squadron Operational Records Books terminology, which records 11 crews bombed on 'Navigational Aids'. This is an unusually high number of G-H aircraft to be detailed by a single squadron with no G-H operational experience. The No.3 Group Operational Records Book reports 11 crews bombed on 'Navigational Aids' to confuse the issue even more. The author believes both seem highly improbable and are more likely to be referring to the crew's dropping on a designated G-H Leader. This is corroborated by the available Flying Log Books.
It was a switch to night bombing the following day when the squadron was detailed for an early evening attack against Koblenz, situated on the banks of the Rhine. It would be another all No.3 Group effort. This operation would be the first occasion that the group would independently mark and attack a target of its own at night. Number 186 Squadron would provide 15 crews. The raid did not begin well. Over at RAF Methwold, 21 crews were cancelled due to a delay in bombing up. The majority were G-H crews.

Form B.690 – November 6th, 1944 (N) : Target : Koblenz : 'Dogfish'

| | | | | | | | |
|---|---|---|---|---|---|---|---|
| F/O | Tait | R.R | | NG148 | XY-B | Main Force | Duty Carried Out. |
| F/O | Wait | C.J | | NG147 | XY-C | Main Force | Duty Carried Out. |
| F/O | Smith | S | | NG140 | XY-F | Main Force | Duty Carried Out. |
| F/Lt | Phillips | T | | NG149 | XY-G | Main Force | Duty Carried Out. |
| F/O | Powers | R.C | | NG175 | XY-J | Main Force | Duty Carried Out. |
| F/O | Gibson | J.H | | NN720 | XY-K | Main Force | Duty Carried Out. |
| Sgt | Cowley | N.C | | HK661 | XY-R | Main Force | Duty Carried Out. |
| P/O | Tonks | J.E | | HK688 | XY-M | Main Force | Duty Carried Out. |
| F/Sgt | Clarson | A.J | RAAF | HK684 | XY-O | Main Force | Duty Carried Out. |
| F/O | Gogler | R.J | RAAF | HK662 | XY-P | Main Force | Duty Carried Out. |
| F/O | Orman | K.G | RNZAF | HK659 | XY-Q | Main Force | Duty Carried Out. |
| F/Sgt | Green | L.A | | HK606 | XY-V | Main Force | Duty Carried Out. |
| F/Lt | Powell | A.C | | LM160 | XY-W | Main Force | Duty Carried Out. |
| P/O | Godfrey | D.F | RAAF | HK613 | XY-Y | Main Force | Duty Carried Out. |
| F/O | Liddell | J.B | | HK622 | XY-Z | Main Force | Duty Carried Out. |

The depleted force of 128 Lancasters departed over Beachy Head and headed out over the English Channel towards Le Touquet south of Boulogne. Time over the target was planned for 19:30 hours, with 186 Squadron's contribution part of the third and final wave. The target would be ground marked if weather permitted with green flares with red stars. If cloud covered the aiming point, Koblenz would be marked using 250lb green and red sky-markers. The weather over England and en route was excellent. This continued over the target, where conditions were perfect. The ground marking force had been briefed to make an exact and careful run into the target. The crew of P/O J.E Tonks had a sharp encounter with a twin-engined JU88 at 17:50 hours while at 10,000 feet. The Combat Report records the following.

> Enemy aircraft first seen on Port beam by Mid Upper, he ordered corkscrew to port, apparently the evasive action was too violent for accurate firing. Both gunner having difficulty with sighting. Fighter broke away astern and was not seen again.

The rear gunner Sgt Woods managed to get off 250 rounds, while the mid upper gunner, Sgt Forshaw just 100 before the fighter was lost from sight. The crew of F/Sgt A.J Clarson RAAF also reported an inconclusive encounter with a JU88 west of Aachen.

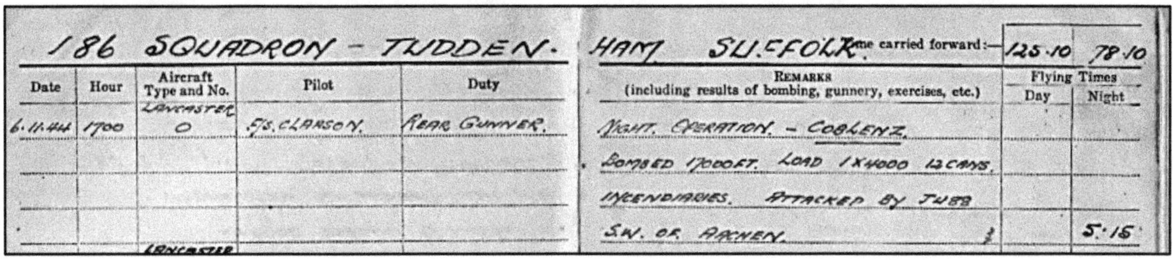
186 SQUADRON - TUDDENHAM SUFFOLK. Time carried forward:— 125.10 78.10

| Date | Hour | Aircraft Type and No. | Pilot | Duty | Remarks (including results of bombing, gunnery, exercises, etc.) | Flying Times Day | Flying Times Night |
|---|---|---|---|---|---|---|---|
| 6.11.44 | 1700 | LANCASTER O | F/S. CLARSON. | REAR GUNNER. | NIGHT. OPERATION. - COBLENZ. | | |
| | | | | | BOMBED 17000FT. LOAD 1X4000 12 CANS. | | |
| | | | | | INCENDIARIES. ATTACKED BY JU88 | | |
| | | | | | S.W. OF AACHEN. | | 5.15 |

Flight Sergeant Gerald McPherson RAAF entry in his Log Book for the encounter with the JU88 on November 6th 1944.

The G-H ground markers were loaded with one bundle of 3 green flares with red stars. These were only to be released with the bomb load if both the bomb aimer and navigator were confident of the accuracy. If for any reason they were not, the markers were to be retained, and the crew were to bomb as per the main force. The attack opened on time. The reception was strong from both the CAT and

MOUSE[4] stations as the early waves began their bomb runs. Koblenz offered only slight resistance with spasmodic heavy flak. There were no searchlights and no fighters. The ground markers were visible as the bombers entered the target area, such were the conditions crews could quickly identify numerous streets and large buildings. The reduction in G-H marker aircraft may have resulted in the crew of F/O J.B Liddle having to orbit the target, *'Target Indicators late in falling. Over the target at 19.27 hours but saw no markers so circled until 19.36 hours and then bombed on markers which appeared'.*
A concentration of markers was seen near the join of rivers Rhine and Moselle, where large swathes of Koblenz was soon on fire. This conflagration attracted the vast majority of the incendiaries, which made up the bulk of the bomb loads. The ordinarily cautious crews were confident that the raid was a total success. At de-briefing, the crews spoke enthusiastically about the destruction over the once beautiful city, F/O R.R Tait, *'Good attack, whole town ablaze. Fires Still visible when 80 miles away.'* Flying Officer C.J Wait bombed from 18,500 feet at 19.29 hours. He reported, *'My bomb aimer reports the best attack I've seen, whole town thoroughly hit'.* Finally, Flight Lieutenant S Smith and crew reported, *'Most successful raid experienced so far. Whole town churned up and fire visible from 200 miles away on return trip'.* The raid was a complete success. The worst affected area was the centre of the city where a large proportion of the built-up area was demolished. The districts of Lutzel and Ehrenbreistein situated where the river Mosel and Rhine join were also hard hit. The town's gas works and main passenger station were both seriously hit and damaged. A reported 58% of the town was destroyed and 25,000 people lost their homes.

The people of the ground. A cheerful bunch of sadly unknown WAAFs and Airmen who worked in the Squadron Stores. Their work may not have been particularly exciting, but it was vitally important to the squadron's success.

4 Cat and Mouse were the code names for the GH tracking station 'Cat' and the GH Releasing station 'Mouse'.

The squadron was not required on the 7th. It came just at the right time. The funeral of Flying Officer W.S Cowan RCAF took place at Brookwood Cemetery, Surrey at 15.00 hours. The service was conducted by Presbyterian Padre, S/Ldr R Moynan. The coffin, draped in a Union flag, was carried by members of the squadron and his crew. A number of wreaths were laid, one from the Officers and men of RAF Tuddenham and strangely one from RAF Station Coningsby, home of No.97 Squadron. A wreath was also laid by Mrs H.R David, of Blackheath, Kent. Finally, the Last Post sounded, concluding a sad day. The squadron was called for yet another early morning briefing on the 8th. The 14 assembled crews were informed that a further effort was required against the Meerbeck synthetic oil plant at Homberg.

Form B.691 – November 8th, 1944 (D) :Target : Homberg : Fischer Tropsch synthetic oil plant:

| | | | | | | | |
|---|---|---|---|---|---|---|---|
| F/Lt | Fleming | A.J | | NG148 | XY-B | Follower | Duty Carried Out. |
| F/O | Tait | R.R. | | NG137 | XY-D | Follower | Duty Carried Out. |
| F/O | Hoskin | F.C | RCAF | HK661 | XY-R | Follower | Duty Carried Out. |
| F/O | Barton | E.E | RAAF | HK688 | XY-M | Follower | Duty Carried Out. |
| F/Sgt | Young | H.S | | HK606 | XY-V | Follower | Duty Carried Out. |
| F/O | Field DFC | E.L | | NG174 | XY-A | Follower | Duty Carried Out. |
| F/O | Phillips | T | | HK684 | XY-O | Follower | Duty Carried Out. |
| P/O | Mason | F.H | | NG146 | XY-E | Follower | Duty Carried Out. |
| F/O | Powers | R.C | | HK662 | XY-P | Follower | Duty Carried Out. |
| W/O | O'Brien | J.D | RAAF | LM188 | XY-S | Follower | Duty Carried Out. |
| F/O | Hanson | R.A | | HK662 | XY-Z | Follower | Duty Carried Out. |
| F/O | Gibson | J.H | | HK650 | XY-T | Follower | Duty Carried Out. |
| F/Sgt | Green | L.A | | LM617 | XY-X | Follower | Duty Carried Out. |
| P/O | Tonks | J.E | | HK659 | XY-Q | Follower | Duty Carried Out. |

Group despatched 136 Lancasters, the oil plant would be attacked in three waves timed between 10:27 hours and 10:42 hours. The force encountered exceptionally high winds of 75 mph from the northwest en route, making time-keeping difficult. Fighter escort was provided by over 150 Spitfires and 68 RAF Mustang IIIs. On this occasion, a number of Mustang squadrons were ordered to sweep broad areas of Germany from Munster to Gutersloh and Koblenz to Frankfurt on the lookout for German fighters. This tactic had been proven to be highly effective when introduced by the US 8th Air Force earlier in the year. The planned route brought the stream into proximity of some heavy flak zones. These zones appeared to engage the various base group formations individually. The strategy was obvious and deadly, concentrate all available flak onto one group at a time in the hope the bombers flying in their Vic formation would need to take evasive action. The Germans were fully aware that any attempt to evade the flak affected accuracy and bombing concentration. The Lancasters of No.33 Base would open the batting. They would provide ten G-H Leaders and twenty followers. Two minutes later, these would be followed by eight G-H Leaders from Methwold with twenty-four followers drawn from No.33 Base. Four minutes after H-Hour, the third and final wave would provide the bulk of the attack. Eight Methwold G-H Leaders would lead thirty-six followers from No.32 Base. During this operation, the responsibility of providing its own Leaders befell No.32 Base, if only on a limited scale. It had previously relied on the regularly criticised squadrons of Methwold. With the G-H sets becoming available, seven G-H equipped Lancasters of No.15 Squadron would lead a small group of twelve followers and makeup part of the final wave, which included No.186 Squadron. A significant break in the cloud cover in the target area enabled crews to confirm that bombs were falling precisely on the target. Flak was accurate and intense, and three crews were hit on the run into the target. Warrant Officer

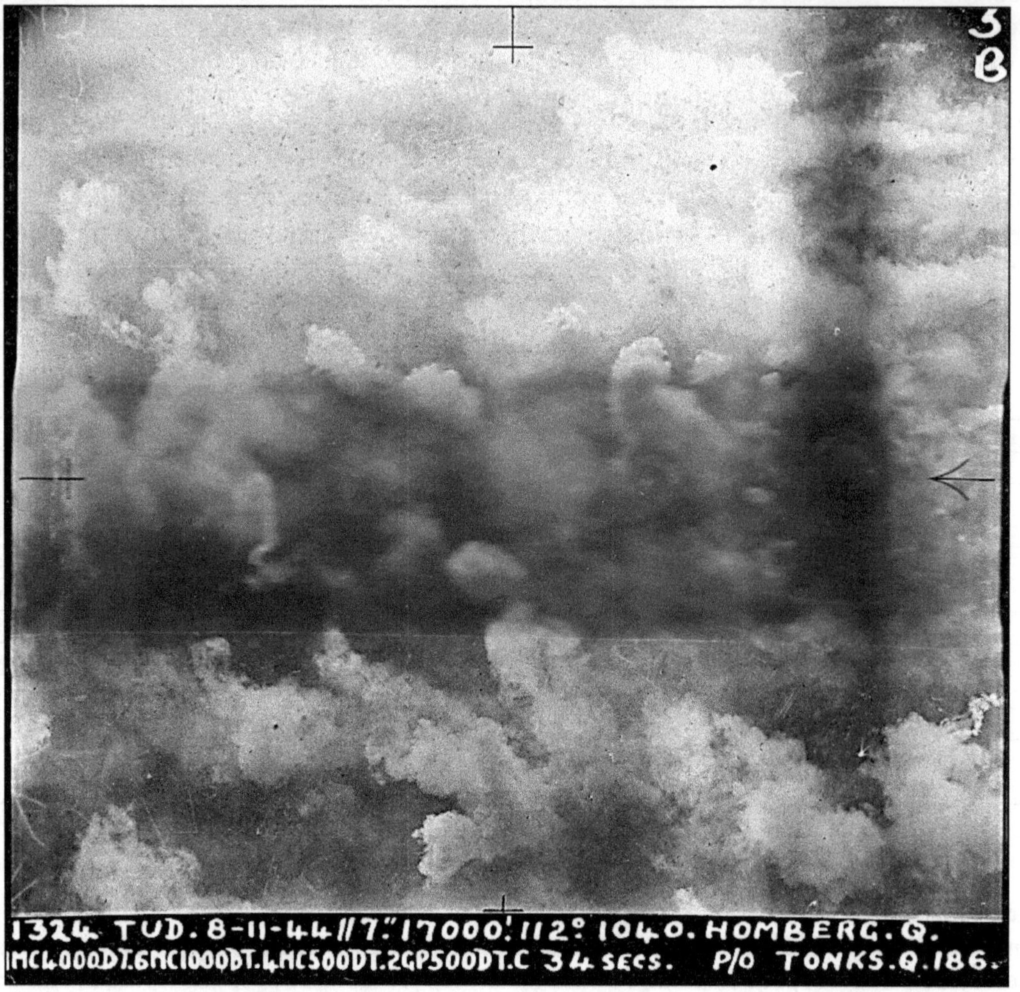


The Fischer Tropsch synthetic oil plant at Homberg is shown covered in smoke in this target photograph taken by the crew of Pilot Officer J Tonks from 17,000 feet at 10:40 hours.

O'Brien RAAF was hit at 10:36 hours. The damage was confined to the fuselage and rudder aboard Lancaster LM188 XY-S. More seriously hit was the Lancaster flown by F/O R.A Hanson. A burst of flak ripped into the port inner engine of HK662 XY-Z, forcing him to feather the engine before it burst into flames. As the squadron started its bomb run, dense smoke rose from the target area. Flying Officer J.H Gibson, on his first operation reported, *'Much smoke, difficult to see the target'*. Flying Officer T Phillips was at 17,000 feet at the controls of Lancaster HK684 XY-O. He submitted the following on return to RAF Tuddenham, *'Well concentrated attack caused large fires, Smoke plumes seen in the vicinity of smokestacks.* The squadron began landing back at base just after midday. Despite the flak opposition, all of RAF Tuddenham's crews return safely.

No.186 Squadron Reported Flak Damage 08/11/1944

| Serial | Code | Damage Reported | Repairs / Notes |
|---|---|---|---|
| HK662 | **XY-Z** | Port Inner engine, port wing. | Repaired on squadron. |
| LM188 | **XY-S** | Fuselage / Rudder. | Repaired on squadron |

New Zealander Ken Orman got himself in trouble with the C/O on the 8th. While taking off for a Fighter Affiliation Exercise at 11:50 hours accompanied by F/O J.B Liddell, his Lancaster, LM160 XY-W swung violently on take-off. Unable to correct the Lancasters swing, the undercarriage collapsed, resulting in the Lancaster coming to rest on the grass adjoining the runway. Thankfully, no one was injured, but Armstrong Whitworth built LM160 was classified as Cat E/FA and written-off. The subsequent investigation squarely blamed the young Kiwi, reporting *'Uneven use of the throttles, high boost caused swing when pilot failed to correct'.* It would appear that the initial classification was changed, LM160 was sent to A.V Roe and, after four months of repair, the aircraft returned to active service in March 1945 briefly with No.300 (Polish) and then No.626 Squadrons.

| Type | Avro Lancaster Mk.I **LM160 XY-W** | Armstrong Whitworth |
|---|---|---|
| Taken on Charge | 15/10/1944 | |
| Cat FA | 08/11/1944 | |
| Struck Of Charge | 16/11/194 | |
| Re-Cat 'B' | A.V Roe | |
| AW/CN | 10/02/1945 | |
| No.300 (Polish) Sqdn | 03/03/1945 | |
| No.626 Squadron | 10/03/1945 | |
| | **CREW** | **Notes** |
| Pilot | F/O K Orman RNZAF & Crew | Safe |
| 2nd Pilot | F/O J.B Liddell. | Safe |

The Cine Gyro Circus arrived from RAF Newmarket on the 8th, the purpose of which was to give the crews practice in Fighter Affiliation, its stay was brief but productive. The Circus was in fact No.1688 Bomber (Defence) Training Flight equipped with a motley collection of ageing Spitfire Mk.II's and V's and Hurricane Mk.II's.

An unknown pilot of No.1688 Bomber (Defence) Training Flight is photographed sitting on the hinged door of his ageing Spitfire Mk.V. The much-unappreciated unit did excellent work.

On the 10th, orders were received that the squadron would be required for a daylight operation directed against the Castrop Rauxel synthetic Oil Plant, but this was subsequently cancelled due to bad weather. It would be another short reprieve as instructions were received on the evening informing the squadron that they would be required to attack the following day. Sixteen Lancasters departed just after

08:00hours in filthy weather. Once airborne the squadron first flew to Bury St Edmunds where they joined 108 other Group Lancasters before heading to Diss then out over the English coast at Orford Ness. Wing Commander Giles DFC was at the controls of Lancaster NN720 XY-K, he was accompanied by the all-NCO crew of F/O J.H Gibson, who sat the operation out. Unlike some

Flying Officer Ken Orman RNZAF was photographed at the controls of Lancaster HK659 XY-Q 'Queenie', his favourite aircraft. The crew had a series of photographs taken in this aircraft.

Commanding Officers who would only operate with the various Section Leaders or their own crew, W/Cdr Giles DFC preferred to fly with individual crews. This instilled them with confidence, especially the recent arrivals. However, what their pilot thought about watching his crew depart is unknown. Flying Officer L Smith DFC was forced to abandon the operation when he suffered oxygen failure aboard Lancaster LM188 XY-S. The crew jettisoned the 4000 pounder and 2 x 500lb bomb east of Southwold before landing at Tuddenham at 10.30 hours.

Form B.693 – November 11th, 1944 (D) :Target : Castrop Rauxel : Oil Plant.

| Rank | Surname | Initial | Airforce | Serial | Code | Role | Results |
|---|---|---|---|---|---|---|---|
| F/Sgt | Cowley | N.C | | NG147 | XY-C | Follower | Duty Carried Out. |
| F/O | Tait | R.R | | NG137 | XY-D | Follower | Duty Carried Out. |
| F/O | Field DFC | E.L | | NG140 | XY-F | Follower | Duty Carried Out. |
| F/O | Phillips | T | | NG149 | XY-G | Follower | Duty Carried Out. |
| F/O | Hoskin | F.C | RCAF | NG175 | XY-J | Follower | Duty Carried Out. |
| W/Cdr | Giles DFC | J.H | | NN720 | XY-K | Follower | Duty Carried Out. |
| F/Sgt | Young | H.S | | HK682 | XY-L | Follower | Duty Carried Out. |
| F/Sgt | Clarson | A | RAAF | HK688 | XY-M | Follower | Duty Carried Out. |
| F/O | Mason | F.B | | HK662 | XY-P | Follower | Duty Carried Out. |

| | | | | | | | |
|---|---|---|---|---|---|---|---|
| F/O | Gogler | R.J | RAAF | HK659 | XY-Q | Follower | Duty Carried Out. |
| S/Ldr | Leyshon AFC | | | HK661 | XY-R | Follower | Duty Carried Out. |
| F/Lt | Smith DFC | L | | LM188 | XY-S | Follower | Duty Not Carried Out. |
| F/Sgt | James | W.C | RAAF | HK650 | XY-T | Follower | Duty Carried Out. |
| F/Sgt | Green | L.A | | HK606 | XY-V | Follower | Duty Carried Out. |
| F/O | Barton | E.R | RAAF | HK680 | XY-H | Follower | Duty Carried Out. |
| F/O | Liddell | J.B | | HK684 | XY-O | Follower | Duty Carried Out. |

A north wind of 60-65 mph meant that the bombers were forced to take a more northerly route than normal on entering the Ruhr. Unusually, the force encountered accurate predicted flak between Arnhem and Emmerich as they entered German airspace above a thick layer of cloud. Flying Officer R.R Tait remarked about this on his return, *'Defences considerably increased especially around Arnhem'*. The final 50 mile run into the target produced almost no opposition. The usual venomous flak was strangely subdued. This however changed dramatically as the first waves began their bomb runs at 11.04 hours. By the time the squadron began depositing their mixed HE loads just 3 minutes later, the flak had almost ceased. Why was unclear, but the crews were not complaining. A series of red markers clearly stood out against the white clouds below. Flying Officer E.L Field experienced two 500lb GP hanging up, which was the only incident in an otherwise routine raid flown by the crew. The Luftwaffe made a brief appearance on this raid in the form of a pair of Bf109's which were observed south of the target area. These were quickly scared off when a squadron of RAF Mustangs raced to engage them. The first crew safely back at Tuddenham was S/Ldr M Leyshon AFC, who touched down at 12.55 hours at the controls of Lancaster HK661 XY-R. Little did he know it would be his 38th and last bombing raid of the war. There was little enthusiasm about the accuracy of the raid, S/Ldr Leyshon AFC reporting, *'Target obscured, bombing probably scattered, straightforward trip'*. This view was echoed by most of the returning crews.[5] Squadron Leader Mervyn Leyshon AFC had suffered from crippling headaches brought on by high altitude flying since his return to operations. Courageously, the young Welshman had tried to fight the pain and discomfort, but the operation to Castrop Rauxel made him realise that he needed to seek professional medical help. A visit to the station MO resulted in Mervyn being sent to see specialists at the RAF Hospital at Ely. Their report was shattering and a bitter blow to Mervyn, who aspired of commanding his own squadron one day. A break from operations for six months was the recommendation. Feeling utterly dejected, he quickly requested an interview with Air Commodore abrasive New Zealander was sympathetic but explained that he could not overrule the medical evidence 'Square' McKee DSO DFC AFC CB in the hope that the recommendation could be changed. The usual abrasive New Zealander was sympathetic but explained that he could not overrule the medical evidence 'and informed the disappointed Mervyn he was to cease operations immediately and was ordered to rest. A solitary crew was detailed and briefed for a minelaying operation on the late evening of the 11th. Mine laying the once staple diet of No.3 Group, had gradually decline from the Group's activities. Australian F/Lt A.J Fleming RAAF would join 9 other group Lancasters to mine the area around Oslo Harbour ( Code name *'Onions'*). Weather was abysmal as the crew first headed towards Cromer then out over the North Sea. Lancaster NG148 XY-B was loaded with five parachute acoustic sea mines. Over the 'Garden area' the weather improved enough for visual confirmation on their position. From 10,000 feet the mines were successfully dropped, the parachutes were observed as the mines slowly floated to the sea below. Other than sleet and an electrical storm the operation did not encounter any opposition

---

[5] The Squadron Operational Records Book records that 11 crews bombed on 'Navigational Aids' and three on flares. Thankfully the Tuddenham Station Records Book finally clarifies the misleading bombed on 'Navigational Aid' statement. This document clearly records that the 11 crews bombed on 'Leaders' while three bombed on flares.

Squadron Leader Mervyn Leyshon AFC is seen here while a Flying Officer. Battling crippling pain, this fearless young pilot did all he could to continue on as Flight Commander. Sadly not even the formidable Air Commodore 'Square' McKee DSO DFC AFC CB would challenge the medical advice from the specialists at RAF Hospital Ely.

Seven hours 14 minutes after departure the crew landed at RAF Tain on the east coast of Scotland, the weather over East Anglia having closed in preventing the crews return.

Form B.694 – November 11th, 1944 (N) :Target : Mining : *'Onions'*

| Rank | Surname | Initial | Airforce | Serial | Code | Role | Results |
|---|---|---|---|---|---|---|---|
| F/Lt | Fleming | A.J | RAAF | NG148 | XY-B | Gardening. | Duty Carried Out. |

The squadron was informed it could stand down on the 12th but was warned that an attack against Wanne Eickel was planned the following day. This stand down gave the crews an opportunity to visit the local pubs or relax in the mess. There was, however no such luxury for the Ground Crews who fussed over their Lancasters in preparation of the operation the following day. There followed two days of frustration, the planned daylight operation against Wanne Eickel was cancelled due to bad weather. The foul weather continued throughout the night, but the optimists at No.3 Group HQ once again informed the squadron to prepare 18 crews for a daylight attack on Soest the following day, the secondary target being Wanne Eickel, Exning was hedging its bets. The weather once again intervened, However, unlike the two previous cancelled operations, the squadron was instructed not to unload the bombed-up Lancasters. Finally, on the 15th, the squadron crews gathered for a mid-morning briefing. The target was a synthetic oil plant at Dortmund.

Form B.696 – November 15th, 1944 (D) :Target : Dortmund : Synthetic Oil Plant.

| | | | | | | | |
|---|---|---|---|---|---|---|---|
| F/Sgt | Cowley | N.C | | NG147 | XY-C | Follower | Duty Carried Out. |
| F/O | Templeton | G.M | RCAF | NG146 | XY-E | Follower | Duty Carried Out. |
| F/O | Smith | S | | NG140 | XY-F | Follower | Duty Carried Out. |
| S/Ldr | Reynolds | P | | NG149 | XY-G | Follower | Duty Carried Out. |
| P/O | Barton | E.R | RAAF | HK680 | XY-H | Follower | Duty Carried Out. |
| F/O | Hoskin | F.C | RCAF | NG175 | XY-J | Follower | Duty Carried Out. |
| F/O | Green | J.H | | NN720 | XY-K | Follower | Duty Carried Out. |
| F/Sgt | Young | H | | HK682 | XY-L | Follower | Duty Carried Out. |
| F/Sgt | Clarson | A | RAAF | HK688 | XY-M | Follower | Duty Carried Out. |
| F/O | Ritson | E.E | | HK684 | XY-O | Follower | Duty Carried Out. |
| F/O | Madden | R.P | RCAF | HK662 | XY-P | Follower | Duty Not Carried Out. |
| F/O | Orman | K.G | RNZAF | HK659 | XY-Q | Follower | Duty Carried Out |
| F/O | Mason | F.H | | HK661 | XY-R | Follower | Duty Not Carried Out |
| F/O | Smith DFC | L | | LM188 | XY-S | Follower | Duty Carried Out |
| F/Sgt | Green | L.A | | HK650 | XY-T | Follower | Duty Carried Out |
| P/O | Godfrey | D.F | | HK606 | XY-V | Follower | Duty Carried Out |
| F/O | Hanson | R.A | | HK613 | XY-Y | Follower | Duty Carried Out |
| F/Sgt | James | W.C | RAAF | HK622 | XY-Z | Follower | Duty Carried Out |

The Lancasters began lifting off from RAF Tuddenham just after midday, joining the squadron after an absence of a few weeks was S/Ldr P Reynolds at the controls of NG149 XY-G. It was no surprise that once over the North Sea, the usually ragtag formation keeping by the group dramatically improved, for this would be one of the deepest penetrations into Germany by the group to date. Disappointingly the squadron notched up two early returns. The first was P/O R.P Madden RCAF aboard Lancaster HK662 XY-P. They suffered a run-away starboard outer prop resulting in the cookie being jettisoned and the crew landing back at base at 14:53 hours. They were followed 28 minutes later by F/O F.H Mason and crew aboard HK661 XY-R. They too had problems with their starboard outer engine due to lack of oil pressure. The Group's 177 Lancasters had a trouble-free flight until the German border. Here the usual

Sadly not the best quality photograph. Pictured here at its RAF Tuddenham dispersal in November 1944 is Lancaster HK680 XY-H 'Happy Harry', the aircraft regularly flown by 22-year-old, Flying Officer Robert Charles Powers RAAF.

heavy flak began to explode in amongst the formations. It was reported as heavy but not remarkably accurate. Time over the target was planned between 15:39 hour and 15:45 hours, the squadron was part of the first wave and would not have the benefit of 'Window' coverage. When dropped in great numbers, it was believed to swamp the German Radar and Radar directed Flak guns with force echoes. New Zealander F/O K.G Orman RNZAF had a lucky escape on his bomb run at 15:40 hours. A burst of flak exploded close enough to Lancaster HK659 XY-Q to lift the heavily ladened aircraft upwards with a massive jolt. Shrapnel ripped into the fuselage, a piece of flak smashed through the windscreen injuring the pilot in the right cheek. Sergeant W Beer was fortunate to survive in the rear turret as a chunk of flak embedded itself in his turret. Thankfully other than the pilot, all the crew and the engines remained undamaged. Cloud over the target area made it impossible to accurately assess the raid, however crews were reasonably confident. Flying Officer J.H Gibson reporting, ' *Concentrated marking'*. Squadron Leader P.Reynolds told the intelligence officer at de-briefing, *'Compact formation suggests that attack may have been fairly concentrated'*.

The last crew to land was F/Sgt W.C James RAAF, who brought Lancaster HK662 XY-Z into land at 17.32 hours. Even before the crews had finished interrogation, orders were received from No.3 Group HQ requesting 18 crews for a daylight raid on the Sterkrade the following day. There would be no early night for the Ground Crews who would be required to work long into the early hours to ensure the squadron provided the number of Lancasters requested. Thankfully, no other aircraft reported damage or malfunctions, apart from the Lancaster of F/O K.G Orman RNZAF and the two early returns. Flying

Officer Ken Orman RNZAF was admitted into the SSQ to have his cheek stitched up. He would be grounded for the next four days.

No.186 Squadron Reported Flak Damage 15/11/1944

| Serial | Code | Damage Reported | Repairs / Notes |
|---|---|---|---|
| HK659 | **XY-Q** | Front and rear fuselage, cockpit. | Repaired on squadron. |

The Group was chosen for a special operation on the 16th. The Sterkrade operation was switched to a tactic operation supporting the American 9th Armies Operation 'Queen'. The Group would provide 183 crews to attack the town of Heinsberg in the North Rhine-Westphalia. Situated close to the Dutch border, this almost untouched town would feel the full force of No.3 Group. Given the close proximity of the American troops, No.3 Group HQ appointed a 'Master Bomber' (Call sign Marlow) in the form of the vastly experienced W/Cdr W.Watkins DSO, DFC DFM Officer Commanding No.15 Squadron based at RAF Mildenhall. Once the assembled force had formed into their various waves, the bombers departed over Orford Ness in terrible weather. The squadron's 18 crews were equally divided over the 2nd and 3rd waves.

Form B.698 – November 16th, 1944 (D) :Target : Heinsberg. Tactical Bombing.

| | | | | | | | |
|---|---|---|---|---|---|---|---|
| F/Lt | Fleming | A.J | RAAF | NG148 | XY-B | Follower | Duty Carried Out. |
| F/Sgt | Cowley | N | | NG147 | XY-C | Follower | Duty Carried Out. |
| F/O | Templeton | G.H | RCAF | NG146 | XY-E | Follower | Duty Carried Out. |
| F/O | Barton | E.R | RAAF | NG140 | XY-F | Follower | Duty Carried Out. |
| F/O | Phillips | T | | NG174 | XY-A | Follower | Duty Carried Out. |
| F/O | Field DFC | E.L | | HK680 | XY-H | Follower | Duty Carried Out. |
| F/O | Hoskin | F.C | RCAF | NG175 | XY-J | Follower | Duty Carried Out. |
| F/O | Gibson | J.H | | NN720 | XY-K | Follower | Duty Carried Out. |
| F/O | Tait | R.R | | HK682 | XY-L | Follower | Duty Carried Out. |
| F/Sgt | Clarson | A | RAAF | HK688 | XY-M | Follower | Duty Carried Out. |
| F/Sgt | James | W.C | RAAF | HK684 | XY-O | Follower | Duty Carried Out. |
| F/O | Madden | R.P | RCAF | HK662 | XY-P | Follower | Duty Carried Out. |
| F/O | Gogler | R.J | RAAF | HK659 | XY-Q | Follower | Duty Carried Out. |
| S/Ldr | Reynolds | P | | LM188 | XY-S | Follower | Duty Carried Out. |
| F/Sgt | Fernley | F | | HK650 | XY-T | Follower | Duty Carried Out. |
| F/Sgt | Green | L.A | | HK606 | XY-V | Follower | Duty Carried Out. |
| F/O | Hanson | R.A | | HK613 | XY-Y | Follower | Duty Carried Out. |
| F/O | Liddell | J.B | | HK622 | XY-Z | Follower | Duty Carried Out. |

The raid could not have started worse when the first G-H marker flares fell well north of the aiming point due to an *'error in miscalculation in the release coordinates'.* No doubt aware of this, W/Cdr Watkins DSO DFC DFM is believed to have ordered his pilot to reduce altitude to assess the situation. This proved his undoing. A Lancaster was observed on fire over the target area with yellow TIs falling from it. Sadly, only W/Cdr Watkins survived. With the 'Master Bomber' shot down there were a few minute's silence, with no instructions, the wayward TI markers attracted a number of bomb loads. It was the timely intervention of the Deputy Master Bomber, F/Lt D Cox ( Call sign Box-Kite), flying with S/Ldr B Payne aboard Lancaster ME844 LS-O that saved Group HQ blushes. However, the issue with misplaced Markers continued when yet more fell south of the aiming point. These were quickly identified and the crews ordered to ignore. At this point, No.186 Squadron began their bomb runs from between 7,000 and 9,000 feet. The first crew to bomb was F/Sgt W.C James RAAF at 15:31 hours, the last was fellow Aussie F/Lt A.J Fleming RAAF at 15.36 hours. Within five short minutes, utter destruction rained down on this one peaceful backwater. Flak was confined to the approach to the target, none of the squadron crews reporting trouble. Flight Lieutenant A.J Fleming RAAF reported, *'TI's were short, but raid appeared concentrated'*. Flight Sergeant N Cowley remarked, '*Master Bomber cancelled the Reds Markers'*. Thankfully, the Deputy Master Bomber, who was circling the target, kept up a barrage of instructions encouraging and coaxing the crews, they in turn were equally up to the task. Flying Officer G.H Templeton RCAF, *'Much smoke, the attack seemed concentrated, bombed on starboard side of smoke as instructed by the Master Bomber.* Fellow Canadian F/O F.C Hoskin RCAF was at 9,000 feet at the controls of Lancaster NG175 XY-J. He was ordered to *'Bomb upwind of smoke, ignore TI markers'*. The encouragement and clear instructions from the Deputy Master Bomber seemed to work. As the crews departed, the northern suburbs of the town were blanketed in smoke, it had been

Photographs taken while on operations are rare. However, this remarkable photograph was taken by the crew of Flying Officer Dennis Godfrey RAAF on a daylight raid over Germany. It shows the crew's mid-upper gunner, Sergeant R.G 'Pat' Patterson perched in his Fraser Nash turret. Note the sunglasses and the Lancaster in the distance.

especially hard hit. Flying Officer R.R Tait and F/O R.P Madden RCAF were last over the town. Tait reported upon his return, '*Town obliterated'* while Madden remarked, *'Town thoroughly plastered'*.
There was a three-day lull on return from Heinsberg, No.3 Group was effectively grounded, although Group had warned of a possible raid on Soest on the 17th. Twelve Lancasters were fuelled and bombed up only for the operation to be cancelled just before briefing. Instructions received from HQ were for the aircraft to remain bombed-up. There was some excitement on the 18th with the appearance of 21 Lancasters from No.1 Group, stormy weather over their Lincolnshire bases preventing their return. Eighteen ABC equipped Lancasters of No.101 Squadron were joined by a crew apiece from 626, 460 RAAF and No.576 Squadron. The influx of over 140 additional airmen put a tremendous strain on the already overcrowded facilities of both the Officers and Sergeants Mess at RAF Tuddenham. On the 19th, the squadron was warned of an impending attack on the Ruhr, which was again cancelled. A follow-up message was received ordering the squadron to prepare 17 crews for a daylight raid on the oil plants at Homburg on the 20th. This loading and unloading and cancelling of operations put a tremendous strain on everyone on the squadron. The Ground Crews had the physical and dangerous

task of loading and unloading ordinance in freezing conditions. For the Aircrew, it was more a battle of the nerves. The mental rollercoaster caused by cancelled raids did little to calm already fraught fears. Just after lunch on the 20th, the first of seventeen squadron Lancasters began taking off from RAF Tuddenham in marginal weather. Their target was the Meerbeck synthetic oil plant. Problems beset the operation from the start. Torrential rain and thunderous clouds made forming up extremely difficult. Finally, a far from compact formation set off from Diss and out over the North Sea. The foul weather continued over Europe with mountainous columns of thunderous clouds reaching up to 24,000 feet and above.

Form B.700 – November 20th, 1944 (D) :Target : Homberg. Moers Meerbeck Fischer Tropsch oil plant. :GQ1511

| | | | | | | | |
|---|---|---|---|---|---|---|---|
| W/Cdr | Giles DFC | J.H | | NG174 | XY-A | Follower | Duty Carried Out. |
| F/Lt | Smith | S | | NG148 | XY-B | Follower | Duty Carried Out. |
| F/Sgt | Clarson | A.J | RAAF | NG147 | XY-C | Follower | Duty Carried Out. |
| F/O | Tait | R.P | | NG137 | XY-D | Follower | Duty Carried Out. |
| F/O | Templeton | G.M | RCAF | NG175 | XY-J | Follower | Duty Carried Out. |
| F/O | Phillips | T | | NG149 | XY-G | Follower | Duty Carried Out. |
| F/O | Tonks | J.E | | HK680 | XY-H | Follower | Duty Carried Out. |
| F/O | Gibson | J.H | | NN720 | XY-K | Follower | Duty Carried Out. |
| F/O | Barton | E.R | RAAF | HK688 | XY-M | Follower | Duty Carried Out. |
| F/Sgt | Young | H.S | | HK682 | XY-L | Follower | Duty Carried Out. |
| F/O | Smith DFC | L | | HK684 | XY-O | Follower | Duty Carried Out. |
| F/O | Madden | R.P | RCAF | HK662 | XY-P | Follower | Duty Carried Out. |
| F/O | Cogler | R.J | RAAF | HK659 | XY-Q | Follower | Duty Carried Out. |
| F/Sgt | Fernley | F | | HK650 | XY-T | Follower | Duty Carried Out. |
| W/O | O'Brien | J.D | RAAF | HK613 | XY-Y | Missing | Duty Carried Out. |
| F/O | Williamson | G.E | RAAF | HK622 | XY-Z | FTR | MISSING |
| F/Sgt | Smith | | | HK606 | XY-V | Follower | Duty Carried Out. |

To make matters worse, and not disclosed at briefing, the crews encountered winds of over 50mph from the southwest. The squadron, part of the second and final wave desperately tried to keep station with their allotted G-H Leader in amongst the clouds. Some were lucky. An unfortunate few lost them in amongst the clouds only to either latch onto another G-H aircraft or take their chance seeing the TI Markers over the target. Within minutes of the start of the attack, two Lancasters are believed to have collided. This tragedy was witnessed by F/O Tonks, *'We saw two Lancasters falling in flames from 20,000 feet at 15.14 hours'*. The loss of the two Lancasters was almost immediately followed by another Lancaster exploding[6]. Flying Officer J.E Tonks at the controls of Lancaster HK680 XY-H was forced to make two bombing runs, he remarked on return, *'Flew over the target twice, but each time bombs failed to release. Changed fuses, tried manual jettison and jettison toggle. All bombs brought back'.* Within a minute, the Lancaster of F/Lt George Williamson RAAF was mortally hit by flak over Baerl and exploded mid-air, there were no survivors from Lancaster XY-Z HK622.

| | | |
|---|---|---|
| Type | Avro Lancaster **Mk.I HK622 XY-Z** | Vickers Armstrong |
| T.O.C | 15/10/1944 via No.90 Squadron | |
| Cat Ac/FB Missing | 20/11/1944 | |
| S.o.C | 30/11/1944 | |
| Total Flying Hours | 116.10 | |
| Take Off Time | 12:37 hours | |

[6] Three Lancasters were lost from No.75(NZ) Squadron. A fourth Lancaster was lost from No.514 Squadron.

| | | |
|---|---|---|
| Bomb Load | 1 x 4000lb + 15 x 500lb | |
| | | |
| | **CREW** | |
| Pilot | F/O George Edward Williamson A426933 RAAF | Coll Grave 29.B.1-16 |
| Navigator | F/Sgt Kenneth Henry Turner 1458457 RAFVR | Coll Grave 29.B.1-16 |
| Bomb Aimer | F/O Edward Winton 153353 RAFVR | Coll Grave 29.B.1-16 |
| Wireless Operator | W/O Arthur Edward Jarvis Stiles A423349 RAAF | Grave 25.G.8 |
| Mid Upper Gunner | F/Sgt Wallace Patrick Burton A432748 RAAF | Coll Grave 29.B.1-16 |
| Rear Gunner | F/Sgt Herbert Keith Coombe A433197 RAAF | Coll Grave 29.B.1-16 |
| Flight Engineer | Sgt Arthur Ernest Piggin 976406 RAFVR | Coll Grave 29.B.1-16 |
| Posted Via | No.15 Squadron | |
| Operations Flown 186 Squadron | 4 | |
| Buried | Reichswald Forest War Cemetery | |

The nerve centre of any RAF Station was the Flying Control. This superb photograph shows RAF Tuddenham. The duty pilot on this day was W/O Reg Poynton DFC (far right) of No.90 Squadron.

The crew had shown remarkable skill in crash landing their badly damaged Lancaster on return from an attack on the very same target on November 2nd. For that action, the pilot was awarded a DFC in December 1944. The citation reads.

> *"In November 1944, this officer was the pilot of an aircraft detailed to attack Hamburg[7]. When approaching the target, the aircraft was hit by anti-aircraft fire. Both the port engines were disabled and only one of the propellers could be feathered. The port petrol tanks were pierced and much of the contents seeped into the wing and fuselage. The aircraft lost height but Flying Officer Williamson continued his run to execute a good bombing attack. Afterwards, course was set for base. The aircraft was still gradually losing height and Flying Officer Williamson was unable to maintain his place with the main bombing force. A little later the aircraft was again hit. The petrol supply was becoming diminished and it was apparent that England could not be reached. Course was altered and eventually FO Williamson effected a masterly landing in a waterlogged field in friendly territory. In most harassing circumstances this officer displayed skill, courage and tenacity of a high standard".*

F/O George Edward Williamson A426933 RAAF

F/Sgt Kenneth Henry Turner 1458457 RAFVR

[7] This is incorrect should be Homburg

F/O Edward Winton 153353 RAFVR

W/O Arthur Edward Jarvis Stiles A423349 RAAF

F/Sgt Wallace Patrick Burton A432748 RAAF

F/Sgt Herbert Keith Coombe A433197 RAAF

Sgt Arthur Ernest Piggin 976406 RAFVR

Some harsh words were directed against the G-H leader of F/O R.P Madden RCAF and his predominantly Canadian crew on return to Tuddenham, *"Leader"? aircraft steering a most erratic course often across the stream and finally away from the target. Bombed last resort target at 15.27 hours'.* The frustration of relying on other squadrons for marking was now becoming an major issue, especially amongst the senior crews eager to show what they could do.

The offending G-H Leader's identity is unknown but was provided by the RAF Methwold based No.149 (East India) or No.218 (Gold Coast) Squadron. Unsurprisingly the accuracy of the raid was impossible to determine given the cloud conditions. Flying Officer R.R Tait reported, *'Probably a scattered attack'.* It was a fair assessment. Obviously aware that the raid was ineffective, the senior Officers at No.3 Group HQ wasted no time preparing for a follow-up attack on the 21st. Once again, the squadron provided 17 crews who began departing just after lunch.

Form B.701 – November 21st, 1944 (D) :Target : Homberg. Moers Meerbeck Fischer Tropsch oil Plant. :GQ1511

| | | | | | | | |
|---|---|---|---|---|---|---|---|
| S/Ldr | Reynolds | P | | NG174 | XY-A | Follower | Duty Carried Out. |
| F/Sgt | Cowley | N | | NG148 | XY-B | Follower | Duty Carried Out. |
| F/O | Wait | C.J | | NG147 | XY-C | Follower | Duty Carried Out. |
| F/O | Tait | R.R | | NG137 | XY-D | Follower | Duty Carried Out. |
| F/O | Phillips | T | | NG149 | XY-G | Follower | Duty Carried Out. |
| F/O | Gibson | J.H | | NN720 | XY-K | Follower | Duty Carried Out. |
| F/O | Hoskin | F.C | RCAF | HK662 | XY-L | Follower | Duty Carried Out. |
| F/Sgt | Clarson | A | RAAF | HK668 | XY-M | Follower | Duty Carried Out. |
| F/Sgt | James | W.C | RAAF | HK684 | XY-O | Follower | Duty Carried Out. |
| F/O | Madden | R.P | RCAF | HK662 | XY-P | Follower | Duty Carried Out. |
| F/O | Gogler | R.J | RAAF | HK659 | XY-Q | Follower | Duty Carried Out. |
| F/O | Templeton | G.N | RCAF | HK661 | XY-R | Follower | Duty Carried Out. |
| F/Lt | Smith DFC | L | | LM188 | XY-S | Follower | Duty Carried Out. |
| F/Sgt | Fernley | F | | HK650 | XY-T | Follower | Duty Carried Out. |
| F/O | Ritson | E.E | | NG293 | XY-U | Follower | Duty Carried Out. |
| F/Sgt | Green | L.A | | HK606 | XY-V | Follower | Duty Carried Out. |
| W/O | O'Brien | J.D | RAAF | HK613 | XY-Z | Follower | Duty Carried Out. |

Thankfully, the weather had improved dramatically from the previous day. Forming up 15,000 feet above Bury St Edmunds the 162 Lancasters of No.3 Group quickly formed into two distinct waves with the squadrons of No.33 Base making up the spearhead. The now familiar landmark of Orford Ness was passed as the heavily laden bombers slowly climbed to their operational altitude. Number 186 Squadron

The sheer size and complexity of the oil refineries in the Ruhr is graphically illustrated in this view of Meerbeck. The miles of pipes, gasometers, oil storage tanks and numerous buildings meant that these targets were vulnerable to attack from the air. Homberg was the most westerly of the vital oil targets in the Ruhr Valley and was frequently attacked by RAF Bomber Command and the US 8th Air Force.

would once again have to rely solely on the accuracy and flying discipline of No.15, No.218 and No.149 Squadron's for bombing.

Over Belgium, the Group picked up the first of its fighter escort. Seven squadrons of RAF Mustangs formed a protective umbrella over the bomber stream. Weather conditions over Homburg were relatively clear, allowing the squadron crews the opportunity to gauge the accuracy or otherwise of their bombing. Flying between 19,000 and 20,000 feet, the bombers encountered *'predicted flak, moderately to intense'*. Not only was the flak more accurate than the previous day, but a number of G-H equipped Lancasters suffered reception issues to their sets at a crucial point in the bombing. None of the No.186 Squadron crews were aware of the drama aboard these 'Leaders' and steadfastly held position. The first crew to bomb and a full seven minutes before the planned start time of 15.07 hours was F/O J.H Gibson at the controls of Lancaster NN720 XY-K. He deposited his 4000 pounder and 16 x 500lb GP while flying behind a G-H Leader from 19,000 feet. Seven minutes after F/O Gibson bombed, it was the turn of 'B' Flights F/Lt L Smith DFC and crew to begin their run into the target. The flak was intense. Flying in the same vic as F/Lt Smith was the crew of W/O J.D O'Brien, who seemed to attract their fair share of flak, which damaged the starboard outer engine of HK613 XY-Y and punched numerous holes into the bomb bay doors. Thankfully, the crew were all uninjured Warrant Officer O'Brien quickly feathered the starboard outer engine, which was now leaving a stream of oily grey smoke as he turned away from the target area. Also hit was F/O R.P Madden RCAF. His Lancaster HK662 XY-P was peppered in both wings and fuselage at 15.10 hours while at 19,000 feet. Flak was sufficiently accurate to upset the bombing of some crews, which resulted in some scattered bombing. Squadron Leader P Reynolds, *'Much smoke over target. Many bombs falling in fields'*. Flying Officer T Phillips was over the target at 15.10 hours. He reported on return, *'Much dense smoke, one large fire seen. Some*

A typical mix of nationalities on the squadron. Here the crew of Flight Lieutenant Les Smith relax outside some Nissen huts. The beautiful Suffolk countryside is evident around RAF Stradihall in this photograph. Centre front row, Flight Lieutenant Sidney Smith (English) - Pilot. Sadly I cannot place the names with the crew, but they are Flight Sergeant Gerry Hernon (English) - Bomb Aimer, Flight Sergeant Eric (Mick) Macminn (Scottish) - Tail Gunner, Sergeant George (Boofhead) Woolhead RAAF (Australian) – Wireless Operator, Sergeant Alex (Mac) McLaren (Scottish) – Mid upper Gunner, Flight Sergeant John Frederick (Slim) Hartford RCAF (Canadian) – Navigator and Flight Sergeant Royston Thom (English) – Flight Engineer.

*overshooting and undershooting bombing'.* More optimistic was the crew of F/Sgt N Cowley and F/O E.E Ritson. Back at debriefing, the Ritson crew reported, *'Town well hit factory was seen to be hit by several sticks of bombs. Some smoke'.* Group HQ once again seemed unimpressed with the results. They reported, *'Bombing was rather scattered, although some fires were started at the plant'.* Nearly fifty Lancasters received varying degrees of flak damage, and three Lancasters, all from 33 Base's 514 Squadron, were shot down. Importantly for No.186 Squadron, all the crews returned safely back to RAF Tuddenham, some, however showing battle scars.

No.186 Squadron Reported Flak Damage 21/11/1944

| Serial | Code | Damage Reported | Repairs / Notes |
|---|---|---|---|
| HK622 | **XY-P** | Both wings, fuselage. | Repaired on squadron. |
| HK613 | **XY-Y** | Bomb doors. | Repaired on squadron |

A few days after this operation, reports began to emerge that the still dangerous German day fighters were poised to counter this operation in strength. A secret report 'Interception and Tactics No.288/44' recorded the following for the attack.

This operation in daylight produced, for the first time in many weeks evidence of a desire on the part of the enemy to oppose Bomber Commands daylight attacks. No.3 Group's target was the oil plant at Homberg, at the western (or Rhine) end of the Ruhr and they were plotted thither from the seaward side of Belgium coast at 14:24 hours, the tracking being accurate and intensive. At 14:00 hours day fighters from the Munster area were assembling in that vicinity, that is to say, 60 miles roughly NE of the bombers target. At 14:56 hours they were ordered to the Recklinghausen area (halfway to the target. Had this order been fully carried out and followed up return route interceptions would have been possible, and the possibility of being done on a future occasion has to be reckoned with. The No.11 Group fighter escort to No.3 Group on this day reported the bomber stream improving from the point of view of protection, individual boxes maintaining good formation on penetration, but there being too much distending of the boxes and some straggling at the rear on withdrawal. It is interesting that on this same day, when the weather generally both here and over Germany was much improved, the US heavy bombers attack Merseburg oil plants and Hannover were met by an exceptionally stiff opposition consisting of 500 plus fighters, and that throughout the day a total of nearly 1,000 fighters were airborne on the western front.

This valuable information was collected by the British "Y" Service, whose role was to monitor German R/T and W/T radio traffic and analyze against existing intelligence data on Luftwaffe unit locations, call-signs, and movements. This information and that provided by ULTRA gave the Allies a tremendous advantage over the Germans. The Nordstern oil plant at Gelsenkirchen was the intended target on the 23rd, the squadron dispatching sixteen crews. Number 186 Squadron would be part of the second wave scheduled to bomb between 15:18 hours and 15:21 hours. The raid would follow an earlier attack by the American 1st Bombardment Division who despatched a number of B17 Flying Fortresses on attacks directed against the oil plant.

A total of 160 Lancasters of No.3 Group climbed into the merk from their East Anglian bases just after lunch. Solid overcast was the Group's most significant challenge once airborne. It caused a few moments of panic as crews anxiously edged their way up into the clear sky at 10,000 feet. Once free of the clouds, the various Base Groups jockeyed into position. Finally satisfied, the armada set off across the North Sea. Leading the force were the squadrons of No.33 Base.

Form B.703 – November 23rd, 1944 (D) :Target : Gelsenkirchen - (Nordstern) Gelsenberg-Benzin A.G Synthetic Oil Plant :GQ1509

| | | | | | | | |
|---|---|---|---|---|---|---|---|
| F/O | Barton | E.R | RAAF | NG148 | XY-B | Follower | Duty Carried Out. |
| F/O | Tait | R.E | | NG137 | XY-D | Follower | Duty Carried Out. |
| F/O | Templeton | G.M | RCAF | NG146 | XY-E | Follower | Duty Carried Out. |
| F/O | Smith | A | | NG140 | XY-F | Follower | Duty Carried Out. |
| F/Lt | Phillips | T | | NG149 | XY-G | Follower | Duty Carried Out. |
| F/O | Powers | R.C | RAAF | HK680 | XY-H | Follower | Duty Carried Out. |
| F/O | Hoskin | F.C | RCAF | NG175 | XY-J | Follower | Duty Carried Out. |
| F/O | Tonks | J.E | | HK682 | XY-L | Follower | Duty Carried Out. |
| F/O | Madden | R.R | RCAF | HK662 | XY-P | Follower | Duty Carried Out. |
| F/Sgt | James | W.C | RAAF | HK661 | XY-R | Follower | Duty Carried Out. |
| F/Lt | Smith DFC | L | | LM188 | XY-S | Follower | Duty Carried Out. |
| F/Sgt | Fernley | F | | HK650 | XY-T | Follower | Duty Carried Out. |
| F/O | Gogler | R.J | RAAF | NG293 | XY-U | Follower | Duty Carried Out. |
| F/Sgt | Green | L.A | | HK613 | XY-Y | Follower | Duty Carried Out. |
| F/O | Orman | K.G | RNZAF | HK684 | XY-O | Follower | Duty Carried Out. |
| F/Lt | Powers DFC | A.C | | HK688 | XY-W | Follower | Duty Carried Out. |

They would be responsible for navigating and leading the stream to the target over 10/10th cloud. Surprisingly, there was no opposition until the bombers entered the Ruhr. Unseen flak defences started putting up accurate predicted flak that seemed to concentrate on the first two waves. Fortunately, none of No.186 Squadron's 16 Lancasters was hit, but the crew F/Sgt W.C James RAAF was particularly lucky. They suffered starboard outer engine failure aboard Lancaster HK661 XY-R 15 minutes before the target. Unwilling to abandon the operation, the crew courageously decided to continue, all the while losing both altitude and speed. They arrived over the aiming point at 15.20 hours at the perilously low height of 12,000 feet, just 2,000 feet above the solid cloud layer and 8,000 feet below 160 plus Lancasters. A concentrated bunch of Red Target Markers were clearly visible against the white clouds as combinations of 'cookies' and 500 pounders disappeared into the overcast. The crews encountered spasmodic but accurate flak from both Wesel and Utrecht on the return flight. All the crews were back over base just after 15:00 hours. At interrogation, the crews gave the poor Intelligence Officer mixed reactions to the raid. Flying Officer R.P Madden RCAF reported *'results fair'*, while others remarked that the marking was exceptionally concentrated.

There was an increase in the number of reported 'Scarecrows' on this operation. Bomber Command aircrew had come to accept and believed that the German defenders were using a shell or some projectile to simulate the effect of an aircraft exploding in mid-air. One assumes for the demoralising effect it would have on aircrew who witnessed such an explosion. The report of 'Scarecrows' would continue until the war's end. Following the Gelsenkirchen raid, the squadron found itself effectively stood down. Other than the customary fighter affiliation and bombing exercises, a period of relative calm settled over Tuddenham. On the 25th, the Squadron was informed it would be required for a small scale attack against Marshalling Yards at Fulda. It was the deepest penetration raid to date and into the very heart of Germany. Situated on the River Fulda, the yards were an important link between Frankfurt and Leipzig. The Squadron Commander briefed fourteen crews early on the morning of the 26th. Unlike previous attacks, No.3 Group would be sending just 75 Lancasters. Fifty would be provided by No.32 Base including 4 G-H equipped Lancasters. RAF Methwolds No.149 and No.218 Squadrons would provide the bulk with 25 G-H crews on this experimental operation.

Given the distance involved, W/Cdr Giles DFC enforced how essential it was to retain a cohesive formation at all times and that everything must be done to ease the task for the fighter escort. All the squadron crews were airborne by 08.00 hours. There was some unease at No.3 Group HQ, as recent raids carried out by the US 8th Air Force had met increased opposition in the same region of Germany. It was just a matter of time before Bomber Command was on the receiving end. The 75 Lancasters flew south to Manston on the Kent coast before turning east towards Germany. Further north, a massive fleet of over a thousand B17 Flying Fortress and B24 Liberator bombers and over 700 US fighters were on their way to attack various targets in central Germany. The small RAF formation picked up its escort of seven UK based RAF Mustang squadrons near Aachen while six squadrons of European based Spitfires would be used to sweep the area north of the planned route.

Form B.706 – November 26th 1944 (D) :Target : Fulda : Railway Centre.

| | | | | | | | |
|---|---|---|---|---|---|---|---|
| F/O | Barton | E.R | RAAF | NG148 | XY-B | Follower | Duty Carried Out. |
| F/O | Tait | R.E | | NG137 | XY-D | Follower | Duty Carried Out. |
| F/O | Templeton | G.M | RCAF | NG146 | XY-E | Follower | Duty Carried Out. |
| F/Sgt | Clarson | A.J | RAAF | NG140 | XY-F | Follower | Duty Carried Out. |
| F/O | Powers | R.C | RAAF | HK680 | XY-H | Follower | Duty Carried Out. |
| W/O | O'Brien | J.D | RAAF | HK688 | XY-W | Follower | Duty Carried Out. |
| F/Sgt | Young | H.S | | HK682 | XY-L | Follower | Duty Carried Out. |
| F/O | Madden | R.R | RCAF | HK662 | XY-P | Follower | Duty Carried Out. |
| F/O | Gogler | R.J | RAAF | HK659 | XY-Q | Follower | Duty Carried Out. |
| F/Lt | Smith DFC | L | | LM188 | XY-S | Follower | Duty Carried Out. |
| F/Sgt | Fernley | F | | HK650 | XY-T | Follower | Duty Carried Out. |
| F/Sgt | James | W.C | RAAF | NG293 | XY-U | Follower | Duty Carried Out. |
| F/O | Hanson | R.A | | HK688 | XY-W | Follower | Duty Carried Out. |
| F/O | Godfrey | D.F | RAAF | HK606 | XY-V | Follower | Duty Carried Out. |

The squadron would be divided between the first two waves timed to attack between 11.04 hours and 11.10 hours. The squadron bombed within a space of three minutes of each other meeting practically no opposition. Due to the extreme range it was no surprise that No.3 Group HQ considered the raid a failure. The G-H signal was faint and faded out completely forcing the crews to either bomb visually or bomb targets of opportunity. For the crews of No.186 Squadron it was yet another disappointing operation, they reported *'Judging by the flares and timing, the attack was scattered'*. The squadron was now making almost daily requests to Exning House for the delivery and installation of G-H sets, and frustration was now setting in. Two crews suffered hang-ups due to icing, with F/Sgt N.C Cowley unwittingly bringing back a 500 pounder to Tuddenham without realising. There would have been a few red faces at debriefing and a few words from the armourers.

While No.3 Group met no opposition, the Americans bore the brunt of the German fighters, losing a sobering 13 B17 Flying Fortress and 21 B24 Liberators. Heavily armed the gunners claimed 19 fighters destroyed. The US fighter escort amazingly claimed the destruction of 109 German fighters!

While half the squadron was over Germany, 41 Lancasters drawn from all three Bases, plus RAF Methwold participated in a daylight exercise code-named "REMOULD". Given the recent resurgence of the German day fighter force, and more ominously, the appearance of German jets, No.3 Group HQ and its counterpart at Fighter Command arranged an extensive Group exercise. The exercise intended to give the escort fighters experience of defending against the new German jet menace. Forty Lancasters, including four from No.186 Squadron, rendezvoused over Newmarket at 10,000 feet and formed up into the standard vic formation. Crews were advised to keep a tight and compact formation throughout the exercise. The route took them first to Newmarket and then onto Lavenham, where they travelled south to Gravesend, Manston, Beachy Head, Red Hill, and then back to Manston. Along the entire route, the formation was escorted by Spitfires. RAF Mustangs would join them over Manston. Here, eight RAF Gloster Meteors of No.616 Squadron made an appearance conducting a series of high--speed attacks. On completion of the 3-hour exercise, the crews turned for home. Other than the staggering speed of the Meteors and the apparent inability of the piston engine Spitfires and Mustangs to engage them, the crews learnt extraordinarily little. But all secretly hoped they would never meet the real thing over Germany. The squadron bade farewell to 'A' Flight Commander S/Ldr M Leyshon AFC on the 26th. After a shorter than prescribed rest period, Mervyn reported to No.19 OTU at RAF Kinloss in January 1945 and would serve in the Senior Flight Commander and Deputy Chief Flying Instructor role. This brave Welshman would see the war out, pounding the windswept runways aboard the units ageing Wellington's. The following was written by Mervyn, who recalls the many trials and tribulations he encountered during his operational career.

*I volunteered for Royal Air Force in September 1939 and was accepted for aircrew training. After 'call up'. I was posted to an Initial Training Wing where I was subjected to numerous medical examinations and tests, basic subject examinations, drilling, cross-country endurance tests and eventually a Selection Board, whose job was to decide on my suitability for aircrew was selected as being suitable for pilot training.*

*My first introduction to an aeroplane was at an Elementary Flying Training school, the aircraft type being the Tiger Moth. Instruction was extremely strenuous and thorough-H in every detail such as circuits and landings, elementary aerobatics, re-starting the engine in flight, recovering from 'spins', action in the event of engine fire, emergency landings in strange fields and cross-country flights by map reading. After a rather hectic testing by the Chief Flying Instructor, I was sent off for the first 'solo' flight, this, without doubt, being the most important and exciting achievement. Sad to say, there were many failures at this stage and then the unfortunates reverted to other aircrew or ground duties. After further instruction in all aspects of flying the time arrived for solo cross-country flights of someone and a half to two hours duration over a planned course, navigation by map reading only these flights were undertaken regularly. Ground instructions and lectures were given in many subjects, Wellington, exercises were carried out in cross-country flying for many hours duration by day and night, bombing from various heights with practice bombs on a special bombing range, air to air firing of guns, fighter affiliation, drills for exit by parachute and dingy (in the event of force landing in the sea) and all the ground subjects were studied to a still more advanced standard and variation.*

*After completion of the OTU Course I was posted to a Wellington Squadron, RAF Stradishall, West Suffolk No.214 Squadron. After completion of the OTU course I was posted ahead of my crew to a Wellington Squadron — sad to relate, my crew flew with another pilot on a mission to Kiel and were all killed in action. After some operations over Europe as a second pilot to an experienced crew, | was promoted a captain of my own crew and aircraft. We took part in raids on the principal targets at the time, January 1941 — August 1941, to Hamburg, Kiel, Brest, Bremen, Cologne, Duisburg, Hamm, Essen, Gelsenkirchen, Dortmund, Dusseldorf, Berlin and others, returning many times. It is of interest to note that the Wellington carried some 4,000 Ibs of bombs with 650 gallons of fuel say to Berlin, and from take-off to landing the flight duration could be near nine hours. Needless to say there were many hazards and dangerous moments, it could be extremely cold at 12,500 feet with no heating and the weather conditions with electric storms and severe icing conditions most unpleasant. The attention from enemy antiaircraft guns of various calibre, search light cones of up to 40 lights and the dreaded enemy night fighter aircraft kept us well awake. The return to base could be a problem - Shortage of fuel, low visibility conditions, sometimes 'bandits' (enemy aircraft) in the area and not forgetting damage to the aircraft caused by enemy action. Unfortunately, casualties during this period became almost unbearable, it has been calculated post war that only one crew in four expected to survive a tour of some 30 operations. Toward the end of my stay at the squadron I received a commission and promoted to the rank of Pilot Officer.*

*The next posting was to an Operational Training Unit as an instructor and | eventually rose through the ranks to a Flight Commander post with the rank of Squadron Leader. During this period we instructed many crews before they departed for various squadrons, many as replacement crews to the Middle and Far Eastern Commands. After D Day I requested a posting to an Operational Squadron for a second tour, this was granted and I proceeded to a Heavy Conversion Unit equipped with the Lancaster four engine bomber. After instruction flying the Lancaster by day and night a crew was selected — a flight engineer being an addition to replace the second pilot. After the conversion period I was posted to a special squadron operating the Gee-H — a navigational and bombing radar aid. This enabled bombing to take place above cloud and in all weather conditions. Many raids were carried out in daytime during this period ahead of the advancing armies and with deeper penetration into enemy territory — mainly synthetic oil refineries and fighter cover protection was available. At this Lancaster squadron I was the Senior Flight Commander with the rank of Squadron Leader and therefore deputy Squadron Commander. A typical day in the life of aircrew would be something like this. Each night's operation commenced for the crews by mid-morning when targets and therefore bomb loads, fuel capacities and a hundred other details were decided and notified to both air and ground crews. Final checks on the technical state of each facet of the aircraft culminated in a night flying test by its crew who promptly notified the ground staff of any snags for immediate rectification. Final briefing of the aircrews involved each man in last minute details on weather expected throughout the operation and on return to base, defences to avoid en route, enemy emergency signals and secondary targets. Throughout these seemingly long preparatory hours the tension inside each aircrew member inexorably mounted in anticipation (only the totally insensitive or unimaginative knew no fear) until the moment of relative relief when finally, we walked or more usually climbed aboard a truck to proceed to the aircraft for the actual flight. Once at dispersal final checks were made and engines ground tested, finally taxiing around the perimeter track to the point of take-off and awaiting 'green' to go. The take-off run began at the end of the runway. Every take off in a maximum loaded bomber was always dangerous, encased in a light metal machine carrying up to 16,000 lbs of explosives, thousands of pounds of highly inflammable petrol and oils. A burst tyre, engine failure, loss of pressure or one second's lack of total concentration could spell instant disaster. Once safely airborne and on course for the objective, the outward leg meant crossing the North Sea before reaching an enemy coastline, usually pre-alerted along its line of flak defences with the ever-present Luftwaffe night fighter force in probable ambush locations just beyond.*

*The flight across enemy-occupied lands meant running a gauntlet of flak, fighters and searchlights which intensified as the bomber made its final approach to the designated target. Once committed to the ultimate bombing run a pilot had to fly straight and level up to the bomb release point - no evading the holocaust of lights and shells reaching up to destroy him, perhaps minutes or seconds during which the bomber was a sitting duck for predicted flak guns aided by radar. Once the bombs had gone a further few seconds of steady course to obtain an aiming point photo then a full boost turn and climb, or dive, out of the hell of probing lights and necklaced streams of multi-coloured tracers and shells. The return flight was no less anxious — three, four or five-hours watching instruments for the first sign of any faltering engines or controls; every mile home could bring further hazards from flak or fighters, while forecasted weather conditions might add complications to an already fraught situation.*

*Once clear of the enemy coast the crew still needed to cross that dreaded North Sea — already a graveyard for hundreds of previous crews who hadn't 'made it'. With that obstacle behind them, the crew still needed to locate their base airfield, or if badly damaged and/or carrying wounded or dead men, the nearest aerodrome to accept them in emergency. Once over base they might still be directed to another airfield due to blocked runways by preceding bombers which had crashed or more often, dense fog nullifying visibility near the ground. Even as a bomber came into land it might become a victim of marauding German fighter intruders seeking scalps from the weary returning bomber streams. On a safe landing and parking of the aircraft, crews were de-briefed and went back to their respective messes relaxing over a fresh egg and bacon meal.*

*To quote Air Vice Marshal D C T Bennett — Air Officer Commanding No 8 Group Bomber Command:*

*"I should point out that the bombing of a German target on one single occasion was equivalent of going through the Battle of Jutland or any other great battle. An ordinary bomber crew in one tour of duty experienced thirty such battles. The contribution of an aircrew member of Bomber Command who completes an operational tour, or died in the process, measured in terms of danger of death. Both in intensity and duration was, in my view, far greater than that of any other fighting man, RAF, Navy or Army."*

*One raid of particular interest —Antwerp had been occupied by the 2" Army on September 2" 1944 but it was useless to the Allies while the Germans occupied Walcharen Island and other fortresses on the mainland at the mouth of the Scheldts. Walcharen Island is almost*

*entirely below sea-level and the water is kept back by a sea wall more than 200 foot thick at its base, tapering upwards until it is 60 feet thick at the top. On this wall and inland, the Germans had a number of powerful batteries which would have made any landing a perilous, if not impossible operation. Bomber Command was required to attack these batteries and breach the sea wall with a view to drowning the batteries inland. Some 300 Lancaster bombers were used. I think we were the first to release our bombs (flying a Lancaster as a Squadron Leader Flight Commander).*
*There was very little enemy opposition from the anti-aircraft batteries or enemy fighters, I did not see any though, they were expected in the area as it was an early morning daylight raid on 2nd October 1944. The two main breaches blown in the dyke were at Westkapelle. Royal Marine Commandos were engaged in the attack at Westkapelle, landing in various types of barges having sailed from Ostend in the early hours of 1st November 1944. There were horrific casualties in these landings and considered by many battle historians to be one of the most important and bloodiest battles in the European Theatre. I was posted back to an Operational Training Unit, reverting to Wellingtons as Senior Flight Commander and for a short period as Chief Flying Instructor. With the ending of the war in Europe, I was responsible for the handing over the airfield to Coastal Command. Throughout my RAF service attended many courses on different subjects connected with the Royal Air Force, the main one being a Senior Commanders course at RAF College Cranwell for a period of 3 months intensive training, and a further course in RAF Law and Administration before being posted as Senior Administrative Officer to a large RAF station and its satellite airfield — something in the order of 3,500 personnel.*

*I was awarded the* ***Air Force Cross****, presented by King George VI and* ***Mentioned in Despatches*** *for distinguished service.*

*None of the flying would have been possible without the skill and devotion to duty of all grades of ground crews and staff.*

His replacement was the experienced F/Lt Arthur Powell DFC. It was an excellent month for Arthur, who had been awarded the DFC at the beginning of the month, and now he commanded his own flight. The citation for his DFC reads.

*Acting Flight Lieutenant Arthur Charles POWELL (54794), R.A.F. 186 Sqn. This officer has completed very many sorties and has displayed great courage and determination in pressing home his attacks. In October 1944, he was pilot and captain of an aircraft detailed to attack a target in the Ruhr area. When approaching the target considerable anti-aircraft fire was encountered and Flight Lieutenant Powell's aircraft was hit. The port inner engine sustained damage, whilst a member of the crew was wounded. Nevertheless, Flight Lieutenant Powell maintained formation and executed a successful bombing run. This officer set a line example of coolness and resolution.*

The important Cologne Kalk Nord Marshalling Yards were the intended target on the 27$^{th}$. The Group would detail 170 crews drawn from all its Lancaster squadrons. Sixteen crews were provided by No.186 Squadron, which included the Squadron Commander and both Flight Commanders.

Form B.707 – November 27th 1944 (D) :Target : Cologne : Kalk Nord Marshalling Yards

| | | | | | | | |
|---|---|---|---|---|---|---|---|
| S/Ldr | Reynolds | P | | NG174 | XY-A | Follower | Duty Carried Out. |
| F/Lt | Fleming | A.J | RAAF | NG148 | XY-B | Follower | Duty Carried Out. |
| F/Lt | Wait | C.J | | NG147 | XY-C | Follower | Duty Carried Out. |
| W/Cdr | Giles DFC | J.H | | NG137 | XY-D | Follower | Duty Carried Out. |
| F/O | Tonks | J.E | | NG146 | XY-E | Follower | Duty Carried Out. |
| F/O | Fields DFC | E.L | | NG140 | XY-F | Follower | Duty Carried Out. |
| F/Lt | Phillips | T | | NG149 | XY-G | Follower | Duty Carried Out. |
| F/O | Powers | R.C | RAAF | HK680 | XY-H | Follower | Duty Carried Out. |
| F/O | Hoskin | F.C | RAAF | NG175 | XY-J | Follower | Duty Carried Out. |
| F/Sgt | Clarson | A.J | RAAF | HK682 | XY-L | Follower | Duty Carried Out. |
| W/O | O'Brien | J.D | RAAF | HK684 | XY-O | Follower | Duty Carried Out. |
| F/O | Madden | R.R | RCAF | HK662 | XY-P | Follower | Duty Carried Out. |
| F/O | Gogler | R.J | RAAF | HK659 | XY-Q | Follower | Duty Carried Out. |
| F/O | Mason | F.H | | LM188 | XY-S | Follower | Duty Carried Out. |
| F/Lt | Powell DFC | A.C | | HK688 | XY-W | Follower | Duty Carried Out. |
| F/Sgt | James | W.C | RAAF | NG293 | XY-U | Follower | Duty Carried Out. |

The force would be divided into two waves, with the No.186 Squadron contingent part of the second wave. Forming up was slow and confusing above Bury St Edmunds, this appeared to unsettle the group, from this point on, the whole operation started to go dramatically wrong.

What followed was recorded in the No.3 Group Head Quarters Records Book, *'This attack seemed spoilt mainly by the navigator in the spearhead lead who led his aircraft through most of the Ruhr defences before getting to the target'.* The formation escorted by seven squadrons of RAF Mustangs and 16 squadrons of Spitfires were engaged continuously by flak as they headed deeper and deeper into the Ruhr. The first wave began bombing just after 15:03 hours. There was no cloud cover but plenty of ground haze. Surprisingly, given the lack of cloud, opposition over the marshalling yards was considered by some returning crews to be more subdued than the run-into target. These views were not shared by 'B' Flight commander, F/Lt A.C Powell DFC and F/O's R.C Powers RAAF, F.H Mason and

*A P51 Mustang Mk.III of No.19 Squadron. With its range and performance, the Mustang would be given the vital role of escorting the Groups lumbering Lancaster's to and from targets in Germany.*

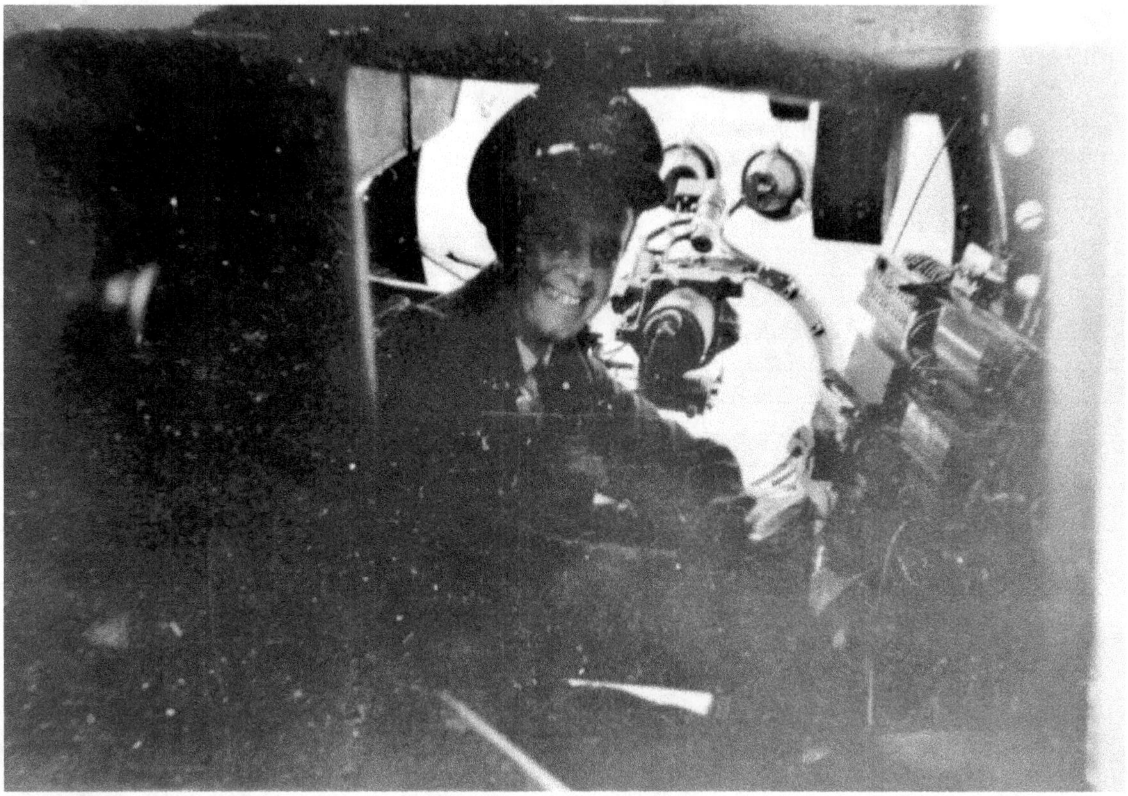

A smiling Pilot Officer Barney Earrey RAFVR Bomb Aimer to Flying Officer Ken Orman RNZAF. He is seen here in his bomb aimers position in Lancaster Q-Queenie.

F/Sgt W.C James RAAF, as each was damaged by flak. The Lancaster of F/O F.H Mason was the worst-hit sustaining coolant failure to the starboard outer engine necessitating its feathering. The starboard wing tanks were holed and leaking. Both bomb bay doors were holed, while the Lancaster's special equipment (H2S) was rendered u/s. A large piece of flak shattered the Perspex roof above the pilot, and numerous holes were punctured along the fuselage of Lancaster LM188 XY-S. The crew on only their third operation nursed the badly damaged Lancaster back to base. Despite the spirited defences, all the squadron crews returned. RAF Tuddenham was informed that a number of aircraft from the Canadian No.6 Group would be diverted that night due to their Yorkshire bases being cloud covered. The already overcrowded Tuddenham would welcome a total of twenty Lancasters from No.431 (Iroquois) Squadron who had just returned from plastering Neuss.

The squadron's Navigation Leader, F/Lt William Earle was London bound on the 28th. He was to attend an investiture at Buckingham Palace to receive his DFM from His Majesty the King. The award was in recognition of his time with No.199 Squadron.

No.186 Squadron Reported Flak Damage 21/11/1944

| Serial | Code | Damage Reported | Repairs / Notes |
|---|---|---|---|
| NG140 | **XY-F** | Reported, but no detail available. | Repaired On Squadron. |
| HK680 | **XY-H** | Reported, but no detail available. | Repaired On Squadron. |
| LM188 | **XY-S** | Extensive damage to fuselage, bomb doors, H2S radome blown out. Starboard inner engine damaged. Starboard wing No.1 fuel tank holed. | Cat Ac/FB. RoS A.V Roe. Returned 16/12/44. |
| NG293 | **XY-U** | Reported, but no detail available. | Repaired On Squadron. |
| HK688 | **XY-W** | Reported, but no detail available. | Repaired On Squadron. |

It was a welcomed return to nocturnal operations on the 29th, with a very early morning attack by an all No.3 Group force against the Ruhr city of Neuss located on the west bank of the Rhine opposite Düsseldorf. While No.3 Group were over Neuss, a force of over three hundred aircraft drawn from 1, 4 and 8 Path Finder Group would simultaneously attack Essen.

Form B.708 – November 29th 1944 (N) :Target : Neuss : Marshalling Yards.

| | | | | | | | |
|---|---|---|---|---|---|---|---|
| S/Ldr | Reynolds | P | | NG174 | XY-A | Main Force | Duty Carried Out. |
| F/Lt | Fleming | A.J | RAAF | NG148 | XY-B | Main Force | Duty Carried Out. |
| F/Lt | Wait | C.J | | NG147 | XY-C | Main Force | Duty Carried Out. |
| F/O | Barton | E.R | RAAF | NG137 | XY-D | Main Force | Duty Carried Out. |
| F/O | Templeton | G.M | RCAF | NG146 | XY-E | Main Force | Duty Carried Out. |
| F/Sgt | Cowley | M.C | | NG140 | XY-F | Main Force | Duty Carried Out. |
| F/Lt | Phillips | T | | NG149 | XY-G | Main Force | Duty Carried Out. |
| F/O | Field DFC | E.L | | HK680 | XY-H | Main Force | Duty Carried Out. |
| F/O | Hoskin | F.C | RAAF | NG175 | XY-J | Main Force | Duty Carried Out. |
| F/O | Tonks | J.E | | HK682 | XY-L | Main Force | Duty Carried Out. |
| F/O | Liddell | J.B | | HK684 | XY-O | Main Force | Duty Carried Out. |
| F/O | Ritson | E.E | | HK662 | XY-P | Main Force | Duty Carried Out. |

Number 3 Group detailed 145 crews, including 12 from No.186 Squadron, led on this occasion by S/Ldr P Reynolds. The operation did not quite go to plan. Number 33 Base was late dropping the Wanganui flares planned for 05:30 hours, and what was dropped appeared scattered. Smoke from the previous night's attack and 10/10th cloud cover appear to have made things challenging for the lead crews, which was surprising given the excellent coverage by the mobile Cat & Mouse Stations. The accuracy of the raid was difficult to appraise.

Returning No.186 crews were, however, not overly impressed. Flying Officer E Ritson was at the controls of Lancaster HK662 XY-P bombed at 05:41 hours, he reported at interrogation, *'Raid scattered, flares dropped late, some over shooting'.* There were three distinct clusters of flares, most crews aimed at the centre of the three more in hope than confidence. Post raid reconnaissance later established that some fresh damage was inflicted on the Marshalling Yards and local industrial areas. However, the Bomber Command Post Raid Report recorded, '*No industries of high priority were effected*'. Given the target and its fierce reputation not a single crew reported any damage. In fact, opposition was described as negligible. Form B.709 arrived at RAF Tuddenham on the afternoon of the 29th, informing the station and its two resident squadrons that they would be required for operations the following day. The Group would divide its force between Bottrop (Welheim) Coking Plant and Osterfeld Benzol Plant. The targets, separated by just two miles, would be attacked by 120 Lancasters who would bomb simultaneously between 13:06 hours and 13-17 hours. Nine crews were detailed and briefed from No.186, their target was the Coking Plant at Bottrop. The first crew aloft was F/O R.A Hanson at 10:46 hours at the controls of Lancaster HK613 XY-X.

Form B.709 – November 30th 1944 (D) :Target : Bottrop (Welheim) Coking Plant. GQ1536

| | | | | | | | |
|---|---|---|---|---|---|---|---|
| Sgt | Saunders | A | | NG137 | XY-D | Follower | Duty Carried Out. |
| F/O | Powers | R.C | RAAF | HK680 | XY-H | Follower | Duty Carried Out. |
| F/O | Field DFC | E.L | | NN720 | XY-K | Follower | Duty Carried Out. |
| F/Sgt | Young | H.S | | HK682 | XY-L | Follower | Duty Carried Out. |
| W/O | O'Brien | J.D | RAAF | HK684 | XY-O | Follower | Duty Carried Out. |
| F/O | Gogler | R.J | RAAF | HK661 | XY-R | Follower | Duty Carried Out. |
| F/O | Hanson | R.A | | HK613 | XY-Y | Follower | Duty Carried Out. |

| | | | | | | | |
|---|---|---|---|---|---|---|---|
| Sgt | Fernley | F | | HK650 | XY-T | Follower | Duty Carried Out. |
| F/O | Godfrey | D.F | RAAF | HK606 | XY-V | Follower | Duty Carried Out. |

Once airborne, the squadron firstly headed towards the market town of Stowmarket located between Bury St Edmunds and Ipswich, where it converged with other squadrons provided by No.32 and No.33 Base. Above this sleepy town, they would attempt to form up behind their G-H equipped Leaders. Number 32 Base would provide 12 G-H aircraft, they would be supplemented by four from RAF Methwold. Once the squadrons had settled into their allotted positions, the whole formation headed towards Orford Ness, on the Suffolk Coast. The Bottrop force attacked downwind from the direction of Cleve. Opposition was once again slight on the run into target and above the Coking Plant. The only danger was from some erratic flying by No.33 Base, who had just delivered their attack on Osterfeld.

While the sixty Lancasters of the Bottrop force were making their attack, a number of Lancaster's from 75(NZ), 115 and 514 Squadrons cut in front and above, causing a certain amount of anxiety and anger amongst the crews. Thick, impregnable cloud covered Bottrop. Only two skippers, F/Sgt F Fernley and Sgt A Saunders, at the helm of Lancaster NG137 XY-D and undertaking his first operation were optimistic about the results, Saunders reporting, *'Thick black smoke billowing from cloud tops just after bombing'.* They were in the minority, the rest of the squadron reported scattered bombing. Only one crew reported damage, F/O D Godfrey RAAF was obliged to feather the starboard outer engine aboard Lancaster HK606 XY-V due to flak. The month of November was not quite over. The squadron was informed that it would be required for an attack on the Urft Dam the following day. Situated near Heimbach, a request from the Americans who were advancing in the region to attack and breach the reservoir dam on the Rur River seemed a strange one, even to the crews of Bomber Command. Regardless, preparations were put in place, aircraft were prepared and the ever willing Groundcrews made sure that the eight Lancasters required were fully serviceable for the following day. It had been another excellent month for the squadron, which was slowly finding its feet. The squadron had flown 237 sorties, pipping No.90, 195 and 218 Squadron by a comfortable margin. With every operation, the squadron's confidence grew, guided by Wing Commander Giles DFC and two very capable Flight Commanders.

A very welcome sight for all, the NAAFI van. A brew could make any situation seem that much better. This photograph shows the NAAFI Van parked in the Sergeant's Mess area. Notice the modern brick-built buildings in the background. Central heating, running hot water was a luxury compared to primitive conditions suffered by No.186 and No.218 Squadrons.

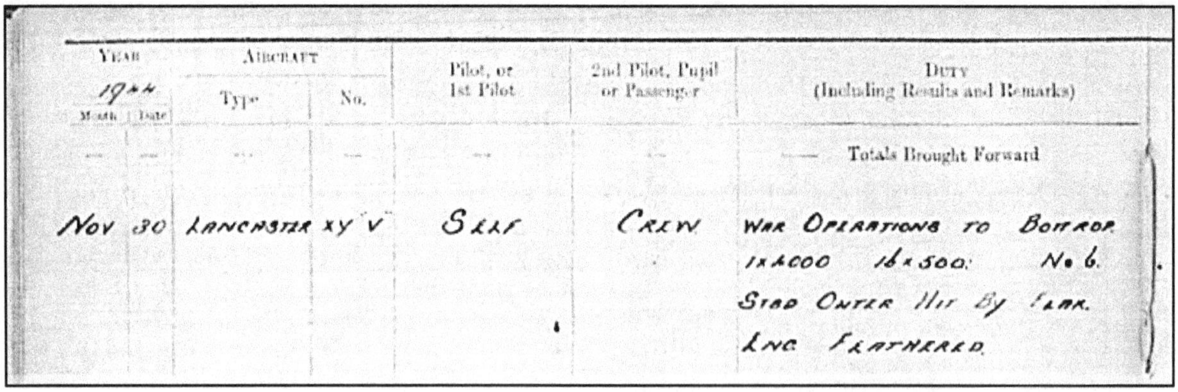

| Year 1944 Month | Date | Aircraft Type | No. | Pilot, or 1st Pilot | 2nd Pilot, Pupil or Passenger | Duty (Including Results and Remarks) |
|---|---|---|---|---|---|---|
| | | | | | | Totals Brought Forward |
| Nov | 30 | Lancaster | XY V | Self | Crew | War Operations to Bottrop 1x4000 16x500. No. 6. Stbd Outer Hit By Flak. Eng Feathered. |

Above: The Log Book entry for Flying Officer D Godfrey RAAF reporting the need to feather the starboard outer engine of Lancaster HK606 XY-V on the Bottrop operation of November 30th. Below: The photograph was taken from the cockpit and shows the offending feathered engine.

Morale on the squadron was excellent. Low losses, substantial gains by the Allied Armies on the Western front, and the German Army's continuing retreat on the Eastern front resulted in an atmosphere of hope that surely the war could not last much longer.

No.186 Squadron Reported Flak Damage 30/11/1944

| Serial | Code | Damage Reported | Repairs / Notes |
|---|---|---|---|
| HK606 | **XY-V** | Starboard Outer engine. | Repaired On Squadron. |

November 1944 : Avro Lancaster Delivery.

| ToC Date | Serial | Code | Maker | Mark | From |
|---|---|---|---|---|---|
| 04/11/1944 | NG293 | XY-U | Armstrong Whitworth | Mk.B.I | Works |
| 25/11/1944 | NG353 | XY-X | Armstrong Whitworth | Mk.B.I | Works |
| 25/11/1944 | NG354 | XY-M | Armstrong Whitworth | Mk.B.I | Works |

# December 1944

## *'German Offensive'*

December 1st, 1944, would see the arrival of two new crews. One was captained by Acting Squadron Leader R.W Bass AFM from the Mildenhall based No.15 Squadron. Robert Bass would replace F/Lt Arthur 'Sandy' Powell DFC as 'B' Flight Commander. Robert's stay on No.15 Squadron had been a brief one. On completion of his conversion at No.3 LFS he was posted to RAF Mildenhall on November 5th, where he joined 'B' Flight. He managed to complete three operations before posting.
The planned attack on the Urft Dam was cancelled, but the squadron was informed that the Dam would be attacked the following day if the weather improved. This, however, changed when Form B.712 arrived from 3 Group HQ, informing the squadron that it would be required for a daylight attack on the Gelsenkirchener Bergwerks A.G Hansa Plant at Dortmund. Eight crews were detailed and briefed including, S/Ldr Bass[8] AFM who would be undertaking his first operation with the squadron.

Form B.712– December 2nd, 1944 (D) :Target : Dortmund : Gelsenkirchener Bergwerks A.G Hansa Plant : GQ1892

| | | | | | | | |
|---|---|---|---|---|---|---|---|
| F/Lt | Fleming | A.J | RAAF | NG148 | XY-B | Follower | Duty Carried Out. |
| F/Lt | Wait | C.J | | NG147 | XY-C | Follower | Duty Carried Out. |
| F/O | Templeton | G.M | RCAF | NG146 | XY-E | Follower | Duty Carried Out. |
| F/Sgt | Clarson | A.J | RAAF | NG140 | XY-F | Follower | Duty Carried Out. |
| S/Ldr | Bass AFM | R.W | | HK661 | XY-R | Follower | Duty Carried Out. |
| F/O | Ritson | E.E | | NG353 | XY-X | Follower | Duty Carried Out. |
| F/Lt | Hunt | E.G | | HK613 | XY-Y | Follower | Duty Carried Out. |
| F/O | Mason | F.H | | HK688 | XY-W | Follower | Duty Carried Out. |

The squadrons of No.3 Group were ordered to rendezvous 10,000 feet above Bury St Edmunds before setting out once again to Orford Ness and the crossing of the North Sea. The Lancasters of No.33 Base would lead the Group along with elements of Methwolds G-H Squadrons. Number 186 Squadron would, together with No.32 Base, make up the second and final wave timed to attack between 14:55 hours and 15:05 hours. The small force of Lancasters was escorted by six squadrons of RAF Mustangs and four squadrons of European based Spitfires. Flying Officer E. Ritson lost the port outer engine aboard Lancaster NG353 XY-Y over the Channel. Nevertheless, showing steely determination, the crew unanimously agreed to continue with the operation. On the run-up to the cloud-covered target, No.186 Squadron encountered spasmodic flak of varying intensity. The crews tucked in behind their allotted G-H Leaders immediately dropped the bombs, and flares emerged from their Leader's bomb-bays. The squadron depositing a total of four x 4000lb, 76 x 1000lb and 16 x 500lb over a five minute period. All the squadron landed safely back at RAF Tuddenham, the last to touch down being F/O E.E Ritson at 15:31 hours. While the squadron was over Germany, Wing Commander Giles DFC and his senior Section Leaders flew to RAF Manston, Kent for a meeting to organise a number of Fighter Liaison Exercises. The raid on Dortmund was a milestone in the Group's involvement with G-H. The Dortmund operation recorded that every G-H aircraft detailed to mark did so successfully. For once, there were no set failures and no issues with the Cat & Mouse tracking stations. This was a tremendous achievement, from the manipulation by the G-H set operators both on the ground and in the air to servicing the temperamental equipment by the radar tradesman.

---

[8] *The Form 540 and 541 are at odds. One shows his rank as Flight Lieutenant , the other Squadron Leader. I have used the S/Ldr rank for this book.*

No.186 Squadrons Leaders. L-R Flight Lieutenant MacDonald RAAF (Radar), Flight Lieutenant Buckland RAF (Air Gunners), Flight Lieutenant Holman RAF (Bomb Aimers), Squadron Leader Reynolds RAF 'A Flight Commander, Wing Commander Giles DFC Commanding Officer, Squadron Leader Bass AFM RAF 'B' Flight Commander. Flight Lieutenant Portway RAF ( Flight Engineers). Front Flight Lieutenant Baxter RNZAF (Wireless Operators) and Flight Lieutenant Earle DFC ( Navigators).

The squadron was stood down on the 3rd, one crew arrived via No.3 LFS based at RAF Feltwell[9]. The lull was a short one. Orders via No.3 Group HQ instructed the squadron to provide 12 crews for an attack on Oberhausen the following day. Sandwiched between Duisburg and Essen and situated on the river Emscher, Oberhausen was the home of the important Ruhrchemie AG synthetic oil plant. Given its location in the Ruhr, it was also equipped with a large modern marshalling yard. The Group detailed a respectable 160 Lancasters. Group rendezvous was once again over the town of Bury St Edmunds. The weather en route was for once as described by the Meteorological Officer back at RAF Tuddenham, solid cloud. The squadron was part of the first wave, briefed to attack between 14:05 hours and 14:08 hours. The Ruhr anti-aircraft made itself known on the run into target. Flak punctured the 10/10th cloud damaging a number of Lancasters, fortunately, none of which were from No.186 Squadron. All twelve crews bombed on their allocated G-H Leader without trouble. The only sign of danger was a few 'Scarecrows'[10] reported over the target area. The operation was considering the target a quiet one.

Form B.713– December 4th, 1944 (D) :Target : Oberhausen : Marshalling Yards

| | | | | | | | |
|---|---|---|---|---|---|---|---|
| F/O | Tait | R.R | | NG137 | XY-D | Follower | Duty Carried Out. |
| F/Sgt | Saunders | A | | NG146 | XY-E | Follower | Duty Carried Out. |
| F/Lt | Smith | S | | NG140 | XY-F | Follower | Duty Carried Out. |
| F/O | Powers | R.C | | HK680 | XY-H | Follower | Duty Carried Out. |
| F/O | Tonks | J.E | | NG175 | XY-J | Follower | Duty Carried Out. |
| F/O | Gibson | J.H | | NN720 | XY-K | Follower | Duty Carried Out. |
| W/O | O'Brien | J.D | RAAF | HK684 | XY-O | Follower | Duty Carried Out. |
| F/O | Orman | K.G | RNZAF | HK659 | XY-Q | Follower | Duty Carried Out. |
| F/O | Liddell | J.B | | NG293 | XY-U | Follower | Duty Carried Out. |
| F/O | Mason | F.H | | HK688 | XY-W | Follower | Duty Carried Out. |
| F/O | Hanson | R.A | | HK613 | XY-Y | Follower | Duty Carried Out. |
| F/Lt | Hunt | E.G | | PD429 | XY-Z | Follower | Duty Carried Out. |

It was the turn of S/Ldr P Reynolds to make the trip south on the 4th for a short detachment to RAF Manston and Fighter Liaison Duties. Bomber Command's preoccupation with dams continued on the 4th. A message from Group HQ informed both No.90 and No.186 Squadron that they would be required for a daylight attack on a new target the following day. The target was the Rur Schwammenauel Dam, again at the behest of the Americans. Built in 1939, the Dam impounds the River Rur to form the Rur Reservoir, which was vital to the industries in both Aachen and Düren. The Urft Dam, which the squadron was initially to attack was bombed by No.1 and 8 PFF Groups on the 2nd without success. Attention now turned towards the Schwammenauel Dam. All they needed was a break in the weather. The fifth crew to be posted onto the squadron in December arrived on the 4th joining 'A' Flight. 'B' Flight's S/Ldr Bass AFM was off to RAF Ingham's Bomber Command Tactical School on the 5th. He would attend No.48 Course, and his departure would once again see the experienced F/Lt 'Sandy' Powell DFC occupy the Flight Commander role.

By the early morning of December 5th, twenty-eight Lancaster crews had been detailed and briefed for the attack, each of Tuddenham's resident squadrons providing 14 crews. Flight Lieutenant A.C Powell DFC was the first away at 09:04 hours at the controls of Lancaster HK688 XY-W. Only 56 Lancasters, all from No.32 Base, would attack the Dam while 94 Lancasters would visit the Marshalling Yards at

[9] *Unlike many of its contemporise within the group the squadron ORB does not record the posting In or Out of crews on the squadron.*

[10] *The term 'Scarecrow' was a generic term used by some Aircrew to describe a fake or dummy explosion to emulate the destruction of an aircraft. Others used the term to describe an aircraft blowing up without any evidence of an attack. The theory was that the Germans were using a new type of shell to simulate a stricken aircraft to demoralise the crews. In fact, what the crews were seeing was the demise of an actual crew. Post-War research confirms that Germany never produced such a shell or device to emulate the destruction of an aircraft.*

Hamm. A 'Master Bomber' code named '*Hotspur*' and 'Deputy Master Bomber' code named *'Hotspur 2'* would control the raid on the Dams. Both are understood to have been provided by 90 Squadron.[11] Unfortunately, a combination of 10/10$^{th}$ cloud and issues with a weak G-H Tracking pulse resulted in the operation being abandoned prior to bombing. The crews jettisoned part of their loads over the North Sea before landing back at RAF Tuddenham. No sooner had the squadrons landed they were informed that with an improvement in the weather they would return the following day.

Form B.714– December 5th, 1944 (D) :Target : Schwammenauel Dam :GO959

| | | | | | | | |
|---|---|---|---|---|---|---|---|
| F/Sgt | Clarson | A.J | RAAF | NG174 | XY-A | Follower | Abandoned. |
| F/O | Field DFC | E.L | | NG148 | XY-B | Follower | Abandoned. |
| F/Lt | Wait | C.J | | NG147 | XY-C | Follower | Abandoned. |
| F/O | Hart | J.H | | NG137 | XY-D | Follower | Abandoned. |
| F/O | Templeton | G.M | RCAF | NG146 | XY-E | Follower | Abandoned. |
| F/Lt | Smith | S | | NG140 | XY-F | Follower | Abandoned. |
| Sgt | Saunders | A | | HK680 | XY-H | Follower | Abandoned. |
| F/O | Madden | R.P | RCAF | HK662 | XY-P | Follower | Abandoned. |
| F/O | Orman | K.G | RNZAF | HK659 | XY-Q | Follower | Abandoned. |
| F/Sgt | Fernley | F | | HK650 | XY-T | Follower | Abandoned. |
| F/O | Godfrey | D.F | RAAF | NG293 | XY-U | Follower | Abandoned. |
| F/Lt | Powell DFC | A.C | | HK688 | XY-W | Follower | Abandoned. |
| F/Lt | Ritson | E.E | | NG353 | XY-X | Follower | Abandoned. |
| F/O | Hanson | R.A | | HK613 | XY-Y | Follower | Abandoned. |

The Rear Gunner aboard Lancaster NG174 XY-A was F/Sgt Gerald McPherson RAAF, he recalls the operation.

> *"We were told at briefing that we would be required to fly at no more than 10,000 feet on this operation, so I decided not to wear my electrically heated suit, which was designed for the low temperatures which were experienced at high altitudes, e.g., 20,000 feet. This, I soon discovered, was a bad decision, because as we crossed the English Channel, the cloud cover forced us to increase our altitude to over 20,000 feet. Consequently, the temperature dropped and as a section of the rear turret's Perspex cover was open to the elements, I felt as if I would freeze to death. My hands were like blocks of ice, and to keep the circulation going I had to bang them hard against the metal uprights of the turret. The operation was aborted because of the heavy cloud cover over the target, and also the proximity of allied troops. Before returning to base, it was necessary for the crews to drop their bomb loads into the Channel, and for the planes to be flying at over 10,000 feet to avoid the percussion effect as the bombs hit the water. There were 180 planes dropping their loads at the same time, and the noise of the explosions all around us made me wonder if we were being shot at, but I was reassured by the pilot that it was only the bombs exploding in the water. I never went on an op without my electrically heated suit again!"* [12]

This would be the first operation flown by the crew of F/O Jack Hart. The crew's Navigator was Sgt Jack Allen. He recalls the weeks and months leading up to this their first operation.

[11] *It is understood the Master & Deputy Master Bombers were provided by 90 Squadron. There is a strong possibility they were F/O's H Floyd and J.W Kaiser RCAF.*

[12] *Via Fay McPherson.*

*It was at 16 O.T.U. where I crewed up with Jack Hart as Pilot, Darby as Bomb aimer, Tony Bath as Rear Gunner, Peter Dangerfield as Rear Upper Gunner, Fred Evens as Engineer and a Flying Officer Davis who had already done a tour in the Middle East. After completing a few operations, he left us, and we had "stand-in" Wireless Operators, including the Australian Evans and a Flight Sergeant Jarvis. We were flying in Wellingtons at Upper Heyford, and in the 15 hrs flying we did as a crew, we had two occasions when one of our engines stopped, and we had to return to base and land on one engine. On September 21st, 1944, we went to 1661 Conversion Unit (RAF Scampton) where we converted from Wellingtons to Stirlings. On November 22nd, we were sent to No.5 LFS based at RAF Syerston for conversion to the Lancaster, which we completed in 17 hours 20 minutes. We were posted to No.90 Squadron on November 30th, 1944 but did no flying as we were almost immediately posted to No.186 at RAF Stradishall.*

The crew of Flight Lieutenant Ted Ritson are seen here having a ride on what appears to be an American Willys Jeep with an unknown Yank driver. Sadly, only three of the crew can be positively identified. Far-right, the crew's Flight Engineer, Flight Sergeant C.J Sharpe RAFVR. The crew's captain, Flight Lieutenant 'Ted' Ritson and sitting behind the Yank, Flying Officer J.R Grey RAFVR, Bomb Aimer.

Early morning mist prevented any flying before midday on the 6th. By mid-afternoon it had dispersed just enough for a number of air tests in preparation of an operation against the Leuna synthetic oil plant at Merseburg that night. Twelve crews were detailed and briefed. It would be the squadron's deepest penetration into Germany since Fulda. Situated some 20 miles west of Leipzig, Leuna was one of the largest synthetic oil plants and the second most extensive chemical organisations in Nazi Germany. Covering over 3 square miles with over of 250 buildings, it was a vast complex employing a staggering 35,000 workers, including 10,000 political and religious prisoners and forced labourers. Such was the factory's importance it had its own flak defences. The 14th Flak Division was responsible for its protection. This was supplemented by more than 19,000 of Leuna's workers, who were members of the air raid protection organisation, which supported an estimated 600 radar-directed guns. It also boasted its own major decoy site with roads, buildings, and factory. One of the first to take-off was S/Ldr

Reynolds who had recently returned from his trip to RAF Manston. Joining No.3 Group's 123 Lancasters were the Lincolnshire based squadrons of No.1 Group which would provide the bulk of the attack with an impressive 291 aircraft. Marking would be provided by No.8 Path Finder Group. That same night over 450 aircraft drawn from No.4 and No.6 RCAF Group would attack Osnabruck, while No.5 Group would provide 265 aircraft for an attack on the Marshalling Yards at Giessen.

Form B.715– December 6th, 1944 (N) :Target : Merseburg : Leuna synthetic oil plant.

| | | | | | | | |
|---|---|---|---|---|---|---|---|
| S/Ldr | Reynolds | P | | NG174 | XY-A | Main Force | Duty Carried Out |
| F/O | Gibson | J.H | | NG148 | XY-B | Main Force | Duty Carried Out |
| F/Sgt | Clarson | A.J | RAAF | NG147 | XY-C | Main Force | Duty Carried Out |
| F/O | Tait | R.R | | NG137 | XY-D | Main Force | Duty Carried Out |
| P/O | Cowley | N.C | | NG146 | XY-E | Main Force | Duty Carried Out |
| F/O | Powers | R.C | | HK680 | XY-H | Abandon | FTR |
| F/Sgt | Fernley | F | | HK659 | XY-Q | Main Force | Duty Carried Out |
| F/Lt | Hunt | E.G | | HK661 | XY-R | Main Force | Duty Not Carried Out |
| W/O | O'Brien | J.D | RAAF | NG293 | XY-U | Main Force | Duty Carried Out |
| F/O | Godfrey | D.F | RAAF | HK606 | XY-V | Main Force | Duty Carried Out |
| F/Lt | Ritson | E.E | | NG353 | XY-X | Main Force | Duty Not Carried Out |
| F/O | Mason | F.H | | HK613 | XY-Y | Main Force | Duty Carried Out |

Once airborne, the squadron crews climbed away and headed towards Reading. No sooner was F/Lt E.C Hunt airborne at 16:42 hours than issues with the starboard inner engine began to cause concern. Very quickly, it was apparent that the priority was to jettison the bomb load as the engine was now misfiring and showing signs of overheating. Unable to climb above 7,000 feet, the crew flew out to sea

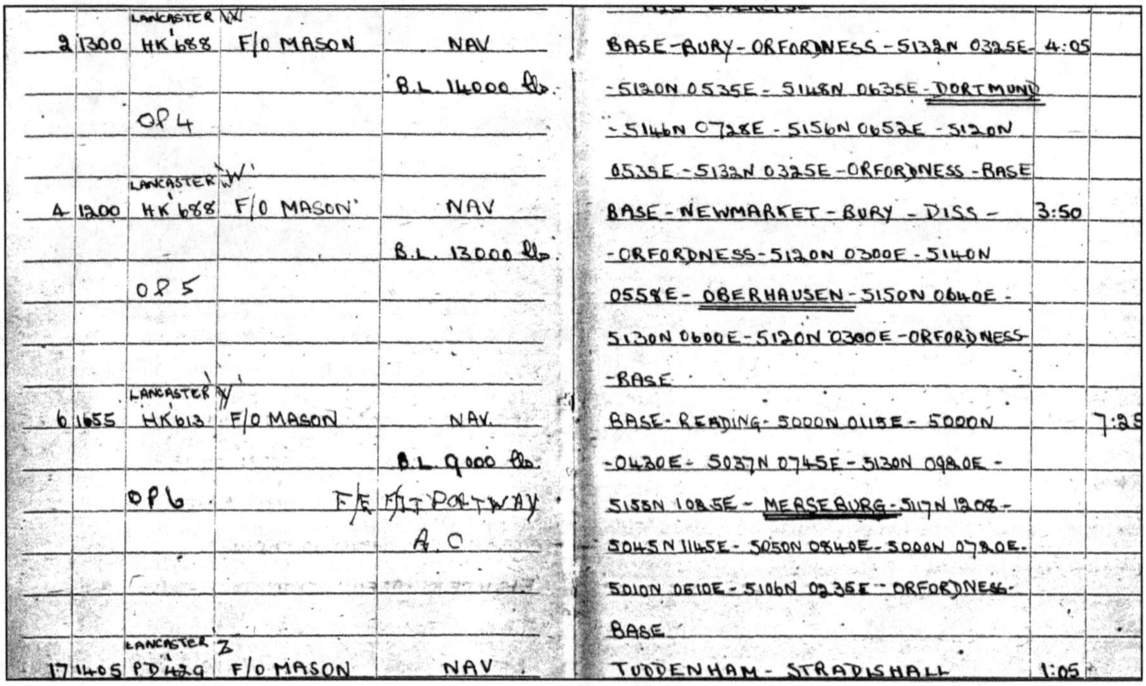
2 1300 LANCASTER 'W' HK688 F/O MASON NAV BASE-BURY-ORFORDNESS-5132N 0325E- 4:05
B.L. 14000 lbs. -5120N 0535E-5148N 0635E-DORTMUND
OP 4 -5146N 0728E-5156N 0652E-5120N
0535E-5132N 0325E-ORFORDNESS-BASE
4 1200 LANCASTER 'W' HK688 F/O MASON NAV BASE-NEWMARKET-BURY-DISS- 3:50
B.L. 13000 lbs. -ORFORDNESS-5120N 0300E-5140N
OP 5 0558E-OBERHAUSEN-5150N 0640E-
5130N 0600E-5120N 0300E-ORFORDNESS-
-BASE
6 1655 LANCASTER 'Y' HK613 F/O MASON NAV BASE-READING-5000N 0115E-5000N 7:35
B.L. 9000 lbs. -0430E-5037N 0745E-5130N 0920E-
OP 6 F/E F/LT PORTWAY A.O 5155N 1025E-MERSEBURG-5117N 1208-
5045N 1145E-5050N 0840E-5000N 0720E-
5010N 0610E-5106N 0235E-ORFORDNESS-
BASE
17 1405 LANCASTER 'Z' PD429 F/O MASON NAV TUDDENHAM-STRADISHALL 1:05

Operation No.6 : The Log Book entry of Sergeant H.F Coleman, Navigator to F/O Mason for the attack on Merseburg. Unusually, the entire route to and from the target is recorded against every raid he undertook. The Squadron Engineering Officer, Flight Lieutenant A.G Portway joined the crew on this occasion.

and jettisoned 8 x 1000lb bombs 40 miles off the coast of Southwold at 17:14 hours. Considerably lighter, and with the defective engine now feathered, the crew made a safe landing at the American bomber base at RAF Knettishall, home of the B17 Fortress equipped 388th Bombardment Group at 18:10 hours. The next crew to abandon was Flying Officer E Ritson due to the failure of the rear turret aboard Lancaster NG353 XY-X to rotate.

Despite both the rear gunner and flight engineer's attempts to rectify, it was soon apparent that to continue into the very heart of Germany without the rear turret was suicidal. Reluctantly the crew flew to the jettison area and landed back at RAF Tuddenham at 18:47 hours. On arrival over the target, the crews were presented with what appeared to be a concentrated mass of Green Stars and Red Markers dropped by the Path Finders. Briefed to bomb in the third and final wave, the squadron arrived over the freezing cloud-covered target at 20:49 hours. Flak was plentiful. One crew, F/O R Tait, was hit while on the bomb run. Damage was concentrated to the rear fuselage of Lancaster NG137 XY-D. Thankfully neither the gunners nor anything vital was hit. A large explosion was witnessed at 20:51 hours, from which dull red fires were observed below the cloud. By 20:54 hours, the last of the squadron had bombed and turned for home. A large red and orange glow was reported to be visible 40 miles on the return route, a testament to the concentrated bombing. It was on the flight home three crews encountered icing problems. Flying Officer J Gibson lost his Air Speed Indicator aboard NG148 XY-B, as did F/Sgt A Clarson RAAF. This crew, flying Lancaster NG147 XY-C, also lost the use of its DR Compass. They landed at the Emergency Landing Airfield at RAF Woodbridge. The worst affected was the crew of F/O R.C Powers at the controls of Lancaster HK680 XY-H. They encountered a severe electrical storm near Le Mans at 23:20 hours. Unable to climb above or fly around the crew flew into the storm. It was a serious mistake. Almost immediately, the controls iced up, making the aircraft unmanageable. Quickly recognising that the Lancaster was doomed, the twenty-two-year-old pilot ordered the crew to bale out.

| | | |
|---|---|---|
| Type | Avro Lancaster Mk.I **HK680 XY-H** | Vickers Armstrong |
| Taken on Charge | 22/10/1944. | |
| Cat E Missing | 08/12/1944 | |
| Struck Of Charge | 17/12/1944 | |
| Total Flying Hours | - | |
| Raids Flown | - | |
| Take-Off Time | 16:45 Hours | |
| Bomb Load | 9 x 1000lb | |
| | | |
| | **CREW** | **Notes / GRAVE** |
| Pilot | Flying Officer R.C Powers RAAF | Bailed-Out - Safe |
| Navigator | Sergeant R.B Best RAFVR | Bailed-Out - Safe |
| Bomb Aimer | Warrant Officer N Latondresse RCAF | Bailed-Out - Safe |
| Wireless Operator | Warrant Officer R.M Evans RAAF ( 418503 ) | Bailed-Out - Safe |
| Mid Upper Gunner | Flight Sergeant W.A.C Hemsley RAFVR | Bailed-Out - Safe |
| Rear Gunner | Flight Sergeant John Skelton DFM RAFVR[13] | X-26-39 |
| Flight Engineer | Sergeant H Short RAFVR | Bailed-Out - Safe |
| | | |
| Posted History | Posted via 15 Squadron 22/10/1944 | |
| Operations Flown | 5 Ops – 15 Squadron. 10 Ops - 186 Squadron. | |
| Buried | **Brussels Town Cemetery** | |

[13] *Awarded DFM while operational with 207 Squadron.*

Flight Sergeant John Skelton DFM RAFVR.

Apart from the experienced second tour veteran, F/Sgt John Skelton DFM, all the crew survived. The unfortunate gunner was found dead in a field by a French peasant. The injured pilot, F/O Powers RAAF, was first admitted to the 8th Army General Hospital based in Brussels before being transferred to the RAF Hospital at Wroughton on December 10th, where he stayed until the 18th. The final details regarding the loss of HK680 are unclear. The Lancaster was reported to have encountered difficulty near Le Mans, southwest of Paris. However, Flight Sergeant J Skelton DFM is buried in Brussel's Cemetery, Belgium and Flying Officer R.C Powers RAAF was hospitalised in Brussels, 150 miles away. And finally, there is the mystery of the crash site. Eighty-eight years after the event, no location is known. Did Lancaster HK680 continue to fly after the crew bailed out and crashed in the sea? We will never know. Robert Powers had a somewhat nomadic career.

He had started his operational career with No.149 (East India) Squadron in September 1943 on completion of his Stirling conversion at No.1651 CU. On January 2nd, 1944, the Australian, having flown four operations as captain, was posted to No.7 Path Finder Squadron based at RAF Oakington. For reasons unknown, he was posted out on January 24th. His next posting was curiously to No.1688 Bomb Disposal Training Flight. In September 1944, he arrived at No.31 Base. On completing his conversion at No.3 LFS, he posted to No.XV Squadron based at RAF Mildenhall. Warrant Officer N.I Latondresse RCAF was flying his first operation with the crew.

The crews began landing at RAF Tuddenham just after midnight. It had been a tough night for Bomber Command, twenty crews failing to return. The losses, although grievous, were by the end of 1944 quickly replaced. Damage to the synthetic oil plant was considerable. The southern area of the complex was particularly hard hit, with a number of refinery buildings and storage holders destroyed. On the 6th, the Squadron Adjutant, F/Lt J.S Walker, departed on some well-earned leave. He was temporarily replaced by F/O B Garland.

No.186 Squadron Reported Flak Damage 06/12/1944

| Serial | Code | Damage Reported | Repairs / Notes |
|---|---|---|---|
| NG137 | **XY-D** | Fuselage. | Repaired On Squadron. |

RAF Tuddenham experienced its first snow on December 7th, keeping the squadron effectively grounded. A heavy frost and snow flurries followed on the morning of the 8th. However, it did not prevent some early morning air-tests. Out at the freezing dispersals, 14 Lancasters were fueled and loaded for a raid directed against the Marshalling Yards at Duisburg. Duisburg had been attacked numerous times since the earliest days of the war by virtue of being the largest inland river port in Europe. This raid would, unbeknown to No.186 Squadron, ultimately have a bearing on its future. Number 31 Base would offer two Lancaster squadrons on operations for the first time. It would join the already established No.32 and No.33 Bases, thus creating No.3 Groups clutch of three. Until recently, No.31 Base with its Base HQ at RAF Stradishall had been used extensively for training and converting the crews of No.3 Group. Re-organisation of the Group in early December would witness the move of No.195 Squadron from RAF Witchford (ex No.33 Base) to RAF Wratting Common with the departure of 1651 HCU. The experienced G-H equipped No.218 (Gold Coast) Squadron moved from RAF Methwold and replaced No.1653 HCU at RAF Chedburgh. Both squadrons would be controlled by No.31 Base HQ at RAF Stradishall, which would continue to organise the Group's conversion and operational needs. Weather on take-off was far from ideal. Within minutes of departure, the Lancasters were shrouded in cloud and light flurries of snow. As the crews steadily climbed away, the cloud slowly dispersed, and the fear of icing gradually disappeared. On this occasion the townsfolk of Bury St Edmunds would hear the monotonous drone of over six hundred Merlin engines as the Groups Lancasters formed up high above them before heading firstly towards Diss, then Orford Ness. Leading the Group's 163 Lancasters were 14 G-H equipped Lancasters of No.218 (Gold Coast) and their No.195 Squadron followers.

Form B.717– December 8th, 1944 (N) :Target : **Duisburg:** Central Station.

| | | | | | | | |
|---|---|---|---|---|---|---|---|
| F/O | Field DFC | E.L | | NG148 | XY-B | Follower | Duty Carried Out |
| F/Lt | Wait | C.J | | NG147 | XY-C | Follower | Duty Carried Out |
| F/O | Tonks | J.E | | NG137 | XY-D | Follower | Duty Carried Out |
| F/O | Templeton | G.M | RCAF | NG146 | XY-E | Follower | Duty Carried Out |
| F/O | Hart | J.H | | NG140 | XY-F | Follower | Duty Carried Out |
| F/Sgt | Saunders | A | | NG149 | XY-G | Follower | Duty Carried Out |
| F/Sgt | Green | T,B | | NG175 | XY-J | Follower | Duty Carried Out |
| F/Lt | Madden | R.P | RCAF | HK662 | XY-P | Follower | Duty Carried Out |
| F/O | Idle | L.A | RNZAF | HK650 | XY-T | Follower | Duty Carried Out |
| F/O | Godfrey | D.F | RAAF | NG293 | XY-U | Follower | Duty Carried Out |
| P/O | Green | L.A | | HK606 | XY-V | Follower | Duty Carried Out |
| F/Lt | Powell DFC | A.C | | HK688 | XY-W | Follower | Duty Carried Out |
| F/Lt | Ritson | E.E | | NG353 | XY-X | Follower | Duty Carried Out |
| F/Lt | Hanson | R.A | | HK613 | XY-Y | Follower | Duty Carried Out |

A fine study of the commissioned Dennis Frederick Godfrey RAAF. His youthful good looks hide a steely determination typical of the Australians on No.186 Squadron. Dennis would quickly rise through the ranks and become one of the squadron's most experienced captains.

The 14 crews of No.186 would join the second wave of the attack, briefed to bomb between 11:04 and 11:06 hours. Flak was reported to be moderate, predicted, and inaccurate. Only one squadron crew reported damage over the target area. Lancaster NG293 XY-U, flown by Australian F/O D Godfrey RAAF, reported superficial damage on return. The biggest problem encountered was severe icing. Flight Lieutenant C Wait had a 1000lb bomb hung-up. Frantic jinking did nothing to dislodge the stubborn bomb. It was only when the crew reduced altitude and reached warmer air that it unexpectedly released, dropping into the bomb bay with a loud thump. The crew quickly opened the bomb bay doors and gratefully watched it disappear below. Flying Officer D Godfrey RAAF had two 1000-pounders refuse to drop when the switches froze aboard Lancaster NG293 XY-Y. No amount of jinking would dislodge them. The crew landed at RAF Mendlesham, still with the bombs on board. Once the crew had cut the engines and opened the bomb bay doors at the dispersal pan, the two offending bombs landed with a thud on the tarmac below! Another crew reporting a hang-up was F/Lt R Hanson. After considerable effort, the pilot finally managed to dislodge an obstinate 1000lb MC bomb after a series of violent and tiring manoeuvres. Flying Officer J. Hart experienced the Flap Selector Lever sticking, resulting in the crew landing at the Emergency Landing Airfield at RAF Woodbridge. The squadron dropped a total of 175 x 1000 pounders on the unfortunate townsfolk of Duisburg. The squadron was stood down on the 9th, but overnight frost did not prevent the Ground Crews from carrying out the various inspections and minor repairs in preparation for a planned raid on Merseburg the following day.

No.186 Squadron Reported Flak Damage 08/12/1944

| Serial | Code | Damage Reported | Repairs / Notes |
|---|---|---|---|
| NG293 | **XY-U** | Fuselage. | Repaired On Squadron. |

This was later cancelled due to weather conditions. Squadron Leader R Bass AFM returned on the 10th and reassumed his 'B' Flight Commander duties. Robert, the son of Ernest and Francis Bass, both Green Grocers, was born on June 1st, 1916, along with his twin brother Frederick. The two boys grew up in the industrial town of Coalville, Leicestershire. In 1930, soon after his 15th birthday, Robert joined the RAF as an apprentice clerk. In October 1940, the then Sergeant Bass was awarded the Air Force Medal. These medals were awarded for *"an act or acts of valour, courage or devotion to duty whilst flying, though not in active operations against the enemy"*. What Robert did, sadly, I have not been able to establish. The first batches of the long-awaited and eagerly anticipated Blind Bombing Aid G-H arrived on the squadron during early December. These first sets, which were arriving at Group in limited numbers, were quickly installed.

The ORB records that on December 10th, 1944, '*one aircraft carried out a special navigation flight*'[14]. Around this time, the squadron was informed that a move was imminent. Number 3 Group had already started reorganising its existing squadrons and airfields, and this new phase would involve No.186 Squadron. The prospect of a move was not one the squadron particularly welcomed. It had come to think of RAF Tuddenham as home. Plans were quickly put in place and implemented, the movement of an operational bomber squadron needed careful preparation. Behind the scenes the ground personnel began organising itself for the forth coming move to RAF Stradishall, the date given was December 16th. The squadrons of No.3 Group were given two separate targets at Osterfeld Sud on the 11th. Ninety-eight crews drawn from No.31 and No.32 Base and RAF Methwold would attack the Marshalling Yards while No.33 Base and its 52 Lancasters would bomb the Coking Plant. Number 186 Squadron would provide 13 crews tasked with destroying the Marshalling Yards. The railway and Marshalling Yards were vitally important to the Germans in the transportation of material and freight, especially coal. It

[14] *Unlike the majority of 3 Group squadrons, 186 would refer to GH as a 'Special Navigational Aid'.*

served primarily as a direct rail connection between the two major marshalling yards of Hamm and Osterfeld Sud to allow long-distance freight trains to avoid the congested Ruhr.

Form B.719– December 11th, 1944 (D) :Target : Osterfeld Sud : Marshalling Yards

| | | | | | | | |
|---|---|---|---|---|---|---|---|
| F/Lt | Smith | S | | NG174 | XY-A | Follower | Duty Carried Out. |
| F/Lt | Field DFC | E.L | | NG148 | XY-B | Follower | Duty Carried Out. |
| F/Sgt | Green | T.B | | NG147 | XY-C | Follower | Duty Carried Out. |
| F/O | Tait | R.R | | NG137 | XY-D | Follower | Duty Carried Out. |
| F/Sgt | Carson | A.J | RAAF | NG146 | XY-E | Follower | Duty Carried Out. |
| F/O | Tonks | J.E | | PD429 | XY-X | Follower | Duty Carried Out. |
| F/O | Gibson | J.H | | NN720 | XY-K | Follower | Duty Carried Out. |
| W/O | O'Brien | J.D | RAAF | HK684 | XY-O | Follower | Duty Carried Out. |
| S/Ldr | Bass | R.W | | HK662 | XY-P | Follower | Duty Carried Out. |
| F/O | Orman | K.G | RNZAF | HK659 | XY-Q | Follower | Duty Carried Out. |
| F/Lt | Hunt | E.G | | HK661 | XY-R | Follower | Duty Carried Out. |
| P/O | Green | L.A | | HK606 | XY-V | Follower | Duty Carried Out. |
| F/Lt | Ritson | E.E | | NG353 | XY-X | Follower | Duty Carried Out. |

The first aircraft slowly climbed away from a freezing RAF Tuddenham at 08:32 hours. At the controls of Lancaster, NG353 XY-X was the experienced F/Lt E Ritson. This would be the crew's 23rd operation since their arrival from No.3 LFS back in September. Almost immediately after take-off, the squadron's Lancasters were cloaked in dense cloud which extended up to 15,000 feet. Even the most experienced crews struggled to locate their G-H Leaders drawn from No.90, No.149 and No.218 Squadron. Any thoughts of forming up into the briefed Vic formation was quickly forgotten. It was a simple case of survival. The main priority was a sharp lookout and avoiding a collision with another Lancaster in the clouds. Confusion reigned above East Anglia as Lancasters carefully groped their way first to the rendezvous point and then the departure point over the north Norfolk coast. Unfortunately, things did not improve over the North Sea. With cloud layers up to 25,000 feet, the already fragmented force was dispersed even more. The formation, especially the spearhead, was badly scattered into individual vics or isolated gaggles of aircraft. Eventually the squadron managed to locate their 'Leaders' and after the initial problems formed up into what F/O E Field reported to be a *'Concentrated stream'*. Flying Officer R Tait and crew were forced to feather the port outer engine aboard Lancaster NG137 XY-D when it started to overheat.

Showing commendable courage, an attribute the squadron Commanding Officer greatly admired, the crew decided to continue the operation on three engines. The dense cloud continued across Europe and resulted in the marshalling yard force being channelled between the towering pillars of cumulonimbus cloud, making the stream narrower and longer than briefed. Barrage flak greeted the crews as they made their run into target just after 11:03 hours. As the first red and green flares ignited, this steadily increased. Despite the excellent work on the part of the G-H Leaders under challenging conditions, the flares were almost immediately swallowed up by clouds making accurate bombing virtually impossible. What followed was a somewhat scattered attack. The whole operation was disappointing from the outset. The relieved crews began landing back at RAF Tuddenham just after lunch. Several crews surprisingly reported that it was *'A straightforward trip'* at de-briefing. This no-nonsense reporting would typify the squadron's attitude throughout the war's final months. Gone were the days of *'jolly good show'* and *'Bang-on old boy'*. These were a new breed of bomber crews. The raid on Osterfeld was the 30th and last operation for the crew of 'A' Flight's, F/Lt Sidney Smith. Their tour had begun in September 1944 with No.90 Squadron on completion of Lancaster conversion with No.3 LFS. They completed 11 operations before transfer to No.186 Squadron. Born in Blyth, Northumberland, in 1919, Sidney was an instrumentation designer for the famous C.A Parsons Ltd, who made turbines and generators and was therefore in a reserved occupation. He successfully applied to join the RAF in 1941 and completed his early training in Canada. On completion of his tour, W/Cdr Giles DFC wrote the following in Sidney's Logbook. *'An above average pilot and an excellent captain of heavy aircraft.'* High praise from a commanding officer who expected total dedication. He would be awarded a DFC in March 1945. The squadron crews awoke the following morning with RAF Tuddenham shrouded by heavy mist and occasional sleet flurries, usually a sign that operations would be scrubbed. However, No.3 Group HQ had other ideas. An early morning briefing would see the squadron supply twelve aircraft for an attack on the Ruhrstahl A.G Steel Works at Witten, located in the south of the Ruhr.

Form B.720 – December 12th, 1944 (D) :Target : Witten : Ruhrstahl A.G Steel Works

| | | | | | | | |
|---|---|---|---|---|---|---|---|
| F/Lt | Wait | C.J | | NG147 | XY-C | Follower | Duty Carried Out. |
| F/O | Templeton | G.M | RCAF | NG146 | XY-E | Follower | Duty Carried Out. |
| F/Sgt | Green | T.B | | NG140 | XY-F | Follower | Duty Carried Out. |
| F/O | Gibson | J.H | | NN720 | XY-K | Follower | Duty Carried Out. |
| F/O | Tonks | J.E | | HK682 | XY-L | Follower | Duty Carried Out. |
| F/Sgt | Clarson | A.J | RAAF | NG354 | XY-M | Follower | Duty Carried Out. |
| P/O | James | J.W | RAAF | HK684 | XY-O | Follower | Duty Carried Out. |
| F/Lt | Hanson | R.A. | | HK662 | XY-P | Follower | Duty Carried Out. |
| F/O | Godfrey | D.F | RAAF | HK659 | XY-Q | Follower | Duty Carried Out. |
| F/O | Idle | L.A. | RNZAF | HK650 | XY-T | Follower | Duty Carried Out. |
| F/O | Gogler | R.J | RAAF | NG293 | XY-U | Follower | Duty Carried Out. |
| F/O | Lindell | J.B | | PD429 | XY-Z | Follower | Duty Carried Out. |

The squadron began to take off just after 11:00 hours and headed for the rendezvous point above Bury St Edmunds. On this occasion, the squadrons of No.32 Base would have the unenviable third and last wave position. Once again No.31 Base was given the responsibility of being first over the target, with No.218 (Gold Coast) Squadron given the added responsibility of heading the stream of 140 Lancasters provided by the group. The group departed over Southwold encountering heavy cloud over the North Sea. Somewhere between forming up over Bury St Edmunds and crossing the Belgian coastal town of Blankenberge, a gap between the leading Lancasters of No.31 Base and the 2nd and 3rd waves of No.33 and No.32 Base developed. The forward formation crossed the Belgium coast just after 13:01 hours. The fighter escort was to be provided by ten squadrons of Spitfires and eight squadrons of RAF Mustangs of 11 Group who took up station over Beringen, Belgium. Unbeknown to the bomber crews, over 100 Bf109s were plotted taking off from various airfields to cover the Essen-Duisburg-Cologne area.

The splintered forward formation comprising of 10 G-H Leaders of No.218 Squadron and 20 followers drawn from No.218 and No.195 Squadrons, plus 10 Lancasters of No.149 (East India) Squadron began experiencing predicted flak from Castrop Rauxel just north of the target on their run into the Witten. Escorted by a solitary squadron of RAF Mustangs, the Lancasters flying between 19,000 and 23,000 feet started their long curved bomb run. Up until this point, other than the gap between the two formations, everything appeared to be going to plan. Then, around 30 miles from the target, menacing black specks started to be seen climbing up through the clouds. At that moment, the intensity of the flak increased. The Lancasters tightened up as much as they dared, wary of the risk that one flak splinter hitting a bomb load of a companion would almost certainly bring them both crashing to earth. The black specks were in fact approximately forty Bf109s from I./JG3, I./JG27 - III./JG27 and IV./JG27 targeted the small, exposed formation. They began their attacks between Bochum Nord and Lutgendortmund.

Above: The Messerschmitt BF109G. Still as deadly as it was over the skies of France in 1939, it, like its British counterpart the Supermarine Spitfire was continuously developed to meet the ever-changing demands placed upon its German pilots.

Below: The Focke Wulf FW190 A8. Together with the BF109 these two fighters became the backbone of the Jagdwaffe. Thankfully encounters with these two deadly foes were few and far between, due in part to the excellent fighter escort provided by the RAF Mustang and European based Spitfire squadrons.

Flying at the rear of the rearmost gaggle was No.186 Squadron, unaware of the frantic action ahead. They had successfully positioned themselves behind their G-H Leaders from No.90 Squadron and were approaching the cloud-covered target unmolested by fighters but bracketed by moderate flak. This rear wave was reported to be compact as the squadron started its bomb run 14:04 hours. By the time the crews of No.186 were over Witten, the German fighters had vanished, brief sightings were reported, but no combats took place. The squadron dropped a total of 11 x 4000 pounders, 98 x 500lb GPs and 70 x Type 14 Clusters almost unchallenged. All returned safely and reported a *'Good concentration of flares and bombing'* at de-briefing. Luck was definitely on the squadron's side during the frantic battle over Germany that afternoon, not a single Lancaster reported damage. A number of diverted aircraft began landing at RAF Tuddenham during the afternoon. One of the airfields equipped with FIDO[15] Tuddenham welcomed a No.115 Squadron Lancaster, a Polish P51 Mustang and six American B17's all of which were unable to land at their home airfields due to low cloud or fog. The forward gaggle of bombers had taken the brunt of the fighter attacks. Number 195 Squadron was the hardest hit, losing four crews, No.218 Squadron lost one crew to fighters, plus a crew ditched enroute home. The RAF Methwold based No.149 Squadron lost two, while No.15 Squadron lost a solitary crew.

[15] *Fog Investigation and Dispersal Operation (FIDO)*

Lancaster NG146 XY-E 'Hullooo There' is the backdrop to a wonderful photograph of the 'A' Flight crew of Flight Lieutenant T.J Tonks and his ground crew. L-R Flight Sergeant E Stockbridge (Bomb Aimer), Sergeant V.O Woods (Rear Gunner), Sergeant H Norman (Flight Engineer), Flight Lieutenant J.E Tonks (Pilot), Sergeant J.H Forshaw (Mid Upper Gunner), Flight Sergeant J.G Mellor (Navigator) and Sergeant L.A Richardson (Wireless Operator).

It had been a bruising encounter and one that would result in many discussions at No.3 Group HQ. All the squadrons of No.3 Group were given the following instructions in the wake of the Witten operation.

1. **The leading base must form a good, solid and recognisable spearhead on which the rest of the group can tighten its formation.**

2. **Bases not in the lead group must leave no gaps between themselves and the formation in front.**

Heavy fog covered much of the region on the 13th, the only activity on the squadron being the welcome return from leave of F/Lt J.S Walker, the Squadron Adjutant. On December 13th, the squadron was ordered to prepare two crews for what was at this time an uncommon operation. A mining operation was planned for the 'Silverthorne' Garden area in the Kattegat Channel. This operation was subsequently postponed due to ropey weather, it was a short reprieve. Number 3 Group had between 1943 and early 1944 bore the brunt of the important, but unglamourous mining offensive. This was primarily due to the gradual removal from the front line of its Short Stirling squadrons due to increasing losses. Now fully equipped with the Avro Lancaster, this type of operation was becoming a rarity.

Form B.722 – December 14th, 1944 (N) :Target : Kattegat Channel : Silverthorne Garden Area

| | | | | | | | |
|---|---|---|---|---|---|---|---|
| F/O | Barton | E.R | RAAF | NG149 | XY-G | Mining | Duty Carried Out. |
| F/O | Hoskin | F.C | RCAF | NG175 | XY-J | Mining | Duty Carried Out. |

No.186 Squadron only undertook one mining raid during the war. Flying Officer Eric Barton RAAF skippered one of the crews involved. This photograph captures five of the crew standing beside Lancaster NG149 XY-G ' George-Giles'. L -R Flying Officer Barton RAAF-Pilot, two ground crew - Sergeant Jack Collins-Rear Gunner. Front row, Flight Sergeant George James - Navigator, ground crew, and Flight Sergeant Jock Macintosh, Bomb Aimer.

On the 14th, Flying Officer Eric Barton RAAF and Canadian F/O F Hoskin RCAF were detailed and briefed for the operation to the Silverthorne Garden area. The first away at 15:11 hours was F/O F

Hoskins RCAF at the controls of Lancaster NG175 XY-J. He was followed four minutes later by F/O Barton RAAF and crew aboard NG149 XY-G. They would be joined by eight other Lancasters from No.3 Group, twenty Halifaxes drawn from No.4 and No.6 RCAF Group, and ten Lancasters from No.5 Group. On departing over Cromer, the two crews kept below 2000 feet as ordered at briefing until they reached the southern tip of Norway, where they quickly climbed to 10,000 feet. At 18:47 hours, F/O Barton RAAF dropped his six mines, confirming his position by H2S on the small Island of Hesselø. Eleven minutes later, the predominantly Canadian crew of F/O Francis Hoskin RCAF dropped their six mines from 10,000 feet on H2S. The two crews landed at RAF Lossiemouth on return. The cold snap continued on the 15th, a heavy overnight frost covered anything exposed. In what was described as 'freezing conditions' the squadron provided twelve crews, including W/Cdr J Giles DFC for a daylight attack on the Marshalling Yards and Railway Workshops at Siegen.

Form B.724 – December 15th, 1944 (D) :Target : Siegan : Marshalling Yards & Workshops

| | | | | | | | |
|---|---|---|---|---|---|---|---|
| F/Lt | Tait | R.R | | NG174 | XY-A | Follower | Abandon. |
| F/O | Templeton | G.M | RCAF | NG146 | XY-E | Follower | Abandon. |
| F/O | Field DFC | E.L | | NN720 | XY-K | Follower | Abandon. |
| P/O | Young | H.S | | HK682 | XY-L | Follower | Abandon. |
| S/Ldr | Bass | R.W | | NG354 | XY-M | Follower | Abandon. |
| W/O | O'Brien | J.D | RAAF | HK684 | XY-O | Follower | Abandon. |
| W/Cdr | Giles DFC | J.H | | HK662 | XY-P | Follower | Abandon. |
| F/Lt | Orman DFC | K.G | RNZAF | HK659 | XY-Q | Follower | Abandon. |
| P/O | Green | L.A | | HK606 | XY-V | Follower | Abandon. |
| P/O | Fernley | F | | HK650 | XY-T | Follower | Abandon. |
| F/Lt | Hunt | E.G | | NG293 | XY-U | Follower | Abandon. |
| F/O | Lindell | J.B | | PD429 | XY-Z | Follower | Abandon. |

Having taken off from Tuddenham's icy runway and reached the assembly point over Bury St Edmunds, the squadron received the order to return to base. The prearranged No.11 Group fighter escort could not take off, their bases cloaked in dense fog. The frustrated crews were directed to a point in the North Sea and then ordered to jettison their 4000lb Cookies retaining their type No.14 Cluster bombs. On December 16th, 1944, the Germans launched a massive offensive through the densely forested Ardennes between Belgium and Luxemburg. Catching the Allies, particularly the Americans unawares, German armoured units poured into Allied-occupied Belgium towards their ultimate goal, the port of Antwerp. Initially sweeping aside any American resistance and taking full advantage of the fog, the German offensive came as a tremendous shock to the overconfident Allied commanders who had been taken entirely by surprise. As a result, panic and retreat swept through the American lines.

The following day, the squadron move was confirmed with the arrival of Administration Instruction Serial No.52/44. The Advance Party, consisting of four officers led by the recently returned Squadron Adjutant, plus three Section Leader representatives, and 78 other ranks including Orderly Room staff travelled to their new station by road. The weather reflected their mood, cold and wet. It was a miserable day to move. On arrival, they quickly set about claiming the various offices housed in No.3 Hangar. That night back at RAF Tuddenham, an impromptu farewell party was organised in the Officers Mess. There was a close bond between No.186 Squadron and its parent squadron. The 186 ORB reporting, *'A grand spirit of fraternity, understanding and co-operation existed at all times with 90 Squadron'.* The

An excellent close-up of Sergeant J.H.W Collins, Rear Gunner to Flying Officer Barton RAAF. Jack Collins has written Jack's Joint on the rear turret of NG149 XY-G 'George-Giles'. Most gunners opted to remove the central perspex panel to improve visibility.

weather had still not improved the following morning when 13 crews took off and made their way individually on the short flight to RAF Stradishall. Conditions were not ideal, heavy cloud and bumpy conditions were encountered. With an improvement in the weather after lunch, Wing Commander Giles DFC led nine Lancasters to RAF Stradishall. Once airborne, the Lancasters formed up into an immaculate formation, with the Canadian C/O out in front. The formation circled RAF Tuddenham for the last time and headed off in style for a new station and a new Base Group, No.31. The departure of the Air Party was immediately followed by the Main Road Party, consisting of 302 Officers and other ranks who headed south to the squadron's new home.

RAF Stradishall was located mainly in the parish of Hundon, south of the A143 road, some 11 miles from Bury St Edmunds. It lay on Suffolk clay, excellent for heavy wheat crops but not for heavy bombers. Despite the extensive under-draining carried out during construction, the glue-like mud that appeared after heavy rain quickly led to RAF Stradishall becoming the first airfield in Bomber Command scheduled for hardened runways. Five spacious Type C hangars, administrative, technical and barrack buildings were built between the bombing circle and the A143. Stradishall officially opened on February 3rd, 1938, although building work was still in progress. The contract to build this then modern station was worth £500,000, a considerable amount to build. It was awarded to Sir Lindsay Parkinson & Co. Ltd. RAF Stradishall would be equipped with three tarmacked runways, 04-22, 07-25 and 14-32, all approximately 1,000 yards long. A total of 24, later increased to 36, hard standings were placed round the encircling perimeter track. Equipped with modern brick built heated offices, spacious administration and accommodation blocks with hot running water and comfortable living quarters made this new airfield in rural Suffolk a much sort after posting. The runways were extended during 1941, 07-25 at the 25 end to 2,000 yards, 14-32 at the 32 end to 1,400 and 04-22 at the 04 end to 1,500 yards. The original hard runways and perimeter track lay within the two public roads running from the A143 to Scotch Corner, but the extensions caused these to be closed. Several pan hard standings were lost during the restructuring leaving 26 intact. To accommodate the ever-increasing numbers of aircraft, 13 loops were added. Three additional hangars were also provided, all T2s, one placed near the end of runway 04 on the 07 side. The other two were in the southeast corner, east of 32. Bomb stores were constructed on farmland to the west of the airfield. From the very outset, RAF Stradishall would play an essential part in No.3 Group's history.

On the afternoon of the 18th, the Rear Party of 30 Officers and other ranks arrived at RAF Stradishall. Once the tons of equipment were safely unloaded by the hard-working Ground Crews, checked in and documented, then carefully stored, the squadron signalled No.3 Group HQ that the move had been successfully completed. The move may have been completed, but there was still a great deal of organising to do before the squadron would once again be operational. All the squadron personnel, especially the diligent ground staff, had made the difficult task of moving the squadron a success and importantly completed on time, a no small achievement. The weather, which had been dreadful throughout the move, finally cleared on the afternoon of 18th, allowing two Lancaster's to take-off for a series of evening Circuit and Landings. Languishing around the airfield were a few battered Short Stirlings, left behind by Stradishall's previous occupiers, No.1657 Heavy Conversion Unit. Only three days prior, on December 15th, 1944, No.1657 disbanded after 27 months of converting crews to the four-engine bomber. Formed on October 6th, 1942, at RAF Stradishall, No.1657, CU was one of the groups most productive conversion units and did much to ensure that the group was provided with well-trained crews. With the transfer of RAF Stradishall to an operational station, No.31 Base would consist of three operational squadrons from this point on. RAF Stradishall, No.31 Base HQ with No.186 Squadron, RAF Wratting Command and No.195 Squadron and finally RAF Chedburgh with No.218 (Gold Coast) Squadron. The former squadrons would consist of three flights, while No.186 would initially remain a two flight squadron. Number 31 Base would have an establishment, on paper, of at least over eighty Lancasters.

There followed two days of dense fog, which was welcomed, affording the squadron time to settle into its new surroundings. On the morning of the 19th, the squadron was informed it would be needed for an early evening operation. The Ground Crews set about preparing 14 Lancasters only for the raid to be cancelled due to fog at 14:08 hours. The following morning the squadron was once again informed to standby despite no improvement in the weather. Once again, the operation was cancelled, much to the frustration of the crews. With the situation in the Ardennes becoming more static, reliable information was gradually reaching the Allied commanders. The railway yards at Trier situated on the southern flank of the German front line was to be attacked. It had become a bottleneck for German reinforcements. Located on the river Mosel, the town's main road led directly to Luxembourg, while Trier was connected to Cologne by an essential and busy railway system.

The squadron detailed 14 crews. However, six were subsequently cancelled. Given the treacherous conditions, it was decided only the more experienced crews would participate. The first crew away at 11:59 hours was S/Ldr P Reynolds at the controls of Lancaster NG174 XY-A. Twelve minutes later the squadron was airborne. Because of the importance of the operation, the squadron Commanding Officer, W/Cdr J Giles DFC was also airborne, flying with him aboard PD429 XY-Z was the Squadron Navigation Leader, F/Lt W Earle DFM. Over 143 Lancasters were to be provided by No.3 Group. However, the weather had other ideas. At RAF Wratting Common, No.195 Squadron only managed to get one crew airborne before the fog made any further attempts to take-off suicidal. The Chedburgh based No.218 (Gold Coast) Squadron provided nine crews. This hastily prepared operation would be No.186 Squadron's first under No.31 Base control and the first that all three base squadrons operated together.

Form B.732 – December 21st 1944 (D) :Target : Trier : Marshalling Yards

| | | | | | | | |
|---|---|---|---|---|---|---|---|
| S/Ldr | Reynolds | P | | NG174 | XY-A | Follower | Abandon. |
| F/Lt | Wait | C.J | | NG147 | XY-C | Follower | Abandon. |
| F/O | Barton | E.R | RAAF | NG149 | XY-G | Follower | Duty Carried Out. |
| P/O | Young | M.S | | HK682 | XY-L | Follower | Duty Carried Out. |
| F/Lt | Hoskin | F.C | RCAF | NG175 | XY-J | Follower | Abandon. |
| F/O | Orman | K.G | RNZAF | HK688 | XY-W | Follower | Duty Carried Out. |
| F/Lt | Hanson | R.A | | HK613 | XY-Y | Follower | Duty Carried Out. |
| W/Cdr | Giles DFC | J.H | | PD429 | XY-Z | Follower | Duty Carried Out. |

The depleted force formed up over the Maze and, once established, headed out across the North Sea. A Master Bomber of No.32 Base had been assigned to direct the attack due to the proximity of Allied ground forces. Each squadron crew would again be required to bomb on a designated G-H Leader. Once above the clouds, the formation was swathed in brilliant sunshine. Six thousand feet below, the whole of Northern Europe was covered in dense clouds and beneath that, freezing fog. With the target blanketed and no possibility of a visual attack, the Master Bomber transmitted over the VHF the code word '*Beetox*' the instruction to carry out a normal G-H attack. All but three crews successfully bombed. Squadron Leader P Reynolds and F/Lt C Wait had the misfortune to follow two G-H Leaders who experienced G-H failure over the target. Flight Lieutenant F Hoskin RCAF abandoned the operation when the bomb release 'tit' malfunctioned aboard Lancaster NG175 XY-J. Brownish smoke had started to rise through the cloud base as the formation turned for home, it had been a textbook G-H operation, and one that only No.3 Group was capable of undertaking in the conditions. Thankfully the weather stayed sufficiently clear for all the crews to land safely back at RAF Stradishall.

The following morning, fog had once again formed over the East Anglian stations. Nevertheless, once again, Bomber Command HQ turned to the G-H equipped Lancasters of No.3 Group. Fourteen crews were detailed and briefed for a return visit to Trier. Despite HQ's confidence, the weather made any attempt to operate impossible. Finally, on the 23rd, the weather began to clear both over the Group's bases, more importantly, over the battlefront. A total of 153 Lancaster crews were detailed and briefed for a mid-afternoon raid on Trier 'A'. 186 Squadron provided 14 crews led away by the quiet and unpretentious 'B' Flight Commander, S/Ldr R Bass AFM. Also airborne was a small force of Lancasters and Mosquitoes of No.8 Path Finder Force. They would bomb the Marshalling Yards at Cologne/Gremburg independently 90 minutes before the Trier force.

## No.31 Base Squadrons December 1944 – May 1945

No.186 Squadron, Avro Lancaster NG354 XY-M RAF Stradishall.

No.195 Squadron, Avro Lancaster LM543 A4-P RAF Wratting Common.

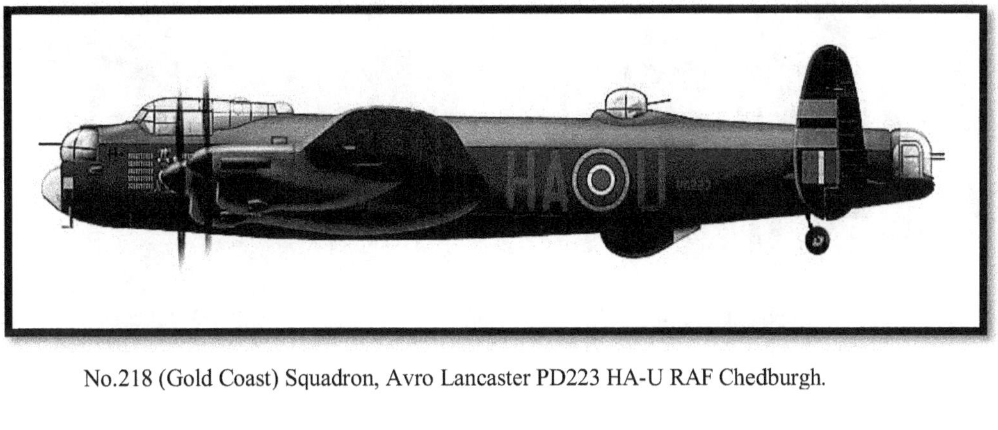


No.218 (Gold Coast) Squadron, Avro Lancaster PD223 HA-U RAF Chedburgh.

Form B.732 – December 23rd 1944 (D) :Target : Trier : Marshalling Yards

| | | | | | | | |
|---|---|---|---|---|---|---|---|
| Sgt | Saunders | A | | NG174 | XY-A | Follower | Duty Carried Out. |
| F/O | Field DFC | R.L | | NG148 | XY-B | Follower | Duty Carried Out. |
| F/Lt | Tait | R.R | | NG137 | XY-D | Follower | Duty Carried Out. |
| F/O | Hart | J.H | | NG146 | XY-E | Follower | Duty Carried Out. |
| P/O | Cowley | N.C | | NG140 | XY-F | Follower | Duty Carried Out. |
| F/O | Gibson | J.H | | NN720 | XY-K | Follower | Duty Carried Out. |
| P/O | Beck | J.A | RAAF | HK684 | XY-O | Follower | Duty Carried Out. |
| F/Lt | Madden | R.P | RCAF | HK662 | XY-P | Follower | Duty Carried Out. |
| F/Lt | Orman DFC | K.G | RNZAF | HK659 | XY-Q | Follower | Duty Carried Out. |
| S/Ldr | Bass AFM | R.W | | HK661 | XY-R | Follower | Duty Carried Out. |
| P/O | Fernley | F | | HK650 | XY-T | Follower | Duty Carried Out. |
| P/O | Gogler | R.J | RAAF | NG293 | XY-U | Follower | Duty Carried Out. |
| P/O | Green | L.A | | HK606 | XY-V | Follower | Duty Carried Out. |
| F/Lt | Liddell | J.B | | PD429 | XY-Z | Follower | Duty Carried Out. |

The squadrons of No.31 Base would make up the third and final wave. The raid would again be controlled by a Master Bomber, on this occasion, New Zealander, Squadron Leader Allan Scott DFC RNZAF (call sign *Steelgrey*) of No.90 Squadron. Once airborne, the crews encountered low freezing cloud, which thankfully quickly dispersed as they headed towards Newmarket, where the three base groups formed up at 10,000 feet. Weather conditions over Trier were ideal. The town was clear of cloud making visual identification of the target possible. The blackened and still smoking town stood out against snow-covered countryside as the first markers fell at 14:28 hours. Seventeen thousand feet above

Sadly a poor quality photograph of the crew of Flight Lieutenant Leonard Arthur Green RAFVR. Leonard and crew would survive their tour on No.186 Squadron. They are standing with their proud Ground Crew in front of Lancaster HK606 XY-V 'Victor'.

Trier, the squadron had unlimited visibility as the red TI markers arched their way towards the target below. Unlike the previous visit, the defenders of Trier put up an intense flak barrage. One of the 19 damaged Lancasters was flown by Pilot Officer L Green. The crew had just dropped their mixed HE load from 17,500 feet when their Lancaster, HK606 XY-V, shook from the impact of an exploding flak burst almost directly under the nose. The prone Bomb Aimer, W/O K Pryor, who had only seconds before watched as his 4000lb Cookie and 14 x 500lb MC hurtled towards Trier, was peppered with flak fragments. Flying Officer E Field DFC had the misfortunate of having his 4000lb Cookie hang-up due to icing. However, not wishing to waste an opportunity, they circled the target and made a second bomb run from 15,500 feet, dropping the cookie at 14.31 hours. The whole town, especially the southern half, was enveloped in explosions. A stick of bombs was seen to straddle and hit the southernmost bridge, while explosions surrounded the northern bridge. Columns of dense white and dark brown smoke radiated from the town, making identifying the individual aiming points difficult for the stragglers. Squadron Leader R Bass AFM flying at 18,000 feet reported at de-briefing, '*Some Red TI's were seen short of the town on the west bank of the river, but the Master Bomber quickly cancelled them out. Southern Bridge was seen to blow up.*' Two crews, F/O J Hart and F/Lt R Tait, reported a large explosion. Tait reported on return, '*Houses seen clearly. Big explosion seen at 14:42 hours, orange in colour with smoke up to 12,000 feet. Good attack*'.

The handling of the raid by the Master Bomber, S/Ldr Eric Scott DFC, was particularly praised. The returning crews appreciated his clear and calm instructions. The group reported one loss, a crew from No.90 Squadron, the victim of flak. However, the Path Finders had encountered German fighters, who tore into the small formation shooting down seven Lancasters and a Mosquito. One of the crews lost was the Master Bomber S/Ldr R.A Palmer DFC & Bar. He would be awarded a posthumous VC for his actions on this raid.

No.186 Squadron Reported Flak Damage 23/12/1944

| Serial | Code | Damage Reported | Repairs / Notes |
|---|---|---|---|
| HK606 | **XY-V** | Forward fuselage, nose. | Repaired On Squadron. |

Fourteen crews were detailed to attack Bonn Hangelar airfield around tea-time Christmas Eve. The target was situated just ten minutes flying time from the German front line. Allied intelligence had reason to believe that the airfield was being used to fly support operations for their ground forces. Adverse weather over East Anglia meant that only No.31, No.32 Base and Methwold could participate. The airfields of No.33 Base were fog-bound. 'B' Flight's Flight Lieutenant R Hanson and crew were the first away at 15:01 hours aboard their regular Lancaster HK613 XY-Y. This was the crew's 17th operation since their arrival in October from No.3 LFS and unlucky 13th aboard Y-York. The Squadron's contribution to the raid would have been reduced if not for the commendable courage of F/O D Godfrey RAAF crew. Prior to take-off, it was discovered that the rear turret aboard Lancaster NG293 XY-U was unserviceable. After a brief discussion between the crew, it was decided to 'press-on'. This attitude was prevalent on No.186 Squadron and expected. The influence of Wing Commander Giles DFC was the deciding factor. He instilled great confidence into crews, and he greatly admired such determination. Flying Officer Godfrey wrote in his Logbook '*Good show by the rear gunner*'. The rear gunner was Sgt Norman Haikney or 'Cisco' to his crew, and a defective rear turret would not spoil his birthday celebrations!

Form B.735 – December 24th 1944 (N) :Target : Bonn/Hangelar : Airfield

| | | | | | | | |
|---|---|---|---|---|---|---|---|
| Sgt | Saunders | A | | NG148 | XY-B | Main Force | Duty Carried Out. |
| F/Lt | Wait | C.J | | NG147 | XY-C | Main Force | Duty Carried Out. |
| P/O | Cowley | N.C | | NG140 | XY-F | Main Force | Duty Carried Out. |
| F/O | Hart | J.H | | NN720 | XY-K | Main Force | Duty Carried Out. |

| | | | | | | | |
|---|---|---|---|---|---|---|---|
| F/O | Young | H.S | | HK682 | XY-L | Main Force | Duty Carried Out. |
| F/O | Barton | E.R | RAAF | NG354 | XY-M | Main Force | Duty Carried Out. |
| P/O | Beck | J.A | RAAF | HK684 | XY-O | Main Force | Duty Carried Out. |
| F/O | Idle | L.A | RNZAF | HK659 | XY-Q | Main Force | Duty Carried Out. |
| F/Lt | Hunt | E.G | | HK661 | XY-R | Main Force | Duty Carried Out. |
| F/O | Green | L.A | | HK650 | XY-T | Main Force | Duty Carried Out. |
| F/O | Godfrey | D.F | RAAF | NG293 | XY-U | Main Force | Duty Carried Out. |
| F/O | Mason | F.M | | HK688 | XY-W | Main Force | Duty Carried Out. |
| F/O | James | J.W | RAAF | NG353 | XY-X | Main Force | Duty Carried Out. |
| F/Lt | Hanson | R.A | | HK613 | XY-Y | Main Force | Duty Carried Out. |

Two 'Aussies' miles from home enjoying the English countryside. Skipper Dennis Godfrey and his Wireless Operator, Pilot Officer Tom Spinks RAAF looking relatively relaxed.

Born in Pallion, Sunderland, on December 24th 1919, the young Norman was a bright young lad and was accepted into the local grammar school. Unfortunately, and typically of the period, there were cost implications, and sadly Norman did not finish off his schooling. Norman did, however, start as an apprentice in one of the many shipyards along the banks of the Wear. He trained as a platter and was responsible for marking out the sheet metal plates for cutting out before the welders and riveters put them together. As this was deemed a reserved occupation, Norman was repeatedly turned down at the local Navy recruiting office and told not to show his face again, or he would spend a night in the cells! Nevertheless, showing that Northern grit, he decided the Navy's loss would be the RAF's gain. The weather was clear over the target area, giving the Group another opportunity to carry out some accurate marking and bombing. The first crew to bomb was F/O F Mason at 18:31 hours, who dropped his mixed HE load on the first salvo of TI clusters. The following crews reported several wayward TI markers near the river, but such was the excellent visibility that these were quickly disregarded. Dense smoke and numerous explosions were reported in the target area, and bombing appeared to be relatively evenly divided between two main groups of markers. The first sign of trouble was the appearance of fighter flares, which hung ominously over the target area. It was no surprise given the clear conditions when tracer fire was observed. German night fighters drawn from NJG.6, and NJG.1 were up and on the prowl. Flying Officer L.A Green had cleared the target area and was at 19,000 feet when in the bright moonlight, the crew's rear gunner, Sgt W Deards, spotted a prowling JU88 night fighter at 16:38 hours. The order to corkscrew starboard was given as the rear gunner opened fire with two short bursts. The JU88 broke away and was not seen again. The returning crews were enthusiastic about the raid, *'A good concentration of flares and bombing'* remarked one crew, while another reported *'Bombs were seen bursting on TI markers'*. Flight Lieutenant R Hanson stated, *'Buildings and hangars on fire'*. These were just a few of the comments at de-briefing, and the crews were correct in their reporting. Extensive damage had been inflicted. The landing ground was blanketed with craters. The large hangar area and the northern dispersal area was particularly hard hit. In addition, a number of hangers and buildings were destroyed or badly damaged. Christmas Day 1944, the sixth Christmas of the war, and No.186 Squadron received orders that it would be required for a mid-afternoon attack on the Gremberg Marshalling Yards at Cologne. Thankfully and to the joy of the crews, this order was cancelled after the briefing at 10:00 hours. The whole station wasted no time celebrating in the customary manner. However, ominously, the crews were warned that they would be required the next day. As was tradition, Officers and Senior NCOs served the Airman's Christmas dinner. The Squadron ORB records, 'Just another instance of Shakespeare's, *"They also serve who stand and wait"*. On the evening, there was a dance in the Officers Mess and much merriment generally in both the Officers and Sergeant's Messes. Boxing Day 1944 was bitterly cold. The early morning fog which blanketed the station had by mid-morning finally started to disperse, it could mean only one thing, operations. With the clear weather still holding over the continent Bomber Command frantically put together a scratch force of bombers to attack German troop and tank concentrations at St.Vith. The fog and freezing weather conditions prevalent over most of England's eastern region was still causing significant problems. Number 3 Group was only able to mobilize 45 aircraft, all of which were provided by No.31 Base. In treacherous conditions, fourteen Lancasters of No.186 Squadron began taking-off from RAF Stradishall's snow covered runway. Aware of the importance of the operation, one of the first names down for the raid was that of the squadron commander, W/Cdr J Giles DFC. This was typical of the Canadian's style of command and the very reason he was held in such high regards.

Form B.740 – December 26th 1944 (D) :Target : St.Vith : Tactical

| | | | | | | | |
|---|---|---|---|---|---|---|---|
| S/Ldr | Reynolds | P | | NG174 | XY-A | Main Force | Duty Carried Out. |
| F/Lt | Wait | C.J | | NG147 | XY-C | Main Force | Duty Carried Out. |
| F/Lt | Tait | R.R | | NG137 | XY-D | Main Force | Duty Carried Out. |
| F/O | Field DFC | E.L | | NG149 | XY-G | Main Force | Duty Carried Out. |
| P/O | Barton | E.R | RAAF | NG175 | XY-J | Main Force | Duty Carried Out. |

| | | | | | | | |
|---|---|---|---|---|---|---|---|
| F/O | Gibson | J.H | | NN720 | XY-K | Main Force | Duty Carried Out. |
| W/Cdr | Giles DFC | J.H | | NG354 | XY-M | Main Force | Duty Carried Out. |
| F/Lt | Madden | R.P | RCAF | HK662 | XY-P | Main Force | Duty Carried Out. |
| F/Lt | Hunt | E.G | | HK661 | XY-R | Main Force | Duty Carried Out. |
| F/O | Fernley | F | | HK650 | XY-T | Main Force | Duty Carried Out. |
| F/O | Idle | L.A | RNZAF | HK606 | XY-V | Main Force | Duty Carried Out. |
| F/Lt | Orman DFC | K.G | RNZAF | HK688 | XY-W | Main Force | Duty Carried Out. |
| F/O | Gogler | E.J | RAAF | HK613 | XY-Y | Main Force | Duty Carried Out. |
| F/Lt | Liddle | J.B | | PD429 | XY-Z | Main Force | Duty Carried Out. |

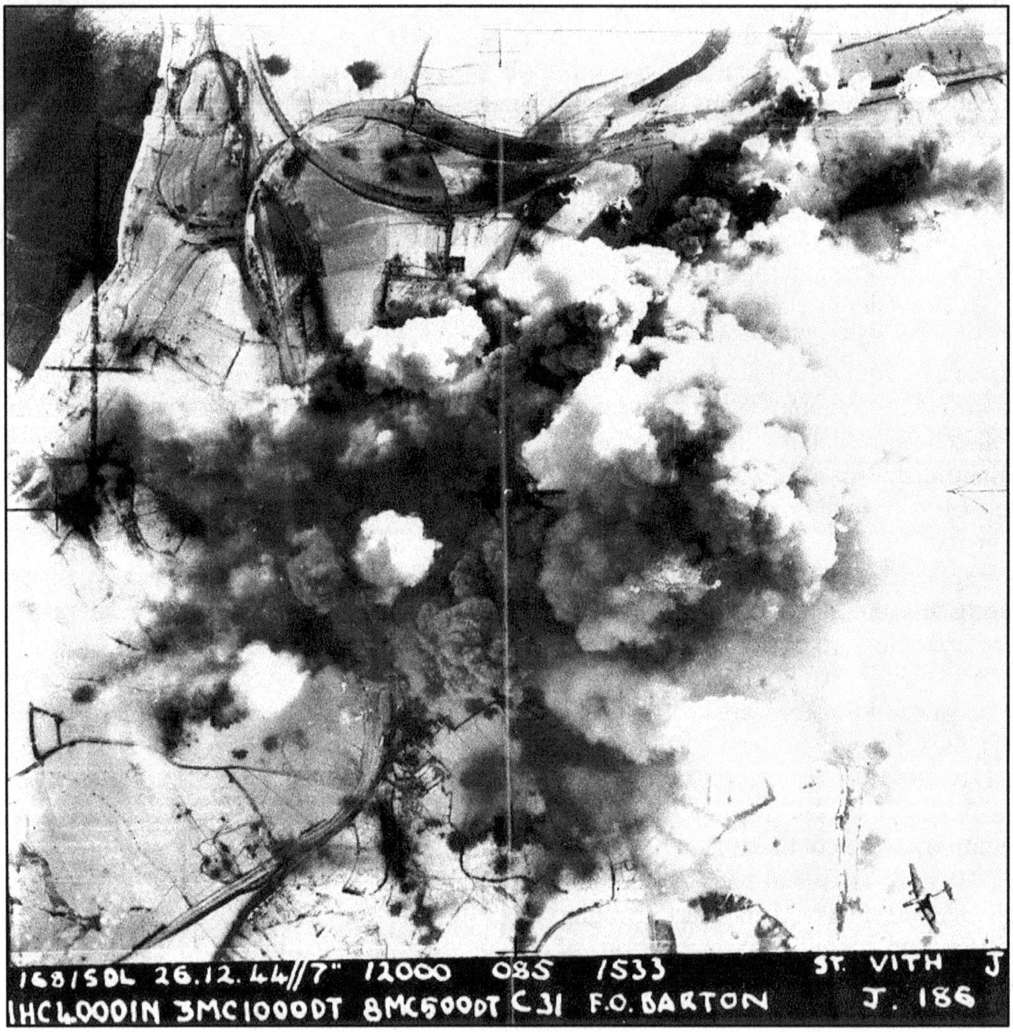


A snow-covered St.Vith. Flying Officer Barton took this target photograph from just 12,000 feet at 15:33 hours. Note the Lancaster well below the briefed bombing height.

The bombers departed over the Straits of Dover and headed towards the Somme. Turning eastwards, the force headed towards the Franco-Belgium frontier, then turned northeast towards St Vith. Over the continent, the bombers encountered patchy fog but thankfully no cloud. Flying between 10,000-14,000 feet, the Lancasters experienced pockets of flak on the route. Bastogne and to its west, the small town of Vielsalm were particularly active and vicious, producing some accurate flak. The 45 Lancasters of

No.31 Base[16] were timed to attack between 15:27 and 15:34 hours. Problems with the initial PFF marking meant that the early waves were ordered to orbit the target by the Master Bomber W/Cdr 'Tubby' Baker DSO DFC of No.635 Squadron. Thankfully opposition was slight as salvo after salvo of red and green markers finally started exploding in the town's centre.

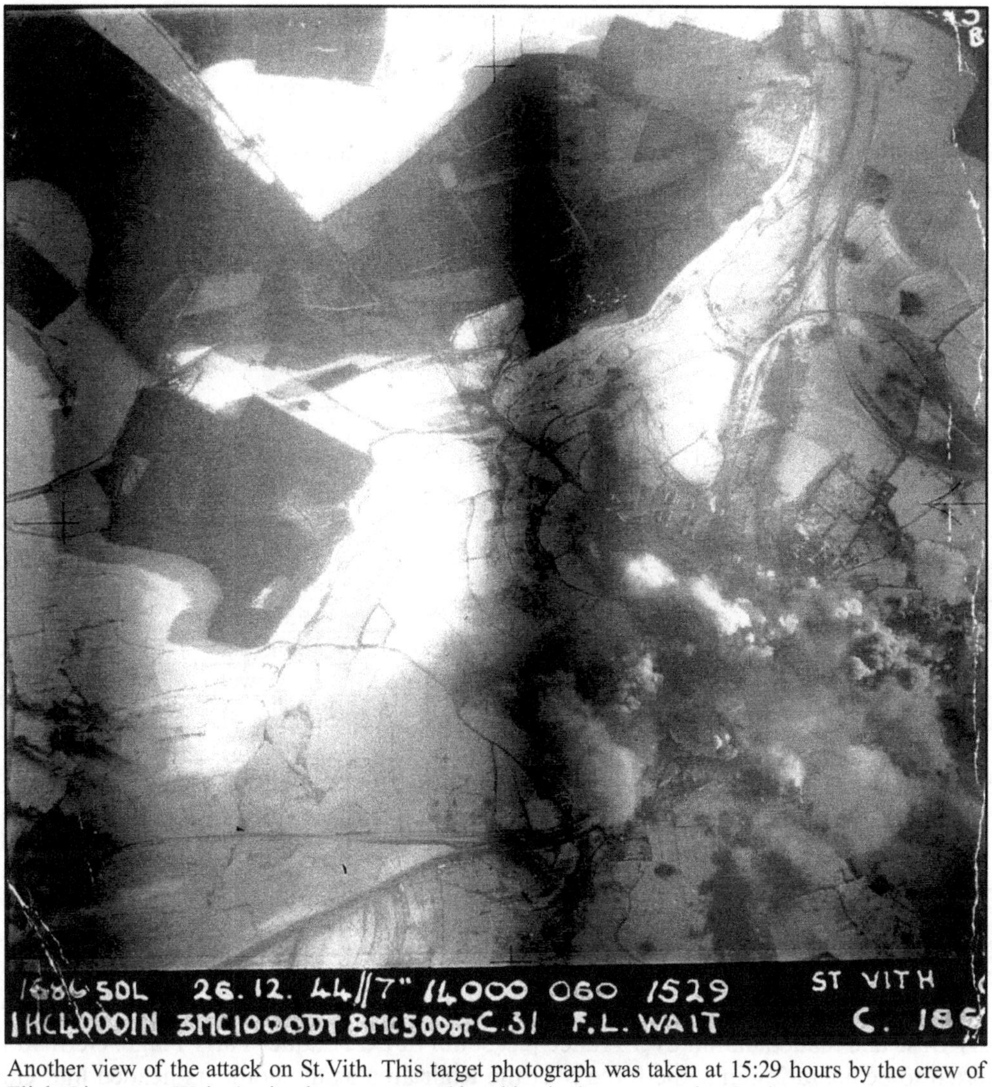


Another view of the attack on St.Vith. This target photograph was taken at 15:29 hours by the crew of Flight Lieutenant Wait. Again, the concentrated bombing in the town can be clearly seen.

Flying Officer J Gibson at the controls of Lancaster NN720 XY-K, *'Target identified visually and on smoke. Bombed 1 second undershot on upward edge of smoke on Master Bombers instructions at 15:36 hours from 10,000 feet. Railway was seen as we approached and own bombs hit railway lines on south edge of town. Town was in ruins. Master Bomber moved attack to loop of railway south of town'.*

Wing Commander J Giles DFC frustratingly had his entire load aboard Lancaster NG384 XY-H hang-up on his first run. He reported on his return, *'Weather clear, target identified on Red TI's and centre of smoke over town. On first run over target bombs hung up, but on second run all bombs went with the exception of 1x 500lb. Bombed first at 15:29 hours, from 14,200 feet and secondary at 15:38 hours from 11,500 feet. Bombs were seen bursting through smoke'.* Bomb load after bomb load exploded in

*[16] No.186 provided 14, No.195 Squadron 17, while No.218 despatched 15 crews.*

the snow-covered town and to the salient to the west where the Germans had concentrated their forces. Encouraged by W/Cdr Baker's 'Good bombing chaps', the crews delivered a devastatingly accurate attack. Smoke covered the town, slowly drifting across the snow and ice-covered countryside. Huge craters in the roads made all routes through St Vith impassable. German sappers, who worked on the St Vith-Malmedy road, stated that it was beyond repair for a distance of two to three miles making vehicular movement impossible. All the squadron aircraft landed safely on return. It was a near thing as the weather took a turn for the worse soon after the last Lancaster landed at 17:11 hours. The groups based in Lincolnshire and Yorkshire were not so lucky, and they were diverted as far as Scotland and Cornwall. The morning of the 27th was again freezing. Overnight frost covered every exposed surface, making it cold to the touch and difficult handle. Despite the conditions Stradishall's Ground Crews fuelled and armed their charges in near-freezing conditions out at the dispersals. An early morning briefing would see fifteen crews briefed for an attack on the Marshalling Yards at Gremberg. This was however, switched to the equally important Marshalling Yards at Rheydt. Joined with, and located south of the city of Mönchengladbach, it was the birthplace of Joseph Goebbels.

Form B.742 – December 27th 1944 (D) :Target : Rheydt : Railway Marshalling Yards : GH609

| | | | | | | | |
|---|---|---|---|---|---|---|---|
| F/O | Field DFC | E.L | | NG148 | XY-B | Follower | Duty Carried Out. |
| F/Lt | Wait | C.J | | NG147 | XY-C | Follower | Duty Carried Out. |
| F/Lt | Tait | R.R | | NG137 | XY-D | Follower | Duty Carried Out. |
| F/O | Cowley | N.C | | NG140 | XY-F | Follower | Duty Carried Out. |
| F/O | Barton | E.R | RAAF | NG149 | XY-G | Follower | Duty Carried Out. |
| F/Lt | Hoskin | F.C | RCAF | NG175 | XY-J | Follower | Duty Carried Out. |
| F/O | Gibson | J.M | | NN720 | XY-K | Follower | Duty Carried Out. |
| F/O | Young | H.S | | HK682 | XY-L | Follower | Duty Carried Out. |
| F/O | James | W.C | RAAF | HK684 | XY-O | Follower | Duty Carried Out. |
| S/Ldr | Bass AFM | R.W | | HK661 | XY-R | Follower | Duty Carried Out. |
| F/O | Green | L.A | | HK606 | XY-V | Follower | Duty Carried Out. |
| F/O | Godfrey | D.F | RAAF | HK688 | XY-W | Follower | Duty Carried Out. |
| F/O | Beck | J.A | RAAF | NG353 | XY-X | Follower | Duty Carried Out. |
| F/Lt | Hanson | R.A | | HK613 | XY-Y | Follower | Duty Carried Out. |
| F/O | Mason | F.H | | PD429 | XY-Z | Follower | Duty Carried Out. |

The crews climbed into a freezing clear blue sky and headed towards Reading, where at 5,000 feet they would form up with No.195 and No.218 Squadrons. Number 31 Base would once again trail behind No.32 and No.33 Bases. The Group despatched a modest total of 91 Lancasters, of which 39 were drawn from No.31 Base and made landfall over France just south of Le Touquet-Paris-Plage. German fighters were reported to be operating in some force over the Ruhr area as the bombers headed into Germany. It was the excellent work of the fighter escort provided on this occasion by the US 9th Airforce that confined the fighters north of the bombers' route, thus giving the force an unmolested run into the target. The Lancasters of No.1 Group would open proceedings followed by No.3 Group. The squadron would be part of the third wave scheduled to bomb between 15:00 hours and 15:03 hours. The spell of good weather continued affording the squadron crews the opportunity of identifying the sprawling Marshalling Yards from over 30 miles prior to bombing. However, it did not prevent some inaccurate Yellow markers from being dropped northeast of the town by Oboe equipped Mosquitos. These wayward markers dropped by the Path Finders attracted some of the earlier waves. It was the timely intervention of the Master Bomber, Squadron Leader Daniel "Danny" Everett DFC of No.35 Squadron who saved the day. Quickly observing the error, he broadcast instructions to the main force to undershoot. He then ordered the aiming point to be remarked. There followed a crescendo of Green and Yellow Markers directly over the aiming point, which attracted most of the participating aircraft. By the time the third and final wave of the attack started, the Marshalling Yards were ablaze. Both 4000lb Cookies and 1000 pounders could be seen exploding, sending up masses of flames and smoke.

The Master Bomber could be heard encouraging the final wave to bomb the Red, Green and Yellow target indicators concentrated over the aiming point. Flying Officer E Field DFC described it as *'Perfect bombing'.* The crew had lost the use of the rear turret a few minutes before the bomb run. Thankfully the fighter escort was out in force. Flight Lieutenant C Wait bombed at 15:00 hours and watched as his 6 x 1000lb + 10 x 500lb MC bombs burst directly across the target. He reported, *'Target should be wiped out.* However, it was not all plain sailing for the crews. 'B' Flight's S/Ldr R Bass AFM was obliged to orbit the target three times before he deposited his all High Explosive load at 15:04 hours. He reported at debriefing, *'Orbited 3 times to avoid other aircraft'.* Flight Lieutenant R Hanson was on his bomb run at 15:03 hours, and with the Target Indicators visible below, the crew's Bomb Aimer F/Sgt S Mullett pressed the 'tit'. To his surprise, nothing happened. The expected jolt as they dropped did not occur. A quick glance into the bomb bay revealed the all HE load had hung up. Undeterred, the crew orbited for a second run, there were still a number of TI's visible as the crew made their second run. They approached the target at 20,000 feet, and once again, the bomb load refused to drop despite a few jinks of the rudder. Most crews would have given up, however, not F/Lt Hanson. Orbiting again, the crew started on a third bomb run, the last few TI's were still burning on the now smoke covered Marshalling Yards. Lining up on the markers, F/Sgt S Mullett pressed the 'tit', and to the crew's dismay, nothing. By now, the frustrated crew realised that a fourth orbit was pushing their luck, so they turned Lancaster HK613 XY-Y for home. They eventually jettisoned the stubborn bombs into the sea without a problem. The crew reported to the Intelligence Officer rather casually, *'It was probably icing'.* At de-briefing four crews reported three or four vertical contrails, the ominous signs of V2 Rocket activity.

That night a Party was held in the Sergeant's Mess, the ORB records, *'Dancing and liquid refreshments! This was hailed as a great success!'* Given the past 72 hours of frantic activity the squadron needed to unwind. With the German railway system at breaking point, Bomber Command continued to pile on the pressure. There were a number of bottlenecks crucial in the transportation and movement of German resources to and from the front. None was more important than the Cologne-Gremburg Marshalling Yards. Situated on the eastern side of Cologne across the River Rhine, the marshalling yards were pivotal for the whole region. A major daylight operation was planned for the afternoon of the 28th. The raid would see No.3 Group's largest effort so far during the month with 170 crews detailed. The armada would form up into the predetermined waves over Brentwood, Essex at 5,000 feet. The squadron along with No.195 and No.218 (Gold Coast) would attack in the second wave.

Form B.743 – December 28th 1944 (D) :Target : Gremburg : Railway Marshalling Yards : GH624

| | | | | | | | |
|---|---|---|---|---|---|---|---|
| Sgt | Saunders | A | | NG174 | XY-A | Follower | Duty Carried Out. |
| F/Sgt | Green | T.B | | NG147 | XY-C | Follower | Duty Carried Out. |
| F/Lt | Tait | R.R | | NG137 | XY-D | Follower | Duty Carried Out. |
| F/O | Templeton | G.M | RCAF | NG146 | XY-E | Follower | Duty Carried Out. |
| F/O | Cowley | N.C | | NG140 | XY-F | Follower | Duty Carried Out. |
| F/Lt | Hunt | E.G | | NG149 | XY-G | Follower | Duty Carried Out. |
| F/Lt | Hoskin | F.C | RCAF | NG175 | XY-J | Follower | Duty Carried Out. |
| W/Cdr | Giles DFC | J.H | | NN720 | XY-K | Follower | Duty Carried Out. |
| F/O | Young | H.S | | HK682 | XY-L | Follower | Duty Carried Out. |
| F/O | Clarson | A.J | RAAF | NG354 | XY-M | Follower | Duty Carried Out. |
| F/Lt | Orman DFC | K.G | RNZAF | HK659 | XY-Q | Follower | Duty Carried Out. |
| S/Ldr | Bass AFM | R.W | | HK661 | XY-R | Follower | Duty Carried Out. |
| F/O | Idle | L.A | RNZAF | HK650 | XY-T | Follower | Duty Carried Out. |
| F/O | Green | L.A | | HK606 | XY-V | Follower | Duty Carried Out. |

| | | | | | | | |
|---|---|---|---|---|---|---|---|
| F/Lt | Madden | R.P | RCAF | HK688 | XY-W | Follower | Duty Carried Out. |
| F/Lt | Ritson | E.W. | | NG353 | XY-X | Follower | Duty Carried Out. |
| F/O | Gogler | R.J | RAAF | HK613 | XY-Y | Follower | Duty Carried Out. |
| F/O | Liddle | J.B | | PD429 | XY-Z | Follower | Duty Carried Out. |

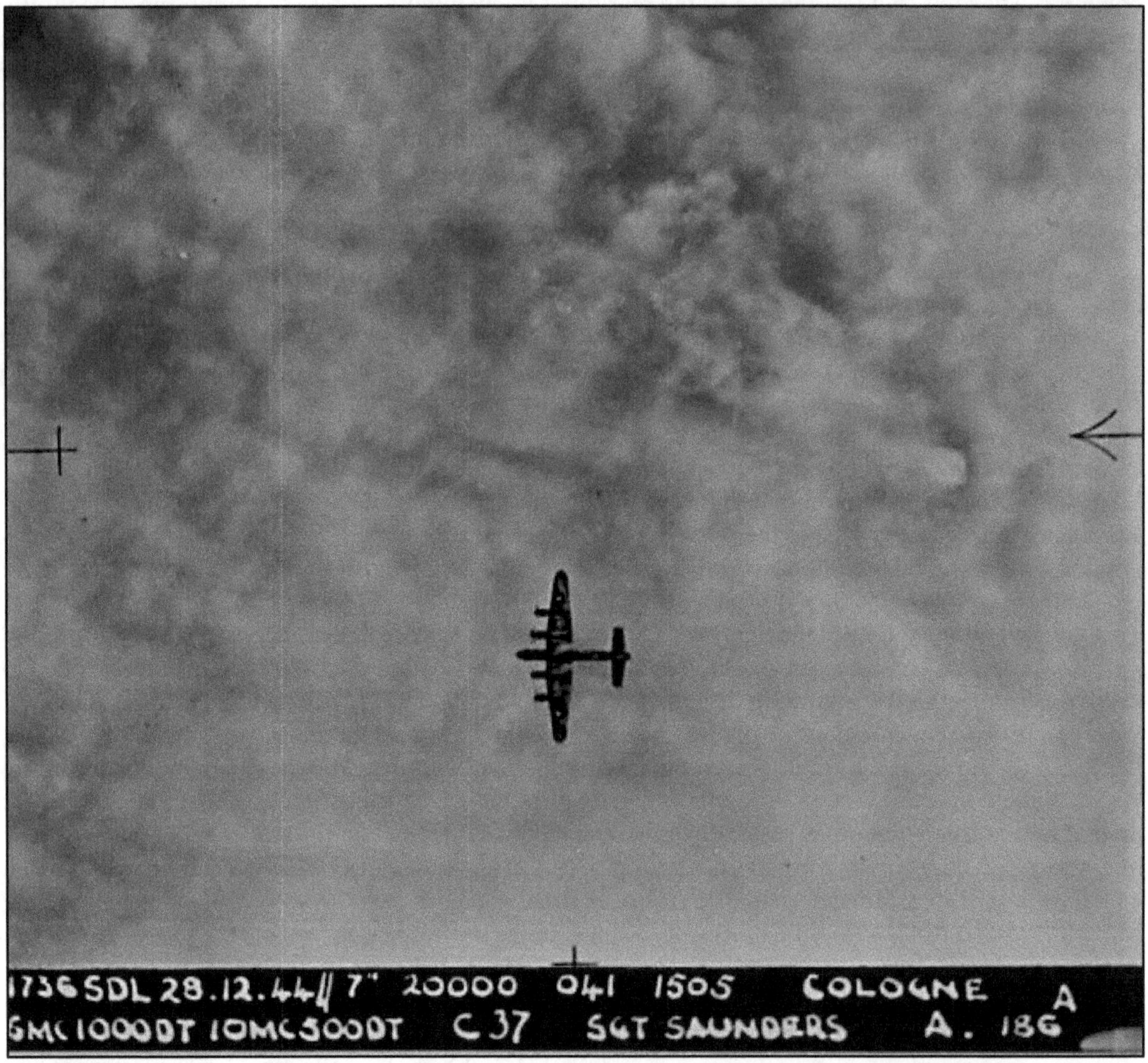


Cologne, December 29th 1944. In this Target Photograph, the crew of Sergeant Saunders captures a Lancaster flying well below them. In instances like this, numerous crews were hit by 'friendly' bombs with tragic results.

The squadron put up a creditable 18 Lancasters, its largest contribution since forming. At the controls of two Lancasters were W/Cdr J Giles DFC and 'B' Flights, S/Ldr R Bass AFM. As usual, the squadron would be employed in the increasingly unpopular follower role. Number 31 Base formation was reported as compact as the squadrons in their vic formations commenced the run into the target, encountering predicted heavy flak. Smoke was already rising through the 10/10th cloud as the Sky Markers and bomb loads started to fall. Wing Commander J Giles DFC was at 20,000 feet at the control of Lancaster NN720 XY-K. The crew dropped on their G-H Leader at 15:06 hours, remarking, *'bombed at same time as a group of aircraft bombed about 400 yards to port, bombs concentrated on flares'.* Squadron Leader R Bass AFM was also at 20,000 feet aboard Lancaster HK661 XY-R, he remarked at de-briefing, *'A mushroom of grey smoke from an explosion, came through the cloud'.*

The squadron dropped a total of 198,000lbs of High Explosive bombs on Gremburg without suffering a single flak hole. It had been a marvellous effort by all concerned. However, the squadron was confident it could do better. Despite the arrival of a handful of G-H sets in mid-December, the squadron still found itself totally reliant on other squadrons for marking and bombing. Number 31 Base's No. 218 was fully equipped, and RAF Wratting Commons No.195 Squadron had been equipped with six sets which had been fitted to the squadron's Lancasters. Number 195 Squadron was deemed ready to start independent marking and bombing. Unfortunately, No.186 had still not been given that opportunity, pressure was once again put on No.3 Group HQ to try and remedy this.

Wing Commander J.H Giles DFC (1st Left) is photographed at No.3 Group's HQ with the AoC, Air Vice Marshal R Harrison CB CBE DFC AFC (Centre). Standing in between is Wing Commander W.J Burnett, Commanding Officer, No.138 Squadron. Standing beside the AoC is No.3 Group's Senior Air Staff Officer, Air Commodore H Kirkpatrick DFC. Also visible is a Royal Navy Liason Officer, Lieutenant Dallas-Smith. Note the horseshoe pinned to the wall map over the Ruhr area.

The Marshalling Yards at Koblenz were the intended target on the 29th, all of the squadron Lancasters were fuelled and bombed up when just after breakfast the squadron was informed it would not be required. Flight Lieutenant F Hoskin RCAF assumed the duties of 'A' Flight Commander with S/Ldr P Reynold's departure for 10 days leave. Francis Hoskin was born in Alberta, Canada but had lived all of his formative years in America. At the age of 19 he returned to Canada and joined the Royal Canadian Air Force. A well-earned day off for the crews followed on the 30th. Apart from an early morning frost, the day was bright and relatively warm, causing the frost and ice to quickly melt. The Ground crews especially would have appreciated a break from the freezing temperatures out at the dispersals and the various maintenance hangars. The last operation for the month was directed yet again against a marshalling yard. This time the target was Vohwinkel. This ultra-modern 2 1/2-mile-long marshalling yard was built west of the main railway station. Fourteen crews were detailed and briefed. The first crew away from RAF Stradishall was 'A' Flight's F/O A Clarson RAAF at 11:30 hours in NG354 XY-M. Number 3 Group despatched a total of 155 Lancasters drawn from all three base groups with No.31

Base providing 53 crews. Bad weather over England and the North Sea initially caused some confusion, but by the time the Group crossed the continent over Boulogne, it had managed to organise itself. Over Boulogne, the Lancasters picked up its escort of eight squadrons of RAF Mustangs and nine squadrons of Spitfires. Weather conditions over Europe were as briefed back at RAF Stradishall, 10/10 cloud the entire route. What was not briefed, however, was the stronger than expected winds, reported to be over 130 mph. This made formation keeping difficult, especially for the followers. As a result, the bomber stream began to lose any coherence and became increasingly splintered.

Form B.746 – December 31st 1944 (D) :Target : Vohwinkel : Railway Marshalling Yards : GH559

| | | | | | | | |
|---|---|---|---|---|---|---|---|
| F/O | Gibson | J.H | | NG148 | XY-B | Follower | Duty Carried Out. |
| F/O | Templeton | G.M | RCAF | NG146 | XY-E | Follower | Duty Carried Out. |
| F/O | Cowley | N.C | | NG140 | XY-F | Follower | Duty Carried Out. |
| F/O | Barton | E.R | RAAF | NG149 | XY-G | Follower | Duty Carried Out. |
| F/Lt | Hoskin | F.C | RCAF | NG175 | XY-J | Follower | Duty Carried Out. |
| F/O | Tonks | J.E | | HK682 | XY-L | Follower | Duty Carried Out. |
| F/O | Clarson | A.J | RAAF | NG354 | XY-M | Follower | Duty Carried Out. |
| F/O | James | J.W | RAAF | HK684 | XY-O | Follower | Duty Carried Out. |
| F/Lt | Madden | R.P | RCAF | HK662 | XY-P | Follower | Duty Carried Out. |
| F/O | Beck | J.A | RAAF | HK650 | XY-T | Follower | Duty Carried Out. |
| F/O | Godfrey | D.F | RAAF | HK606 | XY-V | Follower | Duty Carried Out. |
| F/Lt | Powell DFC | A.C | | HK688 | XY-W | Follower | Duty Carried Out. |
| F/Lt | Ritson | E.E | | NG353 | XY-X | Follower | Duty Carried Out. |
| F/O | Idle | L.A | RNZAF | PD429 | XY-Z | Follower | Duty Carried Out. |

Lancasters jockeyed for position and were altering course constantly in an attempt to keep formation and their allotted G-H Leader insight. The formation met considerable predicted flak from Krefeld and north of Dusseldorf, which continued on the run into the target. The stronger than forecast winds coupled with the intense flak seemed to have unsettled the whole force. Forty-seven Lancasters of No.33 Base opened proceedings at 14:30 hours. Flak was described as accurate and heavy as the second wave of No.31 Base started their bomb runs at 14:31 hours. A number of sky markers were seen 4-5 miles starboard of the aiming point, probably the result of the strong winds. As the squadron crews neared the marshalling yards, which stood out clearly against the white snow-covered countryside, it soon became apparent that the first wave had undershot the aiming point by a wide margin. The main weight of bombs had fallen south-west of the intended target, with a few isolated explosions on the branch line. One squadron Lancaster was hit by flak on the run into target. Flying Officer G Templeton RCAF Lancaster, NG146 XY-E was hit in the port mainplane, outboard of No.3 fuel tank by flak splinters. Thankfully it was the only damage. Most of the squadron managed to keep with their allotted G-H Leaders. Flight Lieutenant F Hoskin RCAF, *'Mainstream of bombers southwest of target, group behind bombing appeared scattered'*. Flying Officer J Beck RAAF delivered his all high explosive load at 14:42 hours, later remarking, *'Bombing did not look good, some aircraft bombing before leaders'*. The crew of Australian F/O D Godfrey RAAF were critical of an unrecorded G-H Leader, *'Leader had a BIG overshoot, so all the followers were the same, Marshalling Yards were not hit!'*. Light snow was falling when the squadron began landing back at RAF Stradishall, it had been a frustrating operation for the squadron crews. The bombing at Vohwinkel was scattered, and No.3 Group HQ conceded that the month's operations ended on a failure. Apart from the failure to destroy the marshalling yards, Group HQ was disappointed and concerned with the crew flying discipline, especially by the lead base group. After leaving the target, the bombers splintered into small groups of aircraft. The operation did little to appease the frustration felt by the squadron having to rely on the marking skill and flying discipline of others. However, there were some encouraging signs of change!

December had been a challenging month. Adverse weather had created numerous problems. Mist and fog had played havoc with planning, resulting in the last minute cancellation of operations and changes of targets. Despite this, No.186 Squadron had flown 202 sorties, dropping in the process 817,47 tons of bombs on German targets. More agreeable was no crews had been lost. Granted, Lancaster HK680 XY-H was missing, but six of its crew were safe. On the last day of the month, three crews were over Rushford Bombing Range, not as expected dropping bombs, but encouragingly flares![17]

Destine for the front, German Tiger tanks are seen here being transported by rail. The German railway system was modern, efficient, and complex in a typical Germanic fashion. As a result, vast quantities of military and civilian material were transported throughout Germany and the occupied territories. Vulnerable to bombing, the Nazis would continually employ slave workers to repair and replace the damaged tracks. The railway system was the very life-blood of Germany. Why it took so long for Bomber Command HQ to realise this is unknown, the US 8th Air Force was fully aware from 1943 onwards.

[17] *The 3 Group Records Book and No.186 Squadron records conflict on the date the squadron received its first GH sets.*

# January 1945

## A New Year and a New Start.

January 1945 started with the best possible news with the arrival of No.3 Group Letter 3G/S.8271/Radar advising the squadron to commence fitting six 'Special Radar Navigational Aids' immediately to its Lancasters. The letter explained that arrangements had been made for sufficient equipment from No.3 Groups Radar Pool to be made available and delivered directly to RAF Stradishall for this purpose. Accordingly, from this date, 186 Squadron would refer to G-H as '*Radar Navigational Aid*' [18]. With the imminent fitting of the G-H sets, orders were also received instructing the squadron to select three experienced crews, consisting of pilot / navigator combination for immediate training. They would be sent to No.3 LFS, RAF Feltwell, to commence training on the intricacies of this temperamental device. Once the first three were trained, they would be followed every two days by two more selected crews, up until12 had received training. Sadly the identity of the first crews to be selected is unknown. To organise the squadron's training, F/O Kenneth Ells arrived from Group HQ.

With the gradual introduction of G-H into the Group in the latter part of 1944, No.3 Group HQ had formed in November 1944 a small G-H Training Flight which worked alongside No.3 Lancaster Finishing School. Before this, crews were trained by experienced tour expired G-H operators. Crews under training would either have to visit a G-H equipped squadron, or the G-H instructors would visit the pupils if sets were available. It was not an ideal set-up, and the creation of the G-H Training Flight went a long way to improve both the standard and speed of training. G-H set training required a minimum of 5 hours of tuition.

While normality rained at RAF Stradishall, things were vastly different on the continent. The German December offensive in the Ardennes had been checked, and the Allies were once again the masters of the air above the battlefield. The initial panic had turned into a determination to retake lost ground and push towards the German frontier. So it came as a rather unpleasant shock that the Germans launched two new operations on the morning of January 1st. At 09:15hrs the Luftwaffe launched Unternehmen Bodenplatte (*Operation Baseplate*), a major campaign against Allied airfields in the Low Countries. Hundreds of planes attacked Allied airfields, taking them completely off-guard, destroying or severely damaging some four-hundred plus aircraft. On the ground, the Americans were once again taken entirely by surprise when the German Army Group G (*Heeresgruppe G*) and Army Group Upper Rhine (*Heeresgruppe Oberrhein*) launched a major offensive against the thinly-stretched 80-mile line of the U.S 7th Army. This offensive, known as Unternehmen Nordwind (*Operation North Wind*), was the last major German offensive on the Western Front. Alarm and disbelief once again swept the Allied command. The news of yet another major offensive by the Germans started to filter through to RAF Stradishall around mid-afternoon. The crews could only listen in disbelief of the destruction being meted out to the Allied bases. Until the pre-Christmas offensive, the British press had almost written off German resistance. A late afternoon briefing would see 14 crews on the Battle Order.

Form B.747 – January 1st, 1945 : (N) Target Vohwinkel : Marshalling Yards – G-H559

| | | | | | | | |
|---|---|---|---|---|---|---|---|
| F/Sgt | Saunders | A | | NG148 | XY-B | Main force | Duty Carried Out. |
| F/Lt | Tait | R.R | | NG137 | XY-D | Main force | Duty Carried Out. |
| F/Sgt | Green | T.B | | LM188 | XY-S | Main force | Duty Carried Out. |
| F/O | Barton | E.R | RAAF | NG149 | XY-G | Main force | Duty Carried Out. |
| F/Lt | Hoskin | F.C.G | RCAF | NG175 | XY-J | Main force | Duty Carried Out. |

[18] *I will continue using G-H.*

| | | | | | | | |
|---|---|---|---|---|---|---|---|
| W/Cdr | Giles DFC | J.H | | NN720 | XY-K | Main force | Duty Carried Out. |
| F/O | Young | H.S | | HK682 | XY-L | Main force | Duty Carried Out. |
| W/O | O'Brien | J.D | RAAF | HK684 | XY-O | Main force | Duty Carried Out. |
| F/Lt | Orman DFC | K.G | RNZAF | HK659 | XY-Q | Main force | Duty Carried Out. |
| S/Ldr | Bass AFM | R.W | | HK661 | XY-R | Main force | Duty Carried Out. |
| F/O | Gogler | R | RAAF | NG293 | XY-U | Main force | Duty Carried Out. |
| F/O | Green | L.A | | HK606 | XY-V | Main force | Duty Carried Out. |
| F/Lt | Powell DFC | A.C | | HK688 | XY-W | Main force | Duty Carried Out. |
| F/Lt | Hanson | R.A.J | | HK613 | XY-Y | Main force | Duty Carried Out. |

The target was again the Marshalling Yards at Vohwinkel. Obviously disappointed by the previous day's attack, Group HQ was keen to make amends. In abysmal visibility, the squadron aircraft began to take off just before 16:00 hours. The bomb aimer aboard S/Ldr Bass's Lancaster was F/O E.J Pope a former London Bobby. Edward John Pope wore on his left breast the crimson and blue striped ribbon of the George Medal, a rarity on the squadron. The award was in recognition of his actions during a bombing raid on London in April 1941. The joint citation reads.

***G.M.** London Gazette 27 June 1941: Sidney Cyril Coomber, Police Constable, Criminal Investigation Department, "D" Division, Metropolitan Police (in a joint citation with W. A. Bailey, Captain, Church Army, Paddington; Police Constable R. G. Grose, "D" Division, Metropolitan Police, and Police Constable E. J. Pope, "D" Division, Metropolitan Police.)*

*'As a result of enemy action buildings were damaged. Detective Constable Coomber and Police Constable Grose entered one house and found several men lying severely injured and one man trapped. They removed all of them to safety and then climbed to the second floor where they were joined by Captain Bailey. Search was made for two men known to be trapped on the premises. After removing a quantity of debris, one man was released and lowered to the ground. The rescuers then climbed to the third floor and eventually located the other man who had apparently fallen through-to the floor below. Coomber, assisted by Bailey, tunnelled under the wreckage while Grose removed rubble passed out to him. In spite of the fact that debris was continually falling around them, and a large slab of stonework was hanging overhead in a dangerous position, they succeeded in releasing the casualty. **Police Constable Pope**, who was on duty nearby, was thrown to the ground by the force of the explosion. He recovered and, after attending to two severely injured victims and helping seven people to safety, he scrambled up to the second floor of a building where a woman was trapped. He made an opening in the wreckage and, by supporting himself with his right hand, gradually lowered himself. After removing debris with his left hand, he was able to extricate the woman, who climbed over his back and was hauled to safety. The rescues were performed while an air attack was still in progress. Huge pieces of masonry and timber were poised in perilous positions, and the danger was further increased by escaping gas and water.'*

On reaching the rendezvous point above Reading, they headed south, crossing the French coast south of Abbeville at 5000 feet. Flying over the Liberated town of Liege, W/J O'Brien RAAF had the misfortune of being hit by American flak. The damage to Lancaster HK684 XY-O was not extensive but did little to promote happy relations with the trigger happy ground troops below. Conditions en route and over the target area were surprisingly clear. The 50 Lancasters supplied by No.31 Base would be divided throughout the raid scheduled to commence at 19:30 hours. A new method of attack was tried on this night which was an all No.3 Group effort. The marshalling yards would have two aiming points marked with G-H Ground Markers. One aiming point would be marked in Red while the other, Green.

On approaching the target at 20,000 feet, the crews could easily pick out the sprawling Marshalling Yards in the light of numerous accurately-placed markers. The planned start time was delayed by five minutes due to stronger forecast headwinds. Flak was moderate over the target area but not troublesome. More worrying was the tell-tale signs of German night fighter activity. No marking was undertaken by No.186 Squadron, whose crews were relegated once again to the purely bombing role. The sky above Vohwinkel was a cauldron of TIs, bursting flak, searchlights and menacing fighter flares. One of the first crews over the target at 19:38 hours was W/Cdr J Giles DFC. He bombed in the centre of three groups of red target indicators and watched as one stick straddled the target. At the controls of Lancaster HK606 XY-V was F/O L Green, who reported, *'Attack well concentrated and target seemed well ablaze. Smoke was seen rising to 5000ft, and at 19:57 hours, two violent explosions were seen, both orange in colour'*. Equally impressed was F/Lt A Powell DFC. He was at the control of HK688 XY-W and reported on return, *'Green TI's were seen cascading but had burnt out before arrival in target area. Bombed on yellow steady fire beside Marshalling Yard. Bombing well concentrated'*. German fighters were active over the target area. One crew was engaged. Flying Officer Rex Gogler RAAF was on his bomb run at 19:43 hours when an FW190 was observed. The following combat report records the events.

> Enemy fighter was first sighted going into the target area, rear gunner ordered corkscrew port. Enemy aircraft lost. Second attack on the bombing run, bomb doors open. Fighter came in from port quarter. Rear gunner immediately ordered corkscrew port, the range being approx 200 yards. Both gunners and fighter opened fire simultaneously, the enemy aircraft firing a short burst that went high over to starboard of bomber. The gunners claim hits on the fighters nose and fuselage. The enemy aircraft dived away to port and was not seen again. Brilliant fighter flares restricted the vision of both gunners.

The lousy weather encountered at take-off had quickly worsened on the squadron's departure. The tired crews now found the whole of East Anglia covered in fog. As a result, the entire squadron was diverted north, ten crews landed at No.4 Group's RAF Linton-on-Ouse, while individual crews managed to find refuge at RAF Holme-on Spalding Moor, RAF East More, RAF Marston Moor and RAF Beighton. The diversion meant that an end of tour celebration in the Messes for the crew of F/Lt Francis Hoskin RCAF was put on hold. The crew who began their tour with No.90 Squadron in September had just returned from their 32nd operation, 23 of which were flown with No.186.

No.186 Squadron Reported Flak Damage 01/01/1945

| Serial | Code | Damage Reported | Repairs / Notes |
|---|---|---|---|
| HK684 | **XY-O** | Wing, and fuselage. | Repaired On Squadron. |

Number 31 Base's Commanding Officer, Air Commodore J Silvester CBE proceeded on nine day's leave on the 2nd, and he was replaced by Group Captain E.C Bates AFC. With improved weather, the diverted crews began arriving back at RAF Stradishall in dribs and drabs. The end of tour celebrations had to be put on hold for one 'B' Flight crew. Flight Lieutenant Robert 'Sandy' Powell DFC and crew had just returned from their 30th and last operation. Born in Rawalpindi, India in 1915, Robert was older than most on the squadron. Their tour started in August 1944 with No.90 Squadron. The diversion meant that only five crews would be available for a long distance attack on the city of Nuremburg.

Form B.748 – January 2/3rd 1945 (N) : Target Nuremberg - 'Greyling'

| | | | | | | | |
|---|---|---|---|---|---|---|---|
| F/O | Templeton | G.M | RCAF | NG174 | XY-A | Follower | Duty Carried Out. |
| F/O | Gibson | J.H.W | | NG354 | XY-M | Follower | Duty Carried Out. |

| | | | | | | | |
|---|---|---|---|---|---|---|---|
| F/Lt | Madden | R.P | RCAF | HK662 | XY-P | Follower | Duty Carried Out. |
| F/O | James RAAF | W | RAAF | PD429 | XY-Z | Follower | Duty Carried Out. |
| F/Lt | Ritson | E.E | | NG353 | XY-X | Follower | Duty Carried Out. |

With numerous crews still diverted or late returning to their parent station, No. 3 Group's contribution was just 95 Lancasters. The Lincolnshire based No.1 Group would contribute a hefty 286 aircraft while the Canadian's of No.6 Group RCAF would provide an additional 54 Lancasters. Marking would be provided by the Path Finders who, given the excellent conditions over this beautiful medieval city, produced some accurate marking. The squadron's five crews were over the target between 19:29 and 19:33 hours. Each was astonished at the intensity of the bombing. Flying Officer Templeton RCAF, *'Bombing well concentrated on markers and the whole town seemed ablaze. Fire visible 200 miles away.* Fellow Canadian, F/Lt R.P Madden RCAF was at 18,000 feet when he dropped his mixed HE and incendiary load at 19:33 hours. He reported, *'Fires were well alight, and the glow was visible over 100 miles on homeward journey.* The raid was an outstanding success. Substantial damage was inflicted, especially to the beautiful old city. Bomber Command HQ claimed that seven important factories were destroyed or badly damaged, including the MANN Diesel Werks and Siemens AG. Also badly hit was the city's main train station and municipal gas works. To the south of the city, the important Nuremberg Marshalling Yards and adjoining workshops took heavy punishment, and 200-300 rolling stock were reported damaged or destroyed.

A photograph that clearly shows the severe conditions the squadron operated in during the winter of 1944/45. Flying Officer J.H. Gibson scrapes off the frost from his cockpit windscreen on a freezing January morning at RAF Stradishall. This is Lancaster NN720 XY-K *'Kautious Kate'.* Note the 17 bomb symbals. This Austin Motors built Lancaster Mk.I had a long career finally being scrapped in 1949.

The crews were awakened early on the 3rd, a daylight attack on the Castrop Rauxel Tar Plant was planned for late morning. The plant which used the Bergius process to produce synthetic oil had miraculously escaped severe damage despite the best intentions of Bomber Command.

Form B.747 – January 3rd, 1945 : (D) Target - Castrop Rauxel : Distillation Plants - 'GQ1531'

| | | | | | | |
|---|---|---|---|---|---|---|
| F/Sgt | Saunders | A | | NG148 | XY-A | Duty Carried Out |
| F/Lt | Tait | R.R | | NG147 | XY-D | Duty Carried Out |
| F/Sgt | Green | T.B | | NG146 | XY-E | Duty Carried Out |
| F/O | Clarson | A.J | RAAF | NN720 | XY-N | Duty Carried Out |
| F/O | Young | N.S | | HK682 | XY-L | Duty Carried Out |
| F/O | Orman DFC | K.G | RNZAF | HK659 | XY-Q | Duty Carried Out |
| F/O | Godfrey | D.F.J | RAAF | HK661 | XY-R | Duty Carried Out |
| F/O | Idle | L.A | RNZAF | LM188 | XY-S | Duty Carried Out |
| F/O | Gogler | R.J | RAAF | NG293 | XY-U | Duty Carried Out |
| F/O | Green | L.A | | HK606 | XY-V | Duty Carried Out |
| F/O | Beck | J.A.G | RAAF | HK688 | XY-W | Duty Carried Out |
| F/Lt | Hanson | R.A.J | | HK613 | XY-Y | Duty Carried Out |

All twelve crews had safely departed by 10:07 hours and, once airborne, headed for No.31 Base rendezvous point over Tonbridge, Kent, where they would form up. The 46 Lancasters provided by No.31 Base would be responsible for attacking Castrop Rauxel. Disappointingly the squadron would once again have to play a secondary role. Number 218 (Gold Coast) Squadron and four crews from RAF Methwolds No.149 Squadron would provide the G-H Leaders. Once assembled, No.31 Base headed directly towards Boulogne. Once crossed, they picked up their Spitfire and Mustang escort. A solid cloud cover prevented the crews from identifying any ground details en route. However, the Lancasters were bathed in brilliant sunshine from a crystal-clear blue sky. The sunshine must have encouraged the crews.

The 46 Lancasters and their G-H Leaders flew towards Germany in a tight and compact gaggle. The G-H Leaders, identified by their two horizontal yellow bars on the rudder, were followed closely by No.186 and No.195 Squadrons flying in the now-familiar vics of three or five. The first red sky markers started to fall at 12:58 hours. Moderate-heavy flak greeted the crews, and almost immediately, two Lancasters were hit. Lancaster NN720 XY-K flown by F/O A.J Clarson RAAF sustained damage to the starboard fuselage, fuel tank and tail. While fellow Aussie F/O D.F Godfrey had a small piece of flak pierce the windscreen of HK661 XY-R. Neither crew sustained any injury. The bombing was once again concentrated, F/Lt R.R Tait reported at de-briefing, *'Concentration of Red TI's seen over target. Bombing seemed very good. Fighter escort excellent'*. On leaving the target, columns of black smoke had started to emerge through the clouds.

No.186 Squadron Reported Flak Damage 03/01/1945

| Serial | Code | Damage Reported | Repairs / Notes |
|---|---|---|---|
| NN720 | **XY-K** | Wing, fuel tank and fuselage. | Repaired On Squadron. |
| HK661 | **XY-R** | Windscreen. | Repaired On Squadron |

On return from Castrop Rauxel, the squadron was warned to prepare for an early morning raid on the Marshalling Yards at Ludwigshafen the following morning. However, overnight snow kept the squadron grounded on the 4th, the arrival of snow meant a night in the Mess. It was, however, just a 24-hour reprieve. Australian rear gunner Gerald McPherson was admitted to the Base Hospital at this

A studio portrait of another of Australia's finest. Alexander Jeffery Clarson strikes a matinee pose. He was another gifted and courageous pilot, which No.186 Squadron seemed to possess in abundance. Alexander, or Jeff would have a few close encounters with the Grim Reaper over his long tour.

time. Gerald recalls what happened and gives a splendid example of W/Cdr Giles DFC no-nonsense style of command and why the crews admiration of this Canadian was so high.

A fresh-faced Jim Mallinson RAAF photographed while still training. He occupied the Mid Upper turret in the crew of A.J Clarson RAAF.

*'Our crew was briefed about 7 p.m. for a daylight raid on Vohwinkel. Due to weather conditions, the take-off time was put back a couple of times and eventually if was announced about 9.30 a.m. that the operation was cancelled, and that crews may now return to their barracks. During this period of delay, all crews had been sitting in warm rooms awaiting developments. When we were released from duty, I felt ill and didn't have the strength to stand up and walk. Our Engineer, Jock, realised I was in trouble and virtually carried me to the base hospital about 300 yards away. He then requested a Corporal to arrange for me to see a doctor. The reply was that sick parade was completed at 9 a.m. Although it was pointed out to the Corporal that I couldn't attend sick parade because all airmen on the intended raid had been held in special rooms until the raid was aborted well after 9 am, he refused to change his initial reply. Jock then helped me back to our barracks about 400 yards away and put me to bed, and covered me with blankets, as he was then well aware that I had a high temperature. That afternoon, our crew was placed on the battle order for an operation that night. Jock then telephoned our pilot in the Officers' quarters to inform him that |I was too ill to fly that night and told him what had transpired at sick quarters that morning. When our pilot informed our Wing Commander of the above facts, I believe that he jumped in his car, raced down to sick quarters, lined up all staff (including doctors) and informed them that if any of his airmen required medical attention at any time, they were to be attended to immediately. He then ordered that a medical officer and ambulance go to my barracks and attend to me promptly. When they arrived, I had a temperature of 104 degrees and I was immediately transferred to the base hospital. I was suffering from tonsillitis and | spent the next week in hospital. I should mention here that Wing Commander Giles, who was a Canadian, was a favourite of all the crews.*

*He was most protective of his personnel and did everything possible to make their time on the Squadron as comfortable as possible. He often took crews on their first operation, and that included ours, as has already been mentioned earlier in this story'.*

The light snow continued throughout the day and into the early hours. A bare-metal B17 Fortress of the 332nd Bomber Squadron, 94th Bomb Group, flown by Captain Robert Voss, made an emergency landing while of an air-test. The freezing conditions prevalent over the region meant while descending in cloud, the plexiglass in the cockpit and nose completely iced over, making forward visibility impossible. However, showing considerable calm and skill, the pilot with his head out of the window and taking the full icy blast of the freezing wind, landed ' The Dorothy Vee' without trouble, although he may have overrun into soft ground.

Freezing visitor. Boeing B17G Flying Fortress *'The Dorothy Vee'* of the 94th Bomb Group based at Bury St Edmunds. Up on an early morning Air-Test the pilot, Col Robert 'Bob' Voss encountered severe icing. Due to the limited visibility, the B17 ended up off the main runway suffering slight damage (Cat E-1).

On the morning of the 5th, RAF Stradishall was blanketed in snow. It was an early start for the Ground Crews, the snow and ice making conditions even more demanding as they fuelled and bombed up 14 Lancasters out at the dispersals in near sub-zero temperatures. The squadron welcomed back S/Ldr Percy Reynolds on the 5th fresh from some well-earned leave, he immediately resumed the 'A' Flight Commander role.

Form B.751 – January 5th, 1945 (D) : Target – Ludwigshafen Marshalling Yards - 'G-H616'

| | | | | | | |
|---|---|---|---|---|---|---|
| F/O | Field DFC | E.L | | NG148 | XY-B | Duty Carried Out |
| W/Cdr | Giles DFC | J.H | | NG137 | XY-D | Duty Carried Out |
| F/Sgt | Saunders | A | | NG140 | XY-F | Duty Carried Out |
| F/O | Barton | E.R | RCAF | NG149 | XY-G | Duty Carried Out |
| F/Sgt | Green | T.B | | NG354 | XY-M | Duty Carried Out |
| F/O | Young | H.S | | HK682 | XY-L | Duty Carried Out |

| | | | | | | |
|---|---|---|---|---|---|---|
| F/Lt | Madden | R.P | RCAF | HK662 | XY-P | Duty Carried Out |
| F/O | Mason | F.H | | HK661 | XY-R | Duty Carried Out |
| F/O | Green | L.A | | NG293 | XY-U | Duty Carried Out |
| F/O | Beck | J.A.G | RAAF | HK688 | XY-W | Duty Carried Out |
| W/O | O'Brien | J.D | RAAF | HK684 | XY-O | Duty Carried Out |
| F/Lt | Orman DFC | K.G | RNZAF | HK659 | XY-Q | Duty Carried Out |
| F/Lt | Ritson | E.E | | NG353 | XY-X | Duty Carried Out |
| F/O | James | W.C | RAAF | PD429 | XY-Z | Duty Carried Out |

Wing Commander J Giles DFC conducted the early morning briefing. It was delivered in his usual no-nonsense manner. He, in turn, was followed by his various section leaders. The final word went to the stand in Base Commander, Group Captain E.C Bates AFC, who reiterated the need for a concentrated formation and flying discipline. Number 3 Group would be out in force, 160 Lancasters would be deployed. Number 31Base providing 46 crews with 8 G-H Leaders, No.32 Base would supply 40 Lancasters and 13 G-H crews, while No.33 Base would produce 56 aircraft backed up by 12 G-H crews. The still independent No.149 Squadron based at Methwold fielded 18 Lancasters, 11 tasked with G-H duties. The G-H role was still frustratingly eluding 186 Squadron.

Unsurprisingly, one of the first crews away was W/Cdr Giles DFC at the controls of Lancaster NG137 XY-D at 10:53 hours. He had borrowed the crew of 'A' Flight's F/Lt C Waits, who sat the operation out and had the unenviable job of waiting for their safe return. Once airborne, the whole force formed up over the market town of Wellingborough before heading towards the French coastal town of Cayeux-sur-Mer. Number 31 Base's squadrons would make up the second wave. Opening the raid and leading the group would be No.33 Base. The whole force flew over the Somme then onto Metz, where it picked up its RAF fighter escort. Unfortunately, soon after crossing the German border, a serious navigational error by the lead crew of No.33 Base meant the entire force overshot the last turning point by nearly ten miles. This was quickly picked up by the proceeding base groups, but the damage had been done.

This error brought the force over a number of heavily defended areas in clear weather. Heavy flak was encountered from both Worms and Mannheim, which did all they could to split up the formation employing intense predicted flak. These were then joined by the flak units at Ludwigshafen. This error in navigation meant that over 80 bombers, half the force reported flak damage during this phase of the attack. Five were from No.186 Squadron. One of the first hit was F/O E Field DFC. Just before bombing, Lancaster NG148 XY-B took the full force of an exploding anti-aircraft shell. In the nose hunched over his bombsight was Australian Bomb Aimer, P/O Wallace Williams RAAF. Fragments of flak burst through the perspex nose, striking the young Aussie knocking him backwards. The aircraft's intercom was damaged, making communication between the crew difficult. The Lancaster's port inner engine was seriously hit, and not wanting to risk a fire, quickly feathered. Also hit was the port outer engine, but this continued giving full revs and giving no sign of trouble. The 29-year-old P/O Williams had been hit by shrapnel in the right arm, but he somehow managed to drop the 1 x 4000lb + 12 x 500lb HE on the G-H dropped flares despite his injury. On clearing the target and without warning, the port outer engine suddenly burst into flames. This, too, was quickly feathered. With only the two starboard engines functioning, and the trimming system iced-up, F/O Field DFC required the help of both the injured Bomb Aimer and the Flight Engineer, Sgt William Enright, to help take the strain on the rudder pedal. It was obvious that the Lancaster would not make RAF Stradishall, so the crew headed towards Belgium. Showing considerable piloting skill and a big dollop of nerve F/O Field brought the Lancaster into land at 16:35 hours on just two engines. They had landed at A-62 Rheims/Champagne airfield, the home of the C-47 Skytrain equipped American 440th Troop Carrying Group. Armstrong Whitworth built Lancaster NG148 was eventually repaired on-site by No.54 MU. It did not rejoin the squadron.

Another crew in trouble was that of F/Sgt A Saunders. They too were hit just before bombing. Heavy flak shooting out the hydraulics and starboard outer engine aboard Lancaster NG140 XY-F. Despite the damage they bombed at 15:10 hours on a G-H Leader who the crew reported was *'some way ahead'*.
'B' Flight's F/Lt E Ritson was hit over the target, a 3" hole punctured the bomb bay doors, thankfully hitting nothing vital. Two other Lancasters were hit but to a lesser extent. Bombing did not appear to be accurate, W/Cdr Giles DFC, *'Marshalling Yards did not seem to be hit, but some good fires were burning around it'*. Flight Sergeant T Green bombed at 15:07 hours, *'Some undershoots were seen, main weight of attack fell on built-up area. Whole town covered in smoke'*. Flight Lieutenant R Madden RCAF at the controls of HK662 XY-P, *'At first the attack was a ¼ of mile east of the target. Some bombing seemed scattered'*. To add to the problems, the Luftwaffe made an appearance. A number of Bf109s arrived over the target as the last wave was bombing, damaging one No.90 Squadron Lancaster before the escorting RAF Mustangs drove them off. Group HQ was confident that the bombing achieved some success, some bombs were seen to explode across the marshalling yards, but a large proportion of the attack fell in the northern suburbs, which by chance was heavily industrialised. All the crews, apart from F/O Field DFC and F/Sgt Saunders landed back at a snow-covered RAF Stradishall. Flight Sergeant Saunders landed Lancaster NG140 XY-F at the emergency landing airfield at RAF Woodbridge at 17:21 Hours. It had been yet another bruising day for the squadrons of No.3 Group. Thankfully No.186 was relatively lucky, over at RAF Wratting Common, No.195 recorded seven damaged Lancasters, while No.218 Squadron reported five. Unsurprisingly, the squadrons of No.33 Base had been severely mauled. The New Zealanders of No.75(NZ) Squadron and No.115 each listed 11 Lancasters damaged, while No.514 Squadron recorded an astonishing 12 aircraft hit.

No.186 Squadron Reported Flak Damage 05/01/1945

| Serial | Code | Damage Reported | Repairs / Notes |
|---|---|---|---|
| NG148 | **XY-B** | Port Outer/inner. Fuselage, and nose. | RoS No.54 MU |
| NG140 | **XY-F** | Hydraulics, Starboard Outer engine. | Repaired on Squadron. |
| HK661 | **XY-R** | Hit but no description. | Repaired on Squadron. |
| NG293 | **XY-U** | Hit but no description. | Repaired on Squadron. |
| NG353 | **XY-X** | Bomb Bay door(s) | Repaired on Squadron. |

The morning of January 6th was freezing, giving the poor ground crews another uncomfortable few hours preparing 12 Lancasters for a daylight operation against Neuss. This operation was however cancelled at 11:00 hours. It was a short stay of execution, as the operation was re-scheduled for that night. Located on the west bank of the Rhine opposite Dusseldorf, Neuss was very much in the front line and played a vital role in the distribution of German military and industrial needs. During the early afternoon, two crews carried out a G-H exercise. However both were unsuccessful. Squadron Leader Robert Bass AFM started his leave on this day, and he was ably replaced by F/Lt Arthur Powell DFC.

Form B.754 (N) – January 6th, 1945 (N) : Target – Neuss Marshalling Yards - 'G-H612A'

| | | | | | | | |
|---|---|---|---|---|---|---|---|
| F/O | Templeton | G.M | RCAF | NG137 | XY-D | Follower | Duty Carried Out. |
| F/O | Hart | J.H | | NG175 | XY-J | Follower | Duty Carried Out. |
| F/Sgt | Green | T.B | | HK682 | XY-L | Follower | Duty Carried Out. |
| F/O | Clarson | A.J | RAAF | NG354 | XY-M | Follower | Duty Carried Out. |
| F/O | O'Brien | J.D | RNZAF | HK684 | XY-O | Follower | Duty Carried Out. |
| F/Lt | Madden | R.P | RCAF | HK662 | XY-P | Follower | Duty Carried Out. |
| F/O | Idle | L.A | RNZAF | HK661 | XY-R | Follower | Duty Carried Out. |
| F/O | Gogler | R.J | RAAF | HK650 | XY-T | Follower | Duty Carried Out. |
| F/O | Green | L.A | | HK606 | XY-V | Follower | Duty Carried Out. |
| F/O | James | W.C | RAAF | HK688 | XY-W | Follower | Duty Carried Out. |

| | | | | | | | |
|---|---|---|---|---|---|---|---|
| F/Lt | Ritson | E.E | | NG353 | XY-X | Follower | Duty Carried Out. |
| F/Lt | Liddell | J.B.M | | PD429 | XY-Z | Follower | Duty Carried Out. |

Two of the Lancasters that reported damage on the previous day's raid were again flying. The damage, obviously minor, had been quickly repaired or replaced. Flying Officer G.M Templeton RCAF led the squadron away just after 15:30 hours. The squadron would be part of a force of 119 Lancasters detailed from No.3 Group. The Group would be joined by the Lincolnshire based No.1 Group, which provided a modest 33 Lancasters. These would bomb on G-H markers provided by No.3 Group. The crews slowly climbed into the freezing night sky and headed south to the town of Reading located west of London.

Sergeant 'Geordie' Beer in Lancaster HK659 XY-Q 'Queenie' rear turret. This photograph clearly shows the Frazer Nash turret fully traversed, giving it an excellent field of fire.

No opposition was encountered en route thanks in part to the shallow penetration and the attack on the Marshalling Yards at Hanau by the Halifaxes No.4 and No.6 RCAF Groups 90 minutes prior. The squadron's 12 crews were evenly distributed over the duration of the raid, timed to start at 18:45 hours. Over the target, flak opposition was slight and offered extraordinarily little problem as the first flares then bomb loads began to fall. Crews were confident that the initial markers were accurate, although the latter marking, and bombing appeared to lose momentum. Explosions and fires were seen below the cloud base as the first wave turned for home. Two distinct groups of fires had taken hold, one larger than the other. One of the first to bomb at 18:45 hours was 'A' Flight F/Sgt Green.

They dropped their all high explosive load from 20,000ft on a bunch of Red Target Indicators. He remarked, *'Some burst were seen around the TI's.'* Three minutes later, things had improved, F/Lt Madden RCAF was at the controls of Lancaster HK662 XY-P, he reported, *' Bombed on Red TI's at 18:48 hours from 20,000 feet. Flares and skymarkers were very concentrated. Red glow of fire seen in target area and bombs bursting in and around the Target Indicators'*. Flying Officer A.J Clarson RAAF who was flying with replacement Rear Gunner, Sgt W.F Upton recalled at de-briefing, '*Good glow below clouds. Red TI's seen in built up area'*.

Several dummy Red TI Markers were reported 5 miles SW of Neuss, but these were ignored and did not appear to lure away crews. Some worthwhile damage was caused to the southern two-thirds of the marshalling yards. Heavy damage was inflicted to the transshipment sheds, large roundhouse, and goods sidings. However, the heaviest bombing was inflicted to the surrounding area where severe damage was caused to a number of industrial factories. RAF Stradishall was visited by a number of distinguished visitors from Iraq on the 6th. Colonel Sami Fatteh, Chief of the Royal Iraqi Air Force and Colonel Arkram Hoshtaq, Director of Civil Aviation and their entourage watched a number of squadron Lancasters taking off and landing on pre-flight air-tests. Squadron Leader Ibraham, RAF Attaché in London, and F/Lt Dickenson, Air Ministry Escort had the job of tour-guides as the party visited first the Briefing Room and then the Intelligence Library before Tea and Dinner. The squadron's effort to get operational on G-H continued on the afternoon of the 7th with four crews airborne. Two crews flew a G-H exercise, while two others carried out a G-H practice bombing exercise over Rushford range. Munich 'A' was the target on the night of January 7th, and only seven crews were detailed. The squadrons of No.3 Group would be divided over three waves with No.31 Base in the 3rd and final wave along with 83 Lancasters of No.1 Group.

Form B.755 (N) – January 7th, 1945 (N) : Target – Munich 'A' - 'G-H606'

| | | | | | | | |
|---|---|---|---|---|---|---|---|
| F/Sgt | Saunders | A | | NG137 | XY-D | Follower | Duty Carried Out. |
| F/O | Barton | E.R | RAAF | NN720 | XY-K | Follower | Duty Carried Out. |
| F/O | Young | H.S | | HK682 | XY-L | Follower | Duty Carried Out. |
| F/O | Templeton | G.M | RCAF | NG354 | XY-M | Follower | Duty Carried Out. |
| F/Lt | Orman DFC | K.G | RNZAF | NG175 | XY-J | Follower | Duty Carried Out. |
| F/O | Beck | J.A | RAAF | HK688 | XY-W | Follower | Duty Carried Out. |
| F/Lt | Liddell | J.B.M | | NG353 | XY-X | Follower | Duty Carried Out. |

Number 5 Group would open proceedings at 20:30 hours. They would mark and bomb independently two hours before the arrival of No.1, 3 and 6 RCAF Groups. The marking for the second phase of the raid would be provided by the Path Finders. A dull red glow could be faintly seen as the main force neared the target, courtesy of No.5 Group. The initial Path Finder marking was spoiled by a fairly thick layer of cloud over the target, the consequence of which was the first sky markers were quickly lost. The first from the squadron to bomb was F/Sgt Saunders at 22:30 hours. He bombed on a bunch of skymarkers just before they were swallowed up by cloud. It was while the crew were on their bomb run that a Ju88 was seen stalking them from below. It was a brief encounter, as the following Combat Report shows.

JU88 was seen flying below our bomber, apparently keeping station at 400 yards. The rear gunner opened fire, and the fighter immediately broke away down, and was not seen again. No claim.

The rear gunner Sgt J.P Doran fired a total of 400 rounds before the JU88 broke away. A matter of just 8 minutes was the difference in the raid appraisal given by two crews on return to RAF Stradishall. The experienced F/Lt K Orman DFC RNZAF was over the target at 22:26 hours.

Flight Lieutenant Eric Hunt was surprisingly entrusted with carrying out the squadron's first G-H operation. Why this relatively inexperienced pilot and his crew were chosen is unclear.

He commented on return, *'Skymarkers were well bunched'*. At 22:34 hours, F/O G Templeton RCAF dropped his single 4000 pounder and 4lb incendiaries. He reported, *'Marking considered poor and scattered, no results seen owing to cloud'*. Leaving the target, a massive explosion was witnessed at 22:59 hours which lit up the clouds below.

The two raids had dealt a devasting blow against this once beautiful city. The glow from the fires could be seen 100 miles from the target. The last crew to land was F/O J. Beck RAAF at 02:42 hours. The squadron dropped a total of 56,800lb of bombs on Munich, which had suffered its last major attack of the war. This would be the 16th and last operation flown by the crew of F/Lt James Liddell. Their application to join the Path Finder's having been successful. On January 19th, 1945, the crew arrived on No.7 Squadron based at RAF Oakington.

Intermittent snow showers kept the squadron on the ground until the 10th, when in-between light snow flurries, five crews managed to complete three G-H exercises and two G-H bombing exercises before the weather once again grounded the squadron. There was a real buzz around the squadron on the 11th. Finally, the squadron would have an opportunity to provide a G-H equipped crew. It was a small contribution but an important development for the squadron's future. The crew given responsibility for marking was 'B' Flight's F/Lt E.G Hunt. Twenty-eight-year-old Eric Hunt had only just arrived on the squadron. He had recently completed No.62 Course with No.3 LFS in November 1944. Eric and his crew were then posted to No.15 Squadron on November 23rd. However, strangely he did not undertake any operations. His posting date to No.186 Squadron is not recorded. The choice of this relatively new and inexperienced crew to carry out the squadron's long-anticipated first G-H raid appears strange. The target for 14 crews was the Uerdingen Marshalling Yards at Krefeld. Situated on a bend on the river Rhine, No.3 Group would dispatch a total of 152 Lancasters drawn from all three Bases.

Form B.756 (D) – January 11th, 1945 (D) : Target : Uerdingen Marshalling Yards at Krefeld - G-H611

| | | | | | | | |
|---|---|---|---|---|---|---|---|
| F/Lt | Wait | C.J | | NG137 | XY-D | Follower | Duty Carried Out |
| F/O | Templeton | G.M | RCAF | NG146 | XY-E | Follower | Duty Carried Out |
| S/Ldr | Reynolds | P | | NN720 | XY-K | Follower | Duty Carried Out |
| F/O | Young | H.S | | HK682 | XY-L | Follower | Duty Carried Out |
| F/O | Clarson | A.J | RAAF | NG354 | XY-M | Follower | Duty Carried Out |
| F/O | James | W.C | RAAF | HK684 | XY-O | Follower | Duty Carried Out |
| F/Lt | Madden | R.P | RCAF | HK662 | XY-P | Follower | Duty Carried Out |
| P/O | Hart | J.H | | NG175 | XY-J | Follower | Duty Carried Out |
| F/O | Mason | F.H | | LM188 | XY-S | Follower | Duty Carried Out |
| F/O | Gogler | R.J | RAAF | NG293 | XY-U | Follower | Duty Carried Out |
| F/O | Green | L.A | | HK606 | XY-V | Follower | Duty Carried Out |

| | | | | | | | |
|---|---|---|---|---|---|---|---|
| F/Lt | Hunt | E.G | | HK688 | XY-W | G-H Leader[19] | Duty Carried Out |
| F/Lt | Ritson | E.E | | NG353 | XY-X | Follower | Duty Carried Out |
| F/O | Fernley | F | | HK613 | XY-Y | Follower | Duty Carried Out |

All the squadron took off without mishap. On reaching the group rendezvous point above Wellingborough, the crews were greeted by clouds extending 3,000 feet above the briefed rendezvous height of 12,000 feet. This resulted in confusion, with squadrons desperately trying to form up in amongst the banks of solid clouds. Finally, and mercifully without any collisions, the three Base formations with Methwold's No.149 Squadron leading set off. In the chaos of forming up over England, three crews found themselves isolated and unable to locate their briefed G-H Leader. Eventually, two crews found sanctuary amongst No.33 Base. Flying Officer Young latched onto a No.514 Squadron G-H aircraft while F/Lt Ritson accompanied a No.75(NZ) aircraft. Flying Officer Mason spent the first half of the raid behind a No.15 Squadron G-H Lancaster of No.32 Base. Thankfully, eight squadron crews found their leaders, who were provided by RAF Chedburgh's No.218 Squadron and the Wratting Common based No.195 Squadron. Soon after forming up at 11:58 hours, the crew of F/O Clarson RAAF found themselves in trouble.

Tucked behind their G-H Leader, their Lancaster NG354 XY-M was caught in its slipstream. The encounter must have been both sudden and violent as the 4000lb cookie fell from its mounting and forced open the bomb doors. The cookie landed harmlessly in a field six miles Northwest of Bishop Stortford. The bomb must have been unarmed as no damage was recorded by the local press! By the time the Group passed over Selsey Bill, the weather had deteriorated even more with flurries of snow and icing and below a solid mass of 10/10th cloud stretched across Europe. Over France, the Group welcomed the appearance of seven squadrons of sleek RAF Mustangs. They quickly organised themselves into a protective umbrella as the formation headed deep into Germany. Number 31 Base was again given the third and final wave position planned to be over the target between 15:03 hours to 15:05 hours. Opposition over the target was reported as light but did not stop Lancaster HK682 XY-L flown by F/O H Young from being hit. The aircraft was holed in several places, and oil started streaming out of the starboard outer engine. The engine was eventually feathered in case of fire. A small number of crews reported fleeting glimpses of the ground. The Australian Bomb Aimer aboard F/O G Templeton RCAF Lancaster, *'Identified a town through gap in clouds, saw a number of bombs bursting in built-up area'*. Flying Officer James RAAF stated, *'A brief glimpse of river and built-up area after bombing but could not pick out target'*. More worrying was F/O Hart's report, *'Air Bomber caught a glimpse of ground with snow-covered fields and a small town a little to starboard.* There were a few conflicting reports on the accuracy, the crew of F/O R Gogler RAAF, *'rear gunner saw target when leaving, and saw hits on it, but Bomb Aimer saw nothing. Some bombers dropped 15 miles short of target'*. Despite the confusion, F/Lt E Hunt reported a successful operation. He reported to the Squadron Intelligence Officer on return, *'Bombed on Radar Navigational Aid at 15:11 hours from 20,000ft. Saw bombs bursting in the centre of a town and identified a railway south of town running East to West. At the time of bombing, there was considerable congestion of aircraft'*.

Regardless of the confusion, one thing was sure, No.186 Squadron had successfully completed its first G-H operation and would from this date on play a full part in the systematic destruction of Germany. While the squadron was over Krefeld, two crews were eagerly carrying out G-H training.

[19] *From this date on I will try and identify all No.186 Squadron GH crews and aircraft.*

No.186 Squadron Reported Flak Damage 11/01/1945

| Serial | Code | Damage Reported | Repairs / Notes |
|---|---|---|---|
| HK682 | **XY-L** | Fuselage, starboard outer engine | RoS by squadron |

The all British crew of Flying Officer Frederick Fernley. They are seen here in front of Lancaster HK613 XY-Y. The crew are L-R Flight Sergeant A.C Grant (Bomb Aimer), Flight Sergeant H Smith ( Mid Upper Gunner), Flight Sergeant E McGarry ( Wireless Operator), Flying Officer F Fernley (Pilot), Sergeant F.B Wilkes (Flight Engineer), Flight Sergeant R.S Needham (Navigator) and Flight Sergeant D.A Morerley (Rear Gunner).

On the 12th, an early morning attack on the chemical works at Grevenbroich was organised, then cancelled at 08:40 hours. This was switched to a night raid against the oil refineries at Misburg, but this too was cancelled at 13:50 hours. The cancellation of operations not only put a tremendous strain on the Ground Crews, especially in the freezing conditions, but it also put a great deal of mental strain on the Air Crews. Having endured the detailed briefings, then the pre-flight checks in the aircraft, plus all the emotional build-up that went with it, the operation was cancelled without warning. It certainly was a roller coaster of emotions for a bomber crew. Number 3 Group's attacks on the German railway system continued on the 13th when 14 crews were detailed and briefed for a daylight G-H attack on the Marshalling Yards at Saarbrucken. Even though the squadron had notched up its first G-H raid, it would find itself once again frustratingly in the follower role.

Form B.759 – January 13th, 1945 (D) : Target : Saarbrucken Marshalling Yards AP 'B' - G-H633

| | | | | | | | |
|---|---|---|---|---|---|---|---|
| F/Sgt | Saunders | A | | NG174 | XY-A | Follower | Duty Carried Out. |
| F/Lt | Wait | C.J | | NG147 | XY-C | Follower | Duty Carried Out. |
| F/O | Gibson | J.H.W | | NG137 | XY-D | Follower | Duty Carried Out. |

| | | | | | | | |
|---|---|---|---|---|---|---|---|
| F/O | Field DFC | E.F | | NG175 | XJ-J | Follower | Duty Carried Out. |
| F/Sgt | Green | T.B | | HK682 | XY-L | Follower | Duty Carried Out. |
| F/O | Idle | L.A | RNZAF | HK684 | XY-L | Follower | Duty Carried Out. |
| F/O | Mason | F.F | | HK659 | XY-Q | Follower | Duty Not Carried Out |
| F/O | Gogler | R.J | RAAF | NG293 | XY-U | Follower | Duty Carried Out. |
| F/O | Fernley | F | | HK606 | XY-V | Follower | Duty Carried Out. |
| F/Lt | Ritson | E.E | | NG353 | XY-X | Follower | Duty Carried Out. |
| F/O | Beck | J.A. | RAAF | PD429 | XY-Z | Follower | Duty Carried Out. |
| F/Lt | Madden | R.P | RCAF | HK662 | XY-P | Follower | Duty Carried Out. |
| F/O | Hart | J.H | | NG146 | XY-E | Follower | Duty Carried Out. |
| F/Lt | Hanson | R.A.J | | HK613 | XY-Y | Follower | Duty Carried Out. |

The squadron, along with No.195 and No.218 Squadrons, would on this occasion be part of the second wave timed to bomb aiming point 'B' between 15:22 and 15:30 hours. Specific orders at briefing had stressed the importance that the followers were not to bomb unless they were formatted on a G-H Leader and could clearly see when his bombs and flare dropped. The previous operation had worryingly witnessed small gaggles of bombers, mostly from No.33 Base bomb independent of G-H Leaders. On reaching the rendezvous point above a cloud covered Brentwood, Essex the 158 Lancasters swiftly formed up. Skirting London's eastern flak defences the force headed towards Tonbridge, Kent then out across the England Channel where they made landfall at Le Touguet. Conditions over the continent were excellent, unlike over England.

The snow-covered countryside was visible below, and above the small force was a clear blue sky and brilliant sunshine. As the squadrons of No.31 Base began their approach, they were confronted with only spasmodic flak at bombing height. The crews could not believe that an important target in Germany offered so little resistance. The previous base group had carried out what appeared to be some accurate bombing. Smoke was seen rising from the target area, and a number of Target Indicators were slowly arching their way towards the Marshalling Yards. The first of the squadron's bombs started to fall at 15:25 hours dropped by F/Lt R.A Hanson, F/Lt R.P Madden RCAF and New Zealander F/O L.A Idle RNZAF. Each bombed on their G-H Leader. The results could not be observed due to a large pall of oily smoke covering the Aiming Point. Flying Officer Mason had the misfortune of being unable to drop his 'cookie' and 14 x 500 pounders when the bomb doors aboard Lancaster HK658 XY-Q failed to open due to hydraulic failure. His troubles were compounded when the port inner engine caught fire and had to be feathered.

The majority of the crews were confident that the raid was a success. Flight Lieutenant E Ritson dropped at 15:26 hours from 18,000 feet, and he reported, *'Bombed on Navigational Aid Leader and falling bombs. Many bombs bursts all over Aiming point 'A' were seen'.* Flying Officer R.J Gogler RAAF, *'Bursts on Aiming Point 'A' a few on 'B' and large clouds of black smoke were seen.* Flight Lieutenant R Hanson was one of the few crews who reported damage to Aiming Point' B', the squadron's intended target, *'Bombed on Radar Navigational Aid Leader and falling bombs. Most of the bomb bursts were on aiming point 'B'. Very few bursting in town'.* Flight Sergeant T.B Green was stationed behind his briefed G-H Leader, Lancaster NF955 HA-A of No.218 Squadron flown by F/O Les Harlow and crew. Immediately his Leader's bombs were observed leaving its bomb bay, Bomb Aimer Sgt K Barkham, lying prone in the nose of Lancaster HK682 XY-L, pressed the 'tit'. Instantly he felt his aircraft lift as the 4000 pound 'cookie' and 12 x 500 pounders fell towards the Marshalling Yards 18,500 feet below. The time was 15:27 hours. There was one moment of danger, not for a crew of No.186 Squadron, but a fellow No.31 Base crew of No.195 Squadron.

GPC G

16.

GPC V STR 2/14 OP OP
T EXEMPT 31 BASE

FROM R.A.F. BASE STATION, STRADISHALL 141700 A
TO H.Q. 3 GROUP
INFO 31 BASE
SECRET QQX BT

SECTION 'A'

3
13 JAN 1945
1 X 4000 HC ( MINOL )
11 X 500 AN-M64- NOSE -3 SECS
1 X 500 MCTD-025

186/C
RR2

LANC MK 1
NG 147

F/P.- H2S MK11-
SAARBRUCKEN /4
11-36 3/4

PB- GH.
F/ LT WAIT 29
1841 C ST MAWGAN

SECTION X'C '

1. PRIMARY
2 7/10- CLEAR OVER ACTUAL TARGET
3 IDENTIFIED TARGET XXX VISUALLY
4 15-25- 20,000- XXX 050-160-
7 GH LEADER HA -B
1.SAW BOMBS BURSTING ON BUILT UP AREAS BLACK SMOKE RISING FROM TARGET . BLUE SMOKE PUFFS SEEN
16 FAILED TO FIND BRIEFED LEADER HA-D AND RVP, SO PICKED BB UP HA-B JUST AFTER CROSSING CONTINETAL CB COAST . FOLLOWED HIM TO TARGET AND BOMBED WITH HIM GEE FIX JUST BEFORE TARGET AT 4912 1/2 M- 0653 E BOMBING SEEMED TOBE ON THE TOWN, AND NOT ON M/Y WHICH APPEARED UNDAMAGED
17 J.K.B.

BT 141700 A
AS
CCC AFTER 7 TO READ 8. NOT 1. AS I HAVE PUT CCC 3 LINE FROM BOTTOM CWA 4912 1/2 N-0653E
FGF BBB

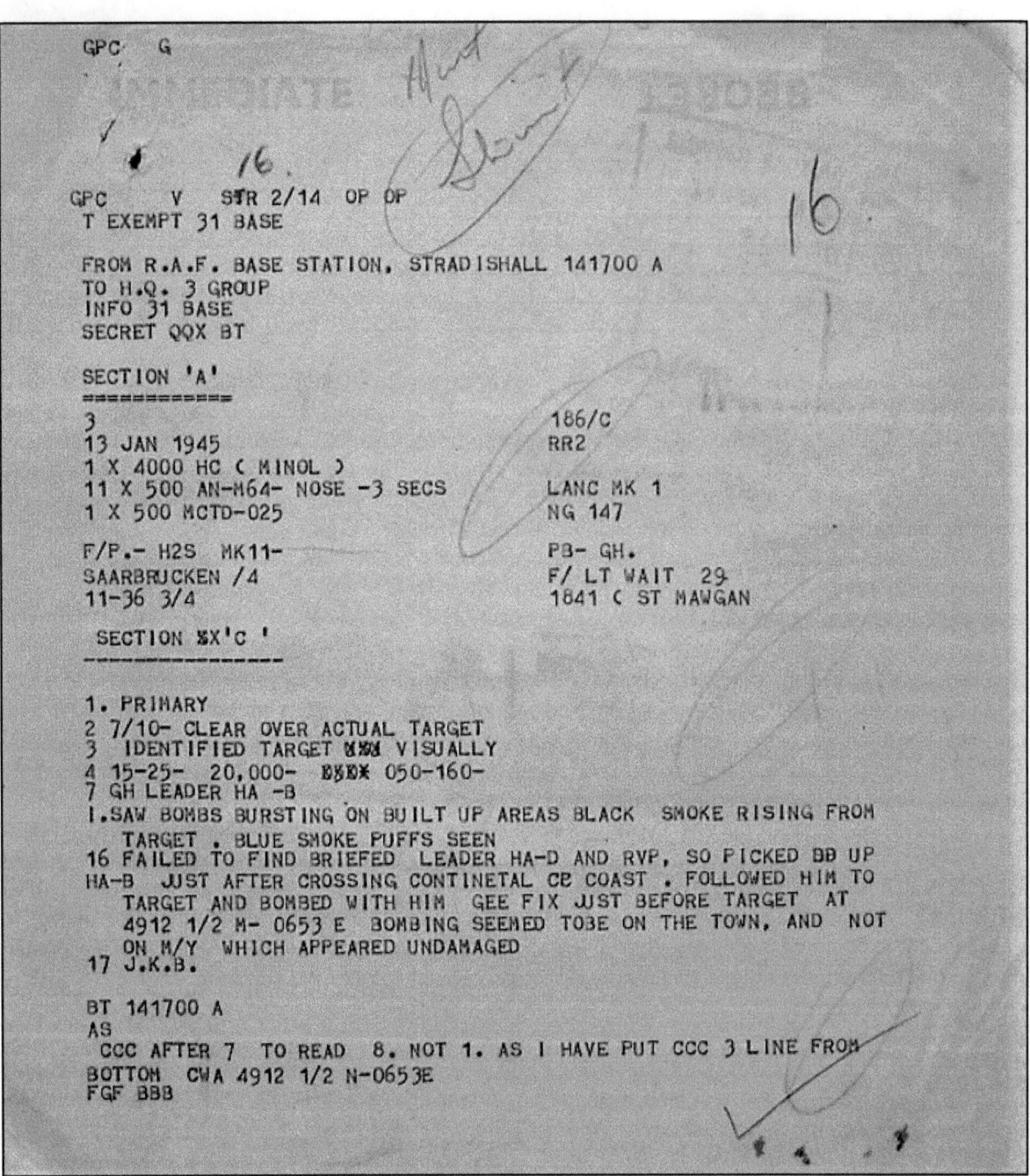

Above: The intelligence report submitted by No.186 Squadron, RAF Stradishall, to No.3 Group HQ for the operation dated January 13th, 1945. Flight Lieutenant Wait and crew submitted this particular report for the operation against Saarbrucken. Note the reference to the crew's allotted G-H Leader. Lancaster HA-D, PB721, this was Flight Sergeant D McClennan. Lancaster HA-B, PD296, was flown by Warrant Officer G.D Evers both of No.218 (Gold Coast) Squadron. Flight Lieutenant Wait was on his 29th operation. Below: The same raid and crew entry in the Squadron ORB.

| | | | | | |
|---|---|---|---|---|---|
| LANCASTER I. | F/L. WAIT C.J. | PILOT | 11.36 | 18.41 | Bomb load 1 X 4000 HC. 11 X 500 AN-M64 and 1 X 500 MC. |
| "C" NG.147. | F/S. BADHAM A.F. | NAV | | | Target SAARBRUCKEN. Weather: 7/10 cloud - clear over actu |
| | F/S. BRIGGS R.J. | A/B | | | target and bombing was carried out on Radar Navigational |
| | F/O. BRITTON G.H. | WO/AIR | | | Aid Leader at 20,000 feet. Bombs were seen bursting on |
| | SGT. THORNE M.V. | M/G | | | built up areas and not on the Marshalling Yards which |
| | SGT. BRAY K.H. | R/G | | | appeared undamaged, although black smoke was seen rising |
| | SGT. HOBSON W.S. | F/E | | | from the target. Blue smoke puffs also seen. Landed at |
| | | | | | ST MAWGAN. |

Flying Officer C Hopkins was at 19,000 feet at the controls of Lancaster NG187 A4-Q,' and he reported, *Weather clear, bombed on G-H aircraft XH/K*[20] *port line abreast. Bombs bursting in target area which was covered in smoke. Just prior to bombing XY/V took up position 400 feet above and slightly to starboard. Thirty seconds before we bombed, he moved into position right above us and released his bombs with a result that we had to take violent evasive action and to be abreast of Leader. HE's passed all around our aircraft and the cookies just behind the aircraft'.* The reckless crew was skippered by F/O F Fernley of No.186 Squadron. Bombers being struck from bombs from above, was on the increase. Crews took a very dim view of this type of flying. They accepted that they had no real control over flak or the elements, but this was avoidable. Thankfully on this occasion, other than a few choice words, no harm was done. All but one crew received a Diversion Message en route home. The Weather, which had been marginal on departure, had now completely closed in. Eight crews managed to land at the Coastal Command station at St Eval, while four dropped in at RAF St Mawgan, Cornwall. Flying Officer F Mason made an emergency landing on three engines at RAF Tangmere at 18:05 hours after jettisoning his bomb load mid-channel. The crew of F/O J Gibson somehow, despite the diversion signal and weather, managed to land back at RAF Stradishall at 17:00. It must have been a very quiet and lonely de-briefing. On inspection of the port inner engine of HK659, it appeared that the issue was caused by the overtightening of the engine block bolts. Group HQ classified the raid as highly successful. The squadron welcomed the return of S/Ldr Bass AFM on this date, and he quickly resumed the 'B' Flight Commander role.

Squadron WAAFs. Their work behind the scenes is all too often overlooked. They were every bit as proud and conscientious as their male counterparts and played a pivotal role in the success of No.186 Squadron and RAF Bomber Command. Sadly, the identity of this smiling group is unknown.

[20] *The crew of F/O George Bates, No.218 (Gold Coast) Squadron*

Other than four fighter affiliation exercises and the now almost daily Radar Navigational exercises, RAF Stradishall was a rather tranquil place on the 14th. It was on this date that Wing Commander Giles DFC took some well-deserved and long overdue leave. 'A' Flight's S/Ldr P Reynolds took over, while F/O E.L Field DFC took over the 'A' Flight Commander duties.

A new name appeared on the Operations board on the morning of the 15th, Erkenschwick, a small Ruhr mining town situated in North Rhine-Westphalia. The target was the Ewald Fortsetzung Colliery and Benzol / Coking Plant. A total of eighty-two Lancasters drawn from both No.31 Base and No.32 Base were given the target to attack between 15:01 and 15:11 hours. Number 186 Squadron would provide 12 crews who began departing just after 11:30 hours. Surprisingly just two G-H crew were provided.

Form B.760 – January 15th, 1945 (D) : Target : Erkenschwick Benzol Plant – GQ1871

| | | | | | | | |
|---|---|---|---|---|---|---|---|
| F/O | Cowley | N.C | | NG147 | XY-C | G-H Leader | Duty Not Carried Out. |
| F/Lt | Wait | C.J | | NG137 | XY-D | Follower | Duty Carried Out |
| F/O | Clarson | A.J | RAAF | NG175 | XY-J | Follower | Duty Carried Out |
| F/O | Field DFC | E.L | | NG149 | XY-G | Follower | Duty Carried Out |
| F/O | Templeton | G.M | RCAF | NG146 | XY-E | Followers | Duty Carried Out |
| F/O | Tonks | J.E | | NG354 | XY-M | G-H Leader | Duty Carried Out |
| P/O | O'Brien | J.D | RAAF | HK684 | XY-O | Follower | Duty Carried Out |
| F/O | James | W.C | RAAF | HK662 | XY-P | Follower | Duty Carried Out |
| F/O | Beck | J.A | RAAF | LM188 | XY-S | Follower | Duty Not Carried Out. |
| F/Lt | Ritson | E.E | | NG293 | XY-U | Follower | Duty Carried Out |
| F/Lt | Hanson | R.A.J | | HK613 | XY-Y | Follower | Duty Carried Out |
| S/Ldr | Bass AFM | R.W | | PD429 | XY-Z | Follower | Duty Carried Out |

The Group rendezvous point was 9000 feet over Braintree, Norfolk. Here they would now carry out the routine forming-up procedure, made easier by low cloud. With No.32 spearheading the small formation, the Lancasters set off firstly to Brentwood then onto Le Gris Nez, on the French coast, steadily climbing to the bombing height of between 20-21,000 feet. The squadron recorded two aborts on this operation. Up until this date, the serviceability rate on the squadron was exceptional, with no aborts in over a month. Disappointingly, one of the early returns was the G-H crew of F/O N. Cowley. Unfortunately, soon after reaching the rendezvous point, the crew experienced problems with the port outer engine aboard Lancaster NG147 XY-C. A green flare was fired, backed up with Aldis signals informing the followers they were experiencing trouble and abandoning the operation. Flying Officer N.C Cowley proceeded to the jettisoning area where 1 x 4000 + 1 x 500 pounder were dropped at 13:32 hours. The crew of F/O J Beck RAAF lost the use of the W/T aboard LM188 XY-S soon after reaching the rendezvous point. They, too, headed for the jettisoning area.

The formation entered German airspace bathed in the winter sun. The sky above was crystal clear, giving the crews unlimited visibility. The white finger-like contrails of the escorting RAF Mustangs stood out against the icy blue sky. Below, Germany was covered with 10/10th stratus with tops up to 10,000 feet. Surprisingly given the conditions and lack of any real opposition, the formation was strung out, forming into a long narrow line with individual vics of three following one after the other. One returning crew member describes the formation like a '*colony of ants on the march*. This resulted in the attack over-running the briefed three-minute duration, it lasted a full ten minutes. There was more

A poor quality photograph of the crew of Flying Officer Donald Roberts standing at a snow-covered dispersal.

disappointment when the squadron's second G-H crew experienced set failure moments before bombing. Up until that point, the crew of F/O Tonks had performed well, F/O G. Templeton RCAF, *'Leader XY-M proved an excellent Leader'*. Little did the Canadian know that F/O Tonks had dropped on a fellow G-H Leader! Returning crews were confident that the raid was a success, target markers were concentrated, and bombing appeared to reflect this. This was the 31st and last operation flown by 'B' Flight's F/Lt Edward Ritson and crew. Their tour began on 'C' Flight of No.90 Squadron in September 1944. The crew of F/O Jeff Clarson RAAF welcomed the return of their Rear Gunner, F/Sgt McPherson, on this raid after his enforced stay in hospital. No crew liked operating with 'spare-bods', especially gunners.

A daylight raid was planned against the Ruhrol A.G synthetic oil plant at Bottrop for the 16th, but this was switched to a late-night take-off operation for twelve crews. The squadron was given a new target, the Krupp Treibstroffwerk G.m.b.H synthetic oil plant at Wanne-Eickel.

<u>Form B.762 – January 16th/17th 1945 (N) : Target : Krupp synthetic oil plant at Wanne-Eickel. GQ1518</u>

| | | | | | | | |
|---|---|---|---|---|---|---|---|
| F/Lt | Tait | R.R | | NG147 | XY-C | Follower | Crashed after take-off |
| F/O | Fernley | F | | NG146 | XY-E | Follower | Duty Carried Out. |
| F/O | Hart | J.H | | NG140 | XY-F | Follower | Duty Carried Out. |
| F/Sgt | Green | T.B | | NG149 | XY-G | Follower | Duty Carried Out. |
| F/O | Gibson | J.H | | NG175 | XY-J | Follower | Duty Carried Out. |
| F/O | Tonks | J.E | | NG354 | XY-M | Follower | Duty Carried Out. |
| F/O | Beck | J.A | RAAF | HK661 | XY-R | Follower | Duty Carried Out. |
| F/O | Gogler | R.J | RAAF | NG293 | XY-U | Follower | Duty Carried Out. |
| F/O | Cowley | N.C | | HK688 | XY-W | G-H Leader | Duty Carried Out. |

| | | | | | | | |
|---|---|---|---|---|---|---|---|
| F/O | Idle | L.A | RNZAF | HK613 | XY-Y | Follower | Duty Not Carried Out |
| F/O | Mason | F.H | | HK684 | XY-O | Follower | Duty Carried Out. |
| F/O | Godfrey | D.F.J | RAAF | HK662 | XY-P | Follower | Duty Carried Out. |

Bomber Command was out in force on this night. 371 bombers were over Magdeburg, and a further 328 were tasked with bombing the Braunkohle-Benzin synthetic oil plant at Zeitz while 231 were given the synthetic oil plant at Brux, Czechoslovakia to blitz. The squadrons of No.3 Group, totalling some 146 Lancasters would be the only group attacking Wanne-Eickel, they were timed to be over the target a 02:15 hours. This was the squadron's first night G-H raid and would be remembered for all the wrong reasons.

Three minutes after take-off, the crew of F/Lt R.Tait crashed near Saxon St, Kirtling Hall between Kedington and Haverhill, about 2 miles southwest of the airfield. In the ensuing explosion and fireball, all the crew were killed. There was considerable damage to local property. It was not surprising with the Lancaster loaded with 1 x 4000lb + 12 x 500lb and fully fueled. Thankfully, there were no civilian injuries reported. A local resident near the crash site reported hearing a heavy bomber approaching at a low level with its *'engines making a strange noise'*. Fortunately for them, it just cleared their rooftop before crashing into an adjacent field. The sleepy Market Town of Haverhill was only a few seconds flying time further on from the crash site. Little did the townsfolk of Haverhill realise how close to disaster they had come. The consequences of the fully-ladened Lancaster crashing into the town would have been catastrophic. Such was the force of the explosion a badly buckled .303 machine gun was found in a nearby stockyard. The scene the Station's Emergency Crash Team arrived at was one of utter destruction. The explosion left a huge crater like hole. The flickering light from the flames reflected on the strips of silver 'window' found eerily swathed over nearby trees and hedges. It was an eerie an shocking sight made even worse by a pall of smoke that hung over the crash site. It was immediately obvious that no one could have survived such a catastrophic crash.

| | | |
|---|---|---|
| Type | Avro Lancaster Mk.I **NG147 XY-C** *'Champagne Charlie'* | Vickers Armstrong |
| Taken on Charge | 07/10/1944 | |
| 'Category' | CAT E/FB 16/01/1945 | |
| Struck Of Charge | 17/01/1945 | |
| Total Flying Hours | Not Recorded | |
| Raids Flown | 33 | |
| Take-Off Time | 23:15 hours | |
| Bomb Load | 1 x 4000lb HC + 12 x 500lb AN-M64 | |
| | | |
| | **CREW** | **GRAVE/CEMETERY** |
| Pilot | Flight Lieutenant Roland Ralph Tait, 179588 RAFVR Age 21. | Sec.K.Grave 1A. Lee (St John Beverley) New Church,Acomn |
| Navigator | Flight Sergeant Thomas Brown Darney, 1676154 RAFVR. Age 21. | Grave 146. Hindley (St.Margaret) Churchyard, Broomley. |
| Bomb Aimer | Flying Officer Herbert Charles Dutfield, 154376 RAFVR. Age 23. Married. | Sec U. Grave 149. Haverhill Cemetery. |
| Wireless Operator | Flight Sergeant Wilfred Sidney Gamble, 2206781 RAFVR. Age 20. | Section D.Grave 38, 12526. York Cemetery, Yorkshire. |
| Mid Upper Gunner | Pilot Officer Gerald Stalker Haslam, 56419 RAF | Sec U.Grave 201. |

| | | |
|---|---|---|
| | Age 26. | Haverhill Cemetery. |
| Rear Gunner | Sergeant Thomas Leslie Lenton, 1622714 RAFVR. Age 21. | Sec F.Grave 38. Ashston-Under-Lyne (Hurst) Cemetery. |
| Flight Engineer | Sergeant Peter Allan Sumpter, 1869349 RAFVR Age 23. | Sec U. Grave 252. Haverhill Cemetery |
| | | |
| Posted History | Posted in from No.3 LFS 06/10/1944 on completion of No.56 Course. Ex No.1653. | |
| Operations Flown | 23 | |
| Buried | *Four crew buried in home towns.* | |

Tragically this was the crews first operation aboard Lancaster NG147, the usual mount of F/Lt Waite. This G-H fitted Lancaster had aborted the Erkenschwick operation with port outer engine trouble on the 15th, when skippered by F/O N Cowley. Flight Lieutenant Tait was an experienced pilot having amassed some 668 Flying hours.

The crew of Flight Lieutenant 'Bob' Tait seen here standing in front of their usual aircraft NG137 XY-D 'Dagwood Special'. The only crewmembers identified are, 1st Left, Sergeant Les Lenton (Rear Gunner), 2nd left Flying Officer Bert Nutfield (Bomb Aimer), 3rd Left, Flight Lieutenant Bob Tait (Pilot), 4th left Sergeant Peter Sumpter (Flight Engineer), 5th left, Pilot Officer Gerry Haslam (Mid Upper Gunner). The rest of the crew were Flight Sergeant Wilf Gamble (Wireless Operator) and Flight Sergeant Tom Darney.

Flight Lieutenant Roland Ralph Tait, 179588 RAFVR

Flight Sergeant Thomas Brown Darney, 1676154 RAFVR.

Flying Officer Herbert Charles Dutfield, 154376 RAFVR.

Flight Sergeant Wilfred Sidney Gamble, 2206781 RAFVR

Pilot Officer Gerald Stalker Haslam, 56419 RAF.

Sergeant Peter Allan Sumpter, 1869349 RAFVR.

Left, The family grave of rear gunner, Sergeant Leslie Lenton. Above, a poor photograph of Leslie while undergoing training.

In a letter to the respected author and historian Jock Whitehouse[21], Sgt Martin Thorne, the mid upper gunner on the crew of F/Lt Waite reported, *'As far as I recall, F/Lt Tait's aircraft went u/s with magneto trouble, and he was given our old hard-worked 'Charlie'.*

Flight Lieutenant Roland Ralph Tait and his crew had completed 23 operations since their arrival from No.3 LFS, with 18 flown aboard NG137 XY-D. The grisly task of recovering the crew's remains could not have been easy given the force of the explosion.

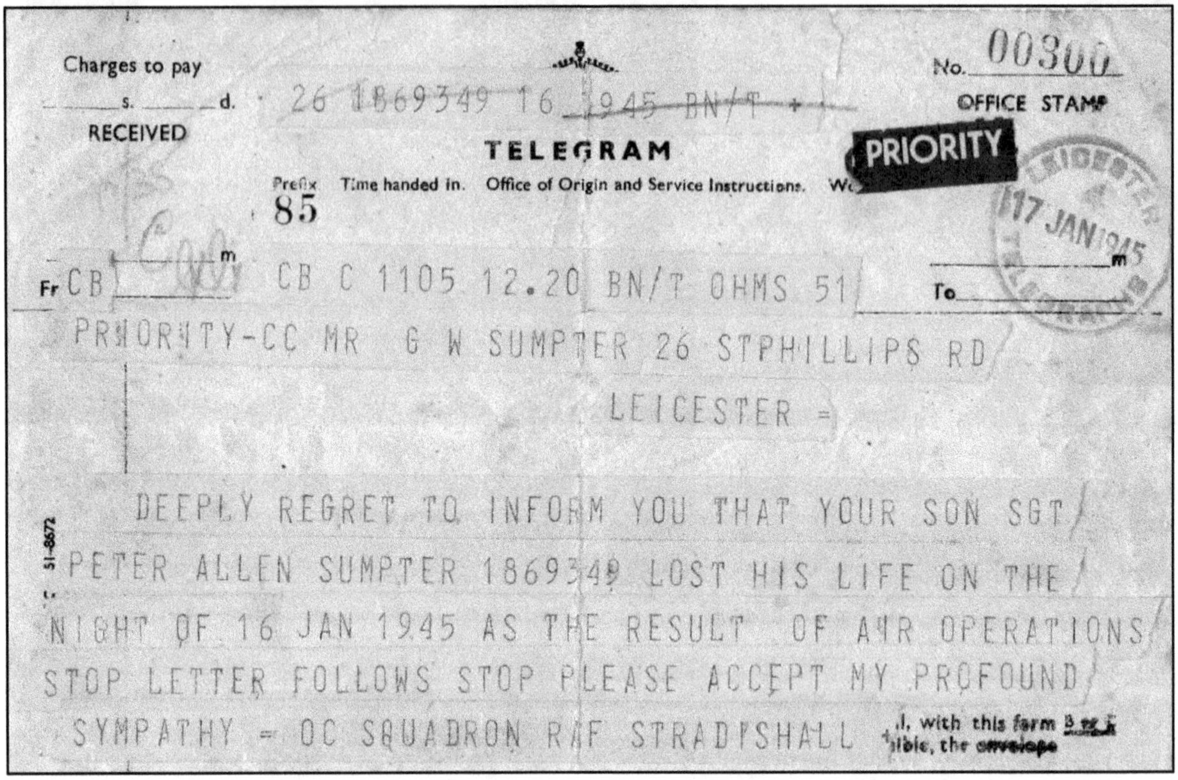

Charges to pay
s. d.
RECEIVED
26 1869349 16 1945 BN/T
No. 00300
OFFICE STAMP
TELEGRAM
PRIORITY
Prefix 85 Time handed in. Office of Origin and Service Instructions.
17 JAN 1945
Fr CB CB C 1105 12.20 BN/T OHMS 51 To
PRIORITY-CC MR G W SUMPTER 26 STPHILLIPS RD
LEICESTER =
DEEPLY REGRET TO INFORM YOU THAT YOUR SON SGT
PETER ALLEN SUMPTER 1869349 LOST HIS LIFE ON THE
NIGHT OF 16 JAN 1945 AS THE RESULT OF AIR OPERATIONS
STOP LETTER FOLLOWS STOP PLEASE ACCEPT MY PROFOUND
SYMPATHY = OC SQUADRON RAF STRADISHALL

The dreaded Telegram would change the lives of so many left behind.

To add to the night's gloom, New Zealander F/O Lawrence Idle RNZAF experienced starboard outer engine trouble aboard Lancaster HK613 XY-Y soon after take-off. It was quickly apparent that the night's operation was over for them. The crew flew to the jettisoning area and, at 23:17 hours, dropped 'safe' the 4000 pounder and 5 x 500lb MC bombs. They landed back at RAF Stradishall at 00:36 hours with 11 x 500 pounders still on board. Scheduled over the target at 02:15 hours and contrary to the briefing from the Met Officer, the squadron found the target covered in a layer of low cloud. Numerous searchlights unable to penetrate the cloud had the effect of illuminating the clouds, producing an unnaturally sinister light above the target. Flak was medium heavy but managed to inflict damage to Lancaster HK661 XY-R crewed by F/O J Beck RAAF, rendering the rear turret unserviceable. Also, hit, but to a lesser extent, was F/Sgt T Green's NG149 XY-G. The explosions of countless four-thousand-pound cookies could be distinguished through the clouds 20,000 feet below. Red and green star flares littered the aiming point, underneath which a large red glow was seen with oily greyish smoke mushrooming through the cloud base. The accuracy of the attack could not be gauged. Photo reconnaissance was not possible until after another attack on February 2/3rd, 1945.

[21] *Mr Jock Whitehouse, Co-author of the book* ***Royal Airforce Stradishall*** *and one of the leading authorities on RAF Stradishall and aviation in East Anglia.*

No.186 Squadron Reported Flak Damage 16/01/1945

| Serial | Code | Damage Reported | Repairs / Notes |
|---|---|---|---|
| HK661 | **XY-R** | Severed external rotation valve. Rear turret U/S. | Repaired on Squadron |
| NG149 | **XY-G** | Damaged, but details not recorded. | Repaired on Squadron |

The tragic deaths of F/Lt R Tait and his crew so near to the station brought the savagery of operational flying that closer to everyone on the station, not that they ever needed reminding.

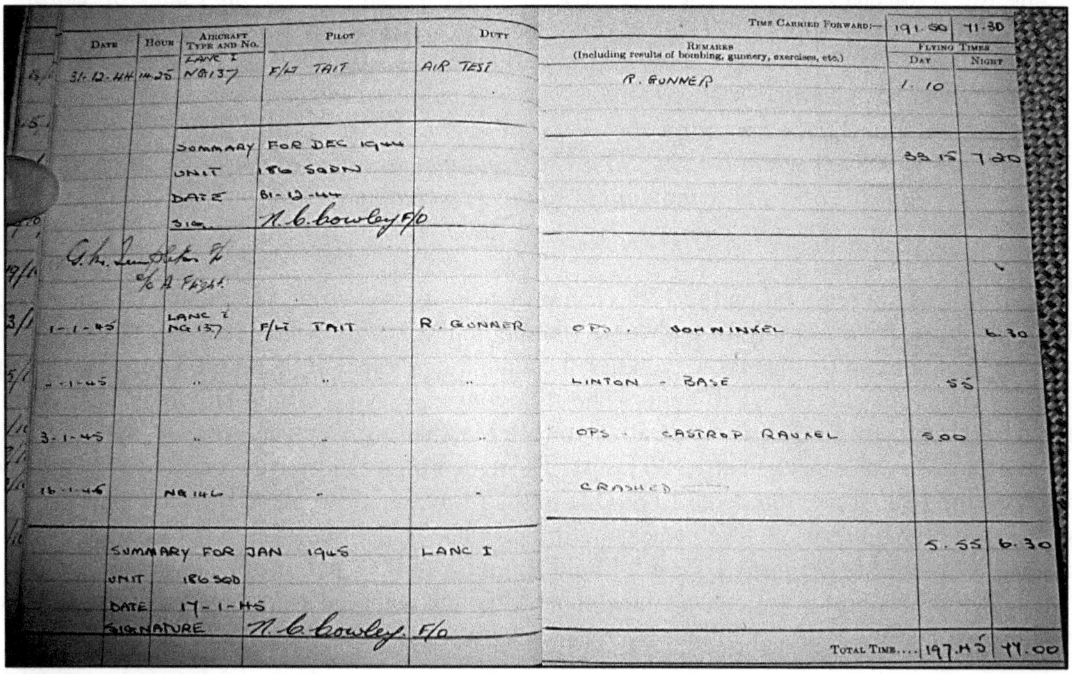

The Flying Log Book of Sergeant Les Lenton. Note that someone has filled in the final operation but recorded the wrong serial NG146!

There was one twist to the tragic events that unfolded on this night. It involved the crew of Australian Jeff Carson. The crew's rear Gunner, F/Sgt McPherson RAAF recalls.

> *'During January 1945, whilst on leave, our wireless operator, Wilbert, became engaged to Elspeth, a young Scottish lass. He eventually returned to the Squadron after availing of an extra day's unauthorised leave. During that day's absence, the crew had to go on a daylight raid to Erkenswick in the Ruhr with a substitute wireless operator. Wilbert was subsequently informed that if another wireless operator was unable to fly on an operation because of illness or absence without leave, he would have to fly as a substitute. If was only a day later, on the 16 of January, that another wireless operator was AWOL, and Wilbert was listed as a replacement for a night operation. The remainder of our crew were having a drink in the Mess as the planes were taking off at about 11 p.m. when suddenly there was a loud explosion and on enquiry, we were told that one of the Lancasters had crashed on take-off, killing all the crew. We were devastated when we learnt that it was the plane in which Wilbert was flying. We then had a "wake" in remembrance of our departed friend and returned to our barracks and bed. Our barracks consisted of a large hall in which about twenty aircrew were housed, and it also had two single rooms at one end. Wilbert, being a Warrant Officer, occupied one of these rooms. Next morning, as we*

*were getting dressed, to our amazement, Wilbert emerged from his room! When we informed him of what had happened the previous night, he went white with shock. He then explained that as he was about to enter the aircraft before take-off, the crew's regular wireless operator appeared and told Wilbert to "nick off" as this was his crew! Wilbert said he didn't need a second bidding, and immediately returned to the barracks and went to bed and was totally unaware that the plane had crashed. On that same morning, all the Australian crew members, except Wilbert, received notification that they had parcels to be collected from the Post Office. Wilbert generally received more parcels than anyone else and was naturally disappointed. Nevertheless, he accompanied me to the Post Office and whilst there enquired of the WAAF if there were any parcels for Warrant Officer Perry. She replied, "Yes, but they are being returned to London because he was killed last night." Wilbert and | immediately realised that no one in Administration had been made aware of the switch of wireless operators the previous night, so we hastily proceeded to the Adjutant's Office to correct the situation. The Adjutant was about to notify Air Ministry of the casualties of the previous night, including W/O W. J. Perry!*

The squadron was not required on the 17th. The only activity was an uncompleted G-H exercise. On the 18th, the weather took a turn for the worse when 60mph freezing winds, hail and thunder battered the airfield. A night raid by nine crews against the synthetic oil plant at Sterkrade Holton was planned but subsequently cancelled at 20.30 hours. The following day, No.3 Group HQ again instructed the squadron to make ready nine crews for an attack on the Marshalling Yards at Stuttgart, but, for a second time, the operation was cancelled at 15:30 hours. The squadron welcomed the crew of Flight Sergeant E Morris on the 19th, fresh from No.3 LFS. Due to the filthy winter weather, the crew had languished at No.3 LFS for the best part of seven weeks before posting. The publication in the London Gazette of a well-deserved DFM to Sergeant T Heard, Flight Engineer to F/Lt Jennings DFC, was announced on the 19th. Thomas had just completed a 30 trip tour. Although recorded as a No.186 award, the incident below and the majority of the operations were flown with No.90 Squadron. The citation reads.

*HEARD, Thomas Edwin. 1087138 Sergeant, No.186 Sqn. This Flight Engineer has carried out his duties with extreme efficiency during his operational tour. On one occasion while the aircraft was running up on the target, the rear gunner was seriously wounded during a sharp surprise attack by an enemy night fighter. Sergeant Heard laboured for a considerable period at 19,000 feet in an effort to extricate the wounded gunner. This he managed to do and then proceeded to administer first aid during the return trip. On another mining sortie when the aircraft was badly damaged by flak before reaching the dropping area, this N.C.O. rendered valuable assistance to his pilot in retaining control of the aircraft, thereby contributing to the successful conclusion of the mission. These incidents are typical of the calm courage and devotion to duty which this N.C.O. has always displayed. He is a good N.C.O. and a fine aircrew member. I recommend that he be awarded the Distinguished Flying Medal.*

The morning of January 20th, 1945, was bitterly cold, every exposed surface was covered in winters icy grip. Once again, Group HQ based at Exning ordered No.186 Squadron to prepare nine crews for another attempt on the Marshalling Yards at Stuttgart. As the morning progressed, snow began to fall. It continued throughout the afternoon until the cancellation signal was finally received at RAF Stradishall at 16:45 hours. The cancellations continued. On the 21st, nine aircraft required, again Stuttgart, cancelled at 17:10 hours. January 22nd was a day of frustration, nine crews were detailed and briefed for an attack on the synthetic oil plant at Sterkrade, only for this to be cancelled at 10:30 hours and rescheduled for that night. This was then switched to a raid directed against Duisburg.

Form B.769 – January 22nd, 1945 (N) : Target : Duisburg (Bruckhausen Benzol Plant) GQ1683(?)

| | | | | | | | |
|---|---|---|---|---|---|---|---|
| F/O | Young | H.S | | NG137 | XY-D | Main Force | Duty Carried Out. |
| F/Lt | Templeton | G | RCAF | NG146 | XY-E | Main Force | Duty Carried Out. |
| F/O | Hart | J.H | | NG140 | XY-F | Main Force | Duty Carried Out. |
| F/O | Field | E.L | | HK682 | XY-L | Main Force | Duty Carried Out. |
| F/O | Gibson | J.H | | NN720 | XY-K | Main Force | Duty Carried Out. |
| F/Lt | Hunt | E.G | | HK661 | XY-R | Main Force | Duty Carried Out. |
| F/O | Green | L.A | | NG293 | XY-U | Main Force | Duty Carried Out. |
| F/O | O'Brien | J.D | RAAF | NG353 | XY-X | Main Force | Duty Carried Out. |
| F/Lt | Orman | K.G | RNZAF | HK613 | XY-Y | Main Force | Duty Carried Out. |

Finally, after what must have seemed an eternity, the first Lancaster took off from RAF Stradishall at 17:02 hours, at the controls was Canadian F/Lt Gordon Templeton RCAF. Once airborne, the crews headed towards Reading before departing over the English Coast near Deal, Kent. The bombers crossed the Belgian coast at Eeklo, 15 miles west of Bruges. Conditions over the continent favoured the defenders. Crystal-clear conditions and bright moonlight was a formula for German opposition. The German border was crossed near the town of Kalderkirchen. The final leg to the target was made all the easier with a snow-covered landscape, making map reading and identification straightforward.

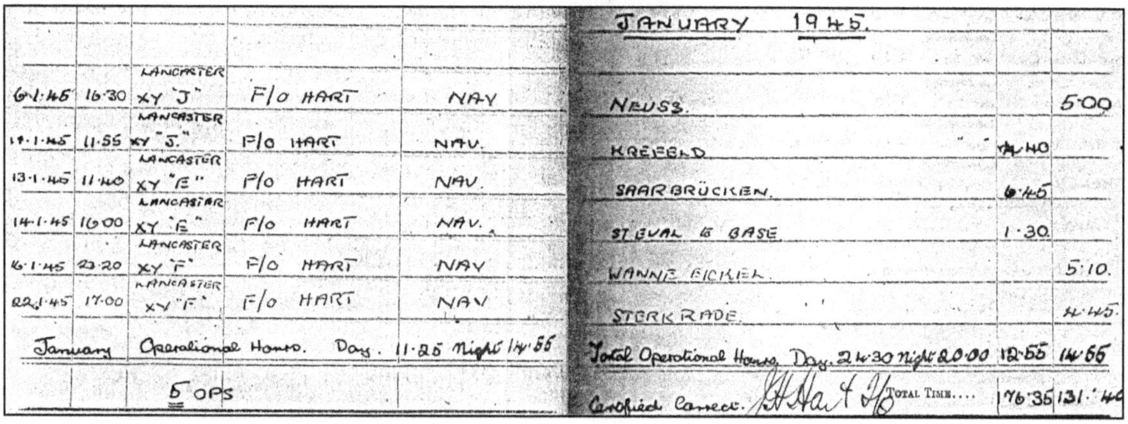
JANUARY 1945.

6.1.45 16.30 LANCASTER XY "J" F/O HART NAV — NEUSS 5.00
11.1.45 11.55 LANCASTER XY "J" F/O HART NAV. — KREFELD 4.40
13.1.45 11.40 LANCASTER XY "E" F/O HART NAV. — SAARBRÜCKEN 6.45
14.1.45 16.00 LANCASTER XY "E" F/O HART NAV. — ST EVAL to BASE 1.30
16.1.45 23.20 LANCASTER XY "F" F/O HART NAV — WANNE EICKEL 5.10
22.1.45 17.00 LANCASTER XY "F" F/O HART NAV — STERKRADE 4.45

January Operational Hours. Day. 11.25 Night 14.55
Total Operational Hours. Day. 24.30 Night 20.00 12.55 14.55
5 OPS
Certified Correct. TOTAL TIME.... 176.35 131.40

A page from the Log Book of Navigator F/O Jack Allan. Recording three daylight and two night trips. The operations were carried out in bitterly cold conditions and often in treacherous flying weather.

Mosquitos and Lancasters of No.8 Path Finder Force would open proceedings followed by the Lancasters of No.3 Group scheduled to bomb between 19:59 and 20:14 hours. They would be followed one minute later by the Lancasters of No.1 Group. The first squadron crew to bomb was F/O Green at 20:02 hours from 21,000 feet. They dropped their all HE load on the main concentration of Red and Green TIs. Visibility was excellent. The River Rhine was clearly seen, as was the explosion of numerous 4000 pounders. Flight Lieutenant E.G Hunt reported, *'several 4000lb bombs were seen bursting in the target area at 20:26 hours'*. Flak was described as moderate to intense. However, it was the searchlights estimated between 40-50 that proved especially troublesome. The crew of F/O J.D O'Brien RAAF reported damage the result of debris from an explosion over the target area, *'At 20:03 hours 'scarecrow' burst at 19,700 feet, but damage was not ascertained'*. This was, in all probability, the end of a No.153 Squadron Lancaster. Flight Lieutenant K Orman RNZAF reported to the Intelligence Officer at de-briefing, *' Three large explosions were seen starboard of aiming point, and on run-up one large explosion was observed. Good fires were burning as aircraft left target area. The glow of the fires could be seen from between 60-70 miles on return to base'*.

No.186 Squadron Reported Flak Damage 22/01/1945

| Serial | Code | Damage Reported | Repairs / Notes |
|---|---|---|---|
| NG353 | **XY-X** | Damaged, but details not recorded. | Repaired on Squadron |

The two Australian Air Gunners of Flight Lieutenant Jeff Clarson RAAF crew. Left, Jim Mallison RAAF Mid Upper, Right, Gerald McPherson RAAF. Both were photographed before their commission.

Wing Commander J Giles DFC returned from leave on the 22nd and reassumed command vice S/Ldr P Reynolds. The same day, the squadron welcomed a new crew, skippered by Scotsman, Sgt Phil Gray, a recent convert from No.1651 HCU at RAF Woolfox Lodge. They had the misfortune to be huddled together awaiting transportation to Stradishall on the snow-covered platform at Haverhill train station at the same time as three coffins of F/Lt Tait's crew were being unloaded for transportation to their hometowns. A group of relatives solemnly watched as the coffins were loaded onto the carriage in the bitter cold. They were being consoled by 'B' Flight Commander S/Ldr Bass AFM. By chance, S/Ldr Bass recognised the freezing crew from his OTU Instructor days and explained to them the tragic circumstances. With the coffins unloaded, the crew were asked if they wanted a lift back to RAF Stradishall in the lorry, which had only minutes before carried the coffins of the unfortunate crew. They declined and chose to wait for the official transport given the situation. It was anything but the start a new crew would want to encounter prior to commencing their operational tour. Flight Sergeant Phil Gray recalls his first impression of his new Commanding Officer, Wing Commander Giles DFC.

*The Winco was quite a character. He regularly flew on ops. himself and is credited with having posed the Group Captain (a by-the-book character) with the ultimatum that he could have one or the other - Ops or bullshit - but not both. They just didn't mix. Apparently the Group Captain wisely chose ops for we had very little trouble from him. I say 'wisely' because if word of any obstruction had filtered back to Air Chief Marshall Harris he may well have dealt with the G/C. in similar fashion to many a German city – and crushed him out of sight.*

The relatives of F/O Duffy, Sgt Sumpter, and P/O Haslam, the oldest man in the crew at just 26, gathered at a snow-covered Haverhill Cemetery for the funeral of their loved ones. The squadron was represented by S/Ldr Bass, F/Lt J Walker and F/O's D Grieg, L Grant, and J. Oyler. At the conclusion of the Full Service, the last post was sounded. One can only imagine the despair and heartbreak of all those present. That same day, at 14:30 hours, the funeral of F/Sgt W Gamble took place at York Cemetery. Flying Officer F Richards represented the squadron on this occasion.

A planned operation to the oil plants at Castrop Rauxel was planned for the 23rd, but was postponed for 24 hours. On the 23rd the private funerals of two of the crew were performed. The funeral of F/Sgt T Darney was conducted at 13:30 hours at Hindley (St. Margaret) Churchyard. While Flight Lieutenant R Tait was buried at St John Beverley New Church at 15:15 hours. The squadron representatives were the recently screened F/Lt C Wait and F/O H Powell.

Pilot, Sergeant Phil Gray and his Flight Engineer, Sergeant Frank Parkhouse.

RAF Stradishall was covered in a thick layer of frost on the morning of January 24th, every exposed surface was coated in its icy grip. Visibility was less than 20 yards, making flying impossible. The postponed attack on Castrop Rauxel was cancelled but the squadron was warned that they would be required the following day. Two hundred miles north, the funeral of Sgt T Lenton took place at 09:15 hours at the Ashston-Under-Lyne (Hurst) Cemetery. Flying Officer G Jepson represented the squadron on this occasion. Nine crews were detailed and briefed for an attack on Krefeld's Railway Marshalling Yards on the 25th, but the freezing fog had other ideas, the operation was cancelled at 09:35 hours.

The squadron Lancasters began to have VHF RT equipment fitted on the 26th. This equipment would allow transmissions between aircraft, essential for the broadcasts by G-H Leaders and with base. On the evening of the 26th, the squadron was instructed that it would be required the following day. The target once again was Krefeld's Marshalling Yards. In freezing conditions, the squadron Ground Crews fuelled and bombed-up ten Lancaster's in semi-darkness and blizzard-like conditions. At 06:45 hours, the news filtered through that the operation was postponed for two hours. Within 15 minutes, this was changed to 'Cancelled'. The recent spate of cancellations had become wearisome. Having trudged to the briefing room, the assembled crews would adorn their flying kit and collect their parachute and then be transported out to a distant dispersal. They now had the unenviable job of waiting, often sitting in their aircraft only for the cancellation signal to arrive. The anti-climax, after so much tension, must have played tremendously on the crew's nerves.

Nine American journalists visited Base HQ on the afternoon of the 27th, accompanied by No.3 Group AoC, AVM R Harrison CB, CBE, DFC, AFC. He was joined by W/Cdr W.T Lawrence, Senior Public Relations Officer at Bomber Command HQ, and No.3 Group's Public Relation Officer, F/Lt S Parkinson. The party were received at RAF Stradishall by Air Commodore J Silvester CBE and Group Captain E.C Bates AFC. In freezing conditions, the assembled group toured the base. It had been planned that the journalists would witness the return of the squadron's Lancasters. However, they made do with watching a Lancaster being bombed up due to the cancellation. Given the weather conditions, they quickly retreated to Flying Control and the Intelligence Library. The tour concluded with dinner in the Officers Mess.

Finally on the morning of January 28th the fog cleared sufficiently to allow ten crews to take-off for a daylight attack on the Cologne/Gremburg Marshalling Yards. One of the crews airborne was W/Cdr J Giles DFC at the controls of Lancaster HK662 XY-P. The squadron would provide just one of 15 G-H crews assigned by No.31 Base. Flying Officer J.E Tonks at the controls of HK668 XY-W would represent the squadron.

Form B.771 – January 28th, 1945 (D) : Target : Cologne/Gremburg Marshalling Yards - G-H624

| | | | | | | | |
|---|---|---|---|---|---|---|---|
| W/Cdr | Giles DFC | J.H | | HK662 | XY-P | Follower | Duty Carried Out |
| F/O | Clarson | A | RAAF | NG140 | XY-F | Follower | Duty Carried Out |
| F/O | Barton | E.R | RAAF | NG149 | XY-G | Follower | Duty Carried Out |
| F/Lt | Gibson | J.H.W | | NN720 | XY-K | Follower | Duty Carried Out |
| F/O | Idle | L.A | RNZAF | NG137 | XY-D | Follower | Duty Carried Out |
| F/O | Fernley | F | | NG293 | XY-U | Follower | Duty Carried Out |
| F/O | Godfrey | D.F.J | RAAF | HK606 | XY-V | Follower | Duty Carried Out |
| F/O | Tonks | J.E | | HK688 | XY-W | G-H Leader | Duty Carried Out. |
| F/O | Mason | F.H | | NG353 | XY-X | Follower | Duty Carried Out. |

The Lancasters of No.31 Base would be in the vanguard of the entire No.3 Group force with No.218 Squadron spearheading. The freezing conditions resulted in the Lancasters Merlin engines leaving long white contrails in the rarified icy conditions. The followers had a particularly torrid time trying to keep their Leader's in sight, blinded by the white vapour trails. Those better positioned had almost limitless visibility as the bombers entered German airspace. The long contrails did little to settle the crews nerves. Thankfully the presence of seven squadrons of RAF Mustangs and nine squadrons of Spitfires helped relieve the tension as the exposed force neared the target in the clear blue sky above Germany.

No flak or fighter opposition was encountered until the bombers were on their curved bomb run into the target, the whole force being timed to be over the target between 14:09 and 14:17 hours. It was then that both heavy barrage flak and predicted flak opened up with uncanny accuracy. To the lead squadrons, it appeared that the flak gunners below had targeted them specifically in an attempt to upset the bomb run. Flying Officer L.A Idle RNZAF was hit at 14:08 hours, but the damage did not stop the crew from dropping on their G-H Leader at exactly 14:09 hours. They watched as their 4000 cookie was seen to explode in the centre of the Marshalling Yards. The next hit was the crew of F/Lt J Gibson at 14:10 hours. Flak punctured the fuselage of Lancaster NN720 XY-K, wounding both gunners and rendering the rear turret unserviceable. Two crews both reported being hit at 14:11 hours. Flying Officer D Godfrey was hit on their bomb run at 20,000 feet. They had lost their G-H Leader and bombed

Avro Lancaster NG149 XY-G *'George Giles'* was photographed just before Flying Officer E.R Barton RAAF and crew took her to Cologne on January 28th 1945. The aircraft sustained slight flak damage over Cologne. Note the 26 bomb symbols.

visually. Australian F/O A Clarson RAAF was also damaged on his run into the target. Despite this, he reported, *'A good attack, at least 80% of bombs appeared on the target'*. Flying Officer R Barton RAAF was over the Marshalling Yards at 14:13 hours. They reported only slight damage to Lancaster NG149 XY-G. Flying Officer J Tonks at the controls of the G-H equipped Lancaster, HK688 XY-W stated on return, *'Target identified on Radar Navigational Aids and visually. Bombing was carried out at 14:10 hours from 20,000 feet. River, town and sidings and Marshalling Yards were seen and there was little activity in the Yards. Ten bombs were seen bursting in the sidings. Bombs appeared concentrated in the yards'*.

Flight Lieutenant J.H Gibson and crew were screened from further operations on return from Cologne. Older than the majority of the pilots on the squadron, the 28-year-old married Brummie had previously served in the British Army. James Gibson had flown all his operations with No.186 Squadron, despite his posting onto No.90 Squadron in September 1944. A sobering 60 Lancasters reported damage on return. At RAF Wratting Common, No.195 Squadron reported seven damaged aircraft, No.218 Squadron registered five, plus two crews missing, both victims of flak.

No.186 Squadron Reported Flak Damage 28/01/1945

| Serial | Code | Damage Reported | Repairs / Notes |
|---|---|---|---|
| NG137 | **XY-D** | Damaged, but details not recorded. | Repaired on Squadron. |
| NG149 | **XY-G** | Damaged, but details not recorded. | Repaired on Squadron. |
| NG140 | **XY-F** | Damaged, but details not recorded. | Repaired on Squadron. |
| HK606 | **XY-V** | Damaged, but details not recorded. | Repaired on Squadron. |
| NN720 | **XY-K** | Both turrets damaged, rear fuselage holed. | Cat Ac/FB. RoS No.54 MU. Returned to unit 22/02/1945. |

It was an early start for the squadron on the morning of the 29th. The first of 12 crews slowly climbed away from a frosty RAF Stradishall at 10:09 hours. It was a beautiful but freezing morning, conditions appeared ideal with a clear blue sky. By 10:29 hours, the last Lancaster was safely airborne and heading towards No.31 Base's rendezvous point west of Colchester. Again No.31 Base found itself in the unenviable third and final wave of the attack. The target was the Krefeld Uerdingen railyards, a vital rail hub between Duisburg and Munchen-Gladbach. Even after five years of almost continuous bombing, the German railway system was still managing to function but on a vastly limited scale. The group detailed 148 Lancasters from all its Lancaster squadrons. The fighter escort would be provided by 96 RAF Mustangs and a single squadron of Spitfires.

Form B.774 – January 29th 1945(D) : Target : Krefeld-Uerdingen Rail Yards - GH611

| | | | | | | | |
|---|---|---|---|---|---|---|---|
| F/O | Marshall | A.N | | NG137 | XY-D | Follower | Duty Not Carried Out. |
| F/O | Green | T.B | | NG140 | XY-F | Follower | Duty Carried Out |
| F/Sgt | Morris | E | | NG149 | XY-G | Follower | Duty Carried Out |
| F/O | Cowley | N.C | | NG175 | XY-J | G-H Leader | Duty Carried Out |
| F/O | Young | H.S | | HK682 | XY-L | Follower | Duty Carried Out |
| F/O | Green | L.A | | HK684 | XY-O | Follower | Duty Carried Out |
| F/Lt | Orman DFC | K.G | RNZAF | HK662 | XY-P | Follower | Duty Carried Out |
| S/Ldr | Bass | R.W | | HK661 | XY-R | Follower | Duty Carried Out |
| F/O | Gogler | R.J | RAAF | HK893 | XY-U | Follower | Duty Carried Out |
| F/O | Beck | J.A.G | RAAF | NG353 | XY-X | Follower | Duty Carried Out |
| F/Lt | Hanson | R.A.J | | HK613 | XY-Y | Follower | Duty Carried Out |
| F/Lt | Hunt | E.G | | PD429 | XY-Z | G-H Leader | Duty Carried Out |

Two G-H Leaders would be provided, with some, if limited, previous experience. The squadron recorded one early return. The squadron recorded one early return. Lancaster NG137 XY-D lost the port outer engine at 11:50 hours. The defective engine was successfully feathered, and the crew made their way to the jettison area. The Cookie and two 500lb GP were jettisoned before F/O Albert Marshall made a safe three-engined landing back at RAF Stradishall at 13:16 hours. Almost a solid layer of cloud en route seemed to hide the bombers from the flak gunners below. Incredibly given their reception the previous day, flak was almost non-existent. Spasmodic heavy flak was encountered but was not considered troublesome. More worryingly as the formation neared the aiming point, the usually spaced base groups appeared to converge and almost overlap. The congestion over the target area was reported by F/O T.B Green, *'Several aircraft narrowly escaped being hit by other aircraft's bombs.'* Flying

Flight Lieutenant C.W Wait and crew. They are seen here in front of their usual aircraft NG147 XY-C *'Champagne Charlie'*. It was this Lancaster that crashed with tragic results on January 16th 1945. The crew L-R Sergeant M.V 'Joe' Thorne (Mid Upper Gunner), Sergeant Arthur Badham (Navigator), Flying Officer C.J 'Jack' Wait (Pilot), Flying Officer George Britton (Wireless Operator), Sergeant W.S Hobson (Flight Engineer). Front row L-R, Sergeant Ken Bray (Rear Gunner) and Sergeant R.J 'Bobby' Briggs (Bomb Aimer). Note the name *'Cecilia'* on the engine, each of which had a women's name starting with a 'C'.

Officer R Gogler RAAF also reported this dangerous situation, *'Something had obviously gone wrong with the timing, great concentration of aircraft over the target'.*

Flying Officer Cowley dropped his all HE load and flares at 13:58 hours. He reported, *'Saw no bombs bursting in town due to a large patch of haze over target. A large cloud of white smoke rose above clouds on leaving target. Seemed a very concentrated attack'.* Flight Lieutenant E. Hunt and his followers dropped at 14:00 hours from the very exact height of 18,359 feet, his assessment of the raid was brief, *Markers very scattered'.* Many crews reported a large white mushroom cloud rising through the clouds over the aiming point. The concerns about the raid's effectiveness would be dispelled when No.3 Group HQ scrutinised the target and post-raid reconnaissance photographs. The raid was a complete success. Heavy damage had been inflicted. Countless rail tracks had been destroyed along the entire length of the yard. A large bridge was hit, destroying two spans while 66 new craters were counted within the yard complex. The raid was an outstanding testament to the No.3 Group's growing confidence. The month of January 1945 had been tough on everyone. The first spell of bad weather was experienced between January 4th and 12th. This was followed by another particularly harsh period from January 20th, which lasted until the end of the month. Snow showers, low clouds, freezing fog and sub-

Sadly, not the best quality photo. Work carried out on the starboard inner Merlin of Flight Lieutenant Ken Orman RNZAF Lancaster, 'Q-Queenie'. Note the extensive exhaust discolouration on the upper wing surface.

zero temperatures played havoc with the squadron and No.3 Group. A number of raids were planned, and crews were briefed only for the raid to be cancelled at the 11th hour. It was challenging and tested the hard-working ground crews. Apart from the tragic accident on take-off on the 16th, the squadron had enjoyed a loss-free month. The squadron was now operational with G-H with six of its Lancaster's equipped. The Finishing School at RAF Feltwell was posting crews already fully trained in its use, and these were supplements by the 'Old-Hands' who carried out the three-day course. Particular praise was directed at the Ground Crews at RAF Stradishall in the Monthly Summary,

*Two stations warrant special attention this month, RAF Stradishall started the new year well by completing seven operations without failures of any kind and ended the month with only three engineering failures – An excellent start for the squadron's first full month under the Stradishall Servicing Wing.*

It was the two men at the helm who had the final say on the month's activities. Group Captain E.C Bates AFC, Station Commander's Summary, January 1945 was if anything brief and to the point.

Bad weather hampered operations. Raids were laid on twenty-four times[22] but only thirteen took off. Of these, 147 sorties were flown. There were no losses due to enemy action, but one aircraft was lost on take-off. There were no accidents and the administration of RAF Shepherds Grove was handed over to No. 38 Group.

[22] *This differs to the Base Commanders report.*

No.31 Base Commander, Air Commodore J Silvester CBE was slightly more descriptive.

January was more a month of hard work than achievement. The weather was generally bad, and of twenty-eight operations detailed only thirteen were carried out. Full use was made of the breaks in the weather and also of our ability to bomb 'invisible' targets. Seven of thirteen attacks were made through-H cloud, with most targets being oil and communications. In spite of the weather, very hard work prevented the airfield from being completely closed. (This MUST be recorded in the Station Diary). There was a lot of snowfall and all worked hard at the 'snow plan'.

Summing up: During the month No. 31 Base detailed 538 aircraft of which thirteen failed to take off. Twenty-three returned early and five failed to return. 2,520 tons of bombs were dropped. Large numbers of 'Failed to Take-Off' were due to two aircraft bogging down at Chedburgh and Wratting Common. (Four FTO from each Base).

January 1945 : Avro Lancaster Delivery.

| ToC Date | Serial | Code | Maker | Mark | From |
|---|---|---|---|---|---|
| 30/01/1945 | HK692 | XY-B | Vickers Armstrong | Mk.B.I | No.90 Squadron |
| 30/01/1945 | HK694 | XY-C | Vickers Armstrong | Mk.B.I | No.90 Squadron |

# February 1945

## *Total Warfare*

The squadron was by February 1945 in excellent shape, commanded by a squadron commander who expected nothing less than total commitment, but was willing to forgo the usual 'bull'. Both morale and confidence throughout the squadron was at a peak. With a hoped-for improvement in the weather, HQ Bomber Command was keen to pile on the pressure against German industry, transportation, and Harris' preference, cities. The squadrons of No.3 would be used increasingly to attack Germany's fragile oil and railway system. By the end of January, 145 G-H sets had been installed throughout the Group. It was a magnificent achievement by the back-room boys, radar mechanics and everyone involved. However, there was a downside. The numbers were close to outstripping the capability of the then existing G-H ground stations, expansion was needed, and quickly. Over the coming months, these attacks on both targets would increase. With German industry vulnerable to daily bombing, Nazi Germany began to disperse its vital factories throughout the shrinking Fatherland by building underground factories. The more the Nazis dispersed, the more they depended on the already fragile railway system. They could not do the same with their synthetic oil and Benzol plants which No.3 Group would systematically destroy over the last few months of the war. By 1945, Albert Speer, the German Minister for Armaments and War Production, viewed the methodical attacks on Germany's oil industry and the resulting fuel shortages as "catastrophic." The squadron welcomed second tour veteran F/O Stuart Brayshaw DFC the last week of January. The 23-year-old married man had started his first tour with No.90 Squadron flying Short Stirlings in the summer of 1943. By December, he had completed a hectic tour. There followed the usual stint instructing with No.1651 HCU. He was awarded his DFC in February 1944. A lot had changed since his first tour, and now he was ready to start again.

The group despatched 160 aircraft against the railway station and marshalling yards at Munchen-Gladbach on the 1st. Twelve were provided by No.186 Squadron, three of which would be G-H Leaders recently adorned with two yellow bars on their rudders.

Form B.776 – February 1st 1945(D) : Target : Munchen-Gladbach Railway Yards – 'Jack'

| | | | | | | | |
|---|---|---|---|---|---|---|---|
| S/Ldr | Reynolds | P | | NG174 | XY-A | G-H Leader | Duty Carried Out. |
| F/O | Marshall | A.N | | NG140 | XY-F | Follower | Duty Carried Out. |
| F/O | Barton | E.R | | NG149 | XY-G | Follower | Duty Carried Out. |
| F/O | Tonks | J.E | | NG175 | XY-J | G-H Leader | Duty Carried Out. |
| F/O | Field DFC | E.L | | NN720 | XY-K | Follower | Duty Carried Out. |
| F/Sgt | Morris | E | | HK682 | XY-L | Follower | Duty Carried Out. |
| F/O | O'Brien | J.D | RAAF | HK684 | XY-O | Follower | Duty Carried Out. |
| F/O | Beck | J.A. | RAAF | HK659 | XY-Q | Follower | Duty Carried Out. |
| F/O | Green | L.A | | HK661 | XY-R | Follower | Duty Carried Out. |
| F/O | Godfrey | D.F.J | RAAF | NG293 | XY-U | Follower | Duty Carried Out. |
| F/O | Brayshaw DFC | S.C | | HK613 | XY-Y | Follower | Duty Carried Out. |
| F/Lt | Hunt | E.G | | PD429 | XY-Z | G-H Leader | Duty Carried Out. |

Flying with S/Ldr Reynolds was RAF Stradishall's Station Commander, Group Captain E.C Bates AFC. Born in Australia in 1906, Eric Cecil Bates joined the RAF in 1930. He served with a number of units in the early 1930s, including the Hawker Hart equipped No.33 Squadron and the Iraqi based No.55 Squadron. In 1938, he was given command of the Bristol Blenheim equipped No.101 Squadron. The following year, in August 1939, he was attached to the RAAF. In 1941 he served in Canada, where he stayed until 1943 when he returned to Britain and joined Bomber Command. Promoted to Group

Captain in January 1944, he was posted to RAF Stradishall as Station Commander. Bomber Command HQ frowned upon their Group Captains flying on operations, but a few keen to experience bombing first hand did. The 39-year-old Aussie was one of them Once airborne, the squadron would rendezvous with No.195 and No.218 Squadron over Hadlow, Kent, before falling in behind the squadrons of No.32 Base which would lead the raid. Almost from the moment the bombers crossed the English coast to the target, no ground detail was observed. Dense 10/10th cloud, with tops up to 14,000 feet blanketed the still snow-covered countryside. As the squadron approached the target on their curved bombing run at 16:28 hours, gaps in the clouds allowed the crews momentary glimpses of what appeared to be rail lines and fires. The G-H crew of S/Ldr Reynolds dropped at 16:28 hours, he remarked on return, *'The ground was seen through a gap in cloud, just before reaching target, but could not identify. Smoke puffs were fairly well concentrated.'* Flight Lieutenant E Hunt at the controls of PD429 XY-Z, another G-H aircraft, bombed at 16:30 hours reported, *'Incendiaries were seen burning in built-up area through gap in cloud. A fairly wide area was alight'.* The final G-H equipped crew was F/O J Tonks which was flying at 19,000 feet when he dropped at 16:31½ hours, *'Bombs fell where blue puffs were concentrated, but there were another cluster ¼ mile to starboard'.* All the crews returned safely to RAF Stradishall, having met practically no opposition. There were mutterings of disgruntlement amongst the squadrons of No.31 Base about the flying discipline of other groups and their apparent refusal to adhere to the

The imposing Wing Commander Alan Cairnes (3rd left) and crew in front Avro Lancaster U *'Karma'*. It is uncertain where this photograph was taken, RAF Stradishall or, more likely, RAF Wratting Common. The crew are L-R, Sergeant C.W Wilkinson (Wireless Operator), Sergeant W Fozard, (Rear Gunner) Wing Commander Cairnes. Sergeant J.C Ward RNZAF (Navigator), Flight Sergeant F Henshaw (Mid upper gunner), and Sergeant O Connolly (Bomb Aimer). Missing from the photo is the Flight Engineer, Sergeant R Sowerbutts.

briefed bombing heights and timing. Lancasters, which should have followed No.31 Base, had been seen flying directly above the second wave, oblivious to the bombers below. On the morning of the 1st, the squadron welcomed one new crew and one on attachment for operational experience. Wing Commander A.E Cairnes captained the latter.

Sergeant Donald Crowe, Rear Gunner. His time on the squadron was measured in just weeks.

Alan Cairnes was new to bomber operations. His path to operational flying started with No.19 OTU at RAF Kinloss in late 1944, flying Whitley's. On completing the course, he and his crew were posted to No.1657 HCU based at RAF Stradishall in November 1944. Bad weather throughout December delayed his subsequent posting to No.3 LFS at RAF Feltwell until January 10th 1945. Wing Commander Cairnes flew his last conversion flight on January 22nd, a 4-hour cross-country and high-level bombing exercise. The crews were given an early briefing on the 2nd, a new name appearing on the Operations Board, Opladen. A district of Leverkusen, its railway workshops were vital in keeping the Cologne to Wuppertal railway running. Twelves crews were detailed before the operation was cancelled at 09:30 hours. It was a short reprieve. The squadron was then informed it would be required that night for an attack on the town of Wiesbaden situated on the right bank of the Rhine River. The town, which boasted the oldest spa in Europe, had been relatively untouched by bombing. The operation would be carried out in conjunction with No.1 and No.6 RCAF Group aircraft. Marking would be provided by the Path Finders. However, G-H equipped aircraft of No.3 Group were ordered to bomb independently and ignore any Oboe markers. The squadrons of No.3 Group would make up the 4th wave. Number 186 Squadron would provide its most significant number of G-H equipped Lancasters to date. These did not carry flares but would bomb on G-H.

Form B.778 – February 2nd 1945(N) : Target : Wiesbaden Town – 'Tope'

| | | | | | | | |
|---|---|---|---|---|---|---|---|
| F/O | Marshall | A.N | | NG146 | XY-E | Bombed on G-H | Duty Carried Out. |
| F/O | Saunders | A | | NG140 | XY-F | Bombed on G-H | Duty Carried Out. |
| F/O | Cowley | N.C | | NN720 | XY-K | Bombed on G-H | Duty Carried Out. |
| F/O | Young | H.S | | HK684 | XY-O | Bombed on G-H | Duty Carried Out. |
| F/O | Green | T.B | | HK662 | XY-P | Bombed on G-H | Duty Carried Out. |
| F/O | Green | L.A | | HK659 | XY-Q | Dropped on TI's | Duty Carried Out. |
| S/Ldr | Bass AFM | R.W | | HK661 | XY-R | Dropped on TI's | Duty Carried Out. |
| F/O | Beck | J.A. | RAAF | NG293 | XY-U | Dropped on TI's | Duty Carried Out. |
| W/Cdr | Giles DFC | J.H | | HK668 | XY-W | Bombed on G-H | Duty Carried Out. |
| F/O | Fernley | F | | NG353 | XY-X | Dropped on TI's | Duty Carried Out. |
| F/Lt | Hanson | R.A.J | | HK613 | XY-Y | Bombed on G-H | Duty Carried Out. |
| F/O | Brayshaw DFC | S.C | | PD429 | XY-Z | Bombed on G-H | Duty Carried Out. |

The squadron began taking off at 21:02 hours. Within 16 minutes, they were all airborne without incident. Despite the excellent weather conditions which favoured the defenders, the squadron reached the target unmolested. Solid cloud over Wiesbaden was causing problems for the Path Finders. The Oboe dropped ground markers were useless in the conditions. Nevertheless, on approaching the target area, the Lancasters of No.3 Group could quickly identify a faint red glow below the clouds. The G-H equipped Lancasters were not hindered by the cloud cover and were confident that their bomb loads at least were dropped over the town. Three 'scarecrows'[23] were seen and reported as the squadron crews started their bomb runs. Fighters were active, one was reported going down on fire at 23:46 hours. Over Wiesbaden, the flak was slight predicted but not reported as troublesome. Opinions varied amongst the returning crews about the accuracy of the raid Flying Officer L.A Green bombed at 23:54 hours on Green TIs, and he reported, *'Target Indicators scattered'*. Flying Officer F Fernley was at the controls of NG353 XY-X. Like F/O Green, he bombed on the Path Finder markers, reporting '*Attack seemed fairly scattered but was in the target area'*. More confident were the G-H equipped crews, F/O Saunders was at 19,500 feet, at 23:59 hours, he dropped his all HE load, they reported on return, *'A big glow was seen under the cloud in the target area, and a pillar of black smoke was seen to rise above the cloud. Bomb flashes below the cloud seemed to cover a wide area. Attack seem concentrated on the*

[23] *The squadron ORB reported these as ' Anti Morale Devices'.*

*town'.* Notwithstanding the crews optimism, No.3 Group HQ reported. The last sentence was obviously meant to antagonise PFF HQ.

> *The attack itself does not appear to have been successful. PFF provided the marking, but G-H aircraft of this group were using their own equipment for bombing. Clouds up to 16,000ft obscure all ground markers, so that crews were forced to bomb on Gee, H2S or D.R. The attack was most likely scattered but successful. G-H ensured that a percentage of the bombs hit the target.*

The raid on this innocuous target had taken a heavy toll, with two of the Group's most capable commanding officers lost. Wing Commander Bannister of No.90 Squadron was killed in a collision over Bury St Edmunds. Thirty-three-year old W/Cdr William Bannister was on attachment to No.90 Squadron from No.32 Base. It was his first operation. Over at RAF Methwold, No.149 Squadron recorded the loss of Wing Commander Leslie Kay DFC and his experienced crew. Leslie Kay had only arrived on the squadron the previous day and was flying as 2nd pilot with F/Lt Button RAAF. Tragically, the Button crew were on their 30th operation of their tour. Wing Commander Kay, a second tour veteran, was one of a handful of air-gunners who became squadron commanders. The following day, fifteen crews were detailed for an early evening attack on the Hansa Coking Plant at Dortmund, it would be an all No.3 Group effort with 150 Lancasters involved from all three Base Groups. The squadron would provide three G-H marker crews.

Form B.779 – February 3rd 1945(N) : Target : Dortmund (Hansa Coking Plant) – GQ1892

| | | | | | | | |
|---|---|---|---|---|---|---|---|
| S/Ldr | Reynolds | P | | NG174 | XY-A | Dropped On TI's | Duty Carried Out. |
| F/Lt | Field DFC | E.L | | HK692 | XY-B | Dropped On TI's | Duty Carried Out. |
| F/Sgt | Morris | E | | HK694 | XY-C | Dropped On TI's | Duty Carried Out. |
| F/O | Saunders | A | | NG140 | XY-F | Dropped On TI's | Duty Carried Out. |
| F/O | Tonks | J.E | | NG175 | XY-J | Bombed on G-H | Duty Carried Out. |
| F/O | Cowley | N.G | | NN720 | XY-K | Bombed on G-H | Duty Carried Out. |
| F/O | Young | H.S | | HK682 | XY-L | Dropped On TI's | Duty Carried Out. |
| F/O | Barton | E.R | RAAF | NG354 | XY-M | Dropped On TI's | Duty Carried Out. |
| F/O | O'Brien | J.D | RAAF | HK684 | XY-O | Dropped On TI's | Duty Carried Out. |
| F/O | Green | T.B | | HK662 | XY-P | Dropped On TI's | Duty Carried Out. |
| S/Ldr | Bass AFC | R.W | | HK661 | XY-R | Dropped On TI's | Duty Carried Out. |
| F/O | Gogler | R.J | RAAF | NG293 | XY-U | Dropped On TI's | Duty Carried Out. |
| F/Lt | Hunt | E.G | | HK668 | XY-W | FTR | Missing |
| F/Lt | Hanson | R.A.J | | HK613 | XY-Y | Dropped On TI's | Duty Carried Out. |
| F/O | Godfrey | D.F.J | RAAF | PD429 | XY-Z | Dropped On TI's | Duty Carried Out. |

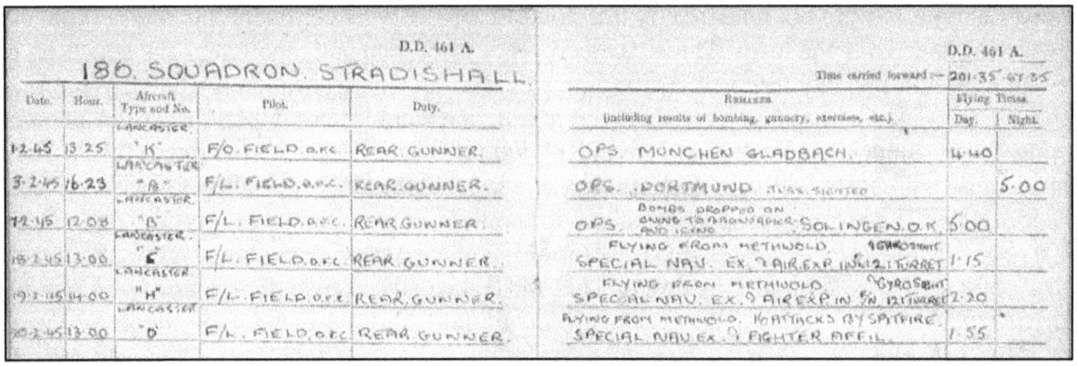
D.D. 461 A.

186. SQUADRON. STRADISHALL.

Time carried forward:— 201.35 67.55

| Date. | Hour. | Aircraft Type and No. | Pilot. | Duty. | Remarks (including results of bombing, gunnery, exercises, etc.) | Flying Times Day. | Flying Times Night. |
|---|---|---|---|---|---|---|---|
| 1.2.45 | 13.25 | LANCASTER "K" | F/O. FIELD D.F.C. | REAR GUNNER. | OPS. MUNCHEN GLADBACH. | 4.40 | |
| 3.2.45 | 16.23 | LANCASTER "A" | F/L. FIELD. D.F.C. | REAR GUNNER. | OPS. DORTMUND [illegible] SIGHTED | | 5.00 |
| 7.2.45 | 12.08 | LANCASTER "B" | F/L. FIELD. D.F.C. | REAR GUNNER | OPS. BOMBS DROPPED ON [illegible] AND ICING SOLINGEN. O.K. | 5.00 | |
| 18.2.45 | 13.00 | LANCASTER "C" | F/L. FIELD. D.F.C. | REAR GUNNER. | FLYING FROM METHWOLD. SPECIAL NAV. EX. & AIR EXP. IN [illegible] TURRET | 1.15 | |
| 19.2.45 | 14.00 | LANCASTER "H" | F/L. FIELD. D.F.C. | REAR GUNNER. | FLYING FROM METHWOLD "GYRO SIGHT" SPECIAL NAV. EX. & AIR EXP. IN [illegible] TURRET | 2.20 | |
| 20.2.45 | 13.00 | LANCASTER "D" | F/L. FIELD. D.F.C. | REAR GUNNER. | FLYING FROM METHWOLD. [illegible] ATTACKS BY SPITFIRE. SPECIAL NAV. EX. & FIGHTER AFFIL. | 1.55 | |

Log Book entry of Rear Gunner, Sergeant C.F Turner. Note the report of a sighting of a JU88 on the operation Dortmund. Also, the exercises completed on the February 18th and 19th in what appears to be the new FN 121 rear turret with the Gyro Gunsight. If this is the case, it would have been the first squadron Lancaster installed with this turret/gunsight combination.

Flight Lieutenant Eric Geoffrey Hunt, RAFVR

Happier times. Eric and his future wife were photographed before qualifying as a pilot.

The G-H equipped crews were prepared for any conditions over the target. Ground Marking was briefed, but if cloud was encountered, emergency Skymarkers were loaded and available. The group had, despite the PFF early reluctance to share information, learned a lot from their Path Finder counterparts.

Time over Target was scheduled for 19:30 hours, the squadrons of No.31 Base were distributed over the entire raid. The weather was clear but affording the crews the unwelcome spectacle of blazing bombers. For the first time in months, searchlights were numerous (reported between 40/50) and working in conjunction with prowling night fighters. Flak was also noticeably more vicious than on previous raids, and a steady barrage of accurate flak was pumped into the sky above Dortmund.

One of the first to bomb was F/Sgt E Morris at 19:35 hours. He reported the first salvo of Target Indicators exploding over the target at 19:29 hours, courtesy of No.32 Base. Flying Officer J Tonks reported, *'The attack seemed good with markers and explosions concentrated. A number of fires burning in the target area'*. The other G-H equipped crew was that of F/O N Cowley at the controls of NN720 XY-K. He stated, *'A good attack, ground markers were concentrated, and fires were started'*. Australian F/O E Barton RAAF was a little more critical, *' One or two markers scattered but generally, there was a good concentration. A triangle of railway lines similar to the north of the target was seen. Explosions took place around the markers, good attack.'* Equally critical was S/Ldr R Bass AFM. He was over the target at 17:38 hours, *'Target indicators were not well placed but bombing good on them. One large orange coloured explosion was seen, and fires with clouds of black smoke was visible on leaving'*.

The 186 Squadron ORB does not report any of its Lancasters in trouble over the target but does record two 'scarecrows'. Over at RAF Wratting Common, two crews witnessed the demise of three Lancasters in quick succussion over the target area. At 19:41 hours, F/Lt K.A Sidford and crew recorded a Lancaster coned by searchlight. The Lancaster desperately took avoiding action but then exploded in a blinding flash. Five minutes later, the crew again had to watch as another Lancaster ablaze from nose to tail plummeted earthwards. No parachutes were observed. Flying Officer K.B Fitton RNZAF of No.195 Squadron also watched as a Lancaster exploded in mid-air, the result of a direct flak hit. Fighters were active and several combats were reported with Bf110s of NJG1 and NJG4. Four Group Lancasters failed to return. One of those that was reported missing was Avro Lancaster HK668 XY-W flown by F/Lt Eric Hunt and crew. The Lancaster and its crew crashed at 19:47 hours near Westerfilde im Wald, some 2 miles East of Castrop Rauxel, killing the entire crew. The cause of loss has not been confirmed, but flak was suspected. The bodies of the young crew, four of which were married were recovered and initially buried in the Principal Cemetery Dortmund (Hauptfriedhof) on February 15th, 1945 in field No.17, Graves 24 (Ross) 25 (Sparkes) 26 (Stainthorpe) 27 (Lowndes) 28 (Jenkins) 29 ( Hunt) and 134 (Webley). Their remains were taken for reburial in the Reichswald Forest War Cemetery between December 1946 and May 1947.

| Type | Avro Lancaster Mk.I **HK688 XY-W** | Vickers Armstrong |
|---|---|---|
| Taken on Charge | 27/10/1944 | |
| 'Category' | FB 'Missing' 03/02/1945 | |
| Struck Of Charge | 09/02/1945 | |
| Total Flying Hours | Not Recorded | |
| Take-Off Time | 16:20 hours | |
| Bomb Load | 1 x 4000lb HC + 6 x 500lb AN-M64 + 6 x 500lb | |
| | | |
| | **CREW** | **GRAVE** |
| Pilot | Flight Lieutenant Eric Geoffrey Hunt, 119119 RAFVR (Married) | 4.E.11. |
| Navigator | Flying Officer Walter Jack Jenkins, 162373 RAFVR. Age 31. | 4.E.10 |
| Bomb Aimer | Flying Officer John Ross, 154224 RAFVR. Age 21. (Married) | 4.E.6 |
| Wireless Operator | Flight Sergeant William Cecil Webley, 1032389 RAFVR. Age 23. (Married) | 18.E.15 |
| Mid Upper Gunner | Sergeant Harrison Stainthorpe, 1594910 RAFVR | 4.E.8 |
| Rear Gunner | Sergeant James Alfred Sparkes, 1867038 RAFVR Age 19. | 4.E.7 |
| Flight Engineer | Sergeant George Edward Lowndes, 1580552 RAFVR. Age 23. (Married) | 4.E.9 |
| | | |
| Posting History | No.1653 HCU-No.3 LFS-Course 62. Posted to XV Squadron 23/11/1944. NFD on posting date No.186. | |
| Operations Flown | 11, plus 1 abandoned. | |
| Buried | Reichswald Forest War Cemetery | |

Flight Lieutenant Eric Geoffrey Hunt, RAFVR.

Flying Officer Walter Jack Jenkins, RAFVR.

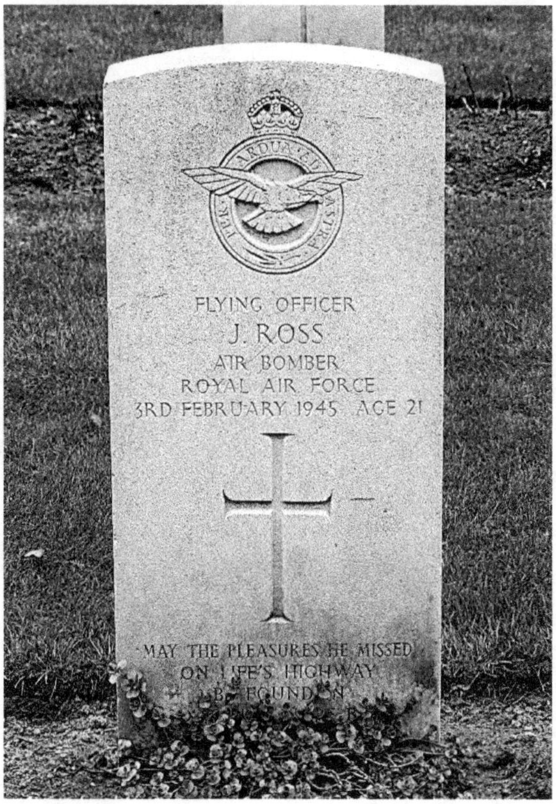


Flying Officer John Ross, RAFVR.

Twenty-one-year-old, John Ross.

Flight Sergeant William Cecil Webley, RAFVR.

Sergeant Harrison Stainthorpe, RAFVR

Sergeant James Alfred Sparkes, RAFVR.

Sergeant George Edward Lowndes, RAFVR.

There was a sense of disbelief around the various Messes that the crew of F/Lt Hunt were reported missing. Born in Huddersfield in November 1917 and one of three brothers, Geoffrey [24] as he was known by his family, was educated at the Merchant Taylors' Boys School in Crosby. Prior to joining the RAF in 1941 he worked for a Hardwood Timber Importers in Liverpool. It is understood that Geoffrey spent the majority of his RAF career as a Flying Instructor. The squadron had not posted a crew 'Missing' since December, and even then, they were reported safe. However, there was still some hope that this could be the case again.

The squadron stood down on the 4th. It allowed the squadron to continue its training on G-H. Two crews successfully completed a G-H exercise, while a solitary crew completed a G-H bombing exercise over Rushford Bombing Range. In addition, two crews were airborne on Fighter Affiliation while a non-G-H crew were over the bombing range at Elmdon. In January, No.186 Squadron had one of the worst records for carrying out Fighter Affiliation Training in the Group with just 22 sorties flown. Thankfully, even worse was No.149 and No.90 with just eight each! Obviously, not impressed, the squadron set about addressing the problem. The primary purpose of this training was to acquaint new pilots with the manoeuvrability of fighters and how importantly, to avoid them. If a bomber crew were to stand any chance of survival, it all hinged on how well the pilot could toss and turn his big bomber around in the sky. Fighter affiliation was generally flown during the day, for obvious reasons, it was safer. Number 3 Group would call upon its own 1688 Flt based at Newmarket for the purpose of fighter affiliation. Equipped with war-weary Hurricanes and Spitfires, they would put the bomber crews through their paces. It took a lot of effort on the part of the pilot to complete the standard corkscrew with a fully-loaded Lancaster. Once the gunners gave the order "corkscrew port or Corkscrew

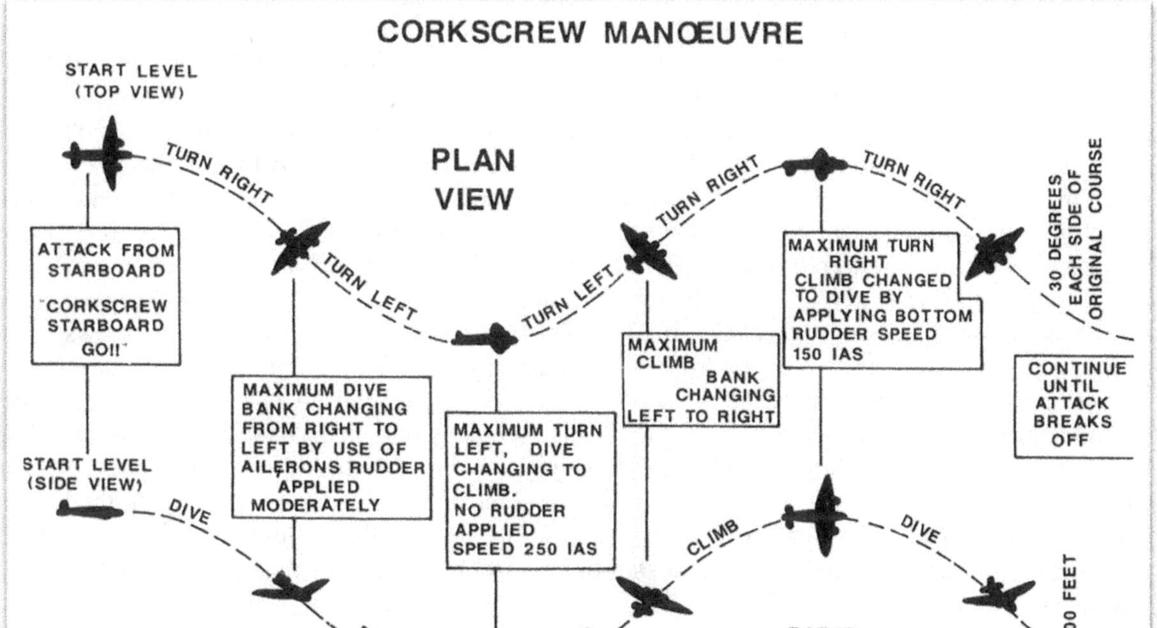


This diagram shows the 'corkscrew' manoeuvre. This example depicts an attack from the starboard side. It would be reversed if the attack came from the port. During the manoeuvre, the pilot was meant to give a running commentary on what he would do next, thus giving both gunners time to make any adjustments or deflection. Although that was the theory, often, the pilot was simply too exhausted to talk. Crews would often practice this manoeuvre time and time again. Their lives depended on it!

[24] *His father, a former Lieutenant in the Royal West Kent Regiment was also named Eric.*

starboard", the pilot would dive to one side or the other, the decision of either port or starboard being made by the gunner based on the direction and angle of the fighter attack. The first action may have been enough to throw the attacker aim off, but maybe not the attacking pilot's ability to keep on the bomber's tail. During the training, the pilots were to put their bombers through a series of climbs and dives, turns to either side, with the whole effect being a roller coaster ride. For the pilot to place the bomber in a corkscrew port, he would have the stick hard forward, foot hard in on the left rudder and wheel entirely over to the left. The pilot would have two other things on his mind regarding the attempt to escape. The pilot also had to ensure that the pattern was not repetitive enough for the fighter to figure out his next move. If this was not enough, the quickly tiring pilot had to keep the swings from port to starboard in equal numbers to help the aircraft on the same heading. The old saying 'practise makes perfect' meant the difference between life and death in Bomber Command. On the evening of the 4th, the squadron was informed it would be required the following night. The target would be Leipzig, in Saxony. A slight haze on the morning of the 5th did not prevent another day of G-H training. Three crews successfully completed a G-H exercise, while another was over Rushford Bombing Range. In the afternoon, twelve squadron Lancasters were fuelled and bombed up for Leipzig. Bomber Command would be out in force. Over 800 aircraft would be involved in what appeared to be an old-fashioned area attack. The No.3 Group Record Book states, *'INTENTION: To destroy the built-up area and associated industries and create maximum administrative disorganisation'.* The twelve crews had been briefed only for Group HQ to cancel the operation at 19:00 hours.

The only activity of the 6th was a solitary G-H exercise, it was the lull before a busy, frustrating and costly 48 hours. Number 3 Group's obsession with the methodical destruction of Hitler's oil production continued on the 7th. The synthetic oil plant at Wanne-Eickel was again chalked up on the Operations Board at Stradishall. One hundred Lancasters drawn from No.31 and No.32 Base would be involved, No.33 Base squadrons being stood down. The day's operation would set a numbers of notable first's for the squadron. The largest contribution of G-H crews, nine in total[25] and the highest number of aborts on one target. The first of twelve Lancasters detailed from RAF Stradishall was airborne at 12:00 hours, at the controls of Lancaster NG146 XY-E was F/O Lawrence Idle RNZAF. A total of nine crews were given the G-H Leader role, of these, five would be undertaking their first G-H Leader operation. Two recent arrivals would be making their operational debut, F/O Preston Hill, and F/O Geoffrey Head. Unusually, the Hill crew were given the G-H Leader role. The Group departed England over Beachy Head, not that any crews could see the chalky headland, or its lighthouse as solid cloud had greeted the squadron almost immediately after take-off. The Met Briefing was wildly off when the crews began encountering an unexpected weather front with clouds up to 24,000 feet, making formation flying almost impossible. With visibility less than 200 yards in places, vigilance was paramount. In between the mountains of billowing freezing cloud, the crews desperately searched for the two yellow horizontal barred rudders of their leaders, or just simply searched for the company of another Lancaster. Apart from the limited visibility, ice was the biggest danger. Freezing ice began to build up on the leading edges or front surfaces of the Lancasters. This build-up would alter the airflow over the wing and tail, reducing the lift, and potentially causing a stall or catastrophic loss of control of the heavily ladened Lancaster.

<u>Form B.781 – February 7th 1945(D) :Target :Wanne-Eickel-Krupp Treibstroffwerk G.m.b.H –GQ1518</u>

| | | | | | | | |
|---|---|---|---|---|---|---|---|
| F/Lt | Field DFC | E.L | | HK692 | XY-B | G-H Leader | Duty Not Carried Out |
| F/O | Hill | P.T | | HK694 | XY-C | G-H Leader | Duty Carried Out |
| F/O | Idle | L.A | RNZAF | NG146 | XY-E | G-H Leader | Duty Carried Out |
| F/O | Tonks | J.E | | NG175 | XY-J | G-H Leader | Duty Carried Out |

[25] *There is some confusion between the ORB and Group Records in relation to bombing technics, ie. On G-H or on Leaders, numbers differ. Also Lancaster NG146 was a G-H equipped Lancaster.*

| | | | | | | | |
|---|---|---|---|---|---|---|---|
| F/O | Cowley | N.C | | NN720 | XY-K | G-H Leader | Duty Carried Out |
| F/O | Hart | J.H | | HK682 | XY-L | Unknown | Duty Not Carried Out |
| F/O | Barton | E.R | RAAF | NG354 | XY-M | G-H Leader | Duty Carried Out |
| F/O | Green | L.A | | HK684 | XY-Q | G-H Leader | Duty Carried Out |
| F/Lt | Orman DFC | L.A | RNZAF | HK659 | XY-O | G-H Leader | Duty Carried Out |
| F/O | Head | G.D | | HK661 | XY-R | Unknown | Duty Not Carried Out |
| F/O | Gogler | R.J | RAAF | NG293 | XY-U | Unknown | Duty Not Carried Out |
| F/O | Beck | A.J | RAAF | HK613 | XY-Y | G-H Leader | Duty Carried Out |

Four crews were forced to abort. Flight Lieutenant E Field DFC abandoned owing to severe icing aboard HK692. The crew bombed the secondary target of Solingen at 15:16 hours. The crew of F/O Jack Hart had experienced problems with their port outer engine soon after take-off but bravely decided to continue with the operation. On entering the mass of freezing cloud, the port outer engine failed completely, and the crew attempted to feather. All but two of the bombs were jettisoned southwest of Brussels. Two remained frozen to their shackles. The port outer engine would not stay feathered and caused considerable drag, and to add to the crew's problems, the port inner engine began to show worrying signs of overheating. Oil was seen pouring out of the engine nacelle. Any thoughts of returning to RAF Stradishall were now out of the question. Cautiously, the crew dropped below the clouds seeking an airfield to landing. They were lucky, visible was the airfield at Ursel [26] Belgium where the crew landed HK682 at 16:21hours. The crew's Navigator Jack Allen recalls the events.

> *This our 10th operation was the first occasion we had any trouble. We were due to bomb Wanne-Eickel. Over Europe we ran into cumulus cloud at about 20,000 ft and lost one of our outer engines. We dived down and returned back out of the cloud at about 15,000 ft. We turned round again and tried to get through the cloud on 3 engines. The other outer engine failed and we were on the two inner engines with a full bomb load. We turned out again and as we were losing height we jettisoned our bomb load. We continued losing height and as we broke cloud at about 2,000 ft. We saw an air strip on which 'Hawkers' were landing and we followed one in. It was an air strip just outside Ghent in Belgium. I had, of course, lost all my instruments when the two outer engines failed and we really had no idea where we were. We were flown back to England via Brussels - Northolt in a Dakota and then to base via Down Ampney in a Lancaster on the February 13th.*

Flying Officer G Head got as far as crossing the German border before he met severe icing. The crew tried to climb above the cloud, but at 20,000 feet and with no sign of clear sky, they turned for home. They jettisoned their entire bomb load at 16:57 hours over the North Sea, landing back at base at 17:38 hours. Australian F/O R.J Gogler RAAF and crew meet the same weather front, they too tried to climb but were forced to concede defeat. The cookie was jettisoned into the Markermeer near the Dutch town of Almere. The remaining 13 x 500 pounders were retained. They landed back at Stradishall at 17:45 hours. As the bomber stream reached Aachen, any resemblance of a formation had been lost in the clouds. The stream now comprised of small groups and isolated vic formations. As they passed between Cologne and Dusseldorf, the entire force was elongated and in disarray. With the stream strung out, the window coverage was greatly reduced. This resulted in the flak defences of the Rhine and Ruhr putting up a steady and accurate barrage, over a third of the bombers being damaged. The usually strong G-H pulse was distinctly weak to add yet more problems to a quickly deteriorating operation. Unbeknown to the crews, a mobile heavy G-H station was experiencing problems. In its place, a smaller version was hastily set up. The result was that the release pulse was feeble, and numerous crews could not get any response from their sets. Flying Officer J Tonks dropped his all HE load on G-H at 15:25 hours. They had flown in almost continuous cloud since entering German airspace, the crew reporting, *'Severe icing,*

---

[26] *Advanced Landing Ground B-67*

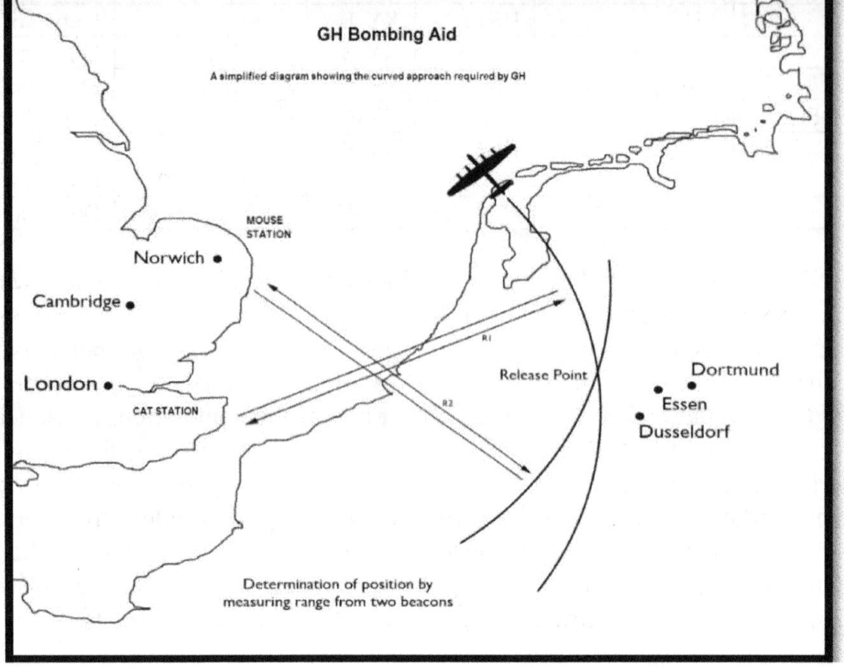


*This simplified diagram taken from an official 3 Group document. By measuring and keeping a fixed distance to a radio station, the bomber could navigate along an arc in the sky. The bombs were dropped when they reached a set distance from a second station. Oboe used very large displays in ground stations to take very accurate measurements but could only direct one aircraft at a time. G-H used much smaller gear on board the aircraft and was somewhat less accurate but could direct as many as 80 aircraft at a time. This operated by sending out two pulses of known timing from ground stations which were picked up by the aircraft and read on an oscilloscope. The timing between transmissions was not fixed and varied from station to station, so the equipment in the bomber had a system that allowed it to adjust for this. The receiver had a local oscillator that provided a time base generator that could be adjusted. When the receiver was first turned on, the pulses from the ground station would move across the display because the two-time bases were not synchronized. The operator then tuned their oscillator until the pulses stopped moving, which meant that the local oscillator was now at precisely the same pulse frequency as that in the ground station. The receiver had two complete systems of this type, allowing the operator to receive signals from two stations and easily compare them and make simultaneous measurements.*

To identify a G-H equipped Leader the aircraft had two yellow horizontal bars applied to the rudders.

Early G-H installation in a Avro Lancasters navigators position.

*and aircraft very unstable'*. Flak shot out the starboard inner engine of F/O L.Idle RNZAF while at 22,000 feet. Although equipped with G-H, the crew bombed on Lancaster XH-F of 'C' Flight, No.218 Squadron flown by F/O K Robertson RAAF. Lawrence Idle flew home to RAF Stradishall on three engines landing at 18:01 hours. Flying Officer N Cowley was over the target at 15:35 hours, *'Nimbus cloud was tops higher than aircraft could climb. Severe icing, unstable. Bombs hung up owing to icing and fell north of target, no results could be seen.'* Despite the issues with the G-H signal, it would appear that some crews at least obtained a strong enough pulse to bomb. Flying Officer E Barton RAAF, *'Identified target on Radar Navigational Aid and bombed at 15:27 hours from 20,000 feet. Met nimbus cloud and could not climb over or go around, severe icing. Seven aircraft were seen bombing at the same time. No results seen owing to cloud'.* The failure of the port outer engine aboard Lancaster HK613 XY-Y flown by F/O A Beck RAAF resulted in the engine being feathered en route home. A subsequent inspection found a defective oil pump was the cause. [27]

The tired crews began landing just after 17:00 hours. It had been a real battle against the elements. It was obvious at debriefing that the raid was a failure. For the participating crews, they were just happy to be safely home. Squadron Leader P Reynolds started his leave on this date. 'A' Flight would be commanded by the experienced F/Lt G Templeton RCAF in his absence.

No.186 Squadron Reported Flak Damage 7/02/1945

| Serial | Code | Damage Reported | Repairs / Notes |
|---|---|---|---|
| NG146 | **XY-E** | Starboard inner engine. | Repaired on Squadron. |

Twelve squadron crews were detailed for a daylight tactical operation against Kleve on the 8th. However, this was cancelled at 01:45 hours as the target had been successfully attacked by No.1 Group the previous day. It was a short reprieve, the squadron was then notified it would be detailed for a night operation directed again the synthetic oil plant at Lutzkendorf, near Halle. This operation was cancelled at 14:00 hours due to poor weather conditions. There followed an agonizing delay for the crews before they were again assembled for yet another briefing. Finally, at 03:36 hours on the morning of February 9th, the first squadron Lancaster departed RAF Stradishall. The target was Krefeld's Marshalling Yards at Hohenbudberg. This was another all No.3 Group operation. A total of 154 Lancasters would be detailed. Twelve crews would be provided by No.186, of which only one, skippered by F/O N Cowley, would be tasked with G-H Marker duties. One crew was withdrawn when the pilot became ill.

Form B.783 – February 9th 1945(N) :Target : Krefeld Marshalling Yards at Hohenbudberg :–G-H622

| | | | | | | | |
|---|---|---|---|---|---|---|---|
| F/Lt | Templeton | G.M | RCAF | NG174 | XY-A | Bombed on TI's | Duty Carried Out |
| F/Sgt | Morris | E | | HK650 | XY-T | FTR | Missing |
| F/O | Barton | E.R | RAAF | NG149 | XY-G | Bombed on TI's | Duty Carried Out |
| F/O | Tonks | J.E | | NG175 | XY-J | Bombed on TI's | Duty Carried Out |
| W/Cdr | Giles DFC | J.H | | NG354 | XY-M | Bombed on TI's | Duty Carried Out |
| F/O | Head | G.D | | HK684 | XY-O | Bombed on TI's | Duty Carried Out |
| F/Lt | Orman DFC | K.G | RNZAF | HK659 | XY-Q | Bombed on TI's | Duty Carried Out |
| F/O | Idle | L.A | RNZAF | HK661 | XY-R | Bombed on TI's | Duty Carried Out |
| F/O | Clarson | A.J | RAAF | NG140 | XY-F | Bombed Visually | Duty Carried Out |
| F/Lt | Mason | F.H | | NG353 | XY-X | Bombed on TI's | Duty Carried Out |
| F/O | Cowley | N.C | | PD429 | XY-Z | G-H Marker | Duty Carried Out |

[27] *This engine failure is not recorded in the Squadron ORB.*

The squadrons of No.31 Base would provide 50 Lancasters and 11 G-H crews. The Lancasters of No.31 Base were scheduled to be over the target area between 06:19 - 06:35 hours. Flying Officer N Cowley, the squadron's sole G-H crew, was loaded with 2 x 250lb Red Sky Markers as well as the usual combination of 4000lb Cookies and 500 pounders.[28] A few seconds later than planned, a number of Green and Red Star markers appeared then started to drift over the aiming point. The group was now fully trained in the art of target marking. Selected G-H crews would be loaded with both Ground Markers and Sky markers depending on the conditions over the target. These crews were specially briefed not to drop TIs or flares unless they were completely satisfied with the G-H signal and their G-H apparatus. If the situation allowed, the overburdened navigator who worked both the G-H apparatus and H2S would, try and obtain an H2S fix for added confirmation, if time permitted. Even then, the semi- redundant bomb aimer would visually confirm what the conditions warranted. Like their Path Finder counterparts, there was a great deal of pressure on them. The outcome of an operation depended on their accurate assessment, and skill.

Eric and his wife were photographed while on leave. Unfortunately, like so many, she would become a widow at an early age.

[28] *This is the first instance that Marker Flares (TI's) are recorded with a bomb load.*

Flight Sergeant Eric Morris, RAFVR. Age 21

The crews scheduled for the opening minutes of the attack found a few misplaced markers north of the marshalling yards and more six miles north. These were quickly discounted as decoys. One of the first over the target was F/O N Cowley at 16:16 hours. The crew identified the aiming point on G-H and dropped their all HE bomb load and two flares from 21,000 feet. The crew reported on return, *'A dull red glow was seen through cloud, probably TI's. Bombing appeared concentrated as the aircraft left target. Aircraft amongst the first on target and therefore few details of attack was seen.'* Close on the heels of F/O Cowley was the Squadron Commanding Officer, W/Cdr Giles DFC. He bombed at 16:23 hours, remarking, *'Attack seemed a good one and well concentrated. Marking was scattered at first but concentrated afterwards.'* Visibility over the Marshalling Yards was excellent, crews reported explosions all around the markers, with one large vivid explosion witnessed at 06:27 hours. German opposition was fierce. A combination of flak and around 50 searchlights greeted the bombers. One crew reported three 'unidentified' fighters over the target, while another reported an aircraft exploding at 06:24 hours with red sky markers and green stars falling from it. Flight Sergeant E Morris was at the controls of Lancaster HK650 XY-T. They were engaged by flak and searchlights soon after bombing, with tragic results. It is understood that the Lancaster exploded mid-air, showering debris over Schwafheim, a built-up area west of the River Rhine and 3 miles southeast of Moers[29]. The main wreckage crashing near Muhlenwinkel. There were no survivors from this all NCO crew.

| Type | Avro Lancaster Mk.I **HK650 XY-T** | Vickers Armstrong |
|---|---|---|
| Taken on Charge | 12/10/1944 | |
| 'Category' | FB 'Missing' 09/02/1945 | |
| Struck Of Charge | 22/02/1945 | |
| Total Flying Hours | | |
| Raids Flown | | |
| Take-Off Time | 03:45 hours | |
| Bomb Load | 1 x 4000lb HC + 12 x 500lb AN-M64 + 1 x 500lb | |
| | | |
| | **CREW** | **GRAVE** |
| Pilot | Flight Sergeant Eric Morris, 1586397 RAFVR. Age 21. (Married) | Coll.Grave 30.F.7-9 |
| Navigator | Sergeant Edward Miles Chetwynd-Stapylton, 191835 RAFVR. Age 20. | 30.F.6 |
| Bomb Aimer | Flight Sergeant Raymond Wellington, 1389461 RAFVR. Age 21. | 30.F.5 |
| Wireless Operator | Sergeant William Stephens, 1590766 RAFVR, Age 19. | Coll.Grave 30.F.7-9 |
| Mid Upper Gunner | Sergeant James Finlayson, 3020199 RAFVR, Age 19. | Coll.Grave 30.F.7-9 |
| Rear Gunner | Sergeant Donald McBean Crowe, 3040754 RAFVR. | Coll.Grave 30.F.7-9 |
| Flight Engineer | Sergeant Albert Stanley Pitt, 1897011 RAFVR. Age 22. | Coll.Grave 30.F.7-9 |
| | | |
| Posted History | No.1657 CU - 06/12/1944 No.3 LFS - 68 Course. Posted No.186 Squadron 19/01/1945. | |
| Operations Flown | 3 | |
| Buried | *Reichswald Forest War Cemetery* | |

*[29] There are conflicting records on the crash location. The MoD record the crash site as Muhlenwinkel.*

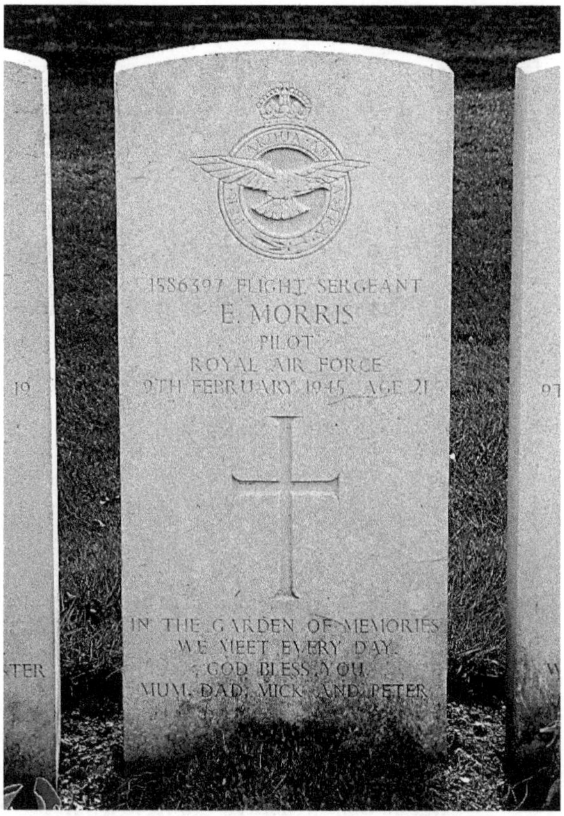


Flight Sergeant Eric Morris, RAFVR.

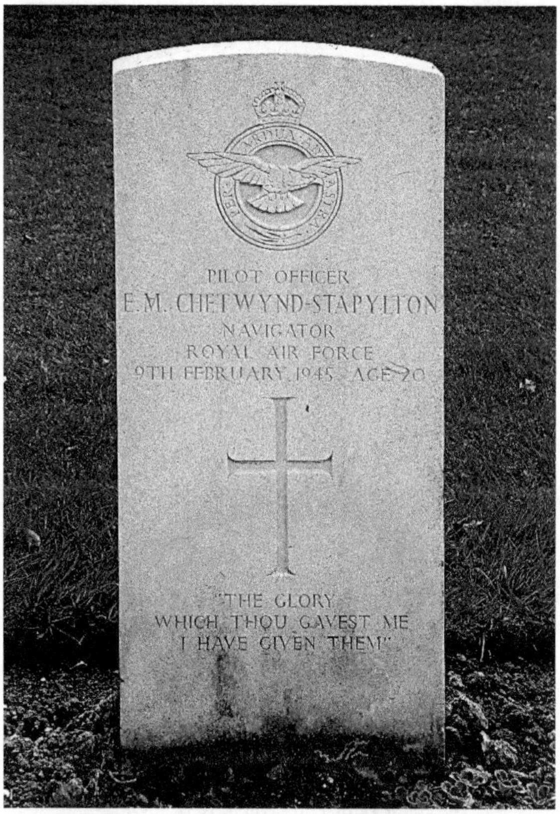


Sergeant Edward Miles Chetwynd-Stapylton, RAFVR.

Flight Sergeant Raymond Wellington, RAFVR.

Sergeant William Stephens, RAFVR.

Sergeant James Finlayson, RAFVR.

Sergeant Donald McBean Crowe, RAFVR.

Sergeant Albert Stanley Pitt, RAFVR.

Those left behind. Left: The parents of Sergeant Donald Crowe visit their son and his crew's grave post-war. Right: The attractive wife of Flight Sergeant Eric Morris was a member of the WAAF.

The bodies of the crew were recovered from the wreckage, but only two could be positively identified. They, plus five unknowns, were buried in the local cemetery at Schwafheim. After the war, the crew were transferred to Reichswald Forest War Cemetery and re-buried in October 1947. The bomber seen on fire at 06:24 hours was, in all probability, the crew of F/Sgt Eric Morris. Eric enlisted in October 1941 in Weston-Super-Mare. After the initial square-bashing, he set sail for America in December 1942, where he would gain his wings. Sergeant Eric Morris arrived back in England ten months later, and like many of his contemporaries, he completed his training serving at No.11 Pilots Advanced Training Unit, No.1531 Beam Approach Training Unit and finally, in May 1944, No.11 Operational Training Unit. While serving with No.11 OTU, Eric would be hospitalised on July 25th. The circumstances of his month-long stay in Halton Hospital are unclear. In October 1944, Eric was promoted to Flight Sergeant. On December 6th, 1944, he and his crew were one of 18 posted to No.3 LFS via No.1657 HCU. Eric was part of No.68 Course, one of the last training courses before No.3 LFS was disbanded on January 31st 1945. Unfortunately, the freezing weather conditions over the Christmas of 1944 meant that it was not until January 19th that Eric and his crew finally arrived on the squadron.

Number 3 Group only lost two crews on this raid. The RAF Mildenhall based No.15 Squadron suffered the other loss. This crew is buried in Brussels. When at Stradishall during the last days of his conversion with No.1657 HCU, Eric wrote home joking about the '*bunch of hooligans'* who were his crew but added that they were a great team who all worked together. In 1987, Mick Carpenter, Eric's half-brother, found the crash site and several German residents who recalled that terrible night. Eric had once suggested to Mick, who served in the Royal Artillery, to transfer to become one of his gunners, but Mick declined. Such is fate.[30]

[30] *Via Jock Whitehouse author of Royal Air Force Stradishall.*

The crew of F/O A Clarson RAAF had successfully bombed at 06:30 hours and were on their way home when at 06:35 hour the crew's mid-upper gunner, F/Sgt J Mallison, spotted a single-engined night fighter on the starboard quarter. The Australian gunner immediately opened fire with a 2-second burst. The fighter quickly disappeared without engaging.

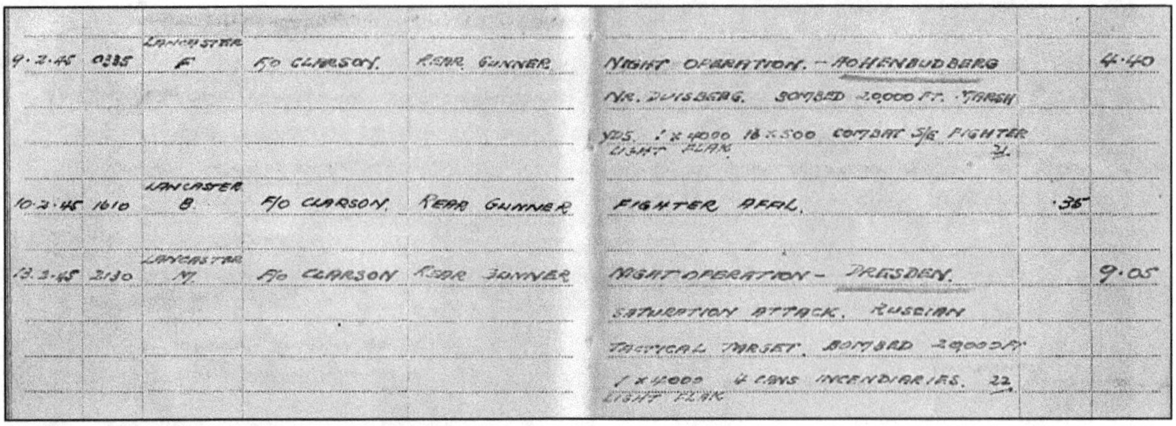

| | | | | | | | |
|---|---|---|---|---|---|---|---|
| 9.2.45 | 0335 | LANCASTER F | F/O CLARSON. | REAR GUNNER | NIGHT OPERATION. – HOHENBUDBERG NR. DUISBERG. BOMBED 20,000 FT. MARSH YDS. 1 x 4000 18 x 500 COMBAT S/E FIGHTER 2. LIGHT FLAK | | 4.40 |
| 10.2.45 | 1610 | LANCASTER B. | F/O CLARSON. | REAR GUNNER | FIGHTER AFFIL. | .35 | |
| 13.2.45 | 2130 | LANCASTER M | F/O CLARSON | REAR GUNNER | NIGHT OPERATION – DRESDEN. SATURATION ATTACK. RUSSIAN TACTICAL TARGET. BOMBED 20000 FT. 1 x 4000 4 CANS INCENDIARIES. 22. LIGHT FLAK | | 9.05 |

Rear Gunner, Gerald McPherson RAAF and his Log Book entry for the attack on Krefeld Marshaling Yards. Of interest is the entry for the Dresden operation. Note the terms 'Saturation attack' and 'Russian tactical target'

On the 10th and then again on the 11th, the squadron was detailed for an attack on Gelsenkirchen. On both occasions, the raid was cancelled. Instead, Radar training and Fighter Affiliation was given priority. Flying Officer John Hart and crew eventually started their return to the squadron on the 11th, having no doubt enjoyed their unexpected stay in Brussels. They were initially collected by P/O Peter Crowden-Longstreath in Dakota FZ613 of No.271 Squadron at Nivelles Airfield (B.75) and then flown to Brussels (B.56). The following day they joined the crew W/O P Bayetto aboard Dakota KG562 of 271 Squadron. After dropping off their cargo at RAF Northolt, they were delivered to RAF Down Ampney at 16:44 hours on the 12th.[31] Squadron Leader Bass AFM, their Flight Commander, collected the crew and flew them back to RAF Stradishall aboard Lancaster NG293 XY-Y on the 13th. Lancaster HK682 would, once repaired, be returned to the squadron on February 26th. On the 13th, and for the third time, the squadron was detailed for a daylight raid directed against Gelsenkirchen. Like the two previous planned operations, it was cancelled mid-morning. On the afternoon of February 13th, 1945, the fourteen crews were assembled in RAF Stradishall's Briefing Room. Joining them was Air Vice Marshal Sir Hugh Lloyd, KBE, CB, MC, DFC, he was accompanied by Air Vice Marshal R Harrison, CB , CBE, DFC, AFC, A.O.C No.3 Group. The target that night would be Dresden, capital of the eastern German state of Saxony. To the assembled crews, their main concern was the range. It would be the furthest penetration into Germany for the squadron to date. The Dresden operation, the first of a series code-named *'Thunderclap'* would make history, sadly for all the wrong reasons. *Operation Thunderclap* had been under discussion within the Allied Command since August 1944. The original plan was to undertake a massive attack on Berlin that would cause catastrophic casualties and shatter German morale. However, on consideration, it was decided that it was unlikely to work. Although initially shelved, the idea was revised in early 1945 by the RAF Director of Bombing Operations, Air Commodore Sydney Bufton. Bufton sent a memo to the Deputy Chief of Air Staff, Air Marshal Sir Norman Bottomley, suggesting a coordinated series of attacks with the objective of bombing the easternmost cities of Germany to disrupt the transport infrastructure behind the Eastern front. It would also graphically demonstrate to the German population in a devastating fashion that the air defences of Germany were now of little substance and that the Nazi regime had failed them. The cities designated for bombing were Berlin, Dresden, Chemnitz and Leipzig. At Yalta, Prime Minister Winston Churchill

[31] *No.271 Squadron all flying from the UK was cancelled on the 12th. Via ORB.*

had promised to do more to support the Soviet forces moving west into Germany and the priority for Thunderclap moved up the timetable of bombing.

Two of Flight Sergeant Phil Gray's crew. Left: The crews Mid Upper Gunner, Sergeant Ivor 'Blondie' Forster in his turret. Right: Wireless Operator Sergeant Harry Jenkinson is looking out of the Astro Dome.

Form B.787 – February 13th 1945(N) : Target : Dresden : 'Chevin 'A'

| | | | | | | | |
|---|---|---|---|---|---|---|---|
| F/O | Brayshaw DFC | S.C | | NG174 | XY-A | Bombed PFF TI's | Duty Carried Out |
| F/O | Young | H.S | | HK692 | XY-C | Bombed PFF TI's | Duty Carried Out |
| F/Lt | Beck | J.A.G | | HK661 | XY-R | Bombed PFF TI's | Duty Carried Out |
| F/Lt | Templeton | G.M | RCAF | NG146 | XY-E | Bombed PFF TI's | Duty Carried Out |
| F/Lt | Marshall | A.N | | NG140 | XY-F | Bombed PFF TI's | Duty Carried Out |
| P/O | Barton | E.R | RAAF | NG149 | XY-G | Bombed PFF TI's | Duty Carried Out |
| F/O | Clarson | A | RAAF | NG354 | XY-M | Bombed PFF TI's | Duty Carried Out |
| S/Ldr | Scott | E.G | | HK684 | XY-O | Bombed PFF TI's | Duty Carried Out |
| F/O | Gogler | R.J | RAAF | HK662 | XY-P | Bombed PFF TI's | Duty Carried Out |
| F/Lt | Orman DFC | K.G | RNZAF | HK659 | XY-Q | Bombed PFF TI's | Duty Carried Out |
| F/O | Saunders | A | | NG175 | XY-J | Bombed PFF TI's | Duty Carried Out |
| F/O | James | W.C | RAAF | NG353 | XY-X | FTR | Missing |
| F/O | Green | L.A | | HK613 | XY-Y | Bombed PFF TI's | Duty Carried Out |
| F/O | Godfrey | D.F.J | RAAF | PD429 | XY-Z | Bombed PFF TI's | Duty Carried Out |

The first away at 21:27 hours was the crew of F/Lt G.M Templeton RCAF aboard Lancaster NG146 XY-E. Once airborne, the crews headed for Reading where they were instructed to circle at 3,000 feet before setting out and steadily climbing to 10,000 feet over the English Channel. Over France, they climbed to bombing altitude. Flying with the squadron for operational experience was the recently posted S/Ldr E Scott and crew. Eric 'Scotty' Scott was an old hand having flown Gloster Gladiators with 112 Squadron in the Middle East in 1940. He was related to the famous Scott of the Antarctic fame. His father was the Reverend Scott, who married his son, and Joan Johnson in June 1940 in St Mary's Elm Church, Ipswich. The first waves over Dresden were almost entirely squadrons drawn from No.5 Group, a group Sir Arthur Harris had a particular fondness for. Number 3 Group would detail 168 Lancasters, of which six would be cancelled due to either mechanical or crew problems, and a further seven would abort. The remaining force would be part of the second raid timed to attack at 01:30 hours, almost 3 hours after Cochrane's No.5 Group. The squadrons crews were evenly distributed over the first two waves timed to bomb between H-Hour + 3 to H-Hour + 6. Navigation to the target on the last leg was straightforward as the fires from the initial attack were visible when still over fifty miles from Dresden. The bombing was carried out on the instructions of the Master Bomber, Squadron Leader Charles Peter De Wesselow, call sign *'Kingcole'* of No.635 Path Finder Squadron. The Master Bomber instructed the main force, code name *'Strongman'* to overshoot the numerous Green TI markers by 1 second. Such was the success of the 5 Group raid Squadron Leader De Wesselow had no option than mark the fringes of the fires below. The whole city was a mass of flames. A large orange conflagration west of the Marshalling Yards was especially evident. The dying city gave little opposition, flak was described as slight/heavy, and no searchlights were reported. Once over the target, the squadron found a number of fires had started to converge. Despite this, they could still identify many prominent landmarks of this once beautiful city. Flight Lieutenant A Marshall arrived over the doomed city early. He reported, *'The target was identified by the fires which resulted from the earlier attack. No markers were seen as the aircraft ran in to attack so the target was orbited once. Still no markers at second run-in so aircraft bombed an undamaged built-up area at the edge of the fires at 01:25 hours'.* Flying Officer D Godfrey RAAF bombed at 01:30 hours, he reported, *'The whole town was burning, and streets were on fire'.* The main opposition was from a few German night fighters who braved the appalling weather conditions on the ground to oppose the raid. For once, the crews were unanimous that the raid was a success and that the Master Bomber and his deputy had done an excellent job. Two bombers were seen to explode over the target area at 01:30 hours and 01:35 hours. The last crew over the target was F/O S Brayshaw DFC at 01:36 hours, he reporting, *'Whole target was heavily covered with fires and bombs could be seen bursting all over it. Thickly built-up area was seen in the light of the fires, seemed an excellent attack'.* The inferno swept across Dresden and was visible 150 miles away on the route home. The crew

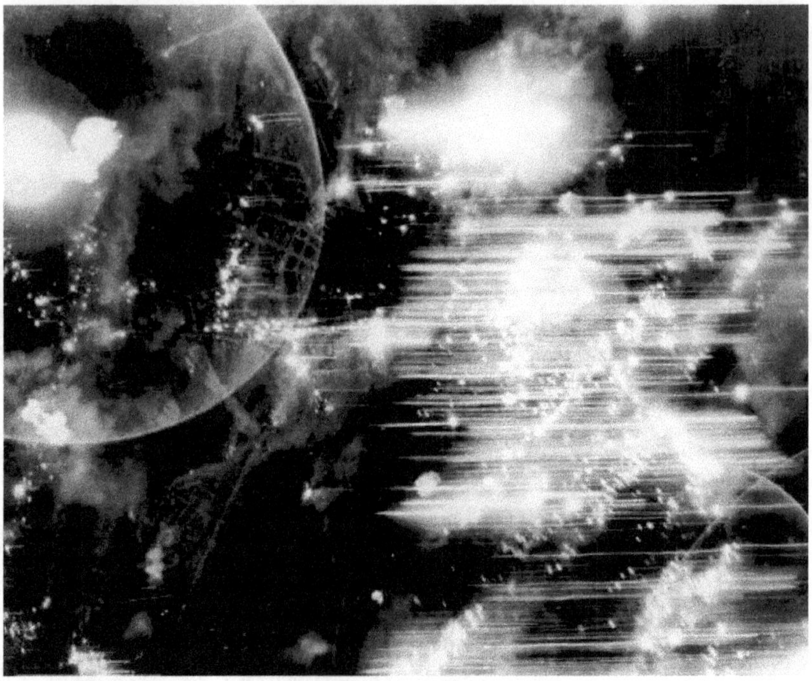

Dresden, February 13th 1945.

of P/O A Green, flying their twenty-eight operation suffered a port inner engine fire at 02:30 hours aboard HK613 XY-Y. Thankfully the fire was extinguished and the smouldering Merlin successfully feathered. It was on the homeward leg of the operation, the squadron reported its only Night Fighter combat. The crew of F/O S Brayshaw DFC were flying at 13,000 feet southeast of Nuremberg over the small town of Freystadt. At 02:38 hours, the crew's mid-upper gunner, F/O C Morrison, saw a JU88 on the starboard quarter. The following brief Combat Report was submitted on return.

> As Lancaster broke cloud the enemy aircraft was seen on the starboard quarter up, range 400+ approx. The order to corkscrew starboard was given as the JU88 turned in to the attack. Mid Upper Gunner fired 100 rounds in 3(three) bursts, no strikes observed. Rear Gunner fired approx 300 rounds, no strikes observed. Enemy aircraft broke away port quarter down, and at a range of 100+ and was not seen again.

Despite what was classified as weak defences, the raid on Dresden claimed another squadron crew. Lancaster NG353 XY-X[32] flown by F/O W James RAAF crashed in Dresden, taking with it its entire crew. There is some confusion regarding the cause of loss. A fighter attack appears to be the probable cause, but this cannot be confirmed. The crew's remains were collected and initially buried in the Johannis Friedhof Cemetery, Dresden. In February 1948, the crew were reinterred in the Berlin 1939-1945 War Cemetery.

| Type | Avro Lancaster Mk.I **NG353 XY-X** | **Armstrong Whitworth** |
|---|---|---|
| Taken on Charge | 23/11/1944 | |
| 'Category' | FB 'Missing' 14/02/1945 | |
| Struck Of Charge | 22/02/1945 | |
| Total Flying Hours | - | |
| Raids Flown | | |
| Take-Off Time | 22.03hrs | |
| Bomb Load | 1 x 4000lb HC + 540 x 4lb Inc + 60 x 40lb 'Type X' | |
| | | |
| | **CREW** | **GRAVE** |
| Pilot | Flying Officer William Charles James A.429965 RAAF. Age 21. | 8.C.11 |
| Navigator | Flight Sergeant Dennis Wood, 1048622 RAFVR | 8.C.12 |
| Bomb Aimer | Flight Sergeant Alfred Leonard Bragg, 1600770 RAFVR. Age 23. (Married) | Joint Grave 8.C.16-17 |
| Wireless Operator | Sergeant Edgar Maurice Holliday, 1817846 RAFVR Age 20. | Joint Grave 8.C.16-17 |
| Mid Upper Gunner | Sergeant Henry Charles Whaites, 1404936 RAFVR Age 22. | 8.C.15 |
| Rear Gunner | Sergeant John Murphy, 1515909 RAFVR | 8.C.13 |
| Flight Engineer | Sergeant John Derek Hall, 1869558 RAFVR, Age 20. | 8.C.14 |
| | | |
| Posted History | No.84 O.T.U – No.1651 HCU – 13/10/1944 No.3 LFS – No.60 Course – No.186 Squadron 25/10/1944. | |
| Operations Flown | 17 | |
| Buried | *Berlin 1939-1945 War Cemetery* | |

[32] *The engines from NG353 were recovered post war.*

Flying Officer William Charles James RAAF.

Flight Sergeant Dennis Wood, RAFVR.

Flight Sergeant Alfred Leonard Bragg, RAFVR.

Sergeant Edgar Maurice Holliday, RAFVR.

Sergeant Henry Charles Whaites RAFVR

Sergeant John Murphy RAFVR.

Sergeant John Derek Hall, RAFVR.

Dresden fatalities. Flight Sergeant William James RAAF is photographed with two of his crew while still training. L-R Sergeant Dennis Wood (Navigator), Flight Sergeant William James RAAF (Pilot) and believed to be the rear gunner Sergeant John Murphy.

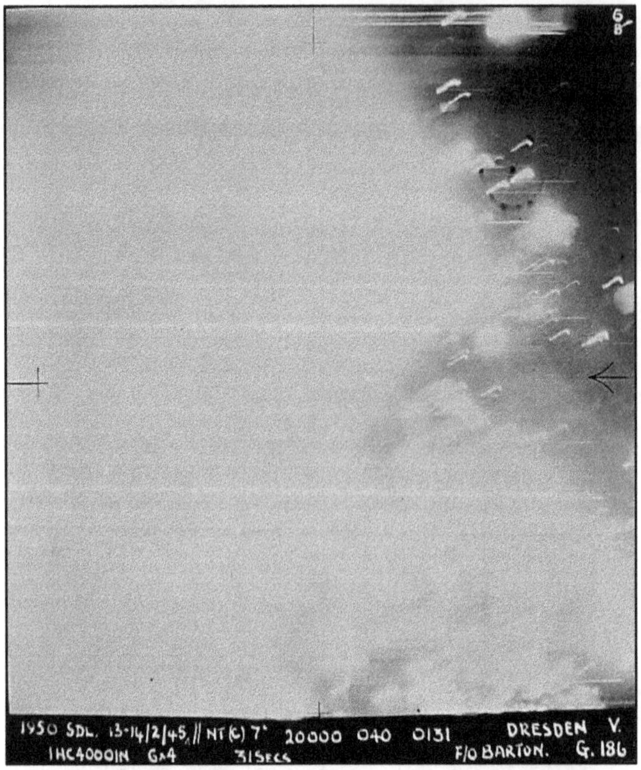


Dresden. This Target Photograph shows almost nothing but flames and smoke over the doomed city. Timed at 01:31 hour and taken by Flying Officer Barton and crew.

The last to land from Dresden in the cold early morning gloom was F/O D.F Godfrey RAAF at the controls of Lancaster PD427 XY-Z at 07.07 hours. They had been airborne for 9 hours and 8 minutes.. Despite the loss of F/O James RAAF and crew, there was an atmosphere of excitement at de-briefing. The feeling amongst the returning crews was that this was something big. There were a few veterans, sadly a small minority on the squadron who had experienced conflagrations on the scale of Dresden. Some had participated in the Battle of Hamburg, but even those realised that this operation had exceeded the devastation meted out almost 18 months prior. Like Hamburg, Dresden would experience a 'firestorm' of almost biblical proportion. The firestorm created by the bombing continued burning for many more days. Eight square miles of the city lay in ruins. Within a few short hours, Dresden would be visited by over 300 B17 Flying Fortress of the US 1st Air Division, who attempted to bomb the marshalling yards through a blanket of smoke. The destruction of the city provoked unease in certain circles in Britain. Once so supportive of Bomber Command's role, the British Press began to voice concerns and questioned if the military force of this scale and destruction was warranted on an already defeated Germany.To maximise the success of Dresden, over 700 aircraft would attack Chemnitz the following night. The third-largest city in Saxony and situated only 40 miles SW of Dresden, it too would feel the destructive force of Bomber Command. Unlike Dresden, it had many large industrial factories, including the important Astra-Werk AG Oil Plant, and a large rail system. The city was often referred to as 'The Saxon Manchester'. Number 3 Group detailed 160 Lancasters on this operation, which like the previous night would attack in two phases. The first phase would see the Halifaxes and Lancasters of No.4 and 6 RCAF Group open proceedings at 20:48 hours. Over two hours later the second phase would commence with Lancasters drawn from No.1 and 3 Groups. The second phase was divided over three waves, No.31 Base would make up the third and final wave and be timed over the target between 00:38 to 00:42 hours. It was another deep penetration into southern Germany and given W/Cdr J Giles DFC preference for flying on all the tough operations. It was no surprise that his name was on the Operations Board. Joining it would be 'A' Flight's S/Ldr P Reynolds who had returned from leave that morning, and S/Ldr E Scott. The raids objective was the same as Dresden. *'TO DESTROY BUILT UP AREA AND ASSOCIATED INDUSTRIES AND RAIL FASCILITIES'*

Form B.788 – February 14th 1945(N) : Target : Chemnitz : 'Blackfin'

| | | | | | | | |
|---|---|---|---|---|---|---|---|
| S/Ldr | Reynolds | P | | NG174 | XY-A | Bombed PFF TI's | Duty Carried Out |
| F/O | Green | T | | HK692 | XY-B | Bombed PFF TI's | Duty Carried Out |
| F/O | Cowley | N.C | | HK694 | XY-C | Bombed PFF TI's | Duty Carried Out |
| F/O | Hart | J.H | | NG146 | XY-E | Bombed PFF TI's | Duty Carried Out |
| F/O | Marshall | A.N | | NG140 | XY-F | Bombed PFF TI's | Duty Not Carried Out |
| W/Cdr | Giles DFC | J.H | | NG148 | XY-G | Bombed PFF TI's | Duty Carried Out |
| P/O | O'Brien | J.D | RAAF | HK684 | XY-O | Bombed PFF TI's | Duty Carried Out |
| F/O | Beck | J.A | RAAF | HK662 | XY-P | Bombed PFF TI's | Duty Carried Out |
| S/Ldr | Scott | E.G | | HK659 | XY-Q | Bombed PFF TI's | Duty Carried Out |
| F/O | Idle | L.A | RNZAF | NG293 | XY-U | Bombed PFF TI's | Duty Carried Out |
| F/Lt | Hanson | R.A | | HK767 | N/K | Taxi Incident | Duty Not Carried Out |
| F/O | Fernley | F | | PD429 | XY-Z | Taxi Incident | Duty Not Carried Out |

The operation started with an uncharacteristic accident. While taxiing, two Lancasters collided in the dark at 19:55 hours, forcing their withdrawal from the operation. Flying Officer Jack O'Brien lifted Lancaster HK684 XY-O into the night sky at 20:07 hours carrying almost exclusively incendiaries. There was one early return, F/O A Marshall and crew had the misfortune of suffering a defective port inner engine southeast of Mannheim. The crew dumped their load on the last resort target and limped for home landing at 02:25 hours. The squadron approached the target from between 19-21,000 feet. It was immediately apparent to the crews that the earlier raid had not achieved the intensity of attack of

A stunning photograph of Flying Officer D.F.J Godfrey RAAF and crew.

Dresden. Unlike the previous night, Chemnitz was obscured by 9/10th cloud. The early flares dropped by the Path Finders were quickly hidden and swallowed up.

The Master Bomber, Flight Lieutenant Duncan McNaughton DFC of No.405 RCAF Squadron codename '*Falstaff*' ordered the main force to bomb on the DR or navigational aids. Crews reported a glow beneath the clouds but were uncertain about the accuracy. Unlike Dresden, the marking appeared scattered. Red and green Skymarkers were observed as were burning target indicators on the ground, F/O J. Hart, *'Marking not good and the raid seemed scattered. Many fires were seen burning within a radius of 10 miles'*. Crews bombed on the glow of flares or the fires below. Wing Commander Giles DFC, *'The target was identified and bombed on skymarkers Red with Green Stars. At 00:44 hours from 19,900 feet. A glow was visible under the cloud, but markers and bombing was very scattered'*. By the time the third and final wave turned for home, there were two distinct fires close together. Although they were not as large as Dresden, they were still visible from almost 50 miles on the return route. The crew of F/O Jack Hart had been given the job of 'Windfinder' for this raid. Selected crews usually positioned at the front of the bomber stream would using both GEE and H2S calculate the found winds over a 30 - 60 minute leg back to Group. Their findings were then relayed to HQ Bomber Command and 'ETA' - the code name for the Met Office HQ at Dunstable. At both places the winds were then plotted on a special diagram board and the mean wind for the 30 minutes calculated using all the reports. These were compared with the forecast wind for that leg and an amendment broadcast would be made if necessary. The objective was to ensure all the aircraft were using the same basic data for navigation. The procedure continued throughout an operation - both out - and in-bound. The idea was introduced during the winter of 1943-44 and brought about an improvement in both navigating and time-on-target. It was Flight Sergeant Jack Allen's job to work both Gee and H2S.

> *We took off at 20.20 in Lancaster XY-E for Chemnitz. I was using both GEE and H2S for navigating and was one of the crews who were to break radio silence and send back reports on the windspeed and direction every hour - which after collecting all the information from so many other crews would be Signalled back to the whole force for them to use. So that the whole force remained together. Unfortunately, on our way out and after having sent only one report, our outer engine which provided the power for the GEE & H2S failed, and I had to complete the 8.30 hr trip on dead reckoning navigation - suffice it to say we got back to base.*

Post-raid reconnaissance later establish that the main weight of bombing fell in open countryside. It was a disappointing result, and the failure lay squarely on the shoulders of the Path Finders. On the plus side, Group recorded the loss of only two crews, both from No.33 Base.

The two Lancasters involved in the taxiing collision caused by confusion over an Aldis lamp signal both required the specialist attention of No.54 Maintenance Unit. Such was the damage that both aircraft would be unavailable for operations until March.

No.186 Squadron Reported Incident / Accident 14/02/1945

| Serial | Code | Damage | Repairs / Notes |
|---|---|---|---|
| HK767 | N/K | Not Recorded | Cat AC/FB –RoS 54 MU-19/02/1945-186 Sqn 08/03/1945. |
| PD429 | **XY-Z** | Not Recorded | Cat AC/GR –RoS 54 MU-19/02/1945-186 Sqn 17/03/1945. |

The squadron enjoyed a well-earned day off on the 15th due to a bank of fog that swept over the region. Wing Commander Giles DFC attended a Master Bomber conference. He did not have to travel far, as it was held in the Ladies Room of the Officers Mess at RAF Stradishall. Unlike Lincolnshire and

Yorkshire based squadrons of Bomber Command, No.3 Group was surrounded by American bomber stations of the US 8th Air Force. It was not uncommon to encounter the natural metal finished American B17 Fortress and B24 Liberator bombers with their colourful tail markings and garish nose art. One such encounter involved Flying Officer A.J Clarson RAAF who was airborne on an early morning Air-Test in Lancaster NG354 XY-M. The crews Rear Gunner, F/Sgt McPherson RAAF takes up the encounter.

> *On 15th February, the crew were instructed to carry out an air test on M for Mike. This exercise involved testing certain working parts of the aircraft following an overhaul by the ground staff. When returning to base after completing the exercise, Jeff spotted an American Fortress bomber flying in the same direction to our starboard. Jeff had been keen on formation flying when he was training on single-engine aircraft, so he and Jock, the engineer, decided to do a little formation flying with the Fortress. He eased up to the Fortress and placed our starboard wing between the wing and the tail of the Fortress. After a few minutes, Jeff feathered one engine, followed shortly by a second engine and, subsequently, a third engine. For about five minutes we flew on one engine in close formation with the Fortress with its four engines. We could see the American airmen looking at us in awe that a Lancaster with one engine operating could keep up with their four-engine aircraft'.*

On the 16th, the squadron was detailed and briefed for an attack on the town of Wesel. Situated on the northern Rhine, the town was an important transportation centre, and sadly for the inhabitants, strategically positioned for the British advance into Germany. Ten crews were detailed and briefed when, unexpectedly, the raid was cancelled at 12:30 hours, at least for 186 Squadron. After the briefing, the weather had quickly deteriorated, fog had swept in, and visibility was down to less than 200 yards.

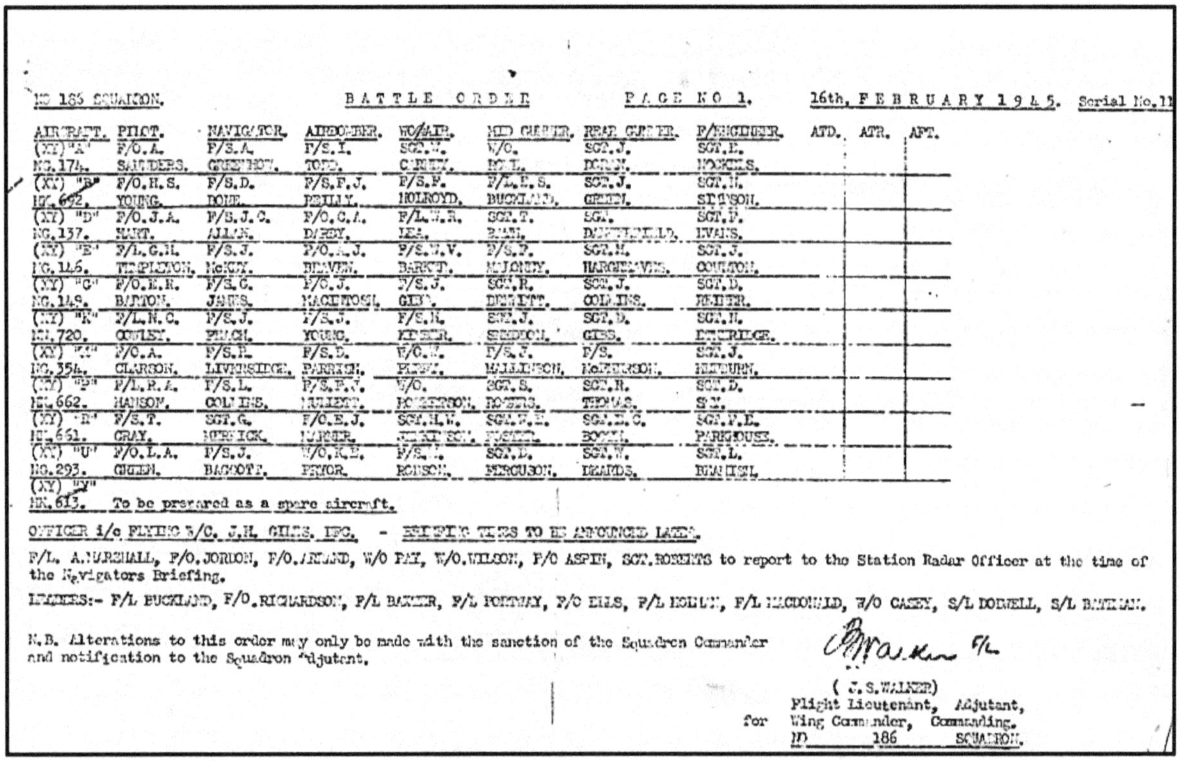

NO 186 SQUADRON. BATTLE ORDER PAGE NO 1. 16th, FEBRUARY 1945. Serial No.1[illegible]

| AIRCRAFT. | PILOT. | NAVIGATOR. | AIRBOMBER. | WO/AIR. | MID GUNNER. | REAR GUNNER. | F/ENGINEER. | ATD. | ATR. | AFT. |
|---|---|---|---|---|---|---|---|---|---|---|
| (XY) "A" NG.174. | F/O.A. SAUNDERS. | F/S.A. GREENHOW. | F/S.I. TODD. | SGT.[illegible] [illegible] | W/O. [illegible] | SGT.J. [illegible] | SGT.E. HOSKINS. | | | |
| (XY) "B" HK.692. | F/O.H.S. YOUNG. | F/S.D. DOHE. | F/S.F.J. REILLY. | F/S.F. HOLROYD. | F/L.E.S. BUCKLAND. | SGT.J. GREEN. | SGT.H. SIMPSON. | | | |
| (XY) "D" NG.137. | F/O.J.A. HART. | F/S.J.C. ALLAN. | F/O.C.A. DARBY. | F/L.W.R. LEA. | SGT.T. [illegible] | SGT. [illegible] | SGT.F. EVANS. | | | |
| (XY) "E" NG.146. | F/L.G.H. TEMPLETON. | F/S.J. McKAY. | F/O.A.J. BEAVEN. | F/S.W.V. [illegible] | F/S.P. MALONEY. | SGT.M. HARGREAVES. | SGT.J. COULTON. | | | |
| (XY) "G" NG.149. | F/O.E.R. BARTON. | F/S.G. JAMES. | F/O.J. MACINTOSH. | F/S.J. GIBB. | SGT.R. DEWITT. | SGT.J. COLLINS. | SGT.D. [illegible] | | | |
| (XY) "K" HK.720. | F/L.N.C. COWLEY. | F/S.J. PEACH. | F/S.J. YOUNG. | F/S.H. [illegible] | SGT.J. SHEDDON. | SGT.D. GIBBS. | SGT.H. ETHERIDGE. | | | |
| (XY) "M" NG.354. | F/O.A. CLARSON. | F/S.R. LIVERSIDGE. | F/S.D. PARRISH. | F/O.[illegible] [illegible] | F/S.J. MALLINSON. | F/S. McPHERSON. | SGT.J. HEPBURN. | | | |
| (XY) "P" HK.662. | F/L.R.A. HANSON. | F/S.L. COLLINS. | F/S.F.[illegible] [illegible] | W/O. ROBERTSON. | SGT.S. ROGERS. | SGT.R. THOMAS. | SGT.D. [illegible] | | | |
| (XY) "R" HK.661. | F/S.T. GRAY. | SGT.G. MERRICK. | F/O.E.J. [illegible] | SGT.H.W. [illegible] | SGT.[illegible] FOSTER. | SGT.[illegible] [illegible] | SGT.F.E. PARKHOUSE. | | | |
| (XY) "U" NG.293. | F/O.L.A. GREEN. | F/S.J. BAGGOTT. | W/O.K.E. PRYOR. | F/S.[illegible] ROBSON. | SGT.D. FERGUSON. | SGT.W. [illegible] | SGT.L. [illegible] | | | |
| (XY) "Y" HK.613. | To be prepared as a spare aircraft. | | | | | | | | | |

OFFICER i/c FLYING W/C. J.H. GILES. DFC. - BRIEFING TIMES TO BE ANNOUNCED LATER.

F/L. A.MARSHALL, F/O.JORDON, F/O.[illegible], W/O FAY, W/O.WILSON, F/O ASPIN, SGT.ROBERTS to report to the Station Radar Officer at the time of the Navigators Briefing.

LEADERS:- F/L BUCKLAND, F/O.RICHARDSON, F/L BAXTER, F/L PORTWAY, F/O ELLS, F/L [illegible], F/L MACDONALD, W/O CASEY, S/L DORWELL, S/L [illegible].

N.B. Alterations to this order may only be made with the sanction of the Squadron Commander and notification to the Squadron Adjutant.

( J.S.WALKER)
Flight Lieutenant, Adjutant,
for Wing Commander, Commanding.
NO 186 SQUADRON.

The raid that never was. Order of Battle for the cancelled Wesel operation of February 16th 1945.

The remainder of the Group's Lancasters, unaffected by the fog, attacked Wesel in clear conditions. The town and railway were seen smothered in bomb bursts. It was the first in a series of devastating raids on this small town. On the 17th, the fog had still not dispersed and effectively grounded the squadron. Independent reports emanating from Germany about Dresden's destruction and the loss of life now began to gain momentum not only in the British press but in America. The unease was made worse by an Associated Press story that the Allies had resorted to terror bombing. At a press briefing held by the Supreme Headquarters Allied Expeditionary Force two days after the raids, British Air Commodore Colin McKay Grierson told journalists:

*First of all, they (Dresden and similar towns) are the centres to which evacuees are being moved. They are centres of communications through which traffic is moving across to the Russian Front, and from the Western Front to the East, and they are sufficiently close to the Russian Front for the Russians to continue the successful prosecution of their battle. I think these three reasons probably cover the bombing.*

One of the journalists asked whether the principal aim of bombing Dresden would be to cause confusion among the refugees or to blast communications carrying military supplies. Grierson answered that the primary aim was to attack communications to prevent the Germans from moving military supplies, and to stop movement in all directions if possible. He then added in an offhand remark that the raid also helped destroy *"what is left of German morale."* It was an unfortunate remark that would have reverberations for years to come long after the conclusion of the bomber offensive.

On February 16$^{th}$, the London Gazette announced the award of no less than seven DFC's to No.186 Squadron. Pilots, S/Ldr Percy Reynolds, and P/O Robert Roach, two Bomb Aimers, Bombing Leader, F/Lt William 'Bill' Holman, and F/O Peter Bray. Two Air Gunners were also honoured, the squadron Gunnery Leader, F/Lt Ernest Buckland, and F/O Leslie Grant. The final award was to F/O Douglas Greig, Wireless Operator.

The morning of the 18th found RAF Stradishall still fog-bound, but a hurried briefing was carried out with a promise of it clearing by mid-day. Accordingly, twelve crews would be detailed for an attack on Wesel. The raid's intention was simple, to create havoc for the Germans by destroying built-up areas and blocking roads and disorganising military movement. One of the twelve was the crew of F/Sgt Phil Gray, who would be undertaking his first operation since his arrival on the squadron on January 22nd. No sooner had the crew arrived than they were posted to RAF Feltwell for an intensive three-day training course on both G-H and H2S. Now, with the training complete, they were ready for operations. With the squadron routinely carrying out G-H operations, it was no surprise that Group HQ was eager to ensure all its crews should be trained on G-H. To this end, a G-H Training Flight was formed on January 29$^{th}$, 1945, under the command of Squadron Leader George Mitchell at RAF Feltwell. The flight's prime role would be to provide training on G-H for both air and ground crews for the Group until the time No.7 Group was in a position to begin training.

Form B.791 – February 18th 1945(D) : Target : Wesel

| | | | | | | | |
|---|---|---|---|---|---|---|---|
| F/O | Saunders | A | | NG174 | XY-A | G-H Leader | Duty Carried Out. |
| F/O | Green | T.B | | HK694 | XY-C | G-H Leader | Duty Carried Out. |
| F/O | Hart | J.H | | NG137 | XY-D | Follower | Duty Carried Out. |
| F/O | Barton | E.R | RAAF | NG149 | XY-G | Follower | Duty Carried Out. |
| F/Lt | Cowley | N.C | | NN720 | XY-K | G-H failure. | Duty Carried Out. |
| F/O | Clarson | A | RAAF | NG354 | XY-M | G-H Leader | Duty Carried Out. |
| F/O | O'Brien | J.D | RAAF | HK662 | XY-P | Follower | Duty Carried Out. |
| F/O | Idle | L.A | RNZAF | HK659 | XY-Q | G-H Leader | Duty Carried Out. |

| | | | | | | | |
|---|---|---|---|---|---|---|---|
| F/Sgt | Gray | P | | HK661 | XY-R | Follower | Duty Carried Out. |
| F/Lt | Hanson | R.A | | NG140 | XY-F | G-H Leader | Duty Not Carried Out. |
| F/O | Green | L.A | | NG293 | XY-U | Follower | Duty Carried Out. |
| S/Ldr | Scott | E.G | | HK613 | XY-Y | Follower | Duty Carried Out. |

A total of 168 No.3 Group Lancasters would attack Wesel between 15:19 and 15:35 hours, No.31 Base would provide 54 aircraft and was scheduled to be the last wave over the target area. Once formed up over Brentwood, Essex, the gaggle of black ant-like bombers departed over Beachy Head with the squadron at the rear of the Armada. As briefed, the crews found the whole of Europe hidden by a carpet of dense white cloud. Above, there was unlimited visibility in a clear freezing sky. An engine fire aboard Lancaster NG140 XY-F at 14:40 hours resulted in the crew of F/Lt R.A Hanson abandoning the operation. The fire, caused by the failure of No.4 cylinder head in the port inner was extinguished and the Merlin feathered. The entire bomb load was jettisoned safe at 51.25N-03.00E at 15:36 hours.

Obviously not a superstitious bunch. Flight Sergeant Phil Gray and his crew are photographed just before their first operation on February 18th, 1945. L-R. Flying Officer Jack Marner (Bomb Aimer), Sergeant Frank Parkhouse (Flight Engineer), Sergeant Harry Jenkins (Wireless Operator), Flight Sergeant Phil Gray (Pilot), Sergeant Ivor Forster (Mid Upper Gunner), Sergeant Gerald Merrick (Navigator), Sergeant Clinton Booth (Rear Gunner).

The group was joined by its fighter escort of four squadrons of Spitfires and five squadrons of RAF Mustangs south of the Belgium cathedral town of Mechelen. With clouds reaching up to 12,000 feet, the formation was initially rather strung out. However, once entering German airspace the three base formations became more compact as predicted flak started exploding amongst the Lancasters. Below the cloud base, three Mustang and three Spitfire squadrons would sweep the route at low level catching unsuspecting German fighters taking off. Over the target, the squadron reported surprisingly little flak opposition. The G-H equipment aboard F/Lt N.C Cowley's Lancaster, NN720 XY-K failed on the run-up to the target. Thankfully, a G-H Leader was in close proximity and the crew bombed with this but retained their 250lb Green TI marker. The most significant danger was the inability of other base groups to keep to the briefed heights, track, and times. Expecting to be the last over target area, the crews were surprised to encounter Lancasters flying both above, and behind them!

Crews also reported seeing a sleek Mosquito a few thousand feet above them over the target area. This was in all probability an aircraft of No.1409 (Meteorological) Flight. Formed on April 1st, 1943, to provide meteorological information for RAF Bomber Command it was equipped with unarmed de Havilland Mosquito aircraft. The Flight undertook long-range meteorological reconnaissance flights codenamed PAMPA (Photo recce And Meteorological Photography Aircraft).From their initial formation the flight proved invaluable.

The squadron was bolstered with the arrival of three new crews on the 18th. One of whom was skippered by New Zealander W/O J.R Marsh RNZAF, who arrived from No.3 LFS. Eleven Squadron crews were briefed for another attack on Wesel on the 19th. Like the previous raid, the No.31 Base Leader role was given to the experienced Flight Lieutenant Frank Blenkin of 'C' Flight of No.218 Squadron based at RAF Chedburgh. The Deputy Base Leader would be given to 218 Squadrons 'A' Flight Commander Squadron Leader John O'Brien, his fifth operation in the role. The role of Base and Deputy Leader had so far eluded No.186 Squadron, but it was just a question of time. The squadron was now fully emersed in G-H techniques and had a number of experienced crews within its ranks.

Form B.792 – February 19th 1945(D) : Target : Wesel

| | | | | | | | |
|---|---|---|---|---|---|---|---|
| F/O | Saunders | A | | NG174 | XY-A | G-H Leader | Duty Carried Out. |
| F/O | Head | G.D | | HK692 | XY-B | Follower | Duty Carried Out. |
| F/O | Young | H.S | | NG146 | XY-E | Follower | Duty Carried Out. |
| F/O | Barton | E.R | RAAF | NG149 | XY-G | Follower | Duty Carried Out. |
| F/O | Clarson | A.J | RAAF | NG354 | XY-M | G-H Leader | Duty Carried Out. |
| F/O | Hart | J.H | | NG137 | XY-D | Follower | Duty Carried Out. |
| F/Lt | Orman DFC | K.G | RNZAF | HK659 | XY-Q | G-H Leader | Duty Carried Out. |
| F/O | Beck | J.A | RAAF | HK662 | XY-P | G-H Leader | Duty Carried Out. |
| F/O | Gogler | R.J | RAAF | NG293 | XY-U | Follower | Duty Carried Out. |
| F/Sgt | Gray | P | | HK661 | XY-R | Follower | Duty Carried Out. |
| F/Lt | Green | L.A | | RF126 | XY-V | Follower | Duty Carried Out. |

The squadron departed just before 14:00 hours. Four of its crews were given the G-H Leader role. There was one moment of danger. While taking off at 13:52 hours, the starboard tyre burst on Lancaster HK662 XY-P, possibly the result of surface debris. Showing extraordinary skill, plus a good dollop of luck, F/O J.A Beck RAAF managed to get the fully-ladened Lancaster airborne. Thankfully, the tyre had burst when the Lancaster had sufficient speed and momentum to clear the end of the runway and gain precious height. It would have been a catastrophe if the tyre had blown seconds earlier. Once airborne, the crew took stock, showing incredible calm and courage they decided to continue with the operation. The next away was Flight Sergeant Phil Gray, who writes about the strain and dangers of taking off fully loaded with high Explosives and fuel.

> *I had experienced no trouble with handling the torque during our conversion, but on this occasion, as we gathered speed I felt the familiar pull to the left. I was a little slow on the rudder and the swing continued but I used all measures available, easing back on the starboard engines and keeping full power on the port, at the same time remembering that we were using up runway fast and 25 was not the longest in the world. The drift continued, and a split-second choice had to be taken, either bash on and hope all would be alright or to throw all the anchors out. Due to the proximity of the fence and our delicate cargo I*

*decided to press on, but our corrective actions had slowed us down, and as we were now well off the centre-line we needed all help to get us off the deck as we were heading for the biggest bloody hangar I had ever seen! It had to be maximum emergency power and to get this we needed to go through the 'gate'. I had classed it as a dire emergency and called to Frank for full emergency power. Like any good engineer Frank's first thoughts were for his poor engines, and only after my frantic yelling of four-letter words were the levers slammed through-H the quadrants. The four thoroughbred engines responded valiantly, and as the Lancaster inched upwards I hauled back on the stick as far as I dared and we staggered over the hangar. There was a quiet amongst the crew, and even 'Blondie' (Ivor Foster) who was a most prolific dispenser of words was stunned into silence.*[33]

Safely airborne, the squadron proceeded once again to the rendezvous point above Brentwood, Essex. Some crews experienced problems finding their Leaders. Flying Officers G.D Head, H.S Young and E.R Barton RAAF could not locate XY-A flown by F/O A Saunders. They instead followed A4-R NG388, a G-H equipped Lancaster of No.195 Squadron flown by 'B' Flight Commander, S/Ldr B.W.R Forster. Interestingly, F/O A Saunders, submitted the following, *'Briefed followers not met at RVP. No other aircraft formed up on us and we bombed alone'.*

Once formed up, the three base groups headed towards Beachy Head. Predictably, No.31 Base would make up the unhealthy final wave with over fifty Lancasters. Unlike the previous day, the crews had the opportunity of making out ground features 19,000 feet below while en route. The squadron entered German airspace unmolested from flak or fighters. Only as the formation started its final leg to target were they engaged. Intermittent predicted flak from Emmerich began to burst around the bombers. The gunners below had gauged the height precisely. The formation keeping by both No.31 Base and the preceding Groups warranted some criticism. Flight Sergeant Gray, *'Formation flying on the way to target was not good'*. At 16:36 hours, the squadron crews began their bomb runs. A plume of dense smoke was already rising 8,000 feet above the town, a testament to the accuracy of the earlier waves. Over the target, the formation seemed to achieve some cohesion, F/O R Gogler RAAF, *'Bombed on Radar Navigation Aids Leader at 16:37 hours from 19,000 feet. Bombs seen falling on the town. Aircraft formation seemed good.'*. A concentrated bunch of Red Sky Marker and the more vivid Blue Sky Markers attracted numerous bomb loads. The ground appeared to vibrate as bomb-load after bomb-load exploded in the town and nearby marshalling yards. The flak may have been slight, but it was accurate. Crews reported the presence of 'scarecrows' over the target area. Flight Lieutenant L.A Green dropped on his G-H Leader at 16:36 hours, *'Bombs were seen falling on the town, Marshalling Yards and the canal.'*

G-H Leader, F/Lt K.G Orman DFC RNZAF was one of the last squadron crews to bomb. On return, he informed the Intelligence Officer at de-briefing. *'Bombed on Radar Navigational equipment at 16:37 hours from 18,700 feet. The aircraft formation over the target was good and bombing therefore concentrated. Bombs were seen bursting on the target, and columns of brownish-grey smoke were rising above the cloud to about 7,000 feet. Sky Markers well concentrated'.* Flying Officer Beck RAAF, who had suffered a burst tyre on take-off, had positioned himself aft of his G-H Leader, F/O A.J Clarson RAAF, at the RVP. Here he stayed until just before the target when he somehow lost his leader. Thankfully in sight was F/Lt Orman DFC RNZAF, who he bombed with. Having successfully bombed the target, the crew of Lancaster HK662 XY-P now had the difficult job of landing with a burst tyre. On selecting the undercarriage lever down, F/O J.A Beck RAAF discovered that the starboard undercarriage would not lock due to a damaged oleo struct. The crew selected to divert to the Emergency Airfield at RAF Woodbridge, where they carried out a belly landing at 18:10 hours.

---

[33] *Used with kind permission of Author Jock Whitehouse.*

Flying Officer James Beck RAAF would be awarded an immediate DFC for his actions on this day, it was the crew's fifteenth operation. Flight Sergeant P Gray suffered both Gee and radio failure on the return trip and was obliged to land at RAF Sudbury at 18:27 hours.

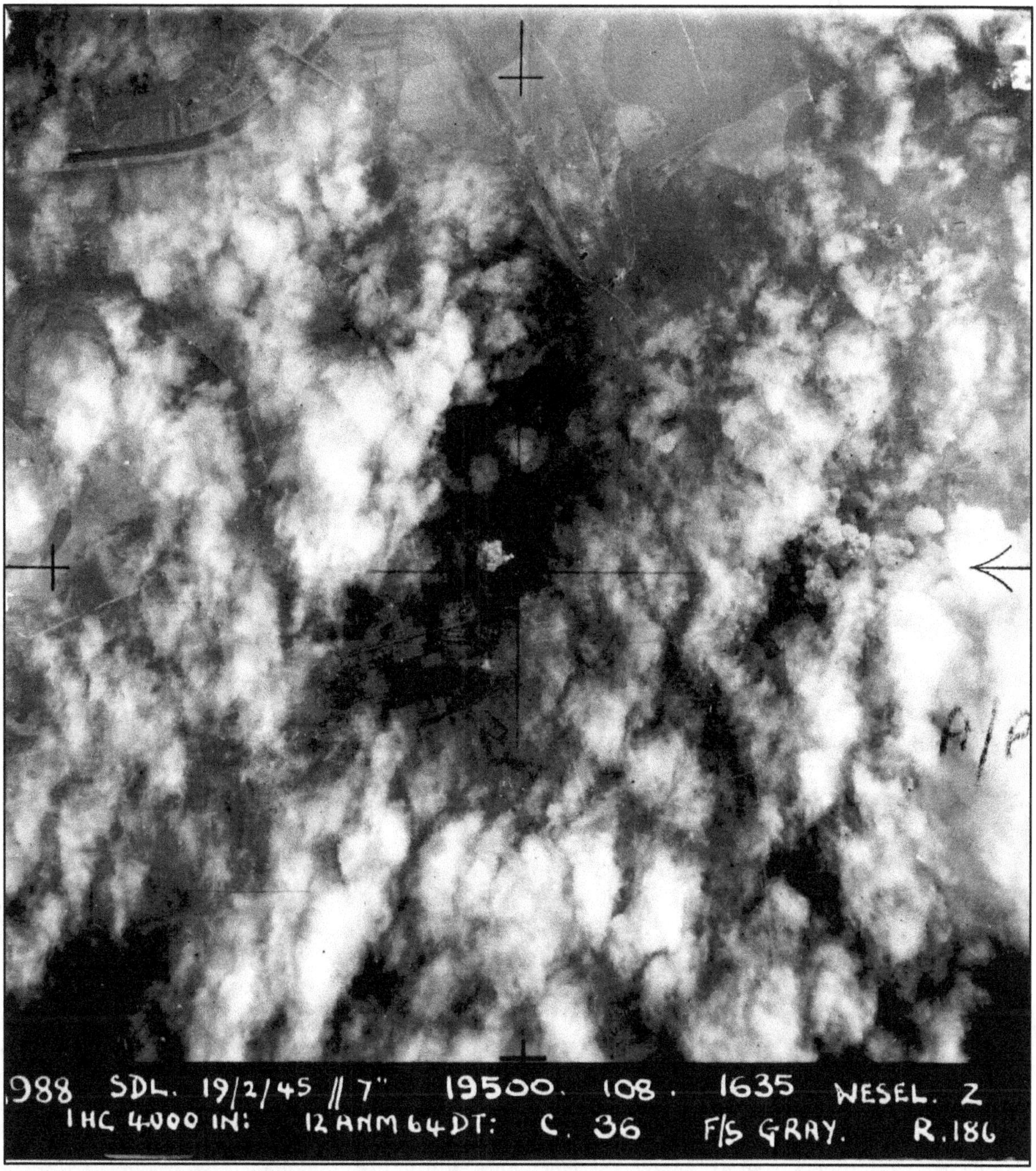


The Target Photograph taken by Flight Sergeant Phil Gray over Wesel, February 19th 1945. Some ground detail, including the Rhine River can be identified. The Aiming Point (AP) is middle right of photograph.

No.186 Squadron Reported Incident / Accident 19/02/1945

| Serial | Code | Damage | Repairs / Notes |
|---|---|---|---|
| HK662 | **XY-P** | Various | Cat B–RiW 24 MU- Did not return to service, |

The damage to Lancaster HK662 was extensive, the aircraft was transferred to the care of No.24 Maintenance Unit where it was Repaired in Works. HK662 did not return to front line service and languished at No.5 MU until Struck off Charge in 1947.

The crew of F/O Jack Hart were posted to RAF Feltwell on the 20th to carry-out G-H Training. Flight Sergeant Allen recalls.

> *We spent three days on what my log book calls "G-H Training". This was "bombing" by photographs Ely Cathedral, Wisbech and actual bombs at Rushford using GEE & H2S navigational aids. It was about this time that our Navigational Leader called me to his office and told me he had put my name forward for a commission so that after I had completed my tour - if I was so lucky, I could stay on the station as Deputy Navigational Leader.*

It was back to area bombing on the night of February 20th. The group would once again join forces with No.1 Group and the Canadians of No.6 RCAF. The target was the industrial area and rail facilities located in the south of Dortmund. The squadron despatched twelve crews.

Form B.793 – February 20th 1945(N) : Target : Dortmund 'Blackfin'

| | | | | | | | |
|---|---|---|---|---|---|---|---|
| F/Lt | Dowley | N.C | | NG174 | XY-A | Bombed TI's | Duty Carried Out |
| F/O | Head | G.D | | HK692 | XY-B | Bombed TI's | Duty Carried Out |
| F/Lt | Marshall | A.N | | NG137 | XY-D | Bombed TI's | Duty Carried Out |
| F/O | Green | T.B | | NG146 | XY-E | Bombed TI's | Duty Carried Out |
| F/O | Young | H.S | | HK661 | XY-R | Bombed TI's | Duty Carried Out |
| S/Ldr | Scott | E.G | | HK659 | XY-Q | Bombed TI's | Duty Carried Out |
| F/O | Gogler | P.J | RAAF | NG293 | XY-U | Bombed TI's | Duty Carried Out |
| W/Cdr | Giles DFC | J.H | | HK801 | XY-S | Bombed TI's | Duty Carried Out |
| F/O | Fernley | F | | HK794 | XY-T | Bombed TI's | Duty Carried Out |
| F/O | Idle | L.A | RNZAF | RF126 | XY-V | Bombed TI's | Duty Carried Out |
| S/Ldr | Bass AFM | R.W | | HK796 | XY-W | Bombed TI's | Duty Carried Out |
| F/Lt | Hanson | A.J | | HK613 | XY-Y | Bombed TI's | Duty Carried Out |

The Lancasters of No.6 Group would open the proceedings at 01:00 hours, bombing between 14-17,000 feet, No.3 Group would immediately follow, bombing from between 18-22,000 feet, while the final wave of No.1 Group would bomb between 13-21,000 feet. As the squadron neared Dortmund, the presence of night fighters steadily increased, and a few combats were reported with flaming bombers easily visible in the inky blackness. Above Dortmund, it was a cauldron of exploding flak, fighter flares and TI markers. The Canadians had produced a conflagration that was plainly visible as No.3 Group started their bomb runs. Large explosions, a massive fire, and Wanganui Flares, which the crews complained were dropped by the Path Finder's much too high, greeted the crews. Flying Officer T Gogler RAAF, '*Bombing well concentrated around Target Indicators and as mass of incendiaries were burning. A good attack. Skymarker burst too high, up at 21,000 feet!*' Flying Officer Idle RNZAF bombed at 01:13 hours from 21,000 feet, '*Tremendous glow of fires illuminated the whole cloud area, fires spread over the whole target area. Concentration seemed excellent.*' It was not all one sided. The returning crews reported four bombers shot down in flames over Dortmund. A large glow under the clouds bore testament to the concentration of bombing. The whole of the southern part of the city appeared ablaze, numerous Sky Markers and TI markers were floating or bursting over the aiming point, it was a classic area attack reminiscent of the raids of 1943. German fighter flares had been seen prior to the target. However it was on the return journey that F/Lt Marshall and crew ran into trouble. Having reduced height to 16,000 feet, the crew were passing over Grietherbusch, 3 miles Southeast of

Emmerich, when the rear gunner spotted an approaching fighter. The following Combat Report was submitted on return.

> Me110 first seen on port fine quarter, range 500 yards coming into attack. The order was given to corkscrew port was given, and rear gunner and mid upper gunner opened fire. The fighter closed in to 200 yards, both gunners continued firing and the enemy aircraft broke away down to port with smoke pouring from the aircraft as it dived away into cloud. Shortly afterwards an explosion on the ground illuminating the clouds. Claimed as PROBABLY destroyed.

The rear gunner, F/O A. Aspin, fired over 1000 rounds, while the mid upper gunner, W/O L. Wilson fired 700 rounds. He reported the fighter as destroyed in his Logbook. The attack on Dortmund appeared, at least to the crews to be an outstanding success. The success, however, came at a cost. Fourteen crews failed to return, none however were from No.3 Group.

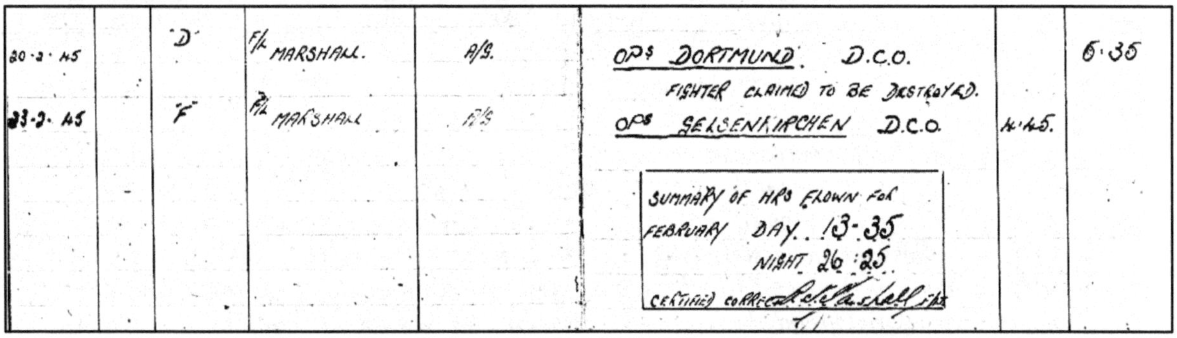

| | | | | | | | |
|---|---|---|---|---|---|---|---|
| 20·2·45 | | 'D' | F/L MARSHALL. | A/G. | OPS DORTMUND. D.C.O.<br>FIGHTER CLAIMED TO BE DESTROYED. | | 6·35 |
| 23·2·45 | | 'F' | F/L MARSHALL | A/G | OPS GELSENKIRCHEN D.C.O | 4·45. | |
| | | | | | SUMMARY OF HRS FLOWN FOR FEBRUARY DAY. 13·35 NIGHT 26·25.<br>CERTIFIED CORRECT | | |

Log Book of Warrant Officer L Wilson claiming the destruction of the fighter.

The London Gazette announced the award of the DFM to Canadian Sgt Robert Hunter RCAF, navigator, who had by this time been repatriated back to Canada. The citation reads.

> *HUNTER, Robert Oliver. Can/R.69301 Sergeant, R.C.A.F, No.186 Sqn.*
>
> *L.G. 20/2/1945. Sorties 25, Flying hours 111.40. Navigator. This N.C.O. has completed many operations, most of these being to German targets. His navigation has always been of a high order while his keenness and devotion to duty has instilled complete confidence in his Captain and crew. One day in October, 1944, he was Navigator in an aircraft detailed to attack Wesseling. Before reaching the target, the aircraft was hit by heavy flak, wounding the rear gunner and damaging the control surfaces of the aircraft. Sergeant Hunter helped to render first aid to the gunner and then calmly continued to navigate the aircraft onto the target and the return journey.*

Sergeant Hunter's skipper was F/Lt A.C 'Sandy' Powell DFC. The squadron was not required on the 21st but warned that it would be required the following day. A number of G-H exercises were flown, and six crews participated in a formation flying exercise. There had been much discussion at Group HQ about the flying discipline over recent operations. It was a common complaint and one that would never be fully resolved despite the best endeavours of the squadron commanders. The squadron received another new crew on this date, Australian W/O Maxwell Onus RAAF from No.1668 HCU at RAF Bottesford.

Number 3 Group would divide its attention on the daylight raid of February 22nd. Eighty-six Lancasters of No.31 and No.32 Base were given the Hibernia AG coking plant at Scholven, Gelsenkirchen to attack. Sixty-one Lancasters of No.33 Base and twenty Lancasters of No.149 Squadron were tasked with attacking the Benzol plant at Osterfeld.

Form B.795 – February 22nd 1945(D):Target : Gelsenkirchen: Hibernia AG coking plant at Scholven,

| | | | | | | | |
|---|---|---|---|---|---|---|---|
| F/O | Saunders | A | | NG137 | XY-D | Follower | Duty Carried Out. |
| F/O | Clarson | A.J | RAAF | NG146 | XY-E | Follower | Duty Carried Out. |
| F/Lt | Marshall | A.N | | NG140 | XY-F | Follower | Duty Carried Out. |
| F/O | Barton | E.R | RAAF | NG149 | XY-G | Follower | Duty Carried Out. |
| F/Lt | Tonks | J.E | | NG175 | XY-J | G-H Leader | Duty Carried Out. |
| W/Cdr | Giles DFC | J.H | | NN720 | XY-K | G-H Leader | Duty Carried Out. |
| F/Lt | Orman DFC | K.G | RNZAF | HK659 | XY-K | G-H Leader | Duty Carried Out. |
| F/Sgt | Gray | P | | HK661 | XY-R | Follower | Duty Carried Out. |
| F/O | Fernley | F | | HK794 | XY-T | G-H Leader | Duty Carried Out. |
| F/O | Gogler | R.J | RAAF | NG293 | XY-U | Follower | Duty Carried Out. |
| F/O | Idle | L.A | RNZAF | RF126 | XY-V | Follower | Duty Carried Out. |
| F/O | O'Brien | J.D | RAAF | HK796 | XY-W | Follower | Duty Carried Out. |

Flight Sergeant Phil Gray describes the briefing for the raid.

*The chatter and banter across the Briefing Room at Stradishall muted and died, all eyes following the Wing Commander of 186 Squadron as he crossed the platform to the blackboard. Always there was a curtain drawn across the face of the board, one of several security measures taken to lessen the chances of our intent filtering prematurely into enemy hands. The door of the room was locked. Service police were stationed all around the complex. Our before Ops meal of eggs, bacon and toast was served in a dining-room right next to the Briefing Room, the two sharing a connecting door. Every public telephone within a wide area around bomber stations 'died' when their squadrons were about to launch an attack, coming back into service when the planes were well on their way to the target. What we were attending was the general briefing. The first briefing, the nuts and bolts preparation by the navigators, had started one hour before, giving them information about weather conditions as well as technical details of tracks to be followed by the whole bomber stream. From all of this, the navigators would work out and plot the courses to be flown, estimating times of arrival at the various turning points.*

*Navigators knew most of the secrets long before the rest of us were allowed into the Briefing Room. To rectify this deficiency, the WingCo pulled the curtain clear of the blackboard. "The Ruhr again, gentlemen" he confirmed, "Gelsenkirchen to be precise. You have good back-up this time. I'm coming with you.' Wing Commander Giles gave the general picture of heights and courses there and back, the strength of the attack, the name of the synthetic oil installation we were aiming to eradicate. The Intelligence Officer told us about possible fighter opposition, and the latest position of the bomb line. This was a line which snaked down through the maps and charts as a parallel to the front line but was always ten miles inside enemy territory. We were not allowed to bomb, or the fighters to strafe, within this sensitive area between the front and bomb lines. The Bombing Leader gave the names of the Gee-H leaders, and the two Lancasters which would fly with them to form V or Vic formations. The lead plane would use specialised radar equipment to pinpoint the precise spot to be bombed. In the final act, of course, Gee-H or not, it was the air bomber of each Lancaster who was responsible for dropping the bombs. Jack brought the fuses of these 500-pounders alive and more or less controlled the bomber on the final run-up to the target. He was also responsible for ensuring that none of the bombs was left hanging stubbornly in the bomb bay. The engineers were told what the petrol load would be and which cross-feed levers to use. The wireless operators were briefed on which channels to monitor on the run to the target, exactly when they could safely start sending out information on the way back and given details about the various emergency frequencies. Then came the Meteorological Officer with the weather details, information vital for the success of the attack and our own survival. The Flight Commanders, 'A' and 'B' Flights, rounded off the briefing with a word for the pilots—'bus drivers' as we were known. We were to fly as tight a formation group as possible. If separated from our Gee-H leader for any reason, we were to try to attach to another leader. If this proved impractical, then we should bomb on our own Gee-H coordinates.*[34]

The squadron provided twelve crews led away by Wing Commander J Giles DFC, who had commandeered the highly-experienced crew of S/Ldr P Reynolds. Once airborne, the crews headed towards the familiar rendezvous point over Reading before heading south towards Beachy Head. The weather was clear with unlimited visibility. A blue sky that seemed never to end was offset by freezing conditions as No.186 Squadron gained altitude. The entire force was routed via Brussels, Nijmegen and then Kleve. When entering the Ruhr, the flak defences opened up with a steady and accurate barrage of heavy flak. It was particularly accurate for the Gelsenkirchen force, who were greeted by a wall of exploding 88mm and 128mm shells. Conditions quickly got worse over the target. The squadron met considerable and sustained opposition from the city below. Having already run the gauntlet, the formation was still reasonably intact until the bomb run. One of the first hit was F/O E.R Barton RAAF. They were hit while still one minute before bombing. The port inner engine was severely hit and immediately burst into flames. Prompt action by the pilot and his flight engineer, Sgt D Reiner, saw the blazing engine feathered. Still, at 20,000 feet, the crew somehow managed to keep formation with their allotted G-H Leader and drop their all High Explosive load at 15:55 hours. It was a tremendous effort by the crew. The next hit was Lancaster XY-E, captained by Aussie F/O Alexander Clarson. They were hit numerous times on the run-in at 20,000 feet resulting in the starboard inner engine being feather on leaving the target area. Over the target, F/Lt Marshall sustained damage to both wings and fuselage aboard NG140 XY-C. One of the most seriously hit was the crew of F/Lt K Orman DFC RNZAF. Three engines were hit, and the rear gunner, Sgt L Sewell, was wounded by flak in the hand. Flying with the crew was the Squadron's Navigational Leader, F/Lt W Earle DFM as an extra navigator. It is understood that this crew were given the Deputy Base Leader Role. Both marking and bombing were reported as accurate and concentrated despite the flak. Wing Commander Giles DFC was on his first G-H Leader operation. He reported, *'Bombs seen exploding on railway lines and black smoke was rising in target area'*. Flight Lieutenant J.E Tonks and crew were equally impressed, *'A good accurate attack. A big sheet of flames was seen in the target area and bombs were seen bursting'*. On leaving the target, the Lancaster flown by F/Sgt P Gray was damaged by barrage flak. Flight Sergeant Phil Gray.

*A box of four ack-ack shells exploded just ahead of our three bombers. My reflexive evasive action to jump the aftermath of the explosions must have been just a wee bit too energetic. I had lost both the cohesion of the formation and my Gee-H leader. I was hanging above the other two bombers like a vulture about to strike. There was no time to regroup, so I elected to go in as a solo.*

The bursting flak smashed the mid-upper turret and wounded the gunner, Sgt I Forster on the cheek. It also severed the port aerial. Flying Officer Barton had already feathered one engine when seven minutes after bombing, he was hit again by flak, this time in the starboard outer. Thankfully, the damage was less severe. The Merlin continued to function despite the temperature registering in the red. Somehow, all the crews safely landed back at RAF Stradishall. The last to land at 17:55 Hours was the squadron C/O, W/Cdr J Giles DFC. The flak over Gelsenkirchen had taken a heavy toll on both No.31 and No.32 Base. The squadrons of No.31 Base reported the following. 186 Squadron, five damaged, 195 Squadron 13 damaged, the RAF Chedburgh based No.218 (Gold Coast) Squadron, five damaged and one loss.

[34] *Ghosts of Targets Past : Phil Gray.*

This was seen to explode over the target area. The Mildenhall based No.15 Squadron recorded 13 Lancasters with varying degrees of flak damage, No.622 a total of nine, while No.90 Squadron got off lightly with only three Lancasters hit. However, there was cause for celebration on return from Gelsenkirchen. The crew of F/O Eric Barton RAAF had just returned from their 35th and last operation. They had started their tour back in October 1944 and had operated continuously since. Eric would, after a spell of leave, be posted to No.27 O.T.U for Instructor duties, and he would be awarded a well-deserved DFC in July 1945.

No.186 Squadron Reported Flak Damage 22/02/1945

| Serial | Code | Damage | Repairs / Notes |
|---|---|---|---|
| NG140 | **XY-F** | Wings/Fuselage. | Repaired on Squadron. |
| NG146 | **XY-E** | Starboard Engine damaged. | Repaired on Squadron. |
| NG149 | **XY-G** | P/O Engine / S/O Engine. | Repaired on Squadron. |
| HK659 | **XY-Q** | Three engines damaged. | Repaired on Squadron. |
| HK661 | **XY-R** | Mid upper turret, aerial. | Repaired on Squadron. |

A poor quality photo of Pilot Flying Officer Donald Roberts and his Navigator, Flight Sergeant John James, posing at the rear of 'A' Flight, Lancaster NG147 XY-A.

It was back to Gelsenkirchen and the flak the following day. One hundred and thirty-three crews were given the Alma Pluto Benzol Plant as their primary target. RAF Stradishall would provide just eight crews, who were led away by S/Ldr E Scott just before midday. That very morning, he had assumed the role of 'B' Flight Commander on the departure of S/Ldr R Bass AFM on leave.

Form B.796 – February 23rd 1945(D) : Target : Gelsenkirchen - Alma Pluto Benzol Plant

| | | | | | | | |
|---|---|---|---|---|---|---|---|
| F/O | Hart | J.A | | NG175 | XY-J | Follower | Duty Carried Out |
| F/Lt | Mason | F.H | | NG354 | XY-M | G-H Leader | Duty Carried Out |
| F/Lt | Cowley | N.C | | NN720 | XY-K | G-H Leader | Duty Carried Out |
| F/Lt | Brayshaw DFC | S.C | | HK684 | XY-O | Unknown | Duty Not Carried Out |
| F/O | Head | G.D | | HK661 | XY-R | G-H Leader | Duty Carried Out |
| S/Ldr | Scott | E.G | | HK801 | XY-S | G-H Leader | Duty Carried Out |
| F/O | O'Brien | J.D | RAAF | NG146 | XY-E | Follower | Duty Carried Out |
| F/O | Godfrey | D.F | RAAF | HK796 | XY-W | Follower | Duty Carried Out |

The Group's rendezvous point was over the village of Canewdon, Essex. Here No.31 Base would again find itself in the unenviable position of tail-end-Charlie, the third and last Base Group. Unfortunately, it was becoming a regular occurrence, much to the displeasure of the crews. Once formed, the group headed south and departed over Beachy Head, East Sussex. Over the Channel, the weather worsened and continued to do so as the group picked up its RAF P51 Mustang escort. Flight Lieutenant S Brayshaw DFC was at 15,000 feet when he lost the port outer engine aboard Lancaster HK684 XY-O a few miles north of Namur, Belgium. The Merlin was quickly feathered, and the crew turned for home, jettisoning the 'cookie' on the way but retaining the 12 x 500 pounders. They landed safely on three engines at 16:45 hours.

The squadrons of No.31 Base had, despite the ever-worsening weather conditions, managed to keep a good formation, but in the towering clouds which in places reached up to 22,000 feet and with visibility down to less than 1000 yards, the Lancasters of No.31 Base had fallen somewhat behind the preceding base formations as the German border was crossed. With the escort also struggling with the weather conditions, the small, isolated group had the company of a solitary squadron of European-based Spitfires. They were on their own as flak started to burst amongst them as they skirted south of Dusseldorf. The squadron started their bomb runs at 15:01 hours. The four selected G-H Leaders reported no problems other than some followers had vanished in the clouds. The G-H pulse was strong as the first Green sky markers started to drop. Due to the abundance of clouds, the accuracy of the raid could not be determined. Most just reported *' No results seen'*. Flight Lieutenant N.C Cowley lost all electrical power aboard NN720 XY-K on the run into the target. However, they did manage to bomb on G-H at 15:02 hours, remarking. *' Saw blue marker puffs in fair concentration but no results of raid seen'*. With no electrics and the W/T unserviceable, the crew wisely opted to land at B.90, a recently laid PSP (Pierced Steel Planking ) emergency strip located outside the village of Petit-Broghel (Kleine-Brogel) Belgium[35] at 15:40 hours. Unlike the previous day, the flak was slight, and no aircraft from the squadron reported damage. Foul weather over East Anglia on return resulted in the crews being diverted. All six crews were diverted north to Cumbria, landing at RAF Crosby-on-Eden located 6 miles northeast of Carlisle. Four crews were detailed and briefed for a daylight raid on Kamen on the 24th, but this was cancelled at 09:30 hours. It would be a short reprieve, the squadron was informed that it would be required the following day morning, and Kamen would be the intended target, weather permitting. During the day, the six diverted crews returned to RAF Stradishall.

Form B.799 – February 25th 1945(D):Target : Kamen: Essener Steinkohle und Harpener Oil Plant. GQ1513.

| | | | | | | | |
|---|---|---|---|---|---|---|---|
| F/O | Fernley | F | | NG147 | XY-A | G-H Leader | Duty Carried Out. |
| F/O | Saunders | A | | NG137 | XY-D | G-H Leader | Duty Carried Out. |
| F/O | Hart | J.H | | HK694 | XY-C | Follower | Duty Carried Out. |

[35] *The ORB incorrectly records France.*

| | | | | | | | |
|---|---|---|---|---|---|---|---|
| F/O | Hill | P.T | | NG140 | XY-F | Follower | Duty Carried Out. |
| F/Lt | Tonks | J.E | | NG175 | XY-J | G-H Leader | Duty Carried Out. |
| F/O | Clarson | A.J | RAAF | NG354 | XY-M | G-H Leader | Duty Carried Out. |
| F/Lt | Sawyer | F.R | | HK802 | XY-L | Follower | Duty Carried Out. |
| F/Lt | Brayshaw DFC | S.C | | HK801 | XY-S | Follower | Duty Carried Out. |
| F/O | Idle | L.A | RNZAF | NG283 | XY-U | Follower | Duty Carried Out. |
| F/O | Beck | J.A | RAAF | RF126 | XY-V | Follower | Duty Carried Out. |
| F/Lt | Mason | F.H | | HK796 | XY-W | Follower | Duty Carried Out. |
| F/Sgt | Gray | P | | HK661 | XY-R | Follower | Duty Carried Out. |

A fine study of the crew of New Zealander Ken Orman RNZAF. The identity of the Lancaster is sadly unknown. L-R Flying Officer Barney Earrey (Bomb Aimer), Flight Sergeant Geordie Bennett (Mid Upper Gunner), Ken Orman (Pilot), Flight Sergeant Geordie Beer (Rear Gunner), Sergeant Len Sewell (Flight Engineer), Flight Sergeant Reg Simon RAAF (Wireless Operator), Unknown, Flight Sergeant Rolly Ward (Navigator).

The squadron departed late morning, climbing into the solid grey overcast. Number 31 Base would provide 46 crews, No.186 was the lead Base Squadrons[36]. They would rendezvous 9,000 feet above Tonbridge, Kent, from where the formation headed south once again towards Beachy Head joining a further 107 Lancasters from No.32 and No.33 Base. The squadron provided just four G-H Leaders, F/O Fernley the least experienced. Cloud was encountered between 6,000 to 10,000 feet with a band of cloud between 20,000 to 22,000 feet. Unlike the previous day, all three Base Groups remained rigidly together. Followers kept formation stepped behind and below their allotted G-H Leaders. A strong tailwind of 65mph aided the formation as it entered the Ruhr. As expected, accurate predicted flak greeted the formation as it passed through the Cologne - Dusseldorf gap. Any stragglers were singled out and received savage attention. The Ruhr flak defences were once again living up to their reputation.

[36] *This is the first occasion that No.186 Squadron is recorded as being Base Leader. No.31 Base ORB. Air14/2583.*

Flying Officer P Hill lost the starboard inner engine aboard Lancaster NG140 XY-F due to an oil leak caused by a connection joint becoming loose. With the engine feathered, the crew could not keep up with their designated G-H Leader. Fortunately, 30 minutes before the target and now at the tail end of the formation, they latched onto an unidentified G-H Leader with whom they bombed at 12:52 hours. Over the target area, a number of Blue Puff Flares were seen. These attracted the majority of the bomb loads. The G-H Leaders had achieved a concentration of markers that resulted in some very accurate bombing. A column of black smoke was seen rising from the target area. Flight Lieutenant Brayshaw DFC bombed at 12:47 hours from 20,000 feet. He reported, *'The target was well hit and many bomb bursts were seen in the blackish smoke which was rising from the target when aircraft left'.*

Only one crew reported flak damage. Flying Officer L Idle RNZAF had two holes in the starboard inner engine nacelle courtesy of the flak defences of Leverkusen. All apart from F/O Hill landed back at RAF Stradishall, Hill and crew opted to land at the Emergency airfield at RAF Woodbridge.

No.186 Squadron Reported Flak Damage 25/02/1945

| Serial | Code | Damage | Repairs / Notes |
|---|---|---|---|
| NG283 | **XY-U** | S/O Engine damaged | Repaired on Squadron. |

The squadron bade farewell to Squadron Leader Eric Scott and his crew on the 25th, promoted to Wing Commander he assumed command of No.90 Squadron based at RAF Tuddenham on the 26th. He would survive the war. It was a mid-morning take-off on the 26th. Twelve crews were detailed and briefed for another daylight operation to the Ruhr. The target was the Hoesch Benzin Plant at Dortmund which produced high quality diesel and lubricating oil.

Form B.800 – February 26th, 1945 (D):Target : Dortmund Hoesch Benzin Plant :GQ1555

| | | | | | | | |
|---|---|---|---|---|---|---|---|
| F/O | Gogler | R.J | RAAF | NG174 | XY-A | G-H Leader | Duty Carried Out. |
| F/O | Green | T.B | | NG146 | XY-E | G-H Leader | Duty Carried Out. |
| F/O | Head | G.D | | HK694 | XY-C | Follower | Duty Carried Out. |
| F/Lt | Tonks | J.E | | NG175 | XY-J | G-H Leader | Duty Carried Out. |
| F/Lt | Sawyer | F.R | | HK692 | XY-B | Follower | Duty Carried Out. |
| F/Lt | Orman DFC | K.G | RNZAF | NG354 | XY-M | Follower | Duty Carried Out. |
| F/O | Fernley | F | | HK796 | XY-W | Follower | Duty Carried Out. |
| F/Lt | Brayshaw DFC | S.C | | HK794 | XY-T | G-H Leader | Duty Carried Out. |
| F/O | Saunders | A | | NG293 | XY-U | Follower | Duty Carried Out. |
| F/O | Beck | J.A | | RF126 | XY-V | Follower | Duty Carried Out. |
| F/Lt | Mason | F.H | | HK801 | XY-S | Follower | Duty Carried Out. |
| F/O | O'Brien | J.D | | HK606 | XY-Z | Follower | Duty Carried Out. |

One hundred and fifty Lancasters were despatched by No.3 Group. The first crew airborne was flown by Brummie, F/Lt J.E Tonks at 10:51 hours. He, like the squadron's three other G-H Leaders, was loaded with 1 x 4000lb + 12 x 500lb MC + 1 x 250lb Red Skymarker Red Puff. As the formation headed towards Germany, they were chaperoned by an impressive 18 squadrons of fighters, 11 RAF Mustang and seven Continent-based Spitfires squadrons. The formation was routed to attack Dortmund from the north. The whole approach to the target was over a solid mass of cloud. The squadrons of No.31 Group kept in reasonable shape as the first bombs started to drop. There was one moment of danger, F/O R Gogler RAAF had the misfortune to be flying directly behind a Lancaster that *'Kept weaving violently and put our aircraft off slightly on the bomb run'.* The identity of the Lancaster is unknown. Flight Lieutenant K Orman DFC dropped his bomb load and Skymarkers at 14:05 hours from 20,000 feet. The crew reported at de-briefing, *'No results visible owing to cloud, but formation over the target was good and attack appeared well concentrated.'* The squadron welcomed back F/Lt Cowley fresh from his enforced stay in Belgium while the squadron was over Germany

Form B.801 – February 27th, 1945 (D):Target : Gelsenkirchen : Alma Pluto Coking Plant: GS555

| | | | | | | | |
|---|---|---|---|---|---|---|---|
| F/O | Hart | J.H | | NG174 | XY-A | G-H Leader | Duty Carried Out. |
| F/Lt | Templeton | G.M | RCAF | NN720 | XY-K | Follower | Duty Carried Out. |
| F/O | Hill | P.T | | HK694 | XY-G | Follower | Duty Carried Out. |
| F/Lt | Cowley | N.C | | NG175 | XY-J | G-H Leader | MISSING |
| W/Cdr | Giles DFC | J.H | | HK802 | XY-L | Follower | Duty Carried Out. |
| F/O | Clarson | A.J | RAAF | NG354 | XY-M | G-H Leader | Duty Carried Out. |
| F/O | Idle | L.A | RNZAF | NG149 | XY-G | Follower | Duty Carried Out. |
| F/Lt | Orman | K.G | RNZAF | HK794 | XY-T | G-H Leader | Duty Carried Out. |
| F/O | Gogler | R.J | RAAF | NG293 | XY-U | Follower | Duty Carried Out. |
| F/Sgt | Gray | P | | RF126 | XY-V | Follower | Duty Carried Out. |
| F/O | Godfrey | D.F | RAAF | HK796 | XY-W | Follower | Duty Carried Out. |
| F/O | O'Brien | J.D | RAAF | HK606 | XY-Z | Follower | Duty Carried Out. |

Daylights. The crew of Flying Officer Dennis Godfrey RAAF are captured in this photograph. Many of the second tour crews who had cut their teeth on nocturnal operations never felt comfortable flying in daylight, preferring the relative safety of darkness. However, during the last six months of the bomber offensive, daylight operations were statistically safer than night operations.

There was no let-up in the attacks on Hitler's oil plants. On the 27th, No.3 Group organised a return trip to Gelsenkirchen and the Alma Pluto Coking Plant. Twelve squadron crews, including the squadron C/O and F/Lt Templeton RCAF, fresh from a spot of leave, were airborne by 11:38 hours, joining a further 134 drawn from all Base Groups. Number 186 Squadron would once again lead the squadrons of No.31 Base. Unfortunately, a problem of timing over England resulted in the stream being split in two on reaching German airspace. The lead group, No.33 Base, was five miles ahead of the following base groups. It was an unhealthy gap that the following groups tried desperately to reduce as they neared the target area. Fortunately, the Luftwaffe day fighters were absent due to the excellent escort provided by the RAF Spitfires and Mustangs. The squadron crews began their bomb runs at 14:28 hours, encountering slight to heavy flak. A number of Blue Sky-markers were already arching over a cloud-covered aiming point when the first bombs started to drop. It was only when the crew of F/Lt N Cowley dropped their bombload and single Skymarker that tragedy struck. Flying Officer K.R Hamilton of No.195 Squadron was flying directly behind F/Lt N.C Cowley. Tucked in close and flying slightly to port of his allocated No.186 Squadron G-H Leader, they were over the target area at 14:30 hours. The small vic formation was bracketed by flak when F/O Ken Hamilton watched helplessly as the Lancaster in front shuddered and immediately burst into flames. The aircraft, Lancaster NG175 XY-J flown by F/Lt N Cowley[37], was seen streaming flames and entering cloud. Three parachutes were observed. The Squadron ORB records the tragic few minutes :

> Aircraft L, C, K, W, A, V,Z, U,M,G and T reported this aircraft dropped all bombs in salvo and about two seconds afterwards, the bombs blew up when they were a thousand feet below. The aircraft then went down in flames. The pilot appeared to be in control, the flames died down about 1000 feet above the cloud, and a parachute came out, and the aircraft turned over and dived into the cloud. Aircraft variously report that 1 to 3 parachutes were seen. One aircraft believed Rear Gunner was clear.

Flying Officer Geoff Clarson RAAF was one of the crews who witnessed the loss of F/Lt N Cowley. They, like the Cowley crew, were G-H Leaders. Rear Gunner, F/Sgt G.M McPherson.

> *As we were over the target, I witnessed a Lancaster on fire about 50 yards away, on our port side, which had been hit by anti-aircraft fire. I recognised the crew, who were all Englishmen. As I watched in horror, the aircraft went into a dive, but the pilot somehow managed to straighten the aircraft out, despite the fact that the cockpit was surrounded by flames. I saw three of the crew bail out before the plane began to spiral downwards, then I lost sight of it. The pilot was a very brave man and gave his life to try to save his crew. Ironically, I had known this man, and I must confess I didn't like him much, as he appeared quite arrogant to me, but obviously he was a man of great courage and his actions changed my opinion of him'.*

Flying in the same formation was F/O Preston Hill at the controls of Lancaster HK694 XY-C. The explosion of the bombs produced a hail of deadly shrapnel, which ripped into anything and anyone in its path. Sitting at the controls of his Lancaster, F/O Hill was struck in his left arm by a piece of shrapnel. Flying Officer F Liles, the bomb aimer, quickly took control and, showing remarkable calm kept the Lancaster steady and in formation. Once attended and his wounds treated, F/O Hill took over and flew the Lancaster back to RAF Stradishall, making a first-rate landing. Flying Officer Preston Hill was awarded an Immediate DFC for his action on this operation. The remaining crews reported that marking and bombing were concentrated. Flight Lieutenant Orman DFC report sums up the operation, *'Bombed on Radar Navigational Aids at 14:30 hours from 21,000 feet. No results seen owing to cloud. Skymarkers Blue were well concentrated'.* The crews began to land back at RAF Stradishall just after 16:00 hours. There would have been only one topic of conversation, the loss of the highly experienced crew of 22-year-old Norman Cowley. Unlike night operations, crews would witness the sickening sight of a Lancaster in its death throes with seven friends on board. It would have been a haunting and horrifying sight. It was the only loss suffered by the group on this operation.

| Type | Avro Lancaster Mk.I **NG175 XY-J** | **Armstrong Whitworth** |
|---|---|---|
| Taken on Charge | 07/10/1944 via 90 Squadron. | |
| 'Category' | FB 'Missing' 14/02/1945 | |
| Struck Of Charge | 08/03/1945 | |
| Take-Off Time | 11.20 hrs | |
| Bomb Load | 1 x 4000lb HC + 11 x 500lb + 1 x500lb MC + 1 x 250lb TI Skymarker Blue Puff. | |

[37] *There are unconfirmed reports that suggest that this was the No.31 Base Leader crew.*

| | CREW | GRAVE |
|---|---|---|
| Pilot | Flight Lieutenant Norman Coatner Cowley, 187512 RAFVR. Age 21. | 20.B.17 |
| Navigator | Pilot Officer John Eric Peach, 191087 RAFVR, Age 22 | 20.B.18 |
| Bomb Aimer | Flight Sergeant John Morrison Young, 648408 RAFVR | PoW Survived War |
| Wireless Operator | Flight Sergeant Harold George Kimber, 1851740 RAFVR | PoW Survived War |
| Mid Upper Gunner | Sergeant James Sneddon, 1823545 RAFVR, Age 23 | 20.D.2 |
| Rear Gunner | Sergeant Douglas James George Gibb, 1656358 RAFVR | 20.D.1 |
| Flight Engineer | Pilot Officer Nigel Paul Etheridge, 190973 RAFVR | 20.D.3 |
| | | |
| Posted History | No.1653 HCU – 07/10/1944 No.3 LFS – No.58 Course – No.186 Squadron 12/10/1944. | |
| Operations Flown | 27 | |
| Buried | *Reichswald Forest War Cemetery.* | |

The grave of 22-year-old Flight Lieutenant Norman Cowley. This young man did all he could to keep his stricken Lancaster stable and airborne to give his crew the best possible chance of survival. But unfortunately, his brave action resulted in just two escaping by parachute.

Left & Above. Pilot Officer John Eric Peach RAFVR.

Above & Right. Sergeant James Sneddon RAFVR

Left & Above. Sergeant Douglas James George Gibb, RAFVR.

Above & Right. Pilot Officer Nigel Paul Etheridge RAFVR.

The crew were originally buried in the Gelsenkirchen – Huellen Cemetery. They were re-buried in the Reichswald Forest Cemetery in May 1947. The squadron welcomed two new crews on the 27th, one was skippered by Warrant Officer Howell. Due to a clerical mix-up by administration the crew had been sent to RAF Tuddenham in the misguided belief that No.186 was still in residence. It was only after a few days of head scratching that the correct posting details were received, and the crew posted at RAF Stradishall. For the fourth day in succession, twelve crews were gathered in the briefing room, where the assembled crews were informed that they were going back to Gelsenkirchen, the target was the Nordstern Benzol and Coke Plant. A total of 157 Lancasters were detailed for this the last raid of the month. Thirty-one Base would provide 48 Lancasters, No.218 Squadron were given the honour of leading the entire force. The crew of Flight Lieutenant Frank Blenkin were given the responsibility of leading the Group while Flight Lieutenant Les Harlow was tasked with Deputy Base Leader. It would be an all No.218 Squadron show on this occasion.

Form B.802 – February 28th, 1945 (D):Target : Gelsenkirchen (Nordstern) Gelsenberg-Benzin A.G Benzol and Coke Plant: GQ1509

| | | | | | | | |
|---|---|---|---|---|---|---|---|
| F/O | Saunders | A | | HK692 | XY-B | Follower | Duty Carried Out |
| F/Lt | Templeton | G.M | RCAF | NG146 | XY-E | Follower | Duty Carried Out |
| F/O | Green | T.B | | NG149 | XY-G | G-H Leader | Duty Carried Out |
| F/Lt | Tonks | J.E | | HK802 | XY-L | Follower | Duty Carried Out |
| F/O | Clarson | A.J | RAAF | NG354 | XY-M | G-H Leader | Duty Carried Out |
| F/O | Idle | L.A | RNZAF | HK684 | XY-O | G-H Leader | Duty Carried Out |
| F/Lt | Brayshaw DFC | S.C | | HK659 | XY-Q | G-H Leader | Duty Carried Out |
| F/Lt | Mason | F.H | | HK801 | XY-S | Follow | Duty Carried Out |
| F/O | Fernley | F | | HK794 | XY-T | G-H Leader | Duty Carried Out |
| F/Sgt | Gray | P | | NG293 | XY-U | Follow | Duty Carried Out |
| F/O | Beck | J.A | RAAF | RF126 | XY-V | Follow | Duty Carried Out |
| F/O | Head | G.D | | HK796 | XY-W | Follow | Duty Carried Out |

Flying with F/O T.B Green aboard NG149 was a second-tour veteran, S/Ldr Ken Dodwell as navigator. His arrival on the squadron and the reason is unknown but believed to be in preparations of a new challenge. A total of 157 Lancasters was detailed for this the last raid of the month. Number 31 Base would provide 48 Lancasters, 15 of which would be G-H Leaders. The squadron would supply five of its most experienced crews. The now-standard procedure of forming up over Tonbridge at 9,000 feet was made more demanding by a band of cloud that reached almost 8,000 feet. This again resulted in the three base formations struggling for position and the G-H followers having difficulties identifying their allotted Leaders. With visibility down to seventy-five yards in places, the crews nervously searched for their correct position within the formation. In an attempt to help with the assembly, experienced crews were selected and given the prestigious role of Base Leader. They would have the sole responsibility of ensuring that the Base, in this case, No.31, arrived at a specific point at an exact time. All the while, they would be running the gauntlet along the forming up route firing off various coloured flares identifying himself as the Base Leader. Finally, the bombers would rendezvous over a predetermined location and often above a blanket of cloud. The Base formation needed to be on time and at the correct altitude and heading as the other two Base groups would be converging on the group rendezvous point. Good timing was essential. The Base Leader and his Deputy Base Leader had to ensure that they positioned themselves and more importantly the Base exactly where ordered. The fighter escort joined the formation just north of Eindhoven as the Lancasters made their run through the Ruhr flak defences. Conditions over the target were not ideal. Individual Lancasters and small groups flying well above the briefed bombing height caused much anxiety to those below. Flight Lieutenant G Templeton RCAF was at 16,800 feet. He reported, *' Stream was straggling. Aircraft from another formation bombed above our formation'*. This was echoed by F/O T Green, he was on his bomb run at

19,500 feet, *'Some aircraft bombed from above 20,000 feet when our Base was bombing'.* Flight Lieutenant J Tonks was another pilot unhappy with the prospect of being hit by 'friendly bombs', he told the Intelligence Officer back at RAF Stradishall, *'Trouble experienced from another squadron which bombed above us at about 20,000 feet'.* Two more squadron crews experienced the danger, F/O A Clarson RAAF, *'About a dozen aircraft bombed above us'*, and finally F/Lt F Mason. He was at 19,500 feet, *'Formation of the base behind caught up with our base and bombed above us at over 20,000 feet, seemed to be 23,000 feet'.* The culprits may have been from No.195 Squadron based at RAF Wratting Common. The Chedburgh based No.218 Squadron experienced the same dangers, but managed to identify the squadron codes, A4! No results were seen except a mushroom of smoke rising above the clouds, crews however were confident about the accuracy of the attack. It was a good raid to finish off a hectic month. The post raid reconnaissance was delayed for a few days due to the weather conditions. However, when the weather did clear an official report was published.

*Very severe damage to the plant can be seen. All four coke ovens batteries are affected, three with direct hits on oven and pipeline disrupted. Both sulphate houses are damaged, both exhauster houses have roofing stripped, gas scrubbers have been damaged and the tar loading area and one gas holder has exploded. The Gelsenkirchen Nordstern 1/2 colliery was modestly damaged, one wing of the cooling tower was destroyed, three wings have roof damage and the railway lines serving the mines to the coke ovens are cut in several places. A pipeline from the coke ovens to the mines is severed. A new installation 500 feet northeast of the sulphate house was heavily damaged, four large buildings, several sheds and a bridge connecting with coke ovens destroyed. Many craters are visible just north of the plant.*

Not the best of photos but one of only three of Flight Lieutenant Ron Hanson. Ron is standing beside a rather sorry looking Lancaster PB509 XY-Y of 'B' Flight. This former No.149 Squadron aircraft started its career back in August 1944. The 149 codes OJ-C have been crudely painted out, and XY-Y applied.

What is remarkable about this raid and many others carried out by the G-H equipped crews of No.3 Group was that the target was covered entirely in 10/10th cloud. The accuracy and damage on this scale would not have been possible six months before. It made a mockery of the boast by Don Bennett of the Path Finders that OBOE was more accurate than G-H and was inferior. On the last day of the month, two new crews joined the squadron, one of which was skippered by Australian F/Sgt Jeffrey Collinson, fresh from No.72 Base.

February had been a demanding month for everyone on the squadron. The loss of three crews was particularly hard, especially when two were well into their operational tours. The squadron flew 191 operational sorties, the lowest sortie rate in the group[38], but only one sortie behind No.90 Squadron. In the process, the squadron dropped a total of 803 tons of bombs on Germany. A total of eleven crews had been posted on to the squadron throughout the month, effectively half the squadron. It was not all briefings and operations, there were some areas where the squadron had pipped its larger squadron rivals. Fighter Affiliation exercises, the squadron had flown 64 sorties, the second highest number in the Group, beaten only by No.195 Squadron who completed 68. It was third place in the monthly Non Visual Bombing exercises held over the North Wotton Bombing Range, fourth in overall hours of Flying Training and 2nd on the Link Trainer.

End of tour photograph. The crew of Australian Eric Barton RAAF pose with their loyal Ground Crew in front of Lancaster NG149 XY-G 'George Giles'. Back Row L-R. Sergeant Jack Collins (Rear Gunner), Flight Sergeant George James (Navigator), Flight Sergeant Jock MacIntosh (Bomb Aimer), Ground Crew, Sergeant Reg Bennett (Mid Upper Gunner), Flight Sergeant John Gibbs RAAF (Wireless Operator). Front row 2nd right, Flying Officer Eric Barton RAAF (Pilot).

Number 31 Base had been chosen to trial the installation of Long Range Petrol Tanks in February. A number of Lancasters had been selected from all three squadrons. Although the trials had not been completed by the end of the month, one obvious problem was quickly found. With the installation of the L.R.P.T, installation of the 4000lb Cookie was impossible. Given this was the staple diet of Bomber

---

[38] *At the end of February the squadrons strength stood at only 20 Lancaster's on two flights.*

Command, it was not a promising start. More promising, and much to the gunner's delight, No.186 Squadron finally received and fitted the new FN 121 turrets. Given the Group's almost exclusive daylight role, the new turret was causing a stir throughout the squadron. Creating even more of a stir was the arrival of a mobile demonstration of the FN82 turret equipped with twin .50 calibre. This mobile demonstration was doing the rounds and touring the No.3 Group stations. The gunners were suitably impressed. The need to improve the defensive hitting power was recognised in 1942 when the Air Staff identified a requirement to fit the then-new Lancaster with a turret armed with more powerful 0.50-inch heavy machine guns. This was, at the time, a priority, *'as soon as possible'* was the instruction. This view was readily supported by Air Marshal Arthur Harris, the commanding officer of Bomber Command. By 1945 the .303 guns were still the standard defensive armament fitted to the Lancasters of No.3 Group despite the Air Staff's mutterings. With daylight operations now the norm, a more powerful turret was urgently required for the gunners, so the appearance of the FN82 could not come quickly enough.

No.31 Base Commanders Summary, February 1945.

**Operations**

Raids were 'laid on' on 23 occasions, and 16 attacks were actually carried out. On these 16 raids 262[39] sorties were despatched. Most of the attacks were on Benzol Plants, but in addition the squadron took part in the big night attacks on Dresden and Chemnitz. Four crews were lost to enemy action.

**Administration**

The usual entertainment and social activities were well attended. The Station W.A.A.F Hockey Team won the Group Competition. During the month the Red Shield Club was opened on the station.

February 1945 : Avro Lancaster Delivery.

| ToC Date | Serial | Code | Maker | Mark | From |
|---|---|---|---|---|---|
| 01/02/1945 | HK767 | XY-A | Vickers Armstrong | Mk.B.I | No.195 Sqn |
| 11/02/1945 | RF126 | XY-V | Armstrong Whitworth | Mk.B.I | Works |
| 13/02/1945 | HK794 | XY-T | Vickers Armstrong | Mk.B.I | Works |
| 18/02/1945 | HK796 | XY-W | Vickers Armstrong | Mk.B.I | No.195 Sqn |
| 18/02/1945 | HK801 | XY-S | Vickers Armstrong | Mk.B.I | No.195 Sqn |
| 18/02/1945 | HK802 | XY-L | Vickers Armstrong | Mk.B.I | Works |
| 23/02/1945 | RA522 | | Metropolitan Vickers | Mk.B.I | Works |
| 24/02/1945 | HK759 | | Vickers Armstrong | Mk.B.I | Flight Trails Vickers |
| 28/02/1945 | RA533 | XY-P | Metropolitan Vickers | Mk.B.I | No.218 Sqn |
| 28/02/1945 | HK804 | | Vickers Armstrong | Mk.B.I | Works |
| 01/02/1945 | HK767 | XY-A | Vickers Armstrong | Mk.B.I | No.195 Sqn |

[39] *These figures are at odds with the Group and Squadron figures.*

# March 1945

## *Daylight Precision Bombing*

The month started with the arrival of yet another crew. March 1945 found the squadron in a positive mood despite the loss of three crews the following month. The departure of a number of tour-expired crews did much to offset the tragic loss of close friends and colleagues. On the continent, the Allied Armies were making steady progress into Germany and the winter grip which had hampered operations was finally coming to an end. With an influx of new crews in the Mess, and new aircraft parked at the various dispersals, the squadron was at its peak in both men and aircraft. The first operation of the month was a daylight raid against the Essener Steinkohle and Harpener synthetic oil plant at Kamen. Given the success of the raid on Nordstern, No.31 Base was again given the lead group role and, to the delight of the Squadron, was given the responsibility of leading the entire group[40].

<u>Form B.803 – March 1st, 1945 (D):Target :Kamen: Essener Steinkohle and Harpener synthetic oil plant : GQ1513</u>

| | | | | | | | |
|---|---|---|---|---|---|---|---|
| S/Ldr | Reynolds DFC | P | | NG174 | XY-A | **GROUP LEADER** | Duty Carried Out. |
| F/O | Head | G.D | | HK692 | XY-B | Follower | Duty Carried Out. |
| P/O | Roberts | D.M | | NG146 | XY-E | Follower | Duty Carried Out. |
| F/O | Hart | J.H | | NG149 | XY-G | Follower | Duty Carried Out. |
| F/Lt | Brayshaw DFC | S.C | | HK802 | XY-L | Follower | Duty Carried Out. |
| F/O | Gogler | R.J | RAAF | HK684 | XY-O | Follower | Duty Not Carried Out. |
| F/O | Saunders | A | | HK659 | XY-Q | G-H Leader | Duty Carried Out. |
| F/Lt | Mason | F.H | | HK801 | XY-S | Follower | Duty Carried Out. |
| F/Lt | Tonks | J.E | | HK794 | XY-T | G-H Leader | Duty Carried Out. |
| F/O | Fernley | F | | NG283 | XY-U | Follower | Duty Carried Out. |
| F/O | Beck | J.A | RAAF | RF126 | XY-V | Follower | Duty Carried Out. |
| P/O | O'Brien | J.D | RAAF | HK606 | XY-Z | Follower | Duty Carried Out. |

A total of 151 Lancasters would be detailed from all three bases. The twelve crews of No.186 Squadron began taking off just before midday. There was just one early return. Flying Officer Rex Gogler RAAF lost the port inner engine aboard Lancaster HK684 XY-O soon after take-off. A plume of oily black smoke poured out of the defective engine, ensuring the crew had no alternative but turn for home. They landed on three engines at 14:06 hours after jettisoning all but six 500 pounders. The role of Group or Base Leader came with a multitude of issues. They would have the sole responsibility of ensuring that the base, in this case, No.31, arrived at a specific point at an exact time. All the while, the Group or Base Leader would be running the gauntlet along the forming up route firing off various coloured flares identifying himself as the Base Leader. The bombers would rendezvous over a predetermined location and often above a blanket of cloud. The base formation needed to be on time and at the correct altitude and heading as the other two base groups would be converging on the group rendezvous point. Good timing was essential. The Base Leader and his Deputy Base Leader had to ensure that they positioned themselves and the Base exactly where ordered. To date, No.186 Squadron had not been given that responsibility. The man chosen to lead was S/Ldr Percy Reynolds DFC, whose experienced crew would be joined by F/Lt Douglas MacDonald RAAF as 2nd Navigator. There was a great deal of pressure placed upon the lead navigator and the deputy lead navigators on operations. Not only did they have the difficult task of threading the bombers between flak zones and heavily defended cities, but they also had the additional responsibility of manipulating the G-H sets and ensuring accurate marking and

*[40] No.31 Base was the lead Base Group on this operation. Information supplied suggests that S/Ldr Reynolds was the No.3 Group Leader. However, this cannot be confirmed.*

bombing. The additional responsibilities had become too much for just one individual navigator. Exning House, No.3 Group's HQ, had issued instructions to all base groups recommending the inclusion of an additional navigator after a few costly navigational errors. With No.31 Base making up the spearhead, No.32 Base quickly positioned itself close behind, and they were eventually followed by No.33 Base, who were more accustomed to leading. With the stream in position, the bombers crossed the North Sea and over Belgium, where the RAF fighter escort would be picked up on the German border. The Lancasters of No.3 Group entered Germany over Twisteden and headed towards the Ruhr, skirting around the flak defences of Duisburg, Essen, and Bottrop. Once over Germany, the weather quickly began to deteriorate. This resulted in the formation becoming slightly separated. It was at the last turning point the raid began to falter. The lead crew, understood to be that of Squadron Leader Percy Reynolds DFC, overshot the last turning point when they failed to pick up the G-H tracking pulse. This error resulted in a number of Lancasters[41] having to circle to reposition themselves for the correct G-H run. Thankfully, the following stream was aware of the error and turned correctly. However, the damage had been done to the lead formation, confusion, and disarray followed. In an attempt to bomb, the forward formation orbited Kamen and converged on the target and the stream from various angles, making matters worse. Both No.195 and No.218 Squadrons were not slow in voicing their irritation at the expense of No.186 Squadron on return. Strangely, and perhaps to hide a few blushes, the No.186 Squadron ORB makes no mention of the error. Group HQ recorded the following.

*Reports of this attack were not encouraging. The bombing was rather scattered. This seems to have been caused by the leading squadron failing to find the tracking pulse and overshooting the turning point just prior to the target. They orbited and converged on the main stream from various angles and broke up the formation.*

The squadron was requested to provide a solitary crew for a night raid directed against German troop and armour concentration close to the area of the forthcoming Rhine crossing, although this order was eventually cancelled at 14:00 hours. The following day, the cathedral city of Cologne was the intended target, specifically German troop positions. This once most-feared of targets was now almost on the front line. The attack would be carried out in two phases. The first phase would see squadrons of No.1,4, and 6 Groups and 8 PFF attack mid-morning. The second phase was an all No.3 Group affair and would include 155 Lancasters of all three Base groups. The squadron would once again provide twelve crews.

Form B.805 – March 2nd 1945 (D):Target :Cologne : German strong points

| | | | | | | | |
|---|---|---|---|---|---|---|---|
| F/O | Clarson | A.J | RAAF | NG174 | XY-A | G-H Leader | Abandoned |
| F/O | Verry | C.C | RNZAF | HK692 | XY-B | Follower | Abandoned |
| F/Lt | Marshall | A.M | | NG146 | XY-E | Follower | Abandoned |
| F/O | Green | T.B | | NG149 | XY-G | Follower | Abandoned |
| F/O | Young | H.S | | HK802 | XY-L | Follower | Abandoned |
| F/Lt | Templeton | G.M | RCAF | RA533 | XY-P | Follower | Abandoned |
| F/O | Idle | L.A | RNZAF | HK659 | XY-Q | G-H Leader | Abandoned |
| F/Sgt | Gray | P | | HK661 | XY-R | Follower | Abandoned |
| P/O | Roberts | D.M | | HK801 | XY-S | Follower | Abandoned |
| S/Ldr | Bass AFM | R.W | | HK794 | XY-T | G-H Leader | Abandoned |
| F/Lt | Hanson | R.A | | HK796 | XY-W | G-H Leader | Abandoned |
| F/O | Gogler | R.J | RAAF | NG293 | XY-U | Follower | Abandoned |

The first crew away from RAF Stradishall at 12:52 hours was F/O L. Idle RNZAF at the controls of Lancaster HK659 XY-Q.

*[41] No.218 (Gold Coast) Squadron report that approximately 14 Lancasters of the lead formation missed the vital last turning point.*

Once airborne, he and the rest of the squadron headed towards the rendezvous point 9000 feet above Tonbridge. It was here that No.32 Base and then No.33 Base took up position astern.

Friends forged in battle. Flying Officer Jeff Clarson RAAF and his Flight Engineer, Pilot Officer James 'Jock' Hepburn.

Flying Office Dennis Godfrey RAAF and Pilot Officer Tom Spinks RAAF, Wireless Operator.

On completing the assembly, which was achieved without any problems due to the excellent weather over England, the whole force headed south to Beachy Head. In the vanguard was the crews' No.31 Base. The fighter escort consisting of six squadrons of Spitfires and two RAF Mustangs took station over Belgium. The weather was ideal. The Lancasters were immersed in bright sunshine as they reached Cologne. Numerous fires were visible raging in the city from the attack carried out by Bomber Command that morning. A cloud of dense black smoke hung over Cologne. It was a pitiful sight. Such was the visibility that the last remaining bridges could be identified, as could the blackened cathedral spires.

Everything seemed to be going to plan. The formation was compact, visibility was excellent, and there was only spasmodic flak on the run-up to target. Unfortunately, a technical problem with the G-H release station resulted in the vast majority of the group bringing home their bombs. The crews had been given strict instructions not to bomb unless G-H was working perfectly. Leading the whole force was No.195 Squadron's S/Ldr B.W.R Forster, who wisely adhered to the orders given at briefing and continued over the doomed city. Due to the fluid nature of the ground situation, HQ Bomber Command was keen that no incidents of friendly bombing occurred. However, a few crews did bomb, but these fell in or just south-east of Deutz. One stick was seen to explode on the west bank of the central road bridge. For the first time in weeks, crews reported fighters. Three FW190s were seen in the target area but did not attack. Having retained their bomb loads, the frustrated crews turned for home. Over the North Sea, each crew jettisoned their 4000 cookie but retained their 500 pounders. Flying on his first operation was F/O Charles Verry RNZAF. He was flying one of the few Lancaster's on the squadron converted to carry the 8000-pound 'super-cookie'. This monster was dropped in the North Sea jettison area at 17:40 hours.

The Lancasters of No.186 Squadron began landing back at RAF Stradishall a little after 18:00 hours. It was a frustrating end to what had promised to be an exciting day. However, fate or the intricacies of G-H had other ideas. The city of Cologne may have escaped, but the squadrons of No.3 Group certainly did not. Cologne had one last defiant attempt defending itself after years of bombing. Twenty-five Lancasters reported flak damage, three from No.186 Squadron. The Mildenhall based No.622 Squadron reported the loss of one Lancaster, which was seen with its port wing on fire spiralling down over the target area, the victim of flak. Cologne fell to the American 3rd Armoured Division four days later.

No.186 Squadron Reported Flak Damage 02/03/1945

| Serial | Code | Damage | Repairs / Notes |
|---|---|---|---|
| HK794 | **XY-T** | Not recorded | Repaired on Squadron |
| NG293 | **XY-U** | Not recorded | Repaired on Squadron |
| HK796 | **XY-W** | Not recorded | Repaired on Squadron |

The squadron was stood down on the 3rd but reported the arrival of three new crews. The squadron provided fourteen crews on a daylight attack against the Marshalling Yards at Wanne-Eickel on the 4th. A total of 128 Lancasters were sent to put even more pressure on the beleaguered German transport system. The bomber stream crossed the Belgium coast in bright sunshine and hugged the recently liberated town of Cleve.

Form B.806 – March 4th 1945 (D):Target :Wanne Eickel : Marshalling Yards: G-H597

| | | | | | | | |
|---|---|---|---|---|---|---|---|
| F/Lt | Tonks | J.E | | NG174 | XY-A | G-H Leader | Duty Carried Out |
| F/Lt | Field DFC | E.L | | HK692 | XY-B | Follower | Duty Carried Out |
| F/O | Head | G.D | | HK694 | XY-C | Follower | Duty Carried Out |

| | | | | | | | |
|---|---|---|---|---|---|---|---|
| F/Lt | Templeton | G.N | RCAF | NG146 | XY-E | Follower | Duty Carried Out |
| F/O | Young | H.S | | HK682 | XY-J | Follower | Duty Carried Out |
| F/O | Hart | J.H | | HK802 | XY-L | G-H Leader | Duty Carried Out |
| F/O | O'Brien | J.D | RAAF | HK661 | XY-R | Follower | Duty Carried Out |
| F/Lt | Brayshaw DFC | S.C | | HK659 | XY-Q | G-H Leader | Duty Carried Out |
| F/O | Godfrey | D | RAAF | HK796 | XY-W | Follower | Duty Carried Out |
| S/Ldr | Bass AFM | R.W | | HK801 | XY-S | G-H Leader | Duty Carried Out |
| F/O | Fernley | F | | HK794 | XT-T | Follower | Duty Carried Out |
| F/O | Perrett | M | | NG293 | XY-U | Follower | Duty Carried Out |
| F/Lt | Green | L.A | | RF126 | XY-V | Follower | Duty Carried Out |
| F/O | Verry | C.C | RNZAF | HK613 | XY-Y | Follower | Duty Carried Out |

Here the escort of 90 RAF Mustangs took up position as the formation swung southeast towards the target area. Like the operation against Kamen, the Group leader, believed to be No.90 Squadron from No.32 Base, overshot the vital last turning point. However, unlike the Kamen attack, the leading formation remained intact and managed to retain a concentrated formation. The crew of F/O C Verry RNZAF lost the starboard outer aboard Lancaster HK613 XY-Y at 13:15 hours. They struggled to keep up with their allotted G-H Leader but valiantly continued with three engines.

Another crew who experienced engine trouble was Australian F/O J O'Brien at the controls of HK661 XY-R. They encountered problems with the Constant Speed Indicator in the starboard outer engine. This also prevented them from keeping formation with their allotted G-H Leader. Despite the problems, both crews successfully reached the target and bombed. Flying Officer O'Brien bombing on the G-H equipped HA-K-PD329 flown by W/O D McClellan RNZAF of No.218 Squadron while F/O Verry bombed on S/Ldr Bass. The crews of No.186 Squadron bombed between 12:27 and 12:29 hours, encountering slight accurate flak. Two crews, however, reported damage, one seriously. Flight Lieutenant John Tonks was hit in several places, rendering the rear turret unserviceable. Thankfully, the rear gunner Sgt Victor Woods was uninjured. Also reporting damage was F/Lt E Field DFC. They were hit just prior to bombing. Most crews agreed that the G-H dropped Blue Smoke Puff markers were compact, and bombing appeared concentrated. The issues with the lead group were reported at de-briefing, F/Lt Tonks, *'Spearhead did not seem to be in the briefed formation, and the leading squadron was too low. The main part of the stream overshot on last turn into target.'* The experienced F/Lt Field DFC, *'Formation seemed well concentrated, but leaders were off-track to port and very late over the target'*. On leaving the target area, the group departed the Ruhr between Krefeld and Dusseldorf. It was a longer than usual route that had long been avoided due to the intensity of the flak defences. With the situation on the Rhine and the Germans in retreat, the opposition here was believed to be lesser than the much-used Dusseldorf - Cologne 'gap'.

No.186 Squadron Reported Flak Damage 04/03/1945

| Serial | Code | Damage | Repairs / Notes |
|---|---|---|---|
| NG174 | **XY-A** | Rear turret, rear fuselage. | FB Cat A/C RoS No.54 Maintenance Unit. Returned 13/04/1945. |
| HK692 | **XY-B** | Not Recorded. | Repaired on Squadron. |

A new modification was introduced to the G-H equipped Lancasters within the group around this time. This new equipment would automatically calculate the ground speed on the bomb run, eliminating any possible error. The new device meant yet more training for the overworked navigators,

*'We had been prohibited from using the new device until fully trained. Consequently, it was necessary to alter our standard procedure on the run up to target. It would now be the navigator's job to call out the number of seconds delay between the warning point and the release point and on zero the bomb aimer could release the bomb load. Up until then, the navigator was in control of the bombing, now the bomb aimer had the satisfaction of pressing the bomb release button himself, the Bombing Union were happy!!' (Navigator, No.31 Base)*

The Schalke Coking Plant at Gelsenkirchen was the name chalked up on the operations board on the morning of March 5th. The squadron would detail fourteen Lancasters, with three flown by recently posted crews on their first operation. One of the crews was skippered by Australian F/O A Gillespie RAAF, who had started his tour on No.622 Squadron in December 1944. On only his second operation against Witten on December 12th he was obliged to make a forced landing behind Allied lines in Belgium with a defective engine. The crew was subsequently flown home by Dakota and for reasons unknown, the crew was then split up.

Left: WAAF Phylis Creed is standing at the Equipment Section and Techincal Section counter at RAF Stradishall. Right: Phylis and WAAF Joan Smith. Note how modern and comfortable the buildings look and the well-managed grass and silver birch trees. It really could not be any further away from the conditions at RAF Chedburgh and RAF Wratting Common.

The crew of F/Lt F. Blenkin of No.218 (Gold Coast) Squadron was given No.31 Base Leader's role, while No.186 Squadron would provide five G-H Leaders. The group rendezvous point was 9000 feet above the now-familiar Tonbridge. On forming up, the stream with No.32 Base leading passed over Beachy Head and again over the English Channel. The formation climbed for altitude, passing through a freezing cloud layer at 14,000 feet. Visibility was poor and made worse by dense contrails forming behind the Lancasters as they slowly reached bombing height of 18,500 feet. Another unexpected layer of cloud was encountered at this altitude, forcing the crews up to 20,000 feet and above. Unfortunately, they encountered stronger than forecast winds at this new height, which resulted in the formation being blown slightly off track.

Form B.807 – March 5th 1945 (D): Target : Gelsenkirchen: Schalke Coking Plant : GQ1829

| | | | | | | | |
|---|---|---|---|---|---|---|---|
| W/O | Cooke AFM | S.F | | HK694 | XY-C | Follower | Duty Carried Out. |
| F/Lt | Templeton | G.N | RCAF | NG146 | XY-E | Follower | Duty Carried Out. |
| F/O | Gillespie | A.P | RAAF | NG140 | XY-F | Follower | Duty Carried Out. |
| F/Lt | Marshall | A.N | | NG149 | XY-G | Follower | Duty Carried Out. |
| F/Lt | Field DFC | E.L | | HK682 | XY-J | Follower | Duty Carried Out. |
| F/O | Clarson | A | RAAF | NN720 | XY-K | G-H Leader | Duty Carried Out. |
| F/O | Young | H.S | | HK802 | XY-L | Follower | Duty Carried Out. |
| F/Lt | Hanson | R.A | | HK659 | XY-Q | G-H Leader | Duty Carried Out. |
| F/Lt | Mason | F.H | | HK801 | XY-S | G-H Leader | Duty Carried Out. |
| F/O | Idle | L.A | RNZAF | HK794 | XY-T | G-H Leader | Duty Carried Out. |
| F/Sgt | Gray | P | | NG293 | XY-U | Follower | Duty Carried Out. |
| F/Lt | Green | L.A | | RF126 | XY-V | Follower | Duty Carried Out. |
| F/O | Gogler | R | RAAF | HK796 | XY-W | G-H Leader | Duty Carried Out. |
| F/O | Forand | J.M | RCAF | HK606 | XY-Z | Follower | Duty Carried Out. |

Joining the crew of F/Lt R.A Hanson was Group Captain C.E Morse. Cyril Morse had spent most of the war in Training Command and was new to operations. Within a few short weeks, he would become Station Commander of RAF Wratting Common. The squadron was on the receiving end of some accurate predicted flak as they entered the Ruhr. This continued all the way to the target. As the stream neared Wesel, the weather cleared for a few minutes giving the flak gunners below an opportunity to engage visually. One of the first hit was F/O A Clarson RAAF. Three minutes before the target flak punctured both No.2 Port fuel tank and No.3 Port Outer fuel tank aboard Lancaster NN720 XY-K. The remaining fuel was quickly transferred for fear of fire. The port wing resembled a colander, but the two Merlins were miraculously undamaged.

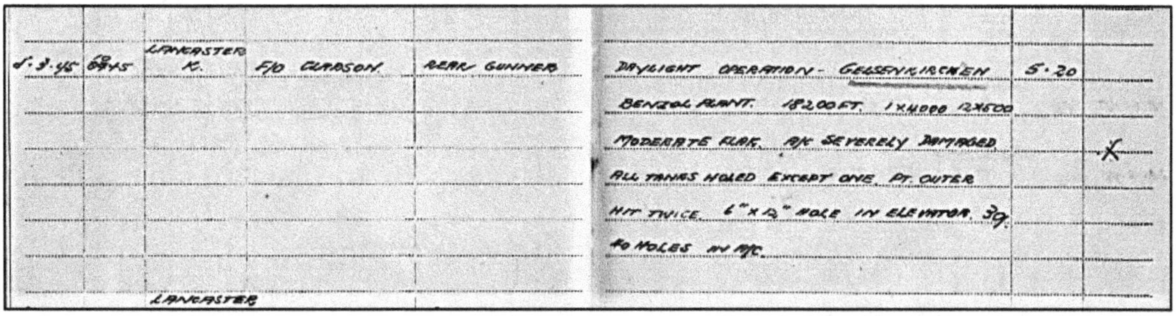

| | | | | | | | |
|---|---|---|---|---|---|---|---|
| 5.3.45 | 10 00 45 | LANCASTER K. | F/O CLARSON | REAR GUNNER | DAYLIGHT OPERATION - GELSENKIRCHEN | 5·20 | |
| | | | | | BENZOL PLANT. 18200 FT. 1×4000 12×500 | | |
| | | | | | MODERATE FLAK. A/C SEVERELY DAMAGED | | X |
| | | | | | ALL TANKS HOLED EXCEPT ONE. PT. OUTER | | |
| | | | | | HIT TWICE. 6"×12" HOLE IN ELEVATOR. 39. | | |
| | | | | | 40 HOLES IN A/C. | | |
| | | LANCASTER | | | | | |

A page from Flight Sergeant G McPherson's RAAF Log Book recording the damage by flak over Gelsenkirchen on March 5th 1945. Gerald kept a very detailed Log Book and recorded many incidents that would otherwise not be recorded in the Operational Records Book.

Flight Lieutenant Field DFC had the electrics cut to his rear turret due to flak fragments. Thankfully, the rear gunner, F/Sgt C.G Turner, was uninjured, but the turret would have to be manually operated if needed in an emergency. Another Lancaster hit over the target was flown by F/Lt G Templeton RCAF. He lost brake pressure and sustained damage to the fuselage aboard Lancaster NG146 XY-E. Over the target area, a Lancaster was seen falling in flames, and four parachutes were reported. Bombing appeared concentrated. However, solid overcast prevented visual confirmation. Flight Lieutenant R Hanson was one of the G-H crews.

He commented on his return, *'No results seen but stream was very scattered and it was impossible to identify spear head'.* His concerns about the formation keeping were echoed throughout the squadron. Flight Sergeant P Gray bombed at 14:13 hours. He commented, *'Stream very scattered although the original base formation were good'.* The recently posted crew of F/O A Gillespie RAAF came in for some well-deserved praise on his return. Soon after take-off, the boost gauge on the port outer engine aboard Lancaster NG140 XY-F became unserviceable. To add to the problems, both the rear and mid-upper turrets were also reported as unserviceable. Nevertheless, showing a certain amount of audacity, they continued onto the target. Canadian F/Lt Gordon Templeton RCAF and crew were the last to land back at RAF Stradishall at 16:18 hours. They circled until all the Lancasters had safely landed before they came into land with no brakes. Once safely down, the crew had reason to celebrate. They had completed their 35th and last operation. Born November 21st, 1921, in Montreal, Canada. Gordon had served pre-war as an Insurance Clark, enlisting in Montreal on April 24th, 1942. He had started his tour back in October. In July 1945, and back home in Canada, he would be awarded a DFC. I have found no citation other than the standard *'In recognition of gallantry and devotion of duty in the execution of air operations against the enemy'.* However, the Canadian historian Hugh Halliday records the following.

Flight Lieutenant Gordon Templeton DFC RCAF.

*This officer has completed many operations against heavily defended German targets in Germany. As captain and pilot he has flown both by day and by night and has always shown fine captaincy. Photographs of the target on some of his sorties have been outstanding and prove that every effort has been made to hit the aiming point, regardless of heavy flak.*

The is also a rather curious comment written by RAF Stradishall's Station Commander dated March 22nd, 1945. It reads, *'An officer whose highly-strung temperament have him a very real appreciation of danger but who, with great courage, coolness and determination completed every mission in a most efficient manner'.*

No.186 Squadron Reported Flak Damage 05/03/1945

| Serial | Code | Damage | Repairs / Notes |
|---|---|---|---|
| NN720 | **XY-K** | Fuel tanks and wings. | Repaired on Squadron. |
| HK682 | **XY-J** | Rear turret. | Repaired on Squadron |
| NG146 | **XY-E** | Hydraulics. | Repaired on Squadron |

The squadron was not required for the raid on the oil refinery at Salzbergen situated on the River Ems on the afternoon of the 6th. It was, however, required for a return to night operations that same night. The squadrons provide eight of its most experienced G-H crews on a two-part attack directed against bridge and troop concentrations at Wesel on the night of March 6th. At what would have been a rather empty briefing room, the eight crews were informed that the operation was in direct support of the Allied ground forces and accuracy was paramount given the close proximity of the Allied front line.

The squadron commander stressed that no bombs were to be dropped unless they were entirely confident that G-H was working perfectly. To maximise the shock effect no markers or flares were to be carried just a single 'cookie' and 14 x 500 pounders. The small force of 39 experienced crews drawn from all three Base Stations departed England over Beachy Head. Each of the Bases was instructed to spread their aircraft across the duration of the No.3 Group attack, timed to commence at 21:01 hours.

Form B.810 – March 6th 1945 (N): Target : Wesel : Tactical Bombing: GQ1829

| | | | | | | | |
|---|---|---|---|---|---|---|---|
| F/Lt | Clarson | A | RAAF | NG354 | XY-M | G-H | Duty Carried Out. |
| F/O | Hart | J.H | | NG137 | XY-D | G-H | Duty Carried Out. |
| F/Lt | Tonks | J.E | | HK802 | XY-L | G-H | Duty Carried Out. |
| F/O | O'Brien | J.D | RAAF | HK684 | XY-O | G-H | Duty Carried Out. |
| F/Lt | Brayshaw | C.S | | HK659 | XY-Q | G-H | Duty Carried Out. |
| F/Lt | Mason | F.H | | HK801 | XY-S | G-H | Duty Carried Out. |
| F/O | Fernley | F | | HK794 | XY-T | G-H | Duty Carried Out. |
| S/Ldr | Bass AFM | R.W | | HK796 | XY-W | G-H | Duty Carried Out. |

On reaching the target, the crews noted the flashes of the exploding cookies. With the G-H pulse signal strong, each crew confidently dropped their all high explosive load onto the shattered town between 21:04 and 21:07 hours. Flight Lieutenant J.Tonks reported, *'Big flashes were seen through cloud over the target'*. Flak over Wesel was reported as slight, although some crews reported seeing combats. It had been an excellent example of G-H bombing. Dessau, the home of aircraft designer Hugo Junkers, was the target on the night of March 7th. Most of the crews had not even heard of this city situated at the junction of Mulde and Elbes rivers. Sandwiched between Berlin in the north and Leipzig in the south, it would be the longest trip to date for many. Due to the distance involved, G-H could not be used. Instead, the Path Finders would mark and control the raid using controlled Newhaven. Despite the arrival of a number of new crews on the squadron during the preceding weeks, it was left to the old hands on this night. Thirteen crews would be detailed and briefed.

Form B.810 – March 7th 1945 (N): Target : Dessau: Associated Industry and Rail Facility.

| | | | | | | | |
|---|---|---|---|---|---|---|---|
| F/Lt | Marshall | A.N | | HK694 | XY-C | PFF Flares | Duty Carried Out |
| F/Lt | Field DFC | E.L | | NG137 | XY-D | PFF Flares | Duty Carried Out |
| F/O | Green | T.B | | NG140 | XY-F | PFF Flares | Duty Carried Out |
| F/O | Head | G.D | | HK682 | XY-J | PFF Flares | Duty Carried Out |
| F/Lt | Tonks | J.E | | HK802 | XY-L | PFF Flares | Duty Carried Out |
| S/Ldr | Reynolds DFC | P | | NG354 | XY-M | PFF Flares | Duty Carried Out |
| F/O | O'Brien | J.D | RAAF | HK684 | XY-O | PFF Flares | Duty Carried Out |
| F/Lt | Brayshaw DFC | S.C | | HK659 | XY-Q | PFF Flares | Duty Carried Out |
| F/O | Idle | L.A | RNZAF | HK661 | XY-R | PFF Flares | Duty Carried Out |
| F/O | Fernley | F | | HK794 | XY-T | PFF Flares | Duty Carried Out |
| F/O | Gogler | R | RAAF | NG293 | XY-U | PFF Flares | Duty Carried Out |
| F/O | Godfrey | D.F | RAAF | RF126 | XY-Y | PFF Flares | Duty Carried Out |
| F/O | Hanson | R.A | | HK613 | XY-Y | PFF Flares | Duty Carried Out |

First away at 17.03 hours was 'B' Flight's F/O R. Hanson at the controls of HK613 XY-Y. He was quickly followed by a further twelve crews who, once airborne, made their way to the rendezvous point above Reading before setting out over the North Sea. A defective rear turret meant that the crew of F/Lt R Hanson were compelled to return early. Despite the rear gunner Sgt R Thomas and the crew's Flight Engineer, Sgt D Smy, attempting to rectify the fault, the crew knew to continue was foolhardy given the distance. They jettisoned the 'cookie' and two 1000 pounders 'safe' and landed back at RAF Stradishall at 19:23 hours.

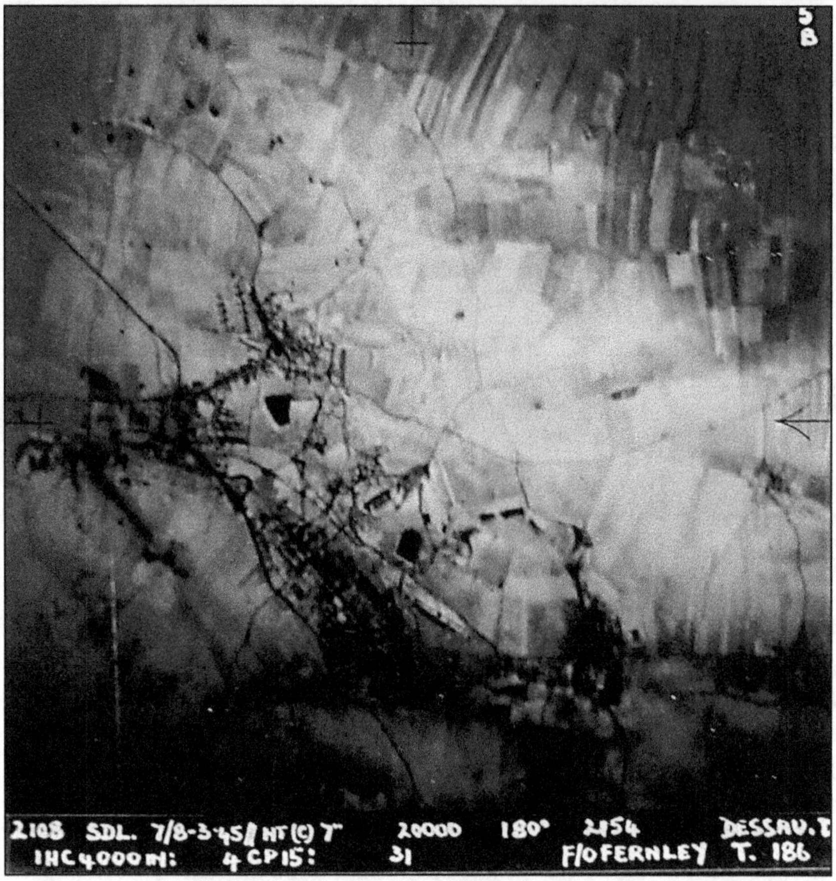


Flying Officer Fernley's Target Photograph taken over Dassau on March 7th 1945. The crew, flying at 20,000 feet, took this photo at 21:54 hours. The still snow-covered landscape is visible, as is plenty of ground detail.

The crews of No.31 Base were part of the first wave timed to attack between 22:00 and 22:04 hours. They would be joined by over 70 Lancasters of No.1 Group and 44 Lancasters of the Canadian No.6 Group. German fighters were active early on, infiltrating the bomber stream prior to the Ruhr and still over 150 miles from the target area. On reaching Dessau, the Master Bomber, Squadron Leader Peter Mellor, call sign 'Zipfast' of No.635 Squadron, began to orbit the city. The planned attack using ground markers was quickly discounted when a cloud layer quickly swallowed up the initial ground marker flares. Squadron Leader Mellor seeing this, immediately ordered the aiming point to be re-marked with sky-markers. This delay would have implications for some of the early arrivals. Two squadron crews had encounters with enemy fighters prior to bombing. The first at 19:50 hours involved the crew of F/O F Fernley. They were north of the target at 20,000 feet when a JU88 was sighted. The following Combat Report was submitted.

> Fighter first seen at 150 yards was recognised as a JU88. As E/A came in towards Lancaster, Mid-Upper gunner opened up with a two second burst. E/A then turned to port and dived down below Lancaster out of sight.

Flying Officer J O'Brien RAAF was just minutes away from bombing when a Me109 was sighted at 21:56 hours. The brief combat report records the following,

| |
|---|
| Fighter came in from port up ahead, Lancaster corkscrewed port as fighter came over top. Mid Upper opened fire with a second burst. The enemy aircraft broke away down to starboard and disappeared. |

Squadron Leader P Reynolds DFC arrived over Dessau at 21:57 hours. His post raid report sums up the frustration of the early arrivals. *'Arrived at 21:57 hours but had to orbit waiting for markers. Master Bomber called for skymarkers, but ground markers could be seen. Someone's inter-com interfered with Master Bomber. Marking was fairly well concentrated but late. Visual on 'U' shaped river obtained and bombed south of it in the fires. Smoke obscured fires which were burning well on leaving the target. Should be a good attack. R/Y aerial was taken away by a Me410 crossing above as aircraft bombed'*. The crew were fortunate to survive on this occasion. Another of the early arrivals was the crew of F/Lt A.N Marshall. They orbited the target twice. The first time they were convinced the Green and Red TIs were dummies, so they chose to ignore them, although they attracted some bombs which appeared to show a forest on fire. Another crew early was that of F/O G Head. They arrived at 21:58 hours and found what they described as *'Rather scattered skymarkers'*. Flight Lieutenant S Brayshaw DFC made an uncharacteristic error by overshooting the target. On his second attempt to bomb, he noted, *'A number of TI's Red around the target were believed to be spoof as they were smaller and darker than ours.'*

The re-marking was completed effectively, and skymarkers began to cascade over the target at 22:00 hours[42]. It was all the first wave needed as bomb load after bomb load started dropping on the town below. Some crews could not hear the Master Bomber's instructions due to an unknown crew broadcasting on VHF. This crew gave a running commentary of the attack, including the Bomber Command broadcast winds and the PFF technique just minutes before H-Hour. Flak was moderate but accurate, but strangely there were no searchlights. There was, however, considerable fighter activity over the target area, and a number of fighter combats were observed. The squadron crews witnessed the destruction of a bomber seen falling in flames in the target area. No parachutes were observed. The Squadron ORB records in a slightly creative fashion the operation.

| |
|---|
| Enemy fighters were active over the target and Me410, Fw190, Me109 and JU88's were identified. Two Combats were reported and one claim for 'Probably Destroyed' was made. One of our aircraft nearly collided with a Me410 and lost it R/T aerial. Generally considered a good attack but the dummy markers received a number of loads. Heavy flak encountered, some of which burst 3 or 4 times – maybe rockets. One 'Scarecrow' ( anti-morale device) was seen. |

The squadron ranks were again bolstered with the arrival of another crew on the 7th. The squadron was stood down on the 8th, but a number of G-H flights were flown in what turned out to be a relatively quiet day after the recent activity.

The attacks on Hitler's oil were still high on the priority list at No.3 Group HQ on the morning of the 9th. Accordingly, the squadron briefed 14 crews for a return visit to the Emscher Lippe Benzol plant at Datteln. The Group would be divided into two groups, each with separate aiming points. Target 'A', the southern aiming point, was allocated to 61 Lancasters of No.32 Base plus 21 Lancasters of No.33 Base. The northern aiming point, Target 'B', would be attacked by No.31 Base's three squadrons which would be led by No.186 Squadron, plus 33 Lancasters from No.33 Base.

Form B.813 – March 9th 1945 (D): Target : Datteln : Emscher Lippe Benzol plant : G-H691B.

| | | | | | | | |
|---|---|---|---|---|---|---|---|
| F/O | Green | T.B | | HK692 | XY-B | Follower | Duty Carried Out. |
| F/Lt | Sawyer | F.R | | HK694 | XY-C | Follower | Duty Carried Out. |

[42] *It would appear the raid started earlier than the planned 22:00 Hours. No.635 PFF dropped their first marker flare at 21:54 hours.*

| | | | | | | | |
|---|---|---|---|---|---|---|---|
| F/O | Hart | J.H | | NG137 | XY-D | G-H Leader | Duty Carried Out. |
| F/Sgt | Rose | B.A | | NG146 | XY-E | Follower | Duty Carried Out. |
| F/Sgt | Hudson | A.L | RAAF | NG140 | XY-F | Follower | Duty Carried Out. |
| F/Lt | Marshall | A.N | | HK802 | XY-L | Follower | Duty Carried Out. |
| F/O | Clarson | A.J | RAAF | NG354 | XY-M | G-H Leader | Duty Carried Out. |
| F/Lt | Hanson | R.A | | HK684 | XY-O | G-H Leader | Duty Carried Out. |
| S/Ldr | Bass AFM | R.W | | HK659 | XY-Q | G-H Leader | Duty Carried Out. |
| F/Sgt | Gray | P | | HK661 | XY-R | Follower | Duty Carried Out. |
| F/Lt | Mason | F.H | | HK794 | XY-T | G-H Leader | Duty Carried Out. |
| F/Lt | Green | L.A | | HK606 | XY-Z | Follower | Duty Carried Out. |
| F/O | Gogler | R.J | RAAF | HK613 | XY-Y | Follower | Duty Carried Out. |
| F/O | Idle | L.A | RNZAF | HK801 | XY-S | Follower | Duty Carried Out. |

The group's rendezvous point was once again above Tonbridge at 9,000 feet. Forming up went without incident as the formation swung south and set off for Boulogne. Flying Officer A Clarson RAAF experienced starboard outer engine failure soon after take-off. The engine was feathered, and after jettisoning the 4000lb Cookie to maintain speed and gain attitude the crew bravely continued onto target.

Flying Officer D Godfrey RAAF and his crew pose at the rear of the G-H equipped Avro Lancaster HK796 XY-W.

Freezing conditions at altitude resulted in white contrails pinpointing the Lancasters progress. A strong fighter escort of 46 RAF Mustangs and 77 Spitfires joined the stream as they neared the German border. Below them was the usual solid mass of impenetrable cloud. The formation passed north of Aachen and then slipped past Bocholt. Accurate intermittent flak was encountered near the beleaguered town of Wesel. Once clear, the formation headed straight to Datteln. The formation that had been relatively poor until then started to become compact as the Lancasters started their curved approach. Number 32 Base and No.33 Base squadrons opened proceedings attacking Aiming point 'A'. Flak accounted for the 32 Base G-H Leader, F/Lt Aldhous MiD whose aircraft Lancaster PA254 WP-A of No.90 Squadron was seen to go down in the target area. This was witnessed by a number of crews.

The squadron crews, five of which were G-H Leaders, approached the target between 18-20,000 feet, encountering only moderate flak. Easily visible against the broken white clouds were a number of concentrated blue puff markers which were slowly floating down over Aiming point 'B'. The first bombs started dropping at 13:57 hours. The G-H crew of F/O Clarson RAAF, who had courageously continued with the raid with three engines, bombed at 13:58 hours from 20,000 feet. His followers tucked close behind watched as his single Blue Skymarker and 15 x 500 pounders added to the destruction meted out below. No results were seen owing to the cloud, but F/O Idle RNZAF reported, *'Brown smoke seen coming through clouds'*. The crews began landing shortly before 16:00 hours. There was once again a reason to celebrate in both Messes on return from Datteln, with the safe return of F/Lt Green and crew at the controls of HK606 XY-Z and F/O Rex Gogler RAAF. Leonard Arthur Green was born in Exeter in 1923. Prior to joining the RAF in September 1941, he worked as an Apprentice Electrician. Now, four years on, he was a battle-hardened bomber pilot who had completed an impressive 37 operations. He would be awarded a well-deserved DFC in July 1945[43]. Twenty-three-year old Australian Rex Gogler RAAF had flown 35 operations. However, unlike Leonard, his tour was not recognised with an award. There was a major development on the squadron on the 9th with the arrival of 'C' Flight of No.90 Squadron. Headquarters No.3 Group Instruction Serial No. 12/45 was received giving instructions of the movement from RAF Tuddenham of 'C' Flight, who would be absorbed into No.186, bringing the squadron up to a 3-Flight Squadron of 30 U.E. aircraft with effect from March 10th. This new Flight 'C' would be engaged in special duties under the command of South African S/Ldr J.H Day DFC. The Lancasters of 'C' Flight would not be coded **XY**, but use the codes **AP**.

John Day had been badly wounded in the left leg on return from an operational sortie with No.50 Squadron in 1941. After many months in hospital, the efforts to save this leg had failed, and it was amputated high-up the thigh. John, an experienced navigator, had a B.Sc. (University of South Africa) and a Ph.D. (Cambridge). In 1943 and while still convalescing he was recruited by Group Captain Dudley Saward to join his staff on the R.D.F Section of Bomber Command HQ. The R.D.F Section was set up to study the use and results of Radio Direction Finding apparatus on operations and strive to achieve better employment of new devices on front line squadrons. The South African was also actively involved in the practical design and development of equipment by T.R.E. This included both *'Liontamer'* a 1 ¼ cm H2S and the 6ft 3cm Mk IVA scanner code-named *'Whirligig'*. John had been sent to America in 1944 to show the Yanks the merits of H2S. On arrival back in England, he joined No.139 Squadron PFF[44] flying operationally to assess the new H2S under operational conditions. With the war in Europe concluding and many new aids still in development, the Air Ministry shifted its focus towards the air bombing war against Japan. Accordingly, a Special Development Flight was formed in the effort to advance the effectiveness of both the Mk.IVA H2S and the Mk.VI H2S for possible use against Japan. Squadron Leader Day DFC was chosen to command this Special Flight, and it was he and his team that arrived at RAF Stradishall. Four specially modified Mk.III Lancasters, SW267, SW269 SW272 and SW275 arrived at RAF Stradishall at around 15:00 hours, completing the short flight from Tuddenham. Squadron Leader Day DFC arrived with the main Road Party later in the day.

Known No.90 Squadron Lancasters transferred to 'C' Flight No.186 Squadron.

| Serial | Via | Date |
|---|---|---|
| LM692 | Via 'C' Flight No.90 Squadron. | March 10th 1945. |
| PB488 | Via 'C' Flight No.90 Squadron. | March 10th 1945. |
| SW267 | Via 'C' Flight No.90 Squadron. | March 10th 1945. |
| SW272 | Via 'C' Flight No.90 Squadron. | March 10th 1945. |
| SW275 | Via 'C' Flight No.90 Squadron. | March 10th 1945. |

[43] *Killed in a flying accident while still serving in the RAF in 1951. The Harvard Trainer he was flying crashed soon after take-off.*
[44] *Would be awarded a Bar to his DFC in April 1945 for his time with No.139 Squadron.*

Just after midday on March 10th, 1945 'B' Flight's F/Lt Kenneth Orman DFC RNZAF was the first away from RAF Stradishall at the controls of Lancaster NG293 XY-U. His target, along with 11 squadron crews, was the Scholvern Buer oil refinery at Gelsenkirchen. The Hydrierwerk Scholven AG in the Gelsenkirchen district of Buer was founded in 1935. The Gelsenberg Benzin AG hydrogenation plant built the following year near the Nordstern mine was by 1944 the most efficient hydrogenation plant on the Rhine and in the Ruhr in terms of capacity and among the five most crucial fuel plants in the Reich. The production from the hydrogenation plants ensured above all the supply of aviation fuel to the Luftwaffe. A total of 155 Lancasters drawn from all three base groups would be involved in the attack, 45 provided by No.31 Base. Squadron Leader J O'Brien of No.218 Squadron would be given the Base Leader role.

Form B.814 – March 10th 1945 (D): Target : Gelsenkirchen : Scholvern Buer oil refinery: GQ1537

| | | | | | | | |
|---|---|---|---|---|---|---|---|
| F/Lt | Field DFC | E.L | | HK692 | XY-B | G-H Leader | Duty Carried Out. |
| W/O | Onus | M.J | RAAF | HK694 | XY-C | Follower | Duty Carried Out. |
| F/Sgt | Hudson | A.L | RAAF | NG140 | XY-F | Follower | Duty Carried Out. |
| F/O | Head | G.D | | NG149 | XY-G | Follower | Duty Carried Out. |
| F/O | Saunders | A | | HK802 | XY-L | G-H Leader | Duty Carried Out. |
| F/O | Beck | J.A | RAAF | RA533 | XY-P | Follower | Duty Carried Out. |
| F/Lt | Orman DFC | K.G | RNZAF | NG293 | XY-U | Follower | Duty Carried Out. |
| W/O | Howell | A.J | RAAF | HK661 | XY-R | G-H Leader | Duty Carried Out. |
| F/O | Fernley | F | | HK801 | XY-S | G-H Leader | Duty Carried Out. |
| F/O | Godfrey | D | RAAF | HK796 | XY-W | G-H Leader | Duty Carried Out. |
| F/O | Forand | J.M | RCAF | HK613 | XY-Y | Follower | Duty Carried Out. |
| F/Lt | Brayshaw DFC | S.C | | HK606 | XY-Z | Follower | Duty Carried Out. |

Flying on their first operation was Australian W/O Maxwell Onus RAAF and crew. The crew's Flight Engineer was Sgt F Winch. Fred Winch was a qualified pilot, but due to the abundance of trained pilots and shortage of postings, he had opted to work on the railways as a fireman instead of kicking his heels awaiting a possible posting. An opportunity to undertake a Flight Engineers Course was willingly taken, and Fred went back to the classroom. He completed this course, and he joined the crew at No.1668 CU. There was a definite Australian influence on the squadron at this time, and this operation typifies their contribution. Five crews were skippered by the men from 'Down-Under'. The mix of British, Australian, New Zealand and Canadian aircrew made Bomber Command tick, and this was especially true on No.186 Squadron. In between operations the crews would often visit the local public houses or travel further afield if on leave. Harrold Peake, navigator to Australian F/Sgt Baker RAAF recalls.

> *We had fairly frequent visits to the Cherry Tree pub for liquid refreshments and in relaxation numerous names and anecdotes (graffiti - expertly executed) were written on the walls and ceiling of the bar by 186 Sqdn. Personally providing a record of squadron activities. Many years ago I called there briefly with my family when returning from a holiday near Yarmouth, but all traces of this graffiti had disappeared.*

The persistent problem of formation indiscipline was once again illustrated on this raid. The attack called for No.32 Base to open the attack followed closely by No.33 Base and then No.31 Base. Over

All smiles for the camera. Flight Sergeant Phil Gray and his crew were obviously in a happy mood when this photograph was taken. Front, Phil, Frank, Gerry and Harry. Top L-R, Clin Jack and Ivor 'Blondie'.

the continent, a gap of almost 4 miles developed between the spearhead and the 3rd and final wave. Somehow in the confusion and in an attempt to reduce the gap a small formation of 40 plus Lancasters of No.33 Base found themselves behind and slightly above No.31 Base.

Warrant Officer A Howell RAAF crew lost the port inner engine aboard Lancaster HK661 XY-R at 15:00 hours, thirty minutes before reaching the target. Gradually losing height the plucky crew decided to continue onto the target. This was becoming a trait on the squadron especially among the Australian skippers. Unable to fly above 13,000 feet, a perilously low altitude, they wisely positioned themselves on the periphery of the stream. Four of the crews remarked about the formation, F/Lt Field DFC *'There were two parallel streams close together. The stream was long and narrow'.* Flight Lieutenant Ken Orman DFC RNZAF, *'Three main groups with long gaps in between.* Flying Officer D Godfrey RAAF had the unnerving experience of finding a Lancaster almost directly above him. He reported upon return, *'Had to move to port of Leader as another aircraft directly above'.* Warrant Officer A.J Howell RAAF found himself almost seven thousand feet below his colleagues. He dropped his all HE load at 15:36 hours on a concentrated bunch of Blue Skymarkers. It was a risky run into the target. With hundreds of bombs dropping, there was a very good chance a 'friendly' bomb could have hit his Lancaster. Thankfully for the crew, their perseverance paid off, and they turned for home without incident. Despite the concerns of the crews, the bombing was extremely accurate, the G-H release pulse was very strong and despite accurate predicted flak, the raid was considered a complete success. Nine Lancasters were damaged by flak, none of which were from 186 Squadron. There was some much needed light entertainment on the evening of the 10th. The Station WAAFs had their first performance of the play "The Mocking Bird". The play was produced and starred officers and airwomen from RAF Stradishall and was a complete success. The only disappointment was that the box office had to turn away too many people on the opening night. One of the recent arrivals was skippered by Australian F/Sgt Les Baker RAAF. Born in November 1922 in York, Western Australia, Les had previously served in the Light Horse Regiment before enlisting in the RAAF. The crew's navigator was Sgt Harold Peake, he recalls his impressions of RAF Stradishall.

> *Always a memorable event were Sergeants' Mess dances with the associated good companionship merrymaking and excellent food prepared by the catering personnel which included the most marvellous trifles. These were occasions for letting ones hair down and getting rid of tensions and not without a certain amount of madness. I still have a black service tie shortened and frayed at the ends caused by 'tie chewing' - a kind of ritual for which I have no explanation, by other revellers. The luxury of the flying breakfast with its attendant bacon and eggs and the combination of eagerness, excitement and apprehension which prevailed in the atmosphere of a crowded briefing room. The de-briefing and interrogation after ops. with the mug of 100% proof rum poured from a stone jar in a wicker basket... In particular the de-briefing after our first Kiel raid on the 9th/10th April on which we apparently bombed a dummy target. I hope it doesn't sound arrogant when I say this was not due to a navigation error, but to an enthusiastic crew being deceived by an excellent imitation set up by Jerry. We subsequently returned very much off track which might have proved to be catastrophic, however, apart from a few red faces, all was forgiven and we went again four nights later with a little more success. Another memory is that of tension created occasionally by the uncertainty of take-off time (if at all) when weather conditions were bad with the possibility of the operation being 'scrubbed as sometimes happened after wakey wakey' tablets had been taken. On such occasions sleep came with some difficulty.*

Bomber Command was out in force on the 11th. 1,079 bombers from all main force groups were airborne, No.3 Group detailing 149 Lancasters, 69 of which were equipped with G-H. The first of the squadron's eleven Lancasters began taking off just before noon. One of the Lancasters was captained by Wing Commander A.E Cairnes. He and his crew had arrived on February 1st, but this would be their first operation. It was some baptism, Essen, Bomber Command's biggest nemesis.

Form B.815 – March 11th 1945 (D): Target : Essen : 'Spratt'

| | | | | | | | |
|---|---|---|---|---|---|---|---|
| W/Cdr | Cairnes | A.E | | PP668 | XY-B | Follower | Duty Carried Out. |
| F/Lt | Sawyer | F.R | | NF146 | XY-E | Follower | Duty Carried Out |
| F/Lt | Tonks | J.E | | NG354 | XY-M | G-H Leader | Duty Carried Out |
| W/O | Onus | M.J | RAAF | NG149 | XY-G | Follower | Duty Carried Out |
| F/O | Green | T.B | | HK802 | XY-L | G-H Leader | Duty Carried Out |
| F/Lt | Marshall | A.N | | HK694 | XY-C | Follower | Duty Carried Out |
| F/Lt | Hanson | R.A | | RA633 | XY-P | G-H Leader | Duty Carried Out |
| F/Lt | Mason | F.H | | HK801 | XY-S | G-H Leader | Duty Carried Out |
| F/Sgt | Gray | P | | HK796 | XY-W | Follower | Duty Carried Out |
| F/Sgt | Collinson | J.J | RAAF | NG293 | XY-U | Follower | Duty Carried Out |
| F/Sgt | Baker | L.G | RAAF | HK613 | XY-Y | Follower | Duty Carried Out |

Two other crews were given Essen as their first operation, and both crews were captained by Australians. Flight Sergeant Jeffrey Collinson RAAF and F/Sgt Leslie Baker[45] RAAF, both recent arrivals from No.72 Base. Once airborne, the eleven squadron crews headed towards the assembly point over Linford, Essex. The raid would take place over five waves with No.3 Group's Lancasters the last over the target area. The attack on Essen would be the largest daylight operation yet undertaken.

The cramped conditions in the Lancaster are evident in this photograph. Flight Engineer Sergeant Len Sewell stands in front of Flight Sergeant Rolly Ward Navigator. Both members of Flight Lieutenant Ken Orman's DFC RNZAF crew.

[45] *F/Sgt Baker RAAF Records show him arriving on the squadron via No.72 Base on March 7th 1945.*

The force flew across Northern France and turned northeast on passing the Julich area. It then turned north again for Dusseldorf and finally towards Essen. The route was flak free until the battlefront when the first black flak bursts punctured the sky. This quickly intensified as the force neared Dusseldorf. All the while, the stream was protected by RAF fighters, with six squadrons of RAF Mustangs providing escort for the entire route. These would be joined by three more Mustang squadrons over the target area. Withdrawal cover was provided by seven squadrons of European based Spitfires, augmented by yet more long-range RAF Mustangs. Number 3 Group's route was slightly different from the other groups due to the curved G-H approach needed. The Group passed over Eschweiler, a district north of Aachen, then onto Essen. The entire route was flown above 10/10th cloud. Once again, the Group's apparent inability to maintain a compact formation was reported. Unhealthy gaps between the three Base groups bringing up the rear guard put yet more strain on the already stretched fighter escort. It was not just No.3 Group having issues, Flight Lieutenant A Marshall reported on return, *'Stream was poor, little resemblance of formation. Three Halifaxes crossed stream'.* As the No.3 Group contingent swept towards Essen, the crews could see a mass of dark brown smoke rising from the target. It was an incredible sight. The closer they got to Essen, the more black and brown smoke columns were seen pushing their way through the white cloud base. The G-H reception was strong as the squadron's crews started their bomb runs at 15:33 hours. The Group was given two separate aiming points to attack, BULLHEAD aiming point 'M' and BULLHEAD aiming point 'E', both with the objective of destroying and disorganising Essen's rail system. A number of what was considered accurate and well-grouped Blue puff skymarkers were bombed by the followers. The two sprog crews bombed behind their G-H Leader at 15:37 hours. Flight Sergeant Collison RAAF reported, *'Stream seemed fairly good, and no aircraft bombed from above.* Flight Sergeant Baker RAAF, on the other hand, reported, *'Stream was straggling, but formation ahead were quite good.* Such was the dilemma experienced by the poor Intelligence Officers back at RAF Stradishall. By the time the Group were over the target, opposition was almost nil. Despite Essen's once fearsome reputation, No.31 Base did not report a single aircraft damaged by flak. All the squadron was safely back at RAF Stradishall before 18:00 hours. This once feared target nestled in the 'Happy Valley' had finally succumbed to the destructive might of Bomber Command. A daylight raid on Dortmund was laid on for the 12th, and the squadron would detail twelve crews. They would join over 1000 bombers over Germany.

Form B.817 – March 12th 1945 (D): Target : Dortmund : Railway disruption.

| | | | | | | | |
|---|---|---|---|---|---|---|---|
| F/O | Saunders | A | | HK767 | XY-A | Follower | Duty Carried Out. |
| W/Cdr | Cairnes | A.E | | PP668 | XY-B | Follower | Duty Carried Out. |
| F/Lt | Brayshaw DFC | S.C | | PP669 | XY-C | Follower | Duty Carried Out. |
| F/Lt | Field DFC | E.L | | NG137 | XY-D | G-H Leader | Duty Carried Out. |
| F/O | Roberts | D.M | | NG146 | XY-E | Follower | Duty Carried Out. |
| F/O | Head | G.D | | NG149 | XY-G | G-H Leader | Duty Carried Out. |
| S/Ldr | Reynolds DFC | P | | HK802 | XY-L | G-H Leader | Duty Carried Out. |
| F/Lt | Tonks | J.E | | NG354 | XY-M | Follower | Duty Carried Out. |
| F/Sgt | Baker | L.G | RAAF | RA533 | XY-P | Follower | Duty Carried Out. |
| W/O | Howell | A.J | RAAF | NG293 | XY-U | Follower | Duty Carried Out. |
| F/O | Godfrey | D.F | RAAF | HK796 | XY-W | G-H Leader | Duty Carried Out. |
| F/O | Fernley | F | | HK794 | XY-T | G-H Leader | Duty Carried Out. |

Number 3 Group would once again be the last group over the target. The entire force was flanked by RAF Mustang and Spitfire escort which reported the presence of two Messerschmitt 262 jet fighters and FW190's. The Path Finders opened proceedings at 16:24 hours. They were quickly followed by No.1 Group, who was followed by the Halifaxes of No.4 Group at 16:35 hours. The Canadians of No.6 Group followed at 16:42 hours, No.5 Group were over the target three minutes later. Then, finally, it was the turn of the G-H equipped squadrons of No.3 Group. Inky black smoke columns were

everywhere, slowly pushing through the 10/10th cloud. One mass of smoke was estimated to be 10-15 miles across. The first of No.186 Squadrons bombs fell at 16:57 hours, within two minutes, the squadron had dropped a total of 131,000lb of high explosive on the city below. Concentrated bunches of red and blue Skymarkers stood out against the white clouds and black smoke. The only crew reporting any damage was that of F/Lt E Field DFC, who was hit by flak over the target area. All the crews apart from W/Cdr Cairnes landed back at RAF Stradishall, unserviceable instruments aboard Lancaster PP668 XY-B forcing the crew to land on F.I.D.O at RAF Tuddenham at 19:03 hours. While both 'A' and 'B' Flights were over Germany, five Lancasters of 'C' Flight, or 'Special Flight' were airborne on a practice flight.

No.186 Squadron Reported Flak Damage 12/03/1945

| Serial | Code | Damage | Repairs / Notes |
|---|---|---|---|
| NG137 | **XY-D** | Note Recorded. | Repaired on Squadron. |

Fourteen crews were detailed for a night attack on the Dortmund Ems Canal on the 13th, but this was subsequently cancelled late afternoon. The crews of 'C' Flight were airborne again during the day, and four Bombing and Gunnery exercises were flown. In London, Squadron Leader R Bass attended an investiture held at Buckingham Palace, where he was presented with the Air Force Medal by His Majesty The King. On return from the Dortmund operation, Australian pilot Les Baker was promoted to the dizzy heights of Pilot Officer, his Navigator was Sgt Harold Peake, who remembers the events.

*One night we went to the Cherry Tree to celebrate Les Baker's commission to P/O, and I recall him placing his new 'cheese cutter' dress cap under the table and during the course of the evening it was used as a receptacle for beer dregs, and as a result it suffered considerable-shrinkage.*

On the 14th, the squadron prepared for a daylight operation directed against the Emscher Lippe (North) Coking plant at Datteln. The man chosen to lead No.31 Base was No.195 Squadron's S/Ldr W.L Farquarson DFC, and his deputy would be F/Lt R.E 'Dinky' Boyd. At RAF Stradishall there was stunned disbelief when the target and route were given during the briefing by W/Cdr Giles DFC. The planners had routed the entire force right through what remained of the Ruhr, exposing it to its formidable flak defences. The assembled crews knew only too well what was awaiting them. In excellent weather all 14 Lancasters from No.186 Squadron took off safely from RAF Stradishall between 13:30 and 13:40 hours.

Form B.817 – March 14th 1945 (D): Target : **Datteln** : Emscher Lippe (North) Coking Plant.

| | | | | | | | |
|---|---|---|---|---|---|---|---|
| F/O | Saunders | A | | HK767 | XY-A | Follower | Duty Carried Out. |
| F/Lt | Marshall | A.N | | PP668 | XY-B | Follower | Duty Carried Out. |
| F/O | Green | T.B | | PP669 | XY-C | Follower | Duty Carried Out. |
| F/Lt | Sawyer | F.R | | NG146 | XY-E | Follower | Duty Carried Out. |
| F/O | Verry | C.C | RNZAF | NG354 | XY-M | Follower | Duty Carried Out. |
| W/O | Onus | M.J | RAAF | NG149 | XY-G | Follower | Duty Carried Out. |
| F/O | Roberts | D.M | | NN720 | XY-K | Follower | Duty Carried Out. |
| F/O | Beck | J.A | RAAF | RA533 | XY-P | G-H Leader | Duty Carried Out. |
| F/Lt | Orman DFC | K.G | RNZAF | HK659 | XY-Q | G-H Leader | Duty Carried Out. |
| F/Lt | Mason | F.H | | HK801 | XY-S | Follower | Duty Carried Out. |
| F/O | Fernley | F | | HK794 | XY-T | G-H Leader | Duty Carried Out. |
| F/Sgt | Gray | P | | NG293 | XY-U | Follower | Duty Carried Out. |
| F/O | Godfrey | D | RAAF | RF126 | XY-V | G-H Leader | Duty Carried Out. |
| F/Lt | Hanson | R.A | | HK613 | XY-Y | Follower | Duty Carried Out. |

Wing Commander John Giles DSO, DFC. Born in 1910 in Shanghai, Wing Commander John Hassel Giles was educated at Victoria High School, British Columbia. He was commissioned in the R.A.F. in 1936. Awarded the D.F.C in August 1943, with No.90 Squadron, he was awarded the D.S.O. in March 1945. Hugely respected by the whole squadron, especially the Australians and Canadians, for this 'No-Bull' approach to command. He would often place himself on the Battle Order when a tough target was planned. Despite squadron commanders' once-a-month operations policy, he regularly flew with inexperienced crews, often without it being recorded in the Operational Records Book. John Giles DSO DFC was one of No.3 Group's and Bomber Command's exceptional squadron commanders. He would retire from the R.A.F in 1960 with the rank of Air Commodore. He died on October 11th 1988.

Once again, the now-familiar rendezvous point above Tonbridge was used before the Group flew south towards the Kent coast departure point. The weather was for once excellent, allowing the crews to see the patchwork countryside below. On crossing the English Channel, the force flew south of Calais and onto Arras. The weather continued to give the crews excellent visibility both above and below. The squadrons of No.3 Group divided their attention between two targets. Target 'A' was the Emscher Lippe Coking Plant at Datteln and target 'B' the Heinrichs Hutte Benzol Plant at Hattingen near Bochum. Target 'A' would be the responsibility of the squadrons of No.31 Base, which would be joined by 15 Lancasters of No.15 Squadron and 13 crews of No.622 Squadron. Target 'B' would be attacked by 60 Lancasters of No.33 Base plus 29 Lancasters of No.32 Base. The bombers flew in one single stream until they passed the small German town of Gemund. Here they split up and headed towards their individual targets. The Datteln force as expected, encountered remarkably accurate heavy flak on the run into the target. For twenty minutes, they were engaged by the defences of Wuppertal, Cologne, and Dusseldorf, and on the run-up to the target, it intensified even more. The old problem of poor formation keeping once again materialised as the whole force headed deeper into Germany. Flying Officer J Beck RAAF was one of the squadron's G-H Leaders, *'Stream was rather straggling, though individual formations were good'* This was confirmed by F/Lt A Marshall, *'Formation poor'* was his observation.

The intensity of the flak meant the initial marking was inaccurate, which was not surprising given the reception. Almost clear sky over Datteln gave the flak defences an ideal opportunity to engage the bombers. This they did with a ferocity that summed up the tenacity of the Luftwaffe Flakkorps. Three crews, F/Lt Sawyer, F/O's Beck and Verry RNZAF were damaged by flak prior to bombing but all three continued with their bomb runs. Over Datteln, several fires and explosions were observed. Flight Lieutenant F Mason witnessed a *'Terrific orange flash suggesting an oil explosion'.* Flying Officer D Godfrey RAAF was at 19,100 feet. He bombed on his G-H set at 16:39 hours. The experienced crew reporting on return, *'Several big explosions were seen around the canal bend north of the target. Seemed a slight overshoot but bombing very concentrated'.* The Lancaster's of F/O's Green and Fernley were peppered with shrapnel over the target area. Thankfully neither crew reported injuries. With the target bombed, the crews had to snake their way through the Ruhr defences back to safety. On this return leg, F/Lt F Mason had the misfortune of being damaged by a salvo of accurate flak with shredded his elevator controls aboard veteran Lancaster HK801 XY-S. The crew were forced to divert to RAF Woodbridge, where a successful landing was made at 18:10 hours.

No.186 Squadron Reported Flak Damage 14/03/1945

| Serial | Code | Damage | Repairs / Notes |
|---|---|---|---|
| PP669 | **XY-C** | Not Recorded | Repaired on Squadron. |
| NG146 | **XY-E** | Not Recorded | Repaired on Squadron. |
| NG354 | **XY-M** | Not Recorded | Repaired on Squadron. |
| RA533 | **XY-P** | Not Recorded | Repaired on Squadron. |
| HK801 | **XY-S** | Elevator / Tail damage | FB CAT Ac. RoS No.54 MU. Rtd 24/03/1945. |
| HK794 | **XY-T** | Not Recorded | Repaired on Squadron. |

The crew's concerns about the route proved correct. Thirty-two bombers reported flak damage attacking the Emscher Lippe Coking Plant at Datteln, with one crew forced to make an emergency landing at Brussels. Worse affected was the force allocated the Heinrichs Hutte Benzol Plant at Hattingen to attack. Thirty-four Lancasters of the 89 despatched were damaged, and one crew was missing. A total of 66 damaged Lancasters returned to the various airfields dotted across East Anglia.

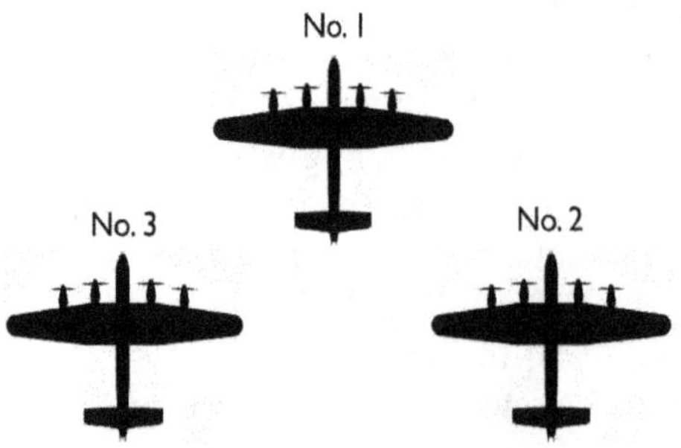


*The group continued to develop the GH Leader formation until VE Day. Above and below are three examples which were used from late 1944 onwards with varying success. The followers would be slightly below that of the GH Leader (No.1) when bombing. Above, the standard Vic formation of three aircraft, No.1 was the GH Leader. This became the generally excepted GH formation with the availability of more GH sets. (**Not to scale via No.3 Group Records**)*

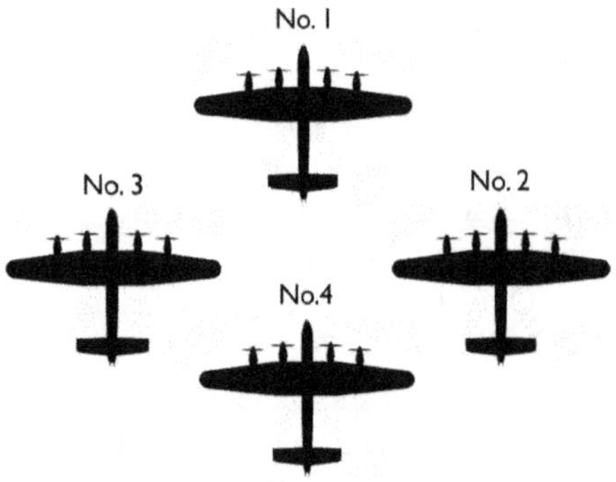


*The four aircraft formation, again No.1 was the GH Leader.*

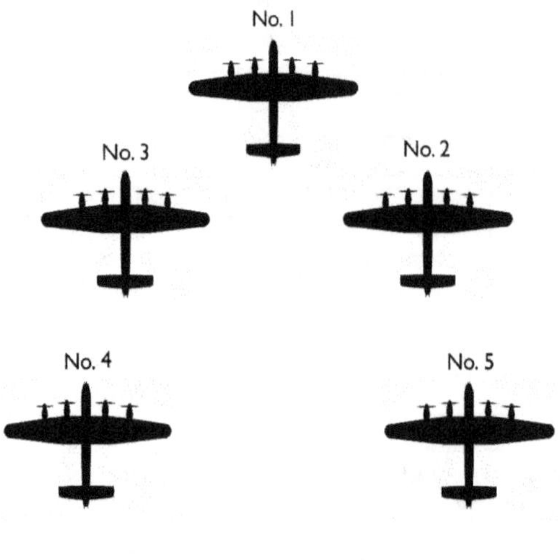


*The five aircraft formation. No.1 was the GH Leader and No.2 the Deputy. This formation proved difficult to maintain and was generally disliked by the crews.*

Early morning fog meant the squadron had a well-deserved day off on the 15th. It was a welcome pause, especially for the ground crews who had the luxury of a few precious hours to carry out essential maintenance and repairs. In their rubber boots, turtleneck sweaters, and sleeveless leather jerkins, they climbed up the scaffolding and clambered over every inch of their charges. Changing props, engines, turrets or patching up the flak holes. Ground crew were masters of improvisation. They needed to be on No.186 Squadron. On the 15th, the squadron was instructed to prepare ten crews for a daylight attack on the Chemical Works at Huls the following day. The Squadron Adjutant, Lt John Walker departed for some well-earned leave on the 15th. He was replaced by New Zealander F/O Frederick 'Fred' Rickard RNZAF.

On the 15th, copies of letters passing between General of the Army, Dwight D Eisenhower and Sir Arthur T Harris, Air Chief Marshal, Commander-in-Chief Bomber Command were received at RAF Stradishall. The following was included in the squadron ORB.

> *Dear Air Chief Marshal,*
>
> *March 6th 1945.*
>
> *I have just returned from a visit in the Julich, Duren, Munchen Gladbach area. As the Allies Armies advance into the former industrialised area of the Rhineland, there are everywhere confronted with the striking effectiveness of the bombing campaigns carried on for years by Bomber Command, and, since 1942, by the 8th Air Force. City by city has been systematically shattered. Against these, our artillery is often used to blast out pillboxes, snappers and hidden tanks, but it could scarcely add to the completeness of the material destruction. Here and there, possibly because of their relative unimportance as an industrial centre, certain towns have been largely spared. These present a remarkable contrast to the ruins of Aachen, Julich, Duren, Cologne and other Rhineland cities that have been targets by our big bombers day after day and night after night-Ht. The effect on the war economy of Germany has obviously been tremendous a fact that our advancing troops are quick to appreciate, and which unfailingly reminds them of the heroic work of comrades in Bomber Command and the United States Air Force.*
> *I should like all your units to know that the sacrifices they have made are today facilitating success on all fronts.*
>
> *Sincerely,*
> *(Signed) Dwight T Eisenhower.*

Harris could have asked for no more from Eisenhower, on March 10th he responded with a letter of his own. In it, he thanked Eisenhower for his tribute and summarized the work of his crews in preparing the way, concluding: '*The reward we have sought is to know that in the ruins of Germany's major war industrial areas the Armies already recognise a major cause of their own comparative immunity from the long drawn agonies and the fearful casualties of the last war'*.

On the morning of the 16th, RAF Stradishall was shrouded in fog, as was most of the region. So it was no surprise when orders arrived at 12:30 hours from No.3 Group HQ, cancelling the planned operation. Operations may have been cancelled, but there was much activity around the station. The station was visited by AVM R Graham CB CBE DSO DSC DFC Commandant of the RAF Staff College and a number of students at 10:00 hours. The group were there to observe first-hand the activities of an operational Bomber Station and squadron. However, these were not the only visitors on the 16th. The recent arrival of 'C' Flight and the importance of its secret work resulted in the visit of Major General Crawford CB MC, accompanied by Group Captain W.P.G Pretty OBE, the Development Director of Radar. Joining them was none other than AVM R Harrison, CB, CBE DFC AFC, AoC No.3 Group. The activities of 'C' Flight were, as far as possible, kept secret. However, the arrival of highly experienced crews and teams of radar 'boffin's and modified Lancaster's was hard to disguise. Nevertheless, security was paramount and many crews, even 50 years after the event, were unaware of the secret development work carried out by 'C' Flight.

Also arriving on the 16th was Wing Commander E.L Hancock and his crew who assumed command of the squadron vice the hugely popular W/Cdr J.H Giles DFC who was posted to Bomber Command HQ. Ernest Hancock was a former member of the Oxford University Air Squadron before being Commissioned into the Volunteer Reserve in December 1936. He joined 609 Squadron at Middle Wallop on 23rd September 1940 under S/Ldr Darley, coming from No.7 OTU. On 5th December, he was promoted to Flight Lieutenant under S/Ldr Robinson and was posted to an OTU (as an instructor) on 23rd January 1941 after just 4 months with 609. Prior to his arrival on No.186 Squadron, he had commanded No.578 Squadron, a H.P Halifax equipped unit of No.4 Group. His time with No.578 started back in September 1944, and by February 1945, he was the commanding officer. How he wangled a posting from 578 to 186 Squadron is unknown. The departure of W/Cdr Giles DFC was keenly felt throughout the squadron. His no nonsense approach and his dislike of 'Bullshit' endeared him to everyone, especially the Australians. He would be a hard man to follow. The squadrons of No.31 Base were given two separate targets on the 17th. Curiously, No.31 Base squadrons would divide it squadrons on two separate targets. Ten squadron crews were summoned for an early morning briefing, they along with No.218 Squadron would join forces with No.33 Base in attacking the Augusta Viktoria Coking Plant at Huls, while No.195 Squadron would attack the Gneisenau Coking Plant at Dortmund with No.32 Base.

<u>Form B.821 – March 17th 1945 (D): Target : Huls : Augusta Viktoria Coking Plant : GS162.</u>

| | | | | | | | |
|---|---|---|---|---|---|---|---|
| F/Lt | Sawyer | F.R | | HK802 | XY-L | Follower | Duty Carried Out. |
| W/Cdr | Cairnes | A.E | | PP668 | XY-B | Follower | Duty Carried Out. |
| W/O | Cooke AFM | S.F | | PP669 | XY-C | Follower | Duty Carried Out. |
| F/O | Tonks | J.E | | NG354 | XY-M | G-H Leader | Duty Carried Out. |
| F/Lt | Brayshaw DFC | S.C | | RA533 | XY-P | Follower | Duty Carried Out. |
| S/Ldr | Bass | R.W | | HK794 | XY-T | G-H Leader | Duty Carried Out. |
| F/Sgt | Holmes | E.O | RAAF | NG293 | XY-U | Follower | Duty Carried Out. |
| F/O | Perrett | M | | RF126 | XY-V | Follower | Duty Carried Out. |
| F/O | Godfrey | D.F | RAAF | HK796 | XY-W | G-H Leader | Duty Carried Out. |
| F/Sgt | Collinson | J.J | RAAF | HK613 | XY-Y | Follower | Duty Carried Out. |

The crews departed RAF Stradishall just after midday. The two bomber streams would again be routed together with No.32 Base spearheading the group. A three-minute gap would separate the formations approaching the targets from the North-West Ruhr. It would appear that No.3 Groups meteorological officer had made a boob of it. Over the continent, the crews encountered unexpected stronger than forecast winds and banks of clouds at 7,000 feet and again between 19,000 and 21,000 feet. The wind, estimated between 60-65mph, could be managed, just. However, the towering clouds presented far more challenging problems. Sandwiched between the cloud layers, the formation began to splinter. The second formation, flying a few minutes behind, had to contend with dense contrails, which made forward observation almost impossible. Crews began to spread out but retained some resemblance of a formation. South of the German town of Kevelaer, the two formations divided. The Dortmund force would attack first at 15:01 hours. Instinctively as the formation neared the target, the Lancasters began to tighten up as they followed the G-H signal pulse. This immediately caused problems for the followers. The vapour trails streaming from the lead formation made life unpleasant for those behind, whose forward vision was now practically nil. Regardless, the squadron somehow remained compact. Flying Officer D Godfrey RAAF, *'Concentration of aircraft over target seemed good despite cloud'*. Wing Commander A Cairnes was close behind his G-H Leader at 20,500 feet. He reported, *'No results seen but several aircraft bombed close by'*. The squadron reported no flak or fighters on return, and not a single crew had observed the target. The squadron provided ten crews on the morning of the 18th. Number 31 Base's No.195 Squadron sat the day's operation out. The squadron was responsible for leading 50 Lancasters drawn from both No.31 and No.32 Base for the attack against Hattingen and the Ruhstahl A.G Heinrichshutte Blast Furnace and Steelworks. The man given the responsibility was S/Ldr P Reynolds DFC. Joining the crew as 2nd Navigator was F/Lt W Earle, DFM Squadron Navigation Leader. The Deputy Lead role was filled by F/Lt A.J Clarson RAAF DFC crew.

Form B.822 – March 18th 1945 (D): Target : Hattingen: Heinrichshutte : GF2234.

| | | | | | | | |
|---|---|---|---|---|---|---|---|
| F/Lt | Field DFC | E.L | | PP668 | XY-B | Follower | Duty Carried Out. |
| F/O | Saunders | A | | NG137 | XY-D | G-H Leader | Duty Carried Out |
| F/O | Head | G.D | | NG146 | XY-E | Follower | Duty Carried Out |
| F/O | Verrey | G | RNZAF | NG140 | XY-F | Follower | Duty Carried Out |
| F/Sgt | Haynes | B.G | | NG149 | XY-G | Follower | Duty Carried Out |
| F/O | Roberts | D.M | | NN720 | XY-K | Follower | Duty Carried Out |
| S/Ldr | Reynolds DFC | P | | HK802 | XY-L | G-H Leader | Duty Carried Out |
| F/Lt | Clarson | A.J | RAAF | NG354 | XY-M | G-H Leader | Duty Carried Out |
| F/O | Beck | J.A | RAAF | RA533 | XY-P | G-H Leader | Duty Carried Out |
| F/Lt | Hanson | R.A | | HK684 | XY-O | Follower | Duty Carried Out |

Sadly a poor quality photograph of the crew of Flight Sergeant B.G.W 'Buss' Haynes. The operation on March 18th to Hattingen was their first of their tour.

Squadron Leader Reynolds DFC was the first away at 11:40 hours at the controls of Lancaster HK802 XY-L. It was a crew brimming with experience, F/O L Grant DFC was the Bomb Aimer, F/O D Greig DFC sat at his wireless set, while in the mid-upper turret perched P/O F Garrett DFM.

For once, everything seemed to go as planned. Forming up was quick and almost effortless. The route to Hattingen was completed without interference and the G-H pulse from the Cat & Mouse Stations was strong. Squadron Leader Reynolds DFC and crew arrived over the target at 20,000 feet meeting accurate predicted flak, which put several holes in the wings and fuselage. He reported at de-briefing, *'Bomber stream quite good over target. Nothing visible above cloud'*. The returning crews were all confident that the operation was accurate. Apart from two Blue Smoke Puffs ½ mile from the target, the markers were well grouped and concentrated. Flight Lieutenant R.A Hanson was forced to feather the port outer engine aboard Lancaster HK684 XY-O due to an oil leak on the return journey while two other crews reported flak damage. One unidentified aircraft burst a tyre on landing.

No.186 Squadron Reported Flak Damage 18/03/1945

| Serial | Code | Damage | Repairs / Notes |
|---|---|---|---|
| HK802 | **XY-L** | Not Recorded | Repaired on Squadron. |
| NN720 | **XL-K** | Not Recorded | Repaired on Squadron. |
| NG146 | **XY-E** | Not Recorded | Repaired on Squadron. |

On March 19th, the Mannesmannrohrenwerke Consolidated Colliery I / IV at Gelsenkirchen[46] was pinned up on the crews' operations board at RAF Stradishall, 79 Lancasters would be involved. Leading the entire force would be No.31 Base's No.195 Squadron's commanding officer, W/Cdr D.H Burnside DFC. The Deputy Group Leader role was given to fellow No.195 Squadron crew, F/Lt L.W Thorne aboard Lancaster PP665 A4-V. What followed was at best shambles. Nine crews would be involved in the events that unfolded.

Form B.823 – March 19th 1945 (D): Target : Gelsenkirchen: Consolidated :GQ1829.

| | | | | | | | |
|---|---|---|---|---|---|---|---|
| F/Lt | Sawyer | F.R | | HK767 | XY-A | Follower | Duty Carried Out. |
| W/Cdr | Cairnes | A.E | | PP668 | XY-B | Follower | Duty Carried Out |
| F/O | O'Brien | J.D | RAAF | PP669 | XY-C | G-H Leader | Duty Carried Out |
| F/O | Hart | J.H | | NG137 | XY-D | G-H Leader | Duty Carried Out |
| F/O | Gillespie | A.P | RAAF | NG149 | XY-G | Follower | Duty Carried Out |
| F/Lt | Tonks | J.E | | NN720 | XY-K | G-H Leader | Duty Carried Out |
| F/Lt | Brayshaw DFC | S.C | | HK802 | XY-L | Follower | Duty Carried Out |
| F/O | Burson | T.R | RNZAF | NG354 | XY-M | Follower | Duty Carried Out |
| F/Lt | Orman DFC | K.G | RNZAF | HK659 | XY-Q | Follower | Duty Carried Out |

Weather conditions over England would again produce confusion. Towering cloud banks reaching up to 10,000 feet above Tonbridge's rendezvous point meant that what should have been a reasonably simple forming up process became chaotic due to individual squadrons disregarding the briefed forming up procedure. As a result, despite W/Cdr Burnsides DFC's best endeavour, a disorganised formation finally headed towards Beachy Head. With No.31 Base leading, the 79 Lancasters made up from both No.31 and No.32 Base eventually crossed the English coast and set off across the Channel. Ahead of them was a towering mass of clouds. It was these that proved the formation's undoing. Somehow in amongst the clouds, both base groups became separated. Eventually, on emerging into a clear sky, it

[46] *The ORB records the target as Schalke, Gelsenkirchen. The 3 Group HQ and Raid reports record Mannesmannrohrenwerke Consolidated Colliery I / IV*

was discovered that No.90 Squadron had somehow manoeuvred itself in front of No.31 Base and was now leading the entire force. Realising their mistake and attempting to get back in position behind No.31 Base, the squadron first orbited Brussels and again over Liege. Frustratingly, most of the following formation faithfully followed, unaware of the mix-up that had unfolded. Upon his return, Flying Officer O'Brien RAAF reported, *'Stream orbited at Brussels and Liege, which made aircraft late on target. Could not see no reason for orbiting as a formation of Fortresses were well below and ahead and did not appear to be causing any obstruction'.* Flight Lieutenant Brayshaw DFC *'Formation was split up owing to the Leaders making two orbits'.* Little did he realise the leaders were the Tuddenham based No.90 Squadron.

The Motor Transport Section at RAF Stradishall circa 1945 poses for a group photograph. Note the number of smiling WAAFs in the photograph. They occupied most roles on the station, often working long, gruelling hours and encountering many dangers.

As the formation passed south of Dusseldorf, the cloud began to break up, and the flak increased. The Lancasters flying between 18,000 - 20,000 feet neared Gelsenkirchen in near-perfect weather. All the while, the flak had intensified dramatically. With No.90 Squadron leading and without the luxury of 'window', the forward formation was given a torrid time. Both barrage and box flak immediately had the correct height as hundreds of flak bursts punctured the sky amongst the bombers. Flying Officer T Burson RNZAF was ten minutes from the target when he was hit by flak. The port outer engine took the full force of an exploding flak shell rendering it unserviceable. Quickly feathered for fear of fire, the crew struggled to maintain formation on their G-H Leader. Thankfully the three remaining Merlins were undamaged and performed flawlessly. Somehow the crew managed to keep close behind their G-H Leader, F/O J.H Hart and drop with him. Making their curved approach, the crews had no option to fly through what appeared to be an impenetrable wall of flak. The clear conditions had one benefit, it allowed the crews to evaluate the accuracy of the bombing. Wing Commander A Cairnes lost his starboard inner engine to flak over the target area. With the engine on fire, the extinguisher button on the instrument panel was quickly pushed, and the engine was, once the fire had been extinguished, feathered. Also hit was F/O O'Brien RAAF. He had his No.3 fuel tank punctured aboard PP669 XY-C[47]. Regardless of the opposition, the squadrons carried out an incredibly accurate raid in the face of intense opposition. Flight Lieutenant Sawyer bombed at 16:15 hours, *'Saw columns of black smoke from*

[47] *The Station Records Books states that seven squadron Lancaster's were hit by flak.*

*target and bombs bursting in a good concentration'.* The target was left bathed in black, and dark brown smoke.

No.186 Squadron Reported Flak Damage 19/03/1945

| Serial | Code | Damage | Repairs / Notes |
|---|---|---|---|
| PP669 | **XY-C** | No.3 Fuel Tank holed. | Repaired on Squadron. |
| PP668 | **XY-B** | Starboard Inner | Repaired on Squadron. |
| NG354 | **XY-M** | Port Outer Engine | Repaired on Squadron. |

The squadron was not required on the 20th. Consequently, it gave most of the squadron personnel a well-earned rest. It was, however, a busy day for training. As usual, 'C' Flight crews were airborne, carrying out various bombing and navigational exercises. They had been aloft almost every day since their arrival. This lull, however, did not stretch as far as the ground crews, who had the crucial task of repairing and patching three damaged Lancasters. On the 21st, No.3 Group HQ switched its attention from oil targets to transportation hubs. Fourteen crews, half of which would be G-H Leaders[48] were detailed and briefed for a midday attack on Munster's marshalling yards. Headquarters decided on two aiming points, Target 'A' was the vital railway viaduct, while Target 'B' was the Marshalling Yards. Number 31 and 32 Base squadrons were allocated target 'B'.

Form B.825 – March 21st 1945 (D): Target : Munster : Railway Junction : G-H472.

| | | | | | | | |
|---|---|---|---|---|---|---|---|
| W/O | Cooke | S.F | | HK767 | XY-A | Follower | Duty Carried Out. |
| F/O | Verry | C.C | RNZAF | PP669 | XY-C | Follower | Duty Carried Out. |
| F/Sgt | Haynes | B.G | | NG146 | XY-E | Follower | Duty Carried Out. |
| F/Sgt | Hudson | A.L | RAAF | NG137 | XY-D | Follower | Duty Carried Out. |
| F/O | Robert | D.M | | NG149 | XY-G | G-H Leader | Duty Carried Out. |
| F/Lt | Clarson | A.J | RAAF | NN720 | XY-K | G-H Leader | Duty Carried Out. |
| F/O | Beck | J.A | RAAF | RA533 | XY-P | G-H Leader | Duty Carried Out. |
| F/O | Forland | J.M | RCAF | HK659 | XY-Q | G-H Leader | Duty Carried Out. |
| F/Lt | Manson | F.H | | HK794 | XY-T | G-H Leader | Duty Carried Out. |
| F/O | Godfrey | D.F | RAAF | HK796 | XY-W | G-H Leader | Duty Carried Out. |
| F/O | Perrett | M | | NG293 | XY-U | Follower | Duty Carried Out. |
| F/Lt | Hanson | R.A | | RF126 | XY-V | G-H Leader | Duty Carried Out. |
| W/O | Howell | A.J | RAAF | HK613 | XY-Y | Follower | Duty Carried Out. |
| F/Sgt | Collinson | J.J | RAAF | PD429 | XY-Z | Follower | Duty Carried Out. |

The squadron found the target free of cloud but partially obscured by smoke due to some accurate bombing by No.32 Group. Nevertheless, crews reported that a vast majority of the bombs appeared to have been accurately dropped on the Marshalling Yards, with the heaviest concentration at the northern end of the complex. A dense plume of smoke covered Munster, numerous fires were observed in the area around. The opposition was again fierce. A very accurate box barrage making life uncomfortable. The crew of F/Lt R Hanson summed up the operation at de-briefing, *'A good attack with bombs falling on the yards and one or two in the town. The south Aiming Point was well attacked. Fires seen burning. Formation good on the run-up to target and while bombing but was in three clusters until 50 miles of the target'* By a miracle, No.186 Squadron only report a single Lancaster damaged.

[48] *The Station Records Books states that seven squadron Lancasters were G-H Leaders. This is at odd with No.3 Group HQ. ( See Map*

No.186 Squadron Reported Flak Damage 21/03/1945

| Serial | Code | Damage | Repairs / Notes |
|---|---|---|---|
| NG146 | **XY-E** | Port Outer Engine. | Repaired on Squadron. |

The Lancasters of No.33 Base had taken the brunt of the flak defences. Upon return, over 50% of the force had sustained damage. The New Zealanders at RAF Mepal reported 13 Lancasters damaged, and Munster's flak claimed two crews, both shot down over the target area, while another was believed to have been lost when hit by falling bombs. The returning crews were confident that the attack was concentrated but raised doubts over the actual target attacked. The concerns were confirmed when No. 3 Group HQ discovered that the G-H coordinates for the two aiming points had inexplicably been reversed and the details for the viaduct given to No.31 and 32 Base, while No.33 Base had been given the Marshalling Yard coordinates. It had been a costly error, especially for the New Zealanders of No.75(NZ) Squadron. The squadron was called upon to attack Bocholt on the 22nd, the intention of which was to destroy enemy troop positions and supplies concentrated in the town. It would be another No.31 and 32 Base operation with No.32 Base taking responsibility for leading the raid. Fourteen crews were airborne from RAF Stradishall by 11:00 hours. It would be this operation where the new Squadron Commander, W/Cdr E.L Hancock would open his batting.

Form B.826 – March 22nd, 1945 (D): Target : Bocholt: Troop Positions.

| | | | | | | | |
|---|---|---|---|---|---|---|---|
| F/O | Head | G.D | | HK767 | XY-A | Follower | Duty Carried Out. |
| F/Lt | Field DFC | E.L | | PP668 | XY-B | G-H Leader | Duty Carried Out. |
| F/O | Hart | J.H | | PP669 | XY-C | Follower | Duty Carried Out. |
| F/O | Gillespie | A.P | RAAF | NG149 | XY-G | Follower | Duty Carried Out. |
| F/Lt | Tonks | J.E | | NN720 | XY-K | G-H Leader | Duty Carried Out. |
| F/O | Saunders | A | | NG140 | XY-F | G-H Leader | Duty Carried Out. |
| F/O | O'Brien | J.D | RAAF | HK684 | XY-O | G-H Leader | Duty Carried Out. |
| F/Lt | Brayshaw DFC | S.C | | RA533 | XY-P | G-H Leader | Duty Carried Out. |
| F/Lt | Orman DFC | K.G | RNZAF | HK659 | XY-Q | G-H Leader | Duty Carried Out. |
| S/Ldr | Bass AFM | R.W | | HK794 | XY-T | G-H Leader | Duty Carried Out. |
| F/O | Burson | T | RNZAF | PD429 | XY-Z | Follower | Duty Carried Out. |
| F/O | Idle | L.A | RNZAF | RF126 | XY-V | Follower | Duty Carried Out. |
| W/Cdr | Hancock | E.L | | HK796 | XY-W | Follower | Duty Carried Out. |
| F/O | Perrett | M | | HK613 | XY-Y | G-H Leader | Duty Carried Out. |

Once all the squadron was safely airborne, they were joined by twenty-nine crews supplied by No.195 and 218 Squadrons. These quickly formed up behind No.186 and headed for the rendezvous point where they took up station behind the 57 Lancasters provided by No.32 Base that would take responsibility for the operation. The ragged formation crossed the Belgium coast and headed towards Namur, where the fighter escort was collected. It was one of those rare days in March when the weather conditions over the continent were ideal, giving the crews unlimited visibility. These conditions reached as far as the target area where the town of Bocholt spread out far below. Ugly columns of black and brown smoke had already risen to 14,000 feet, which, mixed with a smoke screen laid by Allied troops on the front line, produced a scene of utter chaos below. With little opposition, the group carried out a textbook G-H operation. The squadron had a grandstand view of the accuracy of the proceeding bombers. Flight Lieutenant E.L Field DFC, *'Six aircraft bombed short, the remainder were well concentrated. Roads appear very congested'*. Australian F/O J.D O'Brien bombed at 14:06 hours from 19,000 feet, *'Large number of bombs were bursting in town area, but incendiaries fell slightly short. A columns of brownish black smoke rose to a great height and was visible from the coast on return'*.

Bomb load 1 X 4000 HC, 14 X 500 MC.
Target: MUNSTER. Weather: Clear over the target.
Bombed on Radar Navigational Aids leader at 13.15 hours from 18,000 feet. Bombs were well concentrated and light brown smoke rose to 8/9000 feet. Starboard Inner engine was only giving half power and this necessitated cutting corners to bomb with stream.

Bomb load 1 X 4000 HC, 1 X 500 MC, 12 X 500 AN-M64 & 1 X 250 Skymarker Blue. Target: MUNSTER. Weather: Clear over the target. Bombed on Radar Navigational Bombing Equipment at 13.13½ hours from 18,700 feet.
A good attack with bombs falling on the yards and one or two on the town. The South Aiming Point was well attacked. Fires were seen burning. Formation was good on the run-up and while bombing but was in three clusters until 50 miles of the target.

Flight Lieutenant K.G Orman RNZAF had a few uncomfortable moments when an unidentified Lancaster was seen directly above him with its bomb bay wide open while on his bomb run. Despite this, he recorded upon return, *'Smoke was billowing from the centre and north of town as aircraft ran in. East of town did not appear to be receiving any damage apart from one bomb, which appeared to explode there. South was hardly touched, but our bombs should have fallen there. Quite a lot of undershooting to the west of the town'.*

Opposition over Germany was almost non-existent. No squadron crew's reported damage, and all landed safely back at RAF Stradishall just before tea-time. The raid was, despite a few wayward bombs, devastating. The No.3 Group Record Book simply comments, *'A very good attack, centre of the town completely wiped out'.* The bombing had been concentrated and intense. The German defenders were obviously reeling from the bombardment as they put up little resistance as the Army entered the town within a few days.

On the 23rd, the London Gazette announced the award of the DSO to W/Cdr John Giles DFC. Every member of the squadron was delighted with this announcement. It could not have been awarded to a better commanding officer. He was a hardworking, courageous, and gallant leader who had led by example. He expected the very best from everyone on the squadron and got it. Unfortunately, there was no citation with the announcement, but in April 1945, Flight Magazine published the following.

*Since the award of the D.F.C., this officer has led his squadron on many daylight operations with courage and skill. He is an excellent squadron commander, who by his untiring efforts and unswerving devotion to duty, both in the air and on the ground, has set an inspiring example to all, and has materially contributed to the high standard of operational efficiency attained by the squadron.*

The same day, the award of the DFM was announced to airgunner, F/Sgt Dennis Parker, the citation reads.

*This N.C.O. is now on his second tour of operations. He has completed a great many sorties against heavily defended enemy targets and has always shown great determination and courage. His cheerfulness has done much to strengthen the morale of other crews.*

Three pilots were also recognised, Flight Lieutenants Thomas Phillips, Edward Ritson, and Sidney Smith. Also Alan Fleming RAAF. The group was again given a close support role on the 23rd. The penultimate raid on the hapless town of Wesel was to be conducted in preparation for the assault across the Rhine. Eight of the most experience G-H crews were detailed. All would bomb solely on G-H. Each Lancaster was loaded with 13 x 1000 pounders.

Form B.826 – March 23rd, 1945 (D): Target : Wesel : Troop Positions.

| | | | | | | | |
|---|---|---|---|---|---|---|---|
| F/Lt | Sawyer | F.R | | NG137 | XY-D | G-H Bombing | Duty Carried Out. |
| F/Lt | Clarson | A.J | RAAF | NG354 | XY-M | G-H Bombing | Duty Carried Out. |
| P/O | Beck | J.A | RAAF | RA533 | XY-P | G-H Bombing | Duty Carried Out. |
| F/Lt | Orman | K.G | RNZAF | HK684 | XY-O | G-H Bombing | Duty Carried Out. |
| F/Lt | Mason | F.H | | HK794 | XY-T | G-H Bombing | Duty Carried Out. |
| F/Lt | Hanson | R.A | | RF126 | XY-V | G-H Bombing | Duty Carried Out. |
| F/O | Godfrey | D.F | RAAF | HK796 | XY-W | G-H Bombing | Duty Carried Out. |
| F/Lt | Brayshaw DFC | S.C | | PD429 | XY-Z | G-H Bombing | Duty Carried Out. |

At the briefing, the selected crews were informed that troops of the British 2nd Army would be positioned within 1,500 yards from the aiming point and that extreme accuracy was essential. The Group had been specially chosen for the attack. Bomber Command HQ had put its trust in No.3 Group over the Path Finders and No.5 Group to deliver. Group detailed 80 crews, all of which were G-H equipped. The small force would rendezvous 10,000 feet over Tonbridge. Here over the hop-fields of Kent, No.31 Base slipped into position behind No.32 Base, which once again would take responsibility for the raid. The formation passed over Beachy Head on the south coast at 10,000 feet and began the slow climb to bombing height over the English Channel. There was some criticism directed at the flying discipline of the leading squadrons. Wing Commander Burnside DFC, Commanding Officer of No.195 Squadron, reported, '*Base ahead very strung out causing us to overlap their last aircraft*'. These sentiments were echoed by the crews of No.186 and No.218 Squadrons. North of Eindhoven, the formation started their run into the target. As the squadron crews started their curved approach, explosions were seen enveloping the aiming point, at 17:35 hours. The first of the squadrons 117 x 1000 pounders, started to drop onto the town below exactly on H-Hour. Flak opposition was confined to 3 or 4 isolated flak bursts. As the formation left the target area, it turned south, leaving behind a shattered town cloaked in a vast pall of smoke with flames engulfing whole areas of this once beautiful town. Flying Officer Beck RAAF reported, '*Whole area was obscured by clouds of smoke. No bombs were seen to burst outside target area. Bomber stream run was very good. An excellent attack*'. Bomber Command did not let the army down, and No.3 Group certainly did not let Bomber Command down. There was cause for a celebration on return from Wesel. Flight Lieutenant Frederick Mason had just returned from his 25th and last operation of his second tour. His crew would be taken over by Canadian F/O Harold Grass RCAF, another seasoned veteran. The good cheer did not finish there, another crew, and one of the squadron's most experienced would also be celebrating. Flight Lieutenant Roland Hanson and crew had returned from their 37th and last operation since their arrival from No.3 LFS in October 1944. The Wesel raid was their swansong.

Flight Lieutenant Walker, the Squadron Adjutant, returned from leave on the 24th, just in time to pin-up on the squadron notice board the following message from No.3 Group HQ.

> *Commando Force wish to thank Bomber Command very much for the very fine attack. Only one stick of bombs fell away from the aiming point, no damage resulted from this. Wesel was taken with only 36 casualties.*

The squadron was stood down on the 25th. It was just as well, it was a day of heavy rain and storms. The mutual back-patting continued on the 25th with the arrival of the following messages, from Field Marshal Montgomery.

> *To Air Chief Marshal Harris from Field Marshal Montgomery. I would like to convey to you personally and to all in Bomber Command my grateful appreciation for the quite magnificent co-operation you have given us in the Battle of the Rhine. The bombing of Wesel last night was masterpiece and was a decisive factor in making possible our entry into that town before midnight. Please convey my thanks to all your crews and ground staff'*

The C-in-C Bomber Command replied in his usual no-nonsense way.

> *Your message much appreciated by all in Bomber Command. We are glad to have played a direct part in this vital battle and look forward to meeting your further calls as they arise. Best of fortune to you all.*

The 'B' Flight crew of Flight Lieutenant Ron Hanson is standing in front of Lancaster HK613 XY-Y. Note the impressive bomb tally below the cockpit. The Vickers Armstrong built Lancaster was one of the batch transferred from No.90 Squadron in October 1944. Strangely HK613 was again transferred in April 1945 to No.195 Squadron at RAF Wratting Common, where it completed three bombing raids before VE Day.

General Dempsey also wrote to Harris, who penned.

*Thank you very much for a wonderfully accurate bombing last night. The Commanders send thanks and greetings to your crews and greatly appreciate their work.*

Harris's, response was short and to the point.

*Thanks for your message. Let us know whenever and wherever we can help.*

There was an unexpected but welcome lull in operations on return from Wesel. It gave the squadron time to draw breath. As usual 'C' Flight was busy flying secret tests over the flat Fens of East Anglia.

On the 27th, fourteen crews were detailed and briefed for operations. Two separate targets were to be attacked, No.31 Base would provide just two squadrons. Number 186 Squadron would join No.33 Base in attacking the Mansfeld A.G Coke plant at Sachsen located near Hamm. Over at RAF Wratting Common, No.195 Squadron would join forces with No.32 Base in attacking the Klockner Werk A.G Steinkohlenbergwerk (Coking plant) at Konigsborn, also situated a few miles Hamm. The crews of No.31 Base accustomed to flying with their family brothers-in-arms were not altogether pleased with being separated.

Form B.830 – March 27th, 1945 (D): Target : Hamm : Mansfeld A.G Coking Plant : GQ1855.

| | | | | | | | |
|---|---|---|---|---|---|---|---|
| W/O | Cooke | S.F | | HK767 | XY-A | Follower | Duty Carried Out. |
| F/O | Robert | D.M | | PP668 | XY-B | Follower | Duty Carried Out. |
| F/O | Hart | J.H | | PP669 | XY-C | Follower | Duty Carried Out. |
| F/O | Saunders | A | | NF137 | XY-D | G-H Leader | Duty Carried Out. |
| F/O | Gillespie | A.P | RAAF | NG149 | XY-G | Follower | Duty Carried Out. |
| F/Lt | Clarson | A.J | RAAF | NG354 | XY-M | G-H Leader | Duty Carried Out. |
| F/Sgt | Hudson | A.L | RAAF | NG140 | XY-F | Follower | Duty Carried Out. |
| F/O | Beck | J.A | RAAF | RA533 | XY-P | G-H Leader | Duty Carried Out. |
| F/O | Perrett | M | | LM692 | XY-R | Follower | Duty Carried Out. |
| W/O | Howell | A.J | RAAF | NG293 | XY-U | Follower | Duty Carried Out. |
| F/O | Idle | L.A | RNZAF | RF126 | XY-V | G-H Leader | Duty Carried Out. |
| S/Ldr | Bass AFM | R.W | | HK796 | XY-W | G-H Leader | Duty Carried Out. |
| F/O | Burson | T.P | RNZAF | HK613 | XY-Y | Follower | Duty Carried Out. |
| F/Sgt | Collinson | J.J | RAAF | PD429 | XY-Z | Follower | Duty Carried Out. |

After forming up over Tonbridge, both forces departed over Dungeness, the bleak headland on the coast of Kent. North of Aachen, the force rendezvoused with five squadrons of Spitfires and two RAF Mustang squadrons. The entire force skirted south of Cologne, then turned N.N.E towards Hamm. The G-H signals from the mobile ground stations were easily picked up by all five G-H squadron Lancasters affording the crews a smooth and relatively untroubled approach. The target was cloaked in 10/10th cloud, but unlike other bomber groups, it did not have any bearing on the operation's success. Slightly beyond the target, a small number of Red Smoke Puffs were observed, but the crews believed that these were decoys fired from below the clouds. New Zealander F/O L.A Idle was at 18,500 feet. He informed the Intelligence Officer back at RAF Stradishall, *'Huge black patches of smoke were rising to the tops of the white cloud over both aiming points. Bomber stream was fairly good. Attack seemed very concentrated'.* Flak was reported as meagre, resulting in the squadron reporting another clean sheet regarding flak damage. As the force turned north, two columns of oily black smoke began rising through the cloud. The columns were still visible 40 miles away on the return flight. Yet another highly accurate G-H operation was completed and made even more palatable with all the group crews returning. The final few days of March 1945 brought the welcome announcement of four DFCs awarded to the squadron. Flying Officer Frederick Mason and F/O Frank Richardson and two Canadians were honoured. Navigators Warrant Officer Norton James RCAF and P/O John Hartford RCAF. Part of John Hartford's citation reads.

*This officer has completed many operations against heavily defended German targets with excellent results. On one occasion the control surfaces of his aircraft were severely damaged by anti-aircraft fire. With great ingenuity and resource, Pilot Officer Hartford assisted his pilot to improvise repairs with ropes and then navigated the aircraft safely back to base. His excellent navigational skill, determination and devotion to duty at all times have been most noteworthy.*

The NCO were, for once, not overlooked. Crewmates Sgt Leonard Grice, Rear Gunner, and Wireless Operator Sgt Norman Wilman, who flew with F/Lt A.C Powell, received the DFM for their actions on October 30th, 1944. Leonard Grice's citation reads.

*On 30th October, 1944, this N.C.O. was rear gunner in an aircraft detailed to attack Wesserling. Before the target was reached, the aircraft was hit by heavy flak, wounding Sergeant Grice in the leg. Sergeant Grice remained at his post refusing to leave the turret until the aircraft had left the danger area. Sergeant Grice, after three weeks in hospital, returned to the squadron and has now completed his tour of operations.*

One of the Ruhr Valley's many Mine and Coking Plants. Once scorned by HQ RAF Bomber Command, these targets were quickly given priority in 1944. The G-H-equipped squadrons of No.3 Group were tasked to destroy these relatively small and well-defended targets. German mines were more highly mechanised than other European coal producers, allowing them to out-produce their neighbours. In 1938 the German coal output per man-hour exceeded Great Britain by one-third and doubled that of France and Belgium. Germany produced 187.5 million tons of coal between 1938 and 1939, before the invasion of Poland. Coal production increased between 1939-1944, reaching a peak of 268.9 million tons in 1944. This would dramatically fall during the last 12 months of the bomber offensive.

The final days of March 1945 were spent training. This was particularly true of 'C' Flight who had when weather permitted flown on every day since transferring from No.90 Squadron. On the 30th, two more crews arrived, one of which was F/Lt Olaf Cussen DFC & Bar.

In March 1945, No. 3 Group proved its worth as a strategic precision bombing group and a tactical bomber group. The Group flew 23 daylight G-H operations and a solitary night G-H raid throughout the month, inflicting crippling damage to Germany's oil and transportation facilities. The squadron flew 215 sorties, the lowest in the Group for March, dropping 1002.5 tons of bombs on German targets in the process. Despite the arrival of 'C' Flight, the squadron was effectively still only a two flight squadron. Once again, the squadron held its own when it came to training. Over four hundred hours were logged, but they were pipped for 1st place by No.514 Squadron with 431 hours. The squadron's gunners flew the most gunnery practice for March, totaling 160 hours. The crews of 'C' Flight had flown an incredible 287 training hours over the month, far more than some of the Group's three Flight squadrons. The squadron received a staggering sixteen new crews throughout March. Away from the monthly figures, the squadron had suffered no losses despite the intensity of operations. The overworked Ground Crews did themselves proud. Not a single early return was logged throughout the month, a remarkable achievement. March 1945 would record the appointment to commissioned rank on ten airmen. Three Canadians, three Australians and four RAF. Unusually seven were Air Gunners, one of those commissioned was the newly promoted Pilot Officer Gerald McPherson RAAF.

The only cloud over an excellent month was the departure of Wing Commander John Giles DSO DFC. His command style was uniquely Canadian, and his crews worshipped him for it. Flight Sergeant Phil Grey recalls an incident involving the C/O in the Mess.

*Someone, I think it was Wing Commander Giles, jumped onto one of the tables, threw off his jacket, and called for another drink. That drink and still other glasses appeared from the smoky shadows as if by magic. 'Off, off, off,' someone shouted, and everyone else seemed to take up the chant on cue. One by one the WingCo flung off his shoes socks, trousers, shirt, singlet, until he stood there in nothing but his underpants. Drink in either hand, balancing precariously on the table top, the Squadron boss now had his hands outstretched, making zooming noises and diving motions with his arms. The racket was fever pitch, and the flak started to fly around the room. Those of us spread here and there in different parts of the bar bunched newspaper pages into balls, set fire to them, and heaved them at the WingCo. He, in turn, tried to parry and avoid the missiles, still holding the drinks at arm's length. Someone got up on another table, then someone else. Soon we were all over the target again, planes rolling through, flak flying in all directions, only this time there were no losers. No one got shot down. Even at this stage though, anaesthetised by Gilbey's Gin and Johnnie Walker, some sixth sense told us that we had to hurry.*

March 1945 : Avro Lancaster Delivery.

| ToC Date | Serial | Code | Maker | Mark | From |
|---|---|---|---|---|---|
| 01/03/1945 | PP668 | XY-B | Vickers Armstrong | Mk.B.I | Works |
| 01/03/1945 | PP669 | XY-C | Vickers Armstrong | Mk.B.I | Works |
| 10/03/1945 | LM692 | XY-R | A.V Roe | Mk.B.III | No.149 Sqn |
| 10/03/1945 | SW267 | AP | Metropolitan Vickers | Mk.B.I | No.90 Sqn via S.I.U[49] |
| 10/03/1945 | SW272 | AP | Metropolitan Vickers | Mk.B.I | No.90 Sqn via S.I.U |
| 10/03/1945 | SW275 | AP | Metropolitan Vickers | Mk.B.I | No.90 Sqn via S.I.U |
| 10/03/1945 | PB448 | | A.V Roes | Mk.III | No.90 Sqn |
| 11/03/1945 | RF147 | AP | Armstrong Whitworth | Mk.B.I | S.R.U Defford |
| 12/03/1945 | PD429 | XY-Z | Metropolitan Vickers | Mk.B.I | No.106 Sqn |
| 13/03/1945 | RF198 | XY-N | Armstrong Whitworth | Mk.B.III | Works |
| 18/03/1945 | NG284 | | Armstrong Whitworth | Mk.B.I | S.R.U[50] Defford |
| 28/03/1945 | NF995 | XY-B | Armstrong Whitworth | Mk.B.I | No.195 Sqn |
| 31/03/1945 | LL854 | | Armstrong Whitworth | Mk.B.I | No.15 Sqn |
| 31/03/1945 | PB483 | XY-X | A.V Roe | Mk.B.III | No.149 Sqn |
| 31/03/1945 | PB509 | XY-Y | A.V Roe | Mk.B.III | No.149 Sqn |

[49] *S.I.U – Signals Intelligence Unit.*
[50] *S.R.U - Signals Research Unit.*

# April 1945

## *The Final Rounds.*

April 1945 started with the squadron being ordered to prepare for a daylight attack on the Echterdingen airfield at Stuttgart. The construction of this airfield started back in 1936, on a field that was famous locally as the site where Graf von Zeppelin's LZ-4 airship crashed and burned in 1908. Fifteen crews were detailed and brief when at 11:19 hours, the operation was cancelled.

The crew of Wing Commander Ernest Hancock are photographed while operational with No.578 Squadron, an H.P Halifax Squadron of No.4 Group. It would not have been an easy posting for the new Wing Commander. He was following a highly regarded commanding officer. He was an Englishman and a pre-war type. The crew, which he brought with him from No.578 Squadron are L-R Flight Sergeant 'Clem' Abrahams (Wireless Operator), Flight Sergeant Johnny Bellion (Mid Upper Gunner), Flight Sergeant Allan Kilberg (Navigator), Sergeant 'Dicky' Bird (Flight Engineer), Wing Commander Ernest Hancock (Pilot) Pilot Officer William Walker (Rear Gunner), and Flight Sergeant Ken Upton (Bomb Aimer).

On the 2nd, fourteen crews were detailed and briefed for a night attack on Kiel. This, too, was cancelled, much to the crew's annoyance at 15:20 hours. Two scrubs in two days was simply not on! Finally, on the 3rd, the squadron was stood down and put all its energy into training. Squadron Leader Harry Adman's DFC, No.31 Base Bombing Leader, was attached to RAF College Cranwell for a two-day Junior Commanders Course. On the 4th, a daylight attack was planned, but quickly cancelled, followed by the news that a night operation was planned. The target was the partly destroyed synthetic oil plant at Merseburg Leuna. This was one of Germany's largest synthetic oil producers and reportedly one of the most heavily-defended targets in Germany.

Form B.834 – April 4th, 1945 (N): Target : Merseburg Leuna : I.G Farben Leunawerks : GQ1515

| | | | | | | | |
|---|---|---|---|---|---|---|---|
| F/Lt | Field | E.L | | HK767 | XY-A | PFF Lead | Duty Carried Out. |
| F/O | Hart | J.H | | NG137 | XY-D | PFF Lead | Duty Carried Out. |

| | | | | | | | |
|---|---|---|---|---|---|---|---|
| F/O | Gillespie | A.P | RAAF | NG146 | XY-E | PFF Lead | Duty Carried Out. |
| W/O | Onus | M.J | RAAF | NG140 | XY-F | PFF Lead | Duty Carried Out. |
| F/Lt | Marshall | A.N | | NG149 | XY-G | PFF Lead | Duty Carried Out. |
| F/Lt | Sawyer DFC | F.R | | NN720 | XY-K | PFF Lead | Duty Carried Out. |
| F/Lt | Green | T.B | | HK802 | XY-L | PFF Lead | Duty Carried Out. |
| F/Lt | O'Brien | J.D | RAAF | HK686 | XY-O | PFF Lead | Duty Carried Out. |
| F/O | Beck | J.A | RAAF | RA533 | XY-P | PFF Lead | MISSING |
| F/O | Orman DFC | K.G | RNZAF | HK659 | XY-Q | PFF Lead | Duty Carried Out. |
| F/O | Fernley | F | | HK801 | XY-S | PFF Lead | Duty Carried Out. |
| F/O | Burston | T.P | RNZAF | NG293 | XY-U | PFF Lead | Duty Carried Out. |
| F/Sgt | Holmes | E.O | RAAF | RF126 | XY-V | PFF Lead | Duty Carried Out. |
| F/Sgt | Baker | L.G | RAAF | HK796 | XY-W | PFF Lead | Duty Carried Out. |

The fourteen crews departed just before 19:00 hours. It would turn out to be a costly night. The Group despatched 189 aircraft, of which No.31 Base provided a creditable 56 Lancaster crews. The operation would be carried out in conjunction with the Canadians of No.6 RCAF Group and controlled by No.8 Path Finder Force. The Lancasters of No.3 Group would follow the Canadians over the target with the squadron divided over the two waves. Once airborne, the Group's contribution headed for Reading and then out across the North Sea. Below them was a familiar dense layer of cloud. Thankfully, at the briefed bombing altitude visibility was excellent. Despite the excellent visibility, tragedy struck at around 20:20 hours when Lancaster RA533 XY-P flown by Australian F/O James Beck RAAF was struck by Lancaster KO-E HK555 of No. 115 Squadron. The collision gave both crews very little chance of survival as both Lancasters plummeted out of control. Wreckage from both aircraft was scattered between the Waldhof Elgershausen, 7 km south of Sinn, Germany. The only survivor was F/Sgt Alan Bartlett, the crew's Navigator. The bodies of the six crew were initially buried in the local cemetery at Ittenbach. Their bodies were later transferred in June 1947 to the Rheinberg War Cemetery.

| Type | Avro Lancaster Mk.I **RA533 XY-P** | **Metropolitan Vickers** |
|---|---|---|
| Taken on Charge | 28/02/1945 via No.218 Squadron. | |
| 'Category' | FB 'Missing' 04/04/1945 | |
| Struck Of Charge | 05/04/1945 | |
| Total Flying Hours | - | |
| Raids Flown | - | |
| Take-Off Time | 18:47 hours | |
| Bomb Load | 1 x 4000lb HC + 6 x 500lb | |
| | | |
| | **CREW** | **GRAVE** |
| Pilot | Flying Officer James Arthur Gordon Beck, DFC Aus/408434 RAAF. Age 24. | 14.A.20 |
| Navigator | Flight Sergeant Allan Edwin Bartlett, 139906 RAFVR[51] | Survived. |
| Bomb Aimer | Flight Sergeant William George Evans, 196117 RAFVR, age 21. (Promoted to P/O after killed) | 14.B.1 |
| Wireless Operator | Flight Sergeant Sydney Raymond Bacon Aus/423037 RAAF, age 21. | 14.A.10 |
| Mid Upper Gunner | Sergeant Albert Richard Baker, 2210627 RAFVR | 14.A.19 |
| Rear Gunner | Sergeant George Ballinger, 1592037 RAFVR, age 19. | 14.A.18 |

*[51] Allan Bartlett had survived a serious crash landing with No.50 Squadron in February 1944. Sergeant Baker is reported to have fought in the Spanish Civil War.*

| Flight Engineer | Sergeant Peter McNiven, 1826326 RAFVR | 14.B.2 |
|---|---|---|
| | | |
| Posted History | No.29 OTU 30/05/1944 – No.51 Base 10/09/1944 – No.5 LFS 08/11/1944 – No.186 Sqn 01/12/1944 | |
| Operations Flown | 28 | |
| Buried | Rheinberg War Cemetery | |

Flight Sergeant Sydney Bacon RAAF was seen to leave the aircraft by the sole survivor but sadly was found dead in a tree. Flying Officer Beck RAAF was awarded the DFC which was announced in the London Gazetted on April 6th 1945. The following is a report from the survivor.

SECRET.

STATEMENT MADE BY 1399016 FLIGHT SERGEANT BARTLETT A.E. - NAVIGATOR AT R.A.F. STATION [illegible] THIS 12th DAY OF APRIL 1945.

******

On the night of April 4th, 1945, I was Navigator of Lancaster bomber XY "P" of No. 186 Squadron, detailed to attack the LEUNA oil plant at MERSEBURG. The other members of the crew were:-

| | |
|---|---|
| Flying Officer James Beck DFC | Pilot |
| Flight Sergeant William Evans | Bomb Aimer |
| Flight Sergeant Sydney Bacon | Radio Operator |
| Sergeant Peter McNiven | Flight Engineer |
| Sergeant Albert Baker | Mid Upper Gunner |
| Sergeant George Ballinger | Rear Gunner. |

The timing of the attack was such that we were briefed to set course four minutes early and lose any time by carrying out the customary course alterations of 60° Port 120° Starboard 60° Port along a leg of the trip between a point North of [illegible] and a second turning point on the town of [illegible] for the amount of time we required to lose.

The trip proceeded according to plan until we had turned onto this leg, when I realised that I would arrive at [illegible] over five minutes early. I therefore warned the Pilot of my intention to carry out a "dog-leg" for that period of time.

The gunners were also warned, both by the pilot and myself of the necessity for maintaining a careful lookout for aircraft on converging courses and in the course of this manoeuvre they reported aircraft ~~aircraft~~ both to port and starboard, but clear of our own aircraft. We had turned onto the second leg of the "dog-leg" when, at approx. 20.20 hours we were rammed from the starboard by another Lancaster. Visibility at the time was very good, our height and airspeed were as briefed and our course true 116°.

At the impact, the front of the aircraft was smashed in and I felt the gale on my black-out curtain. (The bomb-Aimer was sitting at my side working H2S the rest of the crew were at their usual stations, flight engineer "windowing" from his position).

The aircraft continued in level flight for about six seconds then lost starboard wing and motors and went into a spin to starboard. The lights went out. The pilot gave the order for the emergency abandoning of the aircraft by yelling "Go, Go, Go" over the intercom. I disconnected my oxygen supply, slapped the W/Ops. leg, clippedon my chute and dived towards the escape forward hatch. I brushed past the pilot, who was still attempting to hold the aircraft straight for us to leave. There was a mix-up in the bombing hatch, bomb aimer trying to open it with assistance from the flight engineer, with bales of "window" from the stowage abaft the pilot's position falling down in the hatch. However after a period of time which I judge to be about 15 seconds the hatch was open and I fell through head first, with clouds of "window" brushing my face. I let myself clear of the aircraft, then pulled the rip-cord. My chute opened at once and I felt hardly any shock of opening. I realised my hand was cut but checked up to find if any bones were broken. Since none were, I proceeded to uncross the lift-webs of the chute and attempted to steer the chute towards a fire on the ground (the second Lancaster). However, after about three minutes I made a good landing on the edge of a wood and was hung up in the trees. I operated the quick release and droppedthefew feet to earth. I then headed towards the fire shouting and blowing my whistle to attract the attention of other survivors, as I was aware that I was well behind the path of the American spearheads, and in what I thought was "friendly" territory. However, within ten minutes I was picked up by the combat engineers of the (I think) 360th Battn, who informed me that I was lucky enough to fall on the fringe of a resistance pocket south of [illegible]. They took me to their Colonel, but on the way I stopped to identify thebodies of Bacon and Baker. When I saw the colonel I produced my identity card and asked whether he could spare some men to look for the four crew-men unaccounted for. He at once sent his entire company to search the area east of the wreckage, since I informed him the wind was westerly, and would blow chutes into the woods in that area. He then had me taken to the 67th Evacuation Hospital, attached to the 8th (Golden Arrow) Division, 1st. American Army, where my hand was treated and I was fed and given quarters. Throughout my stay with the American Forces I had every kindness and consideration shown to me and I am very grateful to the staff of this hospital, especially Capt. Larribee, the registrar, who did everything in his power to relieve me of any anxiety and worry.

Flight Sergeant Allan Bartlett, the Navigator and sole survivor from Lancaster RA533 XY-P describes the events of the fateful night his crew met their deaths and how he miraculously survived.

Flying Officer James Arthur Gordon Beck, DFC, RAAF.

The ever-resilient German night fighters, including some jets, were active. Combats were observed, but fortunately, none involved the squadron prior to the target. Three crews experienced engine problems before bombing. Flight Lieutenant O'Brien RAAF lost his starboard inner engine due to an oil leak aboard Lancaster HK684 XY-O at 20:15 hours. The engine was duly feathered, and the crew opted to continue onto the target. Also in trouble was New Zealand F/O Thomas Burston RNZAF. He had problems with the port inner engine aboard Lancaster NG293 XY-U ten minutes before the target. The rapidly overheating engine was feathered, but his problems continued. The port outer engine immediately started showing signs of trouble when it began to lose power preventing the crew from maintaining altitude. But, with the target in sight, they too bravely continued on. At around 22:47 hours, the Lancasters of No.3 Group arrived on the outskirts of Merseburg. They were disappointed to find practically no markers, and those visible were quickly disappearing. Flight Lieutenant E.L Field was forced to feather the port outer engine aboard Lancaster HK767 XY-Y when it started to over-rev while on his bombing run. To add to his problems, the port aileron also became unserviceable, but despite the difficulties, the crew managed to bomb on the centre of a cluster of red and green stars.

One of the first to bomb at 22:50 hours was Flight Lieutenant O'Brien RAAF from 19,500 feet despite losing an engine. Flight Lieutenant T Green was over the target at 22:53 hours, *'Only one bunch of TI's Green were seen when bombing. Skymarkers disappeared on approach and were not backed-up by Path Finder Force'*. Flight Lieutenant F.R Sawyer DFC and crew were convinced that some Skymarkers were spoofs *'thrown up by the enemy'* he reported on return. Flying Officer T Burston RNZAF was the last squadron crew over the target at 23:02 hours, and they deposited their bomb load into the middle of an area well ablaze. The crew of F/Sgt E Holmes RAAF had successfully bombed at 22:56 hours and were now settling down for the long flight home and their bacon and eggs breakfast.

Left & Above : Flight Sergeant William George Evans, RAFVR

Flight Sergeant Sydney Raymond Bacon, RAAF.

Sergeant Albert Richard Baker, RAFVR.

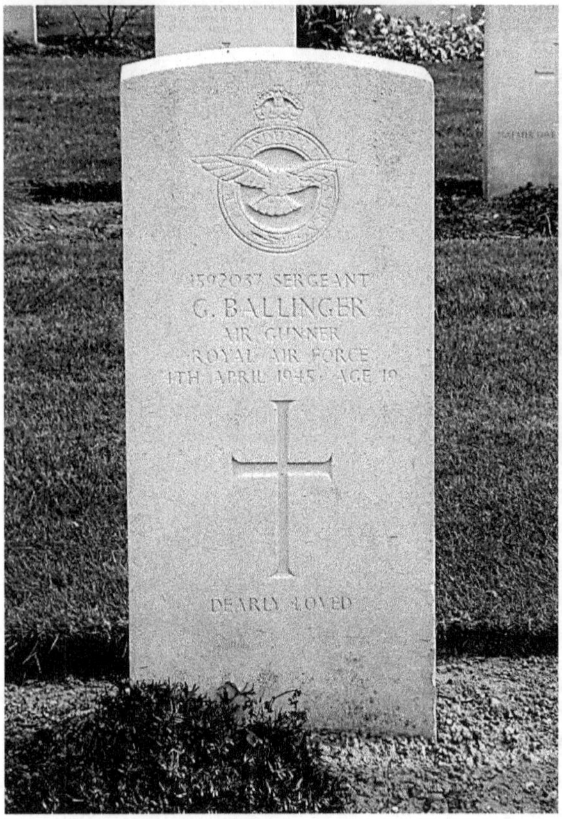


Sergeant George Ballinger, RAFVR.

Sergeant Peter McNiven, 1826326 RAFVR

Having reduced their height by 5,500 feet, the crew were flying over the town of Grossbreitenbach when at 23:15 hours, the rear gunner, Sgt K Cartwright, sighted a twin-engined Me210 fighter. The crew submitted the following Combat Report.

> Me210 first sighted at 400 yards starboard quarter down when order to corkscrew to starboard was given. Fighter closed in, and rear gunner opened fire. No hits were observed, and fighter broke away, port quarter up and was not seen again.

The night's activities were not over. Flight Lieutenant Field was approaching to land when his port inner engine suddenly developed a problem, giving the young pilot no chance of keeping the Lancaster airborne despite his valiant attempts. The impact on the fertile Suffolk soil was quick and catastrophic. The Lancaster came to a shuddering halt, crumpled and broken. The crew miraculously survived, with only two suffering severe injuries. The rear turret had broken off, and the unfortunate gunner, F/Sgt Turner, was found fifty feet away from his turret. On being admitted to the RAF Hospital at Ely, it was discovered he sustained a broken left ankle and femur, facial abrasions and, more seriously, a fractured skull. His injuries were such that he was not expected to survive. It would be 14 months before he had made a full recovery. Less injured was the crew's Flight Engineer, Sgt W.J Enright. Standing beside his skipper, he was flung violently forward on impact and sustained multiple fractures. The shattered Lancaster had been torn apart aft of the mid-upper turret. The nose section had crumpled on hitting the ground, completely ripping off the front turret. The cockpit was torn in half behind the pilot's seat. It was a miracle that anyone survived. Flight Lieutenant Edgar Field DFC would be awarded a Bar for his actions this night. Now accustomed to marking their own targets, the experienced crews were critical of the Path Finders. To add to the problems, they had difficulties hearing the Master Bomber, Wing Commander Hugh 'Speed' LeGood DFC of No.35 Path Finder Squadron Code name ZIP FAST.

| Type | Avro Lancaster Mk.I **HK767 XY-A** | **Vickers Armstrong** |
|---|---|---|
| Taken on Charge | Not recorded on AM Form 78 | |
| 'Category' | CAT E/FB 05/04/1945 | |
| Struck Of Charge | 16/04/1945 | |
| Total Flying Hours | - | |
| Time of Crash | 03:00 hours | |
| Take-Off Time | 18:43 hours | |
| Bomb Load | 1 x 4000lb HC + 6 x 500lb | |
| | **CREW** | **Notes** |
| Pilot | Flight Lieutenant Edgar Field DFC | Survived, minor injuries. |
| Navigator | Flight Sergeant P.A Upson | Survived, minor injuries. |
| Bomb Aimer | Flying Officer G.W Littleboy | Survived, minor injuries. |
| Wireless Operator | Flight Sergeant C.J Morris | Survived, minor injuries. |
| Mid Upper Gunner | Sergeant W.R O'Connell | Survived, minor injuries. |
| Rear Gunner | Flight Sergeant C.F Turner | Survived admitted Ely Hospital. |
| Flight Engineer | Sergeant W.J Enright | Survived admitted Ely Hospital. |
| | | |
| Posted History | Posted via No.3 LFS 20/10/1944 | |
| Operations Flown | 33 | |

The shattered wreckage of Avro Lancaster HK767 XY-A was skippered by Flight Lieutenant Edgar Fields DFC.

Wing Commander Hugh LeGood DFC interestingly reported on his return that in his opinion, the main force bombing was generally poor, and only 25% of the bombs fell in the target area. There was no mention of being late or the lack of markers! The raid inflicted little if any fresh damage on the oil plant. The following day, yet another new name appeared on the Operations Board, Plauen, located in the Lower Saxony region of Germany. Fourteen crews were briefed for a night attack, but this was cancelled at 15:40 hours. On the 6th, the day was spent training. Flight Lieutenant Jack O'Brien RAAF and crew were screened on completion of this operation having flown an impressive 38 raids. What should have been a reason to celebrate turned into a drink to remember and honour the memory of F/O James Becks RAAF on the announcement of his DFC. His Citation reads.

Two more views of the mangled wreckage of Lancaster HK767 XY-A. The crew's survival was a testement to the flying skill of Flight Lieutenant Field DFC and the sturdy construction of the Avro Lancaster,

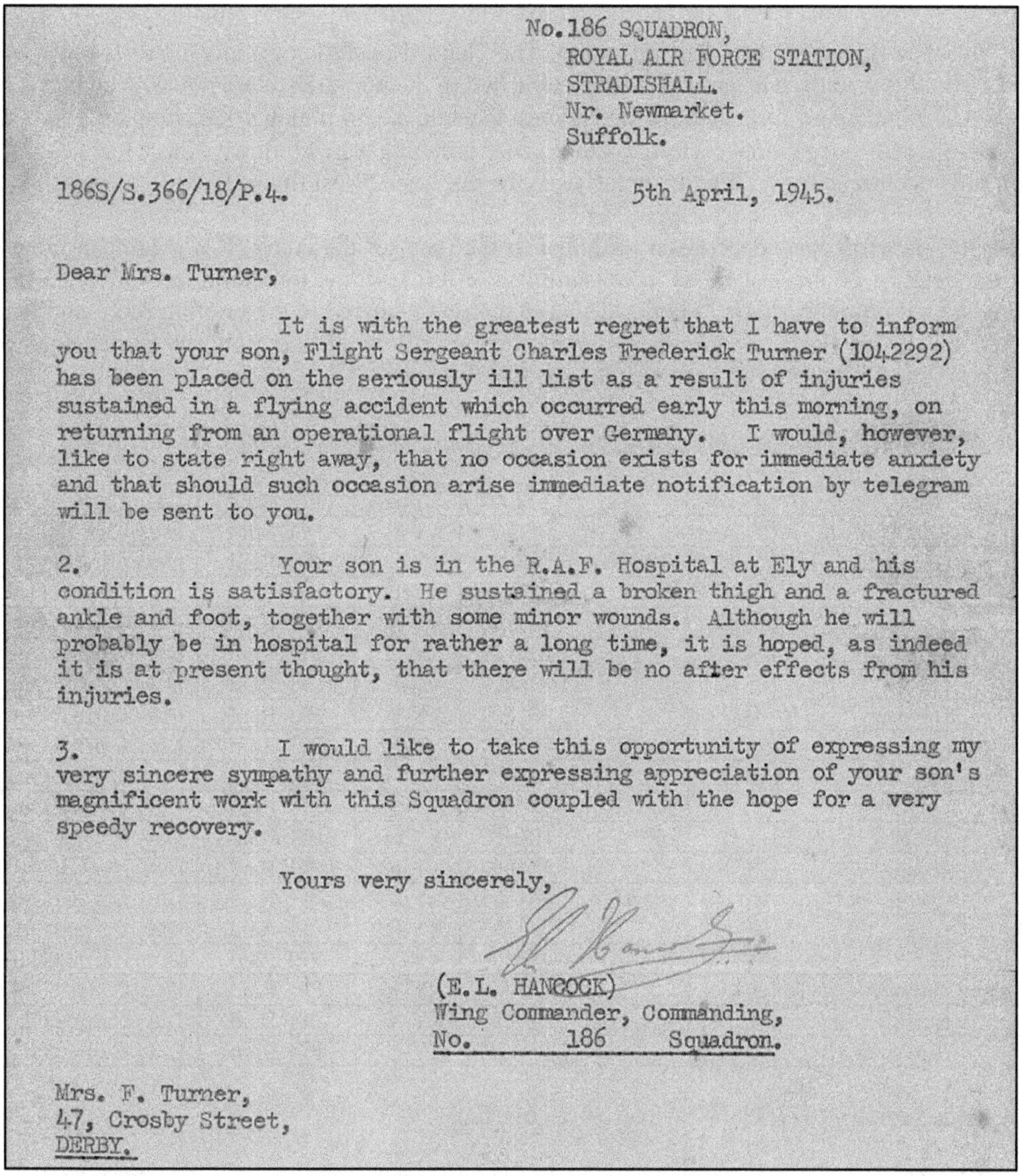
No.186 SQUADRON,
ROYAL AIR FORCE STATION,
STRADISHALL.
Nr. Newmarket.
Suffolk.

186S/S.366/18/P.4. 5th April, 1945.

Dear Mrs. Turner,

It is with the greatest regret that I have to inform you that your son, Flight Sergeant Charles Frederick Turner (1042292) has been placed on the seriously ill list as a result of injuries sustained in a flying accident which occurred early this morning, on returning from an operational flight over Germany. I would, however, like to state right away, that no occasion exists for immediate anxiety and that should such occasion arise immediate notification by telegram will be sent to you.

2. Your son is in the R.A.F. Hospital at Ely and his condition is satisfactory. He sustained a broken thigh and a fractured ankle and foot, together with some minor wounds. Although he will probably be in hospital for rather a long time, it is hoped, as indeed it is at present thought, that there will be no after effects from his injuries.

3. I would like to take this opportunity of expressing my very sincere sympathy and further expressing appreciation of your son's magnificent work with this Squadron coupled with the hope for a very speedy recovery.

Yours very sincerely,

(E.L. HANCOCK)
Wing Commander, Commanding,
No. 186 Squadron.

Mrs. F. Turner,
47, Crosby Street,
DERBY.

The letter sent to the mother of Flight Sergeant Turner, Rear Gunner aboard Avro Lancaster HK766 XY-A informing her that her son was admitted to the RAF Hospital at Ely. Charles would in October 1945 be awarded a DFM for his actions on this and other operations.

*In February 1945, this officer piloted an aircraft detailed to attack Wesel. On the take-off run the tyre on the starboard wheel burst, causing the axle to drag along the runway and break up. The starboard wing dropped and the aircraft swung wildly. Flying Officer Beck succeeded in straightening the aircraft. In gaining height he narrowly missed a hanger. After much difficulty the part of the undercarriage which had not been ripped away was retracted and Flying Officer Beck went on to the target and bombed it. On reaching an airfield in this country after completing his mission he executed a masterly landing with the undercarriage retracted. This officer has completed numerous sorties and has invariably displayed the highest standard of skill and resolution. He is an excellent captain whose finer qualities have been well reflected in the operational efficiency of his crew.*

April 7th was a day of anxiety and frustration. The planned operation against the docks at Kiel was cancelled at 13:00 hours. The target was then switched to the port area of Hamburg, which was again cancelled at 17:40 hours. Despite the cancellations, a hectic day of training was completed. Low-level bombing, Special Navigational exercises, and practice bombing were all flown. These were augmented by the daily occurrence of 'C' Flight aircraft carrying out 'secret' test flights.

On the 9th, the target was once again Kiel, and to the relief of the crews, it was not cancelled. The squadron detailed 20 Lancasters, its most significant effort since its formation in October 1944. The briefing started promptly at 15:30 hours. The 140 aircrew gathered in the briefing room and listened carefully as W/Cdr Hancock gave the assembled crews details on the night's activities against the Deutsche Werkes which would be marked by the Path Finders.

Form B.837 – April 9th, 1945 (N): Target : Kiel : Deutsche Werkes : Minnow 'D'

| | | | | | | | |
|---|---|---|---|---|---|---|---|
| F/O | Head | G.D | | LM697 | XY-A | PFF Raid | Duty Carried Out. |
| F/Sgt | Rose | B.A | | PP668 | XY-B | PFF Raid | Duty Carried Out. |
| F/O | Gillespie | A.P | RAAF | PB139 | XY-C | PFF Raid | Duty Carried Out. |
| W/O | Onus | M.J | RAAF | NG136 | XY-D | PFF Raid | Duty Carried Out. |
| F/Lt | Sawyer | F.R | | NG146 | XY-E | PFF Raid | Duty Carried Out. |
| F/Lt | Marshall | A.N | | NG149 | XY-G | PFF Raid | Duty Carried Out. |
| F/Lt | Green | T.B | | PB488 | XY-J | PFF Raid | Duty Carried Out. |
| F/Sgt | Haynes | B.G | | HK802 | XY-L | PFF Raid | Duty Carried Out. |
| F/Lt | Clarson | A.J | RAAF | NG354 | XY-M | PFF Raid | Duty Carried Out. |
| W/Cdr | Hanock | E.L | | RF198 | XY-N | PFF Raid | Duty Carried Out. |
| F/O | Godfrey | D.F | RAAF | LM543 | XY-P | PFF Raid | Duty Carried Out. |
| F/Sgt | Baker | L.G | RAAF | HK659 | XY-Q | PFF Raid | Duty Carried Out. |
| F/O | Fernley | S | | LM692 | XY-R | PFF Raid | Duty Not Carried Out. |
| F/Sgt | Collinson | J.J | RAAF | HK801 | XY-S | PFF Raid | Duty Carried Out. |
| F/O | Gray | P | | NG293 | XY-U | PFF Raid | Duty Carried Out. |
| F/O | Idle | L.A | RNZAF | RF126 | XY-V | PFF Raid | Duty Carried Out. |
| F/Sgt | Holmes | E.O | | PB483 | XY-X | PFF Raid | Duty Carried Out. |
| F/O | Burson | T.P | RNZAF | PB509 | XY-Y | PFF Raid | Duty Carried Out. |
| F/Lt | Brayshaw DFC | S | | PD429 | XY-X | PFF Raid | Duty Carried Out. |

The recently promoted F/O Phil Gray recalls the briefing.

> *'Kiel, Gentlemen, is your target for tonight.' The Wing Commander gave the initial details of this port on the Baltic Sea, placed approximately 100 kilometres north of Hamburg. 'Geographically,' the WingCo continued, 'it's out on a limb of land, meaning that we can do quite a bit of flying over the North Sea before submitting ourselves to the agony of their ack-ack guns. So try to stay clear of their radar, our altitude on this leg will be 1,500 feet. That's low, and the water's not very far away, so be careful.' Other officers from Met, Armaments, Navigation and Intelligence came forward with their input. Take-off times would be between 2200 and 2210 hours, each bomber loaded with one blockbuster and twelve 500-pound bombs. Fuel load was 1,700 gallons, specific aiming points being warships and shore installations. There will be 584 bombers up there tonight,' Wing Commander Flying concluded the briefing, 'roughly half of them from 3 Group'.*

The once-mighty German fleet was now cowering in Kiel harbour. The heavy cruiser Admiral Scheer, along with the cruisers Admiral Hipper and Emden, had been forced to find refuge in the relative safety of the massive port. The first crew away was 'A' Flight's F/Lt M.J Onus RAAF at the controls of Lancaster NG136 XY-D at 19:22 hours. Seventeen minutes later, the 19th and final crew skippered by the F/Lt F.R Sawyer departed aboard 'A' Flight's Lancaster NG146 XY-E. One crew was withdrawn before take-off. Once safely airborne, the squadron headed north towards the departure point of Whitby on the North Yorkshire coast. For the vast majority of the squadron, this would be their first experience of flying over the inhospitable North Sea and attacking targets located in the northern coastal region of Germany.

The raid would be controlled by the Path Finders and carried out in conjunction with 260 Lancasters of No.1 Group. There was just one early return from the squadron, the crew of F/O F Fernley. Over the North Sea, the starboard inner engine aboard Lancaster LM692 XY-R started to show worrying signs of trouble, firstly with a radiator leak. The engine then caught fire, forcing it to be feathered. Once the fire had subsided, and with the engine feathered, the crew decided to continue on, hoping they could reach the briefed bombing height. However, it was soon evident that this was impossible. The 4000 pounder was jettisoned, and slowly the Lancaster clawed a few extra thousand feet. Unfortunately, despite this gallant effort, the crew wisely jettisoned the remaining bomb load and turned for home, landing on three engines at 00:36 hours. Considering the distance, it is no surprise that fighter opposition was encountered. Both NJG2 and NJG3, old adversaries, were airborne and on the prowl. The first encounter was timed at 22:28 hours. Flying Officer L. Idle RNZAF was approached by a Me410 from the port quarter down. A two-second burst from the rear gunner, Sgt A.G Philery, was sufficient to deter the fighter[52]. The Lancasters of No.3 Group were to bomb Aiming point 'D', the Deutsche Werke. They were equally divided over the two waves timed to bomb between 22:30 and 22:40 hours. Mixed with 238 Lancasters of No.3 Group were sixty aircraft of No.1 Group. The remaining Lancasters of No.1 Group were given AP 'E' to attack.
They would be controlled by Squadron Leader Vivian Owen-Jones of No.582 Path Finder Squadron. On arrival, fighter flares were hanging ominously over the dock area mixed with a steady volume of heavy flak. The Master Bomber for Aiming point 'D' was the experienced Wing Commander Donald 'Tex' McQuoid DFC & Bar of No.405 RCAF Squadron (code name Buzzbomb). With the situation constantly changing over the aiming point, Wing Commander McQuoid's clear and calm Canadian voice could be heard instructing and encouraging the main force to bomb a number of concentrated Green and Red TI markers. The crews were enthusiastic about the raid and marking with excellent visibility over the target and clear instructions from the Master Bomber. Warrant Officer Onus RAAF, *'Markers were punctual, and target clearly identified'* was his report on return. Wing Commander Hancock was over the Docks at 22:35 hours He reported, *'Smoke and flames were seen from own aiming point. Appeared to be a very satisfactory attack'.* A sizeable crimson explosion was witnessed at 22:40 hours, illuminating the dock area. Numerous exploding 'cookies' were seen obliterating the markers. The docks seemed to shudder under the onslaught, and the whole dock area seemed a mass of flames. Flying Officer D Godfrey RAAF was one of the last over the target at 22:44 hours. He had experienced trouble en route to Kiel when his veteran Lancaster LM543 XY-P was unable to climb to the briefed bombing altitude and keep to the speed given at briefing. At just 16,000 feet, the crew were obliged to make a second run over the target. Unfortunately, no markers were available on their first bomb run other than those on the Northern Aiming Point. Thankfully, a few Green TIs were visible on the second run into the target. It was on the return flight that F/Lt A Marshall and crew had the first of two fighter encounters. The first combat was at 23.11 hours at 14,000 feet. An Fw190 was observed on the port quarter down at 300 yards. The rear gunner F/O Aspin gave the order to corkscrew starboard. At the same time, both gunners opened up with a three-second burst which was enough to discourage the German pilot. Thirty minutes later, the crew were at 6000 feet when a JU88 was observed again by the vigilant rear gunner, 600 yards astern. The combat report records the following.

[52] *The Combat Report for this encounter incorrectly records the aircraft as LM692 XY-R.*

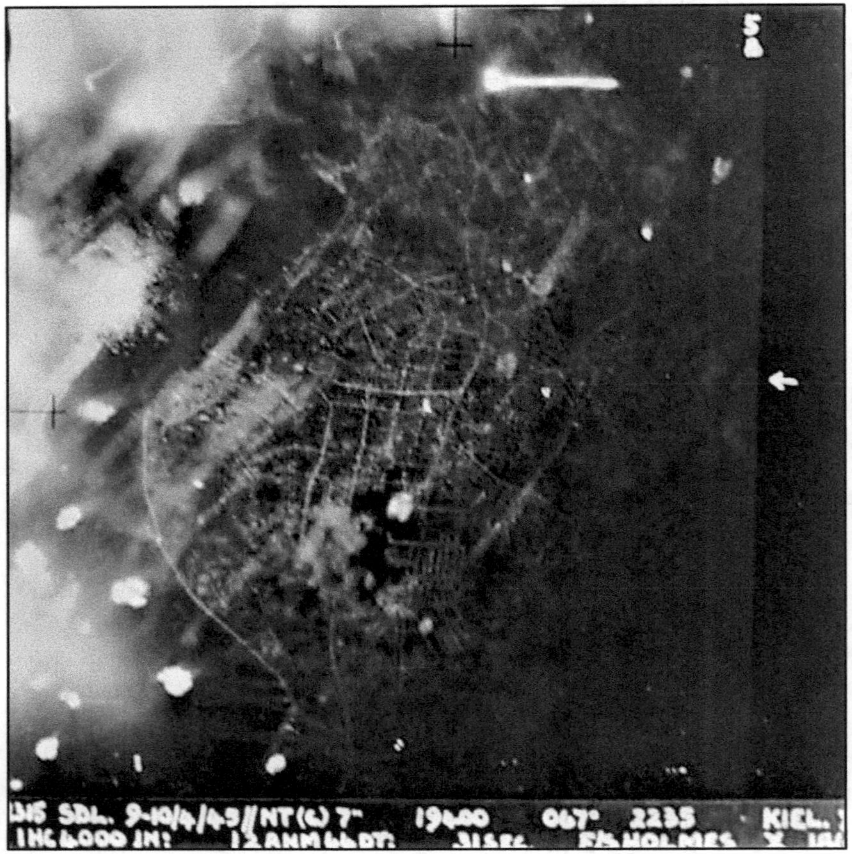


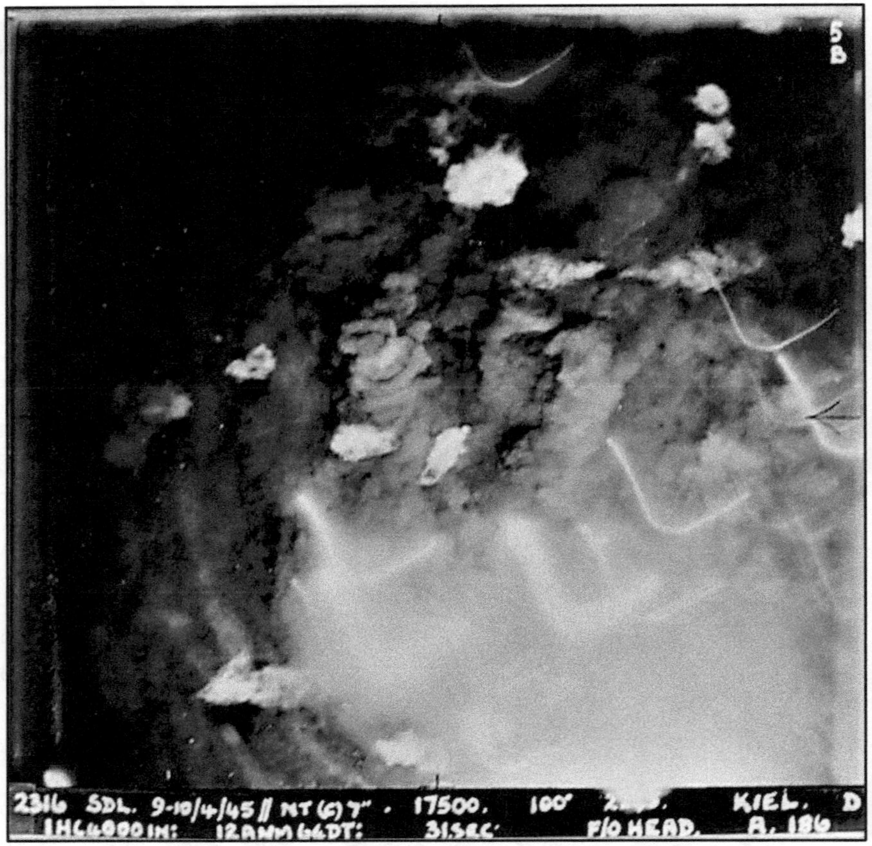


Two Bombing Photographs taken over Kiel on April 9th 1945. Left : photo was taken by Flight Sergeant Holmes and crew on only their third operation. This shows how clear the conditions were when the crew bombed at 22:35 hours from 19,400 feet. It was a very different story ten minutes later when F/O Head and crew arrived over the Aiming Point at 22.45 hours. Dense smoke, searchlights, and explosions cover the target in this photograph, taken from 17,500 feet.

Enemy aircraft was first seen at 500-600 yards dead astern down. He followed the bomber for about 3 minutes closing very slowly. When at 500 yards rear gunner gave the corkscrew starboard and opened fire. Fighter returned fire and closed in to 300 yards before breaking away below bomber. Hits were registered on fighter as he closed in, and as bomber began to weave in order that the crew could search, rear gunner saw a parachute going down.

Post-raid reconnaissance established that the Deutsche Werkes shipyard had been heavily damaged, and the vital transformer station and turbine engine workshops were also severely hit. There were two noticeable successes. Birthed in the Ausrüstungsbecken (fitting out basin) was the mighty Admiral Scheer. The sleek and modern cruiser's first overseas deployment began in July 1936 when she was sent to Spain to evacuate German civilians caught amid the Spanish Civil War. Since then, she had been the scourge of the Royal Navy. Now almost ten years on, she lay capsized. Also damaged was the heavy cruiser Emden which was in the Deutsche Werke dockyard for repairs. It had been a devastating raid. Flight Sergeant Harold Peak, Navigator to F/Sgt Baker RAAF recounts the de-briefing on return from Kiel.

> *The luxury of the flying breakfast with its attendant bacon and eggs and the combination of eagerness, excitement and apprehension which prevailed in the atmosphere of a crowded briefing room. The de-briefing and interrogation after ops. with the mug of 100% proof rum poured from a stone jar in a wicker basket... In particular the de-briefing after our first Kiel raid on the 9/10th April on which we apparently bombed a dummy target. I hope it doesn't sound arrogant when I say this was not due to a navigation error, but to an enthusiastic crew being deceived by an excellent imitation set up by Jerry. We subsequently returned very much off track which might have proved to be catastrophic, however, apart from a few red faces, all was forgiven and we went again four nights later with a little more success as indicated on the Ops. Another memory is that of tension created occasionally by the uncertainty of take-off time (if at all) when weather conditions were bad with the possibility of the operation being scrubbed as sometimes happened after "wakey wakey" tablets had been taken. On such occasions sleep came 'with difficulty after 'scrubbing'.*

One of the most experienced crews on the squadron was deemed tour expired on return from Kiel. Flight Lieutenant Alexander Clarson RAAF had completed 39 operations since his arrival from No.3 LFS in October 1944, 38 as captain and a single operation as second pilot. The 'Clarson Mob' was a mixed bag of five Australians, a Scotsman, and an Englishman, a fairly typical crew line-up on No.186 Squadron, the combination of nationalities brought out the very best in each crew. This, their last operation, was not without its drama and clearly illustrates that survival was sometimes simply down to lady luck.

> *On April, 9th 1945, we were briefed for a night raid on Kiel, a large German naval base. Whilst over the target and just after we had dropped our bombs, we were caught in searchlights and coned by several of them for about 15 minutes. In an endeavour to escape the lights, which turned night into day, Jeff threw the plane around like a fighter plane. Jock subsequently told me that at one stage, the plane was upside down and that if was a remarkable feat by Jeff to get the plane back on to an even keel. After Jeff successfully flew us out of the searchlights, we set sail for the U.K. We were briefed to descend to 7,000 when we crossed the coast of Denmark and to continue to fly back over the North Sea at that height. As we reached the Danish coast, Jeff was obviously tired and stressed and decided to descend to 7,000 feet quickly rather than gradually. In the rear turret, I was aware that we were descending rapidly, when all of a sudden, the tail of the plane started*

*skidding. I instinctively looked down and saw that we were skidding over the body of another Lancaster about 6 to 8 feet below. If was about midnight, but we were so close that I could see the two gunners in their respective turrets. Apparently, during the descent, Jock spotted the other Lancaster directly in our path, and his immediate reaction was to hit Jeff across the chest. Jeff automatically pulled the stick (control column) back and began to climb, and the sudden change of direction made me look down. To this day, | don't know if they saw us. If they didn't, they must have been blind or asleep.*

On return from Kiel, the crew were informed that the operational tour had been lowered to 35 operations. The new Squadron Commander, W/Cdr Hancock, was aware of this reduction before the main briefing. However, when he was made aware that F/Lt Clarson RAAF had already exceeded the new total, he is reported to have replied, *'they are already on the battle order for tonight, leave them there'*. It was a harsh call by the new squadron commander.

The squadron welcomed another second tour veteran on the 8th. Flying Officer T Danvers DFC RAAF and crew joined 'B' Flight. The squadron concentrated on training for the next three days while the Halifax and Lancasters of No.1,4,5 and 6 RCAF Groups attacked Leipzig, Plauen, Nuremberg, and Bayreuth. The squadron was not idle. Sixteen low-level Bombing exercises were flown, four radar flights, two bombing exercises, three Air-to-Air gunnery flights, five cross country and 12 Fighter Affiliation exercises. Plus, 'C' Flight had flown twelve 'simulated' Bombing Exercises. On the 11th, S/Ldr P Reynolds returned from leave and re-assumed his 'A' Flight Commander role. The following day, 'B' Flight's S/Ldr Bass AFC departed on leave. He was replaced, if but temporarily by F/Lt S.C Brayshaw DFC.

On the 13th, the squadron was informed it would be making a return visit to Kiel. Seventeen crews were briefed. On this occasion, the target was aiming point 'Minnow F' situated in the Deutsche Werke Shipyards complex.

Form B.837 – April 13th 1945 (N): Target : Kiel **:** Deutsche Werkes : Minnow 'F'

| | | | | | | | |
|---|---|---|---|---|---|---|---|
| F/Sgt | Rose | B.A | | LM697 | XY-A | PFF Raid | Duty Carried Out. |
| F/Lt | Tonks | J.E | | PB668 | XY-B | PFF Raid | Duty Carried Out. |
| F/O | Gillespie | A.P | RAAF | PB139 | XY-C | PFF Raid | Duty Carried Out. |
| F/O | Verry | C.C | RNZAF | NF146 | XY-E | PFF Raid | Duty Carried Out. |
| W/O | Cooke AFM | S.F | | NG140 | XY-F | PFF Raid | Duty Carried Out. |
| F/O | Roberts | D.M | | PB488 | XY-J | PFF Raid | **Collided on Return.** |
| F/Lt | Green | T.B | | HK802 | XY-L | PFF Raid | Duty Carried Out. |
| F/Lt | Hart | J.H | | NG354 | XY-M | PFF Raid | Duty Carried Out. |
| F/Sgt | Javis | K.W | **2nd Pilot** | | | PFF Raid | Duty Carried Out. |
| F/Lt | Hill | P.T | | RF198 | XY-N | PFF Raid | Duty Carried Out. |
| F/O | Fernley | F | | PB858 | XY-O | PFF Raid | Duty Carried Out. |
| F/O | Gray | P | | LM543 | XY-P | PFF Raid | Duty Carried Out. |
| F/Sgt | Baker | L.G | RAAF | HK659 | XY-Q | PFF Raid | Duty Carried Out. |
| F/O | Grass | H.R | RCAF | RF126 | XY-V | PFF Raid | Duty Carried Out. |
| F/O | Burson | T.P | RNZAF | PB483 | XY-X | PFF Raid | **Collided on Return.** |
| W/O | Howell | A.J | RAAF | PB509 | XY-Y | PFF Raid | Duty Carried Out. |
| F/Lt | Brayshaw DFC | S.C | | PD429 | XY-Z | PFF Raid | Duty Carried Out. |

The relief of being screened from further operations is etched on the smiling faces of each crew member of the Flight Lieutenant Jeff Clarson RAAF seen here with Avro Lancaster NG354 XY-M 'Mike'. They are above L-R Pilot Officer James Hepburn RAFVR (Flight Engineer), Pilot Officer Dennis Parrish RAFVR (Bomb Aimer), Pilot Officer Gerald McPherson RAAF (Rear Gunner), Pilot Officer Ron Liversidge RAAF (Navigator), Pilot Officer Jim Mallison RAAF (Mid Upper Gunner), The Skipper, Flight Lieutenant Jeff Clarson RAAF, and finally, Warrant Officer Wilbert Perry (Wireless Operator).

Number 3 Group despatched a healthy 200 Lancasters, which on this occasion would be joined by the Halifaxes and Lancasters of No.6 RCAF Group. The still dangerous German night fighter units were active both en route and over the target area. The squadrons of No.3 Group would be the first to bomb between 23:30 and 23:38 hours. The flak defences over Kiel were venomous, obviously eager to inflict some retribution over the loss of Admiral Scheer. The crews reported the flak defences as accurate and intense, especially below 19,000 feet. Unlike the previous raid, Kiel was covered entirely in cloud, making visual identification of the aiming point almost impossible. Three of the early crews were obliged to orbit the target. Flight Sergeant B Rose was orbiting at 18,000 feet while being buffeted and engaged by flak. Flying Officer C Verry RNZAF and crew were at 19,000 feet. He was flying with a 2nd navigator, F/Lt D Macdonald. Finally, Warrant Officer Cooke AFM was at 20,000 feet, all eagerly awaiting the appearance of the TI Markers. Crews took a distinct dislike of orbiting targets, especially when fighters were active, and the flak was intense and accurate. With the marking not going to plan, the Master Bomber, Flight Lieutenant George Thorne DFC of No.635 Squadron (call sign Rednose) ordered the main force to bomb the alternative target at 23.24 hours when he was unhappy with the accuracy of the initial marking. Confusion and some desperation were now creeping into the orbiting crews. Some simply bombed the illuminating flares. Flying Officer F Fernley dropped his all High Explosive bombload on a TI cluster at 23:30 hours. On hearing the Master Bomber's broadcast, the crews sought out the secondary target. Thankfully, and in the nick of time, cascading Green TI markers appeared replacing the quickly diminishing illuminating flares, but the damage had been done.

The crews were not overly enthusiastic about the marking or the Master Bomber. Flight Lieutenant J Tonks was at 19,500 ft at the controls of Lancaster PB668 XY-B, *'Master Bomber was difficult to understand'*, F/O J Hart, *'Target Indicators were scattered'*. Flight Lieutenant P Hill DFC, *'Very little marking was visible'* was his opinion on return. The first crew back at RAF Stradishall was F/Lt Tonks, he touched down at 01:53 hours. He was quickly followed by nine crews. The tenth to land was F/O Charles Verry RNZAF, who brought Lancaster NG146 XY-E in at 02:15 hours. At 02:26 hours[53] the inky blackness was momentarily lost when a blinding flash illuminated the Suffolk countryside on the eastern perimeter of the station. The immediately reaction by the Flying Control and those in the circuit was that German Intruders were in the circuit. This was quickly discounted as Flying Control calmly instructed W/O S Cook AFM to land, which he did at 02:28 hours. Scotsman, F/O P Gray, who had landed at 02:12 hours takes up the tragic events.

> *'Fighters around here somewhere'. The lingering silence from the rest of us offered mute agreement. We were quite wrong. As we trooped in from the motor transport wagon, having made our own nerve-tingling filter-in approach and landing, we learned that the tragedy had been self-imposed. One pilot, possibly over-anxious for his steak and eggs, or maybe reduced to a State of couldn't-care-less by six-and-a-half hours of operational night flying, had decided to beat the system by taking a short cut. It was a short cut to Hell. His Lancaster ploughed into another and a full-blooded collision resulted. Throughout the night and all of the following day, the clean-up continued. Ten bodies were found, and there were three survivors, ironically one of these being the pilot who had decided to cut the corner. One aircrew member, the fourteenth, seemed to have vanished completely. By daylight all spare personnel, aircrew and ground crew alike, were linked arm-in-arm in one mighty line, and the countryside was combed in every direction. The result was a negative. The fourteenth flyer could not be found. Not that is, until a week later. When the*

---

[53] *The Stradishall Control Log records the time of the crash as 02:28 hours, RAF Chedburgh Control Log records being asked to attend at 02:20 hours.*

*heavy equipment finally winched up the remains of one of the broken Lancasters, they discovered the missing body, hidden completely by one of the Rolls-Royce Merlin engines.*

Avro Lancaster PB488 XY-J skippered by F/O D Roberts and Lancaster PB483 XY-X flown by New Zealander T. Burson RNZAF had collided in the circuit while circling to land. One crashed instantly into an orchard while the other somehow managed to stagger on until crashing near the village of Cowlinge. The Station's Fire Truck and Rescue vehicles were sent to the crash sites aided by Rescue Teams from RAF Chedburgh. It was the Chedburgh rescuers who found the blazing wreckage of PB483 XY-J, three bodies were recovered, plus three survivors were located. Only one was initially thought would survive. Flight Sergeant Bartlett, the bomb aimer, was rushed to West Suffolk Hospital, but he died of his injuries later that day despite every effort to save the young airman. Flying Officer Burson, and the crew's Wireless Operator miraculously survived almost unscathed. There were no survivors from PB488 XY-J. They had overshot their landing, and while turning away, they were overtaken by PB483 XY-X, which had cut across the airfield at 1000 ft when the collision occurred. As soon as it was daylight, groups of station staff, including a number of aircrew, searched the fields, ditches, and even trees in the hope that the missing seventh crewmember of PB483 could be alive by some miracle but injured. Unfortunately, the search was in vain, as already described by F/O Phil Gray.

| Type | Avro Lancaster Mk.III PB483 **XY-X** | **A.V Roe** |
|---|---|---|
| Taken on Charge | 31/03/1945 via No.149 Squadron | |
| 'Category' | FB Cat E 14/04/1945 | |
| Struck Of Charge | 17/04/1945 | |
| Total Flying Hours | - | |
| Time of Crash | 02:26 hours | |
| Take-Off Time | 20:10 Hours | |
| Bomb Load | 1 x 4000lb HC + 13 x 500lb | |
| | | |
| | **CREW** | **Grave -Cemetery - Notes** |
| Pilot | Flying Officer Thomas Peter Burson NZ424953 RNZAF | Survived. |
| Navigator | Flight Sergeant Francis Michael Hale, 1808291 RAFVR, age 20. | Sec.M Grave 200. Salisbury (London Road) Cemetery. |
| Bomb Aimer | Flight Sergeant William Kenvyn Jack Bartlett, 917435 RAFVR. Age 25 | Survived, died of injuries, 15th. Sec.2 Row.6 Grave 11 Worthing (Durrington) Cemetery. |
| Wireless Operator | Sergeant John Albert Kean | Survived |
| Mid Upper Gunner | Sergeant Robert Cunningham Russell, 1606323 RAFVR | Block.A Row P Grave 8. Horley (St.Bartholemew) New Churchyard. |
| Rear Gunner | Sergeant Jack Vidal Somers, 1589666 RAFVR. Age 20. | Sec U. Grave 202. Haverhill Cemetery. |
| Flight Engineer | Sergeant Ernest Gunner, 1898913 RAFVR. Age 22. | Plot 8.Sec.A Grave 38. Mortlake Cemetery. |
| | | |
| Posted History | Unknown | |
| Operations Flown | 5 | |

Twenty-five-year-old Thomas Burson survived the war and died in New Zealand in 2009, having left the RNZAF in November 1946. Francis Hale's brother, Captain John Hale, was killed in July 1944, fighting in Normandy with the Wiltshire Regiment. To the amazement of the crews gathered in the Mess, Sergeant Kean returned to the squadron the following day, looking remarkably healthy considering the catastrophic crash. When asked about the incident, he just answered, *'It all happened so quickly.*

Sergeant Robert Cunningham Russell, RAFVR

Flight Sergeant William Kenvyn Jack Bartlett, RAFVR

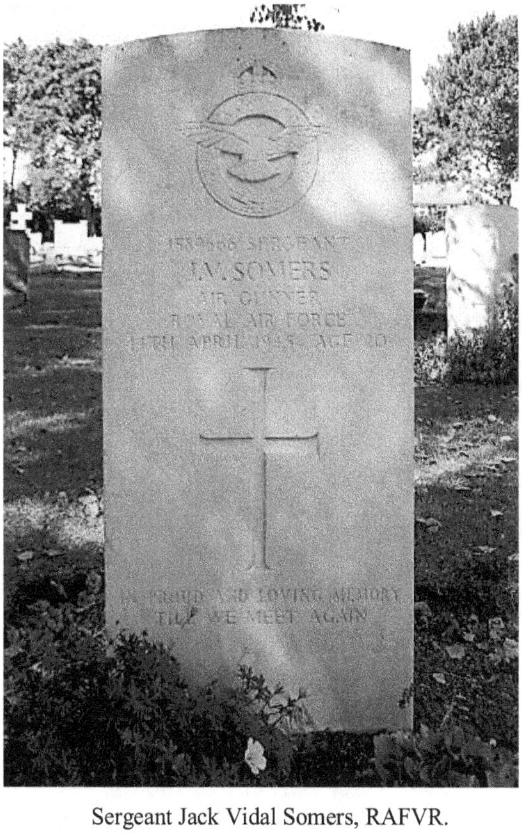

Sergeant Jack Vidal Somers, RAFVR.

Sergeant Ernest Gunner, RAFVR.

Flight Sergeant Francis Michael Hale, RAFVR.

Sergeant Robert Cunningham Russell, RAFVR.

| Type | Avro Lancaster Mk.III **PB488 XY-J** | **A.V Roe** |
|---|---|---|
| Taken on Charge | 10/03/1945 via No.90 Squadron. | |
| 'Category' | FB Cat E 14/04/1945 | |
| Struck Of Charge | 17/04/1945 | |
| Total Flying Hours | | |
| Time of Crash | 02:26 hours | |
| Take-Off Time | 20:17 hours | |
| Bomb Load | 1 x 4000lb HC + 13 x 500lb | |
| | **CREW** | **Grave -Cemetery** |
| Pilot | Flying Officer Donald Michael Roberts, 186931 RAFVR, age 23. | Sec U.Grave 150. Haverhill Cemetery |
| Navigator | Flight Sergeant John Charles James 1684956 RAFVR. Age 22. | Sec 1.R.C Grave 1652 Manchester Southern Cemetery. |
| Bomb Aimer | Flight Sergeant Charles Crooks, 1398447 RAFVR, age 29 (Married) | Sec.G.C Grave 384 Hither Green Cemetery |
| Wireless Operator | Flying Officer William Edward Roberts, 176984 RAFVR, Age 20. | Sec.C. Row A Grave 14 Clewer (Vale End) Churchyard Extension, Clewer. |
| Mid Upper Gunner | Sergeant Harrold Brickell, 2225454 RAFVR, (Married) | Sec L.B Grave 240 Stockport BorouG-H Cemetery |
| Rear Gunner | Sergeant Frederick James Pape, 2225575 RAFVR, age 21. | Sec N.B Grave 180 Halliwell (St Peters) Churchyard |

| | | |
|---|---|---|
| Flight Engineer | Flight Sergeant George Benjamin Whalley, 1587289 RAFVR, Age 21 (Pilot) | Grave 243<br>Killay (St.Hilary) Churchyard. |
| Posted History | Unknown | |
| Operations Flown | 7 | |

Taken only weeks before their death, the crew of Flying Officer Donald Roberts. The crew L-R, Warrant Officer William Roberts (Bomb Aimer), Flight Sergeant George Whalley (Flight Engineer), Flying Officer Donald Roberts (Pilot), Sergeant Harrold Brickell (Mid Upper Gunner), Flight Sergeant John James (Navigator), Pilot Officer Charles Crooks (Wireless Operator), Sergeant Frederick Pape (Rear Gunner). |Below : Flying Officer Roberts at the controls of a squadron Lancaster.

Flying Officer Donald Michael Roberts RAFVR.

Flight Sergeant John Charles James, RAFVR.

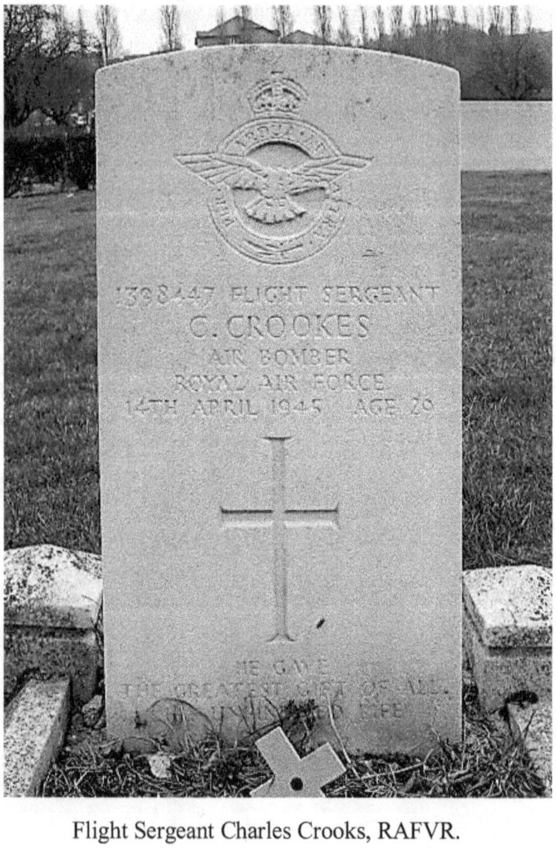


Flight Sergeant Charles Crooks, RAFVR.

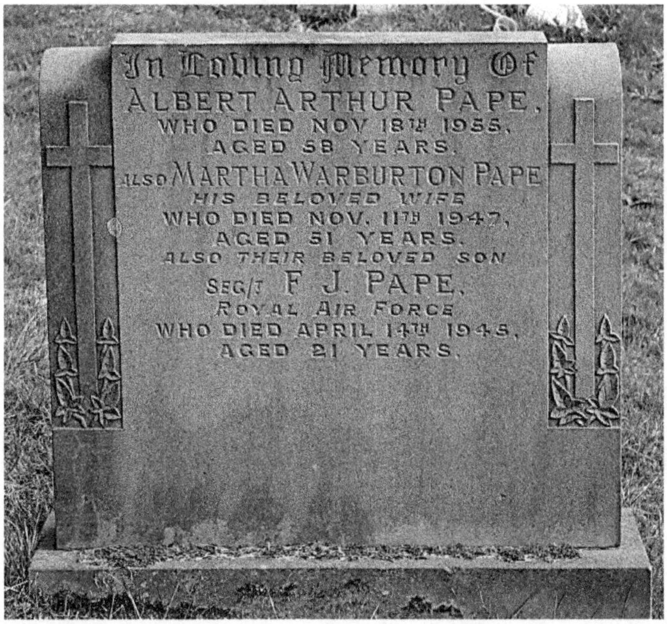


A family headstone, Sergeant Frederick James Pape RAFVR.

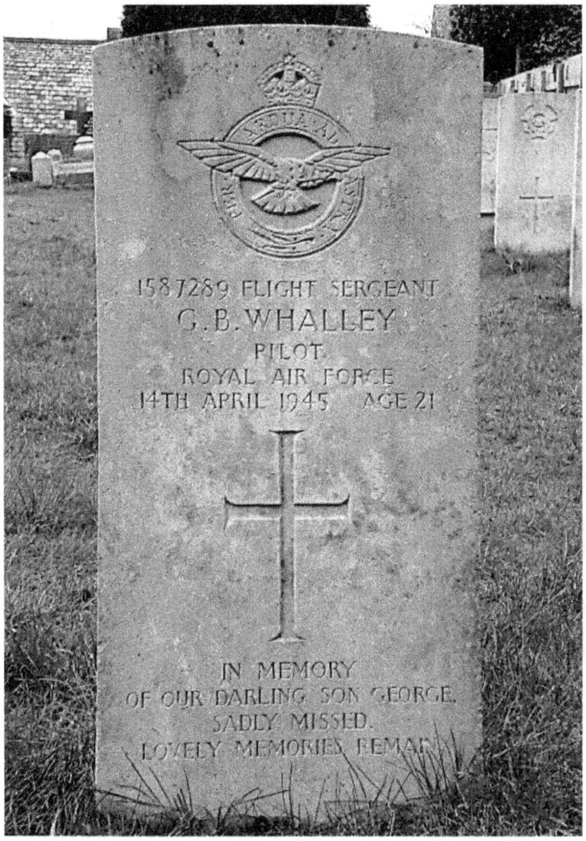

Flight Sergeant George Benjamin Whalley, RAFVR.

Flying Officer William Edward Roberts, RAFVR.

Sergeant Harrold Brickell, RAFVR.

Lancaster PB488 in happier times. This A.V Roe & Co built Mk.III initially served with No.149 (East India) Squadron from August 1944. It was damaged just before Christmas 1944. It spent a few weeks under repair by No.54 MU returning to No.149 in January 1945. In February, PB488 was transferred to No.90 Squadron. It was then transferred to No.186 on March 10th, 1945. The aircraft is seen here with No.149 Squadron. Note the comment above the rear door, 'IS YOUR JOURNEY REALLY NECESSARY?.

The crew's Flight Engineer, F/Sgt Whalley, was a qualified pilot had opted to undertake a Flight Engineers course to get onto a front-line squadron. The parents of Flying Officer D.M Roberts had to endure the loss of three sons. Captain Edward Roberts of the Green Howards was killed on June 10th, 1944, at Anzio. That same month on June 25th, Major Gerald Roberts of the Kings Own Yorkshire Light Infantry was killed in France. The bodies of the young crew were sent home to their hometowns for burial and to be grieved over by their wives and family, all apart from Flying Officer Donald Michael Roberts, who rests in Haverhill Cemetery, Suffolk.

The loss of two crews would have overshadowed the announcement of three DFCs awarded to squadron skippers. Flight Lieutenant Clarence Wait, F/Lt Ralph Madden RCAF, who had just flown his last operation of his tour, and F/O Preston Hill. His citation reads.

*In February, 1945, Flying Officer Hill was pilot and captain of an aircraft detailed to attack Gelsenkirchen. When approaching the target the aircraft was hit by anti-aircraft fire and Flying Officer Hill was wounded in the arm in two places. Blood flowed freely from his badly lacerated wounds but this gallant pilot continued a steady run-in and executed a good bombing attack. Not until he had flown well clear of enemy territory would Flying Officer Hill consent to receive attention. He afterwards flew the damaged aircraft to base and effected a safe landing. This officer set a fine example of courage and fortitude.*

There is no London Gazette citation found for Canadian Madden, but the following is recorded in Air2 held at the National Archives. Born in Saskatchewan, Canada in 1922 he had flown 29 operations with the squadron, plus two with No.90 Squadron in September 1944.

*This officer has completed many operational sorties and has at all times shown determination and splendid captaincy. On more than one occasion his aircraft has been hit by enemy action and once an engine was badly damaged by flak. His courage has been well proved.*

There was an air of anticipation around the station on the 14th. A new target was chalked up on the operations board, Potsdam. Situated amongst a series of interconnecting lakes, Potsdam sat on the banks of the River Havel. It was located just 15 miles southwest of the Nazi capital, Berlin. Every crew was keen to put the target in their logbook, knowing that the war was in its closing stages and the Russians were almost on the outskirts of the capital. Yet, surprisingly, the squadron only provided eight crews.

Form B.841 – April 14th, 1945 (N): Target : Potsdam: Guards Regiment barracks

| | | | | | | | |
|---|---|---|---|---|---|---|---|
| W/O | Cooke | S.F | | LM697 | XY-A | PFF Raid | Duty Carried Out. |
| F/Sgt | Haynes | B.G | | NG140 | XY-F | PFF Raid | Duty Carried Out. |
| F/Lt | Marshall | A.N | | NG354 | XY-M | PFF Raid | Duty Carried Out. |
| F/Lt | Head | G.D | | HK802 | XY-L | PFF Raid | Duty Carried Out. |
| W/O | Howell | A | | PD429 | XY-Z | PFF Raid | Duty Carried Out. |
| F/Sgt | Holmes | E.O | | HK659 | XY-Q | PFF Raid | Duty Carried Out. |
| F/O | Idle | L.A | RNZAF | RF126 | XY-V | PFF Raid | Duty Carried Out. |
| F/Lt | Cussen DFC | O.A | | PB509 | XY-Y | PFF Raid | Duty Carried Out. |

The target were the railway facilities and the former Guards Regiment barracks, which were being used to house military and Nazi personnel. It was the squadron's first visit to the 'Big City' and would, in all probability, be the last. One of the crews briefed was the recently posted Flight Lieutenant Olaf Cussen DFC & Bar. Twenty-nine-year-old Olaf began his operational career with No.58 Squadron before being posted to No.35 Squadron in April 1941, flying the H.P Halifax. In July 1941, he returned to No.58

Squadron after completing six operations in the 2nd pilot role for operational experience. The following year found him undertaking SOE operations with No.161 Squadron flying the Armstrong Whitworth Whitley and Handley Page Halifax. In November 1942, he was the pilot of a Whitley on a transit trip to Gibraltar. On the return flight to RAF Tempsford, persistent engine problems forced the crew to turn back from a position off Cape Finistere and at 09:15hrs, the Whitley forced-landed near Armacao de Pera (Algarve), 40 km NNW of Faro, Portugal. Following a brief spell of internment, Olaf and his crew were flown from Lisbon to Bristol on January 17th, 1943. He was awarded a DFC in April 1943, followed by a bar in November. In January 1944, he was also awarded a MiD. This would be his first operation with the squadron.

The first Lancaster airborne was captained by W/O A Howell at the controls of Lancaster PD429 XY-Z at 18:30 hours. Within six minutes, all the squadron aircraft had departed. Once airborne, No.3 Group's contribution flew to Redhill, from where they headed out over the North Sea and across Belgium. South of Koblenz, the formation turned north, bypassing Kassel and Paderborn before the bomber stream turned onto the final leg into the target. One crew was forced to turn back, F/Lt Cussen DFC and crew experienced port inner engine failure aboard Lancaster PB509 XY-Y. The engine, which had lost oil pressure, was feathered. The crew showed remarkable daring considering it was their first operation, deciding to carry on and try and gain as much altitude as they could out of the remaining three Merlins. Unfortunately, they were unable to climb above 11,000 feet. Realising that it was suicidal to continue, they turned for home over Staufenberg, a small village nestled between Kassel and Gottingen. The time was 21:55 hours. The 'Cookie' was jettisoned, while the 7x500 pounders were brought back to base, where a safe three-engined landing was made at 02:27 hours.

The group was evenly spread over the two waves and were joined once again by Lancasters of No.1 Group. Flying Officer L.A Idle RNZAF was the first over the target at 22:48 hours. He dropped on a number of Red Target Indicators that he described as *' Punctual and well placed'*. Searchlights were active, and seven Lancasters were seen held in their beams, but unusually there was no flak! Flight Sergeant E.O Holmes had a brief but vicious encounter with a single-engined fighter, the rear gunner Sgt Ken Cartwright exchanging fire. No damage was reported, and no claim was made. But the encounter graphically illustrates that the ever-resilient German Night Fighter force was still active and, on the prowl, even during those final desperate weeks of the Third Reich. The squadron came close to losing another crew over Potsdam. Flight Lieutenant Albert Marshall had just dropped his bombs when another Lancaster struck his aircraft at 19,000 feet. The appearance of the Lancaster and its erratic flying gave the crew almost no time to react. The Operational Records Book reports.

> Just after bombing a Lancaster came up from port and below in a steep turn, his propellers hitting the starboard mainplane and rear of starboard outer engine. Damage not ascertained, other aircraft believed to carry on.

The other aircraft was a No.7 Squadron Lancaster, PB582 MG-T flown by S/Ldr K McIntyre RAAF. The No.7 Squadron Operational Records Book strangely does not mention this near-fatal collision! The mid-upper gunner, W/O Len Wilson, *'There was damage to the trailing edge of our wing and belly, but the skipper flew the aircraft home at an angle to make a safe but shaky landing'*. The damage to Lancaster NG354 was such that it required the specialist care of No.54 Maintenance Unit. The Lancaster would return to front line service with the squadron on May 25th. The squadron was instructed to make ready 14 crews for an attack on Leipzig on the night of April 15th. This was eventually cancelled at 13:35 hours. The 16th was another day of training. It also recorded the arrival of another crew fresh from Lancaster Finishing School.

There was cause for celebrations on the 17th, 'A' Flights S/Ldr P Reynolds DFC was posted on completion of his time with No.186 Squadron. Southend born Percy, who had survived a near-fatal crash landing early on in his flying career, had been with the squadron since its formation in October 1944 and was one of the most respected captains on the squadron. He would be awarded a well-deserved Bar to his DFC in September 1945. His replacement was F/Lt Albert Marshall, who was immediately promoted to Acting Squadron Leader. On the same day, the London Gazette announced the award of four DFCs to members of No.186 Squadron. The recipients were Flying Officer Herbert Young, Pilot, Bomb Aimer, F/O John Gray, Navigator P/O William Philpot, both members of F/O Ritson's crew, and Airgunner Warrant Officer Desmond Moverley, Rear Gunner to F/O Fernley. There was just one DFM announced, Flight Sergeant E.J Self, Rear Gunner to Canadian F/O Hoskin RCAF, who had completed a tour of 32 operations. His citation reads.

*This N.C.O. has completed many operations against heavily defended targets. His coolness for operating and coolness in danger have done much to inspire the gunners in the squadron. His devotion to duty is outstanding and he is strongly recommended for the award of the Distinguished Flying Medal.*

Yet another new target was chalked on the operations board on the 18th, Heligoland. The fortress island of Heligoland was located in the Heligoland Bight in the northeastern corner of the North Sea. Bomber Command had a long association with the island going back to 1939. A total of eighteen crews were detailed and briefed. The squadrons of No.31 Base would bomb aiming point 'A', the submarine base, and military installations.

Form B.843 – April 18th, 1945 (D): Target : Heligoland : Submarine Base. GR3429

| | | | | | | | |
|---|---|---|---|---|---|---|---|
| W/O | Cooke AFM | S.F | | LM697 | XY-A | PFF Raid | Duty Carried Out. |
| W/Cdr | Caines | A.E | | PP668 | XY-B | PFF Raid | Duty Carried Out. |
| F/Lt | Hill DFC | P.T | | PB139 | XY-C | PFF Raid | Duty Not Carried Out |
| F/Sgt | Jarvis | K.W | | NG137 | XY-D | PFF Raid | Duty Carried Out. |
| F/Sgt | Haynes | B.G | | NG146 | XY-E | PFF Raid | Duty Carried Out. |
| F/Lt | Tonks | J.E | | NN720 | XY-K | PFF Raid | Duty Carried Out. |
| F/O | Head | G.D | | PD426 | XY-L | PFF Raid | Duty Carried Out. |
| F/Sgt | Rose | B.A | | PB858 | XY-O | PFF Raid | Duty Carried Out. |
| A/S/Ldr | Marshall | A.N | | LM543 | XY-P | PFF Raid | Duty Carried Out. |
| F/Sgt | Baker | L.G | RAAF | HK659 | XY-Q | PFF Raid | Duty Carried Out. |
| F/Lt | Cussen DFC | O.A | | LM692 | AP-R | PFF Raid | Duty Carried Out. |
| W/O | Howell | A.J | RAAF | PB790 | XY-S | PFF Raid | Duty Carried Out. |
| F/O | Fernley | F | | NG148 | XY-T | PFF Raid | Duty Carried Out. |
| F/O | Gray | P | | NG293 | XY-U | PFF Raid | Duty Not Carried Out |
| F/O | Forand | J.M | RCAF | RF126 | XY-V | PFF Raid | Duty Carried Out. |
| F/Lt | Godfrey | D.F | RAAF | PB896 | XY-W | PFF Raid | Duty Carried Out. |
| F/Sgt | Homes | E.O | RAAF | KB475 | XY-X | PFF Raid | Duty Carried Out. |
| F/Lt | Brayshaw DFC | S.C | | PD429 | XY-Z | PFF Raid | Duty Carried Out. |

The first crew aloft was F/Lt S Brayshaw DFC at 10.14 hours at the controls of Lancaster PD429 XY-Z. Once airborne, the squadron headed towards the group rendezvous point 5000 feet above Cromer on the Norfolk Coast. Number 3 Group put up a respectable 255 Lancasters, No.31 Base provided 71 aircraft and its largest contribution to date. Number 32 Base despatched a creditable 102 crews, the squadrons of No.33 Base adding a further 82 crews. Number 32 Base was, by April 1945, the largest of No.3 Group base stations. Five squadrons now operated under the direct control of RAF Mildenhall. The squadrons were No.15, 90, 138, 149 and 622 Squadrons. Weather on the route was free of cloud as the armada of over 900 bombers steadily made their way across the inhospitable North Sea.

One of the last Canadian captains and crew to arrive on the squadron was Flying Officer J.M Forand RCAF. Five crew pose in front of Lancaster NG146 XY-E *'Hullhooo There !!!'* L-R Flight Sergeant D Harris (Wireless Operator), Sergeant J.L Butters (Flight Engineer), Warrant Officer W.F Trivett (Rear Gunner), Sergeant J.S Dugay (Mid Upper Gunner) and finally Flying Officer J.M Forand RCAF (Pilot).

Twelve squadrons of RAF Mustangs provided an escort as the group settled down for the long flight north. At 0300E, the bombers slowly climbed to the bombing height of 15,000-18,000 feet. The squadron frustratingly reported two aborts. The first was F/O P Gray and crew. The constant speed unit of the starboard outer engine aboard Lancaster NG293 XY-U failed almost immediately after take-off. The crew jettisoned their bombs in the Wash. They landed an hour and twenty-nine minutes after take-off. Flight Lieutenant P Hill DFC disappointingly turned back just 75 miles short of the target. An oil leak in the port outer engine, which was noticed while forming up over Cromer, had forced the crew to shut down the engine aboard Lancaster PB139 XY-C. They had hoped that they would be able to slowly

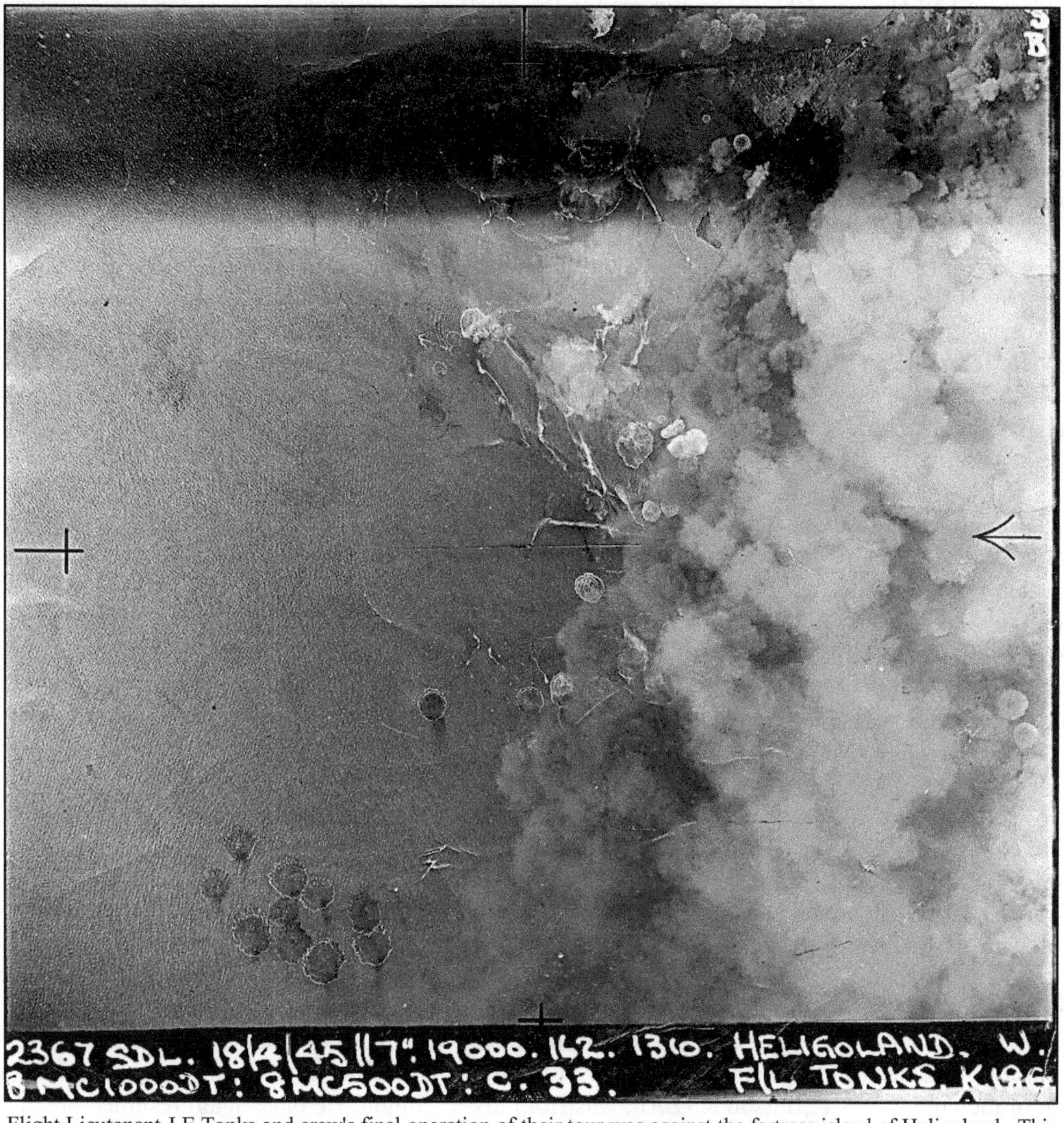


Flight Lieutenant J.E Tonks and crew's final operation of their tour was against the fortress island of Heligoland. This Bombing Photograph clearly shows heavy concentration of bombing on the Aiming Point.

gain height en route. However, with the fortress island just 30 minutes away, they still had not climbed above 9,000 feet. With the best part of 900 bombers above them, they wisely turned back to RAF Stradishall. Number 3 Group would make up the fourth wave scheduled to bomb between 13:05 and 13:15 hours. As the group approached the island, it was immediately evident that visual identification of the aiming point was out of the question. A mass of smoke hung over the island from the previous waves. The only visible landmark was the northern tip of the island. The Master Bomber, Group Captain William Newson DFC of No.405 RCAF Squadron, was clearly heard instructing the group to overshoot the barely visible TI markers by two seconds. The bombing was extremely concentrated except for twelve sticks of bombs that were observed exploding in the sea. The whole island appeared to be blanketed by dense smoke and explosions, as hundreds of 1000 and 500 pounders were seen to explode, obliterating the already hard to distinguish markers. Strangely, not a single 4000lb cookie was dropped by the group. One of the first squadron crews to bomb was F/Lt S Brayshaw DFC at 13:07 hours. He watched as his 8 x 1000lb + 8 x 500lb bombs exploded around a group of Red Target Indicators. Flying Officer J Forand RCAF was over the target are 13:08 hours. Flying with him was the squadron Bombing Leader, F/Lt W Holman DFC. They reported to the Intelligence Officer, *' TI's had disappeared when our aircraft was over aiming point. Thick black smoke obscuring the island almost entirely. Attack seemed good, and only ends of sticks fell into sea'.* Flight Lieutenant O Cussen DFC was at 16,800 feet, a far cry from his low-level clandestine operations with 161 Squadron. He remarked on his return, *'Bombed edge of smoke in accordance with Master Bombers instructions. Bombs appeared to undershoot at start of attack but bombing positions over the target were reasonable. A fierce fire was observed on the North-West tip of island.'.*

There were a few moments of danger when an unidentified Lancaster of No.32 Base flew directly above Flight Sergeant K Jarvis's aircraft and unloaded its entire bombload, narrowly missing the Lancaster a few thousand feet below. This same aircraft was also witnessed by F/O G Head, who was tucked in close behind A/S/Ldr Marshall DFC. The crews turned away from the devastated island. Close on their heels were over 200 Halifaxes which would add more destruction to the island. Wing Commander A Cairnes, *'A black column of smoke could be seen nearly a 1000 miles away, after leaving the target.* [54] There was a reason to celebrate in the various Messes on return from Heligoland. The crew of F/Lt John Tonks had returned from their 36th and final operation. John Tonks, a Brummie, would continue to serve in the RAF until 1955. While the squadron were on their way back from Heligoland, the first of the funerals of the crews killed on the 13th took place. At 14:00 hour at Worthing Cemetery F/Sgt Bartlett was buried. In attendance was F/O A Gillespie RAAF, who represented the squadron. It was back to the more familiar daylight G-H operations on the 19th when a modest force of 50 all G-H equipped Lancasters were detailed to attack Munich's railway transformer station at Munich (Passing). Number 186 Squadron, for some unknown reason, sat this operation out. However, the day would not be wasted. Instead, it would be used to pay respect and say goodbye to seven friends and colleagues.

Two of the crew of F/O Burson RNZAF were buried. At 15:15 hours, the funeral of F/Sgt F Hale took place at Salisbury Cemetery. This was followed at 14:30 hours by the funeral of Sgt Russell at Horley, Surrey. The squadron was represented by F/O's F Audell and R Clarke, respectively. Five of the crew of F/O Roberts were buried in their hometowns. At 12:00hrs, F/Sgt Crookes was buried at Hither Green Cemetery, Orpington. Sergeant Pape was buried at 13:30 hours in St Peters Church, Bolton. Flight Sergeant James had a private burial at 14:00 hours in Manchester's Southern Cemetery. The last two crewmates were laid to rest at 14:30 hours, Sgt H Brickell in Stockport, and Welshman, F/Sgt G Whalley in Swansea. The same day, the squadron welcomed back S/Ldr R Bass AFM from leave. The Flight Commander would have been unaware of the tragedy over the airfield only a few days before. One of the crews, F/O T. Burson RNZAF, was from his 'B' Flight. He once again resumed his Flight Commanders role from F/Lt S Brayshaw DFC, who had assumed the role in his absence.

[54] *This was slightly exaggerated, the distance from base to target was a little over 350 miles.*

Tour Complete. Flight Lieutenant John Tonks and crew pose in front of Lancaster NG146 XY-*E 'Hullhoo There !!!'* .

On the 20th, the squadron was ordered to prepare eleven crews for a daylight attack on the Rhenania-Ossag Oil Plant at Regensburg. Squadron briefing was at 06:10 hours, the squadron would provide just three G-H crews, and for the first and last time, two crews would be skippered by a Wing Commander.

Form B.845 – April 20th, 1945 (D): Target : Regensburg : Rhenania-Ossag Oil Plant :G-H860B

| | | | | | | | |
|---|---|---|---|---|---|---|---|
| F/Lt | Hill DFC | P.T | | NG137 | XY-A | Follower | Duty Carried Out. |
| P/O | Cooke AFM | S | | NG149 | XY-G | Follower | Duty Carried Out. |
| P/O | Rose | B.A | | NN720 | XY-K | Follower | Duty Carried Out. |
| F/O | Head | G.G | | RF198 | XY-N | Follower | Duty Carried Out. |
| F/O | Gray | P | | PB858 | XYO | Follower | Duty Carried Out. |
| F/Lt | Godfrey | D.F | RAAF | HK659 | XY-Q | Follower | Duty Carried Out. |
| F/Lt | Cussen DFC | O.A | | LM692 | XY-R | Follower | Duty Carried Out. |
| F/O | Fernley | F | | PB790 | XY-S | Follower | Duty Carried Out. |
| S/Ldr | Bass AFM | R.W | | RF126 | XY-V | G-H Leader | Duty Carried Out. |
| W/Cdr | Cairnes | A.E | | PB509 | XY-Y | G-H Leader | Duty Carried Out. |
| W/Cdr | Hancock | E.L | | PD429 | XY-Z | G-H Leader | Duty Carried Out. |

Once the crews were safely airborne, they headed towards Tonbridge, joining forces at 5,000 feet with No.218 Squadron and 75 Lancasters drawn from both No.32 and No.33 Bases. It would be No.186 Squadron that would lead No.31 Group's gaggle of 25 Lancasters. Wing Commander Hancock and S/Ldr R Bass were both flying Lancasters equipped with the still relatively new G-H/H2S Mk.III.

Visibility over the target was clear. Despite this, the marking of the lead groups did not impress the crews of 186 Squadron, who reported *'Scattered Blue Puff Markers'*. Thankfully, numerous explosions were seen in the target area and around the circular oil storage tanks. Large explosions were seen in the east of the town and across the river due to some wayward bombing. Two Lancasters were seen in trouble over the target, the apparent victim of flak. Four crews reported a massive explosion between Ingoldstadt and Kosching at 14:05 hours. The explosion produced a mushroom cloud that rose to 10,000 feet. The three G-H crews had differing opinions of the accuracy of the raid. The first to bomb and mark was S/Ldr Bass AFM at 13:58 hours. He reported a *'very good raid'*. The Squadron C/O, W/Cdr Hancock, bombed at 13:59 hours, who informed the Intelligence Officer back at RAF Stradishall, *'Bombs were well concentrated and were seen bursting round oil storage tanks*. Wing Commander Cairnes flying what would be his last operation with No.186 Squadron, was a little more cautious with his assessment, *'Skymarkers Blue Puff were scattered, should be a good attack'*. The squadron bade farewell and good luck to W/Cdr Cairnes on return from Regensburg, he and his crew were posted to No.195 Squadron at RAF Wratting Common where he would take command on the departure of W/Cdr Burnside DFC. Also on the move but under more favourable circumstances were the crews of F/Lt D.F Godfrey RAAF and F/O F Fernley. Both had returned from their last operation. Australian Dennis Godfrey, Frederick Fernley had, along with John Tonks, completed No.60 Course at No.3 LFS and arrived on the squadron on November 1st 1944. Dennis would complete 33 operations while Frederick 36. Both would receive the DFC for their tours.

A stunning photograph of Flight Lieutenant Dennis Godfrey RAAF and his crew aboard Lancaster HK659 XY-Q. In this aircraft, they completed their tour against the oil plants at Regensburg on April 20th, 1945.

The Rhenania-Ossag Oil Plant attack would conclude No.3 Group's operations against Hitler's Oil production. The Group had excelled in the precision bomber role in a relatively short period. Time after time, given the winter conditions over Germany, the Lancaster crews of No.3 Group were called upon to attack important industrial targets hidden by a dense layer of impenetrable cloud. No other bomber Group achieved the same level of accuracy as No.3 Group over a cloud-covered target. Even the Path Finders, and AVM Cochranes fabled specialist No.5 Group were unable to inflict the same level of accuracy and destruction.

Bomber Commands association with oil can be traced back to 1940. However, navigational and bombing aids limitations shifted the emphasis to more profitable targets. With the arrival of Arthur Harris in 1942, oil targets were not even considered. Harris wisely concentrated his forces against German cities with the limited modern equipment at his disposal. However, by June 1943, oil was again on the agenda, if only a relatively low-level priority. By September 1944, the situation had changed dramatically. Germany's reliance on oil was finally acknowledged at the highest level. Attacks on the petroleum industry with particular emphasis on petrol and storage was now prioritised. Germany had virtually no petroleum deposits and little or no natural oil resources at its disposal in the early twentieth century. This all started to change after the Great War. By the early 1930s, with the resurgence of the German military, the country had become increasingly dependent on gasoline and diesel oil engines. The massive increase in tanks, trucks, and aircraft made a plentiful supply of gasoline and oil essential. Moreover, the German Navy increasingly used diesel oil rather than coal as their energy source for their new modern fleet of warships. By the mid-1930s, German ingenuity, especially in the chemical field, meant that companies like IG Farben and Ruhrchemie started industrialising synthetic liquid fuel production. Because of synthetic liquid fuel's high production cost, the industry benefited from the financial incentives the Nazi government offered from December 1933 onwards. Liquid fuel was crucial to Germany's war effort. The synthetic fuel industry became a significant part of Adolf Hitler's Four Year Plan of 1936. By the beginning of the war, Germany produced high-grade aviation gasoline, synthetic oil, synthetic rubber and synthetic methanol. By 1944, the once plentiful supply of oil from the Romanian oil fields had abruptly stopped with the relentless Russian advance. Now deprived, Germany never fully recovered, even with its many oil-producing factories. Romania had developed into Germany's chief overland supplier of oil. From 2.8 million barrels in 1938, Romania's exports to Germany had increased to 13 million barrels by 1941, a level that was essentially maintained throughout 1942 and 1943. Although the exports were almost half of Romania's total production, they were considerably less than the Nazis required. With the capture of the oil fields by the Russians, it was evident that Germany would quickly become reliant on its own production. It was Germany's Achilles heel.

In 1944, the Ministry of Economic Warfare produced a paper listing ten plants in Germany that, between them, had the capability of producing 1,7850,000 tons of oil a year, almost half of Germany's total oil production requirements. One of the leading advocates of attacks on Germany's oil was Air Commodore Sydney Bufton, who pressed for a campaign against Germany's oil production facilities despite mounting opposition. One of the most outspoken and vocal opponents was that of the head of Bomber Command, Air Marshal Sir Arthur Harris. Harris was never convinced that attacks on oil were worthwhile and is on record stating it was just another 'panacea'. More in an attempt to appease the Chief of Air Staff, Air Chief Marshal Charles Portal, the Air Ministry, and the Ministry of Economic Warfare, Harris passed the gauntlet to No.3 Group to destroy Hitler's oil plants. One by one, the plants were destroyed often when blanketed by clouds. These plants often nestled in the very heart of the Ruhr, tested the skill, tenacity and above all, courage of the young crews. The effect of the Group's attacks on Germany's oil production and distribution centres cannot be underestimated. Oil and fuel were the lifeblood of Germany. Without it, they could not wage war. The Chief of Bomber Command never

Appointment to Commission rank was relatively speedy on the squadron, especially if a pilot. However, it was not so quick if you were an Air Gunner. Left - Flying Officer Phil Gray RAFVR. Right- Rear Gunner, Pilot Officer Gerald McPherson RAAF.

accepted that the decision not to attack oil targets sooner was misplaced. However, in his book, The Bomber Offensive, he writes;

> *In the Allied victory over Runstedt's counter-offensive our heavy bombers not only played a most important tactical role, but the results of our strategic bombing were immediately apparent in the enemy's shortage of weapons and fuel. In the last phase of the war Bomber Command, in conjunction with the U.S.A.A.F, carried out a campaign against the enemy's oil supplies which in the spring of 1945 left all the German armed forces without fuel.*

The funerals of the crews killed on the 13th continued on the 20th. Flying Officer D Roberts and Sgt J Somers, a member of F/O Burson RNZAF crew, were laid to rest at 14:15 hours at Haverhill Cemetery, Suffolk. Relatives attended, and a full Services Honours took place, the Last Post being sounded at the end. The squadron was represented by S/Ldr A Marshall and F/Lt's J Walker and G Baxter. In Hammersmith, London, the family and 186 Squadron representative, F/O J Forand, gathered for the private funeral of Sgt E Gunner. Finally, in Windsor, the funeral took place of F/O W.E Roberts at 11.30 hours. One can only imagine the grief of the families, the war was almost over, and here they were standing at the grave of a loved one who came so tantalisingly close to surviving and enjoying the peace they had fought for. Air Commodore J Silvester CBE, Officer Commanding No.31 Base, departed for nine day's leave on the 20$^{th}$. He was replaced by Group Captain C.E Morse, Commanding Officer of RAF Wratting Common.

There was a marked increase in training on the 21st, especially by 'C' Flight. Not to be outdone, both 'A' and 'B' Flights were airborne, undertaking a number of G-H bombing exercises at the bombing range at Elmsdon. The same day, the squadron welcomed another new crew to fill the rapidly swelling ranks of the squadron. April 22nd dawned clear and sunny. Given the success of Bomber Command's attacks against Wesel, it was no surprise when the British Army once again requested RAF intervention. The strongly defended northern coastal port of Bremen was to be attacked by the British XXX Corps, it needed to be softened up prior to the main assault. Bomber Command was given the job. On the late afternoon of April 22nd, 14 Lancasters departed RAF Stradishall. The squadron was part of a force of 197 detailed by No.3 Group. The Group departed over Cromer led by 77 Lancasters of No.32 Base, the squadrons of No.31 Base provided 56 crews while No.33 Base added a further 63 Lancasters. Bremen was to be attacked over six waves by over 700 bombers. Number 3 Group were allocated the 3rd and 4th wave, No.31 and No.32 Base would attack between 18:25 and 18:31 hours while No.33 Base would bomb five minutes later. Their objective was Aiming Point H, the former Focke-Wulf factory, now a defensive strong point.

Form B.846 – April 22nd, 1945 (D): Target : Bremen : GY4773

| | | | | | | | |
|---|---|---|---|---|---|---|---|
| P/O | Onus | M.J | RAAF | LM697 | XY-A | G-H Leader | Duty Carried Out. |
| P/O | Cooke AFM | S.F | | NG140 | XY-F | Follower | Duty Carried Out |
| F/Lt | Sawyer | F.R | | NG149 | XY-G | G-H Leader | Duty Carried Out |
| P/O | Rose | B.A | | NN720 | XY-K | Follower | Duty Carried Out |
| P/O | Haynes | B.G | | PD426 | XY-L | G-H Leader | Duty Carried Out |
| F/Lt | Hill DFC | P.T | | RF198 | XY-N | Follower | Duty Carried Out |
| F/O | Gillespie | A.P | RAAF | PB139 | XY-C | Follower | Duty Not Carried Out |
| F/Lt | Cussen DFC | O.A | | LM543 | XY-P | Follower | Duty Carried Out |
| F/O | Grass | H.R | RCAF | PB858 | XY-O | G-H Leader | Duty Carried Out |
| P/O | Howell | A.J | RAAF | PB790 | XY-S | Follower | Duty Carried Out |
| F/O | Gray | P | | RF126 | XY-V | G-H Leader | Duty Carried Out |
| P/O | Collinson | J.J | RAAF | NG148 | XY-T | Follower | Duty Carried Out |
| F/Sgt | Baker | L.G | RAAF | PB896 | XY-W | Follower | Duty Carried Out |
| W/O | Taylor | A.D | RAAF | JB475 | XY-X | Follower | Duty Carried Out |

One moment of near-fatal drama on take-off was a tyre aboard Lancaster LM543 XY-P bursting just as the heavily-ladened aircraft eased off the tarmac. A few seconds before and the experienced veteran, F/Lt Olaf Cussen DFC & Bar and crew would in all probability have 'brought it'. Flying their first G-H Leader operation was F/O Phil Gray and crew, who writes.

*To add to V-Victors vanity, our bomber was riding along in the number one position, our crew having been given pride of place. We were a Gee-H leader and at the head of the Squadron. Our Lancaster was at the front of four V-formations of three planes each, twelve bombers in all.*

Number 186 Squadron was given the lead squadron role from No.31 Group. The bomber stream flew across the Zuider Zee, where they encountered quickly deteriorating weather with clouds up to 6,000 feet. The squadron lost F/O A.P Gillespie RAAF and crew over Holland with a defective port outer engine. The engine was feathered, and the crew made a successful three-engined landing back at RAF Stradishall. The formation turned northeast towards Wilhelmshaven, where the flak defences were particularly vicious and accurate, forcing the stream, which had up until that point been compact, to split up. The ferocity of flak did not decrease as the force neared Bremen. If anything, it increased in both quantity and accuracy. One Lancaster was seen to be hit and in trouble. The unfavourable weather encountered over Holland had continued to the target, where a solid layer of 10/10th cloud was encountered. With the British XXX Corps less than 2 miles from the aiming point, the Master Bomber abandoned the operation. Neither No.1 nor No.6 RCAF Groups bombed. The cloud, however, did not prevent No.3 Group from carrying out its attack. With G-H stations now located on the continent, a strong G-H pulse was received as the group began their bomb runs. Flying Officer Phil Gray was at the controls of Lancaster RF126 XY-V.

*Bremen was about to make clear, vanity or pride of place counted for nothing in the city's current back-to-the-wall situation. Protectors of the place were well aware that the Allied armies were right at the front door, a fact that seemed to inspire them to cling to. One of my father's prime pieces of advice: "If you have to go down, then make sure that you go down in style". Enemy flak kept pumping up at us during the whole of what was to become one of the longest bombing runs we had ever made, the affair dragging on for close to twenty-five minutes. "You have to give these bastards full marks for sheer tenacity", conceded Ivor from the mid-upper turret. "They know they're whacked, but they just won't lie down.' This attack on Bremen had been designated as a ground-support target, a fact which called for a high measure of accuracy. Our own ground troops were close by, and no doubt reconnaissance units would already be probing into the city suburbs. If we had spread any of our trouble outside the aiming point, we could have ended up bombing our own people.*

The formation was compact over the Aiming Point, and the bombing appeared accurate and concentrated. The few brief glimpses of the ground confirmed that most bombs were on the target. Pilot Officer B Haynes was over the target at 18:32 hours when his mid-upper turret was hit by a piece of flak, smashing the perspex but fortunately completely missing the gunner, Sgt G Middleton. Also hit at 18:32 hours was the Lancaster of W/O A Taylor RAAF. They were hit in both wings, but mercifully the engines and fuel tanks were spared. Flak near Wilhelmshaven brought down a No.514 Squadron Lancaster, while Bremen's defences accounted for a Lancaster of No.622 Squadron. This was seen in trouble, but a number of parachutes were observed. Over 60 Lancasters were damaged by flak, almost one-third of the force sent. Germany was not giving up without a fight.

No.186 Squadron Reported Flak Damage 22/04/1945

| Serial | Code | Damage | Repairs / Notes |
|---|---|---|---|
| **PD426** | **XY-L** | Mid Upper Turret | Repaired on Squadron. |
| **JB475** | **XY-X** | Both wings | Repaired on Squadron. |

The squadron welcomed three more crews on the 22nd, replacing those tour expired. The squadron was stood down on the 23rd. However, it was not idle. A & B Flights flew eight Fighter Affiliation Exercises and three G-H practice bombing flights. 'C' Flight was the busiest, carrying out three Cross Country and two Fighter Affiliation exercises, one local Simulated Bombing exercise, one bombing exercise at Rushford Range and two further Cross Country Flights. Number 31 Base HQ welcomed Captain H Toufanian and Lt A Raffat of the Persian Air Force on the 23rd, who, over the next two days, inspected and observed the day-to-day activities of the squadron and the station. Fourteen crews were detailed and briefed for an early morning G-H attack on the Marshalling Yards at Bad Oldesloe on the 24th. With its essential marshalling yard, this small town was an important link between Hamburg and Lubeck's mighty ports. Number 31 Base was chosen to lead the raid, and No.186 was chosen to lead No.31 Base. They would be joined at 10,000 feet over Southwold by the Lancasters of No.33 Base.

<u>Form B.846 – April 24th, 1945 (D): Target : Bad Oldesloe : Marshalling Yards : GSGS4416</u>

| | | | | | | | |
|---|---|---|---|---|---|---|---|
| F/Lt | Green | T.B | | NG146 | XY-E | Follower | Duty Carried Out. |
| F/O | Gray | P | | NB140 | XY-F | Follower | Duty Carried Out. |
| S/Ldr | Marshall | A.N | | NG149 | XY-G | G-H Leader | Duty Carried Out. |
| W/O | Onus | M.J | RAAF | NG174 | XY-J | Follower | Duty Carried Out. |
| F/O | Gillespie | A.P | RAAF | NN720 | XY-K | G-H Leader | Duty Carried Out. |
| Sgt | Haynes | G.R | | RF198 | XY-N | Follower | Duty Carried Out. |
| F/Lt | Hill DFC | P.T | | PB858 | XY-O | G-H Leader | Duty Carried Out. |
| P/O | Collinson | J.J | RAAF | HK659 | XY-Q | G-H Leader | Duty Carried Out. |
| F/O | Forand | J.M | RCAF | NG148 | XY-T | Follower | Duty Carried Out. |
| F/Sgt | Baker | L.G | RAAF | NG293 | XY-U | Follower | Duty Carried Out. |
| P/O | Howell | A.J | RAAF | JB475 | XY-X | Follower | Duty Carried Out. |
| F/Lt | Cussen DFC | O.A | | PB509 | XY-Y | G-H Leader | Duty Carried Out. |
| F/Lt | Brayshaw DFC | S.C | | PD429 | XY-Z | G-H Leader | Duty Carried Out. |
| F/Lt | Sawyer | F.R | | PB790 | XY-S | ----- | Withdrawn |

One crew was withdrawn before take-off, F/Lt Sawyer reporting his 'Pre-selector' aboard PB790 XY-S becoming unserviceable. The first crew away on this fresh spring morning was F/Lt Stuart Brayshaw DFC at the controls of Lancaster PD429 XY-Z at 06:42 hours. It would be his last operation of his second tour. With No.186 Squadron at the spearhead, the formation departed over Southwold and headed north out over the North Sea towards Holland. The Germans plotted the formation near Den Helder but apparently lost them on turning south-east at Minden. The entire force was routed north of Hanover before heading towards the target. Spasmodic flak was encountered near Ijmuiden and continued up until south of Hamburg. Surprisingly, no squadron aircraft were hit. The squadron provided six G-H Leaders on the squadron's final G-H operation of the European war. All reported excellent G-H reception.

The smiling face of Sergeant Peter Dann seated in his rear turret. Peter was the rear gunner in the crew of Flying Officer M Perrett.

Bombing between 17,400 feet and 20,000 feet, the squadron crews had an unrestricted view of the target below. Flight Lieutenant P.T Hill DFC was at the controls of Lancaster PB858 XY-O, his bomb load of 6 x 1000lb + 10 x 500lb was dropped at 10:37 hours, *'Target well hit and the bombing on the marshalling yards was extremely concentrated'* he reported at de-briefing. Australian F/O A.P Gillespie RAAF and crew were given the G-H Leader position on this operation, their first experience of this demanding role. He reported, *'Followers were picked up at the rendezvous point, who followed and bombed with me'*. The majority of the squadron seemed confident that the attack was successful. It was, in fact, a textbook G-H operation.

As the group turned for home, large fires could be seen across the marshalling yards, and a massive column of smoke drifted slowly towards Hamburg. Pilot Officer P Gray reported, *'Reddish smoke rising*

The remarkably clear conditions over the Marshalling Yards at Bad Oldesloe are captured in this Bombing Photograph taken by the crew of Flying Officer Phil Gray. This was the squadron's last bombing operation.

*from the target'*. Flying aboard F/O Phil Gray's Lancaster was the Squadron Gunnery Leader, F/Lt E Buckland DFC. The crew's usual gunner, Sgt Booth, had reported sick with a throat infection. The only excitement was a brief appearance of a German Messerschmitt Me 262 jet in the target area.The squadron began landing back at RAF Stradishall just after lunch. The honour of making the last operational landing in WW2 fell to the crew of Sgt G.R 'Bill' Haynes, who landed Lancaster RF198 XY-N at 12:59 hours. Little did he or his fellow pilots know that this would be the squadron's final bombing raid of the war. Post raid photo reconnaissance echoed the crew's observations of the raid. The raid was an outstanding success. It was perhaps a fitting end to the squadrons bombing war. The squadron was ordered to prepare fifteen aircraft for operations on the 25th. Although the Squadron ORB does not record details, the Station Records Book does.

*Detailed 15 aircraft to drop urgently needed food supplies to the starving population of that part of Holland still occupied by the Hun. Specific areas were allotted to various aircraft, and the Dutch had been warned to expect this type of transport for the delivery of food supplied and keep a good look out, both for the parcels and being hit by them.*

The operation was eventually cancelled just before take-off. This was first mention in both the Squadron and Station ORB of what would be known as 'Operation MANNA'.

The desperate conditions in northern Holland can be traced back to September 1944. In anticipation of success at Arnhem, the Dutch Government in Exile called on the railway workers to strike, which they did. After the Germans defeated the airborne troops, they took revenge against the civilian population still in their hands. Men were rounded up for slave labour, electricity and gas supplies were severely restricted, partly through lack of fuel, and the transportation of food was forbidden for seven weeks, just as winter was approaching. Railway rolling stock was seized and taken to Germany. The workers maintained their strike, many going into hiding. Initially, the existing food stocks ensured that the shortage did not have an immediate effect. With the onset of winter, this quickly changed. The German embargo was partially lifted in November, allowing only food transported over the numerous canals to be distributed to the now starving Dutch. The country's canals, which had been vital in moving the food began to freeze up, making movement impossible, and the already dilapidated food stocks soon emptied. By early 1945, the situation grew desperate for the three million or more Dutch people still under German control. Prince Bernhard appealed directly to Allied Supreme Commander Dwight D. Eisenhower, but Eisenhower did not have the authority to negotiate a truce with the Germans. The ever-resourceful Prince eventually got permission from British Prime Minister Winston Churchill and American President Roosevelt. Eisenhower immediately had Air Commodore Andrew Geddes DSO begin planning. Allied agents negotiated with Reichskommissar Arthur Seyss-Inquart and a team of German officers. It was agreed that the participating aircraft would not be fired upon within specified air corridors. The squadron parted ways with F/Lt John Walker, Squadron Adjutant, who proceeded on embarkation leave on the 25th. Flight Lieutenant Terrence Capel assumed the role of Adjutant. His first job would be to welcome three recently posted crews. The morning of April 26th started with heavy rain and stormy conditions restricting any activity to a minimum. The foul weather continued on the 27th, cancelling a planned supply dropping operation at 17:35 hours. Stradishall was blanketed by snow on the morning of April 28th, making the conditions even harder for the Ground crews tasked with loading fifteen Lancasters with urgently needed food supplies. Frustratingly, this operation was again cancelled at 15:55 hours due to weather. Finally, once again 15 crews were detailed and briefed despite the clouds and slight snow showers. This time nothing was going to stop them. Each Lancaster was loaded with five parcels.

MANNA : Drop 1 : April 29th, 1945 : Waalhaven Aerodrome Rotterdam

| Rank | Surname | Initial | Airforce | Serial | Code | Drop Zone | Load | Dropped |
|---|---|---|---|---|---|---|---|---|
| P/O | Onus | M.J | RAAF | LM697 | XY-A | Rotterdam | 5 | 4 |
| P/O | Rose | B.A | | NF995 | XY-B | Rotterdam | 5 | 0 |
| F/Lt | Saunders | A | | NG137 | XY-D | Rotterdam | 5 | 5 |
| F/Lt | Sawyer DFC | F.R | | NG146 | XY-E | Rotterdam | 5 | 4 |
| F/Sgt | Jarvis | K.W | | NG149 | XY-G | Rotterdam | 5 | 3 |
| F/O | Hall | M.R | | NG140 | XY-F | Rotterdam | 5 | 4 |
| F/Lt | Hill DFC | P.T | | NG147 | XY-J | Rotterdam | 5 | 4 |
| F/O | Verry | C.C | RNZAF | NN720 | XY-K | Rotterdam | 5 | 5 |
| P/O | Howell | A.J | RAAF | PB790 | XY-S | Rotterdam | 5 | 5 |
| S/Ldr | Bass AFM | R.W | | NG148 | XY-T | Rotterdam | 5 | 5 |
| P/O | Collinson | J.J | RAAF | NG293 | XY-U | Rotterdam | 5 | 4 |
| F/Sgt | Holmes | E.O | RAAF | PB896 | XY-W | Rotterdam | 5 | 3 |
| F/Lt | Cussen DFC | O.A | | RF126 | XY-V | Rotterdam | 5 | 5 |
| Sgt | Haynes | G.R | | PB509 | XY-Y | Rotterdam | 5 | 5 |
| F/O | Forand | J | RCAF | PD429 | XY-Z | Rotterdam | 5 | 4 |
| | | | | | | | **TOTAL** | **60** |

Flying at just 1,500 feet, the bombers raced across the sea in marginal weather. The operation was planned over four waves. Joining the group were 160 Lancasters of the Lincolnshire based No.1 Group. While the formation was over the North Sea, the BBC broadcast a message to the starving Dutch, '*Bombers of the Royal Air Force have just taken off from their bases in England to drop food supplies to the Dutch population in enemy occupied territory*'.

To the delight of the starving Dutch, Lancaster's of No.3 Group fly low over the Dutch countryside on their way to the dropping zones.

The first two waves were made up entirely of No.1 Group, the third consisted of No.33 Base and No.1 Group. The fourth wave was exclusively No.31, and No.32 Base crews were timed to be over the drop zone between 14:12 and 14:30 hours. The squadrons flew low over the flat, featureless, and still potentially hostile Holland. It was an exhilarating experience for the crews accustomed to flying at 18,000 feet and above. With Rotterdam and its vast docks on the horizon, the crews lost altitude to 500 feet and below. The Mosquito Path Finders were to mark the drop zones with Red TI Markers, while on the ground, a large white cross with a red light in the centre and a circle of green lights would designate the dropping areas. The squadron encountered showers and sleet en-route to Rotterdam but was delighted to find the target area clear. A number of crews reported hang-ups, and a few made a second and third run over the release points.

The Dutch people gave the low flying Lancasters a terrific welcome. Flying Officer Hall, *'Hundreds of people were seen in the streets and on roofs around the aerodrome.'* Canadian pilot, F/O J Forand RCAF made two runs over the aiming point and remarked on the dangers the civilians below were placing themselves in, *'On second run crowds of people were rushing to collect the food'.* The returning crew's main concern was that the starving Dutch civilians, in their excitement, chose to ignore the boundary markers set up for their safety and rushed into the drop zone while the low flying Lancasters were still in the process of dropping. As the crews turned for home, it appeared that every Dutch civilian was out waving flags or making gestures to show their gratitude. Once clear of Rotterdam, the squadron regained altitude to 1,500 feet and headed back across the North Sea. Three squadron aircraft reported damage from light flak or rifle fire despite the promises that the bombers would not be fired upon. Pilot Officer Onus RAAF was hit by ground fire emanating from a Pill Box. The disgruntled German's aim was good as damage was inflicted to the starboard outer engine and bomb doors to Lancaster LM697 XY-A. The crew's Flight Engineer, F/Sgt Fred Winch recalls.

> *On our outward leg at about 200 ft. I saw a German soldier aiming a rifle or automatic at us and I remember thinking that he was a bit optimistic thinking he might hit us. He apparently had not been told there was a truce. After we dropped our load I saw engine temperature and oil pressures in, I believe, the starboard inner were wrong. That engine was shut down and the propellor feathered, and we returned to base on three engines. For part of the time we were escorted by a Mosquito[55], the pilot of which feathered one engine in sympathy. We subsequently learned that the oil sump had been punctured by a bullet.*

Lancaster NF995 XY-B was hit by small arms fire. A few holes in the bomb doors and a lucky hit to the undercarriage forced the crew to divert to RAF Woodbridge. Also hit was P/O A Howell RAAF. They watched as three German soldiers took careful aim and fired at their Lancaster, their aim was good as bullet holes in the bomb bay were found on return. The crew remarked, *'Fire not returned!'.*

No.186 Squadron Reported Damage - 29/04/1945

| Serial | Code | Damage | Repairs / Notes |
|---|---|---|---|
| **LM697** | **XY-A** | Fuselage, S/O Engine. | Repaired on Squadron. |
| **NF995** | **XY-B** | Undercarriage, Bomb doors. | Repaired on Squadron. |
| **PB790** | **XY-S** | Bomb doors | Repaired on Squadron. |

The following morning the ground crews busied themselves loading the bomb bays of twelve Lancasters with yet more urgently needed supplies. Two supply lifts were planned. However, the earlier operation by twelve Squadron Lancasters was cancelled due to low cloud and rain. Nevertheless, the squadron would provide 14 Lancasters for the second lift. The Ground Crews who spent the war behind the scenes

[55] *Believed to be Path Finder Mosquito.*

Ground Crew loading panniers with urgently needed supplies.

loading ever-increasing numbers of bombs were out at the dispersals early, ensuring that the panniers were loaded and there were no problems. It was a tremendous thrill to help in a humanitarian capacity for once. Flight Sergeant K Jarvis was the first away at 17:14 hours at the controls of NG146 XY-E. Once again each of the 14 Lancasters was loaded with five packs. While the squadron was preparing to operate, the Adjutant welcomed F/O Phil Lovett RAAF and crew from No.73 Base. They would be one of the last Australian crews posted to No.186 Squadron.

MANNA : Drop 2 : April 30th, 1945 : Rotterdam

| Rank | Surname | Initial | Airforce | Serial | Code | Drop Zone | Load | Dropped |
|---|---|---|---|---|---|---|---|---|
| F/Sgt | Hart | J.H | | NG137 | XY-D | Rotterdam | 5 | 5 |
| F/Sgt | Jarvis | K.W | | NG146 | XY-E | Rotterdam | 5 | 4 |
| P/O | Cooke AFM | S.F | | NG140 | XY-F | Rotterdam | 5 | 4 |
| W/Cdr | Hancock | E.L | | NG174 | XY-J | Rotterdam | 5 | 4 |
| F/O | Verry | C.C | RNZAF | NN720 | XY-K | Rotterdam | 5 | 5 |
| P/O | Rose | B | | PD426 | XY-L | Rotterdam | 5 | 5 |
| F/Lt | Hill DFC | P.T | | RF198 | XY-N | Rotterdam | 5 | 5 |
| F/O | Grindlay | M | | RF126 | XY-V | Rotterdam | 5 | 3 |
| F/Lt | Cussen DFC | O.A | | LM692 | AP-R | Rotterdam | 5 | 4 |
| F/Lt | Fennel DFC | F.W | | NG148 | XY-T | Rotterdam | 5 | 4 |
| P/O | Howell | A.J | RAAF | NG293 | XY-U | Rotterdam | 5 | 4 |

| | | | | | | | | |
|---|---|---|---|---|---|---|---|---|
| F/Lt | Idle | L.A | RNZAF | LM543 | XY-P | Rotterdam | 5 | 5 |
| F/Sgt | Holmes | E.O | RAAF | PB896 | XY-W | Rotterdam | 5 | 5 |
| Sgt | Haynes | G.R | | PB509 | XY-Y | Rotterdam | 5 | 5 |
| | | | | | | | **Total** | **62** |

Two new names appeared on the Op's board for this operation, F/O Grindlay and F/Lt Fennell DFC. Frederick Fennel DFC was a second tour veteran, having completed a tour on Stirlings with No.218 (Gold Coast) Squadron. He had been awarded the DFC for completing an arduous tour in July 1943.

Number 3 Group provided 189 crews that departed England over Orford Ness in heavy rain. Each of the five packs carried contained flour, powdered milk, dried eggs, tinned meat, sugar, tea, potatoes and cigarettes. The Lancasters of No.1 Group were scheduled to drop first and were en-route home when No.3 Group were on their way to the drop zone. This very nearly resulted in a few near mid-air collisions in the limited visibility when a few crews did not keep to the briefed route to and from the drop zones.

On reaching Rotterdam, the crews found the drop zone well marked by Path Finder using the standard TI markers. Heavy rain brought visibility down to 500 yards in places, which added to the congestion over the drop zones and made for yet more near fatal encounters. The smoke from a burning farmhouse, the victim of a few wayward TI markers, did not help matters. Flying Officer C.C Verry RNZAF was able to drop all five panniers but reported, *'Much congestion over drop zone'*. The drop zone also came in for some criticism, F/Lt O Cussen DFC, *'The field had a large ditch running through it which was filled with water many packs fell into it'*. Sergeant G Haynes was also concerned, *'Most containers dropped near aiming point and those that fell in canal picked up by boats. Aiming Point not considered suitable'*.

Pilot Officer A Howell RAAF expressed another concern, *'Panniers covered the field and people including children were seen running amongst the falling packets'*. New Zealander F/Lt L Idle RNZAF experienced another problem frequently encountered by the crews. He was flying at 600 feet when there were two loud thuds. Two packages of sugar had hit Lancaster LM543 XY-P dropped from a Lancaster flying above the briefed altitude. Thankfully, the only damage was some smashed perspex, and a packet of sugar embedded in the buckled leading edge. Pilot Officer S.F Cooke AFM was shot at, a single round hitting the port fin of NG140 XY-F. Once again, some packages hung up, which disappointed the crews immensely. Some crews made three runs over the drop zone, trying desperately to dislodge them despite the limited visibility and congestion. In all, the squadron dropped 62 packages with eight returns. As happy as they were, the returning crews voiced their concerns over the routing and timing. Congestion over the drop zones was one thing, but the near-fatal head-on collision with returning Lancasters of No.1 Group was another. A disastrous encounter had been narrowly averted, just.

No.186 Squadron Reported Damage - 30/04/1945

| Serial | Code | Damage | Repairs / Notes |
|---|---|---|---|
| **NG140** | **XY-F** | Damage to tail fin. | Repaired on Squadron |
| **LM543** | **XY-P** | Wing damaged by falling package. | Repaired on Squadron |

There was yet more good news, Adolf Hitler had committed suicide in his bunker in Berlin. The leadership of Germany's military was handed over to Admiral Karl Donitz. It was perhaps a fitting end to the month. April had been one of mixed contrasts, with independent bombing by G-H in daylight and night operations under the guidance of the Path Finders and humanitarian food dropping to the Dutch.

A G-H equipped Lancaster of No.3 Group flying well below the briefed dropping altitude delivers its supplies. Note the Windmill in the background and the piles of collected supplies in the foreground. The smoke is from PFF Markers Flares.

The last full month of the bombing war had witnessed the squadron wage total war against its enemy with deadly effect. Precision attacks on the last few remaining oil producing factories, or transport centres in Germany went practically unchallenged. A switch to tactical bombing in support of the Army would see the true potential of G-H long dismissed by other group commanders. With a cloud-covered Bremen, only the Lancasters of No.3 Group were able to complete the task with any degree of accuracy. Even at this late stage of the bomber offensive, cloud got the better of the other groups, but not No.3 Group. The attack on Flensburg railway yards and port area on April 23rd by No.5 Group who prided themselves on their skill and accuracy was thwarted by cloud. The AoC of Bomber Command wrote this about No.3 Group in his post war book, 'Bomber Offensive'

> *By October, 1944, a considerable force of Lancasters of No. 3 Group was equipped with G-H, the radar aid which was to be of critical importance in the autumn and winter months. These Lancasters began to operate on a large scale in the middle of October, usually between one and two hundred at a time. By no means all the aircraft were actually equipped with G-H; in fact only about a quarter to a third of the Lancasters in any one operation usually had it, but by flying in formation in daylight this disadvantage was overcome. Three to five aircraft followed a single aircraft equipped with G-H and all the bombs were dropped at the moment when the bombs of the leading aircraft were seen to be released. In case any aircraft should straggle behind or lose formation the G-H aircraft normally dropped coloured smoke puffs so that the stragglers would at any rate have something at which to aim. The vast majority of these G-H attacks were made in daylight and through ten-tenths cloud, but on a few occasions G-H aircraft were used to drop markers by night. An average of three to four attacks a week was kept up by No. 3 Group until the end of the war, and as most of these attacks were made in conditions when no other kind of attack would have been possible, the great access of strength which we gained from the introduction of G-H, and its successful application, may easily be appreciated.*

The commemorative tile was made by the Royal Delft Factory, FOOD, PEACE, FREEDOM. April 29th, 1945 - May 5th, 1945.

The squadron flew a total of 114 sorties. For once, it was not the lowest in the Group. It pipped No.32 Base's No.15, 90 and 622 Squadrons, plus the recently converted No.138 Squadron. The reduction in operations was reflected in the tonnage dropped, only 506 tons being delivered. The squadrons of No.31 Base, No.186, No.195 and No.218 (Gold Coast) undertook a total of 94 'MANNA' operations, five more than the squadrons of No.33 Base but six less than No.32 with its five resident squadrons. Each Lancaster carried five packs[56]. One pack equaled one day's ration for 656 people. The last week of April, No.3 Group dropped 1,091 packages which meant that it fed 715,696 starving Dutchman[57], it was a merciful and rewarding conclusion to the bombing campaign, and every squadron member took great pride in it. With a reduction in operations, there was a marked increase in training. No.186 Squadron topped the month's training hours with a staggering 616 hours flown by day and 41 hours by night. The nearest squadron was No.15, with a 337 hours by day and 46 by night. Sadly, the month would be remembered for the loss of three crews, two due to a momentary lapse in concentration over the airfield. With the war in its final weeks, the losses of these young airmen were hard on those friends left behind, even harder on the families. The loss of F/O Beck RAAF and crew on their 29th operation was especially tragic.

'C' Flight crews continued an almost daily round of practice flights and radar exercises. Unlike 'A' and 'B' Flights, they had flown no offensive operations in April. There was a great deal of excitement amongst the Air Gunner's union in April. An example of the new FN82 rear turret with twin .5inch machine guns did the tour of No.31 Base. None had been fitted to the Group Lancasters despite their limited introduction in No.1 Group and No.5 Group. However, the gunners were impressed with the range and the hitting power over the standard 4 x .303inch fitted to the Groups Lancaster's. By the end of April 1945, No.3 Group reported that 230 Lancasters were fitted with G-H, No.186 Squadron could boast twelve fully operational G-H Lancasters. The squadron welcomed four new crews on April 30th.

[56] *Packs and panniers are both terms used in the document.*
[57] *No.3 Group Monthly Summary of Events for April 1945.*

April 1945 : Avro Lancaster Delivery.

| ToC Date | Serial | Code | Maker | Mark | From |
|---|---|---|---|---|---|
| 03/04/1945 | LM697 | XY-A | A.V Roe | Mk.B.III | No.149 Sqn |
| 04/04/1945 | JB475 | XY-X | Vickers Armstrong | Mk.B.III | No.195 Sqn |
| 04/04/1945 | LM543 | XY-P | Armstrong Whitworth | Mk.B.III | Works |
| 06/04/1945 | RA569 | | Metropolitan Vickers | Mk.B.I | S.I.U |
| 07/04/1945 | PB858 | XY-O | A.V Roe | Mk.B.III | No.195 Sqn |
| 07/04/1945 | PB896 | XY-W | A.V Roe | Mk.B.III | No.195 Sqn |
| 10/04/1945 | RA570 | AP-K | Metropolitan Vickers | Mk.B.I | S.I.U |
| 12/04/1945 | PD426 | XY-L | Metropolitan Vickers | Mk.B.I | No.195 Sqn |
| 12/04/1945 | RA577 | | Metropolitan Vickers | Mk.B.I | S.I.U |
| 13/04/1945 | PB790 | XY-S | A.V Roe | Mk.B.III | No.195 Sqn |
| 23/04/1945 | RA580 | | Metropolitan Vickers | Mk.B.I | S.I.U |

# May 1945

## *Operation MANNA and EXODUS.*

On May 1st, 1945, the chief propagandist for the Nazi Party, Joseph Goebbels, committed suicide on the same day Admiral Karl Donitz broadcast that Hitler was dead. The whole station was in a state of shock, surely now the war would be over. The man who had plunged the world into war was dead. He had taken the coward's way out. Sleet put pay to any early morning flying activity on the 1st. There was, however, no such luxury out at the dispersals. In rotten weather, the ground crews busied themselves loading 70 panniers to 14 squadron Lancasters in between snow flurries and sleet. The target was The Hague, with the drop zone at Ypenburg Airfield. There were a number of new names on the ops board for the operation. By May 1945, there were an estimated 25 plus crews on 'A' and 'B' Flight, not including 'C' Flight. The recent arrivals were especially keen to get involved and put some of their training to good use. One new crew arrived on the squadron on the 1st.

MANNA : Drop 3 : May 1st, 1945 : The Hague : Ypenburg Airfield

| Rank | Surname | Initial | Airforce | Serial | Code | Drop Zone | Load | Dropped |
|---|---|---|---|---|---|---|---|---|
| F/Lt | Sawyer | F.C | | NG146 | XY-E | The Hague | 5 | 4 |
| F/O | Hall | M.R | | NG137 | XY-D | The Hague | 5 | 4 |
| F/O | Grindlay | M | | NG174 | XY-J | The Hague | 5 | 3 |
| F/Lt | Green | T.B | | NG149 | XY-G | The Hague | 5 | 5 |
| F/O | Verry | C | RNZAF | NN720 | XY-K | The Hague | 5 | 5 |
| F/Sgt | Jarvis | K | | PB139 | XY-C | The Hague | 4 | 2 |
| P/O | Cooke AFM | S | | NG140 | XY-F | The Hague | 5 | 3 |
| F/O | Reeve | D.V | | PB858 | XY-O | The Hague | 4 | 4 |
| F/O | Grass | H.R | RCAF | LM692 | XY-R | The Hague | 5 | 3 |
| F/O | Williams | E.S | RAAF | PB790 | XY-S | The Hague | 5 | 4 |
| F/Sgt | Gillespie | B | | NG148 | XY-T | The Hague | 5 | 3 |
| F/O | Forand | J.M | RCAF | RF126 | XY-V | The Hague | 5 | 2 |
| Sgt | Hayne | G.R | | PD429 | XY-Z | The Hague | 5 | 1 |
| P/O | Collinson | J.J | RAAF | PB896 | XY-W | The Hague | 5 | 4 |
| | | | | | | | **Total** | **47** |

The squadron arrived at the drop zone around 15:00 hours, and unlike the previous operation, the visibility was good. A large white cross that had been laid out by the Dutch was easily visible. The Path Finders had accurately dropped a few Red TI Markers but given the conditions they were not needed. Unlike the previous visits, there was a marked decrease in Dutch civilians around the drop zones. What were in abundance were numerous carts neatly lined up, ready to be loaded with the packages. Flight Lieutenant Green was one of the few on the squadron that managed to drop all five packages. His only concern was the *'Stream too concentrated over drop zone'*. Flight Sergeant K Jarvis was at the controls of Lancaster PB139 XY-C. He had the bad luck of dropping only two of his four packages, two being brought back to RAF Stradishall. Equally frustrated was Sgt 'Bill' Hayne. Four urgently needed packages refused to budge aboard Lancaster PD429 XY-Z, the irritated crew landing back at base at 16:17 hours. On the return trip, F/O D Reeve spotted 'GOOD LUCKY TOMMY' painted on the tiled roof of a building. The problems with hang ups resulted in 11 urgently needed packs being brought back to RAF Stradishall. The Ground Crews especially, took this very hard and promised to try and resolve the issue quickly.

Fourteen crews were again detailed and briefed for another supply dropping operation on the 2nd. Number 31 Group would provide 56 Lancasters for a late morning take off. As per the previous day the drop zone was the Ypenburg Airfield. Located close to the coast, the airfield had been closed in 1943 by the Germans fearing it could be used for an airborne landing. By 1944, the airfield had become a storage base for V-1 flying bombs.

The gratitude of the Dutch civilians was expressed in many ways. Here written in the fertile Dutch soil, is a simple message, THANK YOU, BOYS. The crews of No.3 Group were often overwhelmed by their reception.

MANNA : Drop 4 : May 2nd, 1945 : The Hague Ypenburg Airfield

| Rank | Surname | Initial | Airforce | Serial | Code | Drop Zone | Load | Dropped |
|---|---|---|---|---|---|---|---|---|
| F/Lt | Saunders | A | | NG137 | XY-D | The Hague | 5 | 4 |
| P/O | Cooke AFM | S.F | | NG140 | XY-F | The Hague | 5 | 4 |
| F/Lt | Hart | J.H | | Ng149 | XY-G | The Hague | 5 | 5 |
| F/O | Hall | M.R | | NG174 | XY-J | The Hague | 5 | 5 |
| P/O | Rose | B.A | | NN720 | XY-K | The Hague | 5 | 5 |
| F/O | Verry | C.C | RNZAF | PD426 | XY-L | The Hague | 4 | 4 |
| F/Lt | Hill DFC | P.T | | RF198 | XY-N | The Hague | 5 | 5 |
| F/Sgt | Holmes | E.O | RAAF | PB858 | XY-O | The Hague | 4 | 4 |
| F/Lt | Cussen DFC | O.A | | LM692 | AP-R | The Hague | 5 | 5 |

| | | | | | | | | |
|---|---|---|---|---|---|---|---|---|
| P/O | Howell | A.J | RAAF | PB790 | XY-S | The Hague | 5 | 5 |
| F/Lt | Idle | L.A | RNZAF | RF126 | XY-V | The Hague | 5 | 5 |
| S/Ldr | Bass AFM | R.W | | PB896 | XY-W | The Hague | 5 | 5 |
| F/Sgt | Gillespie | P | | PB509 | XY-Y | The Hague | 5 | 5 |
| Sgt | Haynes | G.R | | PD429 | XY-Z | The Hague | 5 | 4 |
| | | | | | | | **Total** | **65** |

Unlike the previous supply operations, each crew would be joined by a Leading Aircraftman passenger. It had been agreed at Group HQ level that the mid-upper gunner could be left behind, and a LAC would take his place. The Station Records Book reports, *'Both the aircrew and the passenger seemed quite thrilled with the novelty'.* What the poor mid-upper gunner thought is not recorded!

Flying between 1,200 and 1,500 feet in daylight over a still occupied Holland was still causing some anxiety amongst the crews. Pilot Officer S Cooke AFM reporting perhaps for future reference, *'A heavy battery of guns was seen at position 52 degrees x 05 degrees North when crossing the coast,'* to the Intelligence Officer on return. Congestion was once again a problem over the aiming point, ensuring the crews kept a vigil both in front and importantly above for any errant Lancasters. Flight Lieutenant A Saunders dropped four of his five packages at 13:04 hours, remarking, *'Packets were seen scattered over centre and Northern parts of airfield'.* Squadron Leader R.W Bass AFM dropped his entire load at 13:07 hours. He commented, *'Load went down on airfield, but some previous aircraft's load fell short and landed in water'.* One Lancaster, flown by F/O W.J Blackman RCAF of No.195 Squadron, was seen to stray off course and enter a restricted area near Vlaardingen. Some red very flares were quickly fired from the ground. Realising the danger, the Canadian quickly turned to starboard and left the area. Sergeant G.R Haynes reported on his return, *'Flags and white sheets were waving on the ground, and a message in white was written on the ground'.* The crew's navigator was a second tour veteran, F/O G Dennis DFC. George Dennis had started his first tour in February 1943 with F/O John Overton on No.90 Squadron flying Short Stirlings. Their stay was brief due to an altercation with the C/O. They were posted to No.218 (Gold Coast) Squadron based at RAF Downham Market in April 1943. In August, they helped form No.623 Squadron. The Overton crew operated with 623 until disbandment in December 1943, when they were posted back to No.218 Squadron. By July 1944, George had completed 33 operations, including 'Operation Gimmer' the D-Day Spoof operation. Yet another new crew arrived on the 2nd. Despite the squadrons commitment to Operation 'MANNA', training continued, especially for 'C' Flight who flew eight training flights on the 2nd.

The squadron was called upon again on May 3rd, with twelve crews being detailed. Yet more new names appeared on the Operations Board. Two of them were second tour veterans, Flight Lieutenant Charles Smith DFC and F/Lt Bruce Rowe-Evans DFC. Charles Smith was awarded a DFC in November 1943 with the Short Stirling equipped No.620 Squadron, while Bruce Rowe-Evans had been awarded his DFC in November 1944 while serving No.115 Squadron. The Lancaster's of 'C' Flight utilised a break in the weather and completed four bombing and four cross country navigational exercises.

MANNA : Drop 5 : May 3rd, 1945 : The Hague Ypenburg Airfield

| Rank | Surname | Initial | Airforce | Serial | Code | Drop Zone | Load | Dropped |
|---|---|---|---|---|---|---|---|---|
| F/Lt | Sawyer | F.R | | NG137 | XY-D | The Hague | 5 | 4 |
| W/O | Mortimer | C.H | | NG140 | XY-F | The Hague | 5 | 5 |
| F/Lt | Smith DFC | C.W | | NG149 | XY-G | The Hague | 5 | 5 |
| P/O | Onus | M.J | RAAF | NG174 | XY-J | The Hague | 5 | 5 |
| F/Sgt | Jarvis | K.W | | NN720 | XY-K | The Hague | 5 | 5 |
| F/Lt | Hill DFC | P.T | | PB139 | XY-C | The Hague | 5 | 4 |
| F/O | Reeve | D.V | | PB790 | XY-S | The Hague | 5 | 4 |

| | | | | | | | | |
|---|---|---|---|---|---|---|---|---|
| P/O | Grass | H.R | RCAF | LM692 | XY-R | The Hague | 5 | 5 |
| F/O | Forand | J.N | RCAF | RF126 | XY-V | The Hague | 5 | 5 |
| P/O | Collinson | J.J | RAAF | PB896 | XY-W | The Hague | 5 | 5 |
| W/O | Taylor | A.D | RAAF | PB509 | XY-Y | The Hague | 5 | 5 |
| F/Lt | Rowe-Evans DFC | B.A | | PD429 | XY-Z | The Hague | 5 | 4 |
| | | | | | | | **Total** | **68** |

The crews reported a high concentration of packages scattered over the airfield, helped by a number of accurately placed Red TI Markers. Several parcels were seen to burst open on landing spreading their contents over a wide area. The numbers of Dutch civilians in the drop zone were again down on the

One of the experienced pilots arriving on the squadron in the last weeks of the war was Flight Lieutenant Bruce Rowe-Evans, DFC. ( 4th from right) He had previously served on No.115 Squadron, where it is understood this photograph was taken.

previous trips, but the crews took great delight in the hundreds of flags and white sheets that marked the route in and out of The Hague. One message read '*TOBAC S.V.P'*. The problems of parcels refusing to drop had still not been fully resolved. However, the number of 'hang-up's was gradually decreasing due to the perseverance of the Ground Crews.

MANNA : Drop 6 : May 4th, 1945 : The Hague Ypenburg Airfield

| Rank | Surname | Initial | Airforce | Serial | Code | Drop Zone | Load | Dropped |
|---|---|---|---|---|---|---|---|---|
| F/O | Levett | P.U | RAAF | PB139 | XY-C | The Hague | 5 | 5 |
| F/O | Danvers DFC | T.C | RAAF | NG137 | XY-D | The Hague | 5 | 5 |
| W/O | Mortimer | C.H | | NG174 | XY-J | The Hague | 5 | 4 |
| F/Lt | Cussen DFC | O.A | | PB509 | XY-Y | The Hague | 5 | 0 |
| W/Cdr | Hancock | E.L | | PB896 | XY-W | The Hague | 5 | 5 |
| W/O | Taylor | A | RAAF | PD429 | XY-Z | The Hague | 5 | 5 |
| | | | | | | | **Total** | **24** |

The squadron's efforts were sufficiently less than the previous trips when only six crews were briefed on the morning of May 4th. Once again, a veteran from the 1944 bomber offensive would make a 'Manna' trip their ticket back into operational life. Flying Officer Thomas Danvers DFC RAAF was an old hand, having started his first tour in September 1943 with No.149 (East India) Squadron. He was awarded a DFC in August 1944 on completion of his tour. The crew of F/Lt O.A Cussen DFC were unable to drop their five parcels due to a mechanical issue aboard Lancaster PB509 XY-Y. However, the crew dropped 200 of their own cigarettes by parachute over the Hague.

MANNA : Drop 7 : May 5th, 1945 : The Hague Ypenburg Airfield

| Rank | Surname | Initial | Airforce | Serial | Code | Drop Zone | Load | Dropped |
|---|---|---|---|---|---|---|---|---|
| F/Lt | Green | T.B | | NG140 | XY-P | The Hague | 5 | 5 |
| S/Ldr | Marshall | A.N | | NG149 | XY-G | The Hague | 5 | 3 |
| F/O | Lovett | P.U | RAAF | RF198 | XY-N | The Hague | 5 | 5 |
| P/O | Turner | T.F | | LM692 | AP-R | The Hague | 5 | 4 |
| F/O | Winfield | H | | PB790 | XY-S | The Hague | 5 | 5 |
| F/Lt | Idle DFC | L.A | RNZAF | RF126 | XY-V | The Hague | 5 | 4 |
| | | | | | | | **Total** | **26** |

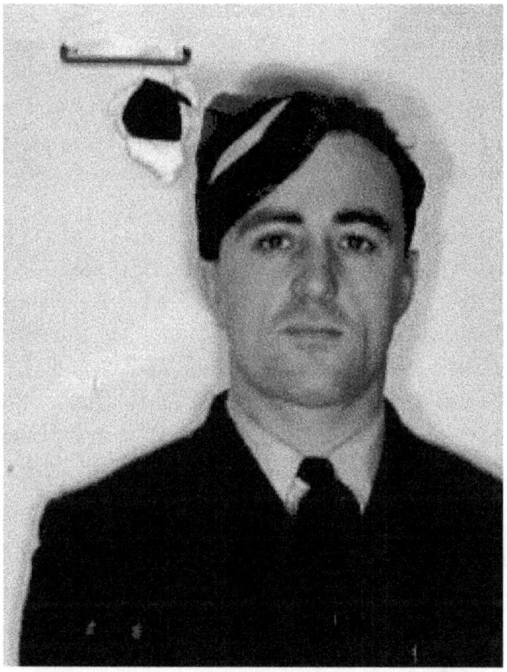

Another pilot with considerable operational experience was Flying Officer Thomas Danvers DFC RAAF. He is photographed here on enlistment.

The aiming point was once again marked by Path Finder TI Markers, which appeared on this occasion to obscure the aerodrome. Squadron Leader A.N Marshall had two hang-ups but was satisfied with the accuracy. They dropped their own chocolate ration over Delft. Two of the participating aircraft, Lancaster RF198 and LM692, were recently modified with a new release mechanism. Flying Officer P.U Lovett RAAF was flying RF198, and his entire load undershot by 200 yards, less one bag of sugar. At the controls of Lancaster LM692, the other modified Lancaster was Pilot Officer T Turner. He dropped his entire load minus a bag of dried eggs at 07:39 hours. On the 6th, 15 Lancasters were prepared and loaded for a supply drop. This was, however, cancelled at 09:50 hours. Closer to home, an investigation by S/Ldr Bass AFM into the circumstances and cause of a mysterious fire in 'A' Flight's Dispersal Hut was carried out throughout the day.

A heavy mist hung over RAF Stradishall on the early morning of the 7th, but would quickly clear by late morning allowing 15 crews to safely take-off just before mid-day.

MANNA : Drop 8 : May 7th, 1945 : The Hague

| Rank | Surname | Initial | Airforce | Serial | Code | Drop Zone | Load | Dropped |
|---|---|---|---|---|---|---|---|---|
| F/O | Haynes | B.G | | LM697 | XY-A | The Hague | 5 | 5 |
| F/O | Perkins | H.G | RAAF | PB139 | XY-C | The Hague | 5 | 5 |
| W/O | Mortimer | C | | NG137 | XY-D | The Hague | 5 | 5 |
| F/O | Cooke AFM | S | | NG140 | XY-F | The Hague | 5 | 5 |
| F/Lt | Hart | J.H | | NG149 | XY-G | The Hague | 5 | 4 |
| F/O | Onus | M | RAAF | NG174 | XY-J | The Hague | 5 | 3 |

| | | | | | | | | |
|---|---|---|---|---|---|---|---|---|
| F/O | Lovett | P.M | RAAF | NN720 | XY-K | The Hague | 5 | 4 |
| F/Lt | Holmes | E.M | | PB858 | XY-O | The Hague | 5 | 4 |
| F/O | Perrett | M | | LM692 | AP-R | The Hague | 5 | 5 |
| F/O | MacDonald | G.W | RAAF | PB790 | XY-S | The Hague | 5 | 4 |
| F/O | Forand | J | RCAF | NG293 | XY-U | The Hague | 5 | 5 |
| S/Ldr | Bass AFM | R.W | | RF126 | XY-V | The Hague | 5 | 4 |
| F/Sgt | Baker | L.G | RAAF | PB896 | XY-W | The Hague | 5 | 5 |
| W/O | Taylor | A.D | RAAF | PD429 | XY-Z | The Hague | 5 | 4 |
| F/O | Gray | P | | NG148 | XY-T | The Hague | 5 | 5 |
| | | | | | | | **Total** | **67** |

During the morning, yet another two crews arrived, making three in just 24 hours. Unfortunately, they would have to wait their turn to get operational. Over The Hague, the Path Finders had marked the drop zone under challenging conditions. A few marker flares landed in a nearby wood setting some trees on fire. Between 13:20 hours and 13:25 hours, the squadron dropped a respectable 67 packs of supplies on the racecourse drop zone. Five Lancasters had the new mechanical dropping device fitted. All but one worked perfectly, although some crews complained that the loads dropped prematurely. The size of the drop zone also came in for some criticism. Flight Lieutenant J.H Hart, *'There was some water on the racetrack as splashes could be seen as the sacks hit the ground. No sacks were seen to burst. The dropping zone was only 300 yards wide, and there was probably some undershooting'.* At 02:41 hours on the morning of May 7th , at SHAEF headquarters in Reims, France, the Chief-of-Staff of the German Armed Forces High Command, General Alfred Jodl, signed an unconditional surrender document for all German forces to the Allies. General Franz Böhme announced the unconditional surrender of German troops in Norway on 7 May. It included the phrase *'All forces under German control to cease active operations at 2301 hours Central European Time on May 8, 1945'.*

May 8th, 1945, the crews awoke to light rain. The squadron would once again be required, eight crews being detailed. After breakfast, the selected crews headed for the briefing held at 11:00 hours. On conclusion and while awaiting transported to the distant dispersals the crews, and all No.31 Base, Stradishall listened over the Tannoy system to two impressive addresses given firstly by the Base Commander, Group Captain E.C Bates AFC followed by Air Commodore Silvester. The elated Base Commander informed everyone the War in Europe was finally over. A massive cheer reverberated around RAF Stradishall. It was hard to contain the joy and sense of euphoria that swept the base. Once the initial shock had sunk in, a one-minute silence was then observed, standing bareheaded and in deep thought. It would have been impossible not to think of friends who had fallen.

The jubilant Aircrew left the briefing rooms and were driven by a fleet of crew buses to their laden aircraft. Unbeknown, this trip, was the last in the 'Manna' programme. The weather reflected the mood of the squadron, it was amazing.

MANNA : Drop 9 : May 8th, 1945 : **VE-DAY** - The Hague Ypenburg Airfield

| Rank | Surname | Initial | Airforce | Serial | Code | Drop Zone | Load | Dropped |
|---|---|---|---|---|---|---|---|---|
| F/O | Gillespie | A.P | RAAF | PB139 | XY-C | The Hague | 5 | 5 |
| F/O | Rose | B.A | | NG137 | XY-D | The Hague | 5 | 5 |
| S/Ldr | Marshall | A.N | | NG149 | XY-G | The Hague | 5 | 5 |
| F/Sgt | Jarvis | K.W | | NG140 | XY-F | The Hague | 5 | 4 |
| F/O | Reeve | D.V | | LM692 | AP-R | The Hague | 5 | 5 |
| F/O | Winfield | H.A | | NG293 | XY-U | The Hague | 5 | 5 |
| F/Lt | Claydon DFC | G.M | | RF126 | XY-V | The Hague | 5 | 5 |
| F/O | Grass | R | RCAF | PD429 | ZY-Z | The Hague | 5 | 5 |
| | | | | | | | **Total** | **39** |

Number 31 Base contributed twenty-four Lancasters on this the final 'MANNA' operation, each squadron providing just eight crews. The sea crossing was made without incident. The stream crossed the coast, and the TI markers dropped by the Path Finders were insight within minutes. The squadron was over the airfield between 13:21 hours and 13:24 hours, dropping 39 urgently needed packages. There were some reports of the packages bursting on impact with the ground. Flying Officer D.V Reeves reported that *'Target Indicators appeared to have set a hangar on fire'*. It was quickly obvious that the Dutch civilians below were aware that the war was over, and at last, they were free. The whole route was a mass of flags. The crowds appeared to be even more enthusiastic. Messages were painted or made with white towels, 'THANK YOU' and 'WELCOME' were observed as the Lancasters raced back to RAF Stradishall. The last Lancaster to land at 14:26 hours was skippered by F/Lt Gordon Claydon DFC and his experienced crew. The crew, which included three holders of the DFCs and one DFM, had previously served on No.15 Squadron. The returning crews and the rest of the Base were in high spirits and were looking forward to celebrating in the customary manner, a Mess Party. However, this was probably dampened a little when, although stood down for 24 hours, they were warned against *'acts of vandalism'*. What this meant is unknown.

The operations carried out to avert the starvation of the brave Dutch were for many of the bomber crews, the pinnacle of their operational tours. Between April 29th and May 8th, 1945, the crews who took part in Operation 'Manna' and not forgetting the Yank effort Operation 'Chowhound' flew almost 5,300 sorties. They dropped up to 11,000 tons of urgently needed supplies (army rations, beans, ship biscuits, cheese, chocolate, cigarettes, egg powder, flour, margarine, condensed milk, spam, tea). Number 186 Squadron had flown a total of 104 sorties and dropped 458 parcels. It was by any standards a marvelous effort by everyone on the squadron. Even though three-quarters of a century has passed by since these events unfolded, the people of the Netherlands have not forgotten the bravery of the young airmen who put their lives on the line to help their parents and grandparents. A Manna monument was inaugurated in 2006 in Rotterdam. Flying Officer Phil Gray, who participated on the May 7$^{th}$ supply operations wonderfully sums up the emotions and what it meant to the crews.

> *Now those huge, mysterious panniers in Stores Section could come into play. Strung along the gaping bomb bay of each Lancaster, the carriers held a load of 7,000 pounds of food. There were sacks of flour, oatmeal, and sugar, huge commercial-size tins of fruit, vegetables and beans, together with tea, coffee, fresh vegetables, and mouth-watering, three-inch-thick, foot-long blocks of manufacturers' chocolate. In essence, there was everything to keep these unfortunate people alive until normality could come trickling slowly back to these vulnerable lowlands of Holland. There was a great feeling of sympathy and consolation about these flights of mercy, all made in the name of Operation Manna. They may have started off tinged with high adventure as the scores of Lancasters roared out over the North Sea at 1,500 feet, easing down to 500 feet for the final run-in, but the mood changed markedly as the drop got underway, as the crews watched the scenes unfolding just outside their windscreens. Men and women—some old, some young, some crippled, some down on their hands and knees—were scrambling to retrieve the commodities being dumped across the few remaining high points of their limited territory. We saw people wave, while others stumbled and fell as they moved over the rough ground. It would have been a hard man indeed who would not have been touched by the emotional scenes taking place not too far below the bombers. I can assure you, without reservation, that I had one hell of a job trying to blink back the tears as I watched one old lady, already down on her knees, hands clasped together and held upwards, face staring towards the sky. Whether she was thanking her Maker, the Lancasters, or both, I will never know. At 150 knots and low-level flight, hers was an image that lasted but a fleeting moment in time*

*for me, a moment that was to be etched deep for the rest of my life.*

The squadron was not required on the 9th. The lack of flying was warmly received, given that the booze-filled festivities in the various Messes continued into the early hours. Four of the squadron's more experienced crews were posted at this time. Flight Lieutenant L.A Idle RNZAF, F/Lt T.B Green, F/Lt F Fernley and F/Lt A Saunders found themselves Yorkshire bound posted to No.76 Squadron on May 10th. Number 76 Squadron had only two days before joined the ranks of RAF Transport Command after admirable work with No.4 Group. The squadron was in the process of converting from the undervalued H.P Halifax to the American Dakota.

On the 10th, a new code name appeared on the Ops Board, 'Exodus'. With the war in Europe over, the repatriation of Allied Prisoners of War was now a priority. With the vast majority of the German and European transportation systems in tatters and the limited availability of Allied transport aircraft, it was decided to utilize Bomber Command's aircraft. This new role had already been discussed at HQ. Number 3 Group's Operations Instruction No.77, dated April 21st, 1945, had calculated that the Avro Lancaster Mk.B.I/III could carry up to 24 passengers plus the usual crew of seven. On May 10th, 'C' Flight lost S/Ldr J.H Day DFC, who took off for some well-earned leave. Command passed, if but temporarily to F/Lt Charles Smith DFC.

May 10th would see the squadron begin the emotional task of bringing back former Prisoners of War, many of whom were suffering from malnutrition after years of captivity. The squadron would supply ten Lancasters. Over at RAF Wratting Command, No.195 Squadron would supply an additional ten crews while the Chedburgh based 218 Squadron provided eleven.

EXODUS : Repatriation Flight 1 : May 10th, 1945 : Juvincourt, France

| Rank | Surname | Initial | Airforce | Serial | Code | Reception A/F | PoWs |
|---|---|---|---|---|---|---|---|
| F/Lt | Hart | J.H | | NG137 | XY-D | RAF Westcott | 24 |
| F/Lt | Sawyer | F | | NG146 | XY-E | RAF Westcott | 24 |
| F/Lt | Hill DFC | P.T | | LM697 | XY-A | RAF Westcott | 24 |
| F/Lt | Millgate DFC | R | RAAF | NG174 | XY-J | RAF Westcott | 24 |
| P/O | Baker | L.G | RAAF | PB858 | XY-Q | RAF Westcott | 24 |
| F/O | Onus | M.J | RAAF | NN755 | XY-Q | RAF Westcott | 24 |
| F/O | Gray | P | | NG148 | XY-T | RAF Westcott | 24 |
| S/Ldr | Bass AFM | R.W | | RF126 | XY-V | RAF Westcott | 24 |
| P/O | Holmes | E | RAAF | PB596 | XY-W | RAF Westcott | 24 |
| F/O | Grass | H.R | | PD429 | XY-Z | RAF Westcott | 24 |
| | | | | | | **Total** | **240** |

As expected, on arrival at Juvincourt, the crews found the whole airfield a mass of dishevelled former PoWs mixed with Air Force and Army personnel trying to process the ever-growing number of aircraft arrivals and troop movement. On landing, the ten Lancasters were quickly loaded, each with 24 PoWs who were recorded as Officers and other ranks. The squadron was at Juvincourt just seventy-five minutes before they were airborne on the 50-minute flight to RAF Westcott. The ORB records the following, *'Behaved with excellent discipline, and there were no cases of air sickness during flight. Many had been prisoners since Dunkirk and were badly clothed. They had recently been well fed by the Americans but had lived in discomfort while at Juvincourt'.*

Juvincourt, France. A bunch of Allied ex PoWs slowly walk towards Lancasters of No.186 squadron. The XY codes can just be seen. The first two aircraft carry the twin yellow bars on the fins, denoting they are G-H Leaders.

Sergeant H Peake was the navigator to Australian P/O Les Baker RAAF, and he recalls the first of his trips during Operation 'Exodus' and what it meant to the crews.

*The 'EXODUS' trips provide me some of the best memories of my service days. We did three of them in May '45. We flew out to the American base at Juvincourt in France to bring back 24 ex-POW's (most of them long term - up to six years) in each Lanc. We flew them back to Westcott, Oakley and Wing (our former 0.T.U.) respectively and returned to base at Strad. The excited anticipation of returning to Britain and home after those long years of captivity, the eager question "Where are we"? of those crowded round the nav table and when shown on the chart that we were approaching the cliffs near Dover the tears of joy that ran down their cheeks as they jockeyed for positions to get a sighting through any aperture they could find. Though we had spent a long time training for comparatively few operations before the end of the war in Europe ended, those three trips alone made it worthwhile.*

The following day, the squadron prepared 15 Lancasters for a return visit to Juvincourt. At the controls of one Lancaster was the Squadron Commander, W/Cdr Ernest Hancock.

EXODUS : Repatriation Flight 2 ; May 11th, 1945 : Juvincourt, France

| Rank | Surname | Initial | Airforce | Serial | Code | Reception A/F | PoWs |
|---|---|---|---|---|---|---|---|
| F/Sgt | Jarvis | K.W | | NG137 | XY-D | RAF Tangmere | 24 |
| F/O | Gillespie | A.P | RAAF | PB139 | XY-C | RAF Tangmere | 24 |
| F/O | Haynes | B.G | | RF198 | XY-N | RAF Tangmere | 24 |
| F/Lt | Sawyer | F | | NG146 | XY-E | RAF Tangmere | 24 |

| | | | | | | | |
|---|---|---|---|---|---|---|---|
| F/O | Cooke AFM | S.F | | NG140 | XY-F | RAF Tangmere | 24 |
| F/O | Onus | M.J | RAAF | NG174 | XY-J | RAF Tangmere | 24 |
| F/O | Danvers DFC | T | | PD426 | XY-L | RAF Tangmere | 24 |
| F/O | Grass | H.R | RCAF | PB858 | XY-O | RAF Tangmere | 23 |
| W/O | Taylor | A | RAAF | NN755 | XY-Q | RAF Tangmere | 24 |
| F/O | Williams | E.S | RAAF | PB790 | XY-S | RAF Tangmere | 24 |
| F/O | Winfield | H.A | | NG148 | XY-T | RAF Tangmere | 24 |
| F/O | Reeve | D.V | | NG293 | XY-U | RAF Tangmere | 24 |
| W/Cdr | Hancock | E.L | | RF126 | XY-V | RAF Tangmere | 24 |
| F/O | Perrett | M | | PB509 | XY-Y | RAF Tangmere | Aborted |
| P/O | MacDonald | G.F | RAAF | PD429 | XY-Z | RAF Tangmere | 24 |
| | | | | | | **Total** | **335** |

The squadron recorded an uncharacteristic early return. Flying Officer M Perritt suffered W/T receiver failure 30 miles south of Calais aboard Avro Lancaster PB509 XY-Y. The crew returned to RAF Stradishall.

Unfortunately, F/O Gillespie RAAF and F/O Cooke AFM were obliged to have tyre changes at Juvincourt, delaying their return flight. The problem was caused by the Pierced Steel Planking, or PSP used at Juvincourt. Excellent for more nimble aircraft, it took a bashing from the 'Heavies' and was prone to warp upwards leaving sharp edges. The issues with tyres continued at RAF Tangmere, where F/O Busteed Gordon William Haynes or 'Buss' had burst a tyre on landing. The Lancaster and the crew were forced to stay overnight. The following day, a spare tyre was flown to RAF Tangmere by F/Sgt Gore Robert Victor Haynes, better known as 'Bill,' aboard PD429 XY-Z. Both 'Bill' and 'Buss' were in fact brothers, the squadron had the rare distinction of having two brothers of the squadron.

Fifteen crews were prepared for a late morning flight to Juvincourt on the 12th, which would be a day of mixed fortunes.

EXODUS : Repatriation Flight 3 ; May 12th, 1945 : Juvincourt, France

| Rank | Surname | Initial | Airforce | Serial | Code | Reception A/F | PoWs |
|---|---|---|---|---|---|---|---|
| F/Sgt | Jarvis | K.W | | LM697 | XY-A | RAF Ford | 24 |
| F/Lt | Gillespie | A.P | RAAF | PB139 | XY-C | RAF Ford | 24 |
| F/Lt | Hart | H.H | | NG137 | XY-D | RAF Ford | Aborted |
| F/Lt | Hill DFC | P.T | | NG146 | XY-E | RAF Ford | 24 |
| F/O | Cooke AFM | S.F | | NG140 | XY-F | RAF Wing | 24 |
| F/O | Onus | M.J | RAAF | NG174 | XY-J | RAF Ford | 24 |
| F/Lt | Smith DFC | C.W | | PD426 | XY-L | RAF Oakley | 24 |
| S/Ldr | Marshall | A.N | | NG149 | XY-G | RAF Ford | 24 |
| P/O | Holmes | E | RAAF | PB858 | XY-O | RAF Ford | Aborted |
| P/O | Baker | L.G | RAAF | LM692 | AP-R | RAF Oakley | 24 |
| P/O | Williams | E | RAAF | PB790 | XY-S | RAF Ford | 24 |
| P/O | Gray | P | | NG148 | XY-T | RAF Ford | 24 |
| F/O | Collinson | J.J | RAAF | NG293 | XY-U | RAF Ford | 24 |
| F/O | Winfield | H.A | | RF126 | XY-V | RAF Oakley | 24 |
| F/Lt | Rowe-Evans DFC | B.A | | PB509 | XY-Y | RAF Oakley | 24 |
| | | | | | | **Total** | **312** |

Juvincourt, France. The Lancasters of No.186 Squadron are parked up and ready for the ex-PoWs

The operations started badly when P/O E Holmes RAAF damaged a tyre on take-off aboard Lancaster PB858 XY-O. Wisely, the crew decided to return to RAF Stradishall, not wanting to risk an accident when fully loaded with PoWs. The early returns continued when the boost on the starboard outer engine aboard Lancaster NG137 XY-O proved an issue while in the circuit over Juvincourt. The crew choose to return to RAF Stradishall and not land and await repairs. The remaining Lancasters landed safely and began loading the PoWs. Eight were loaded and began the flight home. Five, however, were compelled to stay overnight as there were no PoWs ready while the weather remained good over France[58]. The crews, F/Lt's Rowe-Evans DFC, Smith DFC, F/O's Winfield, Cooke AFM, and P/O Baker RAAF would have an opportunity to sample the delights of a liberated France. Navigator aboard LM692 AP-R[59] was Sgt H Peake, who recalls the following.

> *On our second Exodus trip on the 12th May the weather in England clamped down and we had to spend the night on the other side, so the Yanks in their own hospitable way organised transport and took us standing in open trucks (about 60 to a truck) on a hair raising 20Km drive to spend the evening in Rheims, I have recollections of seeing Lady Mountbatten at the Juvincourt base, I think she held a top position with the Red Cross.*

The following morning the crews departed fully loaded, four landing at the reception airfield at RAF Oakley, while F/O Cooke AFM landed at RAF Wing. The flights continued the following day when thirteen crews were detailed. There were thankfully no issues reported. The ORB reported, *'The Prisoners showed good discipline throughout the journey to the reception centre, there were a few cases of air-sickness'*.

---

[58] *Reported in Squadron ORB but at odds with Sgt Peake.*
[59] *One of the rare occasions a 'C' Flight Lancaster is recorded in a log book.*

EXODUS : Repatriation Flight 4 : May 13th, 1945 : Juvincourt, France

| Rank | Surname | Initial | Airforce | Serial | Code | Reception A/F | PoWs |
|---|---|---|---|---|---|---|---|
| F/Lt | Gillespie | A.P | RAAF | PB139 | XY-C | RAF Ford | 24 |
| F/O | Hall | M.R | | NG137 | XY-D | RAF Ford | 24 |
| F/Lt | Sawyer | F.R | | NG146 | XY-E | RAF Ford | 24 |
| F/Lt | Claydon DFC | G.M | | NG149 | XY-G | RAF Ford | 24 |
| F/Sgt | Jarvis | K.W | | PD429 | XY-Z | RAF Ford | 24 |
| F/O | Perkins | H.G | RAAF | NN720 | XY-K | RAF Ford | 24 |
| F/Lt | Plum | F | | NG354 | XY-M | RAF Ford | 24 |
| F/Lt | Hill DFC | P.T | | RF198 | XY-N | RAF Ford | 24 |
| F/O | Reeve | D.V | | PB858 | XY-C | RAF Ford | 24 |
| W/O | Taylor | A.D | RAAF | NN755 | XY-Q | RAF Ford | 24 |
| F/Sgt | Haynes | G.R | | PB790 | XY-S | RAF Ford | 24 |
| F/O | MacDonald | G.W | RAAF | NG148 | XY-T | RAF Ford | 24 |
| F/O | Grass | H.R | RCAF | NG293 | XY-U | RAF Ford | 24 |
| | | | | | | **Total** | **312** |

Number 31 Base provided 46 Lancasters for the repatriation of PoWs on the 14th, with No.186 Squadron providing twelve.

EXODUS : Repatriation Flight 5 : May 14th, 1945 : Juvincourt, France

| Rank | Surname | Initial | Airforce | Serial | Code | Reception A/F | PoWs |
|---|---|---|---|---|---|---|---|
| F/Sgt | Haynes | B.G | | LM697 | XY-A | RAF Ford | 24 |
| F/O | Edwards DFC | D | | PB139 | XY-C | RAF Ford | 24 |
| F/Lt | Hart | J.H | | NG149 | XY-G | RAF Ford | 24 |
| F/O | Onus | M.J | RAAF | NG140 | XY-F | RAF Ford | 24 |
| F/O | Hall | M.B | | PD426 | XY-L | RAF Ford | 24 |
| F/Lt | Hill DFC | P.T | | RF198 | XY-N | RAF Ford | 24 |
| P/O | Holmes | E.O | RAAF | PB858 | XY-O | RAF Ford | 24 |
| W/O | Taylor | A.D | RAAF | NN755 | XY-Q | RAF Ford | 24 |
| F/O | Williams | E.S | | LM692 | AP-R | RAF Ford | 24 |
| F/Lt | Gray | P | | NG148 | XY-T | RAF Ford | 24 |
| F/O | Collinson | J.J | RAAF | NG293 | XY-U | RAF Ford | 24 |
| F/Sgt | Haynes | G.R | | JB475 | XY-X | RAF Ford | 24 |
| | | | | | | **Total** | **288** |

The operation went without any complications, other than a number of PoWs becoming air-sick due to bumpy conditions on the flight home. The Lancasters were cleaned, fueled, and made ready for the following morning when 15 Lancasters would once again be required.

EXODUS : Repatriation Flight 6 : May 15th, 1945 : Juvincourt, France

| Rank | Surname | Initial | Airforce | Serial | Code | Reception A/F | PoWs |
|---|---|---|---|---|---|---|---|
| F/Sgt | Haynes | B.G | | RF198 | XY-N | RAF Wing | 23 |
| F/Lt | Gillespie | A.P | RAAF | PB139 | XY-C | RAF Wing | 24 |
| F/O | Onus | M.J | RAAF | NG137 | XY-D | RAF Wing | 24 |
| F/Lt | Hill DFC | P.T | | NG140 | XY-F | RAF Wing | 24 |
| F/Lt | Sawyer | F.R | | NG149 | XY-G | RAF Wing | 23 |
| F/O | Hall | M.B | | NN720 | XY-K | RAF Wing | 24 |
| P/O | Hudson | A.L | RAAF | PD426 | XY-L | RAF Wing | 24 |
| P/O | Holmes | E.O | RAAF | PB858 | XY-O | RAF Wing | 24 |

| | | | | | | | |
|---|---|---|---|---|---|---|---|
| F/O | Grass | H.R | RCAF | NN755 | XY-Q | RAF Wing | 24 |
| F/O | MacDonald | G.W | RAAF | LM692 | XY-R | RAF Wing | 24 |
| S/Ldr | Bass AFM | R.W | | NG148 | XY-T | RAF Wing | 24 |
| F/O | Collinson | J.J | RAAF | RF126 | XY-V | RAF Wing | 24 |
| P/O | Baker | L.G | RAAF | PB896 | XY-W | RAF Wing | 24 |
| F/O | Winfield | H.A | | JB475 | XY-X | RAF Wing | 24 |
| F/Lt | Milgate DFC | R.F | RAAF | PB509 | XY-Y | RAF Wing | 24 |
| | | | | | | **Total** | **358** |

Flying Officer Phil Gray and crew are ready to fly home to England, a group of ex-PoWs who appear to have a 'Digger' wearing a bush hat amongst them.

The turnaround at Juvincourt and RAF Wing was now almost effortless. Amongst the PoWs deposited at the reception centre were a number of Cypriot soldiers, who still had a long arduous journey ahead of them before they reached home. An oil leak aboard P/O A.L Hudson's Lancaster delayed his return to RAF Stradishall by two hours.

The war may have been over, but the conversion units were still posting crews. Another new crew arrived on the 15th. The squadron had a well-earned day off from the shuttle run on the 16th, not that it was idle. The crews of 'C' Flight continued with their exercises, four completing bombing practice over the bombing range at Wainfleet. Three crews of 'B' Flight completed a Fighter Affiliation exercise. 'A' Flight was also airborne, completing two G-H bombing exercises over Elmdon Ranges and two G-H navigational flights.

It was back to Juvincourt on the 17th. Thirteen crews were detailed and briefed, they would once again join forces with No.195 Squadron, who provided 16 crews and No.218 Squadron, which sent 17 crews. All forty-six Lancasters departed into a clear warm sky.

EXODUS : Repatriation Flight 7 : May 17th, 1945 : Juvincourt, France

| Rank | Surname | Initial | Airforce | Serial | Code | Reception A/F | PoWs |
|---|---|---|---|---|---|---|---|
| F/O | Haynes | B.G | | LM697 | XY-A | RAF Westcott | 24 |
| F/Lt | Sawyer | F.R | | NG146 | XY-E | RAF Westcott | 24 |
| F/O | Hall | M.B | | NG140 | XY-F | RAF Westcott | 24 |
| F/Lt | Gillespie | A.P | RAAF | NG149 | XY-G | RAF Westcott | 24 |
| F/Sgt | Jarvis | K.W | | NG354 | XY-M | RAF Westcott | 24 |
| F/Lt | Smith DFC | C.W | | NN720 | XY-K | RAF Westcott | 24 |
| F/Lt | Forand | J.M | RCAF | PB858 | XY-O | RAF Westcott | 24 |
| F/O | Perrett | M | | LM692 | XY-R | RAF Westcott | 24 |
| F/O | Williams | E.S | RAAF | NG293 | XY-U | RAF Westcott | 24 |
| W/O | Taylor | A.D | RAAF | PB896 | XY-W | RAF Westcott | 24 |
| F/Lt | Gray | P | | JB475 | XY-X | RAF Westcott | 24 |
| F/Sgt | Haynes | G.R | | PB509 | XY-Y | RAF Westcott | 24 |
| W/Cdr | Hancock | E.L | | Rf126 | XY-V | RAF Westcott | 24 |
| | | | | | | **Total** | **312** |

Other than the need to change a tyre aboard NG149 XY-G and an issue with engine trouble aboard F/O M Perrett aircraft, Lancaster LM692 XY-R, the operation was a complete success. The majority of the former PoWs were British. However, several Dominion soldiers were returned, plus three sailors!

Flying Officer M Perrett (Back row centre) and crew.

Twelve crews were detailed for Juvincourt on the 18th, but this was cancelled at 12:45 hours. The squadron welcomed back Squadron Leader J.H. Day DFC from leave that same day. The squadron was stood down on the 19th but informed it would be needed the following day. Fifteen crews were detailed and briefed when the operation was cancelled at 00:15 hours. Air Commodore J Sylvester, No.31 Base Commanding Officer, spent the day at No.3 Group H.Q. with the AoC No.3 Group on the 20th. He was there to discuss honours and awards. On May 21st, Group Captain E.C Bates AFC, Station Commander RAF Stradishall, was flown to Juvincourt to coordinate the organisation of ex-Prisoners of War for evacuation. Information via SHAEF indicated that there were almost 4000 ex PoWs ready to excavate. The crew given the job to fly him is believed to be S/Ldr Marshall aboard Lancaster NG149 XY-G. The crew were to be followed by 18 Lancasters. However, their departure was subsequently cancelled at 14:35 hours. The Station WAAFs had the dubious pleasure of an official visit on May 22nd by Group Officer B Bather from HQ Bomber Command. She was received by No.31 Base C/O Air Commodore Sylvester, who carried out a full inspection of all WAAF sections on No.31 Base along with Squadron Officer E.M Parkhurst. On the 22nd, 15 crews were initially detailed for an early morning take-off.

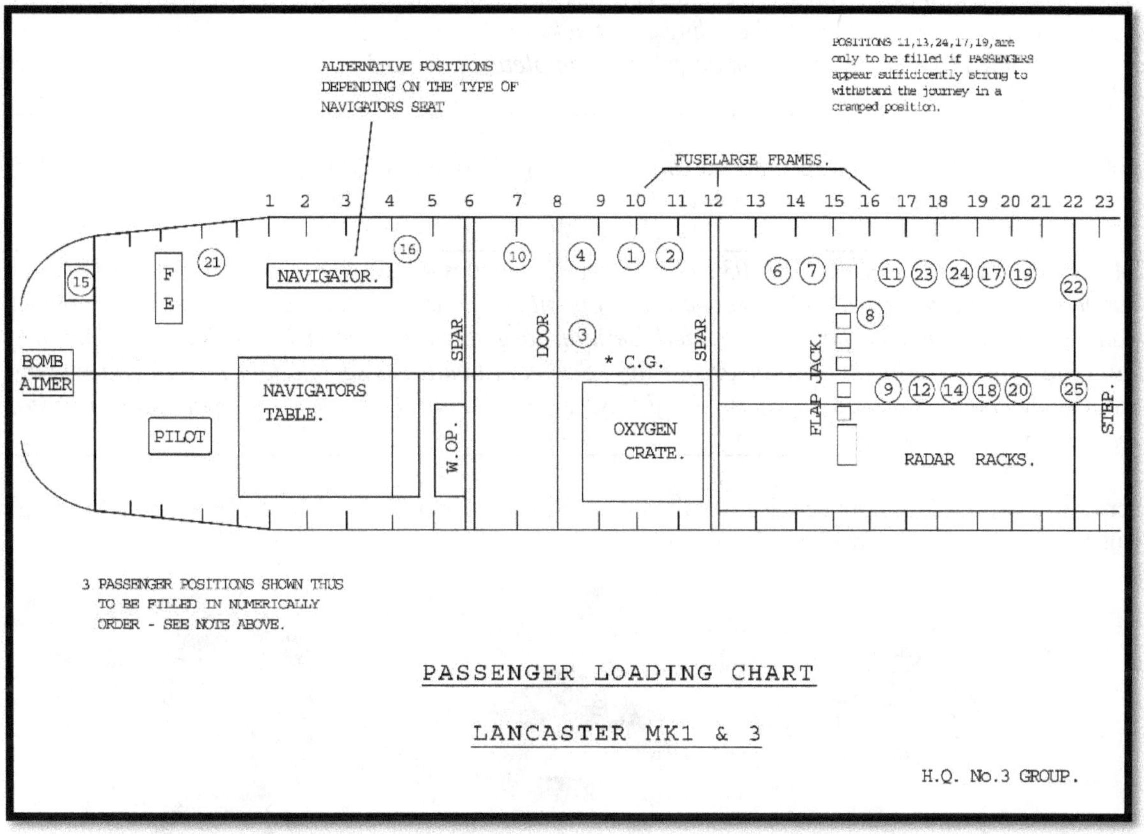


The Loading plane for the Avro Lancaster and bringing home ex-Pows.

This number was reduced when three crews were withdrawn. The remaining twelve Lancasters were fuelled and made ready while the crews completed their pre-flight briefing. Three crews had just managed to get airborne after 09:00 hours when a message was received at 09.06 hours from No.3 Group Controller instructing RAF Stradishall to postpone the operation by one hour. At 10:30 hours, the squadron was instructed to cancel the operation and stand down. The three crews already airborne continued onto Juvincourt as planned.

EXODUS : Repatriation Flight 8 ; May 22nd, 1945 : Juvincourt, France

| Rank | Surname | Initial | Airforce | Serial | Code | Reception A/F | PoWs |
|---|---|---|---|---|---|---|---|
| F/Lt | Hart | J.H | | NG137 | XY-D | RAF Dunsfold | 24 |
| F/Lt | Gillespie | A.P | RAAF | PD426 | XY-L | RAF Dunsfold | 24 |
| F/Sgt | Jarvis | K.W | | NG354 | XY-M | RAF Dunsfold | 24 |
| | | | | | | **Total** | **72** |

The three crews, plus S/Ldr Marshall and his passenger Group Captain Bates returned to RAF Stradishall on the 22nd. Wing Commander E.L Hancock began nine days leave on the 22nd, Command of the squadron was passed to S/Ldr R.W Bass AFM. The London Gazette published details of three awards to members of No.186 Squadron on the 22nd. Two DFM were promulgated, F/Sgt John McFarland, an air gunner for completing 35 operations over two tours. While serving with No.186, he was the Mid-Upper gunner with F/Lt R.A Hanson's crew. His Citation reads.

*McFARLANE, John Reid. 1550041 Flight Sergeant. Sorties 35, Flying hours 242.08. Air Gunner. This N.C.O. has an excellent operational record. On his first tour, he completed many operations against heavily defended targets including 11 attacks on Berlin. Flight Sergeant McFarlane is now on his second tour. His cheerful manner and complete disregard for danger have made him a valuable asset to his squadron.*

Another second tour veteran recognised for completing 43 operations, was fellow air gunner, Flight Sergeant Ralph Lambert, his pilot was F/O H.S Young. The citation of his DFM reads.

*LAMBERT, Ralph Geoffrey. 1811303 Flight Sergeant. Sorties 43, Flying hours 250.32. Air Gunner. Flight Sergeant Lambert is on his second tour of bomber operations. On his first tour, he completed many operations against heavily defended German targets; Berlin he visited twice and Hamburg four times. He also mined the Baltic area. Flight Sergeant Lambert's second tour also includes many heavily defended German Targets. Flight Sergeant Lambert has at all time shown great determination and courage.*

There were two DFC announced, F/Lt Walter Lea, Wireless Operator to F/O J.H Hart and pilot, Flight Lieutenant James Gibson were the recipients.

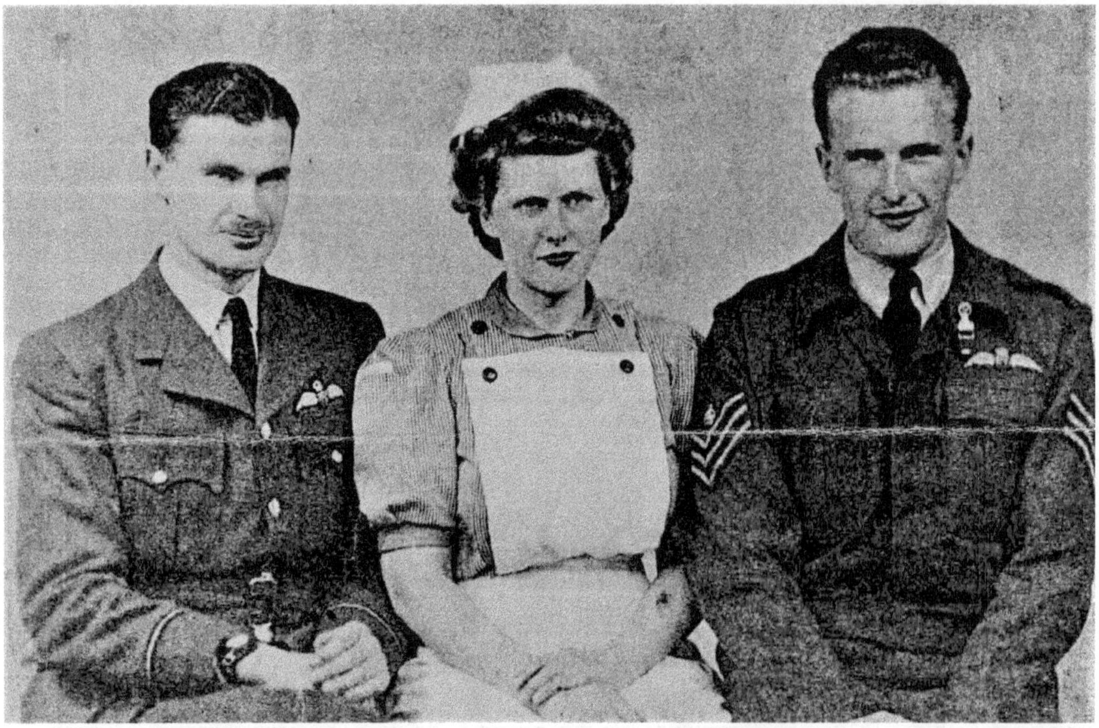

The squadron's two Haynes brothers. On the left, Pilot Officer 'Buss' Haynes, Rosemary Haynes and Flight Sergeant 'Bill' Haynes.

Only seven crews were required on the 23rd. They left just after breakfast in marginal weather conditions. On this date, the first of what would become a popular flight took place. Two crews, one of which was skippered by F/Lt Hart at the controls of NG146 XY-E, would take three passengers on a sightseeing tour of Germany's bombed and blackened cities. These flights would be called 'Baedeker' Tours. These trips were a Command decision to give ground crews and some HQ staff, including WAAFs, the opportunity to see the results of the bomber offensive, which without their dedicated efforts, could never have been maintained. The name 'Baedecker' was deliberately chosen as a reminder that the Germans had used the pre-war 'Baedecker Guide of the United Kingdom' in selecting our most beautiful towns and cities for wanton destruction. Several carefully planned routes overflew many of the main targets.

EXODUS : Repatriation Flight 9 ; May 23rd, 1945 : Juvincourt, France

| Rank | Surname | Initial | Airforce | Serial | Code | Reception A/F | PoWs |
|---|---|---|---|---|---|---|---|
| F/O | Haynes | B.G | | NG137 | XY-D | RAF Dunsfold | 24 |
| F/Lt | Verry | C.C | RNZAF | NG140 | XY-F | RAF Dunsfold | 24 |
| F/O | Onus | M.J | RAAF | PD426 | XY-L | RAF Dunsfold | 24 |
| F/Sgt | Jarvis | K.M | | NG354 | XY-M | RAF Dunsfold | 24 |
| F/O | Holmes | E.O | RAAF | PB858 | XY-O | RAF Dunsfold | 0 |
| F/Lt | Cussen DFC | O.A | | PB877 | XY-R | RAF Dunsfold | 24 |
| P/O | Winfield | H | | NG148 | XY-T | RAF Dunsfold | 24 |
| | | | | | | **Total** | **144** |

There were insufficient ex PoWs for F/O E.O Holmes RAAF and crew, so they returned empty. Flight Lieutenant C Verry RNZAF and crew were forced to stay at RAF Dunsfold due to an oil leak. They returned to RAF Stradishall the following morning. Flight Sergeant Alan Bartlett, the sole survivor from the crew of F/O James Beck RAAF, was airborne for the first time since the tragic collision on April 4th. He completed a 3 ½ hour H2S Cross-Country exercise with S/Ldr Bass AFM. Alan would continue flying with various squadron pilots up until disbandment. What turned out to be the final Exodus operation of the month departed RAF Stradishall just after lunch on May 24th. Eight crews would be involved.

EXODUS : Repatriation Flight 10 ; May 24th, 1945 : Juvincourt, France

| Rank | Surname | Initial | Airforce | Serial | Code | Reception A/F | PoWs |
|---|---|---|---|---|---|---|---|
| F/O | Haynes | B.G | | NN720 | XY-K | RAF Oakley | 24 |
| F/Lt | Fennell DFC | F.W | | NG137 | XY-F | RAF Oakley | 24 |
| F/O | Warren DFC | J.D | | PD426 | XY-L | RAF Oakley | 24 |
| F/O | Rose | B.A | | NG146 | XY-E | RAF Oakley | 24 |
| F/O | Edwards DFC | D.G | | PB877 | XY-R | RAF Oakley | 24 |
| F/Sgt | Haynes | G | | PB794 | XY-X | RAF Oakley | 24 |
| F/Lt | Howell DFC | A.H | | RF126 | XY-V | RAF Oakley | 24 |
| F/O | Winfield | H.A | | NG148 | XY-T | RAF Oakley | 24 |
| | | | | | | **Total** | **192** |

The operation was a complete success, apart from a few cases of air sickness. On the 25th, another award was announced, Air Gunner W/O Joseph Brabazon received the DFC. For the remainder of the month, the squadron would busy itself with the more mundane activities of training or if the weather permitted, 'Baedeker' flights. These were becoming increasingly popular amongst the ground echelon, eager to see firsthand the destructive capabilities of Bomber Command. Flight Sergeant Jack Allen was off to RAF Newmarket. His recommendation for a commission had finally been agreed.

*I was summoned before the Air Vice Marshal at Newmarket where, after a short interview, I was informed that I had been granted a commission.*

There was only one incident on the 'Baedeker' flights. On May 31st, F/Sgt P Gillespie had white smoke pouring from the port inner engine aboard Lancaster PB858 XY-O. The offending engine was feathered, and the crew, plus passengers, returned to RAF Woodbridge landing at 13:02 hours. The same day, W/Cdr E.L Hancock returned from leave.

After a hectic month, the squadron could be justly proud of its involvement in the food drops over Holland and the repatriation of the ex-Prisoners of War. The recently promoted F/Lt Phil Gray movingly writes about these operations. *To us, the crew, it was just another flight, so we helped the soldiers down from the plane, hanging around, possibly to chat. That was our big mistake. To many of these people, this was an overwhelming emotional experience. Some got down on their hands and knees and kissed the concrete, some kissed the grass, others simply burst into tears where they stood, while yet others lay on the grass and sobbed. I was thunderstruck—acutely embarrassed—to say nothing of being near tears myself. Most of all, I was mortified that we had not anticipated these extreme emotions. The Manna runs to Holland had been traumatic, but this was the ultimate emotional confrontation, eyeball to eyeball. We had well and truly blundered. By staying near the plane, we were impinging on privacies we had absolutely no right to share. These were our passengers' personal moments, their time, their experience. That was the important lesson we learned. On all future Exodus trips, the boys and I simply left the plane and walked away, and never, ever looked back. With twenty-four sensitive stomachs sitting in the body of the bomber, even the turns were slow and easy. We had watched our passengers come on board, each one clutching his little bag of glucose sweets, together with one other bag, just in case he was sick. These men were placing their trust in us, and we had no intention of breaking such a confidence. I'm sure every pilot, every crew, if asked, would testify that it was a privilege to have been allowed to take part in Operation Exodus.*

On May 31st, 1945, 14 full crews of 'A' Flight No.218 (Gold Coast) Squadron under the command of Squadron Leader Christopher Martindale were detached to RAF Stradishall for experimental work on H2S. Over the coming weeks, they would work closely with 'C' Flight of No.186 Squadron. Thus ended the last month of the war, it had been a busy one, and the squadron had performed magnificently in its varied tasks. The squadron had flown an impressive 186 sorties, once again exceeding the numbers flown by No.15, 90, 138 and 622 Squadrons. The squadron outshone the rest of the Group in the training programme. A staggering 546.35 hours were flown by day and 49.55 hours by night. The nearest squadron was No.218 with 340.40 hours. These hours were only possible by the endless exercises flown by Squadron Leader Day DFC and his 'C' Flight.

May 1945 : Avro Lancaster Delivery.

| ToC Date | Serial | Code | Maker | Mark | From |
|---|---|---|---|---|---|
| 05/05/1945 | NN755 | | Austin Motors | Mk.B.I | No.115 Sqn |
| 18/05/1945 | PB794 | XY-X | A.V Roe | Mk.B.III | No.195 Sqn |

Six of the crew of New Zealander Ken Orman RNZAF pose on 'Q-Queenie' in the spring sunshine at RAF Stradishall. Ken was awarded a DFC & Bar for his tour on No.186 Squadron.1

# June 1945

## *Peace*

The first week of June consisted of rather tedious training flights, G-H bombing exercises, air-to-air firing, H2S and formation flying. A number of 'Baedeker Tour' flights were once again flown, giving a number of the fortunate ground crew the opportunity to view the shattered cities of Cologne, Bonn, Frankfurt, Kassel, Essen, Duisburg Coblenz, and Dortmund. On the 1st, Squadron Leader R.W Bass AFM, the incumbent 'B' Flight commander, took some well-deserved leave. Flight Lieutenant Olaf Cussen DFC assumed his duties. The same day, the Squadron Adjutant F/Lt T Capel departed on leave. Flying Officer F Miller filled his post.

The same day six Lancaster crews were briefed for an Exodus trip to Juvincourt. Unbeknown to the crews, it would be the last major operation flown.

EXODUS : Repatriation Flight 11 : June 3rd 1945 : Juvincourt, France

| Rank | Surname | Initial | Airforce | Serial | Code | Reception A/F | PoWs |
|---|---|---|---|---|---|---|---|
| F/O | Haynes | B.G | | NG137 | XY-D | RAF Dunsford | 24 |
| F/Lt | Verry | C.C | RNZAF | PB139 | XY-C | RAF Dunsford | 10 |
| F/O | Edwards | D.G | | NG174 | XY-J | RAF Dunsford | 24 |
| F/O | Reeve | D.V | | PB790 | XY-S | RAF Dunsford | 24 |
| F/O | Rose | B.A | | NG148 | XY-T | RAF Dunsford | 24 |
| F/Sgt | Haynes | G.R | | PB896 | XY-W | RAF Dunsford | 24 |
| | | | | | | **Total** | **130** |

This, the last recorded operation in the Squadron Operational Records Book, was the only occasion that both Haynes brothers' Buss' and 'Bill' flew operationally together. It was fitting that it was an Exodus trip bringing home former PoWs. With improvement in the weather, the 'Baedeker' flights, or 'Cook's Tours' as they were also known, were becoming increasingly popular. The Station and Base Commander carried out a detailed inspection of the whole base in preparation for a visit from No.3 Group's AoC on June 5th. Everything was checked and then re-checked. On the 5th, A.V.M. Harrison CB, C.B.E, DFC AFC arrived, and a guard of honour was formed in the pouring rain by cadets attached to the station. After lunch, a full Mustering Parade with 100% attendance was planned. However, the inspection was curtailed due to heavy rain.

The weather cancelled a planned Exodus operation and Baedeker flight on the 6th, and even the ever-reliable 'C' Flight remained grounded. Around this time, the Commonwealth and Dominion crews started their long journey home. The Australians were in the majority. They would be posted first to No. 11 (R.A.A.F.) Personnel Despatch and Reception Centre (P.D.R.C.) before the long voyage home. In true squadron tradition, a leaving party was organised in their honour. This did little to hide the sad fact that the fun-loving opinionated Aussies were never to return. For some crews, the departure of the RAAF meant a large proportion of the squadron were now pilotless. Friendships forged over the skies of Germany were broken, and for many it would be the last time they were united as a crew. Even with the squadron in a peace-time setting, leave was still important and looked forward to. With the populous more relaxed and the anxiety and dangers of a war-time Britain now but a memory, there was an air of optimism sweeping across the country. Romances were rekindled, and marriage proposals that had been put on hold due to the dangers of operational flying were now an everyday occurrence. Following on from the departure of the RAAF personnel, the squadron lost its few Canadians and Kiwis. The loss of the RCAF, RNZAF and RAAF personnel seemed to deflate those remaining. They were always the very life and soul of the squadron. Other than the return of S/Ldr Bass AFM on the 10th, the squadron filled its days with endless exercises. The following day, the squadron's training was stepped up a notch. The squadron was to start an extensive training program. In addition to a new training syllabus, technical experts on the station gave lectures connected to the Far Eastern Theatre of war, plus daily lectures by the Ministry of Information. The crews were informed that the new training syllabus would last six weeks. Two crews undertook bomb touring flights on the 12th along with an aircraft from 'A' Flight of

Two late arrivals on the squadron were Australian Flying Officer Philip Lovett RAAF and Flying Officer Horace Perkins RAAF. Phil Lovett was a pre-war Clerk joining the RAAF in 1941, he arrived at the squadron on April 30th, 1945. Horace Perkins was before enlistment in 1942, a Metro Theatre Manager. He arrived on the squadron on March 10th, 1945.

No.218 Squadron. The three Lancasters and their passengers were routed over the Ruhr Dams. Air Commodore Kirkpatrick CBE, DFC SASO No.3 Group, visited RAF Stradishall on the 13th to see a demonstration in No.1 Hanger of a new supply drop apparatus. This was in all probability in connection with the recent supply dropping operations over Holland. It is presumed that the new apparatus was being assessed for future deployment. The following day, four new British pilots arrived. They would join existing crews who had lost their Commonwealth captains. Nine Lancasters were airborne on the 14th for a squadron formation exercise. Leading would be three 'Special' Lancasters from 'C' Flight. With these *'Liontamer'* equipped Lancaster's with their new H2S radar would come the possible deployment to the Far East be used in a similar fashion to the G-H equipped Lancasters over Germany.

It was the turn of 'A' Flight's S/Ldr Marshall to depart for leave on the 14th. The duties of Flight Commander would pass to F/Lt Frederick Sawyer. On June 16th, the squadron carried out the following exercises or flights. The war may have been over, but the work for the ground crews continued. Below is a typical day's activity for the squadron.

| No. A/C | Flight | Activity |
|---|---|---|
| 2 | 'A' | Bomb Tour of Germany. |
| 4 | 'A' | Fighter Affiliation Exercises. |
| 1 | 'B' | Radar Navigational Aids Photographic Exercise |

| | | |
|---|---|---|
| 3 | 'B' | Cross Country Exercise. |
| 6 | 'A' & 'B' | Practice Night Raids in conjunction with Night Air Defences. |
| 1 | 'C' | Fighter Affiliation |
| 3 | 'C' | Flight, Bombing and Reconnaissance Exercises. |

On one of the 'Cooks Tours' was flown by F/Lt Hart and passengers. They would visit a list of cities that would have put a certain amount of fear into the crews only a few short weeks before. The 6 hour 25-minute flight would visit, Aachen, Duren, Cologne, Bonn, Coblenz, Wiesbaden, Frankfurt, Kassel, Hanover, Hamburg, Bremen, Munster, Dortmund, Gelsenkirchen, Essen, Duisberg and finally Wesel.

Cologne, a target that suffered almost continuous bombing from the earliest days of Bomber Commands bombing war. Colognes, once beautiful gothic Catholic Cathedral with its twin spires, is just a blackened shell. The utter devastation around the Catherdral is evident.

The predictable and everyday routine of training continued. As usual, it was 'C' Flight operating alongside 'A' Flight of No.218 Squadron who were the most active carrying out various 'Radar Research Development Flights'. Not to be outdone and adhere to the new training syllabus, both 'A' and 'B' Flight flew training sortie after training sortie.

Bremen. RAF Bomber Commands first attacked this northern port city in May 1940. Its last raid was in April 1945. Once again, the pre-war vibrant city is in ruins.

On the 18th, two crews completed a 'cook's tour' flight over Germany. The pilot of one of the squadron Lancasters was Wing Commander J Bazin DFC MiD. James Bazin was born in Kashmir, India. He joined the RAF pre-war and saw service as a fighter pilot during the Battle of France and Battle of Britain and is credited with a number of victories. In 1944, he found himself operating with Bomber Command, firstly with No.49 Squadron flying Avro Lancasters. In June 1944, he assumed command

of No.9 Squadron, participating in numerous operations, including two of the attacks on the Tirpitz. He was replaced as C/O in May 1945 and was posted on May 25th to No.31 Base Stradishall.
The Squadron Adjutant F/Lt Terrence Capel's time with the squadron and RAF concluded on the 20th with a posting for discharge. Flight Lieutenant Stephen Tinkler would replace him. It would be a brief appointment. The now daily routine of maintenance and refueling was made all the more pleasant with the warm sunny weather. The Ground Crews especially were not complaining. Hopefully, they had seen the last of the freezing, sub-zero conditions out at the distant dispersals. Squadron Leader A Marshall returned from leave on the 22nd and immediately resumed his 'A' Flight Commander role. Two days later, it was the turn of 'C' Flight's S/Ldr Day DFC to depart on leave. Flight Lieutenant C Smith DFC replaced him. On the same day No.31 Base welcomed Squadron Leader Ron Jell DFC, who took up the Station Administration Officer Duties. By trade, an Air Gunner, his operational career stretched back to September 1939. Up until a few weeks prior, he had commanded 'B' Flight of No.218 (Gold Coast) Squadron.

They are the unsung heroes of any squadron. The hardworking, dedicated, and loyal Ground Crews who applied their trade every day come rain or shine, snow or blizzard. Without them, and the WAAF Bomber Command could never have achieved the success it did. Here members of No.186 Squadron's 'B' Flight pose for a photograph.

A new name, '*Post-Mortem*' appeared on the Op's Board on the 25th and found itself in a number of Log-Books. Fourteen No.186 Lancasters plus seven aircraft from 'A' Flight of No.218 Squadron would be involved. These were the first of a series of investigations into German methods of plotting approaching bomber formations and testing the efficiency of the recently captured German early-warning radar. These flights were given the code name *'Post-Mortem'*. The 'target' was Flensburg. The flights were designed to replicate exactly the methods adopted by Bomber Command as they approached Germany. The whole operation would be observed and monitored by Allied specialists who it was hoped would replicate the system for future defence plans for Great Britain. On the 26th, nine squadron aircraft completed formation trails in conjunction with the Radar Research and Development Establishment (RRDE). The RRDE was a civilian research organisation run by the Ministry of Supply that primarily studied the development of radar for the army. They were based in Malvern, Worcestershire. Their Air Ministry counterparts, who were based in Dorset, were the Telecommunications Research Establishment (TRE). The operation was to determine the efficiency of new radar gun-laying equipment against formations of heavy bombers. Probably with an eye on a permanent career in the RAF, S/Ldr Bass AFM was detached to the School of Administration at RAF Hereford. This non-flying station of the Royal Air Force was situated in the village of Credenhill near Hereford. It was commissioned in 1940 and served as home for a range of training schools from 1940, including Administrative Apprentice training. Flight Lieutenant Olaf Cussen DFC assumed the duties of 'B' Flight Commander. On the 28th, No.218 Squadron was scheduled for a Radio Detection Exercise, but this was subsequently cancelled. The following day it was the turn of No.186 Squadron. They were required to provide eight crews for what was scheduled to be a night time *'Post-Mortem'* exercise. However, take-off was brought forward, and the crews flew out over the North Sea towards Flensburg in blazing sunshine. The last day of June 1945 saw No.186 Squadron stood down, only a solitary aircraft of No.218 Squadron's 'A' Flight was scheduled to fly, but this 'Baedeker' trip was eventually scrubbed due to weather conditions. The dismantling of the squadron had started and begun, a number of crews including that of F/Lt Jack Hart were posted to No.622 Squadron based at RAF Mildenhall. It had been a mixed month for the squadron with training given priority. The new training syllabus in preparation for a possible move to Southeast Asia Command resulted in the squadron flying an incredible 843 hours 5 minutes flying hours by day, plus a further 62 hours, 35 minutes by night, all flown without any reported technical failures, and importantly accident free. The departure of the RAAF, and RNZAF and RCAF personnel was by the end of the month complete. The strength on the station stood at 78 Officers, 196 Warrant Officer / S.N.C.O's and 1297 Other Ranks. There was just one solitary Canadian!

The Station Commander report for June 1945.

*This month, the first after the end of the German War, has seen the training worked up to full pressure, the withdrawal with many regrets of all Dominion aircrew personnel, the commencement with great enthusiasm of the EVT scheme*[60]*, and an all-round Spring cleaning of the Station, which is gradually approaching peacetime standards'.*

The Squadron Operational Records Book finishes abruptly on June 30th, 1945. Why it was not continued is unknown, sadly, which leaves the final few weeks of squadron activity somewhat confusing. The following pages are gleaned from the Station Records Book and various Logbooks.

June 1945 : Avro Lancaster Delivery.

| ToC Date | Serial | Code | Maker | Mark | From |
|---|---|---|---|---|---|
| 29/06/1945 | HK645 | N/K | Vickers Armstrong | Mk.B.I | No.149 Sqn |
| 30/06/1945 | HK652 | N/K | Vickers Armstrong | Mk.B.I | No.149 Sqn |
| 30/06/1945 | HK654 | N/K | Vickers Armstrong | Mk.B.I | No.149 Sqn |

[60] *With the war in Europe nearly over, the Royal Air Force drew up plans to provide training for its personnel which, it was hoped, would help them adapt to civilian life once they left the Service. The RAF Educational and Vocational Training Scheme was launched on a world-wide basis shortly after the defeat of Germany in May 1945. EVT, as it was popularly known, offered a broad syllabus which included courses in subjects such as mathematics, English, French, typing, book-keeping, decorating and citizenship.*

# July 1945

## *Training and the End.*

Two 'Cook's Tour' trips were planned for July 1st and 2nd, both to be flown by two squadron crews. Sadly both were cancelled due to filthy weather. On the 3rd, ten squadron crews were aloft on a Radar Exercise, while two were off to France to ferrying service personnel of B.L.A ( 11 Wing). On July 4th, it was 'A' Flight No.218 Squadron airborne on yet another 'Radar Exercise'. This was followed by a significant *'Post Mortem'* operation on July 5th, which included sixteen Lancasters of No.186 Squadron and 8 Lancasters of 218 Squadron. Their destination was once again Flensburg. It would appear that two crews, F/O Jarvis in Lancaster XY-W and F/Lt Kentish in XY-P, were observed by a 'Mosquito Snoop' [61]aircraft completely disregarding the briefed altitude. Both were observed between 5-6000ft when special instructions called for them to fly at an altitude of 2,000ft. Also caught red-handed was F/O Scholey flying Lancaster JE-C of No.195 Squadron. He was found to be flying at 5,200 feet. Despite the crew's faux pa, the exercise was completed without incident. The crews landed after a 5 ½ hour flight. What was said to the crews on return is unknown!

No.31 Base Stradishall Staff are photographed with the AoC No.31 Base Air Commodore James Silvester (centre front). James Silvester had a long and varied career. In 1914, aged just 16, he joined the British Army and served in the trenches on the Western Front with the Royal Berkshire Regiment. He joined the RAF just before the war's end. Various postings followed, including serving as a Test Pilot in India. In 1939 he briefly commanded No.51 Squadron before a spell at RAF Cranwell and Staff Officer Bomber Operations. In 1941 and now a Group Captian, he served at HQ Bomber Command. In May 1943, he took command of No.31 Base RAF Stradishall. He died in 1956, aged just 58.

---

[61] *Stradishall Operational Log : Air 14/2584*

For the next week, two, sometimes three, crews would carry out a tour of the German cities. The Ruhr Valley was a popular destination. The blackened towns and cities, the very power-house of Germany's industrial might, were a charred wasteland. From just a few thousand feet, the passengers could view the utter devastation that Bomber Command wreaked upon Hitler's 1000 Year Reich during its lengthy and costly bomber offensive. On the 12th, a night Bullseye exercise was flown by eight crews. Some older, more experienced crews could recall these flights as the first steps towards becoming operational while still undergoing training at their OTU or HCU. The rumours that the 'A' Flight detachment would be rejoining No.218 Squadron at RAF Chedburgh had been circulating since the start of the month. The eight Lancasters and 14 crews, plus supporting staff, had formed a close working bond with the members of 'C' Flight. On the 14th, a day of heavy rain and low cloud, the rumours became a reality when the flight under the skilled leadership of S/Ldr Christopher Martindale departed. On the 17th, the expected but still unwelcome news arrived in the form of Authority BC/S.32518/ORG dated July 11th that No.186 Squadron was to disband with the exception of 'C' Flight who would join No.218 (Gold Coast) Squadron at RAF Chedburgh.

There are no records of where the crews of 'A' and 'B' Flight were posted, although some including F/Lt P Gray would end up on No.622 Squadron. Prior to his posting he was given the rather laborious job of dumping unwanted ordinance. He recalls,

> *Our crew, along with several others, had been moved from Stradishall to Mildenhall to take part in the disposal of these incendiary bombs. The memory of Stradishall, and the many happenings, tragedies and histrionics occurring there, would stay with us for the remainder of our lives. Finally, we were switched to the disposal business. It seems our leaders had huge stocks of incendiary sticks, and like ourselves, these bombs had run out of targets and a war in which to manoeuvre. The deadly little inflammable missiles with their fire storms had reduced large tracts of such cities as Hamburg and Dresden to rubble. Now these demonic weapons were to be dumped unceremoniously into the watery wastes of the North Sea. With two flights per day and bombed-up with ten 750-pound canisters of incendiary sticks, our Lancasters were pointed toward the north and given a predetermined Gee-H radar map reference to use as a dropping point.*[62]

Sadly, unlike the majority of No.3 Group squadrons, there was no post-war squadron photograph taken. The squadron, unlike its sister squadron No.195 which was formed just four days before No.186 was never issued a squadron badge. It would seem that the squadron was quickly run-down and any thoughts of recording the squadron's activities for posterity were either quickly dismissed or considered unimportant.

There were no poignant comments in the ORB, disbandment of the squadron was quick and final with no fanfare. Group Captain Bates, Station Commander in his end of month summary writes.

> *On July 17th 'C' Flight of 186 Squadron moved to RAF Chedburgh to continue their special work. The remainder of 186 Squadron was disbanded and its short but **most successful career ended.***

The arrival of 'C' Flight No.186 Squadron did not even merit a mention in the No.218 (Gold Coast) Squadron Operational Records Book. It was no surprise. The squadron was in the middle of a significant re-organisation itself. The only mention of No.186 is in the Chedburgh Records Book, which simply acknowledges its arrival. However, it would be a very brief union. The Station Records then mentions

[62] *P Gray. Ghosts of Targets Past.*

that No.218 (Gold Coast) Squadron was to disband on August 10th 1945. Thus, No.186 Squadron's brief operational existence ended, and its duty was nobly completed.

July 1945 : Avro Lancaster Delivery.

| ToC Date | Serial | Code | Maker | Mark | From |
|---|---|---|---|---|---|
| 25/07/1945 | LM216 | | Armstrong Whitworth | Mk.B.I | No.630 Sqn |
| 27/07/1945 | RF194 | | Armstrong Whitworth | Mk.B.I | No.630 Sqn |

# Post War Awards

The contribution and courage of a number of squadron members were recognised soon after the squadron's disbandment. The allocation of awards within No.3 Group was unlike other more 'glamorous' and publicity-seeking groups less prevalent. It was post war that the squadrons contribution and that of its crews were truly recognized. The following is a list of awards allocated to the squadron.

| Date | Rank | Name | Award |
|---|---|---|---|
| 17/07/1945 | Flying Officer | Eric Reginald Barton | DFC |
| 17/07/1945 | Flight Lieutenant | Gordon McNab Templeton | DFC |
| 20/07/1945 | Pilot Officer | Leonard Arthur Green | DFC |
| 20/07/1945 | Pilot Officer | Kingsley Eric Pryor | DFC |
| 21/09/1945 | Flight Lieutenant | Alexander Jeffrey Clarson | DFC |
| 21/09/1945 | Flight Lieutenant | Jack Dennis O'Brien | DFC |
| 21/09/1945 | Squadron Leader | Percy Reynolds | Bar /DFC |
| 21/09/1945 | Flight Lieutenant | Edgar Leonard Field | DFC |
| 21/09/1945 | Flight Sergeant | Harrold William Beer | DFM |
| 21/09/1945 | Flight Sergeant | Leslie Collins | DFM |
| 21/09/1945 | Flight Lieutenant | Kenneth Gerald Orman | Bar /DFC |
| 21/09/1945 | Flight Lieutenant | Charles Edward Baxter | DFC |
| 21/09/1945 | Flight Sergeant | James Pollock Weir Hepburn | DFM |
| 21/09/1945 | Flight Sergeant | Frederick George Holland | DFM |
| 21/09/1945 | Flying Officer | Arthur Aspin | DFC |
| 25/09/1945 | Flying Officer | Charles John Adam Morison | DFC |
| 25/09/1945 | Pilot Officer | William Alexander Rowe | DFC |
| 25/09/1945 | Pilot Officer | Peter Arthur Upson | DFC |
| 25/09/1945 | Flight Sergeant | Frederick Harold Kempin | DFM |
| 25/09/1945 | Warrant Officer | Frederick Robert Jackson | DFC |
| 25/09/1945 | Flight Sergeant | Cyril John Morris | DFM |
| 25/09/1945 | Warrant Officer | Sidney John Pay | DFC |
| 25/09/1945 | Warrant Officer | Roland Walter Arthur Ward | DFC |
| 25/10/1945 | Flight Sergeant | Charles Frederick Turner | DFM |
| 06/11/1945 | Flight Lieutenant | George Arrand | DFC |
| 06/11/1945 | Flying Officer | Walter Thomas Cooper | DFC |
| 06/11/1945 | Warrant Officer | James McFalls | DFC |
| 06/11/1945 | Flight Lieutenant | Leonard Ernest Jordon | DFC |
| 16/11/1945 | Flying Officer | Frederick Fernley | DFC |
| 16/11/1945 | Warrant Officer | John David Sofin | DFC |
| 16/11/1945 | Flying Officer | John Edward Tonks | DFC |
| 16/11/1945 | Wing Commander | Ernest Lindsey Hancock | DFC |
| 16/11/1945 | Flight Lieutenant | Alfred George Portway | DFC |
| 04/12/1945 | Squadron Leader | Robert William Bass | DFC |
| 04/12/1945 | Flight Lieutenant | Dennis Frederick Godfrey | DFC |

# The Memorial at RAF Stradishall

Unveiled in May 1994 by Marshal of the Royal Air Force, Sir Michael Beetham, GCB, CBE,

DFC, AFC, FRAeS.

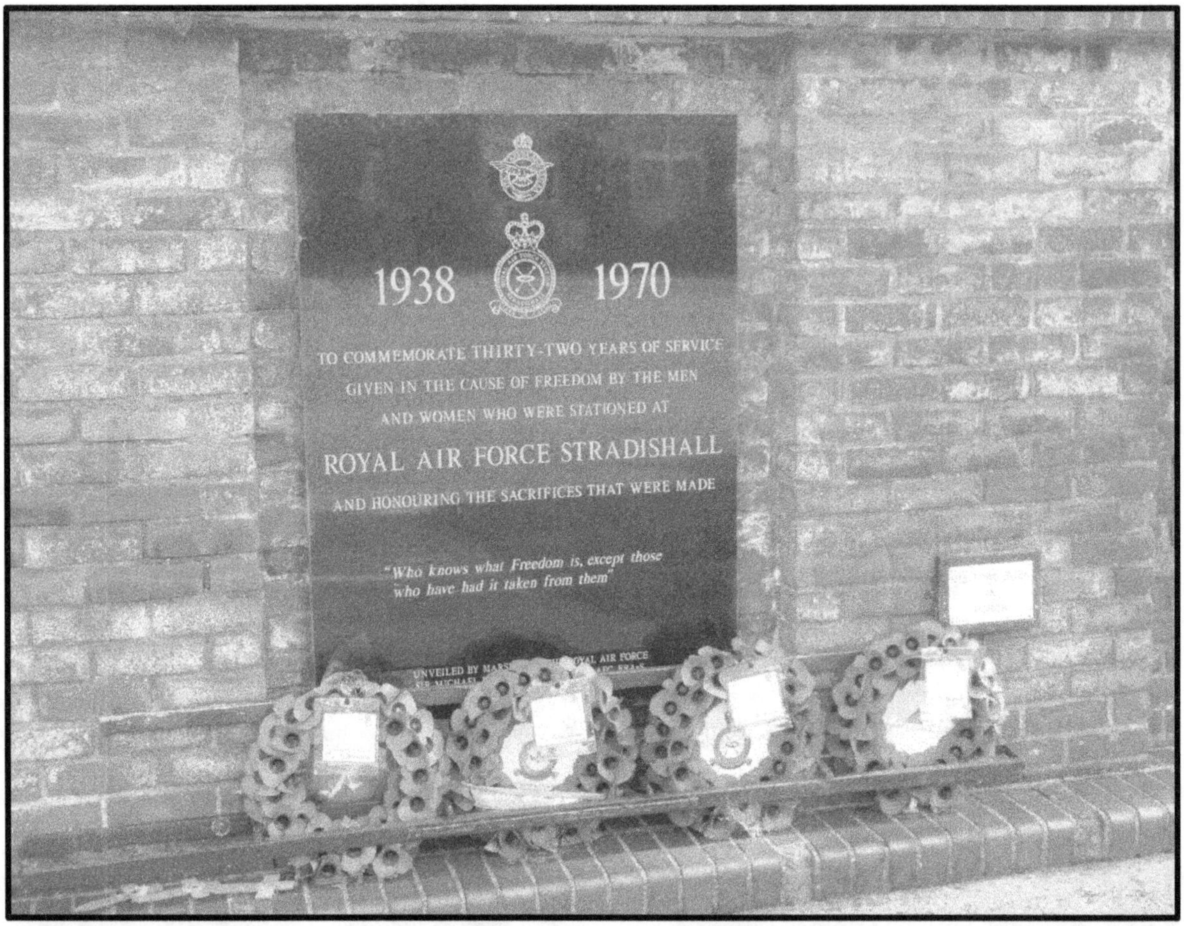
1938
1970
TO COMMEMORATE THIRTY-TWO YEARS OF SERVICE
GIVEN IN THE CAUSE OF FREEDOM BY THE MEN
AND WOMEN WHO WERE STATIONED AT
ROYAL AIR FORCE STRADISHALL
AND HONOURING THE SACRIFICES THAT WERE MADE
"Who knows what Freedom is, except those
who have had it taken from them"

ROYAL AIR FORCE STRADISHALL
1938
1970
BOMBER COMMAND
No 3 GROUP
1938 - 1945 1946 - 1949
TRANSPORT COMMAND
Nos 47 and 48 GROUPS (No 38 GROUP)
1945 - 1946
1961
ROYAL AIR FORCE
Squadrons / Units
9 148 75 150 75(NZ) 254 236
214 Ferry-Flt (1)-419-Flt 138 109
101 1521-BAT-Flt 1657-HCU 186
158 51 35 115 149 207 203-AFS
226-OCU 229-OCU 253 125 245
89 152 263 85 1 54 208
111 56 1-ANS
Royal Air Force Regiment
ATTACHED
Royal Artillery
Royal Engineers
Royal Signals
Cambridgeshire Regiment
Leicestershire Regiment
Suffolk Regiment
4CAACU
N
FLYING TRAINING COMMAND
Nos 25 and 23 GROUPS
1961 - 1970
FIGHTER COMMAND
Nos 11 12 and 81 GROUPS
1949 - 1961

Memorial window, Church of St Margaret's .

www.ingramcontent.com/pod-product-compliance
Lightning Source LLC
Chambersburg PA
CBHW081125170426
43197CB00017B/2758